Consumer Reports®

EXPERT • INDEPENDENT • NONPROFIT

BUYING GUIDE

BEST BUYS FOR 2006

The editors of
CONSUMER REPORTS magazine

Consumers Union • Yonkers, NY

Contents

Shop Smart in 2006

Latest Buying Advice

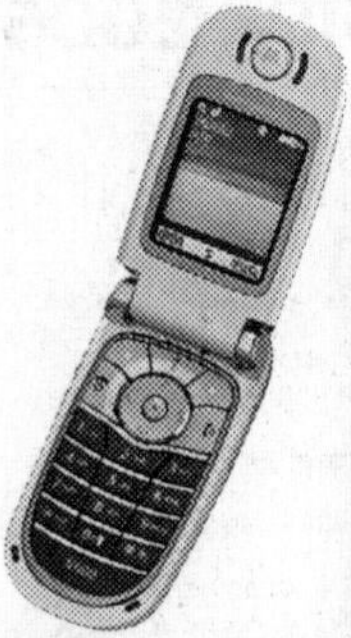

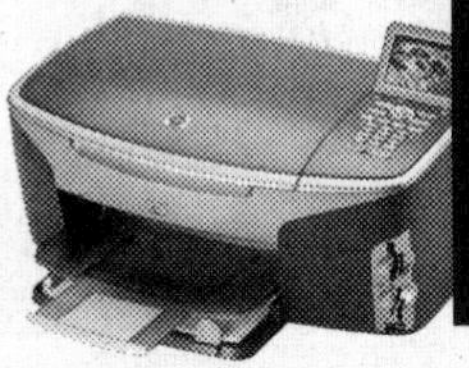

115 COMPUTERS, PHONES, AND PERIPHERALS

Autos

Product Ratings and Reliability

221 PRODUCT RATINGS AND RELIABILITY CHARTS

More Useful Buying Information

CONSUMER REPORTS BUYING GUIDE 2006

Consumer Reports (ISSN 0010-7174) is published monthly, except twice in December, by Consumers Union of U.S., Inc., 101 Truman Avenue, Yonkers, NY 10703-1057. Periodicals postage paid at Yonkers, NY, and at other mailing offices. Canadian postage paid at Mississauga, Ontario, Canada. Canadian publications registration no. 2665247-98. Title Consumer Reports registered in U.S. Patent Office. Contents of this issue copyright © 2005 by Consumers Union of U.S., Inc. All rights reserved under International and Pan-American copyright conventions. Reproduction in whole or in part is forbidden without prior written permission (and is never permitted for commercial purposes). CU is a member of the Consumers International. Mailing lists: CU rents or exchanges its customer postal list so it can be provided to other publications, companies, and nonprofit organizations. If you wish your name deleted from lists and rentals, send your address label with a request for deletion to Consumer Reports, P.O. Box 2127, Harlan, IA 51593-0316. **U.S. Postmaster:** Send address changes to P.O. Box 2109, Harlan, IA 51593-0298. **Canada Post:** If copies are undeliverable, return to Consumer Reports, P.O. Box 1051, STN MAIN, Fort Erie ON L2A 6C7. Back issues: Single copies of 12 preceding issues, $7.95 each; Buying Guide, $10 each. Write Back Issues, Consumer Reports, Customer Relations, 101 Truman Ave., Yonkers, N.Y. 10703. Consumer Reports Buying Guide 2005 (ISBN 0-89043-991-5).

Buying Advice at Your Fingertips

The Consumer Reports Buying Guide 2006 is your handy one-stop source for making intelligent, informed, money-saving purchases for all your home and personal needs. Consult it before you shop, and bring it to the store to help you compare brands. Here's how to make best use of this buying guide:

Begin by learning to protect yourself. An unfortunate byproduct of the information age is identity theft, and you are particularly vulnerable while shopping. **Protect Your Identity in Stores and Online,** on page 7, tells you how to keep your personal data safe while shopping and what to do if you become a victim. You also want to protect yourself from unnecessary expenses, so read **Extended Warranties: A great deal, except for consumers,** on page 15, regarding this kind of coverage.

Whether you shop in stores, through catalogs, or online, arm yourself with time- and money-saving strategies by reading **Shopping Strategies to Get Best Value,** on page 13. This section includes two revealing surveys: **Electronics Retailers Compared** and **Computer Retailers Compared,** about the best places and methods to shop for products.

Once you're familiar with the marketplace for 2006, the **Buying Advice** section, beginning on page 21, gives you guidance from the experts at CONSUMER REPORTS on more than 45 different product categories. From air conditioners and microwave ovens to televisions and washing machines, you'll get invaluable information on what's available, features that count, and how to choose the model that's best for you.

Are you in the market for a car? The **Autos** section contains the latest **Ratings** and information on new and used cars to help you make the right purchasing decision. In addition to reviews of the 2005-06 models, there's a section on the best and worst used cars, as well as reliability ratings for more than 200 models currently in the marketplace.

Product Ratings are given for more than more than 700 models in 24 categories. All of the Ratings now include the highly useful CR Quick Picks. Along with the Ratings you'll find Brand Reliability information for some products and comparison charts that present survey results from thousands of respondents on repairs and problems they've had with various brands in 17 different product categories.

Finally, there's a **Brand Locator** table with information for contacting manufacturers, a list of recent **Product Recalls,** and two indexes to help you find the buying advice you need.

Consumer Reports®

WHO WE ARE

About the Consumer Reports family of products

Founded as a magazine in 1936, CONSUMER REPORTS now brings you its unbiased, trusted information in many formats. Its products and publications include CONSUMER REPORTS magazine; buying guides and magazines from Consumer Reports Publications Development; two newsletters, Consumer Reports On Health and Consumer Reports Money Adviser; and Consumer Reports TV News, a nationally syndicated consumer news service.

ConsumerReports.org offers site subscribers a searchable version of our test findings and advice. Auto prices and custom reports are available through the **Consumer Reports New Car Buying Kit, Consumer Reports Used Car Buying Kit, Consumer Reports New Car Price Service,** and **Consumer Reports Used Car Price Service.** You can find prices, subscription rates, and more information on all these products and services at *www.ConsumerReports.org*. Go to "Bookstore" on the home page. **ConsumerReportsMedicalGuide.org** provides independent health information, including exclusive treatment Ratings and detailed information about prescription drugs, to help consumers with difficult medical decisions.

CONSUMER REPORTS magazine specializes in head-to-head, brand-name comparisons of autos and household products. It also provides informed, impartial advice on a broad range of topics from health and nutrition to personal finance and travel.

CONSUMER REPORTS buys all the products it tests and accepts no free samples. We accept no advertising from outside entities nor do we let any company use our information or Ratings for commercial purposes.

CONSUMER REPORTS is published by Consumers Union, an independent, nonprofit testing and information organization—the largest such organization anywhere in the world.

Since 1936, Consumers Union's mission has been to test products, inform the public, and protect consumers. Our income is derived solely from the sale of our publications and online information and services, and from nonrestrictive, noncommercial contributions, grants, and fees.

Protect Your Identity in Stores and Online

It is hard to go shopping these days without worrying about identity theft. Credit cards, debit cards, personal checks, and registrations can put you at risk of joining the estimated 10 million people who have been victimized in the past year. Fortunately, there are simple steps you can take to reduce your vulnerability to identity theft.

With just a few pieces of personal data—such as a Medicare card and street address—thieves can gain access to your Social Security number, which becomes a golden key, enabling him to open new accounts and start loans in your name.

When the theft is limited to a credit card, the result may be less of a nightmare. The thieves will only be able make charges on that card, and if you act promptly your liability for unauthorized charges is only $50. But fixing the problem can still be a huge hassle. You'll need to call the credit-card company to cancel the unauthorized charges and follow up with a certified letter. You should also closely monitor future credit card statements or get a new card.

How can you prevent someone from stealing your identity? It is not possible to completely insulate yourself, since the companies and agencies that store your data could be hacked or their records could go missing. But there are steps you can take to avoid being a target. Some preventive measures apply to everyone, whether you shop online or off. If you are a frequent online shopper, you will want to lock up your digital data, too. Here's how:

One of the best shields against ID theft is being vigilantly aware of the status of your finances and your credit report.

Keep an eye on your accounts. Monitor the purchases that show up on your monthly statements and watch for unfamiliar purchases. Report suspicious activity to your bank or credit card company immediately so the company can flag your account and halt further purchases.

Watch for monthly utility bills. Check with your utility companies if a bill doesn't arrive on time; for example, thieves who have started receiving cell phone service under your name may have redirected the bills to cover their tracks.

Review your credit reports at least once a year. As of Sept. 1, 2005, everyone in the United States has the right to a free copy of their credit report once every 12 months from each of the three credit reporting agencies—Equifax, Experian, and TransUnion. To order copies of your reports, go to the site authorized by the Federal Trade Commission, *www.annualcreditreport.com,* or call 877-322-8228.

Freeze your credit. Six states have security-freeze laws that require credit reporting agencies to lock up your credit reports upon your request. This prevents anyone from seeing your report without your unfreezing it. Until you lift the freeze, anyone who wants to view your file will be told that the credit reports are unavailable. Typically the creditors will not be able to view your credit report until three or more business days after you have "thawed" your credit. (Hence, this is not a good strategy for people who need instant credit.)

States that currently have security-freeze laws are California, Louisiana, and Nevada, where the law is already in effect; and Colorado, Connecticut, and Maine, where the law goes into effect in 2006. Another three states—Illinois, Texas, and Vermont—require the agencies to institute the freeze for victims only. Washington State has a law that includes people who have been notified of a security breach of their personal information. (For specifics, see the Identity Theft Resource Center's Consumer Guide at *www.idtheftcenter.org/vg124.shtml.*)

Victims of identity theft typically do not pay for security freezes. But nonvictims pay about $10 to $15 per agency; often they must pay a similar fee to lift the freeze.

Gail Hillebrand, a senior attorney for Consumers Union, publisher of CONSUMER REPORTS, notes that a security freeze is more effective than a fraud alert being attached to your account. People who suspect that they are about to become victims of ID theft—perhaps because their personal data were just stolen—can call the credit reporting agencies and request an initial fraud alert. This initial alert lasts for 90 days and requires credit grantors to use reasonable procedures to form a reasonable belief in the identity of anyone trying to open an account with that name or make certain other changes.

Victims of ID theft can get the longer and stronger extended fraud alert which requires potential creditors to contact you

Watch out for credit report scams

Don't be misled into ordering your credit report from scam artists. The Federal Trade Commission is urging people to order their reports only from one official Web site—*www.annualcreditreport.com*. Spoofed sites are already cropping up. In August 2005, the FTC sent warnings to 130 imposter sites that try to sell services such as credit reports, debt analysis, and credit monitoring. The agency is also warning people not to click on e-mail advertisements or pop-ups maintaining that they are an official credit-reporting Web site. They are probably scams.

Don't be tricked into signing up for a fee-based service. Experian, one of the three nationwide credit-reporting agencies, was a target of an FTC complaint for not explaining adequately to customers that they were subscribing to a $79.95 annual membership when they responded to advertisements promising free credit reports. (The company operated the Web sites consumerinfo.com and freecreditreport.com.) In a settlement announced in August 2005, the company was required to refund certain customers, halt deceptive advertising, and pay the FTC $950,000 in what the commission called "ill-gotten gains." If you think you qualify for a refund, go to *www.ftc.gov/freereports* for more information, or call 202-326-3457.

by phone or take reasonable steps to verify your identity. But, Hillebrand said, a fraud alert "is like a yellow light; they can still go through it." By contrast, she said, a security freeze is a stop sign, halting all activity by new creditors until you give the go-ahead.

Keep your data to yourself. Your Social Security number, in particular, should be carefully guarded. Follow these tips:

- Don't keep your Social Security card in your wallet unless you need it that day.
- If you have a Medicare card, be aware that it includes your Social Security number; keep it at home if possible.
- Don't give any personally identifiable information over the phone unless you've initiated the call and you have a trusted relationship with the company.
- Don't use your mother's maiden name as a password hint or identity marker.
- Shield your personal identification number, or PIN, when using an automated teller machine.
- Keep your credit card in your sight when it's being charged. (Unscrupulous employees at restaurants, retail shops, and gas stations have been known to practice "skimming," in which they use a card-scanning device to pull data off your card and sell it on the black market.)
- Shred old documents that include your Social Security number.
- Shred old statements that include your credit- and debit-card numbers.
- Shred credit card offers you get in the mail (and then ask to opt out of telemarketing lists that sell your name and address to credit-card companies).
- Never permit your Social Security number to be written on your checks.
- Avoid using your Social Security number in filling out forms; ask your state if you can substitute another number on your driver's license.

It is relatively safe to shop online, despite what you may hear about computers being hacked and e-mail scams that try to steal your passwords. "We don't have any evidence that online shopping puts anyone at more risk than brick-and-mortar shopping," said Beth Givens, the director of the Privacy Rights Clearinghouse, a nonprofit consumer advocacy group in San Diego.

Most identity thieves obtain information by traditional methods (like stealing wallets), instead of electronically, according to the 2005 Identity Fraud Survey Report co-released by the Better Business Bureau and Javelin Strategy & Research, a company in Pleasanton, Calif., that specializes in research about online financial trends.

But you should still take steps to protect yourself online. Before you head to the online checkout, follow this advice:

Enter payment on secure sites only. Look for the padlock icon (above), or unbroken key at the bottom of your Web browser, which signals that the site will not be transferring your data in plain view over the Internet but will instead encrypt it and transport it over a channel protected from prying eyes. The letters that come before the Web address will also indicate that you are on a secure site. Look for an 's' after the http—https://—in the address bar.

If you use Microsoft's Internet Explorer, sometimes you'll get a pop-up notice (next page) that says you are about to view a page with both secure and nonsecure items. It asks if you'd like to display the nonsecure items. This cryptic message is Microsoft telling you the page has not loaded all of the secure content fully and, according to Microsoft, has nothing

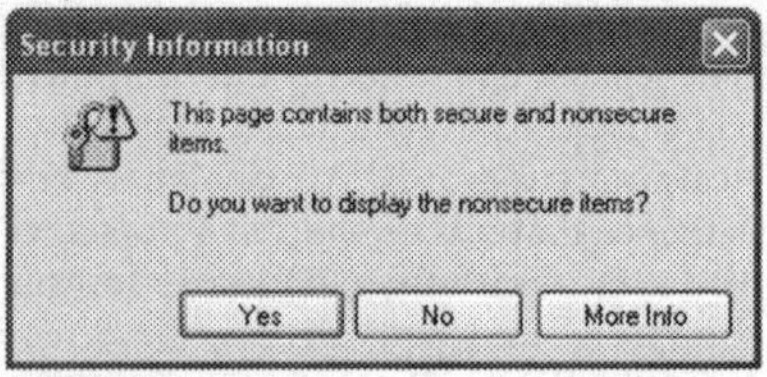

to do with the security of the Web page. Go ahead and choose 'yes'; the page that loads will be secure.

Think carefully about where you store your credit-card number. Many online retailers invite you to add yourself to their databases so you don't have to retype shipping and payment forms every time you buy an item. In addition, services such as the "AutoFill" feature on Google's toolbar enable people to store their credit-card numbers on their own computers so Web forms can be filled out automatically. Are either of these methods safe?

Some security experts say that financial information stored on a personal computer may not be a large risk as long as consumers use firewalls and encryption, the technical word for converting data so that it can be recovered only with a key. Google's "AutoFill" feature, for example, encrypts the credit-card number on your PC so that it cannot be easily read by a hacker.

The practice of keeping credit-card numbers on companies' servers is more worrisome to other privacy experts. "I personally don't like to store my credit-card number on anybody's computer," said Givens, of the Privacy Rights Clearinghouse. "I take the time to type it out." The risk, she said, is that a company's databases could be hacked or dishonest employees could steal the data. In 2005, stories of data breaches were popping up monthly, with tales of tapes gone missing or servers hacked.

But large online retailers, like Amazon .com and Walmart.com, say consumers should be reassured by the measures they take to safeguard credit-card information, which often includes multiple layers of protection, physical security, and encryption. And Richard M. Smith, a security consultant in Boston, points out that large companies may have higher levels of security than what is on your own computer.

Use caution with small stores. Smith sees the biggest risk with little-known companies that may not have the expertise or money to hire information security professionals or install secure sites. Before you enter your credit-card number, look for the padlock icon to ensure security, but also seek signs that the retailer is credible, such as its willingness to display its street address and phone number. (Go to ConsumerWebWatch.org for fraud news about online shops.)

Don't respond to e-mail "phishing" scams. These e-mail messages are designed to fool you into thinking that a legitimate company—like PayPal, eBay, or an online bank—wants you to verify your account. The messages ask you to click on a link and enter your name and password. Don't do it. Scam artists are behind the scenes, collecting that sensitive data.

Never click on a link in an e-mail message that purportedly takes you to a log-in page. Instead, type the Web address of the legitimate company into the Web browser and see if the company is, indeed, asking you to make changes or confirm information in your account. (The chances are slim; the FTC says that legitimate companies don't ask for personal or financial information via e-mail.)

On most computers, you can spot phishing e-mails by moving your cursor over the link in the message and checking the address coding that appears on the screen. The text might say eBay Billing Center, but the Web address behind the link is actually

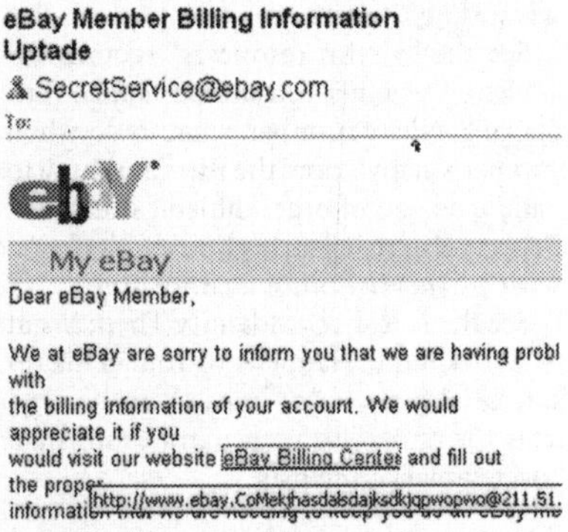
eBay Member Billing Information Uptade
SecretService@ebay.com
To:

My eBay

Dear eBay Member,

We at eBay are sorry to inform you that we are having probl
with
the billing information of your account. We would
appreciate it if you
would visit our website eBay Billing Center and fill out
the proper
informati
http://www.ebay.CoMekthasdalsdajksdkjqpwopwo@211.51.

a series of numbers and letters for a scam artist's Web site (above). When you see messages like this, report them to *spam@uce.gov* or *reportphishing@antiphishing.org*.

Dedicate a credit card for online shopping. You'll be able to easily monitor purchases. And if you have to cancel that card, you have a backup.

Don't use debit cards online. Many debit cards can be used as credit cards, in which case a PIN is not required. If a thief steals the card number, he has access to your checking account and could wipe it out. With a true credit card, you are responsible for no more than $50 in unauthorized charges. With debit cards, your liability is also limited to $50, but only if you notify the financial institution within two business days after learning of loss or theft of your card or code. After that, you could lose up to $500.

If you don't tell the card issuer of an unauthorized transfer that appears on your statement within 60 days after the statement is mailed to you, you could lose all the money in your account, plus the overdraft line of credit, if any. Meanwhile, you may not have access to your account while your bank conducts a fraud investigation. "We've talked to people who have been without their checking account for several weeks," Givens said.

Protect your computer. Install a firewall. (Windows XP and Mac OS have built-in firewalls, so be sure to enable this software.) Use antivirus and antispam software, and sign up for automatic updates. Search for and remove spyware. If you use a wireless network at home, use the router's security features; otherwise anyone in the vicinity with a wireless computer will be able to log on to your network and view your files. If you have a router, change its default password and disable "remote administration" to prevent hackers from seizing control of the router.

Do not open e-mail attachments you weren't expecting, even from someone you know. They could set off a malicious virus that is designed to surreptitiously obtain extra information from your computer.

Be alert to programs that enable people to trade music and other files. File-sharing programs are notorious for hosting spyware that secretly collects information about you, and the files that are shared on the networks may contain nasty viruses. If you do use a file-sharing program—or if your children have installed one—be sure to run antispyware and keep your virus protections up-to-date. Also, be sure that the folders they have elected to "share" with everyone else on the Internet do not contain identifiable personal information. What's more, as with any networked software, the programs could contain security flaws, which hackers could take advantage of to pry into seemingly private files.

Never use shared computers for online shopping. If you fail to log out of, say, your Amazon.com account, the next person to use the computer might see where you went shopping and discover how you filled out online forms (not to mention the chance that someone could continue shopping using your account).

Even if you log out, traces of your activities may be stored in temporary files and in what are called "cookies," tiny bits of information that are left on the hard drive that can be retrieved from hidden folders by people with sophisticated knowledge of computers. A rare but still possible risk is that a crook has installed a piece of software on the computer to record keystrokes, thereby gaining knowledge of all names, credit-card numbers and account passwords that you have typed.

Never use public Wi-Fi hotspots for online shopping. These free wireless networks—often found in coffee shops, city parks, and public libraries—allow people with wireless laptops to go online without having to plug in. But the networks are insecure. If you are using an e-mail account that is unencrypted (as most are), every message you send could easily be watched by tech-savvy strangers.

Change passwords often, use different ones for different accounts, and make them difficult to guess. Yes, it's a hassle to change passwords and try to remember the latest incarnation. But this is a critical part of keeping your online accounts locked up.

WHAT TO DO IF YOU'RE A VICTIM

Go to the following Web sites, which outline how to protect your current assets, lock up your credit and start to regain your good name.

The FTC's identity theft center
www.consumer.gov/idtheft

The first page lists four steps to take immediately, with links to resources like the ID theft affidavit, which may help prove that your accounts have been compromised. Read the report, "Take Charge: Fighting Back Against Identity Theft." It includes tips on how to organize your case.

Identity Theft Resource Center
www.idtheftcenter.org

See the "victim resources" section for advice on whether you should change your Social Security number, what to do when you personally know the thief and how to handle dozens of other difficult situations.

Privacy Rights Clearinghouse
www.privacyrights.org/identity.htm

See the fact sheet, "Identity Theft: What to Do When It Happens to You." This resource also provides links to authorized sites for removing your name from mail and telemarketing lists.

LEARN THE LINGO

A phishing e-mail is a fraudulent message that links to spoofed Web pages, where users are asked to enter passwords—data that is collected by identity thieves.

Secure sites transport data that you've entered on address and credit-card forms over a network that can only be accessed by authorized individuals instead of sending it in plain text over the open Internet. Look for the padlock icon, or unbroken key, at the bottom of your browser and the "https" in front of Web addresses in the address bar.

Skimming is the act of stealing data by running a credit card through an illicit card reader; unscrupulous employees may skim data when processing a payment.

Spam is junk e-mail, including unsolicited offers for legitimate products and fraudulent ones.

A **spoofed e-mail** or **Web site** has been disguised to look official, but it's a fake.

Spyware is a program on your PC that gathers data and may transmit it without your knowledge or consent.

Viruses and **worms** spread through e-mail and are usually activated when an infected attachment is opened. Some seize control of your computer and steal confidential information.

Shopping Strategies to Get Best Values

Are you a careful researcher, someone who takes the time to shop for the best price on whatever you're buying? Perhaps you're a time-saver, looking to get the best price as quickly as possible? Or do you window-shop? Whatever your shopping style, you have lots more choices these days.

While shopping alternatives have grown, the basic rules for smart shopping remain the same: Do your homework and determine the best value for your needs. In this chapter we give you strategies for shopping smart—in the store, online, and by catalog. As you plan your purchases, consult this guide for more than 950 product Ratings (page 221) plus brand reliability information for many products.

STORE STRATEGIES

Traditional retailers are still the principal shopping choice of most consumers. Brick-and-mortar stores allow what online or catalog shopping can't—an in-person judgment of overall appearance and important sensory qualities. Researching your purchase before you set off for the store can pay off in valuable product knowledge, time saved, and,maybe, a lower price.

Specialty stores, special service. Need help selecting a product in a category you're not familiar with? Just want a real person to help you? Smaller stores, such as audio boutiques and Main Street shops, can provide a knowledgeable staff and personal service, including special ordering. These advantages may be offset by higher prices. Determine a fair price before you go, using this guide, the Web, or a retailer's catalog. Then decide how much the personal service is worth to you. Be aware that for some products, such as computers, you can better customize your purchase by buying online. A 2004 CONSUMER REPORTS survey found that people purchasing desktop computers via the Internet or a catalog were generally more satisfied than people who bought them at a brick-and-mortar store.

Bottom-line basics. Is finding the type of product you want at a good price more important than the latest technology and a large selection? Mass merchandisers such as Wal-Mart and Target cover many categories with a selection of moderately priced brands from well-known manufacturers, along with their own store brands. Though these stores usually have liberal return policies, returns may entail time and hassle.

Big stores, big selection. Specialty chains such as Circuit City and Best Buy account for about half of home-electronics sales. Home Depot and Lowe's control one-fourth of the home-improvement product market. CompUSA inhabits strip malls across the country. Sears has a network of stores and a Web site with lots of product choices for major appliances and other home products.

These chains may also feature special services, such as viewing/listening rooms for home-theater demonstrations. And although sales-staff expertise may vary, your questions will usually be answered.

Join the club. If you're willing to be flexible on brand and model, check a warehouse club: Costco, BJ's Wholesale Club, or Sam's Club (Wal-Mart's warehouse sibling). Since those stores emphasize value, not service or selection, expect long lines and little sales help. Prices are consistently low, though not necessarily the lowest.

Clubs charge an annual membership fee (generally $35 to $45). If you don't shop there frequently, that fee can undo much of your savings. But a big saving on a single purchase can pay for your membership. Most clubs will issue a limited-time shopping pass, letting you browse without joining, but you may have to pay a surcharge if you buy goods as a nonmember.

CATALOG STRATEGIES

Catalogs offer selection and convenience, often from established, proven companies with top-notch customer service. And of course they offer 24/7 access. Most catalog merchants are also online.

The catalog-Web connection can give you the best of both venues. You can browse the catalog and then order online using a catalog's "quick search" feature, or call the toll-free number. Online catalogs typically feature more merchandise than expensive-to-mail paper catalogs. Web sites frequently feature lines not available in the paper catalog, online-only sales and bargains, even product-selection tips and detailed en-

Continued on page 20

Did you know?

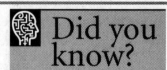

Here are the odds of needing a repair within the first three years.

Product	Repair rate (%)
Desktop PC	37
Laptop PC	33
Lawn tractor and riding mower	29
Refrigerator: side-by-side (with icemaker and dispenser)	28
Self-propelled mower	26
Washing machine	22
Gas range	19
Refrigerator: top- and bottom-freezer (with icemaker)	17
Projection TV	16
Push mower	15
Vacuum cleaner (excluding belt replacement)	13
Dishwasher	13
Clothes dryer	13
Microwave oven (over-the-range)	12
Electric range	11
Camcorder	8
Digital camera	8
Refrigerator: top- and bottom-freezer (without icemaker)	8
TV: 30- to 36-inch	7
TV: 25- to 27-inch	5

Source: Consumer Reports 2004 Annual Questionnaire, based on three-year-old products.

Extended warranties: A great deal, except for consumers

If you've bought anything at an appliance or electronics store in recent years, you've almost certainly been treated to a sales pitch for an extended warranty. But one of our reporters was surprised earlier this year to hear the same spiel at a Toys "R" Us store. The product in question: a $40 scooter.

Needless to say, our reporter scooted out of there without buying the warranty. Had he wished to, however, he could not only have insured the scooter but any number of other products, including skateboards, telescopes, baby strollers, and even DVDs.

Once offered primarily on costly appliances, extended warranties and similar insurance products have now trickled down to just about everything on the shelves. For inexpensive items, they often take the form of a replacement plan that promises to give you a new or rebuilt product, or a store credit, if the unit you bought conks out while the plan is still in effect. For example, for $4.99 our reporter's scooter would have been eligible for a one-year replacement plan, starting when the manufacturer's labor warranty expires.

For higher-priced merchandise you'll usually be offered an extended warranty or service contract that vows to either repair or replace a defective product during the term of the agreement, often one to five years. In some instances, the clock on an extended warranty starts ticking the day you buy the product that you're insuring, even though the manufacturer's warranty is also in effect.

It's little wonder that retailers are enthusiastic about extended warranties and sometimes push their sales staff to pour on the hard sell. When profit margins on the products themselves are being squeezed, extended warranties yield a 40 to 80 percent profit, industry sources say.

So if these plans are a cash cow for retailers, just who's getting milked? You may already know the answer. For years, CONSUMER REPORTS has cautioned against buying this costly and often useless coverage. Survey data from thousands of readers have shown that, in general, extended warranties can cost nearly as much as the average repair—if you ever need a repair at all. As you can see from the box on page 14, many products are unlikely to require repairs within the first three years.

When it comes to some newer technologies, such as flat-panel plasma and liquid-crystal display (LCD) TV sets, however, the decision is more difficult. Preliminary data from our user surveys show no unusual rate of repair for these TVs in the first year, but their long-term reliability is still unknown. Before you say yes to an extended warranty on any product, first see whether your credit or debit card already provides similar coverage.

Such plans, most often found on premium cards, typically lengthen the original manufacturer's warranty by up to one year. If you use a MasterCard, look for Extended Warranty in the card's list of features. Visa calls its program Warranty Manager Service; American Express offer a Buyer's Assurance Plan.

ELECTRONICS RETAILERS COMPARED

Shop big box for price, go local for service

There are numerous retail outfits from which to choose when looking to buy electronic products for your home. In addition to individual and chain stores that specialize in consumer electronics, there are online sources, warehouse clubs, and mega-retailers, such as Wal-Mart, to consider.

What we found

We surveyed our readers in our 2004 annual questionnaire to find out how satisfied they were with their electronics shopping experiences and how they rated stores in terms of Price, Selection, Quality of Product, Service, and Checkout. Nearly, 5000 respondents commented on almost 8,000 electronics purchases. (These are our latest ratings at press time. For an update, please see our newest ratings based on the 2005 Annual Questionnaire in the December issue of Consumer Reports and online at ConsumerReports.org.) Here are some of our other findings from our 2004 survey:

- Amazon.com was the only retailer that excelled in both price and selection, while locally owned independent stores and Ritz Camera were the only two that were rated high for service and checkout.
- The warehouse giants Costco and Sam's Club received high ratings on price, for example, but readers gave them lower marks for service and selection.
- Wal-Mart managed an average score on price, and was rated worse for selection, quality of product, and service.

Guide to the Survey

The Ratings are based on 7,830 store visits by 4,708 respondents who bought any of the following electronics products in 2003 and 2004: camcorders, cameras, DVDs, handheld PDAs, and TVs.

These results from our 2004 online Annual Questionnaire are based on responses from Consumer Reports subscribers and may not reflect the experiences of the general public. There were at least 170 responses for each store.

Reader Score: A score of 100 would mean all respondents had been completely satisfied with their experience; 80 means they were very satisfied, on average; 60, fairly well-satisfied. Differences of less than 6 points aren't meaningful.

Prices, selection, quality of product, service, and **checkout** are based on the percentage of shoppers who rated the chain as excellent or very good on each attribute. These ratings are relative and reflect how each chain compares with the average score.

Electronics retailers

Better ⊜ ⊖ ○ ◒ ● Worse

	Store	Reader score (0–100)	Price	Selection	Quality of product	Service	Checkout
1	**Amazon.com**	91	⊜	⊜	○	-	-
2	**Independent Stores**	88	○	⊖	○	⊜	⊜
3	**Ritz Camera**	87	○	⊖	⊖	⊜	⊜
4	**Costco**	85	⊜	●	○	●	◒
5	**Dell.com**	84	⊖	●	○	-	-
6	**Staples**	81	○	◒	○	○	⊜
7	**Sears**	80	○	○	○	⊖	⊖
8	**Sam's Club**	79	⊜	●	◒	●	◒
9	**Circuit City**	78	○	○	○	○	⊖
10	**Best Buy.com**	76	○	⊖	○	-	-
11	**Best Buy**	76	○	○	○	○	○
12	**Fry's Electronics**	74	○	○	○	●	●
13	**Wal-Mart**	73	○	●	●	●	◒
14	**CompUSA**	72	○	○	○	○	○

COMPUTER RETAILERS COMPARED

Retail stores get lower marks than Web or catalog

It's now common to find fast, powerful, reasonably priced computers virtually everywhere in the marketplace. If you're looking to buy a desktop computer, be sure to check these survey results and Ratings on the best retailers for PCs to insure that you get the model and service that match your personal computing needs.

What we found

According to the survey results, it's generally better to buy a desktop computer from a manufacturer or retail Web site or by mail order than in a store. The representatives tended to be more helpful and the computer selection better. (These are our latest ratings at press time. For an update, please see our newest ratings based on the 2005 Annual Questionnaire in the December issue of CONSUMER REPORTS and online at ConsumerReports.org.) Here are some of our other findings:

- Overall, respondents were less satisfied with their purchasing experiences at retail stores, which were rated relatively low for selection, knowledge, and helpfulness.
- Apple and PC/Mac Connection were the highest-rated vendors in overall satisfaction and garnered top scores on all ratings except prices.
- Wal-Mart and Best Buy were rated lower than most vendors; moreover, Wal-Mart, along with Sam's Club, rated worse on all factors except for prices, on which both stores were rated average.
- Three retailers each scored above average for prices: Costco, a warehouse store; the Web/catalog retailer PC/Mac Connection; and TigerDirect. All manufacturers were rated average for prices, except for Sony, which posted the lowest score of all vendors.

Manufacturers and retail Web sites/catalogs scored at least above average for selection. The one exception was TigerDirect, which was average.

Guide to the Survey

Ratings are based on 43,384 responses from CONSUMER REPORTS subscribers who completed the 2004 Annual Questionnaire online, covering household computers purchased new from 2003 through June 2004. These results are based on CONSUMER REPORTS online subscribers and may not reflect the experiences of the general public. There were at least 163 responses for each vendor.

Manufacturer Direct refers to purchases from the manufacturer through Web or catalog channels only, not stores. **Retail Store** covers in-store purchases only, not those from retailers' Web sites. **Retail Web site/catalog** includes purchases exclusively through Web or catalog channels.

Reader Score: A score of 100 would mean all respondents had been completely satisfied with their experience; 80 would mean they were very satisfied, on average; 60, fairly well-satisfied. Differences of less than 4 points aren't meaningful. **Selection** of PCs (models, price ranges, etc.), **prices, knowledge** of salespeople or customer-service reps, and **helpfulness** or courtesy of employees are relative and reflect how each vendor compares with the average score. (The last two ratings excluded respondents who purchased their PCs online and did not phone or e-mail the vendor.)

Computer retailers

Better ⊜ ⊖ ○ ◒ ● Worse

	Reader Score (0–100)	Selection	Prices	Knowledge	Helpfulness
MANUFACTURER DIRECT					
Apple/iMac	92	⊜	○	⊜	⊜
IBM	86	⊖	○	⊜	⊜
Dell	84	⊜	○	⊖	○
HP	83	⊖	○	⊖	○
Gateway	83	⊖	○	⊖	○
Sony	82	⊖	●	-	-
Compaq	81	⊖	○	○	○
RETAIL STORE					
Costco	82	●	⊖	●	◒
Micro Center	81	○	○	⊖	○
Office Depot	80	●	○	○	○
Sam's Club	79	●	○	●	●
Staples	77	●	◒	○	○
Circuit City	76	◒	◒	○	○
Fry's Electronics	75	○	○	◒	●
CompUSA	74	○	◒	○	○
Best Buy	73	○	○	○	◒
Wal-Mart	73	●	○	●	●
RETAIL WEB SITE/CATALOG					
PC/Mac Connection.com	91	⊜	⊖	⊜	⊜
CDW.com	87	⊜	○	-	-
PC/Mac Mall.com	84	⊜	○	⊖	○
TigerDirect.com	83	○	⊖	-	-

"-" Indicates insufficient sample.

largements of product photos. Habitués of online catalog venues can snap up specials and closeouts before items go out of stock.

Ordering from a catalog over the phone or the Web is usually quick, but popular items can still be on back-order, even if they seemed to be in stock when you placed the order. If you don't receive your purchase within the promised time, check back. And before you order, check shipping fees—they can vary widely and add significantly to the cost of the order.

WEB STRATEGIES

You can hunt down just about anything on the Web, from potato chips to vacation homes, but you'll find that some items are more e-commerce-compatible than others. Books, music, videos, DVDs, and computer software are big online successes because they're standardized products, and no bricks-and-mortar store is able to stock every title. Branded electronics items also lend themselves to online shopping because it's handy to select them by manufacturer and specific features. Shipping is another important factor: Small, lightweight purchases—books as opposed to, say, refrigerators—are top online sellers.

Perhaps even more than for buying, the Web is immensely useful for researching a purchase. Information that would previously have taken many hours and many phone calls (if it could be found at all) is now available via a simple click of your mouse. Thus armed, you can make better decisions about where to buy, what to buy, and how much to pay.

BUYING THROUGH AUCTIONS

Internet auction sites deal in just about anything people want to sell. Though sellers provide descriptions (and, often, digital images), details about flaws and condition may be fuzzy. Except for sites operated by retailers or businesses, most auction sites do not verify the condition of an item—or whether it really exists. That's why you should read the seller's description for details about an item's condition and value, return policy, warranty information, and promised delivery date, plus an address and telephone number.

Buyers should consider insuring expensive items and be sure that sellers ship packages in a traceable manner to help ensure a successful transaction. If a seller fails to deliver or misrepresents an item, eBay, the largest Internet auction site, will reimburse buyers for up to $175 of their loss. The site also offers links to third-party companies that provide authentication and grading services.

If you purchase something at an auction site, use a credit card (not a debit card) or work out terms with an online escrow service, such as Escrow.com, which processes transactions. (Fees are based on the amount of the transaction, method of payment, and, sometimes, shipping costs.)

At pick-your-own price sites, you name a price for, say, airline tickets, hotels, or a mortgage, and merchants come to you. Priceline originated this type of "reverse auction." The catch: You must provide a credit-card number up front. If Priceline finds the item at your price, your credit card is charged immediately, usually with no cancellation option. Nor can you request a specific brand.

For airline tickets, you are only allowed to make one bid within a seven-day period for the same itinerary; for hotel rooms, within a three-day period. Simply changing your bid amount is considered a duplicate bid and will be rejected automatically. Id you want to immediately big again, you must be willing to change, say, your departure date or hotel quality level.

Home Entertainment

Home Entertainment: Digital Dominates

Digital technology is now found in virtually all the hardware and software for creating, storing, and viewing images and sounds, from music to TV service and sets through cameras and camcorders. Especially notable is the digital dominance of cameras, with digital models now outselling film models.

In some other products, however, analog alternatives are proving to be very resilient. Even as most households are now renting their movies on DVD, VHS tape remains the primary medium for recording TV programs. Sales of high-definition TVs are booming, but a surprising proportion of HDTV owners do not subscribe to a level of digital TV service that takes full advantage of their set. And despite the continuing rise of digital music, fueled by the iPod MP3-player phenomenon, some music lovers continue a retro cult worship of the vinyl LP.

Here are other notable trends in today's home entertainment and imaging marketplace:

Rising quality levels. The benchmark specifications associated with quality continue to rise, especially in video and imaging. More and more televisions are high-definition-capable, meaning they'll display images created with 1,080 (or usually 720) lines rather than the less dense 480-line format of standard-definition images. In digital cameras, entry-level models offer 4 megapixels of image resolution, and many offer 5 or more MP. Camcorders are now almost entirely digital, with image quality that's consistently above that of analog camcorders.

An escalation of format wars. The spread of digital technology has not, alas, led to a notable reduction in the number of proprietary (and noncompatible) transmission and storage formats for content. Digital cameras still use a bewildering number of different storage media. If you own an iPod, with its iTunes software, you can't easily transfer a favorite song to a friend's MP3 player of another brand. DVD recorders employ an alphabet soup of formats—from DVD-RAM to DVD-R, DVD+R, DVD-RW, and more. The imminent arrival of high-definition DVDs should be cause for celebration but will instead likely continue a format war that has some manufacturers and movie studios backing the HD-DVD format and others the rival Blu-Ray format.

Continuing price reductions. As the newest technologies mature, prices continue to drop, inducing the holdouts among consumers to acquire them. The least expensive digital cameras now start at less than $200 or so. HDTVs have continued to drop in price, and digital recorders have now dropped to $200 or so.

CAMCORDERS

Fine picture quality and easy editing have improved the functionality of these moviemakers, especially for digital models.

Those grainy, jumpy home movies of yesteryear are long gone—replaced by home movies shot on digital or analog camcorders. You can edit and embellish the footage with music using your computer, then play it back on your VCR; you can even send it via e-mail.

Digital camcorders, now the dominant type, generally offer very good to excellent picture quality, along with very good sound capability, compactness, and ease of handling. Making copies of a digital recording won't result in a loss of picture or sound quality. You can even take rudimentary still photos with some digital camcorders.

Analog camcorders, now a small part of the market, generally have good picture and sound quality and are less expensive. Some analog units are about as compact and easy to handle as digital models, while others are a bit bigger and bulkier.

WHAT'S AVAILABLE

Sony dominates the camcorder market, with multiple models in a number of formats. Other top brands include Canon, JVC, Panasonic, and Samsung.

Most digital models come in the MiniDV format. Formats such as the disc-based DVD-RAM and DVD-R have also appeared. Some digital models weigh as little as one pound.

MiniDV. Don't let their small size deceive you. Although some models can be slipped into a large pocket, MiniDV camcorders can record very high-quality images. They use a unique tape cassette, and the typical recording time is 60 minutes at standard play (SP) speed. Expect to pay $6.50 for a 60-minute tape. You'll need to use the camcorder for playback—it converts its recording to an analog signal, so it can be played directly into a TV or VCR. If the TV or VCR has an S-video input jack, use it to get a high-quality picture. Price range: $350 to more than $2,000.

Digital 8. Also known as D8, this format gives you digital quality on Hi8 or 8mm cassettes, which cost $6.50 and $3.50, respectively. The Digital 8 format records with a faster tape speed, so a "120-minute" cassette lasts only 60 minutes at SP. Most models can also play your old analog Hi8 or 8mm tapes. Price range: $350 to $800.

Disc-based. Capitalizing on the explosive growth and capabilities of DVD movie discs, these formats offer benefits tape can't provide: long-term durability, a compact medium, and random access to scenes as with a DVD. The 3¼-inch discs record standard MPEG-2 video, the same format used in commercial DVD videos. The amount of recording time varies according to the quality level you select: from 20 minutes per side at the highest-quality setting for DVD-RAM up to about 60 minutes per side at the lowest setting. DVD-RAM discs are not compatible with most DVD players, but the discs can be reused. DVD-R is supposed to be compatible with most DVD players and computer DVD drives, but the discs are write-once. We paid about $25 at a local retailer for a blank DVD-RW. Price range: $700 to $1,000.

Most analog camcorders now use the Hi8 format; VHS-C and Super VHS-C are fading from the market. Blank tapes range in price from $3.50 to $6.50. Analog camcorders usually weigh around 2 pounds. Picture quality is generally good, though a notch below that of digital. Price range: $225 to $500.

FEATURES THAT COUNT

A flip-out **liquid-crystal-display (LCD) viewer** is becoming commonplace on all but the lowest-priced camcorders. You'll find it useful for reviewing footage you've shot and easier to use than the eyepiece viewfinder for certain shooting poses. Some LCD viewers are hard to use in sunlight, a drawback on models that have only a viewer and no eyepiece.

Screens vary from 2½ to 4 inches measured diagonally, with a larger screen offered as a step-up feature on higher-priced models. Since an LCD viewer uses batteries faster than an eyepiece viewfinder does, you don't have as much recording time when the LCD is in use.

An **image stabilizer** automatically reduces most of the shaking that occurs from holding the camcorder as you record a scene. Most stabilizers are electronic; a few are optical. Either type can be effective, though mounting the camcorder on a tripod is the surest way to get steady images. If you're not using a tripod, you can try holding the camcorder with both hands and propping both elbows against your chest.

Full auto switch essentially lets you point and shoot. The camcorder automatically adjusts the color balance, shutter speed, focus, and aperture (also called the "iris" or "f-stop" with camcorders).

Autofocus adjusts for maximum sharpness; **manual focus override** may be needed for problem situations, such as low light. (With some camcorders, you may have to tap buttons repeatedly to get the focus just right.) With many models, you can also control exposure, shutter speed, and white balance.

The **zoom** is typically a finger control—press one way to zoom in, the other way to widen the view. The rate at which the zoom changes will depend on how hard you press the switch. Typical optical zoom ratios range from 10:1 to 26:1. The zoom relies on optical lenses, just like a film camera (hence the term "optical zoom"). Many camcorders offer a digital zoom to extend the range to 400:1 or more, but at a lower picture quality.

For tape-based formats, analog or digital, every camcorder displays **tape speeds** the same way a VCR does. Every model, for example, includes an SP (standard play) speed. Digitals have a slower, LP (long play) speed that adds 50 percent to the recording time. A few 8mm and Hi8 models have an LP speed that doubles the recording time. All VHS-C and S-VHS-C camcorders have an even slower EP (extended play) speed that triples the recording time. With analog camcorders, slower speeds worsen picture quality. Slow speed usually doesn't reduce picture quality on digital camcorders. But using slow speed means sacrificing some seldom-used editing options and may restrict playback on other camcorders.

Disc-based formats have a variety of modes that trade off recording time for image quality.

Quick review lets you view the last few seconds of a scene without having to press a lot of buttons.

For special lighting situations, preset **auto-exposure** settings can be helpful. A "snow & sand" setting, for example, adjusts shutter speed or aperture to accommodate high reflectivity.

A **light** provides some illumination for close shots when the image would otherwise be too dark. **Backlight compensation** increases the exposure slightly when your subject is lit from behind and silhouetted. An **infrared-sensitive recording mode** (also known as night vision, zero lux, or MagicVu) allows shooting in very dim or dark situations, using infrared emitters. You can use it for nighttime shots, although colors won't register accurately in this mode.

Audio/video inputs let you record material from another camcorder or from a VCR, useful for copying part of another video onto your own. (A digital camcorder must have such an input jack if you want to record analog material digitally.) Unlike a built-in microphone, an **external microphone** that is plugged into a microphone jack won't pick up noises from the camcorder itself, and it typically improves audio performance.

A camcorder with **digital still capability** lets you take snapshots, which can be downloaded to your computer. The photo quality is generally inferior to that of a still camera.

Features that may aid editing include a **built-in title generator,** a **time-and-date stamp,** and a **time code,** which is a frame reference of exactly where you are on a tape—the hour, minute, second, and frame. A **remote control** helps when you're using the camcorder as a playback device or when you're using a tripod. **Programmed recording** (a self-timer) starts the camcorder recording at a preset time.

HOW TO CHOOSE

Pick your price range and format. The least-expensive camcorders on the market are analog. All the rest are digital.

Once you've decided which part of the price spectrum to explore, you need to pick a specific recording format. That determines not only how much you'll be spending for tapes or discs but also how much recording time you'll get. The tape-based formats are typically superior in picture quality.

With analog, you can get 120 to 300 minutes of recording time on a Hi8 cassette; with the S-VHS-C or VHS-C formats, you can get only 30 to 120 minutes.

With digital formats that use MiniDV, Digital 8, or MicroMV tapes, you can get at least 60 minutes of recording on a standard cassette. MiniDV and D8 cassettes are the least expensive and easiest to find.

Digital DVD camcorders from Panasonic and Hitachi can accommodate DVD-RAM discs, which can be reused but aren't compatible with all DVD players. All brands also use DVD-R, one-use discs that work in most DVD players. The standard setting yields 60 minutes of recording; the "fine" setting, 30 minutes.

Shop smart

The recording format you choose will determine how much you'll be spending for tapes or discs and how much recording time you'll get.

If you're replacing an older camcorder, think about what you'll do with the tapes you've accumulated. If you don't stay with the same format you've been using, you will probably want to transfer the old tapes to an easily viewed medium, such as a DVD.

If you're buying your first camcorder, concentrate on finding the best one for your budget, regardless of format.

Check the size, weight, and controls. In the store, try different camcorders to make sure they fit your hand and are comfortable to use. Some models can feel disconcertingly tiny. (You'll need to use a tripod if you want rock-steady video, no matter which camcorder you choose.) Most camcorders are designed so that the most frequently used controls—the switch to zoom in and out, and the record button—fall readily to hand. Make sure that the controls are convenient and that you can change the tape or DVD and remove the battery.

Check the flip-out LCD viewer. Most

measure 2.5 inches on the diagonal, but some are larger, adding about $100 to the price. If the viewer seems small and difficult to use or suffers from too much glare, consider trading up to a similar model or a different brand to get a better screen.

Think about the lighting. A camcorder isn't always used outdoors or in a brightly lit room. You can shoot video in dim light, but don't expect miracles. In our tests, using the camcorders' default mode, most produced only fair or poor images in very low light. Many camcorders have settings that can improve performance but can be a challenge to use.

Related CR Report: November 2005
Ratings: page 226
Reliability: page 228

DIGITAL CAMERAS

Digital photography allows you to be more easily involved in the creation of the print than film photography.

Digital cameras, which employ reusable memory cards instead of film, give you far easier creative control than film cameras can. With a digital camera, you can transfer shots to your computer, then crop, adjust color and contrast, and add textures and other special effects. Final results can be made into cards or T-shirts, or sent via e-mail, all using the software that usually comes with the camera. You can make prints on a color inkjet printer, or by dropping off the memory card at one of a growing number of photofinishers. You can upload the file to a photo-sharing Web site for storage, viewing, and sharing with others.

Like camcorders, digital cameras have LCD viewers. Some camcorders can be used to take still pictures, but a typical camcorder's resolution is no match for a good still camera's.

WHAT'S AVAILABLE

The leading brands are Canon, Fujifilm, Hewlett-Packard, Kodak, Olympus, and Sony; other brands come from consumer-electronics, computer, and traditional camera and film companies.

Digital cameras are categorized by how many pixels, or picture elements, the image sensor contains. One megapixel equals 1 million picture elements. A 3-megapixel camera can make excellent 8x10s and pleasing 11x14s. There are also 4- to 8-megapixel models, including point-and-shoot ones; those are well-suited for making larger prints or for maintaining sharpness if you want to use only a portion of the original image. Professional digital cameras use as many as 14 megapixels. Price range: $200 to $400 for 3 megapixels; $250 to $400 for 4 and 5 megapixels; $300 to $1,000 for 6 to 8 megapixels.

FEATURES THAT COUNT

Most digital cameras are highly automated, with features such as **automatic exposure control** (which manages the shutter speed, aperture, or both according to available light) and **autofocus.**

Instead of film, digital cameras typically record their shots onto **flash-memory cards.** Compact Flash and SecureDigital (SD) are the most widely used. Once quite expensive, such cards have tumbled in price—a 128-megabyte card can now cost less than $20. Other types of memory cards used by cameras include MemoryStick, SmartMedia and xD-picture card. A few cameras, mainly some Sony models, use 3¼-inch CD-R or CD-RW discs.

To save images, you transfer them to a computer, typically by connecting the camera to the computer's USB or FireWire port or inserting the memory card into a special reader. Some printers can take memory cards and make prints without putting the images on a computer first. **Image-handling software,** such as Adobe Photoshop Elements, Jasc Paint Shop, Microsoft Picture It, and ACDSee, lets you size, touch up, and crop digital images using your computer. Most digital cameras work with both Windows and Macintosh machines.

The file format commonly used for photos is JPEG, which is a compressed format. Some cameras can save photos in the uncompressed TIFF format, but this setting yields enormous files. Other high-end cameras have a RAW file format, which yields the image data with no processing from the camera and is also uncompressed.

Digital cameras typically have both an **optical viewfinder** and a small color **LCD viewer.** LCD viewers are very accurate in framing the actual image you get—better than most of the optical viewfinders—but they use more battery power and may be hard to see in bright sunlight. You can also view shots you've already taken on the LCD viewer. Many digital cameras provide a video output, so you can view your pictures on a TV set.

Certain cameras let you record an audio clip with a picture. But these clips use additional storage space. Some allow you to record limited video, but the frame rate is often slow and the resolution poor.

A **zoom lens** provides flexibility in framing shots and closes the distance between you and your subject—ideal if you want to quickly switch to a close shot. The typical 3x zoom on mainstream cameras goes from a moderately wide-angle view (35 mm) to moderate telephoto (105 mm). You can find cameras with extended zoom ranges between 8x and 12x, giving added versatility for outdoor photography. Other new cameras go down to 24 or 28 mm at the wide-angle end, making it easier to take in an entire scene in close quarters, such as a crowded party.

Optical zooms are superior to **digital zooms,** which merely magnify the center of the frame without actually increasing picture detail, resulting in a somewhat coarser view.

Sensors in digital cameras are typically about as light-sensitive as ISO 100 film, though some let you increase that setting. (At ISO 100, you'll likely need to use a flash indoors and in low outdoor light.) A camera's **flash range** tells you how far from the camera the flash will provide proper exposure: If the subject is out of range, you'll know to close the distance. But digital cameras can tolerate some underexposure before the image suffers noticeably.

Tech tip

Optical zooms are superior to digital zooms, which merely magnify the center of the frame without actually increasing picture detail, resulting in a somewhat coarser view.

Red-eye reduction shines a light toward your subject just before the main flash. (A camera whose flash unit is farther from the lens reduces the risk of red eye. Computer editing of the image may also correct red eye.) With **automatic flash mode,** the camera fires the flash whenever the light entering the camera registers as insufficient. A few new cameras have built-in red-eye correction capability.

Some cameras that have powerful telephoto lenses now come with **image stabilizers.** These compensate for camera shake, letting you use a slower shutter speed than you otherwise could for following movement. But an image stabilizer won't compensate for the motion of subjects.

Most new 6- to 8-megapixel cameras come with full **manual controls,** including independent controls for shutter and aperture. That gives serious shutterbugs control over depth of field, shooting action, or shooting scenes with tricky lighting.

HOW TO CHOOSE

The first step is to determine how you will use the camera most of the time. Consider these two questions:

How much flexibility to enlarge images do you need? If you mainly want to make 4x6 snapshots, a camera with 3- or 4-megapixel resolution will be fine. Such a camera will also make an 8x10 print of an entire image without alteration that looks as sharp as one from a 6- or 8-megapixel model. But to enlarge the image more or enlarge only part of it, you'll want a 6- to 8-megapixel camera.

How much control do you want over exposure and composition? Cameras meant for automatic point-and-shoot photos, with a 3x-zoom lens, will serve snapshooters as well as dedicated hobbyists much of the time. The full-featured cameras in the 6- to 8-megapixel range offer capabilities that more-dedicated photographers will want to have. Two of the more important capabilities are a zoom range of 5x to 10x or more, which lets you bring distant outdoor subjects close and also lets you shoot candid portraits without getting right in your subject's face, and a full complement of manual controls that let you determine the shutter speed and lens opening.

Once you've established the performance priorities that you need from a camera, you can narrow your choices further by considering these convenience factors:

Size and weight. The smallest, lightest models aren't necessarily inexpensive 3-megapixel cameras. And the biggest and heaviest aren't necessarily found at the high end. If possible, try cameras at the store before you buy. That way, you'll know which one fits your hand best and which can be securely gripped. In our tests, we have found that some of the smallest don't leave much room even for small fingers.

Battery type and life. All digital cameras run on rechargeable batteries, either an expensive battery pack or a set of AAs. In our tests, neither type had a clear performance advantage. The best-performing cameras offer upward of 300 shots on a charge, while the worst manage only about 50. We think it's more convenient to own a camera that accepts AA batteries. You can buy economical, rechargeable cells (plus a charger) and drop in a set of disposable lithium or alkaline batteries if the rechargeables run down in the middle of the day's shooting.

Camera speed. With point-and-shoot cameras like the ones we tested, you must wait after each shot as the camera processes the image. Most models let you shoot an image every few seconds, but a few make you wait 5 seconds or more. They may frustrate you when you're taking photos in sequence.

Your other cameras. If you're adding a camera to your lineup or trading up to a more versatile model, look first for one that's compatible with the other cameras. If it is, you can share memory cards and batteries. Designs within a camera brand line are often similar. So staying with the brand you have lowers the learning curve on the new camera for family members who switch between cameras.

Related CR Report: November 2005
Ratings: page 241
Reliability: page 246

DVD PLAYERS

These devices play high-quality videos and CDs, and prices are lower than ever.

The DVD has come to dominate video even more quickly than the CD conquered audio in the 1980s. Along with changing what we watch—discs rather than tapes—DVDs are changing how we watch. The digital format makes it easy to go directly to desired sections of a movie, and the picture and sound quality surpass what you'll get with a videotape. One DVD can store a complete two-hour-plus movie with a Dolby Digital or DTS soundtrack containing up to eight audio channels. There's also room for extra material such as multiple languages, behind-the-scenes documentaries, and commentary by the director or actors.

High-definition DVD players are expected to hit the market by the beginning of 2006.

DVD players can play standard audio CDs, and some models fully support DVD-Audio or SACD, two competing high-resolution audio formats offering multichannel sound.

While DVD players are playback-only devices, DVD recorders record as well as play. Prices of recorders have dropped considerably in the past few years, with entry-level models now selling for less than $200.

WHAT'S AVAILABLE

Apex, Panasonic, Sony, and Toshiba are among the biggest-selling brands of DVD players. Virtually all new DVD players are progressive-scan models. When used with a conventional TV, these players provide the usual high DVD picture quality. With a TV that can display high-definition (HD) or enhanced-definition (ED) images, image quality is slightly better. (That's because HD and ED sets support the player's progressive-scan 480p mode, drawing 480 consecutive lines on the screen. By comparison, with a conventional TV, every other line is drawn and then interlaced or combined, a resolution referred to as 480i.) A player can be connected directly to your TV for viewing movies or routed through your receiver to play movies and audio CDs on your sound system. Progressive-scan models come in single-disc and multidisc versions. The few nonprogressive-scan players now on the market are mostly single-disc models; those tend to be the cheapest type.

Single-disc consoles. Even low-end models usually include all the video outputs you might want. Price range: less than $60 to more than $300.

Multidisc consoles. Like CD changers, these players accommodate more than one disc at a time, typically five. DVD jukeboxes that hold 400 or so discs are also available. Price range: $100 to $800.

Portables. These DVD players generally come with a small wide-screen-format LCD screen and batteries that claim to provide three hours or more of playback. Some low-priced models don't come with a screen; they're intended for users who plan to connect the device to a television. You pay extra for portability either way. Price range: $150 to $800.

FEATURES THAT COUNT

DVD-based movies often come in various formats. **Aspect-ratio control** lets you choose between the 4:3 viewing format of conventional TVs (4 inches wide for every 3 inches high) and the 16:9 ratio of newer, wide-screen sets.

A DVD player gives you all sorts of control over the picture—control you may never have known you needed. **Picture zoom** lets you zoom in on a specific frame. **Black-level adjustment** brings out the detail in dark parts of the screen image. If you've ever wanted to see certain action scenes from different angles, **multi-angle capability** gives you that opportunity. Note that this feature and some others work only with certain discs.

A DVD player enables you to navigate the disc in a number of ways. Unlike a VHS tape, most DVDs are sectioned. **Chapter preview** lets you scan the opening seconds of each section or chapter until you find what you want; a related feature, **chapter gallery,** shows thumbnails of section or chapter opening scenes. **Go-to by time** lets you enter how many hours and minutes into the disc you'd like to skip to. **Marker functions** allow easy indexing of specific sections.

To get the most from a DVD player, you need to hook it up to the TV with the best available connection. A **composite-video connection** to the TV can produce a very good picture, but there will be some loss of detail and some color artifacts such as adjacent colors bleeding into each other. Using the TV's **S-video input** can improve picture quality. It keeps the black-and-white and the color portions of the signal separated, producing more picture detail and fewer color defects than composite-video.

Component-video, sometimes not provided on the lowest-end models, improves on S-video by splitting the color signal, resulting in a wider range of color. If you connect a DVD player via an S-video or component connection, don't be surprised if you have to adjust the television-picture setup when you switch to a picture coming from a VCR or a cable box that uses a **radio-frequency** (RF, also called antenna/cable) connection or a composite connection.

Two newer outputs found on some players, **Digital Video Interface (DVI)** and **High Definition Multimedia Interface (HDMI),** are intended for use with digital TVs with corresponding inputs. They may be used to pass digital 480p and upconverted higher-resolution video signals. These connections potentially allow the content providers to control your ability to record the content.

Another benefit of DVD players is the ability to enjoy movies with **multichannel surround sound.** To reap the full sound experience of the audio encoded into DVD titles, you'll need a Dolby Digital receiver and six speakers, including a subwoofer. (For 6.1 and 7.1 soundtracks, you'll need seven or eight speakers.) **Dolby Digital decoding built-in** refers to a DVD player that decodes the multichannel audio before the audio receiver; without the built-in circuitry, you'd need to have the decoder built into the receiver or, in rare instances, use a separate decoder box to take advantage of the audio. (A Dolby Digital receiver will decode an older format, Dolby Pro Logic, as well.) Most players also support **Digital Theater System (DTS)** decoding for titles using that six- or seven-channel encoding format. When you're watching DVD-based movies, **dynamic audio-range control** helps keep explosions and other noisy sound effects from seeming too loud.

In addition to commercial DVD titles, DVD players often support playback or display of numerous other disc formats. They include CD-R/RW recordings of standard audio CDs; the recordable DVD formats DVD+R/RW, DVD-R/RW, and DVD-RAM; Video CD (VCD); and DVD-Audio and Super Audio CD (SACD). They can also play CD-R/RW discs containing MP3 and Windows Media Audio (WMA) files and JPEG picture files. Make sure a model you're considering plays the discs and formats you use now or may want to use in the future.

DVD players also provide features such as **multilingual support,** which lets you choose dialog or subtitles in different languages for a given movie. **Parental control** lets parents "lock out" films by their rating code.

HOW TO CHOOSE

Buy a progressive-scan model unless the lowest price is your highest priority. Although you won't see progressive-scan picture quality on a conventional analog TV, it's worth spending a little extra for a progressive-scan player if you might get a digital (probably HD) TV at some point. You'll have a wider choice of products as well, since almost all new players are progressive-scan. It's definitely worth getting a progressive-scan player for use with a digital TV, which is capable of displaying the smoother picture these players can deliver.

Choose a multidisc model if you want continuous music. A single-disc player is fine for movies and CDs one at a time. If you want this to be your main music player, consider a multidisc player. Note, though, that multidisc models are typically about 1 to 2 inches taller and 6 to 7 inches deeper than single-disc players.

Make sure there are enough connections of the types you want. Virtually all DVD players now have outputs for optimal connection to most TV sets. A few players have DVI or HDMI connectors that are compatible with some new TVs, though these don't necessarily offer improved picture quality. If you want to use digital-audio connections from the DVD player to a receiver, make sure the DVD player's digital-audio outputs match the receiver's inputs. Some receivers use a coaxial input; others, an optical input. If you have an older receiver that lacks 5.1 surround-sound decoding, look for a player with a decoder for Dolby Digital.

Consider which, if any, special playback formats matter. All DVD players can play prerecorded DVDs and CDs. Most models also play several types of discs you record yourself, such as DVD-R, DVD+R, and CD-R/RW. Most can read DVD+RW, but the ability to read DVD-RW discs depends on how they were recorded. Some can also play DVD-RAM discs. Most models play CD-audio and MP3 music recorded on discs you burn yourself. You'll need to shop around more if you want to play Windows Media Audio (WMA) files, video CD, and high-resolution SACD and DVD-Audio discs in their original format.

Do you want to present slide shows on your TV? Then choose a model that can read the memory card for your camera or JPEG image files from a digital camera or scanner that you have burned onto a disc.

Related CR Report: November 2005

HOME THEATER IN A BOX

All-in-one systems that hook up to your TV and DVD player can minimize the setup hassle.

Good speakers and the components for a home-theater system cost less than ever. But selecting all those components can be time consuming, and connecting them a challenge—even for audiophiles. You can avoid some hassle by buying an all-in-one "home theater in a box" system that combines a receiver with a speaker set, wiring, and often a DVD player. Unless you're very demanding, you'll compromise little on quality.

WHAT'S AVAILABLE

Panasonic and Sony are among the best-selling brands in the market. Home-theater packages include a receiver that can decode digital-audio soundtracks and six to eight compact, matched speakers—two front, one center, two to four surround speakers for the rear, and a subwoofer. You also get all the cables and wiring you need, usually color-coded and sometimes labeled for easy setup. Most systems now include a progressive-scan DVD player (either a separate component or one built into the receiver) and a powered subwoofer. Price range: $275 to $1,000 for typical systems with a DVD player and powered subwoofer, and $2,000 or more for systems aimed at audiophiles.

Tech tip

To reap the full sound experience of the audio encoded into DVD titles, you'll need a Dolby Digital receiver and five speakers, and a subwoofer.

FEATURES THAT COUNT

The receivers in home-theater-in-a-box systems tend to be on the simple side. They usually include both Dolby Digital and DTS decoders. Controls should be easy to use. Look for a front panel with displays and controls grouped by function and labeled clearly. An **onscreen display** lets you control the receiver via a television screen.

Switched AC outlets let you plug in other components and turn on the whole system with one button. The receivers have about 20 or more **presets** you can use for AM and FM stations. Most receivers also offer a **sleep timer,** which turns them on or off at a preset time. **Remote controls** are most useful when they have clear labels and different-shaped and color-coded buttons grouped by function. A universal remote can control a number of devices.

A component-video output on the receiver that can connect to a relatively high-end TV allows for better picture quality if you choose to switch video signals through your receiver; however, not many receivers have such an output. Instead, most have S-video output, which is better than a composite-video or RF (antenna) connection.

Look also for an S-video input, which lets you pipe signals from an external DVD player, digital camcorder, or certain cable or satellite boxes through the system. Any player that you might want to connect will need the same digital-audio connections, either optical or coaxial, as those of the included receiver. And if you want to make occasional connections at the front—perhaps for a camcorder or an MP3 player—you'll need front-panel inputs.

DSP (for digital signal processor) modes use digital circuitry to duplicate the sound measurements of, say, a concert hall. Each mode represents a different listening environment. A **bass-boost switch** amplifies the deepest sounds.

A **subwoofer** may be powered or unpowered. Either type will do the job, but a powered subwoofer provides more control over bass and lets a powered receiver drive the other speakers.

An **integrated DVD player,** available with some models, typically has fewer features than does a stand-alone DVD player. Features to expect are **track programmability** (more useful for playing CDs than DVDs), **track repeat,** and **disc repeat.** If you want more features, a stand-alone DVD player may be the wiser choice.

HOW TO CHOOSE

Decide whether you want a DVD player. If not, you may save money by buying a system without one. If you want a DVD in the bundle, consider whether you need a multidisc model that will provide uninterrupted play of music CDs and DVD movies. Most systems have a progressive-scan player. Those offer regular DVD picture quality when used with a conventional TV but can deliver a smoother image when paired with a TV capable of displaying high-definition (HD) signals. Some bundled DVD players offer support for multichannel DVD-Audio and SACD music discs, although not in their original, high-resolution format.

Do you want a separate DVD player or one integrated with the receiver? Systems with separate DVD players and receivers tend to offer fuller functionality and more connections than those that integrate both units in one box. Integrated units are somewhat simpler to set up, but they tend to be bulkier and may not allow you to connect video devices other than a TV to the receiver. Any other devices would have to be hooked up directly to the TV.

Make sure there are enough inputs. Most home-theater systems have enough audio and video inputs for an external DVD player, a VCR, a CD player, and a cable box or satellite receiver. See if a model you're considering has enough of the type of inputs you want, given that each type is capable of conveying a different level of video quality. With audio inputs, there are two points to check. Choose a model that matches the output on your CD or DVD player, digital-cable box, or satellite receiver. If you want to connect a turntable, you'll need a phono input—hard to come by. And if you want to make occasional connections at the front—perhaps for a camcorder or an MP3 player—you'll need front-panel inputs.

Get features that suit your needs. With any system, you can be assured of basics such as AM/FM tuners and Dolby Digital and DTS surround-sound support. You almost always get Dolby Pro Logic II, which offers basic surround sound from TV and VHS programs and music CDs.

Features such as front-panel inputs and onscreen displays for making adjustments on the TV screen are less common than on component receivers, so make sure a system has what you want. A few models offer newer Dolby and DTS surround formats that process 6.1 or 7.1 channels. Those formats aren't widely used in movies at this point but could become more common in the future.

Shop smart

Controls should be easy to use. Look for a front panel with displays and controls grouped by function and labeled clearly.

Related CR Report: November 2004

MP3 PLAYERS

These devices let you play music you've either downloaded from the Web or "ripped" from your own CD collection.

Portable MP3 players store digital music in their internal memories, on removable storage media, or a combination of both. You don't buy prerecorded discs or tapes but instead create your own digital files on a computer using software often supplied with a player. You can convert music from your favorite audio CDs, tapes, and even records to digital files—a process known as ripping—or download music from the Internet. In either case you can listen to the files on your computer or transfer them to a portable MP3 player so you have music to go.

The term MP3 has become shorthand for digital audio of every stripe, but it's actually just one of the formats used to encode music. The abbreviation stands for Moving Pictures Expert Group 1 Audio Layer 3, a file format that compresses music to one-tenth to one-twelfth the space it would take in uncompressed form. Other encoding schemes include Windows Media Audio (WMA), the most widely supported; Advanced Audio Codec (AAC), and Adaptive Transform Acoustic Coding (ATRAC), a proprietary format used by Sony products. Most MP3 players can handle formats in addition to MP3, typically WMA. Plus the software that comes with them may convert incompatible files into formats the player can handle.

Despite copyright-infringement lawsuits by the music industry, free music-sharing Web sites carry on. Online music stores, led by Apple's iTunes, allow users to download music legally for a fee. Downloaded songs from contemporary artists typically cost less than $1 per song, or $10 for an entire album. Copy-protection measures prevent these songs from being shared with other people over a network and limits the number of times users can transfer them to MP3 players or burn them onto CDs. That limitation is typically three to 10 times, depending on the service. Other legal online music sources include BuyMusic (WMA), Musicmatch (WMA), and Napster (WMA), retailers such as Wal-Mart (WMA), as well as electronics giant Sony (ATRAC). Some of these sites also offer subscription-based services, typically less than $10 per month, that allow you to listen to music on your computer in real time (streaming). Downloading music that you transfer to an MP3 player or CD costs extra, but fees are generally lower than the ones for non-subscribers.

One caveat of these services is that their copy-protected songs won't work with all players. Also keep in mind that managing MP3 files and using an MP3 player is still more demanding than using an audio CD player.

WHAT'S AVAILABLE

Major brands include Apple, Archos, Creative Labs, Dell, iRiver, Panasonic, Rio, Samsung, and Sony. Other, smaller brands are on the market as well. MP3 playback has been incorporated into other handheld portable products, including CD players, MiniDisc players, cell phones, and personal digital assistants (PDAs).

Flash-memory players. These are solid-state devices with no moving parts, which eliminates skipping, even on a bumpy road or during a grueling jog. They're also the smallest and lightest category, which makes them easier to carry around. Sizes range from as small as a thick matchbook to the size of a large pocket watch. Weight usually ranges from about 1 to 3 ounces. Most of the players have 128 or more megabytes (MB) of internal memory; 256 MB can hold about four hours of MP3-formatted music (about 60 songs) recorded at a CD-quality setting. You can fit more music into memory if you compress songs into smaller files, but that may result in lower audio quality.

Some flash-memory players also have expansion slots to add more memory via card slots or "backpack" modules on the player. Common expansion memory formats include Compact Flash, MultiMedia, Secure Digital, and SmartMedia. Sony players may use a MagicGate MemoryStick, a copyright-protected version of Sony's existing MemoryStick media. Memory-card capacities range from about 32 MB to 1 gigabyte (GB). Memory costs have gradually dropped. Price range: about $100 to $200 for the player; $25 to $40 for a 64-MB memory card.

Hard-disk players. These devices have a hard drive that can hold hundreds and even thousands of songs. Storage capacity can reach 80 gigabytes (GB), enough for more than 1,000 hours of music. But often that extra capacity translates into a bulkier, heavier player. Some are bigger than a portable CD player and weigh up to a pound. Hard-disk players hold about 20 GB of music files, are about the size of a deck of cards, and typically weigh half a pound. Smaller still are microdrive players, which tend to be palm-sized and weigh about a quarter-pound. Their drives typically provide about 4 to 6 GB of storage, but that's still enough room for many hours of continuous music. Some also have memory-card slots to transfer files. Price range: $180 and up.

Disc players with MP3 compatibility. Flash-memory and hard-disk portable players aren't the only way to enjoy digital music. Many of today's portable CD and MiniDisc players can play digital music saved on their discs, and may support the copyright-protected formats from online music stores. Controls and displays are comparable to portable MP3 players, and you can group songs on each disc according to artist, genre, and other categories. A CD, with its 650- to 800-MB storage capacity, can hold more than 10 hours of MP3-formatted music at a CD-quality setting. You can create MP3 CDs using your PC's CD burner.

Sony's MiniDisc players, the other disc option, generally have smaller dimensions than portable CD players. MiniDiscs are smaller, removable optical disks protected by a plastic case, similar in size and shape to a 3.5-inch floppy disk. They can be recorded over many times. According to Sony, models that accept a Hi-MD disk can store up to 45 hours of music. Price range: $100 to $200 for players; 50 cents to $4 for blank CDs; $1.50 to $7 for MiniDiscs.

FEATURES THAT COUNT

Software and hardware. Most MP3 players come with music management software to convert your CDs into the audio playback format the player can handle. You can also organize your music collection according to artist, album, genre, and a variety of other categories, as well as create playlists to suit any mood or occasion. All come with software to help you shuttle music between your PC and the player via a Universal Serial Bus (USB) or FireWire connection. All players work with Windows PCs, and many support the Macintosh platform.

Shop smart

Some convenient features include an FM radio tuner and a built-in microphone or line input for recording, as well as adapters or a line output for patching the player into your car or home audio system.

Player upgradability. On most models, the firmware—the built-in operating instructions—can be upgraded so the player does not become obsolete. Upgrades can add or enhance features, fix bugs, and add support for other audio formats and operating systems.

Display. Most MP3 players have a liquid crystal display (LCD) screen, sometimes a color one, that allows you to view the song title, track number, amount of memory remaining, battery life indicator, and other functions. Some displays present a list of tracks from which you can easily make a selection, while others show only one track at a time, requiring you to advance through individual tracks to find the desired one.

On some of the models you can access the player's function controls via a wired or infrared remote control.

Sound enhancement. Expect some type of equalizer, which allows you to adjust the sound in various ways. A custom setting via separate bass and treble controls or adjustable equalizers gives you the most control over the sound.

Playback controls. Volume, track play/pause, and forward/reverse controls are standard. Most portable MP3 players let you set a play mode so you can repeat one or all music tracks, or play tracks in a random order, also referred to as "shuffle" mode. An A-B repeat feature allows you to set bookmarks and repeat a section of the music track.

Useful extras. In addition to playing music, most MP3 players can function as external hard drives, allowing you to shuttle files from one PC to another. Some allow you to view text files, photos, and videos on their LCD screens. Other convenient features include an FM radio tuner, a built-in microphone or line input for recording, as well as adapters or a line output for patching the player into your car's audio system.

HOW TO CHOOSE

Because digital music players are still a relatively new market, new portable models with more features and greater capabilities are continually coming out. Decide how much you're willing to spend on a unit you may want to replace in a year or two. Here are some considerations before you buy:

Be sure your computer can handle it. Make sure any player you're considering is compatible with your Windows or Macintosh computer (including the version of the operating system your computer uses). Keep in mind that some operating system upgrades can exceed the price of a player. Your computer must have USB or FireWire ports. Consider high-speed Internet access if you plan on downloading much of your music. Also keep in mind that getting started can be tricky with some players. An older computer may not recognize the player, so you may have to seek help from the manufacturer.

Weigh capacity vs. size. Some MP3 players can serenade you for weeks without repeating a tune—a great feature to have on long excursions but perhaps not as necessary on short visits to the gym. Consider a flash-memory model if a lower price, smaller size, less weight and long playback time are more important to you than a vast selection of tunes. Look for flash models that can accept external memory cards to expand song capacity. If you have a large music collection that you want to keep with you, determine whether a hard-disk player may make more sense. However, a hard-disk player is generally more complicated to manage than a flash-memory player—and more vulnerable to damage if dropped. For some, navigating through the menus or directories (folders) of songs may also take longer.

Hard-disk players range in size, generally in step with capacity. So-called microdrive players are about the size of a credit card, and a 4-GB model can hold about 1,000 songs, whereas models with 20-GB hard disks are about the size of a deck of cards and can hold about 5,000 songs.

Consider download choices. Be aware that online music sources are limited with some models. For example, iPods and Sony players only work with one online music store. Owners of players that support the copy-protected WMA formats, like those from Creative, Rio, and RCA, have access to the greatest number of online stores, and, often, the best deals. Some players won't play music purchased from any online store. Downloading "free" music from such online sources as peer-to-peer Web sites is another option. But you risk a copyright-infringement lawsuit by the music industry. You'll also increase your exposure to a host of nasty computer viruses and spyware programs that tend to hitch rides on songs swapped on these sites.

Also, note that with most players, you have choices when it comes to software for recording (ripping) music. You can use the software that comes with your computer or player, such as Apple iTunes, Musicmatch, Napster, or Windows Media Player, or download other freeware or shareware applications. If the program has the software plug-in for your player, you can transfer the music to your player directly; otherwise you'll need to use the program that came with your player to perform the transfer.

Ensure upgradability. Regardless of which player you choose, look for one with upgradable firmware for adding or enhancing player features, as well as accommodating newer encoding schemes or variations of compression. Firmware is coded instructions in read-only memory. Upgrading firmware can be a time-consuming and sometimes risky process. MP3 players use several methods for upgrading; one method, which executes the upgrade file on the computer while the player is still attached, can cause permanent damage to the player if there's even a slight interruption during execution. Upgrades can be found at the manufacturer and music-management software application Web sites.

Consider power consumption and battery type. With any portable device, batteries are a consideration. Our tests found a wide variation among the players. Depending on the player settings, some will run out of power after only five hours of play, while others can play music for more than 70 hours before their batteries give out. Flash-memory players tend to have longer playback times than hard-disk players. Many flash memory players use AA or AAA batteries and can accept either standard alkaline or rechargeable batteries—convenient when electrical outlets are hard to find. Other players use a rechargeable nonstandard "block-" or "gumstick-" shaped nickel metal-hydride (Ni-MH) or lithium-ion (Li-ion) removable battery, which is both more expensive and harder to find. Many hard-drive players use a nonremovable rechargeable battery. When the battery can no longer hold a charge, the player has to be sent back to the manufacturer for service—a costly procedure if the product is no longer under warranty.

Consider ergonomics and design. Whichever type of MP3 player you choose, make sure you'll be comfortable using the device. Look for a display and controls that are easy to read and that can be worked with one hand. Because sizes and shapes vary widely, check to see that the player fits comfortably in your pockets, and that it's easy to fish it out when you need to access controls.

Related CR Report: November 2004

RECEIVERS

For a home-theater surround-sound system, look for a receiver that can decode both Dolby Digital and DTS soundtracks.

The receiver is the brain of a home-entertainment system. It provides AM and FM radio tuners, stereo and surround sound, and switching capabilities. It's also the heart of the setup. Most of the devices in a home-entertainment system connect to it, including audio components such as speakers, a CD player, cassette deck, and turntable, as well as video sources such as a TV, DVD player, VCR, and cable and satellite boxes. Even as receivers take on a bigger role in home entertainment, they're losing some audio-related features that were common years back, such as tape monitors and phono inputs. Manufacturers say they must eliminate those less-used features to make room for others.

WHAT'S AVAILABLE

Sony is by far the biggest-selling brand. Other top-selling brands include Denon, JVC, Kenwood, Onkyo, Panasonic, Pioneer, RCA, and Yamaha. Most models now are digital, designed for the six-channel surround-sound formats encoded in most DVDs and some TV fare, such as high-definition (HD) programming. Here are the types you'll see, from least to most expensive:

Stereo. Basic receivers accept the analog stereo signals from a tape deck, CD player, or turntable. They provide two channels that power a pair of stereo speakers. For a simple music setup, add a DVD or CD player to play CDs, or a cassette deck for tapes. For rudimentary home theater, add a TV and DVD player or VCR. Power typically runs 50 to 100 watts per channel. Price range: $125 to $250.

Dolby Pro Logic. Dolby Pro Logic, Pro Logic II, and Pro Logic IIx are the analog home-theater surround-sound standard. Receivers that support it can take a Dolby-encoded two-channel stereo source from your TV, DVD player, or hi-fi VCR and output it to four to six speakers—three in front, and one to three in back. Power for Dolby Pro Logic models is typically 60 to 150 watts per channel. Price range: $150 to $300 or more.

Dolby Digital. Currently the prevailing digital surround-sound standard, a Dolby Digital 5.1 receiver has a built-in decoder for six-channel audio capability—front left and right, front center, two rear, and a powered subwoofer for low-frequency, or bass, effects (that's where the ".1" comes in). Dolby Digital is the sound format for most DVDs, HDTV, digital cable TV, and some satellite-TV broadcast systems. Newer versions of Dolby Digital add one or two back surround channels for a total of seven-channel (6.1) and eight-channel (7.1) sound, respectively. To take advantage of true surround-sound capability, you'll need speakers that do a good job of reproducing full-spectrum sound. Dolby Digital is backward-compatible and supports earlier versions of Dolby such as Pro Logic. Power for Dolby Digital receivers is typically 75 to 150 watts per channel. Price range: $200 to $500 or more.

DTS. A rival to Dolby Digital 5.1, Digital Theater Systems also offers six channels, and newer versions have additional rear channels. It's a less common form of digital surround sound that is used in some movie tracks. Both DTS and Dolby Digital are often found on the same receivers. Power for DTS models is typically 75 to 150 watts per channel. Price range: $200 to $500 or more.

THX-certified. The high-end receivers that meet this quality standard include full support for Dolby Pro Logic, Dolby Digital, and DTS. THX Select is the standard for components designed for small and average-sized rooms; THX Ultra is for larger rooms. Power for THX models is typically 100 to 170 watts per channel. Price range: $500 to $2,500 and up.

FEATURES THAT COUNT

Controls should be easy to use. Look for a front panel with displays and controls clearly labeled and grouped by function. **Onscreen display** lets you control the receiver via a TV screen, a squint-free alternative to using the receiver's tiny LED or LCD display. **Switched AC outlets** (expect one or two) let you plug in other components and turn the whole system on and off with one button.

Remote controls are most useful when they have clear labels and buttons that light up for use in dim rooms. It's best if the buttons have different shapes and are color-coded and grouped by function—a goal seldom achieved in receiver remotes. A **learning remote** can receive programming data for other devices via their remotes' infrared signal; on some remotes, the necessary codes for other manufacturers' devices are built-in.

Input/output jacks matter more on a receiver than on any other component of your home theater. Clear labeling, color-coding, and logical groupings of the many jacks on the rear panel can help avert glitches during setup such as reversed speaker polarities and mixed-up inputs and outputs. Input jacks situated on the front panel make for easy connections to camcorders, video games, MP3 players, digital cameras, MiniDisc players, and PDAs.

A stereo receiver will give you audio inputs and no video jacks. Digital receivers with Dolby Pro Logic will have several types of video inputs, including composite and S-video and sometimes component-video. **S-video** and **component-video jacks** allow you to route signals from DVD players and other high-quality video sources through the receiver to the TV. Digital receivers also have **analog 5.1 audio inputs.** These accept input from a DVD player with its own built-in Dolby Digital decoder, an outboard decoder, or other components with multichannel analog signals, such as a DVD-Audio or SACD player. This enables the receiver to convey up to six channels of sound or music to your speakers. Dolby Digital and DTS receivers have the most complete array of audio and video inputs, often with several of a given type to accommodate multiple components.

Tone controls adjust bass and treble, allowing you to correct room acoustics and satisfy your personal preferences. A **graphic equalizer** breaks the sound spectrum into three or more sections, giving you slightly more control over the full audio spectrum. Instead of tone controls, some receivers come with tone presets such as Jazz, Classical, or Rock, each accentuating a different frequency pattern; often you can craft your own styles.

Tech tip

To take advantage of true surround-sound capability, you'll need speakers that do a good job of reproducing full-spectrum sound.

DSP (digital signal processor) modes use a computer chip to duplicate the sound characteristics of a concert hall and other listening environments. A **bass-boost** switch amplifies the deepest sounds, and **midnight mode** reduces loud sounds and amplifies quiet ones in music or soundtracks.

Sometimes called "one touch," a **settings memory** lets you store settings for each source to minimize differences in volume, tone, and other settings when switching between sources. A similar feature, **loudness memory,** is limited to volume settings alone.

Tape **monitor** lets you either listen to one source as you record a second on a tape deck or listen to the recording as it's being made. **Automatic radio tuning** includes such features as seek (automatic searching for the next in-range station) and 20 to 40 **presets** to call up your favorite stations.

To catch stations too weak for the seek

mode, most receivers also have a **manual stepping knob** or buttons, best in one-channel increments. But most models creep in half- or quarter-steps, meaning a lot of button tapping to find the frequency you want. **Direct tuning** of frequencies lets you tune a radio station by entering its frequency on a keypad.

HOW TO CHOOSE

First, don't assume that pricey brands outperform less costly ones. We've found fine performers at all prices. Points to consider:

How many devices do you want to connect? Even low-end digital receivers generally have enough video and audio inputs for a CD or DVD player, a VCR, and a cable box or satellite receiver. Mid- and high-priced models usually have more inputs, so you can connect additional devices, such as a camcorder, a digital video recorder such as a TiVo box, or a game system.

The number of inputs isn't the only issue; the type also matters. Composite-video inputs, the most basic type, can be used with everything from an older VCR to a new DVD player. S-video and component-video inputs are used mostly by digital devices such as DVD players and satellite receivers. If you have such digital devices or may add them, get a receiver with a few S-video and/or component-video inputs. Both can provide better video quality than composite-video.

All these video inputs require a companion audio input. The basic left/right audio inputs can be used with almost any device to provide stereo sound. A turntable requires a phono input, which is available on fewer models than in years past.

To get multichannel sound from DVD players, digital-cable boxes, and satellite receivers, you generally use a digital-audio input. With this input, digitally encoded multichannel sound is relayed on one cable to the receiver, which decodes it into separate channels. The input on the receiver must be the same type—either optical, the more common type, or coaxial—as the output on the other device. You usually must buy cables, about $10 and up, for digital-audio, S-video, and component-video connections. You often have to buy speaker cables as well.

What kind of sound do you want from movies? All new digital receivers support Dolby Digital and DTS, the surround-sound formats used on most movies. Both provide 5.1 channels. Most receivers also support Dolby Pro Logic, Pro Logic II, and sometimes Pro Logic IIx. If you want the latest type of surround sound, look for a receiver that supports Dolby Digital EX and DTS-ES. These offer 6.1 or 7.1 channels, subtly enhancing the rear surround. Fairly few movies using these formats are available, but offerings should increase.

What kind of music do you like? Any receiver can reproduce stereo from regular CDs. Most models have digital signal processing (DSP) modes that process a CD's two channels to simulate a sound environment such as a concert hall. For multichannel music from SACD or DVD-Audio discs, get a receiver with 5.1 analog inputs.

How big is your room? Make sure a receiver has the oomph to provide adequate volume: at least 50 watts per channel in a typical 12-by-20-foot living room, or 85 watts for a 15-by-25-foot space. A huge room, plush furnishings, or a noisy setting all call for more power.

Is the receiver compatible with your speakers? If you like to blast music for hours on end, get a receiver rated to handle your speakers' impedance. Most receivers are rated for 6-ohm and 8-ohm speakers. If used with 4-ohm speakers, such a receiver could overheat and shut down or be damaged.

Is it easy to use? Most receivers have legible displays and well-labeled function buttons. Some add an onscreen menu, which displays settings on your TV screen. An auto-calibration feature adjusts sound levels and balance to improve the surround effect. Models with a test-tone function for setting speaker levels help you balance the sound yourself.

Two tips: When deciding where to place your receiver, allow 4 inches or so of space behind it for cables and at least 2 inches on top for venting to prevent overheating. If setting up a home theater is more than you want to tackle, consider calling in a professional installer. Retailers often offer an installation service or can refer you to one.

Related CR Report: December 2004

SETTING UP A HOME THEATER

Adding surround sound to a TV can transform the viewing and listening experience even more than buying a bigger set. Most TV sound can be improved by adding external speakers; a pair of self-powered speakers is a simple, easy way to do that. But for a real home-theater experience, you need a big TV, a video source, a surround-decoding receiver/amplifier, and five speakers plus a subwoofer. Following is an overview of the whole system.

HOW SURROUND SOUND WORKS

Surround sound adds more channels to the familiar two-channel stereophonic sound for stronger movie-theater realism, allowing additional speakers to carry the multichannel sound found on movies.

What you'll hear depends on three things: the format used for the source (a TV show or DVD, for instance), the software decoder (on the receiver or DVD player) used to decipher the format, and the number of speakers you have. If your gear lacks the latest, most sophisticated decoder, it can still handle a TV broadcast or DVD, but it will do so with fewer audio channels and less dramatic effect. Conversely, state-of-the-art hardware can play older material only because new decoders are generally backward-compatible with early formats. Again, you'll hear fewer channels.

The following is a rundown on the major formats:

Dolby Surround, an early version of surround sound, is an analog encoding scheme used mostly for VHS movies and TV shows. It combines four channels into stereo soundtracks. With no decoder—say, on a TV—you'll hear stereo.

With a **Dolby Pro Logic** decoder, you'll hear four channels: left, right, center (unlike Dolby Surround), and one limited-range surround channel. A newer version, **Pro Logic II,** has the same left, right, and center channels but also has two discrete, full-range surround channels for a total of five channels. Most new receivers have Pro Logic II; older models may have only Pro Logic. You'll need four or five speakers for optimal sound.

The next step up is **Dolby Digital,** a digital encoding scheme that's also called Dolby Digital 5.1. Like Pro Logic II, it has full-range left and right channels in front and rear plus a center channel; it adds a subwoofer channel for deep bass (called ".1" because it's limited to low-frequency effects). Dolby Digital is used on digital media, such as DVDs, digital cable, digital broadcast TV, and satellite transmissions. Virtually all new receivers and some DVD players have Dolby Digital decoders. You'll need five full-range speakers and a subwoofer for optimal sound.

DTS (Digital Theater Systems) is a rival to Dolby Digital, also with six channels. It's offered on most new receivers and on some DVD players. It calls for the same speaker setup as Dolby Digital.

Dolby Digital EX and **DTS-ES** are "extended surround" formats that add either a center-rear surround channel or an extra pair of rear-surround speakers that go behind the listener. With Dolby Digital EX, the two flavors are referred to, respectively, as Dolby Digital 6.1 (with three surround speakers) and 7.1 (with four surround speakers). Both formats are still relatively new and not widely used on either equipment or programming. At this stage, they are mostly for video enthusiasts. With them, you'll need seven or eight speakers to achieve the full effect.

THX is a certification that indicates a multichannel audio product has passed certain performance and ergonomic tests and can process sound to simulate movie-theater acoustics.

CONNECTING THE COMPONENTS

The way you connect your video and audio equipment can affect the quality of the sound and images you receive. Here's what you need to know about each.

Video connections. Even the best TV set won't live up to its potential without a high-quality video source and a high-quality connection. As described below, TV sets can have four different types of inputs, each of which accepts a specific kind of signal. Most sets 27 inches and larger have an RF antenna/cable, composite-video, and S-video input; a component-video input is found mostly on higher-end models.

Antenna/cable input, sometimes called a VHF/UHF input. This is the most common connection. It's the easiest connection to use because it's the only one that carries both sound and picture on one cable—in this case, the familiar coaxial cable. (The other video inputs carry only the picture, requiring the use of a separate pair of audio inputs to carry the sound.) The antenna/cable input is used with video sources such as antennas, cable boxes, and VCRs.

Composite-video input. This offers a step up in quality. It uses a single standard RCA-style jack—a round jack (frequently yellow) with a single pin—to pass video signals. Two separate RCA jacks (frequently red and white) are used to pass the stereo audio signals. Most video sources—including cable boxes and VCRs, as well as DVD players—have a composite-video connection.

S-video input. A round jack with four pins, it accepts even better-quality signals. This input separates the signal into two—color and luminance (black and white)—which improves the image quality. This can be used to connect your TV to DVD players, satellite receivers, and digital-cable boxes, as well as digital, S-VHS, or Hi8 camcorders.

Component-video input. A three-cable connection found on some higher-end TVs, this carries potentially the best-quality signals. It separates the video signal into three signals, two color and one luminance. This input is used primarily with DVD players. On HD-ready sets, this input is specially designed to handle signals from HDTV tuners, cable boxes, satellite receivers, and progressive-scan DVD players.

Some TVs come with more than one S-video, composite-video, or component-video input, letting you connect several devices. On many TVs, a composite-video or S-video input is on the front of the set for easy access.

Audio connections. The picture is obviously only half the story. You will also need to hook up your sound equipment. To obtain the audio from a device such as a VCR, DVD player, cable or satellite receiver, or camcorder, you generally connect one or a pair of **audio inputs** to your receiver, which routes sound to the speakers. Stereo analog audio inputs are labeled L and R for left and right. Newer multichannel receivers will also have **coaxial** or optical digital-audio inputs for providing surround sound; some have both. These are used for connecting a DVD player and some digital-cable and satellite receivers. Be sure that the receiver's input matches the output of any device you want to connect—in other words, to use an optical output on the DVD player, you will need to have an optical input on the receiver. Aftermarket converter boxes are also available.

To output the sound, every multichannel receiver will have at least six speaker terminals so it can accommodate a surround-sound system with six speakers. You don't have to use all six terminals—you can use only two for a stereo setup, for instance. Most receivers also have a **subwoofer preamp out,** an output that carries unamplified low-frequency signals to an active (powered) subwoofer.

Some receivers come with **5.1 inputs,** six connectors that accept multichannel analog audio signals that another device—such as a DVD player that has a built-in Dolby Digital or DTS decoder, or that plays DVD-Audio or SACD discs—has already decoded through a process that splits a signal into six or more audio channels. The inputs are typically marked Front L and R, Rear (or Surround) L and R, Center, and Subwoofer (which also may be labeled LFE, for low-frequency effects).

User manuals should be able to take you through much of the setup process. Hang on to them. Give yourself easy access to the back of the receiver and other components. You will need good lighting to read the labeling on the back panels, so have a flashlight ready. Connect audio devices first, using the cables that came with each component.

To connect speakers, you typically strip off enough insulation from the ends of the wires to connect them, without shorting, to adjacent wires. Observe proper polarity; a speaker, like a battery, has "+" and "–" terminals. (The insulation of one wire in each pair should have a distinguishing feature, such as color or striping.) Reversing polarity will cause a loss of bass or other frequencies.

You can plug almost all of your components into a two-prong AC power strip—preferably one with surge suppression. The exceptions are the three high-powered devices—the TV, receiver, and powered subwoofer. Plug those into the wall or into a three-prong AC power strip. Or you can plug all of your components into a power control center, which handles the entire system and can include surge suppression.

Tech tip

The type of connections you use to connect your video and audio equipment can affect the quality of the sound and images you receive.

ARRANGING THE EQUIPMENT

The trick in setting up a home theater is arranging components in a way that maximizes their capabilities. The room you choose has a fundamental bearing on sound quality. For the best sound, try to strike a balance between acoustically "live" (bare floor and walls) and "dead" (carpeted floor and curtained walls).

Upholstered furniture, wall hangings, and stocked bookshelves can help deaden the front of a room, where the TV is. The back of the room, where the rear-channel speakers are, should be live. The size and shape of room also matter. A 17x11-foot room with an 8-foot ceiling is good. A square room can make bass sound boomy or uneven.

Make sure your room has enough distance between you and the TV for comfortable viewing. The ideal for viewing a conventional, 30- to 40-inch set is 8 to 12 feet, which gives your eyes enough distance to knit the scan lines into a unified picture. But a high-definition TV screen has no visible scan lines, so you can sit closer. Allow at least 5 feet for a 36-inch or smaller set, 6 to 9 feet for larger screens. For analog sets larger than 40 inches—flat-panel or projection sets—figure on sitting more than 10 feet away. Another way of looking at it: The bigger the room, the bigger the TV can be.

Receivers generate more heat than other audio and video components, so they need to go on the top of the stack or on their own shelf, with at least a couple of inches of head space and a path for the heat to escape. If a receiver's surface becomes hot to the touch, try one of the following: turn down the volume; provide more cooling, perhaps with a small fan; use speakers with a higher impedance; or play only one set of speakers at a time.

MATCHING SPEAKERS & RECEIVER

Speakers and the receiver must match in two ways: power and impedance.

Power. Generally, the more power (measured in watts) that a receiver delivers, the louder you can play music, with less distortion. Each doubling of loudness uses about 10 times as much power. Most models these days provide plenty of power—at least 60 watts per channel.

Here's a quick guide to power requirements for various room sizes: 80 to 100 watts per channel for a large living room (15x25 feet or more with an 8-foot ceiling); 40 to 80 for an average living room (12x20 feet); 20 to 40 for a bedroom (12x14 feet). A "live" (echoey) room will need less power than a "dead" (muffled-sounding) room.

Impedance. Materials that conduct electrical current also resist the current's travel to varying degrees. This resistance, or impedance, is measured in ohms. Standard speaker impedance is 8 ohms, which all receivers can handle. Many speakers have an impedance as low as 4 ohms, according to CONSUMER REPORTS tests. All else being equal, 4-ohm speakers demand more current than 8-ohm speakers. The use of the former generally doesn't pose a problem at normal listening levels but may eventually cause a receiver to overheat or trip its internal overload switch when music is played very loud. Before buying 4-ohm speakers to regularly play loud music, check the manual or back panel of your receiver to confirm that it's compatible.

Some speakers overemphasize various frequencies when placed against the wall or tucked in a bookshelf. Manufacturers' recommendations can help you decide on the optimal placement in your particular room.

Speakers are sold as pairs for traditional stereo setups, and singly or in sets of three to six for equipping a home theater. To keep a balanced system, buy left and right speakers in pairs, rather than individually. The center-channel speaker should be matched to the front (or main) speakers. For the best effect, the rear speakers should also have a sound similar to the front speakers.

The best position for the main front speakers is roughly an equilateral triangle whose points are the left speaker, the right speaker, and you, the listener. Try to place them at about the same height as your ears as you sit. The center speaker should be atop or below the TV and aligned with, or only slightly behind, the main speakers. The left and right surround speakers can be placed alongside the seating, facing each other or the back wall. The subwoofer can go anywhere convenient—under a table, behind the sofa. Watch out for corners, though. They accentuate the bass, often making it unacceptably boomy.

THE FINE-TUNING

You can optimize the system by properly setting audio levels and taking advantage of some of your components' features.

DVD audio settings. A DVD player can output each disc's audio signal in a number of ways. The raw "bitstream" signal is undecoded; use this setting if your receiver decodes Dolby Digital and DTS audio. If you have only a digital-ready (or DVD-ready) receiver and your DVD player has a built-in Dolby Digital or DTS decoder, use the "analog 6-channel output" setting, which outputs decoded audio to the receiver. And if you have only a stereo receiver or TV (or just stereo speakers), set the DVD player for "analog 2-channel"—this downmixes the multiple channels into two.

Subwoofer adjustments. Most powered subwoofers have two controls: cutoff frequency and volume level. The former is the frequency above which the subwoofer won't reproduce sound. If your main speakers are regular, full-range types (not satellites), set the subwoofer to the lowest setting, typically 80 hertz. If they're satellites with no woofers, see the manual regarding of set up the satellite and subwoofer combination. Adjust the subwoofer's volume so its contribution is noticeable but subtle.

Receiver settings. With your receiver's user manual as a guide, adjust the receiver speaker by speaker, according to each speaker's size, distance from the listener, and sound level relative to the other speakers. With most audio systems, you should be able to sit where you will be listening and make the proper adjustments by using the receiver's remote control.

Related CR Report: November 2004

TV SETS

Flat panels, rear-projection sets, conventional TVs—you have more (and better) viewing choices than before, including HD models, at ever-lower prices.

There's never been more variety in TV types, sizes, and shapes than there is right now. If you'd love a flat-panel set that's only a few inches thick, an LCD or plasma TV might be right for you. Want a really big picture? You can get a 60-inch or larger screen on a rear-projection TV. And a front projector can fill screens stretching 100 inches or more. Meanwhile, conventional TVs with picture tubes, the kind of set you've been watching for years, are still big sellers, and many offer outstanding performance. No matter which type of TV you choose, it's likely to cost less than it did just a few months ago.

WHAT'S AVAILABLE

In most TV categories, high-definition (HD) TVs using digital technology represent the majority of new models. The analog TVs that have been the standard since the 1950s are becoming scarcer as manufacturers shift their focus to HDTVs, and broadcasters move toward digital broadcasts.

HD offers the best video experience you can get at home, with noticeably clear, sharp, lifelike images. That's because these digital sets are designed to display the visual detail contained in HD signals. Most HD signals have resolution of 1080i (1,080 lines scanned in two passes then interlaced to form an image) or 720p (720 lines scanned progressively, in one sweep). New, high-priced TVs designed for an even more detailed HD format—1080p, for 1,080 lines scanned progressively—have started to hit the market. They could raise the bar for picture quality, but they're not likely to become mainstream until there's enough TV programming that uses this high resolution.

Shop smart

Many TVs with larger screen sizes must now have built-in tuners to comply with government regulations, and smaller sets must begin offering tuners within the next year or two.

Enhanced-definition (ED) TVs are a step down from HD. These sets display 480p resolution (480 lines scanned progressively). Most are LCD or plasma. Many, but not all, ED sets can convert HD signals to a format they can handle, but picture quality won't match that of true HD.

The standard-definition signals that are still used for most TV broadcasts contain up to 480 lines that are drawn onscreen in two passes, odd and even, then interlaced to make a complete image. This resolution is called 480i.

To receive high-quality HD signals, digital TVs need a digital tuner. Some models, called integrated HD sets or HDTVs, have a built-in digital tuner that can decode HD signals pulled in off-air via antenna. But the built-in tuner can't unscramble HD signals sent via cable or satellite. For that, they need an external device: an HD-capable cable or satellite box, or a smart card that replaces a cable box.

Sets with no built-in digital tuner, called HD-ready TVs or HDTV monitors, also require an HD-capable cable box or satellite receiver. The main difference from an integrated set is that they need a set-top box to receive over-the-air broadcast signals via antenna. They also cost less than integrated sets. EDTVs also come with and without digital tuners. The days of HD-ready and ED-ready TVs are numbered, though. TVs with larger screen sizes must now have built-in tuners to comply with government regulations, and smaller sets must begin offering tuners within the next year or two.

Here are the types:

Picture-tube sets. Conventional TVs that use picture tubes called CRTs (cathode-ray tubes) still offer the best combination of performance and value, and they've established a good track record for reliability. Most picture-tube TVs have a screen that measures 13 to 36 inches diagonally, so they're not big by today's standards. On analog sets, the screens are squarish, with an aspect ratio of 4:3, meaning they're four units wide for every three units high. HD sets of this type have either a 16:9 wide screen with proportions similar to that of a movie-theater screen or a 4:3 screen.

Generally, the larger the screen, the higher the price, and the more features and inputs for other video devices. Slimmer sets are arriving as manufacturers address a major objection to picture-tube TVs—their roughly 2-foot depth. The thinner models are about 16 inches deep. Price range: 13-inch sets start at $75 or so; 27-inch sets start at about $250; 32-inch sets start at about $400; 36-inch sets start at $500. HD sets cost about $200 more than analog models.

LCD flat panels. LCD TVs are lightweight and only a few inches thick. Most have screens that measure between

13 and 37 inches diagonally, although there are some 45-inch sets coming on the market. These TVs can stand on a table or be wall-mounted; small sets can be suspended under a cabinet. LCD TVs come in both 4:3 and 16:9 screen shapes and in conventional analog (typically only the smaller sizes), ED, and HD models. All LCD TVs use the same technology as flat-panel computer monitors. The best can display very good picture quality. A bright, smooth image is created by a combination of a white backlight and thousands of LCD pixels that open and close like shutters. Slow pixel response may make fast-moving images appear fuzzy, and the image may dim somewhat as you angle away from the center of the screen.

Some new models have improved on both counts. Many LCD models have inputs enabling them to serve as both a computer monitor and a TV. In the largest sizes, LCD sets are more expensive than other types of TVs. Because LCD TVs haven't been in widespread use for very long, long-term reliability is still a question. Preliminary data are encouraging, showing a low repair rate during the first year of use. Price range: about $600 and up for 14-inch or 15-inch models, $1,000 and up for 20-inch models, and up to $2,000 or more for a 32-inch model.

Plasma flat panels. Also renowned for their thin profile, plasma displays tend to be bigger than LCD models, with 42-inch and 50-inch sets among the more popular sizes. They're not as light as LCDs, but you can get special hardware that enables them to be wall-mounted. All plasmas are widescreen models; both HD and ED versions are available. Images are created by thousands of pixels containing gas that is converted into plasma by an electrical charge. That results in a bright, colorful display, even in light-filled rooms. The best plasma TVs are capable of excellent picture quality. The shiny surface can produce annoying reflections in bright lighting. Most plasma displays come with a TV tuner and speakers, but with some sets these components must be purchased separately.

Because plasma TVs are fairly new, long-term reliability is still a question. Preliminary data are encouraging, showing a low repair rate during the first year of use. Price range: about $2,300 and up.

Rear-projection TVs. Rear-projection TVs using CRT technology are the most affordable jumbo TVs on the market. Screens typically measure 42 to 60-plus inches diagonally, though there are a few sets with even larger screens. HD sets are becoming the norm as analog models are being phased out. Most rear-projection TVs have 16:9 screens. These sets use three small CRTs, which makes them big (24 to 30 inches deep) and heavy (sometimes more than 200 pounds).

Picture quality in most rear-projection TVs can be good and occasionally is very good, but it falls short of most other types of TVs, even with HD programming. Also, the image appears dimmer as your position angles away from the center of the screen. Survey data indicates a higher rate of repair than for conventional TVs. Price range: HD-capable sets start at about $1,800.

Microdisplays. A newer class of rear-projection set creates images using LCD, DLP (digital light processing), or LCoS (liquid crystal on silicon) technology. These sets are much slimmer and lighter than CRTs, as well as more expensive. All are HD-capable digital sets with wide screens measuring 40 to 70 inches or so; LCoS sets are as large as 82 inches. The best are capable of very good picture quality. But LCD- and LCoS-based models often can't render deep black. With DLP sets, some viewers perceive flashes of color called the rainbow effect, which can be troubling. Microdisplays will become even more dominant before long, as manufacturers stop making CRT-based rear-projection TVs. Because these TVs are fairly new, long-term reliability is still a question. Preliminary data shows a higher repair rate during the first year of use for these sets than for LCD and plasma TVs. Price range: $2,500 and up.

Front projectors. Technically display devices rather than TVs, front projectors can give you by far the largest images—up to 200 inches, measured diagonally. These units require a separate screen (or a smooth wall) as a display surface, and you can vary the picture size by moving the projector closer to the screen or farther back and using the zoom control. Consequently, you're not locked into a specific screen size, as you are with every other type of TV. You also need a tuner (such as a cable or satellite box) and generally have to provide speakers as well. These are best viewed in dark rooms, and usually require some sort of installation.

Front projectors use the same microdisplay technologies as their rear-projection cousins: LCD, DLP, and LCoS. While they're not the best choice for typical everyday viewing, front projectors are the best way to get top-quality images in a size that brings the movie-theater experience home. Price range: $1,500 to $5,000.

FEATURES THAT COUNT

Practically all new TVs have a **flat screen**, which reduces reflections, and **picture-in-picture** (PIP), which lets you watch two shows simultaneously, or keep a program playing in a small box while exploring the onscreen program guide. **Motion compensation** is a useful feature that can improve the smoothness of movies played on standard (not progressive-scan) DVD players. This feature is sometimes referred to as **3:2 pulldown compensation** or by brand-specific names such as CineMotion.

The **aspect ratio**, or width-to-height ratio, is of special importance when choosing an HD set. Some have a squarish 4:3 aspect ratio like that of a conventional TV. Wide-screen sets have a rectangular 16:9 (or 15:9) shape that more closely resembles a movie-theater screen. TV programming is usually formatted for a 4:3 screen, but more programmers are adopting the 16:9 format. Many cinematic movies are 16:9; some have an even wider format.

Content formatted for one type of screen has to be modified to fit the other, so you may see dark bars to the left and right or top and bottom unless you use a stretch or zoom control. Most HDTVs are wide-screen models. You'll find 4:3 screens only on some picture-tube and LCD HDTVs.

Stretch and zoom modes will adjust the image size to better fill the screen shape. This helps to reduce the dark bands that can appear above, below, or on the sides of the image if you watch content formatted for one screen shape on a TV that has the other shape. (The picture may be distorted or cut off a bit in the process of stretching and zooming.) Those bars make the picture slightly smaller and over time can leave ghosted images on the screens of plasma sets and CRT-based rear-projection TVs. This "burn-in" is also a risk with any images left on the screen for long periods—say, from a stock ticker or a channel logo.

On CRT-based projection sets, **auto convergence** provides a one-touch adjustment to automatically align the three CRTs for a sharp, accurate image. It's much more convenient but perhaps not as thorough as manual convergence, which can be time-consuming.

Most TVs have a number of different **inputs** for connecting other components.

Antenna/cable, or **radio frequency (RF)** inputs are the most basic; the next step up is **composite video. S-video inputs** let you take advantage of the superior picture quality from a satellite system, a DVD player, or a digital camcorder. **Component-video inputs** offer even better quality, useful with equipment such as most DVD players, high-definition satellite receivers, and cable boxes.

In addition to those TV connections, most HD-capable sets have a **Digital Visual Interface (DVI)** or **High-Definition Multimedia Input (HDMI)**. These provide a digital connection to digital devices and may allow content providers to control your ability to record certain content. DVI inputs carry only video; HDMI inputs carry audio and video on one cable.

VGA input lets the TV accept signals from a computer. For a camcorder or video game, a **front-mounted A/V input** is helpful. **Audio outputs** let you direct a stereo TV's audio signal to a receiver or self-powered speakers. A **headphone jack** lets you watch (and listen) without disturbing others.

HOW TO CHOOSE

Strongly consider HD. Digital HDTVs can display sharper, finer images than conventional analog TVs, especially with HDTV programming, but even with standard TV programming or DVD movies. Even with standard (non-HD) signals from a good cable connection, a satellite signal, or a DVD player, the picture quality can be better than a conventional set's. But with a poor signal, like the worst channels from cable, an HDTV can make the images look worse. The digital circuitry can't always know how to interpret the noise from the real signal.

If you're at all serious about TV or DVD viewing, we strongly recommend you consider an HDTV—especially if you're looking at a big-screen set. Even if there isn't yet enough HD programming to suit you, it's likely there will be during the life of the TV.

Decide on a screen size. TVs with small screens (less than 27 inches) are more likely to come without all the bells and whistles of larger sets. A notable exception: Most LCD sets fall into this size range, and they may be more fully featured. Medium screens—27 to 36 inches—are the best sellers, so the category has a large number of choices in terms of features, price, and brand. Large screens—40 to 82 inches—are generally plasma or rear-projection models; there are some LCDs in the 40- to 50-inch range, but they're very expensive.

Most big-screen sets are HDTVs. Keep in mind that a jumbo set is likely to look even larger and more overwhelming in your home than it did on a spacious showroom floor. In the same vein, consider whether you want thick or thin. LCD and plasma flat-panel TVs are the trimmest and the priciest; rear-projection and picture-tube TVs are the bulkiest and cheapest. Rear-projection microdisplays, using the new technologies, are a middle ground on size and price.

Lean toward a wide screen. Most HDTVs have wide screens, but some picture-tube and LCD models have squarish 4:3 screens. Our advice: Go wide. Most DVD movies and some HDTV programs are formatted for a 16:9 wide screen, and they'll look better on this type of screen. With more TV content going wide-screen, a 16:9 set will make even more sense as time goes on. A regular screen with the familiar 4:3 aspect ratio is the only choice for analog TVs.

Choose the technology. TVs using the familiar picture-tube technology are the least-expensive option, and these still offer the best picture quality, but the maximum screen size is limited to 36 inches. The best LCD, plasma, and rear-projection sets are capable of displaying very good HD images, but you have to be selective. Consider the pros and cons outlined above in making your choice. Be sure to view the sets for yourself to see which you prefer.

Decide between an HD-ready set and an integrated HDTV. HD-ready sets cost less than integrated HDTVs, and there's no reason to pass them by. The only plus to an integrated HDTV is that it can get broadcast HD signals via antenna; with cable or satellite, you need a box with either type.

Digital-cable-ready, or DCR, TVs are a newer type of HDTV. These can receive some digital-cable programming with no additional devices. To get premium cable and HD, you must get a CableCard from the cable company and put it in a slot on the TV. DCR sets command a premium, but don't pay extra just to lose the cable box. Current CableCard setups are one-way and don't provide an interactive program guide, video-on-demand, or pay-per view ordering via the remote. For those, you'll still need a cable box. Second-generation DCR TVs and CableCards offering two-way capability should be here soon.

Consider an analog TV for casual use. While standard-definition TVs can't match HD for picture quality, some offer fine picture quality that may suit you fine. Only firsthand experience will enable you to decide whether the HD improvement is worth the extra cost. Though HD sets cost less than they used to, they still command a premium—usually hundreds more than a comparable analog set. If you're a casual viewer and top quality isn't a must, a low-priced analog picture-tube set would be the best choice for a midsized set, while a small LCD would be a good choice for a kitchen or bedroom.

Related CR Report: November 2005
Ratings:
LCD: page 303
Picture-tube: page 308
Plasma: page 316
Rear-projection: page 320
Reliability (picture-tube): page 315

Kitchen, Bath, and Laundry

Kitchen, Bath & Laundry: More Style for Less Money

Creating the kitchen or bath of your dreams is more affordable than you may think. Manufacturers are adding upscale-looking style features like stainless-steel surfaces to midrange kitchen appliances. For the bath you'll find lower-priced whirlpools, glass vessel sinks, and other fixtures that sport a high-end look. Meanwhile, competition among big-box retailers has helped drive prices down in many categories. For example, countertops made of marble, limestone, and granite are becoming less expensive. Other news of note:

The best doesn't always cost the most. In cabinets, price doesn't guarantee performance. While premium cabinets do indeed withstand heat, water, moisture, and other abuse best overall, we found some strong lower-priced performers. You'll find more low-priced basic cabinets with pull-out shelves and full-extension drawers.

"Faux pro" gas ranges, with powerful cooktops, convection ovens, and the stainless-steel look of pro-style, are now available for a modest $1,000 or so. Some faux pro and even mainstream models priced as low as $400 did better in our rigorous cooking tests than pro-style models costing thousands. In the electric range market, smoothtops dominate over coil models.

Appliances sport new features. Refrigerators are taking on new shapes and configurations. Armoire-style french-door refrigerators, with double doors on the refrigerator compartment atop a drawer-style freezer, are big sellers. Slim, cabinet-depth refrigerators that mimic the built-in look are also catching on. Features continue to evolve; water dispensers are showing up in lower-priced models, selling for about $700. There's also a continuing trend toward quieter operation.

Dishwashers are adding new features like high-pressure "turbo" wash options to save time or clean tough, baked-on grime. You'll find dishwashers for as little as $350 that offer stainless-steel exteriors, dirt sensors, and other options once found only on pricier machines. We found many test models were excellent in the basic task of washing.

With toilets, price doesn't correlate with performance. Many models costing $200 to $300 outperformed higher-priced models. Pressure-assisted toilets excel in flushing power, but they can be noisier.

Adjustable showerheads are full of new features like variable spray settings and dozens of spray channels for wide water distribution. Our testers preferred this traditional style to new, oversized rainshower fixtures, which deliver a less-powerful spray and can cost far more.

Top- and front-loading washing machines that employ new, more efficient technology now account for about 30 percent of purchases. The best offer very good washing, gentle action, ample capacity, water and power efficiency, and quiet operation. But you'll pay from $800 to $1,500 for these machines, at least twice the price of many traditional top-loading washers. Among dryers, sensors that can tell a load's dryness are now standard; they do a better job than old-style thermostats.

COOKTOPS & WALL OVENS

Separate appliances give you the flexibility of two cooking areas, with burners placed just about anywhere you want. You also have the option of cooking with gas, electricity, or induction.

Like ranges, cooktops come in electric and gas versions. More consumers go for electric than gas, generally opting for glass ceramic smoothtops. There are fewer coil models from which to choose, but you may want to consider one if price is more important than style. Gas cooktops come in several types, including stainless-steel models with pro-style controls and hefty grates, and gas-on-glass models with burners on a glass ceramic surface. Cooktops with a porcelain enamel top are the lowest priced.

Gaggenau, Viking, and other brands are also introducing stand-alone induction cooktops, which cook via glass-covered magnetic coils that send nearly all of their heat to the pan, rather than the cooking surface. Besides heating faster than gas or electric cooktops, induction models respond instantly to the controls, but they require magnetic cookware to work.

Because about one-third of cooktops and wall ovens are sold as part of a kitchen makeover, style sells. More and more of the appliances have sleek, flush surfaces that are easy to clean or stainless-steel skins that let you easily mix and match brands.

Flexibility is the biggest reason to forgo the typical range and buy a separate cooktop and wall oven instead. However, the two appliances usually cost more than a similar range. Our tests show that you can bring home a pair of fine performers for about $1,300 for a 30-inch electric cooktop and electric oven. A smoothtop range with similar performance would cost about half that. But if you want more than four pots going at once, it won't cost you too much to upgrade from a 30-inch cooktop with four burners or elements to a 36-inch model with five or six. In most cases, the difference is $100 to $400.

WHAT'S AVAILABLE

Frigidaire, GE, Jenn-Air, Kenmore (sourced from others), KitchenAid, Maytag, and Whirlpool are the leading makers of cooktops and wall ovens. Mainstream brands have established high-end offshoots, such as Kenmore Elite, GE Profile, and Whirlpool Gold. High-end, pro-style brands include Bosch, Dacor, GE Monogram, KitchenAid Pro-Line, Thermador, Viking, and Wolf.

Cooktops. You can install a cooktop on a kitchen island or other location where counter space allows. As with freestanding ranges, cooktops can be electric coil, electric smoothtop, or gas. Cooktops add flexibility since they can be located separately from the oven. Most are 30 inches wide and are made of porcelain-coated steel or glass ceramic, with four elements or burners. Some are 24 or 36 inches wide, depending on the number of burners.

Modular cooktops let you mix and match parts—removing burners and adding a grill, say—but you pay a premium for that added flexibility. Preconfigured cooktops are less expensive. Price range: electric cooktop, $150 to $1,000; gas cooktop, $200 to $1,500; induction cooktop, $2,000 and up.

Wall ovens. These can be single or double, electric or gas, self-cleaning or manual, with or without a convection setting. Width is typically 24, 27, or 30 inches. They allow you to eliminate bending by installing them at waist or eye level, though you can also nest them beneath a countertop to save space. Price range: $350 to more than $2,500 for double-oven models; figure on about $300 extra for convection.

FEATURES THAT COUNT

On electric cooktops. Consider where the controls are located. On most electric cooktops, controls take up room on the surface. Some models have **electronic touchpads,** however, allowing the cooktop to be flush with the counter.

Coil elements, the least expensive electric option, are easy to replace if they break. Spending $200 more will buy you a smoothtop model.

Most smoothtops have **expandable elements**—also called **dual elements**—which allow you to switch between a large, high-power element and a small, low-power element contained within it. Some smoothtops also include a **low-wattage element** for warming plates or keeping just-cooked food at the optimal temperature. Some have an elongated "bridge" element that spans two burners—a nicety for accommodating rectangular or odd-shaped cookware. And many have at least **one hot-surface light**—a key safety feature, since the surface can remain hot long after the elements have been turned off. The safest setup includes a dedicated "hot" light for each element.

Many electric cooktops have one large, **higher-wattage element** in front and one in back. An **expanded simmer range** in some smoothtop models lets you fine-tune the simmer setting on one element for, say, melting chocolate or keeping a sauce from getting too hot.

On gas cooktops. Most gas cooktops have four burners in three sizes, measured in British thermal units per hour (Btu/hr.): one or two medium-power burners (about 9,000 Btu/hr.), a small burner (about 5,000 Btu/hr.), and one or two large ones (about 12,500 Btu/hr.). We recommend a model with one or more 12,000 Btu/hr. burners for quick cooktop heating. Some have a fifth burner instead of a center island. On a few models, the burners automatically re-ignite.

For easier cleaning, look for **sealed burners.** Gas ranges typically have knob controls; the best rotate 180 degrees or more. Try to avoid knobs that have adjacent "off" and "low" settings and that rotate no more than 90 degrees between High and Low.

Spending more gets you either heavier **grates** made of porcelain-coated cast iron or a sleek **ceramic surface**—also called **gas-on-glass**—and **stainless-steel** accents, along with a low-power simmer burner with an extra-low setting for delicate sauces (though other burners often are capable of simmering).

On ovens. An oven's usable capacity may be less than what manufacturers claim because they don't take protruding broiler elements and other features into account.

A **self-cleaning cycle** uses high heat to

burn off spills and splatters. An **automatic door lock,** found on most self-cleaning models, is activated during the cycle, then unlocks when the oven has cooled. Also useful is a **self-cleaning countdown** display, which shows the time left in the cycle.

Higher-priced wall ovens often include **convection,** which uses a fan and, sometimes, an electric element to circulate heated air. CONSUMER REPORTS tests have shown that this mode cut cooking time for a large roast and, in some cases, baked large cookie batches more evenly because of the circulating air. A few electric ovens have a low-power **microwave feature** that works with bake and broil elements to speed cooking time further. The GE Advantium over-the-range oven uses a **halogen heating bulb** as well as microwaves. Another cooking technology, Trivection, uses regular thermal heating, convection, and microwave energy to cut cooking time. Trivection is available in some top-of-the-line GE Profile and Monogram ovens. Though very good overall, it's very pricey.

A **variable-broil** feature in most electric ovens offers adjustable settings for foods such as fish or thick steaks that need slower or faster cooking. Ovens with **12-hour shutoff** turn off automatically if you leave the oven on for that long. But most models allow you to disable this feature. A **child lockout** allows you to disable oven controls for safety.

Manufacturers are also updating oven controls across the price spectrum. **Electronic touchpad controls** are common. A **digital display** makes it easier to set the precise temperature and keep track of it. A **cook time/delay start** lets you set a time for the oven to start and stop cooking; remember, however, that you shouldn't leave most foods in a cold oven very long. An **automatic oven light** typically comes on when the door opens, although some ovens have a switch-operated light. A **temperature probe,** to be inserted into meat or poultry, indicates when you've obtained a precise internal temperature.

Oven windows come in various sizes. Those without a decorative grid usually offer the clearest view, although some cooks may welcome the grid to hide pots, pans, and other cooking utensils typically stored inside the oven.

HOW TO CHOOSE

Cooktop/wall oven or a range? With a cooktop/wall oven combo, you can put the appliances pretty much anywhere in the kitchen and mount the oven at a convenient height. Choose a range if you want it to be the centerpiece, as a professional-style model would be.

Installing separate appliances is more work. Electric wall ovens and cooktops each need their own electrical circuit and are best installed by a professional.

Shop smart

If you want more than four pots going at once, it won't cost you too much to upgrade from a 30-inch cooktop with four burners or elements to a 36-inch model with five or six.

Gas or electric? If you have gas service, you might want to use both fuels. Electric wall ovens generally have a larger capacity than gas ones, and they're easier to install. With cooktops, the quick response of a gas flame might better suit your style of cooking. Gas performs very well in our tests. We have found, however, that electric cooktops tend to boil water faster and simmer sauces better.

Consider cleanup and safety. To minimize the parts you need to clean around, look for a smooth-surface cooktop and an oven with a covered bottom heating element and smooth touchpad controls.

Cooktops stay hot for a while after you turn off the heat. Since smoothtops blend into the surrounding counter, children and unwary adults could get burned. For safety, smoothtops have lights to signal which element is still hot.

Related CR Report: November 2005
Ratings: page 234

DISHWASHERS

Models selling for as little as $350 or so can excel at washing dishes, but they may not measure up to costlier models in quietness, water and energy usage, or features.

Spend $300 to $400 and you can get a dishwasher that does a good job cleaning dirty dishes without prerinsing, but with a bit of noise. To get the best of everything—cleaning prowess plus the quietest operation, convenience features, water and energy efficiency, and designer styling—you'll have to spend $600 or more.

A dirt sensor, once a premium feature, is now becoming standard, even on lower-priced models. Sensors are designed to adjust the water used and the length of the cycle to the amount of soil on dishes.

WHAT'S AVAILABLE

Frigidaire, GE, Maytag, and Whirlpool make most dishwashers and sell them under their own names, associated brands, and sometimes the Sears Kenmore label. Whirlpool makes high-end KitchenAid, low-end Roper, and many Kenmore models. Maytag makes the high-end Jenn-Air, midpriced Amana, and low-priced Admiral dishwashers. GE offers a wide range of choices under the GE label and also makes the value-priced Hotpoint. Asko, Bosch, and Miele are high-end European brands; Bosch also makes Siemens models. Haier is an import from China; Fisher & Paykel is from New Zealand.

Most models fit into a 24-inch-wide space under a kitchen countertop and are attached to a hot-water pipe, drain, and an electrical line. Compact models fit into narrower spaces. If you have the room, it's now possible to get a wider, 30-inch dishwasher from Dacor, although you'll pay a hefty premium. Portable models in a finished cabinet can be rolled over to the sink and connected to the faucet. A "dishwasher in a drawer" design from Fisher & Paykel (also available from KitchenAid) has two stacked drawers that can be used simultaneously or individually, depending upon the number of dishes you need to wash. Price range: $200 to $1,300 (domestic brands); $350 to $2,000 (foreign-made brands).

FEATURES THAT COUNT

Most models offer a choice of at least three **wash cycles**—Light, Normal, and Heavy (or Pots and Pans)—which should be enough for the typical dishwashing jobs in most households. A few brands, including Kenmore (Sears), now offer power-washing features designed to remove heavy soil such as baked-on brownie batter. Kenmore's Turbo Zone has a section that's exposed to high-pressure washing to handle extra-dirty dishes. It worked well in our tests.

Rinse/Hold lets you rinse dirty dishes before using the dishwasher on a full cycle. Other cycles offered on many models include **Pot Scrubber, Soak/Scrub,** and **China/Crystal,** none of which we consider crucial for most consumers. Dishwashers often spray water from multiple places, or "levels," in the machine. Most models typically offer a choice of **drying** with or without heat.

Some dishwashers use **filters** to keep wash water free of food that can be redeposited on clean dishes. Most such models are self-cleaning: A spray arm cleans residue from the coarse filter during the rinse cycle, and a food-disposal **grinder** cuts up large food particles so they can be washed down the drain. Some of the more expensive dishwashers have a filter that you must pull out and clean manually; these are usually quieter than those with grinders. If noise is a concern, see if better **soundproofing**—often in the form of hard, rubbery insulation surrounded by a thick fiberglass blanket—is available as a step-up feature.

A **sanitizing wash** or **rinse option** that raises the water temperature above the typical 140° F doesn't necessarily mean improved cleaning. Remember, the moment you touch a dish while taking it out of the dishwasher, it's no longer sanitized.

Most dishwashers have **electronic touchpad controls.** On more expensive models, controls may be fully or partially hidden, (or integrated) in the top edge of the door. The least expensive models have mechanical controls, usually operated by a dial and push buttons. Touchpads are the easiest type of control to wipe clean. **Dials** indicate progress through a cycle. Some electronic models digitally display time left in the wash cycle. Others merely show a "clean" signal. A **delayed-start** control lets you set the dishwasher to start later, for example, at night when utility rates may be lower. Some models offer **child-safety features,** such as locks for the door and controls.

Most dishwashers hold cups and glasses on top, plates on the bottom, and silverware in a basket. **Racks** can sometimes be adjusted to better fit your dishes. On some units, the top rack can be adjusted enough to let you put 10-inch dinner plates on both the top and bottom racks simultaneously, or it can be removed entirely so very tall items will fit on the bottom.

Other features that enhance flexibility include **adjustable** and **removable tines,** which fold down to accommodate bigger dishes, pots, and pans; **slots for silverware** that prevent "nesting"; **removable racks,** which enable loading and unloading outside the dishwasher; **stemware holders,** which steady wine glasses; clips to keep light plastic cups from overturning; and **fold-down shelves,** which stack cups in a double-tiered arrangement.

Tech tip

Dishwashers with adjustable racks and fold-down tines are better if you want to wash oversized platters or odd-shaped serving pieces.

Stainless-steel **tubs** should last virtually forever, but even plastic tubs generally have a warranty of 20 years, much longer than most people keep a dishwasher. Light-colored plastic may discolor, especially from tomato sauce, but there's otherwise no advantage to stainless. Dishwashers with stainless-steel tubs typically cost $500 and up.

If you want a front panel that matches your cabinets, you can buy a kit compatible with many dishwashers. Some higher-priced models come without a front panel so you can choose your own, usually at a cost of several hundred dollars.

HOW TO CHOOSE

Our tests over the years have shown that most new dishwashers will do a great job cleaning even the dirtiest dishes without pre-rinsing, which wastes lots of water. But they differ in appearance, noise, loading, energy efficiency, and features. Here are points to consider when choosing a dishwasher:

Don't settle for drab design. Like other kitchen appliances, dishwashers are becoming more stylish. White is still the dominant color, followed by black and bisque; stainless steel is an increasingly common option. (Keep in mind that stainless, while trendy, often shows fingerprints and smudges.) The least-expensive stainless-finished dishwashers generally cost about $400, but you might find one on sale for closer to $300. If you want your appliances to blend in with the cabinetry, buy a dishwasher that can be fitted with a custom front panel.

All but the lowest-cost new models have a one-piece door without a separate bottom panel, creating a clean look that eliminates a dirt trap. Some higher-priced models have most or all controls hidden along the top edge of the door. That makes for a smooth, sleek exterior, but the small labels can be hard to read and the small buttons hard to operate.

Nix the noise. To ensure that the after-dinner cleanup won't drown out the TV or conversation, check the Ratings for a dishwasher judged excellent or very good for noise. You might have to pay $600 or more to get one of the quietest models, which is barely noticeable when running.

Decide whether a self-cleaning filter is a must. Most dishwashers have self-cleaning filters, which can add to noise. The Asko, Bosch, Fisher & Paykel, Haier, Miele, and Siemens models we've tested have filters you clean yourself. That isn't a big deal: You simply remove the filter and rinse it off, typically every week or two. A clogged filter could affect wash performance.

Look for loading flexibility. Any dishwasher can fit 10 typical place settings of dishes, glasses, and cutlery, but those with adjustable racks and fold-down tines are better if you want to wash oversized platters or odd-shaped serving pieces. In some machines, adjustable parts are color-coded. If you often host large dinner parties, you might want a model that adjusts to fit dinner plates on the top and bottom racks at the same time.

Consider the cost of use. Most of the energy a dishwasher uses goes to heating the water. Water usage, and thus the operating costs, vary greatly from model to model. In our recent tests, water usage ranged from about 3½ to 12 gallons a load. Energy costs to heat the water and run the machine could vary by up to $65 a year for the tested models, depending on rates in your area. Over its lifetime, a more efficient model could be a better buy than a lower-priced model that is less energy-efficient.

Don't get hung up on dirt sensors. Generally, all but the lowest-priced and some of the highest-priced new dishwashers have sensors. In our tests, some sensors couldn't differentiate between slightly and very dirty dishes, so the machines used more water than needed. Also, the cycles on sensor models were about 20 minutes longer than on machines without a sensor. Some Kenmore dishwashers have a second sensor that adjusts the water level to the load size. It cut water usage slightly in our tests.

Don't pay more for special cycles. As mentioned previously, the three basic wash cycles—Light, Normal, and Pots and Pans—are adequate for most chores. Rinse and Hold is handy if you want to delay washing until there is a full load. Settings such as China and Sanitize don't add much, in our opinion.

If speed matters, check cycle time. The normal cycle (including drying time) ranges from about 80 minutes to 150 minutes, but longer cycles don't necessarily clean better. In our tests, models with cycle times of about 100 minutes did just as thorough a job as others that took 145 minutes.

Consider the cost of delivery and installation. Installation can run $100 to

$200 or more. Sears, which sells roughly 35 percent of all dishwashers, typically charges $130 to install a new unit and remove your old one.

Related CR Report: March 2005
Ratings: page 247
Reliability: page 251

DRYERS

On the whole, clothes dryers do a good job. More sophisticated models dry your laundry with greater finesse.

Dryers are relatively simple. Their major differences are how they heat the air (gas or electricity) and how they're programmed to shut off once the load is dry (thermostat or moisture sensor). Gas models typically cost about $50 more than electric ones, but they're usually cheaper to operate.

CONSUMER REPORTS has found that dryers with a moisture sensor tend to recognize when laundry is dry more quickly than machines that use a traditional thermostat. Because they don't subject clothing to unnecessary heat, moisture-sensor models are easier on fabrics. And since they shut themselves off when laundry is dry, they use less energy. Sensors are now offered on many dryers, including some relatively low-priced ones. Thermostats are generally available only on the most basic dryers.

WHAT'S AVAILABLE

The top four brands—GE, Kenmore (Sears), Maytag, and Whirlpool—account for more than 80 percent of dryer sales. Other brands include Amana (made by Maytag), Frigidaire (made by Electrolux), Hotpoint (made by GE), and KitchenAid and Roper (both made by Whirlpool). You may also run across smaller brands such as Crosley, Gibson, and White-Westinghouse, all of which are made by the larger brands. Asko, Bosch, Miele, and Siemens are European brands. Fisher & Paykel is from New Zealand, LG and Samsung from Korea, and Haier from China.

Full-sized models. These models generally measure between 27 and 29 inches in width—the critical dimension for fitting into cabinetry and closets. Front-mounted controls on some models let you stack the dryer atop a front-loading washer, but shorter people may find it difficult to reach the dryer controls or the inside of the drum. Full-sized models vary in drum capacity from about 5 to 7½ cubic feet. Most dryers have ample capacity for typical wash loads. A larger drum can more easily handle bulky items such as queen-size comforters. Buying a more expensive model may get you more capacity and a few extra conveniences. Price range: electric, $200 to $1,000; gas, $250 to $1,100.

Space-saving models. Compacts, exclusively electric, are typically 24 inches wide, with a drum capacity roughly half that of full-sized models—about 3½ cubic feet. Aside from their smaller capacity, they perform much like full-sized machines. They can be stacked atop a companion washer. Some compact dryers operate on 120 volts, while others require a 240-volt outlet (as do full-sized electric dryers). Price range: $200 to about $1,400.

Another space-saving option is a laundry center, which combines a washer and dryer in a single unit. Laundry centers come with either gas or electric dryers. There are full-sized (27 inches wide) or compact (24 inches wide) models available. The dryer component of a laundry center typically has a somewhat smaller capacity than a full-sized dryer. Laundry centers with electric dryers require a dedicated 240-volt power source. Price range: $700 to $1,900.

FEATURES THAT COUNT

Full-sized dryers often have two or three **auto-dry cycles,** which shut off the unit when the clothes reach the desired dryness. Each cycle might have a **More Dry** setting to dry clothes completely, and a **Less Dry** setting to leave clothes damp for ironing, plus gradations between those two extremes.).

Most dryers have a separate **temperature control** that allows you to choose a lower heat for delicate fabrics, among other things. An **extended tumble** setting, sometimes called Press Care or Finish Guard, helps to prevent wrinkling when you don't remove clothes immediately. Some models continue to tumble without heat; others cycle on and off. An **express-dry cycle** is meant for drying small loads at high heat in less than a half hour. Large loads will take longer. **Touchpad electronic controls** found in higher-end models tend to be more versatile than mechanical dials and buttons—once you figure them out, that is. Some models allow you to save favorite settings that you use frequently. Some high-end dryers have a display with a progression of menus that enable you to program specific settings for recall at any time. Such menus can be time-consuming (and sometimes confusing) to navigate, but they may allow custom programming or offer detailed help and information otherwise available only in the manual.

Tech tip

Dryers with a moisture sensor tend to recognize when laundry is dry more quickly than machines that use a traditional thermostat.

A **top-mounted lint filter** may be somewhat easier to clean than one inside the drum. Some models have a **warning light** that reminds you to clean the lint filter. It's important to clean the lint filter regularly to minimize any fire hazard and to maintain the dryer's efficiency. It's also advisable to use metal ducting (either rigid or flexible) instead of plastic or flexible foil. Plastic or foil ducts can create a fire hazard if they sag and clog with lint, causing lint to build up in the dryer, where it can ignite. You should clean the ducts out at least once a year.

Most full-sized models have a **drum light,** making it easy for you to spot stray items that may be hiding in the back. Some models allow you to raise or lower the volume of an **end-of-cycle signal** or shut it off. A **rack** included with many dryers attaches inside the drum and is intended to hold sneakers or other items that you want to dry without tumbling. Models with **drop-down doors** in front may fit better against a wall, but **side-opening doors** may make it easier to access the inside of the drum.

HOW TO CHOOSE

Consider gas. Both gas and electric dryers perform comparably, our years of testing show. Gas dryers cost about $50 more than comparable electric models, but the likely savings in fuel costs should more than make up the difference in the long run. An electric dryer requires a 240-volt outlet, a gas dryer a gas hookup. If you have both, don't rule out the gas model simply because it costs more. (CONSUMER REPORTS now tests only electric dryers, which account for about 80 percent of the models sold, but equivalent gas models are listed in the Ratings.)

Insist on a moisture sensor. As noted earlier, overdrying can damage or shrink fabrics, and moisture sensors can minimize that possibility. Sensors are available on about half the dryers on the market, including most priced above $350. Whether a specific model has a sensor or thermostat may not be obvious from labeling or controls. Check the literature, visit the manufacturer's Web site, or pick a highly rated dryer that we've tested.

Don't get hung up on capacity. Manufacturers describe dryer capacity (as they do washer capacity) with terms such as extra large, super, and super plus. The differences aren't meaningful for everyday use. Most full-sized dryers can hold a typical wash load. If you want to dry big, bulky items, choose a model judged excellent for capacity in our Ratings.

Start in the middle. When using an automatic setting rather than a timed one (which we generally recommend), set the control to the midpoint and raise or lower it as needed. Using More Dry routinely can overdry clothes and waste energy. Use Less Dry to leave clothing damp for ironing. Don't worry about knowing when an automatic cycle is done: If you don't hear the buzzer, an extended tumble without heat prevents wrinkles if you don't remove clothes immediately.

Don't pay for unnecessary extras. Higher-priced dryers may offer a dozen or so choices, including specialty cycles such as "speed dry" (15 minutes of high heat, for example). These can usually be replicated with standard settings. A choice of heat level, timed and auto-dry, and a few fabric types (regular/cotton and permanent press/delicate) is usually plenty. Touchpads look impressive and may allow you to save custom settings but don't improve performance. Nor do stainless-steel tubs, unlike in washers.

Get a quiet dryer for living areas. If your dryer will be near the kitchen or a bedroom, look for a model judged very good or excellent for noise.

Related CR Report: February 2005
Ratings: page 252
Reliability: page 257

FOOD PROCESSORS & MIXERS

Match the machine to the way you prepare foods. You may find you need more than one.

Which food-prep appliance best suits your style and the foods you prepare? Food processors are versatile machines that can chop, slice, shred, and purée many different foods. Mini-choppers are good for small jobs such as mincing garlic and chopping nuts. Hand mixers can handle light chores such as whipping cream or mixing cake batter. And powerful stand mixers are ideal for cooks who make bread and cookies from scratch.

WHAT'S AVAILABLE

Dominant brands are Black & Decker, Cuisinart, Hamilton Beach, and KitchenAid.

Food processors. Several brands have introduced multifunction models designed to do the job of two or more machines—for instance, an interchangeable food-processor container and a glass blender jar and blade. Either attachment fits on the motorized base.

Another design trend is a mini-bowl insert that fits inside the main container for preparing smaller quantities of food. Newer designs tend to be sleek, with rounded corners. Price range: $30 to $450.

Stand and hand mixers. KitchenAid owns about half the stand-mixer market; GE, Hamilton Beach and Sunbeam are the next best-selling brands. Black & Decker, GE, Hamilton Beach, KitchenAid, and Sunbeam are the dominant brands among hand mixers. The big push in mixers is for more power, which is useful for handling heavy dough. You'll find everything from heavy-duty models offering the most power and the largest mixing bowls to light-service machines that are essentially detachable hand mixers resting on a stand. Models vary in power from about 200 to 800 watts. Sales of light-duty, convenient hand mixers have held their own in recent years. Price range for stand mixers: $60 to $500; price range for hand mixers: $25 to $100.

FEATURES THAT COUNT

Food processors. All have a clear plastic **mixing bowl** and lid, an S-shaped metal **chopping blade** (and sometimes a duller version for kneading dough), and a plastic **food pusher** to safely prod food through the feed tube. Some models have a wider tube so you don't have to cut up vegetables—such as potatoes—to fit the opening. One speed is the norm, plus a **pulse setting** to control processing precisely. Bowl capacity ranges from around 3 cups to 14 cups (dry), with most models holding 6 to 11 cups. A **shredding/slicing disk** is standard on full-sized processors. Some come with a **juicer attachment. Touchpad controls** are becoming more commonplace, too.

Shop smart

A midsized food processor model, around 7 cups, is likely fine for most tasks.

Mini-choppers look like little food processors, with a capacity of 2 to 3 cups, but they're for small jobs only, like chopping small quantities of nuts or half an onion.

Mixers. Stand mixers generally come with one **bowl** and either single or paired **beaters, whisks,** and **dough hooks.** Some mixers offer options such as **splash guards** to prevent flour from spewing out of the bowl, plus **attachments** to make pasta, grind meat, and stuff sausage. Stand mixers generally have 5 to 16 speeds; we think five or six well-differentiated settings is enough. You should be able to lock a mixer's power head in the Up position so it won't crash into the bowl when the beaters are weighed down with dough. Conversely, it should lock in the Down position to keep the beaters from kicking back when tackling stiff dough.

Just about any hand mixer is good for nontaxing jobs such as beating egg whites, mashing potatoes, or whipping cream. The slow-start feature on some mixers prevents ingredients from spattering when you start up, but you can achieve the same result by manually stepping through three or so speeds. An indentation on the underside of the motor housing allows the mixer to sit on the edge of a bowl without taking the beaters out of the batter.

HOW TO CHOOSE

Food processors & choppers

Consider capacity. Food-processor capacity ranges from about 3 to 14 cups. (Those are manufacturers' figures; we've found that processors typically hold a cup or two more or less than claimed.) Choppers, which are designed expressly for small jobs, hold about 1 to 3 cups.

If you regularly cook for a crowd or like to whip up multiple batches of a recipe, you might appreciate the bigger, 11- to 14-cup units. However, they tend to be pricier and heavier than smaller versions and take up more counter space. A midsized model (around 7 cups) is likely fine for most tasks.

Note that even big food processors can handle small jobs such as chopping half an onion. But using a chopper makes cleanup easier.

Don't focus on speeds. Food processors typically have two settings: On and Pulse, which allows you to run the machine in brief bursts for more precise processing control. Choppers typically have one or two Pulse settings (High and Low). Those are really all the speeds you need. Some machines have a few extra speeds (a Dough setting on some high-end processors, for example), but we haven't found that they perform much better.

Note feed-tube size. Some processors have wider feed tubes than others, which can save you the effort of having to cut potatoes, cucumbers, and other big items.

Expect to pay more for kneading prowess and quiet operation. The models we tested that cost $55 or less strained and jumped while kneading dough. They also made quite a racket, where most of the higher-end models we tested were quiet. Choppers can be noisy but are used briefly.

Stand & hand mixers

Decide how much mixer you need. Just about any stand or hand mixer will do for all those simple mixing and whipping chores. But if you're a dedicated baker, you'll probably want to invest in a heavy, powerful stand mixer, because it can knead even two loaves' worth of bread dough with ease.

Downplay wattage and number of speed settings. Manufacturers stress wattage and number of speeds, but neither figure necessarily translates into better performance. For example, some stand mixers have as many as 16 speeds; some hand mixers have 9. We think 5 or 6 well-differentiated speeds are sufficient. The slower the lowest speed, the better; slow speeds prevent spattering.

Speeds should be clearly indicated. With some of the inexpensive hand mixers we tested, the switch you use to select speeds didn't line up well with the speed markings.

Consider size and weight. Hand mixers should feel well-balanced and comfortable to hold; most that we tested did. Size and weight can be a concern with stand mixers—some weigh more than 20 pounds—but their heft gives them the stability to handle tough jobs.

Make sure you will have enough clearance if you plan to keep the mixer on a counter below a cupboard.

Consider beater style and motion. Most of the top-performing hand mixers have wire beaters without the thick center post found on traditional-style beaters. The wire beaters performed well and were easier to clean.

Light-duty stand mixers typically have stationary beaters and a bowl that sits on a revolving turntable. The bowl sometimes needs a push to keep spinning.

Related CR Report: December 2003

FREEZERS

Chest freezers cost the least to buy and run, but self-defrost uprights are the winners for convenience.

If you buy box loads of burgers at a warehouse club or like to keep a few weeks' worth of dinner fixings on hand, the 4- to 6-cubic-foot freezer compartment in most refrigerators may seem positively Lilliputian. A separate freezer might be a good investment.

WHAT'S AVAILABLE

Most freezers sold in the U.S. are from one of three companies: Frigidaire, which makes models sold under the Frigidaire, GE, and Kenmore labels; W.C. Wood, which makes models sold under its own name as well as Amana, Magic Chef,

Maytag, and Whirlpool; and Haier, a Chinese manufacturer, which has become a major player in the freezer business in recent years. Haier is now the leading supplier of compact-sized freezers sold under its own name and some under the Amana, Kenmore, GE, and Maytag brands.

There are two types of freezers: chests, which are essentially horizontal boxes, with a door that opens upward; and uprights, which resemble a single-door refrigerator. Both types are available in self-defrost and manual-defrost versions.

In recent tests, we found models of both types that failed to keep food frozen.

Manual-defrost chests. These freezers vary most in capacity, ranging from 4 to 25 cubic feet. Aside from a hanging basket or two, chests are wide open, letting you put in even large, bulky items. Nearly all the claimed cubic-foot space is usable. The design makes chests slightly more energy-efficient and cheaper to operate than uprights. Cooling coils are built into the walls, so no fan is required to circulate the cold air. Because the door opens from the top, virtually no cold air escapes when you put in or take out food.

A chest's open design, however, does make it hard to organize the contents. Finding something can require bending and, often, moving around piles of frozen goods. If you're short, you may find it difficult to extricate an item buried at the bottom (assuming you can remember it's stashed there). A chest also takes up more floor space than an upright. A 15-cubic-foot model is about 4 feet wide by 2½ feet deep; a comparable upright is just as deep but only about to 2½ feet wide.

Defrosting a chest can be a hassle, especially if it's fully loaded or has a thick coating of ice. You have to unload the food, keep it frozen somewhere until the ice encrusting the walls has melted, remove the water that accumulates at the drain, then put back the food. Price range: $150 to $500.

Self-defrost chests. This type of chest freezer is relatively new to the marketplace and, except for defrosting, has the same advantages and disadvantages as a manual-defrost chest freezer. Self-defrosting involves heaters that turn on periodically to remove excess ice buildup, eliminating a tedious, messy chore but using extra energy. Because of the circulating fan, self-defrost models are somewhat noisier than manual-defrost chest freezers. Price range: $250 to $700.

Manual-defrost uprights. These freezers have a capacity of 5 to 25 cubic feet, of which some 15 percent isn't usable. They cost less to buy and run than self-defrost models but aren't as economical as chests. Unlike their self-defrost counterparts, they don't have a fan to circulate cold air, which can result in uneven temperatures. Defrosting is quite a chore with some. The metal shelves in the main space are filled with coolant, so if you're not careful scraping off the ice you can damage the shelves. What's more, ice tends to cling to the shelves, so defrosting can take up to 24 hours.

Other models have a "flash" defrost system that heats the cooling coils to quickly melt any frost. There's no need to scrape, but, as with any freezer, you must empty the contents before defrosting. Because a manual-defrost upright's shelves contain coolant, they can't be adjusted or removed to hold large items. Price range: $170 to $700.

Self-defrost uprights. These models (sometimes called frost-free) have from 11 to 25 cubic feet of space. Like a refrigerator, they have shelves in the main compartment and on the door; some have pull-out bins. This arrangement lets you organize and access contents but reduces usable space by about 20 percent. Interior shelves can be removed or adjusted to fit large items. When you open the door of an upright, cold air spills out from the bottom while warm, humid air sneaks in at the top. That makes the freezer work harder and use more energy to stay cold, and temperatures may fluctuate a bit. These models compensate by using a fan to circulate cold air from the cooling coils, which are located in the back wall.

A self-defrost model costs about $20 a year more to run than a similar-sized manual-defrost model. For many people, the convenience may be worth the extra cost. Self-defrosting models are a bit noisier than manual-defrost models, an issue only if they're located near a living area rather than in the basement or garage. While freezers of old weren't recommended for use in areas that got very hot or cold, current self-defrost models should work fine within a wide ambient temperature range—typically 32° F to 110° F. Price range: $350 to $800.

FEATURES THAT COUNT

While freezers are simpler than some other major appliances, there are several features worth looking for. **Interior lighting** makes it easier to find things, especially if you place the freezer in a dimly lit area. A **power-on light,** indicating that the freezer has power, is helpful. A **temperature alarm** lets you know when the freezer is too warm inside, such as after a prolonged power outage. (If you lose power, don't open the freezer door; food should remain frozen for about 24 to 48 hours.)

A **quick-freeze** feature brings the freezer to its coldest setting faster by making it run continuously instead of cycling on and off; that's handy when you're adding a lot of food. The **flash-defrost** feature on some manual-defrost upright freezers can make defrosting easier and faster.

HOW TO CHOOSE

Figure the capacity you need. This will depend on the size of your family and its fondness for frozen foods. Freezers are available in four general sizes: compact (5 cubic feet), small (6 to 9 cubic feet), medium (12 to 18 cubic feet), and large (more than 18 cubic feet). Aside from hanging baskets, chest freezers are wide open so that almost all of the claimed space is usable. Upright freezers have shelves and pull-out bins. These make it easier to organize and reach contents but reduce usable space by up to 20 percent.

> **Tech tip**
> Self-defrosting freezers eliminate a tedious, messy chore but use extra energy.

Weigh manual vs. self-defrost. Manual-defrost freezers, either chest or upright, are generally quieter and more energy-efficient than self-defrosting models of the same type. But manually defrosting a freezer is a lot of work and can take up to 24 hours.

Consider local power problems. If the area where you live is prone to brownouts or power failures, a chest freezer will be the better choice.

Check the controls and lights. Easy-to-reach controls make adjusting the temperature simple. An interior light makes it easier to find foods, especially if the freezer is in a dimly lighted area. A power-on light on the outside of the freezer lets you see at a glance that the freezer is on. That way you don't have to open the unit to check, letting cold air out.

Related CR Report: October 2005
Ratings: page 258

MICROWAVE OVENS

You'll see larger capacity, sensors that detect doneness, and stylish designs.

Microwave ovens, which built their reputation on speed, are also showing some smarts. Many automatically shut off when a sensor determines that the food is cooked or sufficiently heated. The sensor is also used to automate an array of cooking chores, with buttons labeled for frozen entrées, baked potatoes, popcorn, beverages, and other common items. Design touches include softer edges for less boxy styling, hidden controls for a sleeker look, stainless steel, and, for a few, a translucent finish.

WHAT'S AVAILABLE

GE leads the countertop microwave-oven market with approximately 25 percent of units sold, followed by Sharp. Other brands include Panasonic, Emerson, and Kenmore. GE also sells the most over-the-range models.

Microwaves come in a variety of sizes, from compact to large. Most sit on the countertop, but a growing number sold—about 13 percent—mount over the range. Several brands offer speed-cooking via halogen bulbs or convection. Speed-cook models promise grilling and browning, though results can vary significantly depending on the food. Manufacturers are working to boost capacity without taking up more space by moving controls to the door and using recessed turntables and smaller electronic components.

Microwave ovens vary in the power of the magnetron, which generates the microwaves. Midsized and large ovens are rated at 900 to 1,500 watts, compact ovens at 600 to 800 watts. A higher wattage may heat food more quickly, but differences of 100 watts are probably inconsequential.

Some microwave ovens have a convection feature—a fan and, often, a heating element—which lets you roast and bake, something you don't generally do in a regular microwave. Price range: $40 to $250 (countertop models); $150 to $500 (over-the-range); $250 to $700 (convection or halogen-bulb countertop or over-the-range).

FEATURES THAT COUNT

On most, a **turntable** rotates the food so it will heat more uniformly, but the center of the dish still tends to be cooler than the rest. With some models, you can turn off the rotation when, for instance, you're using a dish that's too large to rotate. The results won't be as good, however. Some models have replaced the turntable with a rectangular tray that slides from side to side to accept larger dishes. Most turntables are removable for cleaning.

You'll find similarities in **controls** from model to model. A **numeric keypad** is used to set cooking times and power levels. Most ovens have **shortcut keys** for particular foods, and for reheating or defrosting. Some microwaves start immediately when you hit the shortcut key, others make you enter the food quantity or weight. Some models have an **automatic popcorn feature** that takes just one press of a button. Pressing a **1-minute** or **30-second key** runs the oven at full power or extends the current cooking time. Microwave ovens typically have a number of **power levels.** We've found six to be more than adequate.

A **sensor** helps prevent over- or undercooking by determining when the food is done based on infrared light or the steam emitted by food. The small premium you pay for a **sensor** is worth it. A few ovens have a **crisper pan** for making bacon or crisping pizza, since microwave cooking without the special pan leaves food hot but not browned or crispy.

Over-the-range ovens vent themselves and the range with a **fan** that has several speed settings. Typically the fan will turn on automatically if it senses excessive heat from the range below. Over-the-range microwaves can be vented to the outside or can just recirculate air in the kitchen. If the oven is venting inside, you'll need a **charcoal filter** (sometimes included). An over-the-range microwave generally doesn't handle ventilation as well as a hood-and-blower ventilation system because it doesn't extend over the front burners.

Tech tip

Six power levels is more than adequate for microwaves.

HOW TO CHOOSE

Decide which type meets your needs. Countertop models cost the least and are best for kitchens with lots of counter space. Compact models can cost as little as $30. Midsized and large models have more capacity and features, though most eat up 1½ to 2 feet of length of countertop space. You can hang some countertop models below a cabinet, though doing so often leaves little space below the microwave oven.

You're likely to consider an over-the-range oven only if you're replacing one or remodeling your kitchen. While they save counter space, installation is an added expense and often requires an electrician. What's more, they can't vent steam and smoke from a range's front burners as well as the range hoods they replace.

Choose convenience, not clutter. There's little reason to buy a microwave without a sensor, which shuts off oven power when it senses the food is hot; sensor models begin at about $85. But you may want to avoid ovens with an array of shortcut and defrost settings for foods you don't eat.

Keep convection in perspective. Browning and crisping via convection are great if you use a microwave as a second oven. But if you're buying one mostly for heating and defrosting, consider a lower-priced nonconvection model.

Be wary of capacity claims. Oven makers often measure corner space you can't use; actual space can be 50 to 60 percent less than they claim. Check whether a large platter fits an oven you're considering.

Related CR Report: February 2005
Ratings: page 275
Reliability: Page 279

RANGES

Choices can be confusing, but you don't have to spend top dollar for impressive performance with high-end touches.

If you're in the market for a range, you're faced with several choices. You can buy a freestanding range that combines a cooktop and oven, or you can buy a separate cooktop and wall oven. The oven can be equipped with a convection feature. If you have access to a gas hookup, you need to decide whether you want gas, electricity, or a combination of the two.

All of these choices bring innovations and upgrades as competition among manufacturers heats up. Electric ranges now include traditional coil and newer smoothtop models where the heating elements are below a ceramic glass surface. Both offer quick heating and the ability to maintain low heat levels. Gas ranges use burners, which typically don't heat as quickly as electric elements, despite increasingly higher power—measured in British thermal units per hour (Btu/hr.). Even the highest-powered burners tend to heat more slowly than the fastest electric coil elements, sometimes because the heavy cast-iron grates that typically come with them slow the process by absorbing some of that heat. But you can see how high or low you are adjusting the flame.

You'll also see more high-end or "professional-style" gas ranges with beefy knobs; heavy cast-iron grates; thick stainless-steel construction; and four or more high-powered burners. These high-heat behemoths can easily cost $2,000 or more and typically require a special range hood and blower system, along with special shielding and a reinforced floor in some applications. But because the look is so popular, you'll find a growing number of stoves that include stainless trim and other pro-style perks for far less.

Shared characteristics between electric and gas ranges are also a growing trend. Some gas models have electric warming zones. Convection features are available on both gas and electric ranges. More and more manufacturers are offering dual-fuel gas ranges, which pair a gas cooktop with an electric oven. These cost about $1,000 and up.

WHAT'S AVAILABLE

GE, Kenmore (sourced from others), Frigidaire, Maytag, and Whirlpool are the leading makers of ranges, cooktops, and wall ovens. Other major brands include Amana, Hotpoint, Jenn-Air, and KitchenAid. Mainstream brands have established high-end offshoots, such as Kenmore Elite, GE Profile, and Whirlpool Gold. High-end, pro-style brands include Bosch, Dacor, GE Monogram, KitchenAid Pro-Line, Thermador, Viking, and Wolf.

Freestanding range. These ranges can fit in the middle of a kitchen counter or at the end. Widths are usually 20 to 40 inches, although most are 30 inches wide. They typically have oven controls on the backsplash. Slide-in models eliminate the backsplash and side panels to blend into the countertop, while drop-ins rest atop toe-kick-level cabinetry and typically lack a storage drawer. Most mainstream ranges now include a self-cleaning feature and—for gas models—sealed burners, which keep crumbs from falling beneath the cooktop. On the higher end of the scale, electric models have one or more expandable electric elements, and gas models have two or more high-powered burners, a convection oven, and warming drawers. Price range: $250 to $1,600.

Shop smart
More and more manufacturers are offering dual-fuel gas ranges, which pair a gas cooktop with an electric oven.

Pro-style range. Bulkier than freestanding ranges, these gas models can be anywhere from 30 to 60 inches wide. Larger ones include six or eight burners, a grill or griddle, and a double oven. Many have a convection feature, and some have an infrared gas broiler. While you usually don't get a storage drawer, more pro-style stoves now include a self-cleaning oven and sealed burners. Price range: $2,000 to $5,000.

FEATURES THAT COUNT

On all ranges. Look for easy-cleaning features such as a **glass** or **porcelain backguard,** instead of a painted one; **seamless corners** and **edges**, especially where the cooktop joins the backguard; a **warming drawer** for convenience; **six or more oven-rack positions** for flexibility; and a **raised edge** around the cooktop to contain spills. Note, though, that a range's usable capacity may be less than what manufacturers claim because they don't take protruding broiler elements and other features into account.

On electric ranges. Consider where the **controls** are located. Slide-in ranges have the dials on the front panel, while freestanding models have them on the backguard. Some models locate controls to the left and right, with oven controls in between, giving you a quick sense of which control operates which element. But controls clustered in the center stay visible when tall pots sit on rear heating elements.

Coil elements, the most common and least expensive electric option, are easy to replace if they break. On an electric range with coil elements, look for a **prop-up top** for easier cleaning, and **deep drip pans** made of porcelain to better contain spills and ease cleaning.

Spending $200 more will buy you a **smoothtop** model; most use radiant heat.

Some smoothtops have **expandable elements**—also called **dual elements**—which allow you to switch between a large, high-power element and a small, low-power element contained within it. Some smoothtops also include a **low-wattage element** for warming plates or keeping just-cooked food at the optimal temperature. Some have an elongated **"bridge" element** that spans two burners—a nicety for accommodating rectangular or odd-shaped cookware. And many have at least one **hot-surface light**—a key safety feature, since the surface can remain hot long after the elements have been turned off. The safest setup includes a dedicated "hot" light for each element.

Most electric ranges have one large, **higher-wattage element** in front and one in back. An **expanded simmer range** in some electric models lets you fine-tune the simmer setting on one element for, say, melting chocolate or keeping a sauce from getting too hot.

On gas ranges. Most gas ranges have four burners in three sizes, measured in British thermal units per hour (Btu/hr.): one or two medium-power burners (about 9,000 Btu/hr.), a small burner (about 5,000 Btu/hr.), and one or two large ones (about 12,500 Btu/hr.). We recommend a model with one or more 12,000 Btu/hr. burners for quick cooktop heating. Some have a fifth burner instead of a center island. On a few models, the burners automatically reignite.

For easier cleaning, look for **sealed burners**. Gas ranges typically have **knob controls**; the best rotate 180 degrees or more. Try to avoid knobs that have adjacent "off" and "low" settings and that rotate no more than 90 degrees between High and Low.

Spending more gets you either heavier **grates** made of porcelain-coated cast iron or a **sleek ceramic surface**—also called **gas-on-glass**—and **stainless-steel accents,** along with a **low-power simmer burner** with an extra-low setting for delicate sauces (though other burners often are capable of simmering).

On pro-style ranges. These models have four or more brass or cast-iron burners, all of which offer very high output (usually about 15,000 Btu/hr.). The burners may be nonsealed, with hard-to-clean crevices, though sealed burners are appearing on some models. Large knobs are another typical pro-style feature, as are **continuous grates** designed for heavy-duty use. The latter, however, can be unwieldy to remove for cleaning.

A **self-cleaning cycle** uses high heat to

burn off spills and splatters. Most ranges have it, although some pro-style gas models still don't. An **automatic door lock**, found on most self-cleaning models, is activated during the cycle, then unlocks when the oven has cooled. Also useful is a **self-cleaning countdown display**, which shows the time left in the cycle.

Higher-priced ranges often include **convection**, which uses a fan and, sometimes, an electric element to circulate heated air. CONSUMER REPORTS tests have shown that this mode cut cooking time for a large roast and, in some cases, baked large cookie batches more evenly because of the circulating air. A few electric ovens have a low-power **microwave** feature that works with bake and broil elements to speed cooking time further. Another cooking technology, called **Trivection**, uses regular thermal heating, convection, and microwave energy to cut cooking time. Trivection is available in some top-of-the-line GE Profile and Monogram ranges. Though very good overall, Trivection is very pricey.

A **variable-broil feature** in some ranges offers adjustable settings for foods such as fish or thick steaks that need slower or faster cooking. Ranges with **12-hour shut-off** turn off automatically if you leave the oven on for that long. But most models allow you to disable this feature. A **child lockout** allows you to disable oven controls for safety.

Manufacturers are also updating oven controls across the price spectrum. **Electronic touchpad controls** are common. A **digital display** makes it easier to set the precise temperature and keep track of it. A **cook time/delay start** lets you set a time for the oven to start and stop cooking; remember, however, that you shouldn't leave most foods in a cold oven very long. An **automatic oven light** typically comes on when the door opens, although some ovens have a switch-operated light. A **temperature probe**, to be inserted into meat or poultry, indicates when you've obtained a precise internal temperature.

Oven windows come in various sizes. Those without a decorative grid usually offer the clearest view, although some cooks may welcome the grid to hide pots, pans, and other cooking utensils typically stored inside the oven.

HOW TO CHOOSE

Think about your cooking. If you often cook for a crowd, look for at least one high-powered element or burner and a large oven. Indeed, you'll find more mid-priced gas ranges with the ultrahigh heat once exclusive to pro-style stoves. High-heat burners can be useful for searing, stir-frying, or heating large quantities. Ranges with convection can speed roasting a little. Models that excelled in broiling produced burgers seared on the outside and cooked quickly and evenly.

Think hard before buying a pro-style range. For most consumers, pro-style ranges aren't the best choice. In our tests, they did no better than conventional ranges. Some pro-style models lack common features, and some models have a higher repair rate.

Consider the fuel. Electric surface elements tend to heat faster and maintain low heat better. But a gas flame makes it easier to see the heat level. Either type is capable of very good performance. A dual-fuel range combines an electric oven and gas cooktop.

Balance convenience and durability. Electric smoothtops are pretty easy to clean, but they require a special cleaner. They can be damaged by a dropped pot or sugary liquids. Coil tops aren't as susceptible to such harm, but they require more cleaning time.

Keep high-tech in perspective. Ranges with special baking modes may not outperform conventional models. Touchpad oven controls are more precise than knobs. But front-mounted touchpads can be bumped and reset by accident, so see if the controls are logically placed and visible while you're cooking.

Related CR Report: November 2005
Ratings: page 288
Reliability: page 292

REFRIGERATORS

Get ready for more choices as refrigerator manufacturers refine existing designs and reprise old ones in the name of style and convenience.

If you're shopping for a new refrigerator, you're probably considering models that are fancier than your current fridge. The trend is toward spacious models with flexible, more efficiently used storage space. Useful features such as spillproof, slide-out glass shelves and temperature-controlled compartments, once found only in expensive refrigerators, are now practically standard in midpriced models. Stainless-steel doors are stylish, but they add to the cost. Bottom freezer, French-door models offer the convenience of a full-width refrigerator at eye level with the style and narrow door swing of a side-by-side. Built-in refrigerators appeal to people who want to customize their kitchens and are willing to pay thousands of dollars for the custom look. Some mainstream cabinet-depth models offer a built-in-style look for less.

Replacing an aging refrigerator may save you in electric bills since refrigerators are more energy-efficient now than they were a decade ago. The Department of Energy toughened its rules in the early 1990s and imposed even stricter requirements in July 2001 for this appliance, which is among the top electricity users in the house.

WHAT'S AVAILABLE

Only a handful of companies actually manufacture refrigerators. The same or very similar units may be sold under several brand names. Frigidaire, General Electric, Kenmore, and Whirlpool account for about three-quarters of top-freezer sales. For side-by-side models, those brands and Maytag account for more than 80 percent of sales. Brands offering bottom-freezers include Amana, Fisher & Paykel, GE, Jenn-Air, Kenmore, KitchenAid, LG, Maytag, Samsung, Sub-Zero, Thermador, and Whirlpool. Mainstream companies have introduced high-end brand lines such as Electrolux Icon, GE Monogram and Profile, and Kenmore Elite. These brands cover built-ins: GE (Monogram and Profile), Jenn-Air, KitchenAid, Sub-Zero, Thermador, and Viking. You can get built-in-style or "cabinet-depth" models from Amana, Electrolux, Frigidaire, GE, Jenn-Air, Kenmore, KitchenAid, LG, Maytag, and Whirlpool.

Top-freezer models. These are generally less expensive to buy and more space-efficient than comparably sized side-by-side models. Widths typically range from about 30 to 33 inches. The eye-level freezer offers easy access. Fairly wide refrigerator shelves make it easy to reach the back, but you have to bend to reach the bottom shelves and drawers. Claimed, labeled capacity ranges from about 10 to 25 cubic feet. With top-freezers, the usable capacity is typically about 80 percent of its nominal capacity, according to our measurements. Price range: Most cost $300 to $800.

Bottom-freezer models. A small but growing part of the market, these put frequently used items at eye level. Fairly wide refrigerator shelves provide easy access. Though you must bend to locate items in the freezer, even with models that have a pull-out drawer, you will probably do less bending overall because the main refrigerated compartment is at eye level. Bottom-freezers are a bit pricier than top-freezers and offer less capacity relative to their external dimensions because of the inefficiency of the pull-out bin. Widths typically range from 30 to 36 inches. Claimed capacity is up to 25 cubic feet, nominally, and usable space is a bit less than with top-freezers, but more than offered by side-by-sides. French-door models are increasingly available. Price range: Most cost $600 to $1,200; French-door type, $1,500 to $2,000.

Shop smart

Usable space is always less than claimed capacity.

Side-by-side models. These are by far the most fully featured fridges, most often equipped with through-the-door ice and water dispensers—among the most requested consumer features—as well as temperature-controlled bins and rapid ice-making cycles. Their narrow doors are handy in tight spaces. High, narrow compartments make finding stray items easy in front (harder in the back), but they may not hold wide items such as a sheet cake or a large turkey. Compared with top- and bottom-freezer models, a higher proportion of capacity goes to freezer space. Side-by-sides are typically large—32 to 36 inches wide, with claimed capacity of 20 to 30 cubic feet. About 65 percent of that space is usable. They're much more expensive than similar-sized top-freezer models and are less efficient in terms of energy use, as well as space. Price range: Most cost $800 to $2,000.

Built-in models. These are generally side-by-side and bottom-freezer models. They show their commercial heritage, often having fewer standard amenities and less soundproofing than lower-priced "home" models. Usually 25 to 26 inches front to back, they fit nearly flush with cabinets and counters. Their compressor is on top, making them about a foot taller than regular refrigerators—an issue if you have overhead cabinets. Most can accept extra-cost front panels that match the kitchen's décor. Side-by-side models in this style are available in 42-inch and 48-inch widths (vs. the more typical 36-inch width). You can even obtain a built-in pair: a separate refrigerator and freezer mounted together in a 72-inch opening. Price range: Most cost $4,000 to $6,000.

Cabinet-depth models. These freestanding refrigerators offer the look of a built-in for less money. They are available mostly in side-by-side styles, with some top- and bottom-freezers available. Many accept extra-cost panels for a custom look. Cabinet-depth models have less usable space than deeper freestanding models and cost more. Price range: $1,500 to $3,000.

FEATURES THAT COUNT

Interiors are ever more flexible. **Adjustable door bins** and **shelves** can be moved to fit tall items. Elevator shelves can be cranked up and down without removing the contents. Some **split shelves** can be adjusted to different heights independently. With other shelves, the front half of the shelf slides under the rear portion to provide clearance.

Shelf snuggers—sliding brackets on door shelves—secure bottles and jars. A few models have a wine rack that stores a bottle horizontally.

Glass shelves are easier to clean than wire racks. Most glass shelves have a raised, sealed rim to keep spills from dripping over. Some slide out. **Pull-out freezer shelves** or bins improve access. An alternative is a bottom-freezer with a sliding drawer.

More models have replaced mechanical controls with **electronic touchpads.** Some have a digital display that shows the temperature setting; a few show the actual temperature, which is more useful.

A **temperature-controlled drawer** can be set to be several degrees cooler than the rest of the interior, useful for storing meat or fish. Crispers have controls to maintain humidity. Our tests have shown that, in general, temperature-controlled drawers work better than plain drawers; results for humidity controls are less clear-cut. See-through drawers let you see at a glance what's inside.

Curved doors give the refrigerator a distinctive profile and retro look. Most manufacturers have at least one curved-door model in their lineups.

Step-up features include a **variety of finishes and colors.** Every major manufacturer has a stainless-steel model that typically costs significantly more than one with a standard pebbled finish. Some brands offer fingerprint-resistant stainless with clear coatings, while other brands have faux stainless that resists prints. Another alternative is a smooth, glass-like finish.

Most models have an **icemaker** in the freezer or give you the option of installing one yourself. Typically producing several pounds of ice per day (although some produce 10 pounds or more), an icemaker reduces freezer space by about a cubic foot. The ice bin is generally located below the icemaker, but some new models have it on the inside of the freezer door, providing a bit more usable volume. **Through-the-door ice-and-water dispensers,** a side-by-side staple, have been hard to come by on top- and bottom-freezers. More of those models have added water dispensers inside the fridge in recent years, and some now have through-the-door water dispensers—icemakers are still in the freezer.

With many models, the icemaker and/or water dispenser includes a **water filter,** designed to reduce lead, chlorine, and other impurities in ice and/or drinking water. An icemaker or water dispenser will work without one. You can also have a filter installed in the tubing that supplies water to the refrigerator.

Once a refrigerator's controls are set, there should be little need to adjust temperature. Still, accessible controls are an added convenience.

HOW TO CHOOSE

Size is likely to be more important than style or price, since most new refrigerators must fit in the same space as the old one. So begin by measuring the available space, including the space you'll need to open the door wide enough to pull out bins and drawers if there's a wall on the hinge side of the door. Also measure doorways and halls through which the refrigerator must pass when delivered.

Then choose a type that fits your space, needs, and budget. Once you've decided on a type, keep these shopping tips in mind:

Look for space-stretching features. A fridge's claimed capacity lists raw volume, including space taken up by lights, hardware, and unreachable nooks. Top- and bottom-freezers give you more storage for their size than side-by-sides. Some 30-inch-wide, 18-cubic-foot top-freezers we tested have about 15 cubic feet of usable space—nearly as much as some 36-inch-wide, 25-cubic-foot side-by-sides. With any fridge, look for features that maximize space, such as split shelves and cranks for adjusting shelf height. Pull-out shelves provide access to the back of the fridge and freezer. In bottom-freezers, full-extension drawers help you find items in the rear.

Consider costs and reliability. Most new refrigerators cost about $40 to $70 a year to run, based on average energy rates, but up to twice as much in the priciest markets. Top- and bottom-freezers are typically more efficient than side-by-sides. To get the most bang for the buck, pick a model that scored well for energy efficiency in our tests.

Weigh the likelihood of repairs as well. Some brands have been more reliable than others, and an icemaker and ice-and-water dispenser increase the chance that a fridge will need repair. As a group, built-ins appear to have had higher repair rates than freestanding models.

Listen up. Any new refrigerator is likely to be quieter than an older one. If your kitchen is a gathering spot, look for a model that did very well in our noise tests.

Keep styles coordinated. If you want the fridge to blend in with cabinetry, consider a built-in or cabinet-depth model that accepts custom panels. If you're mixing stainless-steel and metallic look-alikes, make sure any difference in the finishes doesn't bother you.

Related CR Report: July 2005
Ratings: page 293
Reliability: page 302

SHOWERHEADS

For a quick rinse, any old showerhead will do the job. But if you want a pounding stream of water to jump-start your morning or a gentle spray to help you unwind at day's end, the right showerhead is a must.

With hundreds of models on the market, from old-fashioned wall-mounted showerheads to oversized rain-shower styles to shower towers, there's bound to be a fixture to suit your style. Most sell for less than $100, though you can spend $1,000 for elaborate fixtures in expensive finishes. Considering the low cost and easy installation of most, getting a new showerhead is a great way to rev up a bathroom.

WHAT'S AVAILABLE

The big names include American Standard, Delta, Kohler, Moen, and Waterpik. Other manufacturers include Peerless, Pollenex, and Price Pfister.

Adjustable showerheads. These give you multiple settings so you can choose the strength of flow, from nice and easy to a vigorous massage. Levers, push buttons, and dials are designed to make it easy to change spray settings on adjustable models. Most are low-priced and easy to install. But style isn't their strong suit, and sometimes the most forceful settings can be noisy and too intense. Some can be hard to adjust, especially with wet hands. Price range: $25 to $175.

Rainshower. These stylish showerheads are best for those who want a soft, soothing shower. The fixtures have diameters of 6 to 12 inches or more, so they deliver a wider spray that covers more of the body at once. They're very quiet when in use, but most have only one setting, which may not be strong enough to quickly rinse off soap or shampoo or to provide an invigorating feel. You might need more room for one if it needs to be mounted directly overhead to function properly. Some may require additional plumbing parts or special installation. Price range: $30 to $500.

Shower towers. These elaborate models are best for creating a spalike experience without the cost and mess of behind-the-wall plumbing work, but they're pricier than showerheads and more complex to install.

They do use lots of water—up to 2.5 gallons per nozzle per minute, requiring a larger water heater or a separate, dedicated unit. The volume of water could overwhelm a septic system. Lower-cost models don't offer much. Price range: $200 to $2,500.

FEATURES THAT COUNT

Some improvements in showerheads include dozens of **spray channels** for wide water distribution and **anticlog nozzles** to combat hard-water deposits. Some models come in **handheld** versions, which adds flexibility.

Today's shower fixtures come in a range of styles, from traditional to contemporary. Chrome remains the best-selling finish, but brass, brushed nickel, and other trendy finishes are often available at higher prices.

HOW TO CHOOSE

While style may sway you, be sure to consider these performance factors:

Choose an adjustable fixture for spray options and oomph. Adjustable showerheads generally have three or more settings, ranging from a gentle mist to a needle-like spray and a pulsating massage. Continuously variable settings let you choose anything in between. Many of these models can deliver a forceful water flow.

Consider a rainshower fixture if you want a soft shower and stylish design. The eye-catching design of rainshower heads may appeal to style-conscious users. Most rainshower heads have only one setting that's described as a "cascade" or "downpour" by marketers. But on all but a few, we found the flow to be gentle and not very forceful—"wimpy" in the words of our testers. That can be relaxing, but it takes effort to rinse off soap and shampoo. Because many rainshower models are mounted directly above you, they extend farther from the wall and aren't suited to small areas. Also, the overhead position makes it hard to keep your hair dry.

Beware of water pressure. Almost all the adjustable and rainshower models we tested can deliver the government-mandated maximum of 2.5 gallons per minute when the water pressure is 80 pounds per square inch (psi). However, many homes with a municipal water supply have lower pressure, so the stream from the showerhead will be weaker. Also ask a plumber whether adjusting or replacing your pressure regulator might help.

> **Tech tip**
>
> Many homes with a municipal water supply have lower pressure, so the stream from the showerhead will be weaker.

Look for easy-to-use adjustments. With wet, soapy hands and water dripping into your eyes, you don't want to fumble with adjustments. Try setting the showerheads in the store to see how easy it is to change the spray setting and to adjust the height or angle of the showerhead. For maximum flexibility, consider a handheld model that can be set in a wall bracket or removed to focus the spray.

Consider installation. Even if you are only slightly handy, adjustable showerheads and most rainshowers are a do-it-yourself project. Think twice about heavy rainshower heads that require additional support or extra hardware for proper installation.

Choose a model that works with your water hardness. Many U.S. households have hard water, which contains a high percentage of calcium carbonate. This leaves a chalky buildup on fixtures, tiles, and doors, and can clog a showerhead's nozzles. Many had a plastic face or rubbery nozzles that were easier to clean and less likely to clog than all-metal showerheads.

Be choosy if you like it hot. Some showerheads aerate the spray to make it feel more substantial, but that cools the water by about 15 degrees before it hits your back. To compensate, you have to adjust the mix of hot and cold water using the shower controls.

Related CR Report: August 2005

TOILETS

Even the utilitarian commode is getting a revamp as toilet manufacturers strive to make this most basic of bathroom elements more accommodating.

Some of the first low-flush toilets on the market earned a reputation for being problematic because they required two or more flushes to do their job—and often clogged in the process. Many of the newer models that were tested work quite well on a single flush. But there are large differences in performance—even within a given brand.

Trends include more comfort-height models, which raise the rim from the usual 14 inches to as much as 17 inches above the floor. The added height makes getting on and off easier, especially for aging baby boomers, who have helped boost sales to roughly twice what they were in 2001. But their added comfort is likely to appeal to younger buyers, too. Added efficiency is another selling point as major brands attempt to improve upon the 1.6 gallons per flush that has been the legal threshold since 1994. A growing number of models with dual-flush technology use a mere 0.8 gallons for liquid-waste removal.

WHAT'S AVAILABLE

Most major manufacturers offer an extensive array of models in different designs and colors and in a range of prices. Within types, more money does not buy better performance, just more upscale design.

Pressure-assist. These toilets create the most flushing power, as pressure created when water displaces air within a sealed tank causes the water to thrust waste forcefully out through the bowl. They work very well as long as household water pressure is at least 25 pounds per square inch. They're best for large families, kids, and heavy use, where clogs are likeliest. But they tend to be pricey and noisy. Their raucous whoosh can be disconcerting, especially near bedrooms. Price range: $225 to $300 for most.

Vacuum-assist. A vacuum chamber inside the tank works like a siphon to pull air out of the trap below the bowl so that it can quickly fill with water to clear waste. These toilets are best for close quarters where quietness counts. But while some vacuum models performed well in past tests, the latest we tested had far less flushing power than pressure-assisted toilets yet typically cost as much. Fewer vacuum models sold also means fewer choices. Price range: $225 to $300 for most.

Gravity. These rely on water dropping from the tank into the bowl and trap to move waste down the drain. Pressure as low as 10 pounds per square inch is adequate, since gravity does all the work. They're best for those who want a quiet, proven design or have low water pressure. But models that approach pressure-assisted performance typically cost just as much, while lower-priced models often aren't up to the job. Price range: $150 to $300 for most.

FEATURES THAT COUNT

Bathroom remodeling is the most common reason to buy a new toilet. Depending upon the configuration of the new bathroom, you may want a round-front or elongated **bowl.** A round-front style is generally a better choice for a small bathroom than an elongated one. Two-piece designs, with a tank that bolts onto the bowl, are less expensive than one-piece designs. Toilets are available in several different "rough-in" dimensions—the clearance to the back wall needed to connect to the water line. The most common rough-in is 12 inches.

HOW TO CHOOSE

Many toilets are replaced as part of a bathroom makeover. But if you're simply replacing a broken gravity toilet, consider having it fixed, especially if you bought it after 1994. A new flapper valve (about $5) or new fill valve (about $15) solves most problems and is easy to install. Once you've decided to buy a new toilet, begin by considering the bathroom's location. If it's near a kitchen or other living area, or your home is small, you're likelier to prefer a quieter toilet.

After you've chosen the type you want, pressure-assisted, vacuum-assisted, or gravity, keep these shopping tips in mind:

Check your water pressure. Before buying a pressure-assisted toilet, be sure that your home has the water pressure it requires. You can check your home's water pressure yourself with a $10 gauge that connects to an outdoor spigot. You'll need at least 25 pounds per square inch for the toilet; allow a little extra to compensate for pressure drops from the spigot to the toilet. If you need to adjust your water pressure, don't go above 80 psi, which can harm toilets and other fixtures.

Consider your cleaning. Most toilets use a two-piece design with a separate tank and bowl; the seam between the two tends to trap grime. One-piece models from Eljer, Kohler, Toto, and others add style while eliminating the seam. But most we tested cost $400 or more.

Choose colors with caution. More models now are available in glacier blue, peach bisque, and other hues. But as with the avocado green and harvest gold that graced '70s kitchens, some could make your bathroom look dated over time.

Decide on a shape. Toilets with a round bowl take the least room and accept the widest variety of seats. If you have the space, consider models with elongated bowls, which are more stylish and allow a longer seat that provides more room and support for a variety of users.

Check the date. Manufacturers often change a toilet's design without changing the model name. An example is the Briggs Classic Vacuity 4200, a top-scoring vacuum model in 2002. A revised version of that model performed much worse in our current tests. Toilets typically have a date stamped inside the tank. Most models we tested were made in 2004.

Check the specs on gravity models. Gravity toilets rely on a flush valve to discharge water from the tank and into the bowl. Beefier valves 3 to 3¼ inches wide deliver more thrust in our tests than gravity models with 2-inch valves. Ask to see the manufacturer's specifications for the flush valve when considering a gravity toilet.

Related CR Report: August 2005

WASHING MACHINES

Front-loaders tend to give you the best of everything, but traditional top-loaders offer the best value.

You'll find more variety in the washing-machine aisle when you visit an appliance store these days. Traditional top-loaders with agitators are going strong, but front-loading washers are gaining ground, thanks to their very good washing performance, large capacity, water and energy efficiency, and quiet operation.

Despite the advantages of front-loaders, many Americans still prefer a top-loading design. Manufacturers have responded with washers that promise some of the advantages of front-loaders in a top-loader. Models include the Calypso from Whirlpool and Kenmore, the GE Harmony, and the Maytag Neptune TL. This new breed of washer replaces the usual vertical agitator post with different mechanisms to circulate laundry. The design increases capacity and reduces water and energy usage.

Washing machines of all types are becoming more energy-efficient. New, stricter Department of Energy standards regarding energy and hot-water use and water extraction became effective in January 2004, and standards will become even more stringent in 2007. Many front-loaders and some top-loaders already meet the 2007 requirements.

WHAT'S AVAILABLE

The top four brands—GE, Kenmore (Sears), Maytag, and Whirlpool—account for more than 80 percent of washing-machine sales. Other brands include Admiral and Amana (made by Maytag), Frigidaire (made by Electrolux), Hotpoint (made by GE), and KitchenAid and Roper (both made by Whirlpool). You may also run across smaller brands such as Crosley, Gibson, and White-Westinghouse, all of which are made by the larger brands. Asko, Bosch, Miele, and Siemens are European brands. Fisher & Paykel is imported from New Zealand, LG and Samsung from Korea, and Haier from China.

Traditional top-loaders. Traditional top-loaders fill the tub with water, then agitate the clothing. They use more water than other types of washers, and thus consume more energy to heat the hot water. They also extract less water from laundry during the spin cycle, which results in longer drying time and higher energy costs. Because they need to move the laundry around to ensure thorough cleaning, these machines hold about 12 to 16 pounds, which is less than large front-loaders and top-loaders without agitators in the center of the tub.

On the plus side, top-loaders make it easier to load laundry and to add items midcycle. You can also soak laundry easily. This type of machine has the shortest cycle times and is the only one that gives the best results with regular detergent. But most top-loaders are noisier than front-loaders, and there's a risk of loads getting unbalanced. Price range: $200 to $650.

High-efficiency (HE) top-loaders with new wash systems. The GE Harmony and the Calypso models from Kenmore and Whirlpool have a "wash plate," rather than an agitator, to move clothes around. The Maytag Neptune TL has discs that lift and tumble laundry. Washing performance is usually better than with regular top-loaders, and capacity is generally larger as well.

These top-loaders work somewhat like front-loaders, filling partially with water and spinning at very high speeds. Most are more efficient with water and energy than regular top-loaders, but the high spin speeds that reduce drying time (and energy consumption) tend to make clothing more wrinkled. These machines work best with low-foaming, high-efficiency detergent. Price range: $900 to $1,300.

Front-loaders. Front-loaders get clothes clean by tumbling them in the water. Clothes are lifted to the top of the tub, then dropped into the water below. They fill only partially with water and then spin at high speed to extract it, which makes them more efficient with water and energy than regular top-loaders. Most handle between 12 and 20 pounds of laundry. Like HE top-loaders, front-loaders wash best with low-sudsing detergent. Many front-loaders can be stacked with a dryer to save floor space. Price range: $600 to $1,600.

Space-saving options. Compact models are typically 24 inches wide or less (compared with about 27 inches for full-sized washers of all types) and they can wash 8 to 12 pounds of laundry. A compact front-loading washer can be stacked with a compact dryer. Some compact washers can be stored in a closet and rolled out to be hooked up to the kitchen sink. Price range: $450 to $1,700.

Washer-dryer laundry centers combine a washer and dryer in one unit, with the dryer located above the washer. These can be full-sized (27 inches wide) or compact (24 inches wide). The full-sized models hold about 12 to 14 pounds, the compacts a few pounds less. Performance is generally comparable to that of full-sized machines. Price range: $700 to $1,900.

FEATURES THAT COUNT

A porcelain-coated steel **inner tub** can rust if the porcelain is chipped. Stainless-steel or plastic tubs won't rust. A stainless-steel tub can withstand higher spin speeds, which extract more water from laundry and speeds drying. A porcelain top/lid resists scratching better than a painted metal one.

Controls should be legible, easy to push or turn, and logically arranged. High-end models often have **touchpad controls;** others have traditional **dials.** Touchpad controls tend to be more versatile; for instance, you may be able to save favorite settings that you use frequently. Some high-end models have a display with a progression of menus. Such menus can be time-consuming to navigate, but they may allow custom programming or offer detailed help information otherwise available only in the manual. A plus: **lights** or **signals** that indicate the cycle.

On some top-loaders, an **automatic lock** during the spin cycle keeps children from opening the lid. Front-loaders lock at the beginning of a cycle but can usually be opened by interrupting the cycle, although some doors remain locked briefly after the machine stops.

Front-loaders and some top-loaders set **water levels** automatically, ensuring efficient use of water. Some top-loaders can be manually set for four or more levels; three or four are probably as many as you would need.

Most machines establish wash and rinse temperatures by mixing hot and cold water in preset proportions. For incoming cold water that's especially cold, an **automatic temperature control** adjusts the flow for the correct wash temperature. This feature is useful if your incoming water is very cold or if your washer is a long way from the water heater.

Some models allow an extra rinse, which can help for those sensitive to detergent residue, or an extended spin to remove more water from laundry. A **time-delay feature** lets you program the washer to start at a later time, such as at night, when your utility rates are low. **Automatic dispensers** for bleach, detergent, and fabric-softener release powder or liquid at the appropriate time in the cycle so they work effectively. Bleach dispensers also prevent spattering.

HOW TO CHOOSE

For best high-end performance, go with a front-loader. If you're willing to spend $1,000 or so, at this point we'd steer you to a front-loader. The best front-loaders offer very good washing, ample capacity, and quiet operation. The front-loading design has been around for a while, and Frigidaire, GE, and Kenmore front-loaders have a good track record for reliability. (Note that numerous readers have reported that their front-loading washers developed mold or a musty smell. Leaving the door ajar between uses and using chlorine bleach occasionally should help.)

Think twice about new-technology top-loaders. Even though some top-loaders have done well in our tests, they're not among our top picks. The Kenmore Calypso was one of the more repair-prone top-loaders, and it left garments tangled and wrinkled in our tests. The GE Profile Harmony and Maytag Neptune TL are too new to have reliability data, and neither was very gentle on clothes.

Get a conventional top-loader for good performance at a modest price. If you want a less expensive machine that's decent across the board, consider a familiar top-loader. Even though these machines aren't as exciting as newer types, they offer decent washing for as little as $500 or less, and there's a large selection of reliable brands. A model judged good or very good for washing should be fine for all but very soiled laundry and should satisfy most consumers.

Consider energy usage. Our tests for energy efficiency differ from those used to determine the government's Energy Star eligibility, giving more weight to performance with maximum loads. As a result, some Energy Star models haven't scored that well for energy efficiency in our Ratings.

Decide if noise is an issue. If you plan to install a washer in a laundry room near the kitchen or a bedroom, we strongly recommend one judged very good or excellent for noise. Front-loaders as a group tend to be very quiet; some top-loaders are as well.

Weigh the value of pricey extras. The more features a washer has, the more it usually costs. Don't buy an expensive model just to get four or more water levels, dozens of cycle and setting combinations, or dedicated cycles for fabrics such as silk. The basic cycles and settings can handle most washing needs, and you can replicate most special cycles with buttons or dials. An electronic touchpad may allow custom programming, but it can also be more confusing to use, especially at first. Unless you insist on the same style, there's no need to match a washer and a dryer. If your old dryer still works fine, don't think you have to replace it when you buy a new washer.

Use the proper detergent. Any washing machine will do a better job if you use a good detergent. For traditional top-loaders, regular detergent is fine, and that's what we used. With front-loaders and high-efficiency top-loaders, you'll get the cleanest clothes with special low-sudsing detergent; that's what we used for these machines. In fact, using regular detergent can cause excessive sudsing in HE washers. Not only is it hard to rinse clothing, but the foam can cause problems with the washer. There are fewer HE products to choose from than with regular detergent, and they cost about 5 to 10 cents more per load than regular detergent. Consider the cost and convenience of ongoing detergent purchases when you're buying a washer.

Related CR Report: February 2005
Ratings: page 332
Reliability: page 338

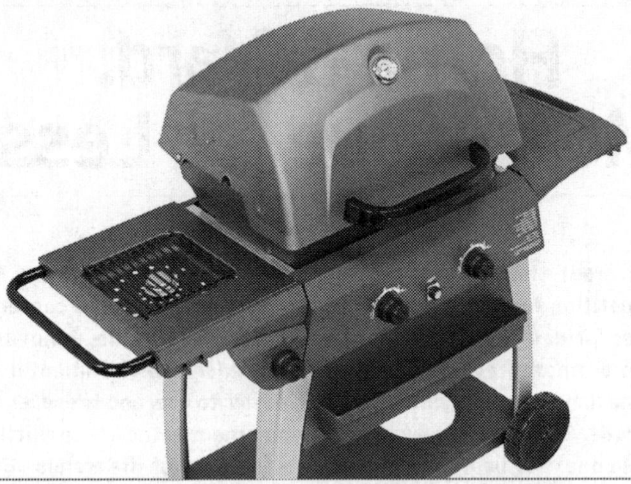

Home and Yard

Home & Yard: More Value for Less

It's a great time to buy products for your home and yard. Fierce competition from the major retailers and big-box home centers has driven prices down in many categories. Meanwhile, innovations, often prompted by tougher state and federal environmental rules, are making home and yard gear safer, easier to use, and friendlier to the environment. So buying a new piece of equipment rather than putting up with an old one may be a good move. Here are some of the trends you'll be seeing in stores this year:

Easier, cheaper mowing. You can pick up a well-equipped automatic-drive lawn tractor for less than $1,000—several hundred dollars less than you would have paid a few years ago. Tractors and mowers are also benefiting from retail competition among Home Depot, Lowe's, and Sears. You'll find easy-to-use clutchless hydrostatic transmissions on a growing number of ride-on mowers and tractors. All of these machines stop the blade when you leave the seat. Most tractors now let you mow in reverse by flipping a safety switch, and walk-behind mowers are easier than ever to start.

Gas grills get more affordable. You'll be pleasantly surprised when you check the price tags on gas grills. Some of the best we tested cost less than $200, and you can start adding features like side burners and up to four main burners before you hit the $300 price range.

Room air conditioners improve. You'll discover that room air conditioners are more energy-efficient, feature-laden, and quieter than the older models. Features such as remote controls and relatively precise electronic temperature controls are available on even the smallest units.

Balance selection, service, and price. In addition to fueling price-cutting competition, the large chains such as Sears and Wal-Mart usually include a wide array of lower-priced brands. Home centers such as Home Depot and Lowe's offer a mix of low-priced, midpriced, and upscale brands. Local hardware stores and other independent dealers tend to carry midpriced and higher-priced brands. Independent stores often offer a level of service that mass merchandisers and home centers don't.

Home and yard products are also sold over the Internet, through sites such as Amazon.com, Homedepot.com, Lowes.com, and Sears.com. Such online sites can be useful, especially as research tools, but there's still a lot to be said for taking a trip to the local hardware store or home center. You can't beat hefting a vacuum cleaner or rolling a mower to see if it feels right in your hands.

AIR CONDITIONERS

Falling prices make individual room air conditioners an inexpensive alternative to central-air systems for cooling one or two rooms.

Once a high-priced convenience, relatively precise electronic controls with digital temperature readouts have replaced vague "warmer" and "cooler" settings on a growing number of lower-priced air conditioners. Added efficiency is also trickling down the price scale. No longer are models that use the least electricity the priciest. Most models in our recent tests have a higher Energy Efficiency Rating (EER) than the federal government requires. To have Energy Star status, brands must meet or exceed 10.7 EER. This means a model is at least 10 percent more efficient than the standard. The minimum EER for air conditioners below 8,000 British thermal units per hour (Btu/hr.) is 9.7; the minimum is 9.8 for those with 8,000 to 13,999 Btu/hr.

WHAT'S AVAILABLE

Fedders, GE, Haier, Kenmore (Sears), LG, Maytag, and Whirlpool are the leading brands. You'll find cooling capacities that range from 5,000 Btu/hr. to more than 30,000 Btu/hr. The majority of room air conditioners in stores are small and midsized units from 5,000 to 9,000 Btu/hr. Large models (9,800 to 12,500 Btu/hr.) can also be found. Price range: about $100 to $600 (small to midsized, depending mostly on cooling capacity); $200 to $800 (large).

FEATURES THAT COUNT

An air conditioner's exterior-facing portion has a **compressor, fan,** and **condenser,** while the part that faces a home's interior contains a fan and an **evaporator.** Most room models are designed to fit double-hung windows, though some are built for casement and slider windows and others for in-wall installation.

Most models have adjustable vertical and horizontal louvers to direct airflow. Many offer a **fresh-air intake** or **exhaust setting** for ventilation, although this feature moves a relatively small amount of air. An energy-saver setting on most units stops the fan when the compressor cycles off. **Electronic touchpad** controls and **digital temperature readouts** are also common. A **timer** lets you program the unit to switch on (say, a half-hour before you get home) or off at a given time. Most models also include a **remote control.** Some models install with a **slide-out chassis**—an outer cabinet that anchors in the window, into which you slide the unit.

The latest feature on air conditioners is a big new plug to help prevent fires. The plug shuts down power when it senses that the air conditioner cord is damaged. The new plugs are known by different names, including **leakage current detection interrupters (LCDI)** and **arc shields.** They have test and reset buttons like those on bathroom and outdoor outlets. The plugs are required by Underwriters Laboratories on units made after July 2004.

HOW TO CHOOSE

These are things to consider:

Assess your room size. A general rule is that 5,000 to 6,000 Btu/hr. models cool rooms 100 to 300 square feet; 7,000 to 8,200 Btu/hr. models cool rooms 250 to 550 square feet; and 9,800 to 12,500 Btu/hr. models cool rooms 350 to 950 square feet. Room construction, climate, and other factors also affect your choice.

Consider window location. To direct

air to the center of the room for uniform cooling, does the air conditioner need to blow more air to the left or right? Most units do a better job directing air in one direction or the other, in part because of the design of the model's internal fan.

Look for third-party certification. When assessing EER, look for a certification sticker from the Association of Home Appliance Manufacturers (AHAM) or the Canadian Standards Association (CSA). An energy-efficient unit will not only help the environment but may also qualify for rebates in some areas; see the Energy Star Web site, at *www.energystar.gov*, for details.

Don't buy features you don't need. Low-profile models take up less space in your window and can direct air up, not just side-to-side, but they are pricier.

Clean it periodically. With any model, clean the filter biweekly or as needed. Where possible, hose off the back of the unit if debris has clogged cooling coils.

Related CR Report: July 2005
Ratings: page 223

CIRCULAR SAWS

Circular saws are a mainstay for quickly cutting the two-by-fours and plywood used in many popular home-improvement projects.

After drills, circular saws are the most common power tool in a home workshop. Battery-powered saws offer go-anywhere convenience, but there's a reason you aren't likely to see professional carpenters using them: Plug-in saws are far more capable.

WHAT'S AVAILABLE

Black & Decker, Bosch, Craftsman (Sears), DeWalt, GMC, Makita, Milwaukee, Porter-Cable, Ryobi, and Skil brands account for most of the circular saws sold.

Corded models. These models run on an electric motor that can range from 10 to 15 amps. The higher the amps, the more power you can expect. Most models are oriented so the motor is perpendicular to the blade. Corded models outperform cordless models by a wide margin with up to seven times the speed and power of cordless saws. Price range: $30 to $175.

High-torque worm/hypoid geared models. In this design, the motor is parallel to the blade. That gives a saw more twisting power, or torque, making the blade less likely to bind in dense or thick wood, though sawing tends to be slower since the blade speed is reduced. Pros like them, but they're heavy and offer little advantage for most users. Price range: $150 to $175.

Cordless models. These range from 14.4 to 24 volts. They usually have a smaller blade than corded models, and their run time is limited by their battery. Price range: $100 to $420.

FEATURES THAT COUNT

Every saw has a large main handle and a stubby **auxiliary handle;** the main handle incorporates the saw's on/off switch. Some saws include a **safety interlock**, a second switch you have to press to turn on the motor. This adds a level of safety by preventing accidental start-ups, but can make the saw awkward to use.

Inexpensive saws have a stamped-steel base and thin housing; pricier models use thick, rugged material, such as reinforced steel, that stands up to hard use. A blade with two dozen large teeth cuts fast but can splinter the wood; a blade with 40 or more teeth gives a cleaner cut. The thinner the blade, the faster the cut.

Bevel adjustment is used to change the angle of the cut from 0 to 45 degrees or more for some saws. The **depth adjustment** changes the blade's cutting depth. A circular saw works best when the teeth just clear the bottom of the wood. A **visible blade**, one that's located to the left of the motor or a notch in the upper blade guard, helps you see the blade and your cutting mark without leaning over the saw. Because the motor on worm-drive saws is parallel to the blade, it's easier to see your cutting mark—one reason pros like worm drives. Many models include a **laser guide**. But the feature is of limited use. You still have to draw a line and use a steady hand. And a laser is useless when you saw outdoors in bright sunlight.

A **spindle lock** keeps the blade from spinning while you change blades. A **blade brake** stops the blade quickly when you release the trigger. The **dust chute** directs the sawdust away so you can see what you're doing. A 9- or 10-foot power cord can make an extension cord unnecessary. Even if you need one, the extra length of the saw cord keeps the cord junction away from your work.

HOW TO CHOOSE

Decide the kind of work you'll do. For occasional light cutting, most any saw is fine. For heavy use or for cutting hard or thick wood, you want a saw with speed and power, such as the top-rated models. Speed also affects safety; you're more likely to push a slow saw, dulling the blade quickly and overheating the motor, or making the saw jam or kick back.

Try it out in the store. Design points that can make a saw easy to use include a visible blade and cutting guide, a blade that's simple to change and to adjust for depth and angle, good balance, a comfortable handle, and a handy on/off switch. How well the saw is constructed impacts its potential for a long, trouble-free life. It should have durable bearings, motor brushes that are accessible for servicing or replacement, a heavy-duty base, and rugged blade-depth and cutting-angle adjustments.

Most new saws now come with carbide-tipped blades. Steel blades are slower than carbide-tipped blades and wear out faster. If your current saw has a steel blade consider replacing it with a carbide-tipped blade when the steel blade wears out. Be sure to match the number of teeth with the material you want to cut; a blade for plywood, say, has more teeth than one for rough cutting.

Safety counts. All the saws are loud enough when cutting to warrant hearing protection. All kick up a lot of chips and dust, so safety glasses or goggles are advised.

Related CR Report: August 2005

DECK TREATMENTS

Deck treatments that retain their appearance the longest are the ones that are the most like paint. Widely advertised clear finishes don't provide long-term protection.

Lumber, like skin, doesn't fare well when it's left unprotected. The sun's ultraviolet rays are always on the attack. Rain and sun alternately swell and dry wood, eventually causing it to crack and split. Moisture promotes the growth of mold and mildew. Even redwood, cedar, and pressure-treated wood can benefit from a protective coat. Our tests show that many clear deck treatments usually don't offer more than a year of protection before their appearance has visibly degraded.

WHAT'S AVAILABLE

Major brands include Ace, Behr, Benjamin Moore, Cabot, Flood, Glidden,

Olympic, Sherwin-Williams, Sikkens, Thompson's, and Wolman. There are also many smaller, specialized brands.

Clear finishes are generally water-repellent, but they don't provide protection from ultraviolet and visible light. They let the wood's natural grain show through but allow the wood to turn gray. Semitransparent finishes contain some pigment but still allow the wood grain to show. Opaque stains completely mask wood grain and are also known as solid finishes. Price range: $10 to just over $50 per gallon.

FEATURES THAT COUNT

Deck treatments may be **alkyd-based (solvent)** or **latex-based (water)**. Most alkyd-based products require cleanup with mineral spirits, but a few can be cleaned with water. Latex-based products clean up with water. Linseed oil and tung oil, once common binders in wood coatings, have largely been replaced by synthetic resins. These new formulations are typically described as preservatives, protectors, stabilizers, repellents, sealers, cleaners, restorers, or rejuvenators.

HOW TO CHOOSE

Make an opaque treatment your first choice, as it retains its appearance the longest. Because an opaque deck treatment should last for two to three years, it's also more economical in the long run. After several coatings, however, an opaque finish can build up a film layer that may require more extensive preparation—such as scraping or sanding—for subsequent coats. Special precautions, such as the use of goggles, gloves, and respirators, are necessary when scraping or sanding pressure-treated wood due to the presence of toxic substances. Consider a semitransparent treatment if you want the wood grain to show. Be aware that if you choose a clear deck treatment, you'll likely be doing the job over again within a year.

Related CR Report: July 2005

DRILLS, CORDLESS

Many 14.4-volt drill/drivers pack all the power you need for a wide variety of chores. And higher-voltage drills can cost little more than less capable, lower-voltage models.

Battery packs with higher voltage and capacity allow today's cordless models to run longer and more powerfully per charge. The best can outperform corded drills and handle decks and other big jobs with minimum battery recharging. Recent tests also show that you don't have to spend $200 or more to get very good performance. Some models in the 14.4- to 18-volt range that cost around $100 perform nearly as well as the most expensive drills.

You'll also see more impact drivers. While similar to conventional drill/drivers, impact drivers emphasize added tightening and loosening power, courtesy of a spinning internal hammer that strikes an anvil attached to the chuck to boost twisting force. Besides being lighter and smaller (most use 12- or 14.4-volt batteries), impact drivers don't twist in your hands under load. But they tend to be slower at drilling and require special drill bits for that task. Those we've tested have also been loud enough to require hearing protection.

WHAT'S AVAILABLE

Black & Decker and Craftsman (Sears) are the major brands. Along with Ryobi and Skil, they're aimed primarily at homeowners. Bosch, DeWalt, Hitachi, Makita, Milwaukee, Ridgid, and Porter-Cable offer pricier drills designed for professionals.

Most 9.6-volt models cost less than $100. At about three pounds, they weigh half as much as some 18-volt models. But unless you value low weight and low cost over performance, you're likely to be disappointed with a 9.6-volt drill. Many 12- and 14.4-volt models also sell for less than $100, and are more capable. Price ranges: Figure on about $40 to $100 for 9.6-volt drills, $50 to $130 for 12- volt drills, $60 to $200 for 14.4-volt models, and about $100 to $300 for 18-volt models.

Cordless impact drills are made by the same manufacturers who make conventional drill/drivers. While many cost $200 or more, as with regular drills, you'll find capable models for around $100.

FEATURES THAT COUNT

A **"smart" charger** recharges a drill's battery in about an hour or less, compared with three to five hours or more for a conventional charger. Smart chargers also extend battery life by adjusting the charge as needed. Most smart chargers switch into a maintenance or "trickle-charge" mode as the battery approaches full charge. One drill has a dual charger that charges two batteries at once.

Most cordless drills 12 volts and more have **two speed ranges**: low for driving screws, high for drilling. Low speed provides more torque, or turning power, than the high-speed setting, which is useful for drilling holes. Most models also have a **variable speed trigger**, which can make starting a hole easier, and an **adjustable clutch**, which lowers maximum torque to avoid driving a screw too far into softwood or wallboard, or mangling its head.

Most drills have a **⅜-inch chuck**, but some higher-voltage models have a ½-inch chuck, which can accommodate drill bits up to a ½ inch. (Large diameter bits with a reduced shank will fit in smaller chucks.) Today's models are also reversible, letting you more easily remove a screw or back a drill bit out of a hole.

Still other features make some drills easier to use than others. Some models have a second handle that attaches onto the side of the drill so you can use two hands for better control when driving large screws, for example. All but the least expensive drills come with two batteries, letting you use one while the other charges.

Most cordless drills run on nickel-cadmium (NiCad) batteries, which can be recharged hundreds of times. Once they're depleted, though, NiCads must be recycled, since cadmium is toxic and can leach out of landfills to contaminate groundwater if disposed of improperly. Incineration can release the substance into the air and pose an even greater hazard to the environment.

A few models run on nickel-metal-hydride (NiMH) batteries, which don't contain cadmium and are friendlier to the environment. In recent tests, CONSUMER REPORTS found that some NiMH-powered models ran longer than many 18-volt and 14.4-volt NiCad-powered as those models yet weighed about the same.

Some drills are bundled with other cordless tools and sold as kits. The package typically includes a circular saw, a reciprocating saw, and—often—a flashlight and carrying case. Some kits are a relatively good deal. But as our reports have shown, cordless circular saws tend to be far weaker than corded models. And some kits are merely a collection of mediocre tools.

HOW TO CHOOSE

High value in the 14.4- to 18-volt category means there's little reason to buy a 12- or 9.6-volt drill/driver. You won't save much money, and power and run time are lower. You'll also find lower-voltage drills that combine ample drilling and screwdriving power for larger household projects without being too heavy for smaller ones.

Determine how much voltage you're likely to need for the drilling and screwdriving tasks you do most. Then ask yourself these questions while you're shopping for a new drill:

Are high-end brands worth it? High voltage isn't the only mark of a capable drill. You can buy an 18-volt drill with a ½-inch chuck for thicker bits, versus the usual ⅜-inch chuck, letting you drill larger holes. But you may not want to pay the $200 or more typical for most cordless drills with that feature if your home to-do list doesn't include larger projects or heavier-duty drilling.

Shop smart
High voltage isn't the only mark of a capable drill.

How much are replacement batteries? A cordless drill's battery can be discharged and recharged roughly 500 times before it must be replaced. While batteries can last five years or more, frequent use can deplete them sooner. At $20 to $80 each for many of the batteries that power drills, replacing them can cost as much as buying a new cordless drill tasks.

Battery replacement may be less of a concern if you're buying a $250 drill you plan to keep for a while. And for models that cost less than $100, simply replacing the drill may make more sense than buying a new pair of batteries. Otherwise, consider battery cost along with the drill.

Are you buying other cordless tools? You're likely to be tempted by multi-tool kits, which cost far less than you'd pay for the tools separately, since the tools in each kit are powered by the same batteries and charger. But these kits can be less of a bargain than they seem; performance of some of the tools they include, particularly circular saws, has been mediocre in our tests, and you may not use all of them.

Related CR Report: May 2004

GRILLS, GAS

Many people are choosing models that do more than just grill. Go high-end, and you can pay as much as you would for a pro-style kitchen range.

Getting a good grill is becoming easier and cheaper as competition heats up; some of the best we tested cost $200 or less. You'll also find $500 grills with the added style, space, and convenience of the much pricier models.

Stainless steel tops the list of high-end features that are moving down the price spectrum. Many lower-priced models now have at least some stainless trim, while midpriced models typically feature more of it as manufacturers find ways to offer the shiny metal for less.

You'll also find more grills that cost $1,000-plus as kitchen-range brands such as Frigidaire and Viking move onto the patio. At the other extreme, manufacturers are introducing more small, portable grills as they cash in on the popularity of tailgating.

WHAT'S AVAILABLE

Char-Broil, Coleman, Kenmore (Sears), and Weber account for more than 60 percent of gas-grill sales.

Basic grill. These grills are ideal for barbecuers who want a good small or medium-sized grill without the frills, for serving four to six people. Features include a painted cart and cast-aluminum firebox and hood; thin porcelain-steel grates; a side burner for some; more stainless trim as you spend more. But most of these grills lack premium, coated cast-iron or thick stainless grates; burners with long warranties; rotisseries; and trays that hold wood chips for smoking. Many carts have only two wheels and lack drawers and other features. Price range: $100 to $300.

Midpriced grill. Grills in this price range are the best choice for most outdoor cooks. Options include medium-sized grills with more features and, increasingly, large models that can cook enough for 15 people. Features include longer-warranty burners; premium grates; higher-heat, recessed side burners; an electronic igniter; a rotisserie or smoker tray; more stainless; double doors. But some carts have only two wheels. Many midpriced models have premium grates or burners with long warranties, but few have both. Price range: $300 to $500.

High-end grill. Best for those who want a more-stylish medium-sized or large grill that can serve up to 15 people. Features include those on midpriced grills plus mostly or all-stainless construction; lifetime burner warranties; more burners with more heat; a fully rolling cart; better storage space. Paying $1,000 or more often buys a toe-kick that hides the wheels. But based on our tests, paying more than $1,000 for a high-end model usually doesn't buy you better grilling. Price range: $500 to $1,000-plus.

FEATURES THAT COUNT

Most cooking **grates** are made of porcelain-coated steel, with others made of the somewhat sturdier porcelain-coated cast iron, bare cast iron, or stainless steel. A porcelain-coated grate is rustproof and easy to clean, but it can eventually chip. Bare cast iron is sturdy and tends to sear impressively, but you have to season it with cooking oil to fend off rust.

The best of both worlds: Stainless steel is sturdy and resists rust without a porcelain coating. Cooking grates with wide, closely spaced bars tend to provide better searing than grates with thin, round rods, which may allow more food to fall to the bottom of the grill.

Grills are mounted on a **cart,** usually made of painted steel tubing assembled with nuts and bolts. Higher-priced grills have welded joints, and some have a cart made of stainless steel. Pricier grills often use 300-series stainless steel, which includes nickel and has more corrosion-fighting chromium than less-expensive, 400-series stainless. Manufacturers often use the cheaper stuff to cut costs. A stainless grill that is magnetic is made of the less-expensive material. Carts with two wheels and two feet must be lifted at one end to move; better are two large wheels and two casters or four casters, which make moving easier. Wheels with a full axle are better than those bolted to the frame, which can bend over time.

Gas grills generally have one or more **exterior shelves,** which flip up from the front or side or are fixed on the side. Shelves are usually made of plastic, although some are made of cast aluminum or stainless steel, which is more durable. (Wood shelves are the least sturdy and tend to deteriorate over time.) Most grills have **interior racks** for keeping food warm without further cooking. Another plus is a **lid** and **firebox** made of stainless steel or porcelain-coated steel, both of which are more durable than cast aluminum.

Still other features help a grill start more easily and cook more evenly. An example is the **igniter,** which works via a knob or a push button. Knobs emit two or three sparks per turn, while push buttons emit a single spark per push. Better are **battery-powered electronic igniters,** which produce continuous sparks as long as the button is held down. Also look for **lighting holes** on the side of or beneath the grill, which are handy if the igniter fails and you need to use a wooden match or propane lighter to start the fire.

Most gas grills have steel **burners,** though some are stainless steel, cast iron, or cast brass. Those premium burners typically last longer and carry warranties of 10 years or more. Many grills have three or more burners, which can add cooking flexibility. A **side burner,** which resembles a gas-stove burner and has its own heat control, is handy for cooking vegetables or sauce without leaving the grill. Other step-up features include an **electric rotisserie,** a **fuel gauge,** a **smoker drawer,** a **wok,** a **griddle pan,** a **steamer pan,** a **deep fryer,** a **nonstick grill basket,** and one or more high-heat **infrared burners** in place of the conventional type.

Tech tip

Main burners warranted for 10 years or more are likely to last longest.

Most gas grills also use a cooking medium—a metal plate or metal bars, ceramic or charcoal-like briquettes, or lava rocks—between the burner and grates to distribute heat and vaporize juices, flavoring the food. Our tests have shown that no one type is better at ensuring even heating.

Gas grills sometimes include a **propane tank;** buying a tank separately costs about $25. Some grills can be converted to run on natural gas or come in a natural-gas version. The tank usually sits next to or on the base of the grill and attaches to its gas line with a handwheel. All tanks must now comply with upgraded National Fire Protection Association standards for overfill protection. Noncompliant tanks have a circular or five-lobed valve and aren't refillable, although they can be retrofitted with a three-lobed valve or swapped for a new tank at a hardware store or other refilling facility.

HOW TO CHOOSE

Most gas grills should perform at least adequately at your next alfresco feast. As with indoor ranges, some models do so with more style and panache.

Consider your cooking. Grills with wide or thick stainless or cast-iron grates tend to be best at searing and browning quickly to seal in juices—essential for meats and fish. Wide grates also leave the wide grill marks barbecue buffs crave. But heavy grates can take longer to heat up.

Take a head count. If you often entertain large crowds, look for a large grill with lots of grilling, shelf, and storage space.

Inspect the burners. These distribute the gas and flames. They're also the most-replaced part. Main burners warranted for 10 years or more are likely to last longest. Recessed side burners are also a plus, since some can accept a griddle and others include one. If you don't cover your grill, look for a side burner with its own cover.

Check the construction. Make sure the rolling cart that supports the firebox and lid doesn't rattle when shaken. If you want a stainless-steel grill and you're picky about stains, look for stainless fasteners and better, 300-series stainless (bring a magnet to the store). Or consider buying a grill made with the cheaper, 400-series stainless and protecting it with a cover (about $40 to $50).

Related CR Report: June 2005
Ratings: page 260

HUMIDIFIERS

Using a humidifier can help ease dry skin and other problems associated

with dry air. But choosing one involves trade-offs among efficiency, cost, noise, and convenience.

Who needs a humidifier? Anyone who suffers from uncomfortably dry or itchy eyes, throat, or skin, or whose asthma is a problem indoors during the heating season. Ideally, the indoor humidity should be 30 to 50 percent. But that level can drop significantly in winter, since cold air holds less moisture, and heating it makes it even dryer.

Humidifiers have improved over some earlier models, which spewed white dust in our tests. But that doesn't mean they all work equally well. What's more, CONSUMER REPORTS tests show that manufacturer claims can be a poor guide to how well a humidifier will work; several small tabletop models fell well short of their claimed output and may not raise the humidity to the desired level.

WHAT'S AVAILABLE

Major humidifier brands include Bemis, Bionaire, Emerson, Holmes, Honeywell, Hunter, Kaz, Kenmore, Lasko, and Sunbeam.

Humidifiers come in three major configurations:

Tabletop. These cost the least and are fine for single rooms. Tabletop humidifiers include evaporative models, which use a fan to blow air over a wet wick, and warm-mist models, which use a heating unit to boil water before cooling the steam. However, smaller tanks need to be refilled more frequently. Evaporative models are noisy; warm-mist models are costly to run. Price range: $40 to $100.

Console. With larger tanks that require less refilling, console models are a suitable choice for humidifying multiple rooms. Console humidifiers are also efficient and can be placed unobtrusively. But all use evaporative technology and are relatively noisy. The larger the tank, the more difficult it will be to handle. Price range: $80 to $140.

In-duct. These whole-house humidifiers are convenient, quiet, and efficient, making them the least expensive to operate. Most are evaporative bypass units, which tap into the air supply and return ducts. Some are warm-mist; others are nebulizers, which use a spray technology. In-duct humidifiers can be used only with forced-air heat. While inexpensive to operate, they're the most expensive to buy and often require professional installation. Price range: $90 to $200, plus $100 to $150 more to install.

FEATURES THAT COUNT

A good portable model should offer relatively easy carrying, filling, cleaning, and wick replacement. Also look for easy-to-use controls and tanks that fit beneath faucets. Some portable models can be programmed to turn on automatically.

HOW TO CHOOSE

Decide the size you want based on how many rooms you need to humidify. Before buying a portable model, be sure you're willing to take the trouble to clean and disinfect it regularly to prevent mold and mildew. Otherwise, consider an in-duct humidifier, which is plumbed into the water supply and drainpipes, needn't be refilled, and has an easy-to-change filter that requires attention only once or twice a year.

Then keep these considerations in mind as you shop:

Be sure it has a humidistat. Whether it's dial or digital, a humidistat controls humidity levels and shuts the humidifier off when the set level is reached. Models without a humidistat can allow humidity levels to rise high enough to form condensation on windows and other cold surfaces. Overhumidification can also lead to mold and bacteria growth. Humidistats that display room humidity levels and settings are best.

Also be aware that some humidistats aren't accurate or reliable. And most portable humidifiers won't let you set humidity levels below 30 percent. When outside temperatures drop below 20° F, even a 30-percent indoor humidity level can lead to window condensation. Be sure to lower humidity levels as outdoor temperatures drop.

Noise level. Consider a warm-mist tabletop if quietness counts. All warm-mist humidifiers were quieter than evaporative models; some made little or no noise beyond mild boiling and hissing sounds. By contrast, comparably sized evaporative humidifiers generated 45 to 50 decibels on low settings—about as much noise as a small air conditioner—and emitted more than 50 decibels on high. At 80 decibels on its high setting, one model proved as raucous as a loud vacuum cleaner.

For larger areas, consider buying a noisier console model and locating it away from sleeping areas; the water vapor travels quickly through the home air and will still benefit remote bedrooms if doors remain open for air exchange. While you could alternatively buy several warm-mist tabletop models, doing so costs more.

Factor in the running costs. In-duct systems and other evaporative models deliver the most energy efficiency. While initially pricey, in-duct humidifiers are likely to cost the least over time; you can easily spend $350 per year to run four tabletop models compared with just $28 for one in-duct model.

Consider your water. Some humidifiers have lower output with hard water. Nonetheless, you'll find tabletop, console, evaporative, and warm-mist humidifiers that perform well under those conditions.

Related CR Report: October 2004

LAWN MOWERS

Practically any mower will cut your grass. But you'll get better results with less effort if you choose a machine based on your lawn size, mowing preferences, and budget.

Mowing options range anywhere from $100 manual-reel mowers to tractors that cost $4,000 or more. If you have a small yard, a manual-reel or electric walk-behind mower is probably fine. Gasoline-powered walk-behind mowers are appropriate for most lawns up to about a half-acre. If your lawn is larger, you might appreciate the ease and speed of a ride-on lawn tractor.

Compared with cars, gasoline-powered lawn mowers produce a disproportionate amount of air pollution. Federal regulations aimed at reducing smog-producing mower emissions have made today's gas-powered mowers cleaner than old ones—something to consider if you're now using an older mower.

WHAT'S AVAILABLE

Manual-reel mowers are still made by a few companies. Major brands of electric mowers include Black & Decker and Craftsman (Sears). Of all brands, Craftsman sells the most gasoline-powered walk-behind mowers. Other less expensive, mass-market brands include Bolens, Murray, Yard Machines, and Yard-Man. Pricier brands, traditionally sold at outdoor power-equipment dealers, include Ariens, Cub Cadet, Honda, Husqvarna, John Deere, Lawn-Boy, Snapper, and Toro. Several of those brands are now available at large retailers, including Home Depot and Lowe's.

Which type is best for your lawn? Here are the basics about each to help you decide:

Manual-reel mowers. Pushing these

simple mowers turns a series of curved blades that spin with the wheels. Reel mowers are quiet, inexpensive, and nonpolluting. They're also relatively safe to operate and require little maintenance other than periodic blade adjustment and sharpening. On the downside, our tests have shown that cutting performance is typically mediocre, and most can't cut grass higher than 1½ inches or trim closer than 3 inches around obstacles. Some models have cutting swaths just 14 to 18 inches wide—another drawback. Consider them for small, flat lawns a quarter-acre or less. Price range: $100 to about $400.

Electric mowers. These push-type, walk-behind mowers use an electric motor to drive a rotating blade. Both corded and cordless versions start with the push of a button. They produce no exhaust emissions, and, like reel mowers, require little maintenance aside from sharpening. Most offer a side or rear grass catcher, and many can mulch—a process where clippings are recut until they're small enough to hide unobtrusively within the lawn. But electrics are less powerful than gas mowers and less adept at tackling tall or thick grass and weeds. What's more, their narrow, 18- to 19-inch swaths take a smaller bite than the 21-inch swath found on most gas-powered mowers.

Both corded and cordless electrics have other significant drawbacks. Corded mowers limit your mowing to within 100 feet of a power outlet—the typical maximum length for extension cords. Cordless versions, while more versatile, weigh up to 30 pounds more than corded models and typically mow just one-quarter to one-third acre before their sealed, lead-acid batteries need recharging. Both types of electrics are mainly suitable for small, flat lawns of a quarter-acre or less. Price range: corded, $125 to $250; cordless, $400 or more.

Gas-powered walk-behind mowers. These include push mowers and self-propelled models with driven wheels. Most have a 4.5- to 6.5-hp four-stroke engine and a cutting swath 21 or 22 inches wide, allowing you to cover more ground with each pass, and handle long or thick grass and weeds. All can mow as long as there's fuel in the tank. But gas mowers are relatively noisy and require regular maintenance.

Most gas mowers provide three cutting modes: bagging, which gathers clippings in a removable catcher; side-discharging, which spews clippings onto the lawn; and mulching, which cuts and recuts clippings until they're small enough to settle and decompose within the lawn.

Consider a push-type model for mowing relatively flat lawns of about a quarter-acre or for trimming larger lawns. Choose a self-propelled model for hilly lawns or lawns of a half-acre or more. You might also choose a self-propelled mower if you mostly bag clippings; a full bag can add 20 or 30 pounds to the mower's weight. Price range: push-type, $150 to $400; self-propelled, $200 to $900.

FEATURES THAT COUNT

For electric mowers. A sliding clip **electric cord keeper** (holder) helps ease turns when using corded mowers by allowing the cord to move from side to side. Some have a **flip-over handle** you move from one end of the mower to the other as you reverse direction, say, at the end of a row.

For gas-powered mowers. Some models have a **blade-brake clutch system** that stops the blade but allows the engine to keep running when you release the handlebar safety bail. This is more convenient than the usual **engine-kill system,** which stops the engine and blade and requires that you restart the engine. An **overhead-valve engine** tends to generate less pollution than a traditional **side-valve** engine and is often quieter.

With most gas mowers, you press a small rubber bulb called a **primer** to supply extra fuel for cold starting. Some now use a manual choke that automatically shuts off. An **electric starter** is easier to use than a recoil starter, though it typically adds $75 to the price. Most mowers with a **recoil starter** are easier to start than they once were, however.

Some self-propelled mowers have just **one speed,** usually about 2½ mph; others have **several speeds** or a **continuous range,** typically from 1 to 3½ mph. Driven mowers also include **front-drive** and **rear-drive** models. Rear-wheel-drive models tend to have better traction on hills and with a full grass-collection bag. Mowers with **swivel front wheels** offer the most maneuverability by allowing easy 180-degree turns. But on some, each front casterlike wheel must be removed to adjust cutting height.

You'll also find several different deck choices. Most are steel, although some mowers offer **aluminum** or **plastic** decks, which are rustproof; plastic decks also resist dents and cracks. Nearly all mowers now have **tool-free cutting-height adjusters,** which raise and lower the deck with wheel-mounted levers. Some let you adjust cut height with only one or two levers, rather than having to adjust each wheel. Most models also allow you to change mowing modes without tools, although a few still require wrenches and, rarely, a blade change. A few models have a **variable-mode lever** that lets you mulch some of the clippings and bag the rest. Some models use a **side-bagging deck design,** where a side-exit chute routes clippings into a side-mounted bag or out onto the lawn—or is blocked with a plate or plug for mulching.

Mowers with a **rear-bagging deck** tend to cost more, but their rear-mounted bag holds more than side bags and eases maneuvering by hanging beneath the handlebar rather than out to the side. The rearward opening is fitted with a chute for side discharging or a plug for mulching.

HOW TO CHOOSE

You'll see lots of competent choices for mowing the typical quarter- to half-acre lawn. Here are the most critical points to consider as you shop:

Pick your power. Gasoline-powered mowers continue to perform best overall, especially in long or dense grass. Self-propelled models are best for larger or hillier terrain, while lighter push models are fine for smaller, flatter lawns or for trimming. On the downside, gas models of both types are relatively noisy, create exhaust emissions, and require periodic tune-ups. Most also require pull-starting.

Electric mowers are quieter and create no exhaust emissions. They also free you from fueling and engine maintenance, and start with the push of a button. But even the best corded electric mowers aren't as powerful as gas models. Cordless models free you from the tether and tangles of a power cord. But they're pricey and have limited run time before their batteries need recharging.

Manual reel mowers are another clean and quiet option, since they rely solely on people power to move their spiral-shaped mowing blades. Most models are relatively inexpensive (about $130 to $200). But some can be hard to push. And those in past tests couldn't match a power mower's cut quality.

Pick your mowing mode. Most walk-behind mowers can mulch, bag, or side-discharge clippings. But not all mowers handle all three modes equally well. Choose a model that scored well in the mowing mode you use most. If you bag most clippings, you'll probably prefer a self-propelled mower, since a full bag can make push types a handful, especially uphill.

Check the drive control. Most self-propelled mowers have two controls: a blade-engagement bail you must hold against the handlebar and a bail for adjusting the speed. Some new models now use a short lever that allows you to engage and vary ground speed by squeezing it with the right hand.

Those we tested worked well. But some levers can be stiffer than others—a potential problem for some users, since all require constant pressure to keep the machine moving. As with all controls, see if you can try such levers before buying.

Don't get bowled over by big names. You'll find a Honda engine on even more non-Honda walk-behind lawn mowers this year as Craftsman, Lawn-Boy, Yard-Man, and other brands use Honda's premium image to give their machines some added cachet. These newer engines aren't the commercial-grade versions that made Honda's reputation for durability, however. While those we tested performed well, so did the more-plebeian Briggs & Stratton and Tecumseh engines on many other machines.

Don't count horses. High horsepower is another rallying cry at the store and online. Many of the mowers we tested now have up to 7 hp on tap. But mowers with at least 5.5 hp performed just as well overall as higher-horsepower models.

Related CR Report: June 2005
Ratings: page 263
Reliability: page 269

LAWN TRACTORS

If your lawn is larger than a half-acre, a ride-on lawn tractor could be your best option.

Heated competition among the big-box stores has lowered the price of a well-equipped automatic-drive tractor to as little as $1,000 or so. That's several hundred dollars less than comparable machines from only a few years ago.

Big-name brands are also piling on premium features as they trade some of the profit margins they enjoyed at the corner mower shop for the added volume of home centers and large retailers like Sears, which together sell nearly 70 percent of lawn tractors.

WHAT'S AVAILABLE

Lawn tractors now dominate the rise-on marketplace, with some models available for less than the cost of a riding mower. (Keep in mind, though, that a bagging kit will typically add another $250 to $400 to the total cost). Tractors can accept light-duty attachments to plow, tow a cart, or clear snow. Lower prices and versatility help explain why lawn tractors have become far more popular than riding mowers.

Tight-turning riders are a growing alternative. Also known as zero-turn-radius models, these let you steer by pushing or pulling levers, each controlling a driven rear wheel. The advantage is added maneuverability in tight spots and around obstacles. But you pay a premium for agility and faster cutting. Price range: riding mowers, $1,000 to $2,000; lawn tractors, $1,000 to $2,500; tight-turning riders, $2,500 to $7,000 and beyond.

FEATURES THAT COUNT

Lower-priced models are **gear-driven** and require a shift lever and combination brake/clutch to change speed. Spending more will buy you a model with a **clutchless automatic drive,** which allows even more convenient, continuously variable speed changes via a **hydrostatic transmis-**

sion or a **continuously variable transmission (CVT)**. Most models have a **translucent fuel tank,** making it easy to check fuel level. Some have a **fuel gauge** and **cup holders.** Still others provide cruise control to rest your foot on long runs and an electric **power takeoff (PTO)** switch to engage the cutting blades, instead of a manual lever.

HOW TO CHOOSE

Wide-swath mowing at a reasonable price makes lawn tractors an appealing choice if you have a half-acre or more of lawn. Falling prices for tractors also help explain why small, rear-engine riders are nearly extinct.

Keep these points in mind as you shop:

Determine the mowing you'll do. All tractors can side-discharge clippings, the mode most people use. Many include a mulching plate that seals the deck so clippings are cut finely and deposited into the lawn rather than on it. But a kit for bagging clippings typically costs hundreds of dollars extra. Before paying more for that bagging, be sure that the model you're considering did well in that mode and that you will use it.

Pick your retailer. Most of the brands we tested are now at major retailers as well as dealers. Big-box stores tend to have the lowest prices. But dealers typically offer more personalized service, setup, and instruction. John Deere, Poulan, and Yard Machines are at Home Depot. Bolens, Cub Cadet, Husqvarna, and Troy-Bilt are sold at Lowe's. Sears sells Craftsman and Husqvarna, and Wal-Mart has Yard Machines and Yard-Man.

Don't count horses. Some models now pack 20 hp or more. Higher horsepower doesn't guarantee more performance, however; models with as little as 17 hp mowed as well as brawnier models.

Play it safe. Use common sense when mowing. Wear ear plugs or muffs; all of the machines we tested emitted more than the 85 decibels at which we recommend hearing protection. Don't mow on grades steeper than 15 percent. Look behind you when you mow in reverse.

Related CR Report: May 2005
Ratings: page 270
Reliability: page 274

MATTRESSES

Once you've settled on the size you need, shop around for the firmness and feel you like. Try each top choice for 15 minutes in the store.

Shopping for a mattress can be a nightmare. The reason is that shoppers are flying blind. It's hard to tell one box of metal, foam, fuzz, and fabric from another, making you vulnerable to a sales pitch. Model names differ from store to store, making it impossible to comparison shop. And prices vary so much that the $1,300 mattress set you look at one day can cost $2,600 the next.

From years of bashing and dissecting, we know that all but the cheapest mattresses are apt to be sturdy, but there are no reliability data for specific models or even brands. The bottom line is that despite the claims you'll hear, there is no best bed for everyone. You'll need to spend time finding the mattress that's most comfortable and supportive for you. The good news is that trying a mattress for 15 minutes in a store can predict long-term satisfaction.

WHAT'S AVAILABLE

Innerspring mattresses are the most widely sold type. Sealy, Serta, Simmons, and Spring Air are the top-selling brands. Highly hyped alternatives to conventional innersprings include Duxiana (springs galore, in layers), Select Comfort (air-filled, with adjustable firmness for each partner), and Tempur-Pedic (polyurethane "memory foam"). Price range: $500 to more than $5,000.

FEATURES THAT COUNT

Most stores have a cutaway or cross-section of at least some of the mattress sets on display. Here's what matters:

Ticking, the outermost layer, is typically polyester or cotton-polyester. On fancier mattresses, you'll see plush fabrics such as fancy damask, jersey knit, microsuede, wool, cashmere, and silk. None of this matters. What does? The stitching that binds the ticking to the top padding can affect feel. If you like a deep, cushiony sensation, look for a large quilt pattern. A smaller pattern tends to squeeze down top padding, creating a slightly firmer feel. Some ticking includes silk, which adds to the price but provides no real benefit.

Top padding generally consists of one or more types of polyurethane foam, with or without polyester batting. Polyester batting provides a soft feel and makes a mattress more breathable, allowing perspiration to dissipate quickly. Look for a mattress with polyester; more than an inch, and it's apt to sag eventually. In foam layers, look for latex, which is soft, supportive, and resilient, and visco-elastic "memory foam," which conforms to your body and can help keep you from feeling motion on the other side of the bed. Convoluted foam ("egg crate") feels softer than a straight slab of the same type of foam.

Coils provide the main support, and all the hyped types—whether Bonnell (in an hourglass shape), continuous wire, or individually pocketed—are up to the task. The wire's gauge is what counts. Heavier-gauge coils can provide a stiffer suspension. Lighter-gauge coils usually lend a springier feel.

For **extra support,** some manufacturers beef up certain areas by using more closely spaced coils, slabs of stiff foam around edges and between coils, or thicker wire. Stiffer edges make for a solid place to sit and tie your shoes, and keep you from feeling as if you'll roll off. Salespeople are also quick to point out extra support at the mattress's head, foot, or center. Among big-name mattresses with extra-support zones: Simmons BackCare and Sealy BackSaver.

There's nothing springy about **foundations;** they simply provide support. Manufacturers often deliver the same foundation with various models within their lines, regardless of price. If you buy an ultrathick mattress, consider pairing it with a "low profile" foundation, 4 to 6 inches thick, instead of the usual 10 inches or so. That way, you won't need a stepladder to climb into bed.

HOW TO CHOOSE

Consider an innerspring first. A conventional innerspring mattress is the most common choice and often the least expensive. Memory foam, which was developed to protect astronauts against g-forces, is heat-sensitive and conforms to your body. Tempur-Pedic is the big name, but there are other brands. Not all memory foam feels the same, and it can take time to get used to. A third option: an inflatable mattress that lets you choose a different firmness for each half of the bed. Select Comfort is the major brand.

Decide where to shop. Buy at a store, not online or over the phone, unless you've already tried the identical mattress in a store. Department stores have frequent sales and lots of brands, but can be somewhat crowded, cluttered, and short on sales help. Bedding stores such as Sleepy's and

1-800-Mattress, and furniture stores such as Seaman's, offer plenty of variety and are often less crowded.

Understand the name game. Manufacturers usually modify any innerspring mattress they make for different sellers, changing the color, padding, quilting pattern, and so forth. Then each seller can call the mattress by a different name. Consumers are the losers. Since such mattresses are at least somewhat different, and the names vary, you can't comparison-shop. (A big chain such as Sears or Bloomingdale's has the same model names for the same beds at all of its stores, but usually at the same price.)

Shop smart

You'll just have to try a mattress for 15 minutes in a store in order to figure out if it's right for you.

Some bedmakers provide helpful information on their Web sites. Go to *www.simmons.com*, for example, and you'll uncover basics about the company's flagship Beautyrest lines, the Classic, World Class, and Exceptionale. You'll see those names wherever you find Beautyrest, and all beds in each line share attributes.

Choose the right firmness. Don't rely on names: Levels are described differently. One company's ultraplush might be another's supersoft. Orthopedists once recommended sleeping on an extremely firm mattress, but there's little evidence to support that view.

Do the 15-minute in-store test. Don't be embarrassed to lie down on lots of mattresses in the store. Salespeople expect it. Wear loose clothes, and shoes that you can slip off. Spend at least five minutes on each side and your back (your stomach, too, if that's a preferred position).

Assess your need for a new box spring. Foundations can sell for as much as the mattress they're sold with, even though they're generally just a wood frame enclosing stiff wire and covered with fabric matching the mattress's.

We found that companies frequently pair the same foundation with mattresses in different price ranges. You might save by buying a higher-priced mattress with a lower-priced foundation. Once the bed is made, no one will know. If your current foundation is only a few years old, with no rips, warps, creaks, or "give," consider using it with a new mattress. If the old box has bouncy springs instead of stiff wire, it needs to be replaced.

Be wary of "comparables." If you like a mattress at one store and ask elsewhere for something similar, you're likely to be steered toward a same-brand mattress that's supposed to have the same construction, components, and firmness. It's unlikely. Manufacturers don't publish a directory of comparables.

Don't count on warranties. They cover defects in materials and workmanship, not comfort or normal wear. They're typically in effect for 10 years; Duxiana, Select Comfort, and Tempur-Pedic are in effect for 20. Some warranties don't cover full replacement value; an annual usage charge is deducted from the current retail price.

When you make a claim, the store or manufacturer sends an inspector to your house. You'll need to show your receipt. If you say the bed has sagged, the inspector checks whether the dip is below the allowable limit, 1½ inches. A company will void a warranty if you remove the "do not remove" tag, if the mattress is soiled, or if it has uneven support from foundation or frame.

Wait for a sale, and bargain. Specialty mattresses usually have a set price, but you can save at least 50 percent off list price for an innerspring type. Ads for "blowout" sales make such events seem rare. They aren't. If the price is good, buy; if not, wait. An advertised "bargain" may not be all it seems, so read the fine print.

Related CR Report: June 2005

MINI-TILLERS

Mini-tillers aren't just for ardent gardeners. The best of these machines can handle more-pedestrian chores such as tearing away crabgrass and whisking away weeds far more quickly and easily than a spade or hoe.

Several new models add faster starts and more digging power, courtesy of a four-stroke engine like the kind on mowers. They also run cleaner, since four-stroke tillers produce fewer exhaust emissions than two-stroke models—a prime reason most two-stroke tillers are not certified for stricter California emissions standards. Yet at about $300, most of these cleaner machines cost only slightly more than two-stroke models.

You'll also find plug-in electric tillers, along with tiller attachments that replace the bottom half of the shaft on some string trimmers.

WHAT'S AVAILABLE

Half of all tillers are sold by Home Depot (Honda, Yard Machines), Lowe's (Troy-Bilt), and Sears (Craftsman). Other brands include Mantis, Ryobi, and Toro.

Gas mini-tillers. Gas models are best for planting shrubs, reseeding lawn patches, and tending areas smaller than 300 square feet. Most four-stroke models are easier to start and handle, and most have a swath 9 to 10 inches wide. Gas models do require maintenance, though, and tend to be louder and heavier than electrics. Two-stroke models require mixing gas and oil. All gas-powered tillers are noisy; all the gasoline-powered tillers and trimmer-driven machines we tested produced noise levels at or above the 85 decibels at which we recommend hearing protection. Price range: $150 to $400.

Electric mini-tillers. If you're near an outlet and have lighter-duty tasks, this kind should do the trick. Most are lighter and quieter than gas tillers, and all free you from fueling, pull-starting, and engine tune-ups, and produce no exhaust emissions. Most have a swath 9 to 10 inches wide. Most, however, just don't perform as well as gas models. Be careful of the power cord, which can get caught in the tines or damage fragile plants. Electric tillers are quiet by comparison; the quietest emitted just 68 decibels at ear level, making it quieter than many vacuum cleaners. Price range: $150 to $300.

Trimmer-based tillers. These models are right if you already own a string trimmer and care mostly about light-duty weeding. These replace the line head on trimmers that take attachments. Most swaths are 9 to 10 inches wide. On the downside, they do does tend to be heavy, poorly balanced, and short on performance. Dedicated tillers are a better bet. Price range: about $90 for the tiller; $80 to $200 for the trimmer.

Larger tillers. These are the bigger machines, best for reseeding a large lawn, deeper tilling jobs in harder or rockier soil, and tending areas that are larger than 300 square feet. Most have a swath 14 to 21 inches wide. But size can also be a drawback: They're heavy, bulky, and pricey. The largest can also be hard to handle. Consider renting as an option if you're only going to use it occasionally. Price range: $600 to $2,000; about $60 per day to rent one.

FEATURES THAT COUNT

A **four-stroke engine** typically starts with fewer pulls and delivers more power at lower speeds. It also produces fewer emissions than a two-stroke and requires no fuel-mixing. Tillers with clevis pins at the outsides of the tines, rather than within, make it easier to remove tines to clear a jam or narrow the tilling width. A **handle-mounted switch** lets you stop the engine or motor quickly from the operator's position. Models with an effective **drag stake** help keep the moving tines from pulling the tiller forward too fiercely as you work. Good ones are long enough to penetrate the soil. Some tillers use a relatively short stake or a roller. **Transport wheels** let you roll, rather than carry, a tiller to and from the garage or shed. If the ground is too rough for wheels, look for a **lift handle,** which makes carrying easier. **Angled tines** tend to be better for mixing soil. **Pointed tines** reduce pulling effort and are often better at sod-busting.

Shop smart

Be sure that any mini-tiller is reasonably easy to lift and rolls smoothly on its wheels.

HOW TO CHOOSE

Mini-tillers have grown in sales as lot sizes and gardens have shrunk. But they aren't for everyone. You're likely to prefer renting or even buying a larger tiller for yard projects beyond 300 square feet or for rocky soil. You may also prefer the added control of hand tools for jobs smaller than 100 square feet.

If you've decided advantages outweigh disadvantages, keep these points in mind as you shop:

Determine how you'll use it. The best of these machines excel at tilling, sod-busting, and weeding. But you may be willing to trade some performance in one or more of those areas for a lower price or an electric's push-button starting.

Look for convenience. Features that make some tillers easier to use include a four-stroke engine for gas models, along with easy tine removal and wheels for all tillers. Also be sure that any tiller is reasonably easy to lift and rolls smoothly on its wheels. Check, too, that the handlebar is wide enough to allow both elbows to clear your sides when you pull back on the machine—something you'll do often while working as the tines pull the tiller ahead.

Consider repairs down the road. Some retailers have service agreements with local dealers, as do brands such as Hoffco, which are sold by manufacturers. Before buying, ask which dealer will provide your service. Then call or visit the dealer to get a sense of whether you'll be treated as well as customers who bought their machines at that dealer.

Think twice about add-ons. With some tillers, you can buy dethatchers, edgers, aerators, and other attachments for roughly \$40 to \$100 each. As with tiller attachments for trimmers, however, we've typically found these add-ons less effective than dedicated machines.

Keep it safe. Wear goggles and boots, along with hearing protection when using a gas tiller. And keep children and pets away while you work.

Related CR Report: March 2005

PAINT, EXTERIOR

The best paint can improve your home's appearance and protect it from the weather for about nine years.

While a fresh coat of paint on the siding and trim will give your house curb appeal, exterior paint isn't just for show. It provides an important layer of protection against moisture, mildew, and the effects of the sun.

WHAT'S AVAILABLE

Major brands include Ace, Behr (sold at Home Depot), Benjamin Moore, Dutch Boy, Glidden, Sears, Sherwin-Williams, True Value, and Valspar (sold at Lowe's). You'll also see many brands of paint sold regionally.

Exterior paints come in a variety of sheens. The dullest is flat, followed by low-luster (often called eggshell or satin), semigloss, and gloss. The flatter finishes are best for siding, with the lowest-sheen variety the best choice if you need to mask imperfections. Glossy paint is most often used for trim because it highlights the details of the woodwork and the paint is easy to clean. Price range: $15 to $40 a gallon.

HOW TO CHOOSE

Our tests of exterior paints are very severe, exposing painted panels on outdoor racks angled to catch the maximum amount of sun. One year of testing is approximately equal to three years of real-life exposure. Generally, most paints will look good for at least three years, and some should look good for about six. Most also do a good job of resisting the buildup of mildew and preventing the wood from cracking. To determine the best paint for your home, consider the following tips:

Buy the best. Our tests have found that the grade of paint matters. "Good" or "economy" grades don't weather as well as top-of-the-line products. Using a cheaper grade of paint means you'll spend more time and money in the long run because you'll need to repaint more often. "Contractor" grades of paint that we've tested in the past also tended to be mediocre.

Consider where you live. Paints of any color accumulate dirt over time. The top-rated paints tended to resist it better than the others; darker colors hide it better. Mildew can be a problem in damp areas, from rainy Seattle to steamy Tampa, or on any house that gets more shade than sun. Baking in bright sun can change even the best-quality pigments. Blues and yellows are the most likely to change.

Don't overlook the prep work. Be sure you scrape, sand, and clean the siding thoroughly before applying the paint. Good preparation makes any paint last longer. And plan to apply two coats.

Related CR Report: June 2005

PAINT, INTERIOR

Plenty of high-quality, durable wall paints are available to brighten your rooms. And you won't need to endure as many fumes as in years past.

A fresh coat of paint is an easy, inexpensive way to freshen a room. Today's paints are significantly better than their predecessors of even a few years ago in several important respects: They spatter less, keep stains at bay, and have ample tolerance for scrubbing. They also resist the buildup of mildew (important if you're painting a kitchen, a bathroom, or a basement room that tends to be damp). Some are labeled low-VOC (volatile organic compounds).

WHAT'S AVAILABLE

The major brands include Ace, Behr (sold at Home Depot), Benjamin Moore, Dutch Boy, Glidden, Kilz (sold at Wal-Mart), Sears, Sherwin-Williams, and American Tradition by Valspar (sold at Lowe's). You'll also see designer names such as Martha Stewart and Ralph Lauren, as well as many brands of paint sold regionally.

You'll find several types of paints for interior use. Wall paints can be used in just about any room. Glossier trim enamels are usually used for windowsills, woodwork, and the like. Kitchen and bath paints are usually fairly glossy and formulated to hold up to water and scrubbing and to release stains. Price range: $10 to $35 per gallon.

FEATURES THAT COUNT

Paint typically comes in a variety of sheens—**flat, low luster,** and **semigloss.** The degree of glossiness can be different from one manufacturer to another. Flat paint, with the dullest finish, is the best at hiding surface imperfections, but it also tends to pick up stains and may be marred by scrubbing. It's well suited for formal living rooms, dining rooms, and other spaces that don't see heavy use.

A low-luster finish (often called eggshell or satin) has a slight sheen and is good for family rooms, kids' rooms, hallways, and the like. Semi-gloss, shinier still, usually works best on kitchen and bathroom walls and on trim because it's generally easier to clean. Low-luster and semigloss paints look best on smooth, well-prepared surfaces, since the paint's shine can accentuate imperfections on the wall.

Most brands come in several tint bases—the uncolored paint that forms the foundation for the specific color you choose. The tint base largely determines the paint's toughness, resistance to dirt and stains, and ability to withstand scrubbing. The colorant determines how much the paint will fade. Whites and browns tend not to fade; reds and blues fade somewhat; bright greens and yellows tend to fade a lot.

HOW TO CHOOSE

Begin with the gloss. The gloss level will affect your perception of the color. Flat paints and textured walls absorb light, so colors seem darker. Glossy paints and smooth surfaces reflect, so colors look brighter.

Choose a color. Take advantage of the various color-sampling products and computer programs to get the color you think you want. Most manufacturers now sell small samples of many paint colors, so you can test a paint without having to buy large quantities. Manufacturers also offer large color chips or coupons, which are easier to use than the conventional small swatches. Sunlight and room light can affect your perceptions, so check samples on different walls or at different times of day.

Fluorescent light enhances blues and greens but makes warm reds, oranges, and yellows appear dull. Incandescent light works with warm colors but might not do much for cool ones. Even natural sunlight changes from day to day, room to room, and morning to night.

Many aspects of paint performance depend on the quality of the base and not on the particular color. We test each brand's pastel and medium bases as well as white. So if you want a medium or dark color, it won't matter whether it's red or blue or something in between. Its performance should track with our findings.

Buy the top of the line. The paints we test represent the top of each manufacturer's line. Over the years, we have found that lower grades—typically dubbed good, better, or contractor grade—do not perform as well. If a top-line paint will cover all but the darkest colors in two coats, lower-quality paints might need three or four coats. That makes them a poor value. But plan on two coats even with a top-rated paint for best coverage.

Match a paint's strong points to the room's use. Here are the most important considerations:

- Stains are more of a problem with flat paints.
- Heavily used rooms need a paint that can stand up to scrubbing. Our tests show that paints in every gloss level can per-

form well in this regard. Some semi-gloss paints may change sheen when scrubbed.

• Mildew can grow in any warm, humid room, not just a bathroom or kitchen. Paint with high mildew resistance won't kill existing mildew (you must clean it off with a bleach solution), but it will slow new growth.

• Sticking can occur with glossier paints long after they've dried. Books seem glued to shelves, and windows become hard to open. Most of the glossy paints we tested did not have that problem.

Related CR Report: September 2005

POWER BLOWERS

The best electric handheld blowers outperform their gas counterparts and cost less. But they aren't any quieter, and the power cord can be a hassle.

These miniature wind machines take some of the effort out of sweeping and cleaning fallen leaves and other small yard and driveway debris. Many can also vacuum and shred what they pick up. But practically all available models still make enough noise to annoy the neighbors. Indeed, some localities have ordinances restricting their use.

WHAT'S AVAILABLE

Mainstream brands include Black & Decker, Craftsman (Sears), Homelite, Ryobi, Toro, and Weed Eater. Pricier brands of gas-powered blowers include Echo, Husqvarna, John Deere, and Stihl. As with other outdoor power tools, gas and electric blowers have their pros and cons. You'll also find variations among gas-powered models. Here are your choices:

Electric handheld blowers. Designed for one-handed maneuvering, these are light (about 7 pounds or less). Many are also relatively quiet, produce no exhaust emissions, and can vacuum and shred. Some perform better than handheld gas-powered models, although mobility and range are limited by the power cord. Price range: $30 to $100.

Gasoline handheld blowers. These perform like the best electrics but aren't restricted by a cord. As with other gas-powered equipment, tougher regulations have reduced emissions. Manufacturers have also quieted some models in response to noise ordinances. But all are still loud enough to warrant hearing protection. Other drawbacks include added weight (most weigh 7 to 12 pounds) and the fuel-and-oil mixing required by the two-stroke engines most gas models use. A few blowers have a four-stroke engine that burns gasoline only, though they tend to be heavy for this group. Price range: $75 to $160.

Gasoline backpack blowers. At 16 to 25 pounds, these are double the weight of handheld blowers, which is why you wear rather than carry them. But the payoff with most is added power and ease of use for extended periods, since your shoulders support their weight. Hearing protection is strongly recommended. Backpack blowers don't vacuum. And they can be expensive. Price range: $170 to $420.

Gasoline wheeled blowers. These offer enough oomph to sweep sizable areas quickly. All use a four-stroke engine that requires no fuel mixing. But these machines are large and heavy, and require some effort to push around. They also cost the most and tend to be hard to maneuver, which can make it difficult to precisely direct leaves and other yard waste. Count on using hearing protection. Price range: $400 to $800.

FEATURES THAT COUNT

Look for an easy-to-use **on-off switch** and multiple speeds on electric blowers, a **variable throttle** you can preset on gasoline-powered models, and a convenient **choke** on gas-powered units. Varying the speed lets you use maximum force for sweeping and minimum force around plants. Blowers that excel at cleaning or loosening debris usually have **round nozzle blower tubes; oblong** and **rectangular nozzles** are better for moving or sweeping leaves. A bottom-mounted **air intake** is less likely to pull at clothing.

A **control stalk** attached to the blower tube of backpack models improves handling, while an **auxiliary handle** on the engine or motor housing of a handheld blower makes it easier to use—provided the handle is comfortable. Other useful features on gas-powered models include a **wide fuel fill** and a **translucent fuel tank,** which shows the level inside. An **adjustable air deflector,** found on most wheeled blowers, lets you direct airflow forward or to the side.

HOW TO CHOOSE

For sheer power, you can't go wrong with any of the backpack or wheeled blowers and several of the handheld models we tested. There's more to blowers than air power, however. The best in each group also proved easier to handle and control. And some are less noisy than others. Here's what else to think about as you decide which model to buy:

Consider what you'll clear. If it's mostly fallen leaves or grass clippings, choose a model judged very good or excellent in our sweeping tests.

Handheld models that vacuum are also handy for cleaning between shrubs, though their small reduction ratios and bags are impractical for vacuuming larger areas or leaf piles. If embedded leaf fragments are a frequent problem, look for a machine that did well at freeing tenacious debris in our loosening tests.

Consider what you can handle. High performance and low weight at a relatively low price make electric blowers your first choice if arm fatigue or low arm strength is a factor. Backpack blowers put their added weight on your back, not your arms, and provide more air power, though at a much higher price.

Wheeled blowers deliver the most air power, thanks to their larger fans and higher-horsepower engines. But because they lack the drive systems available on mowers, moving these 100-plus-pound machines requires plenty of push, especially uphill. Wheeled blowers also require about 8 square feet of storage space.

Consider your neighbors and their peace and quiet. While none of these blowers is quiet, several can move lots of debris with a bit less noise. Regulations typically limit blowers to 65 decibels at 50 feet. About a third of all the models we tested should meet that standard, and they were judged very good or excellent in that performance category.

Related CR Report: September 2003

POWER SANDERS

These smooth operators save time and effort. More convenience and safety features for less money help account for their growing popularity.

Some of the latest power sanders can skim off as much wood in 5 minutes as you could in 30 minutes of continuous sanding by hand. Many are easier to use than older models. And nearly all have a dust bag—important considering the health risks of inhaling wood dust.

That and prices as low as $20 help explain why annual sales recently jumped 15 percent to 2.3 million. Homeowners are driving much of that growth as they use power sanders for everything from refinishing a desk to building a picnic table.

WHAT'S AVAILABLE

Major brands include Black & Decker, Craftsman, Dewalt, Makita, Porter Cable, Ryobi, and Skil. You'll find four major types of power sanders at the store:

Random-orbit. Best for versatility, these can do some rough sanding and most finish sanding, which helps explain their large share of the market. The round pad moves in a random ellipse to help prevent gouges. Price range: about $20 to $100.

Finishing. Best for small to moderate-sized tasks, finishing sanders have squared-off pads that can reach into corners. The most popular type along with random-orbit models, finishing sanders can handle a variety of homeowner tasks. Price range: about $20 to $70.

Belt. Best for smoothing doors, tabletops, and other large or uneven areas, a belt sander has a pulley-driven loop that removes more wood in less time than other sanders. But it isn't meant for small-area or finish sanding. Price range: about $50 to $200.

Detail. Best for sanding around chair spindles, moldings, and other tight spots, most detail sanders have triangular pads that are good for corners. Some also come with finger-shaped pads for sanding around slots and grooves. But none are meant for rough-sanding or large areas. Price range: $30 to $50.

FEATURES THAT COUNT

An attached **dust bag** captures dust routed into it via holes in the pad but requires frequent emptying. A **vacuum connection** lets you attach a wet/dry vac for more thorough dust-collecting, though the hose may hamper maneuverability and handling.

Random-orbit and detail sanders use a **hook-and-loop** system to attach the sanding pad. Many finishing sanders have a **lever-and-clip** system. And all finishing sanders can be converted to **pressure-sensitive adhesive pads.** All belt sanders use a **flip-out lever** and **tracking control** to lock the sandpaper loop in place.

Many models of all types can be gripped securely with one or both hands for added ease and stability. A **two-handed grip** is especially important for a belt sander's heavier-duty rough sanding, as is a large front grip that keeps hands well spaced to ease larger jobs. Some belt sanders can be secured to a bench with the belt facing upward—convenient for two-handed shaping where you hold the wood against the spinning belt, rather than the belt against the work piece.

Many belt sanders allow you to adjust tracking with a **knob** or **thumbscrew** instead of a screwdriver to move the paper nearer to one edge or the other. Many also have a **trigger lock** that can be locked in the On position with one hand.

Most finishing sanders with a dust bag or vacuum connection include a template for punching the pattern for the dust-routing holes in replacement sandpaper.

Variable speed adds control by letting you sand more slowly and carefully.

A **long cord** lets you dispense with an extension cord near an electrical outlet. A **carrying case** makes storage easier and neater.

HOW TO CHOOSE

Lots of choices for power sanders mean more considerations when shopping. Here are some of the major features you should be thinking about:

Decide how you'll use it. Determine which of the four types of power sanders meets your needs. If you're buying just one sander, you'll probably prefer a random-orbit or a finishing sander, which offer the most versatility.

If you're buying a finishing sander, choose a one-quarter-sheet model for mostly small jobs and a larger, one-third-sheet model for the occasional tabletop.

Consider your strength. A heavier sander tends to remove more wood in less time, since more weight helps the sander contact the wood more effectively. While the added heft isn't an issue with most types of sanders, it could be with belt sanders, some of which weigh 11 pounds or more. Particularly for belt-type sanders, try lifting and holding the sander at the store. Then choose the heaviest model you can handle comfortably.

Check the grip. For added control, especially with larger, harder-working models, make sure the sander is easy to grasp with one or both hands.

Look for a bag and a vac connection. Many sanders now include at least one of these features. But most of the low-cost models lack an attached dust-collection bag, a port for connecting a wet/dry vacuum hose, or both.

A vacuum connection is especially important. Besides capturing dust more thoroughly than a bag, attaching a wet/dry vacuum helped speed sanding with several models we tested.

Look for easy paper changes. Even small projects may require that you replace the sandpaper several times. The hook-and-loop pads now common on random-orbit and detail sanders are the easiest to change. Some sanders of other types also make changing the sandpaper relatively convenient.

Related CR Report: January 2004

PRESSURE WASHERS

Professional cleaning at a do-it-yourself price has helped move pressure washers beyond the tool-rental shop and into your local home center.

Pressure washers use a gas engine or electric motor, pump, and concentrating nozzle to boost water pressure from your garden hose as much as 60 times. That lets them blast away deck mildew, driveway stains, and other grunge a hose can't touch while cleaning chairs, siding, and other items more quickly and easily than you could with a scrub brush.

For as little as $90 for electric machines and $300 for gas, owning one is a tempting alternative to renting one for $50 to $90 per day.

Lower prices and less upkeep explain why 60 percent of buyers choose an electric pressure washer. But gas machines have roughly twice the cleaning power, which is the main reason you'll see fewer plug-in models at the big-box stores where most pressure washers are sold.

WHAT'S AVAILABLE

You'll find models from Black & Decker, Campbell Hausfeld, Craftsman, Excell, Honda, Husky, Karcher, and Troy-Bilt.

Gas-powered washers. If you need to quickly clean large areas, such as decks or siding, or want to whisk away gum, tree sap, and other tough stains, a gas-powered model is right for you. Water pressure is typically measured in pounds per square inch (psi). Gas-powered models typically put out 2,000 to 2,800 psi of pressure compared with 1,000 to 1,700 psi for electric models. Much higher pressure allowed the top-performing gas machines to clean a grimy concrete patio three times faster than the fastest electrics. Gas models are relatively noisy and heavy, though, and they require tune-ups. Pumps must be winterized with antifreeze in colder areas, since gas machines should not be stored inside a home. Remember that more power raises damage and injury risks. Gas models require more caution and control than the electrics to avoid splintering and etching wood and other soft surfaces. Price range: $200 to $500.

Electric washers. Electrics are best for small decks and patios, furniture, and other smaller jobs that emphasize cleaning over stain removal. They're relatively light and quiet, require little upkeep, and create no exhaust emissions. They start and stop via a trigger and are small enough to be stored indoors without winterizing. But less pressure means slower cleaning compared with gas models. Wands and nozzles are less-sturdy plastic, rather than metal. And of course you'll need to be near an outlet. Price range: $90 to $180.

FEATURES THAT COUNT

A **soap tank** saves you the hassle of using separate containers. **Tool and cord storage** is a plus, as are **wheels** for heavier models. **Adjustable nozzles** are more convenient than replaceable nozzles; a twist is all it takes to change spray width or pressure. But replaceable nozzles let you customize the spray pattern with specific spray angles.

HOW TO CHOOSE

Any of the pressure washers we tested can handle decks, walks, and other typical cleaning tasks. They're also forceful enough to harm a car's paint, which is why we suggest using a hose for cars.

If you decide that a pressure washer's benefits outweigh its risks, then keep these tips in mind when you're shopping in the store:

Don't buy solely on specs. Retailers and manufacturers often push lofty numbers for water pressure and volume. Some talk about "cleaning units," which are simply the pressure multiplied by the volume.

Faster is noisier. All the gas pressure washers we tested produced at least 85 decibels (dBA), the threshold at which we recommend hearing protection. Electric models averaged 78 dBA when running and are silent with their triggers released, since doing so stops the motor.

Related CR Report: July 2005

SNOW THROWERS

Bigger, better, and easier to use describe the latest of these labor-saving machines.

Some of the newest snow throwers are larger, more capable, and easier to control. Many models also cost less, thanks to price pressure from major retailers such as Home Depot, Lowe's, and Sears, which now account for about 60 percent of total sales.

Two-stage models are the largest of these machines. Unlike smaller, single-stage models, which rely solely on a rubber-edged auger to move and disperse snow, as well as to provide some pulling power, two-stage models add drive wheels and a fanlike impeller to help disperse what they pick up.

You needn't buy the biggest snow thrower to get competent clearing. Honda and Toro are among the brands with single-stage models that rival some larger machines yet weigh far less and require less storage space. Manufacturers are designing these more-capable models for homeowners with smaller driveways as well as for women, who make at least part of the buying decisions in more than 30 percent of snow-thrower purchases.

Other advances include easier steering and chute controls. You'll also find easy-handling electric models, which may be sufficient for smaller driveways.

WHAT'S AVAILABLE

Major brands include Ariens, Craftsman (Sears), Honda, John Deere, Simplicity, Toro, Troy-Bilt, Yard Machines, and Yard-Man. While two-stage snow throwers all have a gas engine, single-stage models are sold in both gas and electric versions. Here are the pros and cons of each:

Shop smart

Always use a fuel stabilizer in snow throwers. It will help them start after long periods of sitting idle.

Two-stage gas. Best for long, wide, or hilly driveways, with a typical snowfall over 8 inches. They're essential for gravel driveways, since the auger doesn't contact the ground. All offer electric starting and have driven wheels, an auger that gathers snow, and an impeller to throw it. Some clear a swath 28 to 30 inches wide. But two-stage gas models are relatively heavy, take up as much space as some lawn tractors, and require regular engine maintenance. Those without trigger drive releases can be hard to maneuver. Price range: $600 to $2,100.

Single-stage gas. Best for flat, midsized paved driveways and walks, with typical snowfall less than 8 inches. They're lighter and easier to handle, and take up about as much storage space as a mower. Most offer electric starting. But they're a poor choice for gravel, since the auger contacts the surface and can throw stones. Most clear a 20- to 22-inch swath. All lack drive wheels and require engine maintenance. The auger's limited drive action isn't enough for steep hills and can pull from side to side. Price range: $300 to $900.

Single-stage electric. Best for short, flat driveways or decks and walks, with snowfall 4 inches or less. Single-stage electric models are the lightest, smallest, and easiest to handle and store. They're also less noisy than gas-powered models, and their electric motors free you from fueling and other engine maintenance. But they're as unsuited to gravel driveways as single-stage gas snow throwers. Their small, 11- to 18-inch swath slows clearing. Electric machines also trade engine fueling and maintenance for the hassle of a power cord. Price range: $100 to $300.

FEATURES THAT COUNT

A **one-handed drive/auger control** on two-stage models lets you engage the drive-wheel and auger-control levers with one hand, leaving the other free to control the chute. A growing number of new two-stage machines use **handlebar-mounted trigger releases** that ease steering by letting you quickly disconnect either or both wheels from the transmission on the fly, rather than having to stop and move a pin or lever at a wheel.

A **dead-man control** is an especially critical safety feature. It stops the spinning auger and, on two-stage models, the impeller when the handlebar-grip controls are released. Also look for a **clearing tool**—typically a plastic stick that is attached to the machine so it's handy for safely clearing clogs in the discharge chute or auger housing. Use a wooden broom handle, never hands or feet, on models without the tool.

Some snow throwers let you quickly

change the chute direction and height of thrown snow via a **single-lever joystick** on two-stage machines or a long handle you can reach from the operator's position on single-stage models. That's easier than wrestling with two separate controls on many two-stage snow throwers or the stiff, awkward discharge-chute handle on many single-stage models.

All electric models turn on with a switch, though most gas-powered models now offer **plug-in starting**—handy if you're near an outlet. All two-stage snow throwers have a four-stroke engine that requires periodic oil changes. Some single-stage models use a two-stroke engine that requires no oil changes, but entails mixing oil with the fuel. All gas snow throwers must meet the same emissions standards. **Headlights** for night use are an added nicety you'll now find on many two-stage machines.

HOW TO CHOOSE

Snow-throwing may be easier than shoveling, but it's still harder than using a self-propelled mower. Consult a doctor before buying a snow thrower if you have hypertension, diabetes, or heart disease. Also consider having your driveway plowed if it's especially long and two or more cars wide. If a snow thrower meets your needs, match the type to your space and climate and then consider these tips.

Try the controls. Independent dealers and even big-box stores typically have floor samples. Along with trigger releases on two-stage models, look for electric starting. Also be sure you're comfortable with the handle height and the chute adjustment, which you'll use frequently.

Don't get hung up on power claims. You'll find two-stage snow throwers with engines that boast 11 horsepower or more. But higher power claims don't necessarily mean more performance; some less-powerful machines in our most recent tests cleared snow on a par with the highest-horsepower models.

Some manufacturers and retailers are also pushing Briggs & Stratton engines vs. the usual Tecumseh powerplants. We found that the Tecumseh engines on most of these machines performed competently.

Don't get dazzled by drive speeds. Most two-stage machines have five or six forward speeds—useful for going slowly through heavy snow to prevent clogs, or quickly when returning to the garage. While the seven forward speeds on some two-stage models sound like a plus, we found them within the typical range for six-speed models.

Related CR Report: October 2004

STRING TRIMMERS

An electric model can do a good job for many trimming tasks. But for tall grass and weeds, you'll need a gasoline-powered string trimmer.

A string trimmer can pick up where a lawn mower leaves off. It provides the finishing touches, slicing through tufts of grass around trees and flowerbeds, straightening uneven edges along a driveway, and trimming stretches of lawn your mower or tractor can't reach. Gasoline-powered models can also whisk away tall grass and weeds.

Faster starts, fewer tangles, and easier handling are among the string-trimmer features you'll find as manufacturers improve these tools. Models from Craftsman (Sears), Troy-Bilt, and others now start with one or two pulls, thanks to a new starting system. Tangled and jammed-up cutting string can be avoided with a fixed-line head that uses two precut pieces of cutting line; the system is available for Echo and Craftsman models. And trimmers are now more than 1 pound lighter than the ones we tested only a few years ago—they're now 11 pounds, on average.

WHAT'S AVAILABLE

Black & Decker, Craftsman (Sears), Toro, and Weed Eater are the major brands of electric string trimmers, while Craftsman, Homelite, Ryobi, Troy-Bilt, and Weed Eater are the big names in gas-powered models. Leading high-end brands of gas trimmers include Cub Cadet, Echo, Husqvarna, John Deere, and Stihl.

Shop smart

Before you buy, adjust the front handle for comfort and hold the trimmer in the cutting position with both hands to gauge weight and balance.

Gasoline-powered trimmers. These are better than electrics at cutting heavy weeds and brush, and are often better at edging—turning the trimmer so its spinning line cuts vertically along a walk or garden border. They also go anywhere, so they're the best choice if you'll be trimming far from a power outlet. On the downside, gas trimmers are heavier than electrics, weighing about 10 to 14 pounds. Most have a two-stroke engine that requires a mixture of gas and oil. These tend to pollute more than a four-stroke engine that uses gasoline only, and entail pull-starting and regular maintenance. And gas-powered trimmers are noisy enough to make hearing protection necessary. Price range: $50 to $200. Most models, however, cost from $70 to $150.

Electric-corded trimmers. These are the least expensive and usually the lightest; many weigh only about 5 pounds. Some work nearly as well as gas trimmers for most trimming. All are quieter and easier to start than gas trimmers—you simply push a button rather than pulling a starter cord. The power cord does limit your range to about 100 feet from an outlet. Models with the engine at the bottom of the shaft can be more difficult to manage than those with the engine located at the top, near the handle. And even the most powerful models are unlikely to handle the tall grass and weeds that the best gas-powered trimmers can tackle. Price range: $20 to $100.

Electric battery-powered trimmers. Cordless trimmers combine the free range of gas trimmers with the convenience of corded electrics: less noise, easy starting and stopping, no fueling, and no exhaust emissions. But they're weak at cutting and run only about 15 to 20 minutes before the on-board battery needs recharging, which can take up to a day. They also tend to be pricey and heavy for their size (about 10 pounds). Some models have the motor at the bottom of the shaft, where it can be even harder to handle than the lighter corded versions. Price range: $30 to $100 or more.

FEATURES THAT COUNT

All trimmers have a **shaft** that connects the engine or motor and controls to the trimmer **head,** where the plastic lines revolve. **Curved shafts** are the most common and can be easier to handle when trimming up close. **Straight shafts** tend to be better for reaching beneath bushes and other shrubs, or if you are taller. Some models have a **split shaft** that comes apart so you can replace the trimmer head with a leaf blower, edging blade, or other yard tool, though we've found that most of these attachments aren't very effective.

Gas-powered trimmers have their engine on top, which helps balance the load.

Most electric models have their motor on the bottom, at the cutting head, though a few have a **top-mounted motor.**

Most gas-powered trimmers have two **cutting lines,** while most electrics use just one, which means they cut less with each revolution. Most gas and electric trimmers have a **bump-feed line advance** that feeds out more line when you bump the trimmer head on the ground; a blade on the safety shield cuts it to the right length. Models with a **fixed-line head** use two strips of line instead of a spool, which eliminates tangles and jammed line.

Most gasoline models use **two-stroke engines,** which burn lubricating oil with the gasoline. Some trimmers use inherently cleaner **four-stroke engines,** but these tend to weigh and cost more. Corded and battery models typically use a 1.8- to 5-amp motor.

To start most gas trimmers, you set a **choke** and push a **primer bulb,** then pull a starter rope. On most models, you have to pull, prime, and adjust the choke several times before the engine starts. But some models have an easy **three-step starting system** that reduces the hassles and starts quicker.

On most gas trimmers, a **centrifugal clutch** allows the engine to idle without spinning the line—safer and more convenient than models where the line continues to turn. On trimmers without a clutch (usually less-expensive models), the string is spinning while the engine is running. Electric-trimmer lines don't spin until you press the switch.

Some models make edging more convenient with a **rotating head** that puts the trimmer head in the vertical position. Heavier-duty models often offer a **shoulder harness,** which can ease handling and reduce fatigue. Other convenient features include easy-to-reach and easy-to-adjust switches, comfortable handles, and—on gas models—a **translucent fuel tank.**

HOW TO CHOOSE

You don't have to invest in a pricey, professional-grade trimmer unless you need its metal-blade capability for cutting saplings and other woody waste. Most of the gas trimmers and even some electrics we tested can handle the grass and tall weeds that account for most trimming.

Determine whether a gas-powered or electric trimmer fits your needs. Then keep these points in mind while shopping at the store:

Consider the landscape. Trimmers with a straight shaft can reach beneath shrubs more easily and are less likely than curved-shaft ones to spatter you with clippings. Curved-shaft trimmers trade those benefits for easier maneuvering and, often, less weight—a plus for shorter users and those with less arm strength.

See how it feels. While a lighter trimmer tends to reduce fatigue, weight isn't the whole story. Good balance can be just as critical. To check it, adjust the front handle for comfort and hold the trimmer in the cutting position with both hands. Its weight should feel evenly distributed or slightly heavier at the top.

Also check that all the controls are smooth and easy to reach. If you're left-handed, make sure a gasoline-powered trimmer you're considering has a deflector that routes the hot exhaust gases rearward. Most now include one.

Consider your neighbors. If they're close by, you may want to choose a corded or cordless electric trimmer. Nearly all the ones we tested are significantly less noisy than gasoline-powered models. If you opt for gas, protect your ears with earmuffs or plugs.

Related CR Report: June 2004

VACUUM CLEANERS

Fancy features and a high price don't necessarily mean better cleaning. You'll find plenty of less-flashy performers at a reasonable price.

Which type of vacuum cleaner to buy used to be a no-brainer. Uprights were clearly better for carpets, while canisters were the obvious choice for bare floors. That distinction has blurred somewhat as more upright models clean floors without scattering dust and more canisters do a very good job with carpeting. Central vacuum systems, an increasingly popular third option, add a measure of convenience, along with higher prices.

You'll also see a growing number of features such as dirt sensors and bagless dirt bins, but some of those features may contribute more to price than to function, while other, more essential features may be missing from the least-expensive models. And while cordless and even robotic vacuums have joined your list of choices, neither have been top performers so far.

WHAT'S AVAILABLE

Hoover, the oldest and largest vacuum manufacturer, is a division of Maytag and offers roughly 75 models priced from $50 to $400 as well as central vacuum systems priced higher. Many of Hoover's conventional models are similar, with minor differences in features; the "variety" is mostly in the marketing and retailer distribution. Some Hoover machines are made exclusively for retail chain stores. Kenmore is the biggest name for canister models, accounting for about 25 percent of U.S. sales.

Other players include Dirt Devil, which sells uprights and canisters as well as stick brooms and hand vacuums; Eureka, which offers low-priced models, central vacs, and high-end Electrolux-branded models; Bissell, a mostly mass-marketed brand; Dyson, a British brand, which recently introduced a canister to its brightly colored lineup; and brands such as Miele, Panasonic, Samsung, Sanyo, Sharp, and Simplicity, which are likely to be sold at specialty stores. Higher-priced Aerus (which also makes central vacs) and Oreck models are sold in their own stores and by direct mail, while upscale Kirby and Rainbow models are still sold door-to-door.

Along with a vacuum's brand, your choices include several types:

Uprights. These tend to be the least expensive. Their one-piece design also makes them easier to store than canister vacs. A top-of-the-line upright might have a wider cleaning path, be self-propelled, and have a HEPA filter, dirt sensor, and full-bag indicator. Price range for most: $50 to $400.

Canister vacuums. These tend to do well on bare floors because they allow you to turn off the brush or use a specialized tool to avoid scattering dirt. Most are quieter than uprights, and their long, flexible hose tends to make them better at cleaning on stairs and in hard-to-reach areas. The added clutter of the loose hose and wand makes canisters somewhat harder to store, however. While canister vacs still tend to cost the most, you'll find a growing number of lower-priced models. Price range for most: $150 to $500.

Central vac systems. They clean like a canister vac without your having to push, pull, or carry the motor and body around. They're also relatively quiet and require less-frequent emptying. But they're the most expensive option, and generally require professional installation. The 35-foot hose can be cumbersome, and there's no place to carry tools while you work. Price range: $500 to $1,250 for the unit including tools, plus $300 to $750 to install.

Stick vacs and hand vacs. Whether corded or cordless, these miniature vacuums typically lack the power of a full-sized vacuum cleaner. But they can be handy for small, quick jobs. Price range: $20 to $100.

FEATURES THAT COUNT

Typical attachments include **crevice** and **upholstery tools.** Most vacuums also include **extension wands** for reaching high places. A **full-bag alert** can be handy, since an overstuffed bag impairs a vacuum's ability to clean.

Lately, many uprights have adopted a **bagless** configuration with a **see-through dirt bin** that replaces the usual bag. Performance has improved for bagless vacs, though emptying their bins can raise enough dust to concern even those without allergies. You'll also find dirt-collection bins on most stick vacs and hand vacs. Some of these have a **revolving brush,** which may help remove surface debris from a carpet. Stick vacs can hang on a hook or, if they're cordless, on a wall-mounted charger base.

Canister vacuums we've tested have a **power nozzle** that cleans carpets more thoroughly than a simple suction nozzle. Look for a **suction-control feature;** found on most canisters and some uprights, it allows you to reduce airflow for drapes and other delicate fabrics. On uprights, also look for an **on/off switch for the brush** if you plan to use attachments. Stopping the brush protects the user from injury, the power cord from damage, and your furnishings from undue wear. Some uprights automatically stop the brush when the handle is in the "up" position.

Most canisters and a few uprights have a **retractable cord** that rewinds with a tug or push of a button—a plus, considering the 20- to 30-foot length for most. Another worthwhile feature is **manual pile-height adjustment,** which can improve cleaning by letting you match the vacuum's height to the carpet pile more effectively than machines that adjust automatically. While a self-propelled mode takes the push out of more and more uprights, it can make them heavier and harder to transport.

Midpriced **accessory kits for central vacs** typically include an electrically powered cleaning head—a must for carpets—as well as a floor brush, crevice tool, upholstery brush, dusting brush, and extension wands. Spending more gets you more tools, a premium powerhead, and a longer hose. A sound-deadening **muffler,** installed in the exhaust air pipe near the central-vac base unit, comes on some models but can be added to any model for about $10 to $25. Most central vacs have a **suction switch** at the wand's handle so you can turn the vacuum unit on and off where you're standing.

Shop smart

Most vacuums include a narrow crevice tool, a small brush for upholstery, and a round one for dusting—enough for most users.

Some vacuums have a **dirt sensor** that triggers a light indicator when the concentration of dirt particles in the machine's air stream reaches a certain level. But the sensor signals only that the vacuum is no longer picking up dirt, not whether there's dirt left in your rug. That can result in your vacuuming longer and working harder with little or no more cleanliness.

You'll also hear lots of claims about **microfiltration,** which typically uses a bag with smaller pores or a second, electrostatic filter that supplements the standard motor filter in an attempt to capture fine particles that may pass through the bag or filter and escape into the air through the exhaust. Some vacuums have a **HEPA filter,** which may benefit someone with asthma. But many models without a HEPA filter have performed just as well in CONSUMER REPORTS emissions tests, since the amount of dust emitted depends as much on the design of the entire machine as on its filter.

A vacuum's design can also affect how long it lasts. With some uprights, for example, dirt sucked into the machine passes through the blower fan before entering the bag—a potential problem because most fans are plastic and vulnerable to damage from hard objects. Better systems filter dirt through the bag before it reaches the fan. While hard objects can lodge in the motorized brush, they're unlikely to break the fan.

HOW TO CHOOSE

Some of the best vacuums cost $350 or less. But you might be willing to spend more for models with other strengths. Here's what to think about at the store:

Match the vacuum to your cleaning. Most uprights are still better than canisters for carpets. They also cost less and are easier to store. Canisters tend to be better for cleaning drapes, upholstery, and under furniture, and they are more stable on stairs.

Consider suction. Look for models that performed well in our airflow tests if you often clean with tools. These maintained more suction through the hose as they filled with dust, reducing the need to change bags and empty bins.

Pick your features. Models with bags tend to hold more than bagless vacs and create less dust when emptying. A brush on/off switch allows you to turn off the brush on floors and delicate rugs, and reduces dust and the risk of thrown objects when using tools. Manual pile-height adjustment can improve carpet cleaning by letting you raise or lower the powerhead.

Don't be dazzled by gadgets. Most vacuums include a narrow crevice tool, a small brush for upholstery, and a round one for dusting—enough for most users. Hand tools with powered brushes tend to add little over nonpowered tools when removing pet hair from upholstery.

Try before buying. Weight can be critical if your arms aren't strong or your home has more than one level. Self-propelled uprights ease pushing and pulling, though their added heft makes lifting and storing more challenging.

Protect your ears and lungs. Vacuums that scored a poor in our noise tests produced the 85 decibels or more at which we recommend ear protection. If you're sensitive to dust, choose a model that scored well in emissions. Also consider avoiding bagless models or wearing a dust mask when emptying their bins.

Related CR Report: October 2005
Ratings: page 324
Reliability: page 331

Computers, Phones, and Peripherals

Computers, Phones, & Peripherals: Portable and Versatile

Multi-tasking on the go continues to get easier as cell phones take on new roles and improved wireless networks untether laptop computers. Meanwhile, the power and versatility of today's laptops equal that of desktop computers. Both types have become cheaper, faster, and easier to use with improved features for listening to music, editing digital photos and movies, and creating your own CD and DVDs. Among the trends that are changing computers, phones, and related gear:

Portable functions merge. It's getting tough to decide what to call that little box in your hand. The newest generation of cell phones goes beyond voice and text messaging to allow you to check your e-mail, browse the Web, play games, and take photos. Some even record short videos, and models that double as a full-fledged MP3 players are coming onto the market.

Some of the latest personal digital assistants (PDAs) are combined with cell phones so you can make voice calls or directly connect to the Internet via a wireless Internet service provider.

Cordless phones adopt cell features. Cordless phones are borrowing more and more from their wireless cousin, the cell phone. Features that have migrated to some cordless models include phone books, distinctive ring tones, color displays, and the folding flip-phone design for easy pocketing. A few new cordless models tap into your cell-phone services too.

Desktops move into the den. Some new high-end desktop computers are designed to be the hub of a home media center. The new models include larger hard drives and additional bays for other drives that can be devoted to heavy-use tasks such as TV-program storage and DVD creation.

Tech support still disappoints. Our reader surveys have been showing a decline in satisfaction with computer tech support since the early 2000s, and it continues to be one of the lowest-rated services we evaluate. (See page 232 for our survey results.)

Apple continues its lead in tech support while other brands show only so-so performance. The biggest complaint is that support people simply can't solve the problem. Either they don't seem knowledgeable or they have trouble communicating clearly, our readers say. Online or e-mail support also doesn't measure up. Of those who tried to find support information on the company's Web site, more than 66 percent said they left empty-handed. Nearly 30 percent said they followed instructions that didn't work. Of those who used e-mail for support, 9 percent said they never received a reply. Almost half of those who got an answer said it was of no help.

CELL PHONES

Complex pricing schemes and incompatible technologies can make it hard to find the right calling plan and handset.

There are now more than 190 million cell-phone subscribers, more than one per household, on average. A small but steadily growing number of people use a cell phone (a.k.a. a mobile phone) as their only phone. Phone manufacturers and wireless-service providers are promoting new generations of equipment that let users do much more than merely make phone calls.

Despite its popularity, wireless service has a reputation for problems: dead zones, where you can't get service; calls that inexplicably end in midconversation; inadequate capacity, so you can't put a call through when you want; hard-to-fathom calling plans; and errors in bills. Problems like those are why one-third of the cell-phone users we've surveyed say they're seriously considering a switch of carrier.

Switching is now much easier than ever, thanks to the government mandate on local number portability. However, keep in mind that the phones themselves aren't portable. If you switch carriers, expect to buy a new phone.

WHAT'S AVAILABLE

The cell phone itself is only part of what you need. You also have to sign up for service with a wireless provider and choose a calling plan. You can find phones in many outlets, including independent wireless retailers, electronics stores, and Web sites.

The providers. The major national companies are Cingular (which merged with AT&T Wireless), Nextel, Sprint PCS (which is in the process of merging with Nextel), T-Mobile, and Verizon Wireless. There are also numerous local or regional providers.

You'll often find phones described as tri-mode, dual-band, tri-band, or multinetwork. Those terms describe the ways a phone can connect to one or more wireless networks. Here are the specifics:

- Tri-mode phones can access a digital network in two frequency bands and older analog wireless networks.
- Dual-band phones can connect to a digital network, but in two different frequency bands. GSM providers often use the term 850/1900 MHz instead of dual-band.
- Multinetwork phones are compatible with more than one digital network, often in two frequency bands. Some can also access analog networks. Samsung offers a multinetwork world phone. It uses CDMA technology in the U.S. and GSM technology outside the U.S. It's sold by Verizon as the Samsung SCH-A70 and by Sprint as the IP-A790.
- Tri-band or "world phones" operate on GSM networks in both the U.S. and abroad. Those with 850/1800/1900 MHz capability can operate on two bands domestically and one internationally. Those with 900/1800/1900 MHz capability operate on one band in the U.S. (1900 MHz) and two bands internationally.

The calling plans. Most providers offer a range of plans based around a "bucket" of calling time minutes. The more minutes in the bucket, the more the plan costs you each month. However, the total number of minutes isn't the most important figure. Some of those minutes may be good anytime, others available only on nights and weekends; if you exceed the allotment of minutes, you'll be charged 20 to 50 cents per minute, depending on the plan. Cingular and Sprint let you avoid wasting unused minutes by either rolling them over to the next month or adjusting your monthly quota. Most plans require you to sign a one- or two-year contract and levy a hefty fee if you want to cancel before the contract expires.

Prepaid plans can be a good alternative if you're averse to a long-term contract. Many wireless providers, as well as Virgin Mobile, Liberty Wireless, Metro PCS, and Tracfone, offer prepaid calling. You pay in advance for airtime minutes, which typically last 45 to 60 days before they expire.

Tech tip

Most cell phones have a vibrating alert or a flashing light-emitting diode to let you know about an incoming call, useful when you're in a meeting or at the movies.

The phones. Some are simple rectangles with a display window and keypad on the front. But most have a flip-open cover to protect the keys. The major phone manufacturers are UTS-Starcom (formerly Audiovox), Kyocera, LG, Motorola, Nokia, Panasonic, Samsung, Sanyo, and Sony-Ericsson. Light weight is pretty much standard. All the newer phones can send and receive text messages up to 160 characters long to or from any other cell-phone user, and most phones now come with a full-color display. Phones equipped with cameras allow you to send and receive picture messages from other people, even if they're not on your network. You'll also see phones that can play games, are integrated with a digital camera, offer wireless Internet access, or that are combined with a personal digital assistant (PDA).

FEATURES THAT COUNT

Some cell-phone makers and service providers are offering so-called **3G service,** which enhances the speed of data transfer. 3G services deliver reasonably fast, secure connections to the Internet and allow you to use the cell phone for playing and downloading audio and video, multimedia messages, and e-mail.

Among basic cell-phone features, look for a **display** that is readable in both low- and bright-light conditions. Be sure it's easy to see the battery-life and signal-strength indicators and the number you're dialing. The **keypad** should be clearly marked and easy to use. **Single-key last-number redial** is useful for dropped calls or when you're having trouble connecting. Most phones these days have **voice dial**, which lets you dial someone's phone number by speaking their name. But the number and name have to be in your phone's contact list, and you have to program each voice dial name—a time-consuming process. **Voice command**-enabled phones don't require training. You can dial anyone's number in your contact list, and even dial a number not in the list by speaking the digits.

In addition to ringing, most handsets have a **vibrating alert** or a flashing light-emitting diode to let you know about an incoming call, useful when you're in a meeting or at the movies. Handiest is an **easy-to-mute ringer,** which switches from ring to vibrate when you press and hold one key. **Volume controls** on the side let you change the earpiece volume level without moving the phone too far from your ear. You can't do that if the volume controls are on the keypad. A **speakerphone** boosts the earpiece volume and microphone sensitivity, so you carry on a conversation without having the phone against your ear.

Some cell-phone models include a **headset.** That capability is sometimes demanded by various local laws for drivers using cell phones. A **standard headset connector** (also known as a 2.5-mm jack) is the most common type of headset connector. Phones with this connector are compatible with a wider variety of wired headsets. If you frequently use a headset but hate fussing with cords, consider a phone with **Bluetooth voice** capability, which allows you to use a cordless headset. Not all phones with Bluetooth are equal. **Bluetooth data** lets you transfer pictures and contacts, etc. to other Bluetooth-enabled devices like printers, PDAs, and computers. Bluetooth data capability is found on GSM phones but not on CDMA phones.

Many CDMA phones have **analog backup** capability, which may be important if you travel through rural areas or places where your digital carrier doesn't provide service. Phones with analog capability can sometimes connect in places where digital-only phones cannot.

Phones vary widely in keypad design and readability of screen displays, as well as in the ease of using the function menu or performing such basic tasks as one-button redial and storage of frequently called numbers for speed-dialing later. It's important to handle a phone in the store before you buy, to be sure that its design and your fingers are well-matched.

HOW TO CHOOSE

Begin by selecting a service. Finding good service where you want it can be a challenge. The best way is to ask your friends and business associates—people who literally travel the same roads you do—how satisfied they are with their cell-phone service. In addition, keep in mind that Verizon Wireless has consistently come in first in CONSUMER REPORTS satisfaction surveys and so is worth considering first, if it's offered in your area.

Choose a calling plan. You need to determine when and where you'll be using a cell phone most in order to select a plan that's right for you. As a rule, a national calling plan (which typically eliminates extra long-distance charges or fees for "roaming" away from your home calling area) is worth considering first, even if you don't travel often. With a regional plan, roaming charges can add up if you make calls too far away from your home.

If two or more family members use cell phones, consider a family plan that lets up to four people share a large monthly pool of minutes for a small additional monthly charge. If you aren't sure how many minutes of phone time you'll use in a month, choose a plan with more minutes than you think you will use. It's often better to let minutes go unused than to have to pay stiff per-minute charges if you exceed your allotment.

Select a phone. You can spend as little as $20 or as much as $600 on a cell phone. You need to begin your selection in the right price tier. Once you've settled on a price range, follow these steps:

- First look for practical features. Cameras, games, music players, and the like are appealing, fun, and even useful for some people. However, features such as a folding case, volume controls on the side, and an easy-to-mute ringer will prove useful every day.
- Hold the phone. In the store, take the phone in your hand and make sure you can comfortably access most keys with one hand. Try to make a test call and access the menu items on a working demo. We've found that phones with radical shapes can be difficult to use. So are keys that are small, oddly shaped, or arranged in unusual patterns, especially if you're trying to dial a number in dim light.
- Check the display. Most color screens

perform well in dim light, but some are hard to see in daylight. Try the phone outside or under bright light. In our tests, phones that display incoming and outgoing numbers with large black fonts against a white background were the easiest to read under most conditions. Also make sure indicators such as battery life and signal strength are clearly visible.

• Consider insuring pricey phones. All major carriers provide insurance that covers lost, stolen, or damaged phones, typically for about $4 to $5 a month, with a $35 to $50 deductible. At those rates, it wouldn't pay to insure a low-priced phone. But if you paid $200 or more, then insurance may be worth considering. Some insurance plans require a police report. Damaged phones are replaced, often with a refurbished model.

Related CR Report: February 2005
Ratings: page 229

CORDLESS PHONES

Two noteworthy trends: Phones use higher frequency bands, and a growing number can handle multiple handsets from a single base.

It's easier than ever to have a phone wherever you want one. The newest breed of cordless phones lets you put a handset in any room in the house, even if no phone jack is nearby.

However, manufacturers still offer a bewildering array of phones: inexpensive models that offer the basics; multihandset, full-featured phones with a built-in answering machine; single-line and two-line phones; digital and analog phones, and different frequency bands. In many instances, a phone will have a phone-answerer sibling. Many phone-answerers come in a phone-only version. If you have a cordless phone that's several years old, it's probably a 900-MHz phone. Newer phones use higher frequencies, namely 2.4 or 5.8 GHz. They aren't necessarily better than the older ones, but they may provide more calling security and a wider array of useful capabilities and features.

WHAT'S AVAILABLE

AT&T, Bell South, GE, Panasonic, Uniden, and VTech account for more than 70 percent of the market. VTech owns the AT&T Consumer Products Division and now makes phones under the AT&T brand as well as its own name.

The current trends include phones that support two or more handsets with one base, less expensive 2.4- and 5.8-GHz analog phones, and full-featured 2.4- and 5.8-GHz digital phones. Some of the multiple-handset-capable phones now include an additional handset with a charging cradle. About a third of the cordless phones sold include a digital answering machine.

A main distinction among cordless phones is the way they transmit their signals. Here are some terms you may see while shopping and what they mean for you:

Analog. These phones are the least expensive type available now. They tend to have the better voice quality and enough range to let you chat anywhere in your house and yard, or even a little beyond. They are also unlikely to cause interference to other wireless products. But analog transmission isn't very secure; anyone with an RF scanner or comparable wireless device might be able to listen in. Analog phones are also more likely than digital phones to suffer occasional static and RF interference from other wireless products. Price range: $15 to $100.

Digital. These offer about the same range as analog phones, but with better security and less susceptibility to RF interference. And, like analogs, they are unlikely to cause interference to other wireless products. Price range: $50 to $130.

Digital spread spectrum (DSS). A DSS phone distributes a call across a number of frequencies, providing an added measure of security and more immunity from RF interference. The range may be slightly better than that of analog or digital phones. Note that some DSS phones—usually the 2.4-GHz or the multiple-handset-capable phones with handset-to-handset talk capabilities—use such a wide swath of the spectrum even in standby mode that they may interfere with baby monitors and other wireless products operating in the same frequency band. Price range: $75 to $225 (for multiple handset systems).

Frequency. Cordless phones use one or two of the three available frequency bands:

- 900 MHz. Some manufacturers still make inexpensive, 900-MHz phones, usually analog. They are fine for many households, and still account for about one-quarter of the market.
- 2.4 GHz. The band most phones now use. Unfortunately, many other wireless products—baby monitors, wireless computer networks, home security monitors, wireless speakers, microwave ovens—use the same band. A 2.4-GHz analog phone is inherently susceptible to RF interference from other wireless devices, and a 2.4-GHz DSS phone may cause interference in other products. However, DSS phones billed as "802.11-friendly" are unlikely to interfere with wireless computer networks.
- 5.8 GHz. The band that newer phones use. Its main advantage: less chance of RF interference because few other products currently use this band.

Some phones are dual-band, but that only means they transmit between base and handset in one band and receive in another; you can't switch to or choose one band or another.

FEATURES THAT COUNT

Standard features on most cordless phones include **handset** earpiece **volume control, handset ringer, last-number redial,** a **pager** to locate the handset, a **flash button** to answer call waiting, and a **low-battery indicator.**

Some phones let you support two or more handsets with just one base without the need for extra phone jacks. Additional handsets including the charging cradle are usually sold separately, although more phones are being bundled with an additional handset and charging cradle.

An **LCD screen,** found on many handsets and on some bases, can display a personal phone directory and useful information such as the name and/or number dialed, caller ID, battery strength, or how long you've been connected. **Caller ID** displays the name and number of a caller and the date and time of the call if you use your phone company's caller ID service. If you have caller ID with call waiting, the phone will display data on a second caller when you're already on the phone.

A phone that **supports two lines** can receive calls for two phone numbers—useful if you have, say, a business line and a personal line that you'd like to use from a single phone. Some of the phones have two ringers, each with a distinctive pitch to let you know which line is ringing. The two-line feature also facilitates conferencing two callers in three-way connections. Some two-line phones have an **auxiliary jack data port** to plug in a fax, modem, or other phone device that can also be useful.

A **speakerphone** offers a hands-free way to converse or wait on hold and lets others chime in as well. A base speakerphone lets you answer a call without the handset; a handset speakerphone lets you chat hands-free anywhere in the house as long as you stay within a few feet of the handset.

A **base keypad** supplements the keypad on the handset. It's handy for navigating menu-driven systems, since you don't have to take the phone away from your ear to punch the keys. Some phones have a **lighted keypad** that either glows in the dark or lights up when you press a key, or when the phone rings. This makes the phone easier to use in low-light conditions. All phones have a handset **ringer,** and many phones have a base ringer. Some let you turn them on or off, adjust the volume, or change the auditory tone.

Tech tip

Phones that use 5.8-GHz bandwidth have less chance of RF interference because few other products currently use this band.

Many cordless phones have a **headset jack** on the handset and include a **belt clip** for carrying the phone. This allows hands-free conversation anywhere in the house. Some phones have a headset jack on the base, which allows hands-free conversation without any drain on the handset battery. Headsets are usually sold separately for about $20.

Other convenient features include **auto talk,** which lets you lift the handset off the base for an incoming call and start talking without having to press a button, and **any key answer.**

Some phones provide a **battery holder for battery backup**—a compartment in the base to charge a spare handset battery pack or to hold alkaline batteries for base-power backup, either of which can enable the phone to work if you lose household AC power. Still, it's wise to keep a corded phone somewhere in your home.

Some multiple-handset-capable phones allow conversation between handsets in an intercom mode and facilitate conferencing handsets with an outside party. In intercom mode, the handsets have to be within range of the base for handset-to-handset use. Others lack this handset-to-handset talk capability; they allow you to transfer calls from handset to handset but not to use the handsets to conference with an outside caller. Still other phones allow direct communication between handsets, so you can take them with you to use like walkie-talkies. Some phones can register up to eight handsets, for instance, but that doesn't mean you can use all eight at once. You might be able to use two for handset-to-handset intercom, while two others conference with an outside party.

HOW TO CHOOSE

Decide how much hardware you need. The basic options are a stand-alone phone, a phone with a built-in answerer, or a phone that supports multiple handsets from one base. A stand-alone phone is best suited for small families or people in a small apartment with little need for more than one phone. The built-in answerer, a common choice, adds a big measure of convenience. A multiple-handset phone is good for active families who need phones throughout the house; this type of phone lets you put handsets in a room that doesn't have a phone jack.

Select the technology and frequency band. A 900-MHz phone should suit most users, but that type may be hard to find because 2.4- and 5.8-GHz models dominate. You're likely to find the widest range of models and prices with 2.4-GHz phones. But if you want to minimize problems of interference with other wireless products, look to a 5.8-GHz or 900-MHz phone. Analog phones, apt to be less expensive than digital, are fine for many people. But if privacy is important, choose a DSS or digital phone.

To be sure you're actually getting a DSS or digital phone for its voice-transmission security, check the packaging carefully. Look for wording such as "digital phone," "digital spread spectrum (DSS)" or "frequency-hopping spread spectrum (FHSS)." Phrases such as "phone with digital security code," "phone with all-digital answerer," or "spread spectrum technology" (not digital spread spectrum) all denote phones that are less secure.

Phones that use dual-band transmission may indicate the higher frequency in a larger print on the packaging. If you want a true 2.4- or 5.8-GHz phone, check the fine print. If only the frequency is prominently shown on the package, it's probably analog.

Settle on the features you want. You can typically expect caller ID, a headset jack, and a base that can be wall-mounted. But the features don't end there for both standalone phones and phone-answerers. Check the box or ask to see an instruction manual to be sure you're getting the capabilities and features that matter to you. As a rule, the more feature-laden the phone, the higher its price.

Performance variations. CONSUMER REPORTS' tests show that most new cordless phones have very good overall voice quality. Some are excellent, approaching the voice quality of the best corded phones. In our latest tests, most fully charged nickel-cadmium (Ni-Cd) or nickel-metal hydride (Ni-MH) batteries handled eight hours of continuous conversation before they needed recharging. Most manufacturers claim that a fully charged battery will last at least a week in standby mode. When they can no longer hold a charge, a replacement battery, usually proprietary, costs about $10 to $25, and may be difficult to find. Some phones use less-expensive AA or AAA rechargeable batteries. (To find a store that will recycle a used battery, call 800-822-8837.)

Give the handset a test drive. In the store, hold the handset to your head to see if it feels comfortable. It should fit the contours of your face. The earpiece should have rounded edges and a recessed center that fits nicely over the middle of your ear. Check the buttons and controls to make sure they're reasonably sized and legible.

Don't discard the corded phone. It's a good idea to keep at least one corded phone in your home, if only for emergencies. A cordless phone may not work if you lose electrical power, and a cell phone won't work if you can't get a signal or the circuits are full. A corded phone draws its power from the phone system and can function without household AC power.

Related CR Report: October 2005
Ratings: page 237

DESKTOP COMPUTERS

Even the least-expensive desktop machines can deliver impressive performance.

The desktop computer has become just another appliance you use every day. Replacement sales—not first-time purchases—now drive the computer market. Fully loaded desktops selling for less than $800 are common, even among established brands.

WHAT'S AVAILABLE

There are dozens of companies vying to put a new desktop in your home. Dell, eMachines, Gateway (which merged with eMachines in 2004), Hewlett-Packard (which merged with Compaq in 2002), IBM, and Sony all make machines that use Microsoft's dominant Windows operating system. Apple is the sole maker of Macintosh models. Small mail-order and store brands cater to budget-minded buyers. Price range: $400 to $3,000.

FEATURES THAT COUNT

The **processor** houses the "brains" of a computer. Its clock speed, measured in gigahertz (GHz), and the chip's design, termed "architecture," determine how fast the chip can process information. In general, the higher the clock speed, the faster the computer. But not always, since different chip families attain different efficiencies.

Manufacturers of Windows machines generally use 1.6- to 3.8-GHz processors with one of the following names: Intel's Pentium or Celeron, or AMD's Athlon or Sempron. Celeron and Sempron are lower-priced processors that equal higher-priced chips in many respects. Intel now assigns "processor numbers" to its chips, de-emphasizing clock speed, while AMD uses a "speed rating" number. Apple's Macintosh machines use 1.25- to 2.7-GHz PowerPC G4 or G5 processors, which are manufactured by IBM.

Apple has announced that they will begin a transition to Intel processors in 2006. The system architecture of some families of chips allows them to be as fast as or faster than others with higher clock speeds, so speed comparison by the numbers can be misleading.

All name-brand computers sold today have at least 256 megabytes (MB) of RAM, or **random access memory,** the memory the computer uses while in operation. **Video RAM,** also measured in megabytes, is secondary RAM that works with the **graphics processor** to provide smooth video imaging and game play.

The **hard drive** is your computer's long-term data storage system. Given the disk-space requirements of today's multimedia games, digital photos, and video files, bigger is better. You'll find hard drives ranging in size from 40 to 300 gigabytes (GB).

A **CD-ROM** drive has been standard on most desktops for many years. Commonly supplied now is a CD-RW (CD-rewriteable) drive, also known as a "burner" that lets you create backup files or make music compilations on a compact disc. A **DVD-ROM** drive brings full-length movies or action-packed multimedia games with full-motion video to the desktop. It complements the CD-RW drive on midline and higher-end systems, allowing you to copy CDs directly between the two drives.

A DVD drive will also play CDs and CD-ROMs. Combo drives combine CD-writing and DVD-playing in a single drive, saving space. The newest in this family, rapidly becoming a common choice, is the **DVD writer,** which lets you transfer home-video footage to a DVD disk, or store as much data as six CDs.

There are three competing, incompatible DVD formats—DVD-RW, DVD+RW, and DVD-RAM—as well as drives that can create dual-layer DVDs that store twice as much. Some drives can write in more than one format, but all can create a disk that will play on stand-alone DVD players.

Almost gone is the **diskette** drive, where 3.5-inch diskettes are inserted. Most PCs don't have such a drive built in, because it only allows you to read or store relatively small amounts of data. Many people use a CD-RW as a large "diskette" drive to back up or transport files. Many PCs now come with a digital camera memory-card reader that can also serve for file transfer. You can also get external drives or use a USB memory module that holds much more than a diskette.

The computer's **cathode ray tube (CRT)** or flat-panel **liquid crystal display (LCD)** monitor contains the screen and displays the images sent from the graphics processor—internal circuitry that creates the images. Monitors come in sizes (measured diagonally) ranging from 15 to 21 inches and larger. Seventeen-inch monitors are the most common.

Apple's eMac and iMac come with built-in monitors, its Mac Mini without one. LCD displays are now the most popular, taking less space and using less power than CRTs. Better LCD displays can use a Digital Video Interface (DVI) connection, found on many newer PCs.

The critical components of a desktop computer are usually housed in a case called a **tower.** A **minitower** is the typical configuration and can fit either on top of or under a desk. More expensive machines have a **midtower,** which has extra room for upgrades. A **microtower** is a space-saving alternative that is usually less expensive.

All-in-one computers, such as the Apple iMac, have no tower; everything but the keyboard and mouse is built into a small case that supports the monitor. Apple's Power Mac line of computers has a tower. Apple's newest model, the Mac Mini, has a space-saving design that puts everything but the monitor, keyboard, and mouse in a case about the size of a hardcover book. An "entertainment PC"—one with a TV tuner built in—comes in a case that is more like an audio or video component, made to fit in with other home-entertainment devices.

A **mouse,** a small device that fits under your hand and has a "tail" of wire that connects to the computer, moves the cursor (the pointer on the screen) via a rolling ball or a light sensor on its underside. Alternatives include a trackball, which is rolled with the fingers in the direction you want the cursor to go; a pad, which lets you move the cursor by sliding a finger; a tablet, which uses a penlike stylus for input; and a joystick, used to play computer games.

Most computers come with a **standard keyboard,** although you can also buy one separately. Many keyboards have **CD (or DVD) controls** to pause playback, change tracks, and so on. Many also have keys to facilitate getting online, starting a search, launching programs, or retrieving e-mail. There are also wireless keyboards and mice that let you move about as you type.

Shop smart

The bigger the hard drive, the better for the long term. You'll find hard drives ranging in size from 40 to 300 gigabytes (GB).

Computers for home use feature a **high-fidelity sound system** that amplifies music from CDs or downloaded music files, synthesized music, game sounds, and DVD-movie soundtracks. Speaker systems with a subwoofer have deeper, more powerful bass. Surround-sound systems can turn a PC into a home theater. Some computers come with a **microphone** for recording, or one can be added.

PCs come with a modem to allow a dial-up Internet connection. **Parallel** and **serial ports** are the traditional connections for printers and scanners. Universal serial bus (USB) ports are designed to replace parallel and serial ports and provide a connection to many other devices. **FireWire** or **IEEE 1394 ports** are used to capture video from digital camcorders and other electronic equipment. An **Ethernet port** or **wireless network card** lets you link several computers in the household to share files, a printer, or a broadband Internet connection. An **S-video output jack** lets you run a video cable from the computer to a television, which lets you use the computer's DVD drive to view a movie on a TV instead of on the computer monitor.

Media Center PCs have a TV tuner and a remote control, making them a complete entertainment system. They can also record TV programs, just like a DVR (digital video recorder, such as TiVo).

HOW TO CHOOSE

First, decide whether to upgrade your current computer. Upgrading, rather than replacing it, may make sense if your additional needs are modest—a second hard drive, say, because you're running out of room for digital photos. Adding memory or a CD burner is usually more cost-effective than buying a whole new machine. If your PC has become unreliable, your want list is more demanding, or there's software you must run that your system is not up to, a new PC is the logical answer.

Consider a laptop. A desktop computer typically costs hundreds less and is easier to upgrade, expand, and repair. It usually offers better ergonomics, such as a more comfortable keyboard, bigger display, and enhanced audio. But a laptop merits consideration if portability and compactness are priorities.

Pick the right type of desktop. Most manufacturers offer several lines at different price points. Budget computers are the least expensive, yet they are suitable for routine work, such as e-mail, word processing, and Web surfing. You can also do photo editing. Workhorse computers cost a few hundred dollars more but are faster, more versatile, and upgradable. They can run complex 3-D games and edit video. All-in-one models have most of the components in a single case. And entertainment or media PCs include TV tuners, a remote control, and software that give them the functions of a DVR.

Choose by brand. Our surveys have consistently shown notable differences in reliability and technical support among computer brands. And some brands are generally more expensive than others. Those factors could help you decide which of two similarly equipped computers is the better buy.

Choose between preconfigured and custom built. You can buy a PC off the shelf in a store or via the Web, configured with features and options the manufacturer pitches to average consumers. Or consider purchasing a desktop that you configure to order, either online or in a store. When you configure a computer to order online, onscreen menus typically show you all the options and let you see how a change in one option affects the overall price.

Related CR Report: September 2005
Reliability: page 232

HOME NETWORKING

If you have broadband Internet service and more than one computer in your home, there's growing reason to link them to create a home network.

A network allows a single broadband account to be shared throughout the home. Unfortunately, such networking is impractical with dial-up Internet service—one of several reasons you might want to consider broadband.

WHAT'S AVAILABLE

Home networking is getting a boost from improvements in the range, speed, and cost of wireless networks. If you own a laptop computer that has wireless capability, a wireless network now allows you to surf the Web at broadband speeds from most places in your house, yard, or apartment. Leading brands of wireless routers include D-Link, Netgear, and Linksys. Wired networking is far from obsolete, however, since it still provides the most secure and reliable connections. Indeed, for many households the best solution for sharing a broadband connection—or a printer, music files, or digital photos—among multiple computers might be a network that includes both wired and wireless.

Ethernet, or wired, networks. Wired networks are very secure by themselves, with no special security measures necessary. They are reliable, and usually immune to interference. They offer the fastest data transfer—up to 94 megabits per second for the common 10/100 type, enough for virtually any data application.

One drawback is that you can't easily move your computer around the home. Routing cables throughout the home can be a hassle or expensive. Price range: $50 to $100 for one router and a cable to connect two fairly new computers. Also, there might be additional costs for routing cable through the home.

Wi-Fi, 802.11g (wireless). There are no cables to connect or rout with a wireless network, and there are minimal installation costs. Mobility is the key—the wireless network supplies signals virtually anywhere around the home. You will need to take additional steps in terms of security, without which your data are vulnerable to hackers. Thick walls can reduce signal strength, which might vary in different areas of the home or even within a room. Wi-Fi networks might interfere with cordless phones, baby monitors, and other wireless devices. These networks are only 25 percent as fast as Ethernet, but they're still fine for typical networking uses, such as Web surfing and e-mail. Price range: $200 or less for a router and client cards to allow two computers to use the network wirelessly.

HOW TO CHOOSE

Plan your network. You'll probably want to locate the router near the source of your broadband service—usually a cable or DSL modem. The router and the modem will be connected by an Ethernet cable. But the connections between the router and the computers in the network might be either wired or wireless.

Choose a wireless router. That is the official term for the models that support both Ethernet and Wi-Fi. Even if you don't need wireless capability now, acquiring it costs little extra (perhaps $10 or so) compared with a wired model, and might spare your having to replace the router if you want to add a wireless device to it in the future.

Stick with the 802.11g wireless standard. Wi-Fi is continually evolving, with new standards designed to increase broadcast range and speed, thus increasing the network's ability to handle new types of information. The name of the standard is usually listed on the router's package, as a letter suffix to the technical term for Wi-Fi, which is 802.11. Currently the most common standard is known as 802.11g. We think it's the best choice for most people.

The 802.11g networks we tested all had sufficient range and speed to provide coverage throughout most homes. The data speeds we measured fell short of the standard speed for 802.11g. But all routers were much faster than the typical speed of a broadband Internet connection.

If you already have a wireless network

that uses 802.11a or 802.11b, two older standards, consider upgrading only if you find the range, speed, or reliability of your network wanting.

At the other end of the spectrum are routers that use early variants of the latest Wi-Fi standard, 802.11n. Frequently referred to with terms such as "MIMO," "Super G," or "pre-n," such models might not be compatible with the actual "n" standard, which is due in late 2006. They also require that you buy matching networking adapters, even for computers with built-in 802.11g capability.

Consider one of these new routers only if you have range problems that can't be solved in other ways. In our tests, they were better at penetrating walls than 802.11g routers, and some offered data speeds that were twice as fast. But they were just as likely to interfere with (or receive interference from) cordless phones and other devices.

Tech tip

A wireless network means you will need to take additional steps in terms of security, without which your data are vulnerable to hackers.

Consider whether and how you'll share a printer. A network lets you avoid the cost of putting a printer in every room by sharing one. To do this, you can use a printer with built-in network capability.

It's possible to share a non-networked printer by attaching it to the network via a print server, a device that costs $70 to $100 and is the size of a large paperback. There may be issues of interference with some printer-management software, however. Any PC connected to a printer can also serve as a print server for the other computers on the network, though you must leave that computer on when you're printing.

Consider networking issues for other devices. An increasing number of devices that typically connect to a single computer—PDAs, printers, and video-game consoles—are now Wi-Fi compatible. If you plan to connect any of them to your network, make sure they're compatible with the network security you set up.

Check whether you need to buy adapters. Every computer on your network will require an adapter to allow it to communicate with the network; the question is whether it already has one built in. If you're using Ethernet to connect a computer bought within the past three years or so, the adapter will most likely be built into the unit. The same applies to recent-vintage laptops, which should have built-in 802.11g capability.

If you need to buy a network adapter for your desktop, you can choose either an internal PC-card version, which requires opening the computer case for installation, or a USB version, which plugs into a USB port. Laptops can use either a PCI-card or USB adapter. In all cases, the cost should be no more than $60.

Resist professional installation help. Computer retailers might try to sell you on professional installation for your new network, starting at a cost of $150 or so. But wiring aside, today's networks are so easy to set up that you shouldn't take them up on their offer if you're comfortable with technology.

Network gear usually comes with instructions and access to free 24/7 technical support. And you can always come back to the retailer for help in troubleshooting the network if necessary.

Shop by return policy. For all your best efforts, the network equipment you've bought might not be compatible with your home. For example, your walls and floors might be especially resistant to wireless transmission (which might be the case if they have a lot of moisture, metal, or other highly conductive material in them). Before you buy, check the store's return policies. Consider a retailer with a generous one.

LAPTOP COMPUTERS

A longtime companion at work, school, and on the road, the laptop has finally come home.

Laptops account for about 25 percent of sales. It's not hard to understand why. Small screens and cramped keyboards have been replaced by bigger, crisper displays and more usable key layouts. Processors have caught up in speed, and innovative new processors provide some real advantages. Fast CD and DVD recording drives are common, as are ample hard drives. And a growing interest in wireless computing plays to the laptop's main strength: its portability. A laptop is the most convenient way to take full advantage of the growing availability of high-speed wireless Internet access at airports, schools, hotels, and even restaurants and coffee shops.

The Centrino technology that's central to Intel's newest laptop processors has wireless capability built in, and delivers commendably long battery life. The thinnest laptops on the market are less than an inch thick and weigh just 2 to 5 pounds. To get these light, sleek models, however, you'll have to pay a premium and make a few sacrifices.

WHAT'S AVAILABLE

Dell, Gateway, Hewlett-Packard, Compaq (now owned by HP), IBM, Sony, and Toshiba are the leading Windows laptop brands. Macintosh laptops are made by Apple. Laptops can be grouped into several basic configurations:

Budget models. These have slower processors and lower screen quality than others but are suitable for routine office work and home software. Price range: $800 or less.

Workhorse models. These have faster processors and more built-in devices, so there's less need for external attachments. They're not lightweight or battery-efficient enough for frequent travelers. Price range: $1,000 and up.

Slim-and-light models. These are for travelers. They can be less than an inch thick and weigh as little as 3 or 4 pounds. They generally require an external drive to read DVDs or burn CDs. Price range: $1,500 and up.

Tablet-style. These sit in your hands like a clipboard and have handwriting-recognition software. Some convert to a "normal" laptop with a keyboard. Price range: $1,800 and up.

FEATURES THAT COUNT

A **diskette drive** has become a rare option in laptops. As an alternative, you can use a **USB memory drive** (about $20 and up), which fits on a keychain and holds as much data as numerous diskettes. Or you can save files on a writeable CD or camera **memory card**. Most laptops have slots that can read one or more types of memory cards.

Windows laptops generally have a 1.5- to 3.5-GHz processor. Pentium 4 processors have the higher speed ratings; the new Pentium M and Celeron M processors have a slower rated speed but actually perform on a par with other processors. Macintosh Power PC processors are measured on a different basis altogether. In short, the different types of processors make direct speed comparisons difficult, but any type of processor is likely to deliver all the speed you'll need.

Laptops come with a 40- to 160-gigabyte hard drive and 256 megabytes or more of random access memory (RAM) and can be upgraded to 1 gigabyte or more.

Today's laptops use a rechargeable lithium-ion battery. In CONSUMER REPORTS tests, batteries provided 2 to 5 hours of continuous use when running office applications. (Laptops go into sleep mode when used intermittently, extending the time between charges.) You can extend battery life somewhat by dimming the display as you work and by removing PC cards and turning off wireless devices when they aren't needed, or by using basic applications only. Playing a DVD movie uses more battery power than usual, but any laptop should be able to play a movie through to the end.

A laptop's **keyboard** can be quite different from that of a desktop computer. The keys themselves may be full-sized (generally only lightweight models pare them down), but they may not feel as solid. Some laptops have extra buttons to expedite your access to e-mail or a Web browser or to control DVD playback. You can attach an external keyboard, which you may find easier to use.

A 14- to 15-inch **display**, measured diagonally, should suit most people. A few larger models have a 16- or 17-inch display. A resolution of 1,400x1,050 (SXGA+) pixels (picture elements) or more is better than 1,024x768 (XGA) for viewing the fine detail in photographs or video but may shrink objects on the screen. You can use settings in Windows to make them larger. Many models are now offered with a display that has a "glossy" surface instead of a dull one. Those look better in bright ambient light, as long as you avoid direct reflections.

Most laptops use a small **touch-sensitive pad** in place of a mouse—you slide your finger across the pad to move the cursor. You can also program the pad to respond to a "tap" as a "click," or to scroll as you sweep your index finger along the pad's right edge. An alternative pointing system uses a pencil-eraser-sized **joystick** in the middle of the keyboard. You can attach an external mouse or trackball if you prefer.

Laptops usually include at least one **PC-card** slot for expansion. You might add a wireless network card or a digital camera memory-card reader, for example, if those are not built in. Many laptops offer a connection for a docking station, a $100 or $200 base that makes it easy to connect an external monitor, keyboard, mouse, printer, or phone line. Most laptops let you attach these devices anyway, without the docking station. An external display lets you set up your workspace more ergonomically. At least two **USB ports**, for easy hookup of, say, a printer, digital camera, or scanner, is standard. A **wired network (Ethernet) port** is common, as is a FireWire port for digital-video transfer. Many models have a standard or optional internal **wireless-network ("Wi-Fi") adapter**. The **infrared port** found on a few models can be used to synchronize data wirelessly between the computer and a personal digital assistant (PDA).

Laptops typically come with less software than desktop computers, although almost all are bundled with a basic home-office suite (such as Microsoft Works) and a personal-finance program. The small **speakers** built into laptops often sound tinny, with little bass. Headphones or external speakers deliver much better sound.

HOW TO CHOOSE

Decide if a laptop is right for you. If you're on a tight budget and aren't cramped for space, a desktop computer may still be OK. It's also best for heavy users who spend hours at the computer each day. Otherwise, consider a laptop.

Windows vs. Macintosh. Many people choose Windows because it's what they've always used. Apple's iBook will suit you if you're interested in photo editing, music, video, and other multimedia applications. In recent subscriber surveys, CONSUMER REPORTS has found Apple laptops to be among the most reliable and Apple technical support to be top-notch. Apple computers are also less susceptible to most viruses and spyware than Windows-based computers. The Apple PowerBook is relatively expensive as laptops go, however.

Buy à la carte. Dell and Gateway pioneered the notion that every computer can be tailored to an individual buyer's needs, much like choosing the options for a car. This configure-to-order model is now common practice for laptops as well as desktops.

You can also purchase a pre-configured computer off the shelf. (You can do the same online if you opt for the default choices of equipment the manufacturer offers.) That's fine if you don't have very strict requirements for how a laptop is outfitted or if you want to take advantage of an attractive sale.

Configure-to-order menus show you all the options and let you see how a change in one affects the overall price. You may decide to use a less-expensive processor, for example, but spend more for wireless capability or better graphics. Configure-to-order will often give you choices you won't get if you buy off the shelf. And configure-to-order means less chance of overlooking important details. But be sure to double-check your choices before ordering and look for unwanted items that some manufacturers include by default.

Downplay the processor speed. Speed is no longer the be-all of personal computers. For years, processors have delivered all the speed most people need. That's still very much the case. Spend the money on more memory instead. A Pentium 4 processor with a speed of 2.4 GHz and a Pentium M at 1.4 GHz earned the same speed score in our tests. The different types of chips now on the market make direct speed comparisons difficult.

Look closely at warranties and insurance. Get the longest manufacturer's warranty you can afford; many offer one or two years above the basic one-year warranty, for a price. If you intend to travel a lot, buy screen insurance from the manufacturer. If you take full advantage of the manufacturer's warranty and insurance, you won't need an extended warranty from the retailer.

Related CR Report: September 2005
Reliability: page 232

MONITORS

Prices are dropping for larger CRT monitors, and for flat-panel LCD displays that free up space on your desktop.

Deciding whether to buy a flat-panel LCD or a standard, fairly fat CRT monitor comes down to this: Do you need more space on the surface of your desk or on the screen? If freeing up space on your desk is the priority, an LCD is the clear choice. But since LCDs are costly, you might still opt for a CRT. Desktop computers and monitors are often sold as a package. Still, some people buying a new desktop decide to hold on to their old monitor. Others choose to buy a new monitor for their existing computer.

WHAT'S AVAILABLE

Apple, Dell, eMachines (which merged with Gateway in 2004), Gateway, Hewlett-

Packard (which merged with Compaq in 2002), IBM, and Sony all market their own brands of monitors for their computers. Other brands of monitors, such as CTX, Envision, Mitsubishi, NEC, Philips, Samsung, and ViewSonic are sold separately. Many brands are manufactured on an outsource basis.

CRT monitors. These typically range from 17 to 22 inches. To reduce glare, some CRTs have flattened, squared-off screens (not to be confused with flat-panel LCD screens). The nominal image size—the screen size touted in ads—is generally based on the diagonal measurement of the picture tube. The image you see, called the viewable image size (VIS), is usually an inch smaller. Thus a 17-inch CRT has a 16-inch VIS. As a result of a class-action lawsuit, ads must state a CRT's VIS as well as its nominal image, but you may have to squint at the fine print to find it.

Generally the bigger the screen, the more room a CRT takes up on your desk, with depth roughly matching nominal screen size. "Short-depth" models shave an inch or more off the depth. A 17-inch monitor, the most frequent choice these days, has almost one-third more viewable area than the 15-inch version now vanishing from the market. The larger size is especially useful when you're using the Internet, playing video games, watching DVD movies, editing photos, or working in several windows.

If you regularly work with graphics or sprawling spreadsheets, consider getting a 19-inch monitor. Its viewable area is one-fourth larger than a 17-inch model's. A short-depth 19-inch model doesn't take up much more desktop space than a standard 17-inch.

Aimed at graphics professionals, 21- and 22-inch models provide ample viewing area but they gobble up desktop space. Price range: $100 to $200 (17-inch); $175 to $300 (19-inch); $500 to $1,000 (21- to 22-inch).

Flat-panel LCD monitors. These began to outsell CRT monitors in 2003. Because these monitors have a liquid-crystal display rather than a TV-style picture tube, they take up much less desktop space than CRTs. They operate with analog or digital input, or both. Unlike a CRT, the nominal and the viewable image sizes of a flat-panel LCD are the same. Desktop models typically measure 15 inches diagonally and just a few inches deep, and weigh around 15 pounds, compared with 30 to 50 pounds for a CRT. LCDs with a screen 17 inches or larger are available, but they are still somewhat pricey. Wide-screen LCDs with a 17-inch VIS, specially designed for watching wide-format videos, are also available. These screens have an aspect ratio of 16:9, like those found on most digital TVs, and they're also fairly pricey.

Flat-panel displays deliver a very clear image, but they have some inherent quirks. Their range of color is a bit narrower than that of CRT monitors. And you have to view a flat-panel screen straight on; except for wide-screen models, the picture loses contrast as you move off-center. Fine lines may appear grainy. In analog mode you have to tweak the controls in order to get the best picture, but we have seen some improvements lately regarding the narrow angle. Price range: $300 to $450 (15-inch); $300 and up (17- to 18-inch).

FEATURES THAT COUNT

A monitor's **resolution** refers to the number of picture elements, or pixels, that make up an image. More pixels mean finer detail. Most monitors can display at several resolutions, generally ranging from 640x480 to 1,600x1,200, depending on the monitor and the graphics card. An LCD usually displays a sharper image than a CRT of comparable size when both are viewed at identical resolutions. But that's only if the LCD is set to its "native" resolution—1,024x768 pixels for a 15-inch screen; 1,280x1,024 or 1,400x1,050 for a 17-, 18-, or 19-inch model. On both types of monitor, the higher the resolution, and the smaller the text and images, so more content fits on the screen. Bigger CRT screens can handle higher resolutions and display more information.

Dot pitch, measured in millimeters, refers to the spacing between a CRT's pixels. All else being equal, a smaller dot pitch produces a more detailed image, though that's no guarantee of an excellent picture. In general, avoid models with a dot pitch larger than 0.28 mm.

A CRT requires a high **refresh rate** (the number of times per second the image is redrawn on the screen) to avoid annoying image flicker. In general, you'll be more comfortable with a 17-inch monitor with a refresh rate of at least 75 hertz (Hz) at the resolution you want. For a 19-inch monitor, you may need an 85-Hz rate to avoid eyestrain, especially at higher resolutions. Refresh rate isn't an issue with flat-panel displays.

Monitors have controls for **brightness** and **contrast.** Most of them also have controls for **color balance** (usually called color temperature), **distortion,** and such. Buttons activate onscreen controls and menus.

Bigger CRTs use a considerable amount of juice: about 80 watts for a typical 19-inch model, between 65 and 70 watts for a 17-inch model, and about 20 watts for a 15-inch flat-panel LCD, for example. Most monitors have a sleep mode that uses less than 3 watts when the computer is on but not in use.

Some monitors include a **microphone,** integrated or separate **speakers,** or **composite-video inputs** for viewing the output of a VCR or camcorder.

Plug-and-play capability makes it fairly simple to add a new monitor to an existing computer.

HOW TO CHOOSE

Decide between LCD and CRT monitors. If your computer's monitor is hogging the top of your desk, you can reclaim much of that space by replacing it with an LCD. But doing so will cost you about $200 to $300 more than if you bought a new CRT monitor. And LCD screens have an inherent shortcoming: The image appears to fade as you move left, right, up, or down. However, most LCD monitors in our recent tests had a wider viewing angle than we've seen in the past. If space isn't an issue but budget is, a CRT monitor is a good choice. Because CRTs deliver truer color and render fast-moving objects better, they are a superior choice for photographers, designers, and gamers.

Shop smart

Decide if you need desk space or screen space when deciding on the style of monitor to buy.

Settle on size. For most people, a 15-inch LCD monitor or a 17-inch CRT is big enough. Larger monitors are best suited for people who need to show photo enlargements or who regularly display multiple windows on the screen.

Consider helpful features. A monitor you can raise or lower can compensate for a desk that's too high or low. It's a feature found on some LCD monitors, but not on CRTs because they're so heavy. Some monitors can be rotated 90 degrees, from a landscape to portrait orientation, with the image automatically adjusting itself. That can be handy for viewing photos and Web pages. Also, look for conveniently placed controls that adjust contrast, brightness, and other settings that affect image.

Look for a long warranty. Many monitors, both LCDs and CRTs, come with a three-year warranty on parts and labor. A warranty that long is worth looking for, especially when purchasing a more expensive model.

Related CR Report: June 2005

PDAS

Besides serving as an address book, calendar, and to-do list, many personal digital assistants offer multimedia functions.

PDAs can store thousands of phone numbers, appointments, tasks, and notes. All models can exchange, or synchronize, information with a full-sized computer with PIM (personal information management) software. To do this, you connect the PDA to your computer via a cradle or cable. For models that run on rechargeable batteries, the cradle doubles as a charger. Infrared, Bluetooth, and Wi-Fi let you synchronize with a computer without wires or a cradle.

Most PDAs can be made to work with both Windows and Macintosh computers, but PDAs with the Pocket PC operating system usually require third-party software for Macs. PDAs with Wi-Fi (wireless) capability can access the Internet. Those without can as well with the addition of a separately purchased modem. Most PDAs can record your voice, play videos, display digital photos, and hold maps, city guides, and a novel.

WHAT'S AVAILABLE

Most PDAs on the market are the familiar tablet-with-stylus types that feature a squarish display screen, a design pioneered by Palm Inc. (now called Palm). Today the main choices are models that use the Palm operating system (OS)—mostly PalmOne models—and Pocket PC devices from companies such as Dell and Hewlett-Packard. The latter use a stripped-down version of Microsoft Windows. A few PDAs use a proprietary operating system. Kyocera, Nokia, Samsung, and Sony Ericsson offer units that combine a cell phone and a PDA.

Palm OS systems. Equipped with software to link with Windows and Macintosh computers, Palm units have a simple user interface. You use a stylus to enter data on the units by tapping an onscreen keyboard or writing in a shorthand known as Graffiti. Or you can download data from your computer. Most Palm OS-based PDAs can synchronize with a variety of desktop e-mail programs, such as Outlook, Outlook Express, and Eudora. Most Palm models come with VersaMail, software good at handling e-mails with attachments. And all include Palm desktop, a basic PIM application for exchanging information with your desktop PC. Palm OS units are easy to use, although navigation between different programs is cumbersome because of the operating system's "single-tasking" nature.

Most Palm OS models make it difficult or impossible to replace the battery yourself. And beyond the warranty period, you can't be sure the manufacturer will do it for you.

Most Palm OS models have expansion slots that let you add memory or attach separately purchased accessories. All Palm OS-based PDAs can be enhanced by adding third-party software applications—the more free memory that a model comes with, the more software it can accommodate. There is a large body of Palm OS-compatible freeware, shareware, and commercial software available for download at such sites as *www.palmgear.com*. Many Palm models come with Documents To Go—word-processing and spreadsheet software similar to that used in Pocket PCs but more versatile. Price range: about $100 to $800.

One of PalmOne's top-of-the-line models, the Tungsten T5, combines a Palm OS-based PDA with many of the best features of the Pocket PC operating system. When it's connected to a Windows PC, you can drag and drop files to the T5's built-in "flash drive," even on PCs that don't have Palm's desktop software installed.

Pocket PC systems. These resemble Palm OS-based models but are more like miniature computers. They have a processor with extra horsepower and come with familiar applications such as a word processor and a spreadsheet. Included is a scaled-down version of Internet Explorer, plus voice-recording and perhaps some financial functions. The included e-mail program handles Word and Excel attachments easily. Also standard is an application that plays MP3 music files.

As you might expect, all the application software included in a Pocket PC integrates well with the Windows computer environment. You need to purchase third-party software to use a Mac. And you'll need Microsoft Office programs such as Word, Excel, and Outlook on your computer to exchange data with a PDA. All Pocket PCs include a copy of Outlook for use as a PIM application. Pocket PCs have a color display and rechargeable lithium-ion batteries. Unlike most Palm OS-based PDAs, replacing the battery of most Pocket PCs is usually straightforward. Price range: $200 to $700.

FEATURES THAT COUNT

All PDAs have the tools for basic tasks: a **calendar** to keep track of your appointments, **contact/address software** for addresses and phone numbers, **tasks/to-do lists** for reminders and keeping track of errands, and a calculator. A **notes/memo function** lets you make quick notes to yourself. Other capabilities include **word-processing, spreadsheet,** and **e-mail functions.** A **voice recorder,** which uses a built-in microphone and speaker, works like a tape recorder. **MP3 playback** lets you listen to digital-music files stored in that format, and a **picture viewer** lets you look at **digital photos.** A few models also include a built-in **digital camera** and **keyboard.**

A PDA's **processor** is the system's brain. In general, the higher the processing speed of this chip, the faster the PDA will execute tasks—and the more expensive the PDA will be. But higher-speed processors may require more battery power and thus deplete batteries more quickly. Processing speeds are 16 to 600 megahertz (MHz), and models typically have 8 to 64 megabytes (MB) of user memory. Even the smallest amount in that range should be more than enough for most people.

> **Tech tip**
>
> The higher the processing speed of the chip, the faster the PDA will execute tasks–and the more expensive it will be.

Nearly every PDA offers an **expansion slot** for some form of removable memory card: CompactFlash, MultiMedia card (slots also accept SecureDigital cards), or Memory Stick. Models with two expansion slots can accommodate a **peripheral device,** such as a **Wi-Fi wireless networking card,** as well as removable memory. If you plan to transfer photos from a digital camera to your PDA, make sure the two devices use the same type of card.

Some PDAs offer **wireless connectivity.** Models with a capability known as **Bluetooth** can connect wirelessly over short distances to a properly equipped computer or peripheral such as a printer or modem. Models with Wi-Fi can connect over medium distances to a Wi-Fi-enabled home network or to the Internet at "hotspots" in certain airports, coffee shops, and hotels.

A PDA combined with a **cell phone** can

make voice calls or directly connect to the Internet via a wireless Internet service provider. It's possible for a single PDA to have more than one of these types of wireless connectivity.

HOW TO CHOOSE

Consider your ties to a computer. Pocket PCs provide a Windowslike interface that allows simple PC-to-PDA file transfer with drag-and-drop capability. They're also more convenient than Palm OS models for setting up a Wi-Fi (wireless) e-mail connection. Most have replaceable batteries, along with accessible flash memory to which you can back up data.

Palm OS models run a wider range of third-party software applications than do Pocket PCs. For the basics, they're still easier to use. While all PDAs can sync with Macintoshes, only Palm models do so out of the box. The Missing Sync (available at *www.markspace.com*) and PocketMac (*www.pocketmac.net*) connect a Pocket PC to a Mac. Both are priced under $50.

Small size vs. extra features. As a rule, a model with a larger display or physical keyboard won't be the lightest or smallest. A PDA with two slots for memory and peripherals is more expandable but will tend to be larger.

Related CR Report: July 2004
Ratings: page 280

PRINTERS

New, inexpensive inkjets print color superbly, and they do it faster than ever. Laser printers excel at printing black-and-white text.

Inkjet printers are now the standard for home-computer output. They can turn out color photos nearly indistinguishable from lab-processed photos, along with banners, stickers, transparencies, T-shirt transfers, and greeting cards. Many produce excellent black-and-white text. With some very good models going for less than $200 inkjets account for the vast majority of printers sold for home use.

Laser printers still have their place in home offices. If you print reams of black-and-white text documents, you probably need the quality, speed, and low per-copy cost of a laser printer.

Printers use a computer's microprocessor and memory to process data. The latest inkjets and lasers are so fast partly because computers themselves have become more powerful and contain much more memory than before.

WHAT'S AVAILABLE

The printer market is dominated by a handful of well-established brands. Hewlett-Packard is the market leader. Other major brands include Brother, Canon, Epson, and Lexmark.

The type of computer a printer can serve depends on its ports. A Universal Serial Bus (USB) port lets a printer connect to Windows or Macintosh computers. A few models have a parallel port, which lets the printer work with older Windows computers. All these printers lack a serial port, which means they won't work with older Macs.

Inkjet printers. Inkjets use droplets of ink to form letters, graphics, and photos. Some printers have one cartridge that holds the cyan (greenish-blue), magenta, and yellow inks, and a second cartridge for the black ink. Others have an individual cartridge for each ink. For photos, many inkjets also have additional cartridges that contain lighter shades of cyan and magenta inks; some have added red, gray, blue, or green inks.

Most inkjets print at 2½ to 11 pages per

minute (ppm) for black-and-white text but are much slower for color photos, taking 1½ to 21 minutes to print a single 8x10. The cost of printing a black-and-white page with an inkjet varies considerably from model to model—ranging from 3 to 7.5 cents. The cost of printing a color 8x10 photo can range from 80 cents to $1.50. Price range: $80 to $700.

Laser printers. These work much like plain-paper copiers, forming images by transferring toner (powdered ink) to paper passing over an electrically charged drum. The process yields sharp black-and-white text and graphics. Laser printers usually outrun inkjets, cranking out black-and-white text at a rate of 12 to 18 ppm. Black-and-white laser printers generally cost about as much as midpriced inkjets, but they're cheaper to operate. Laser cartridges, about $50 to $100, can print thousands of black-and-white pages for a per-page cost of 2 to 4 cents. Color laser printers are also available. Price range: $150 to $1,000 (black and white); $400 and up (color).

FEATURES THAT COUNT

Printers differ in the fineness of detail they can produce. **Resolution,** expressed in dots per inch (dpi), is often touted as the main measure of print quality. But other factors, such as the way dot patterns are formed by software instructions from the printer driver, count, too. At their default settings—where they're usually expected to run—inkjets currently on the market typically have a resolution of 600x600 dpi. For color photos the dpi can be increased. Some printers go up to 5,760x1,440 dpi. Laser printers for home use typically offer 600 or 1,200 dpi. Printing color inkjet photos on special paper at a higher dpi setting can produce smoother shading of colors but can slow printing significantly.

Most **inkjet printers** have an ink monitor to warn when you're running low. Generic ink cartridges usually cost less, but most produce far fewer prints than the brand-name inks, so per-print costs may not be any lower. And print quality and fade-resistance may not be as good.

Shop smart

Be wary of off-brands of replacement inks; we have found brand-name cartridges to have better print quality overall, and per-page costs are often comparable.

For **double-sided printing,** you can print the odd-numbered pages of a document first, then flip those pages over to print the even-numbered pages on a second pass through the printer. A few printers can automatically print on both sides, but doing so slows down printing.

HOW TO CHOOSE

Be skeptical about advertised speeds. Print speed varies depending on what you're printing and at what quality, but the speeds you see in ads are generally higher than you're likely to achieve in normal use. You can't reliably compare speeds for different brands because each company uses its own methods to measure speed. We run the same tests on all models, printing text pages and photos that are similar to what you might print. As a result, our scores are realistic and can be compared across brands.

Don't get hung up on resolution. A printer's resolution, expressed in dots per inch, is another potential source of confusion. All things being equal, the more ink dots a printer puts on the paper, the more detailed the image. But dot size, shape, and placement also affect quality, so don't base a decision solely on resolution.

Consider supply costs as well as a printer's price. High ink-cartridge costs can make a bargain-priced printer a bad deal in the long run. Shop around for the best cartridge prices but be wary of off-brands; we have found brand-name cartridges to have better print quality overall, and per-page costs are often comparable.

Glossy photo paper costs about 25 to 75 cents a sheet, so use plain paper for works in progress and save the good stuff for the final results. We've gotten the best results using the recommended brand of paper. You may be tempted to buy a cheaper brand, but bear in mind that lower-grade paper can reduce photo quality and may not be as fade resistant.

Decide if you want to print photos without using a computer. Printing without a computer saves you an extra step and a little time. Features such as memory-card support, PictBridge support (a standard that allows a compatible camera to be connected directly to the printer), or a wireless interface are convenient. But when you print directly from camera to printer, you compromise on what may have attracted you to digital photography in the first place—the ability to tweak size, color, brightness, and other image attributes. And with a 4x6 printer, you give up the ability to print on larger media.

Weigh convenience features. Most printers make borderless prints like those from a photo developer. This matters most if you're printing to the full size of the paper, as you might with 4x6-inch sheets. Otherwise you can trim the edges off.

If you plan to use 4x6-inch paper regularly, look for a printer with a 4x6-inch tray, which makes it easier to feed paper of this size. With these small sheets, though, the cost per photo may be higher than ganging up a few images on 8½ x11-inch paper.

With some models, if you want to use the photo inks to get the best picture quality, you have to remove the black ink cartridge and replace it with the photo-ink cartridge. Then you have to replace the black for text or graphics. This can get tedious. Models that hold all the ink tanks simultaneously eliminate that hassle.

Consider connections. Printers with USB 2.0 ports are now fairly common. However, they don't enable much faster print speeds than plain USB. All new computers and printers have either USB or USB 2.0 ports, both of which are compatible. Computers more than six years old may have only a parallel port.

Decide whether you need scanning and copying. A multifunction unit provides scanning and color copying while saving space. The downside is that multifunction units' scanners may have lower resolution than the latest stand-alone scanners. Stand-alone scanners are best for handling negatives and slides. And if one part of the unit breaks, the whole unit must be repaired or replaced.

Related CR Report: May 2005
Ratings: page 284

SCANNERS

A scanner is a simple, cheap way to digitize images for printing, editing on your computer, or sending via e-mail.

You don't need a digital camera to take advantage of the computer's ability to edit photos. Continuing improvements in scanners have made it cheaper and easier to turn photos into digital images that you can enhance, resize, and share. And flatbed scanners are no longer restricted to printed originals. Our tests show that the best flatbeds are now a match for pricey film scanners when it comes to digitizing slides and negatives. That's no small accomplishment, reflecting improvements to the resolution that new scanners deliver and better accessories to hold film strips or slides securely for sharp, accurate scans.

WHAT'S AVAILABLE

A number of scanners come from companies, including Microtek and Visioneer, that made their name in scanning technology. Other brands include computer makers and photo specialists such as Canon, Epson, Hewlett-Packard, and Nikon.

Which type of scanner you should consider—flatbed, sheet-fed, or film—depends largely on how you will use it. If you're short on space, consider a multifunction device.

Flatbed scanners. More than 90 percent of the scanners on the market are flatbeds. They work well for text, graphics, photos, and anything else that is flat, including a kindergartner's latest drawing. Flatbeds include optical-character-recognition (OCR) software, which converts words on a printed page into a word-processing file in your computer. They also include basic image-editing software. Some stores may throw in a flatbed scanner for free, or for a few dollars extra, when you purchase a desktop computer.

A key specification for a scanner is its maximum optical resolution, measured in dots per inch (dpi). You'll pay more for greater resolution. Price range: less than \$100 for 600x1,200 dpi; \$100 to \$500 for models with greater resolution.

Sheet-fed models. Sheet-fed models can automatically scan a stack of loose pages, but they sometimes damage pages that pass through their innards. And they can't scan anything much thicker than a sheet of paper (meaning an old photo might be too thick). This type of scanner is often the one that comes as part of a multifunction device that can also print, send, and receive faxes. An increasing percentage of multifunction devices, however, include a flatbed scanner. Sheet-fed scanners also use OCR software. Price range: \$100 to \$600.

Film scanners. Serious photographers may want a film-only scanner that scans directly from an original slide (transparency) or negative. Some can accept small prints as well. Price range: \$400 to \$800.

FEATURES THAT COUNT

While the quality of images a scanner produces depends in part on the software included with it, there are several hardware features to consider.

You start scanning by running **driver software** that comes with the scanner or by pressing a preprogrammed button. Models with buttons automate routine tasks to let you operate your scanner as you would other office equipment. On some models you can customize the functions of the buttons. Any of these tasks can also be performed through the scanner's software without using buttons. A **copy/print button** initiates a scan and sends a command to print the results on your printer, effectively making the two devices act as a copier. Other button functions found on some models include **scan to a file, scan to a fax modem, scan to e-mail, scan to Web, scan to OCR, cancel scan, power save, start scanner software,** and **power on/off.**

You can also start the driver software from within an application, such as a word processor, that adheres to an industry standard known as TWAIN. A scanner's driver software allows you to **preview** a scan on-screen and crop it or adjust **contrast** and **brightness.** Once you're satisfied with the edited image, you can perform a final scan and pass the image to a running program or save it on your computer. You can make more extensive changes to an image with specialized **image-editing software.** And to scan text from a book or letter into a word-processing file in your computer, you run **OCR software.**

Many documents combine text with graphic elements, such as photographs and drawings. A handy software feature that's found on many scanners, called **multiple-scan mode,** lets you break down such hybrids into different sections that can be processed separately in a single scan. You can designate, for example, that the sections of a magazine article that are pure text go to the OCR software independently of the article's graphic elements. Other scanners would require a separate scan for each section of the document.

Tech tip

In our recent tests, the fastest scanner took about 10 seconds to scan an 8x10-inch photo at 300 dpi, while the slowest needed about 40 seconds.

Some flatbed models come with **film adapters** designed to scan film or slides, but if you need to scan from film or slides often, you're better off getting a separate film scanner.

HOW TO CHOOSE

Consider how much resolution you need. If you want a scanner solely for printed originals, look mainly at models that deliver 1,200 dot-per-inch (dpi) resolution; they are generally the least expensive models. You can always set a scanner to work at less than its maximum resolution. In fact, most scans of photos, graphics, and text need only 150 to 300 dpi. (For images to be viewed onscreen, 75 dpi will suffice.) Higher-resolution scans take longer and create bigger files, but usually add little.

For film and negatives, you'll want resolution of at least 2,400 dpi. Such a high setting is needed to capture enough detail so that an image created from a 35mm original can be enlarged.

When comparing specs, focus on the native optical resolution. It's more important than the "interpolated" or "enhanced" resolution, which comes in handy only when scanning line art.

Consider color-bit depth for film. If you plan to make enlargements of prints or to scan negatives or slides, pay attention to a specification known as color-bit depth. The greater the color-bit depth (24-bit is basic, 48-bit is tops), the better the scanner can differentiate among subtle gradations of light and dark.

Consider a multifunction unit. If you won't make heavy demands on a scanner (for instance, you cannot scan film or slides) and you need a general-use printer, especially for a tight space, a multifunction printer/scanner/copier may serve.

Don't sweat quality and speed. The majority of the scanners we recently tested were judged very good based on their ability to reproduce a color photo at maximum optical resolution. The rest were judged good, which means their scans were less crisp with less-accurate colors.

Speed matters if you expect to be scanning regularly. In our recent tests, the fastest took about 10 seconds to scan an 8x10-inch photo at 300 dpi, while the slowest needed about 40 seconds.

Don't sweat the software. All the scanners we recently tested came with software for scanning, image editing, and optical character recognition (which lets you scan text directly into a word-processing program). Some had software for making digital photo albums or other projects. All models also included software, often built into the hardware, that can repair image flaws caused by damaged originals.

Related CR Report: May 2005

Autos

What's New for Cars in 2006

Among the more than 240 models on the market, there are about 45 that are new or have received a major redesign. Designated as 2006 or early 2007 models, they will be introduced throughout the year against a backdrop of several ongoing trends in the automotive market:

• **Higher gasoline prices** are fueling a growing interest in fuel-efficient vehicles, and have led to a drop in sales of big SUVs.

• **More models are being offered with hybrid drivetrains.** Some hybrid models provide significantly better fuel economy than their conventional counterparts; others focus more on performance, providing quicker acceleration but with only moderately better fuel economy.

• **Automakers continue to introduce car-based SUVs and tall wagons** that provide similar benefits to conventional SUVs along with typically better handling, ride comfort, and fuel economy.

New and redesigned cars. With gasoline prices high, many car buyers are thinking small. And they'll now have more choices in the small-car category. Honda, for instance, released a redesigned Civic this fall. In addition to the standard sedan and coupe versions, the Civic line includes a sportier Civic Si Coupe and a new hybrid version that should provide even better fuel economy than the previous Civic Hybrid. California consumers can also buy a natural-gas-powered Civic that can be fueled off of a home gas supply.

In early 2006, Honda will also introduce its new four-door Fit hatchback. Expected to cost about $14,000, it looks like the Scion xA but, with a taller roofline, will offer much more interior room.

In the spring of 2006, Toyota will introduce the 2007 Yaris hatchback, which replaces the Echo. The Yaris line will include two- and four-door models.

Among midsized sedans, Ford Motor Company is releasing the Ford Fusion, Mercury Milan, and Lincoln Zephyr this fall. This trio is based on the Mazda6 and will be priced in the low $20,000 range. In spring 2006, Toyota will release a redesigned Camry as a 2007 model. A hybrid version of the four-cylinder model is also expected.

New SUVs, wagons, and trucks. As sales of large SUVs decline, automakers seem to be providing a stream of new small and midsized car-based minivans and wagons. This fall, for instance, Mazda introduced the Mazda5, a small minivan-like hatchback that's based on the excellent Mazda3. It includes sliding side doors and a third-row seat, and can seat six people. Mazda will also release a midsized car-based SUV called the CX-7 in late 2006, which is based on the Mazda6 sedan.

The new Dodge Caliber, due in early 2006, is a small five-door hatchback that will replace the Neon. In spring 2006, Toyota will roll out a new version of its popular RAV4 compact SUV. It's expected to have a larger, more luxurious interior. In late 2006, Acura will release its first small SUV, the RDX. It will share the same platform as the next-generation Honda CR-V and likely be powered by a V6 engine.

Ford will introduce the Ford Edge and Lincoln Aviator car-based SUV twins later in 2006. Based on the Mazda6 sedan, we expect them to offer better fuel economy and performance than the Ford Explorer. Ford will also release a redesigned Explorer Sport Trac crew-cab pickup, which is expected to be longer, wider, and lower than the previous version; offer an optional V8 engine; and have independent rear suspension for better ride and handling.

Meanwhile, General Motors will introduce new versions of its large pickups and SUVs, including the Chevrolet Avalanche pickup, the Chevy Silverado and GMC Sierra pickup twins, the Chevrolet Tahoe and GMC Yukon SUV twins, and the larger Chevy Suburban and GMC Yukon XL twins. Full-hybrid versions of the Chevrolet Tahoe and GMC Yukon are also expected.

A new wave of hybrids. In addition to the hybrid versions of the redesigned Chevrolet Tahoe, GMC Yukon, Honda Civic, and Toyota Camry mentioned above, there will be several more hybrids released over the coming months. First on the market this fall will be the Mazda Tribute and the Mercury Mariner, which are essentially twins of the Ford Escape. We got 26 mpg overall in the Escape Hybrid, which is significantly better than the 18 mpg we'd recorded in the conventional V6 Escape.

Ford will also introduce hybrid versions of the new Ford Fusion and Mercury Milan sedans. Next fall, GM will release a hybrid version of the small Saturn Vue SUV.

In addition to the RX400h SUV, released in spring 2005, Lexus will introduce a hybrid version of its GS300 sports sedan in spring 2006, called the GS450h. Lexus claims the hybrid will offer the power of a V8 with the fuel economy of a V6.

The problem with new models. As tempting as it may be to buy a new or redesigned model, think twice. CONSUMER REPORTS' auto-reliability surveys show that most newly designed models have more problems in their first model year than in the model year before or in the model years that follow. We recommend waiting a year or two before buying a new design to give the automaker time to work out the bugs.

This year, we studied our reliability data for 79 models—44 redesigned and 35 all new—that were introduced in the 2000 through 2002 model years and compared the reliability of the first-year models with those of the following two model years. More than half had noticeably fewer problems in their second model year and about two-thirds had fewer problems in their third model year than in the model year in which the new design was introduced. Problems dropped 20 percent, from 41 per 100 vehicles in their first model year to 33 and 29 in the second and third model years.

We also compared redesigned models with those from the year before—the last year of the previous design. About two-thirds of them averaged 44 percent more problems than did the prior year's design.

If you must buy soon, and a new model is clearly the best choice, we recommend buying from a manufacturer with a proven reliability record. While problems can still increase in the first model year, overall their problem rates are lower than others.

5 STEPS TO GET THE RIGHT CAR AND BEST PRICE

Buying a new car can be an exciting time. But many people are intimidated by the dealership experience, including the price negotiations and the high-pressure sales tactics that can be used to manipulate you into spending more than you need to. Others find it confusing and frustrating to try to pick the right vehicle from the more than 240 models on the market.

To ensure that you get the right vehicle at the best price, you need to be an informed buyer. That means investing time in research and preparation. The car-buying process can be boiled down to five steps:

- **Get the right information** to narrow your choices and make a smart decision.
- **Check out the cars** by doing a thorough test drive.
- **Set a target price** and learn the value of your trade-in.
- **Shop for financing before you deal** by comparing terms and interest rates, and getting preapproved for a loan.
- **Get the best deal** by contacting dealerships, comparing offers, and using a proven negotiating strategy.

Step 1: Get the right info

To accurately compare vehicles and determine the best one for your needs, you need to get as much information as you can about any models you're considering. Fortunately, the Internet makes that easy to do. But, just as cars can vary greatly in quality, so can sources of information. The key is knowing what to look for and the best sources from which to get the information. Here, we list some of the major areas in which you should compare models you're considering.

AUTO MANUFACTURER WEB SITES

Use these sites to get basic information, such as which models and trim levels the manufacturer offers, available features and options, and to look up specifications, retail pricing, warranties, and the locations of dealerships. Most sites also let you compare vehicles and "build your own car," giving you a retail price for your individual configuration. That doesn't guarantee, however, that you'll find a vehicle configured the way you want it on a dealership's lot. Keep in mind, too, that the main purpose of these sites is to promote their own products, so the model information is the same as advertising.

VEHICLE RATINGS

CONSUMER REPORTS Ratings (see page 177) can help you hone your list of vehicles by giving you a quick look at how tested vehicles compare with their competitors in several areas. The Ratings chart also shows you which vehicles meet our stringent requirements to be recommended.

MODEL REVIEWS

Reviews give you an in-depth perspective of a vehicle's performance, comfort and convenience, and overall driving character, as well as insight into deficiencies that might not be apparent on a test drive. Because different sources have varying points of view, we recommend reading a variety. But keep in mind that most are in publications or on Web sites that are supported by automaker advertising, and no one wants to bite the hand that feeds them.

So you may not find hard-hitting analysis or insight into safety or reliability issues. Only a few do their own instrumented testing, which allows more accurate comparisons between different vehicles.

CONSUMER REPORTS conducts the most comprehensive auto-test program of any U.S. publication or Web site. It differs from those of other reviewers in several significant ways, including the fact that we don't accept advertising, we buy all of our test vehicles from dealerships, just like you do, and we conduct more than 50 individual tests and evaluations on each vehicle over several months and thousands of miles.

Summary reviews of all models are included in the model profiles that begin on page 154. Full road-test reports and test results are included in CONSUMER REPORTS magazine and are available to subscribers of ConsumerReports.org.

RELIABILITY

A vehicle's reliability can have a huge effect on how satisfied you'll be with your car over the years, and it can significantly affect its resale value. Reliability, however, is a difficult and expensive quality to evaluate because the information has to come from vehicle owners; the more, the better. CR provides the most comprehensive reliability information available to consumers. Our 2005 subscriber survey, for instance, drew responses on more than one million vehicles, the most ever.

FUEL ECONOMY

The fuel economy figures printed on a vehicle's window sticker and in automaker advertising and brochures are estimates based on a test created by the U.S. Environmental Protection Agency (EPA). You can access the list of these figures at *www.fueleconomy.gov.* In CR's extensive real-world fuel economy testing, however, we've found that the EPA estimates are often much higher than you're likely to get in normal driving. You can get a more accurate figure for vehicles that we tested by referring to the Vehicle Ratings chart (page 177).

SAFETY RATINGS

Several different elements affect a vehicle's overall safety capability.

Crash tests: Frontal- and side-impact crash tests are conducted by the Insurance Institute for Highway Safety (IIHS; *www.iihs.org)* and the National Highway Traffic Safety Administration (NHTSA; *www.safercar.gov).* CR provides a single overall crash protection rating for many models, based on our assessment of government and insurance-industry tests. See the Vehicle Ratings chart on page 177.

Accident avoidance: A vehicle's ability to help you avoid an accident is just as important as its ability to protect you in a crash. For every accident there are numerous near misses that statistics don't reflect. Several factors contribute to a vehicle's accident-avoidance capability, with the two most important being braking and emergency handling. To see CR's accident-avoidance rating on all tested vehicles, see the Vehicle Ratings chart on page 177.

Rollover resistance: Rollover accidents account for about 33 percent of all vehicle-occupant deaths, and are of particular concern with taller vehicles, such as SUVs and pickups. To help consumers compare vehicles, NHTSA provides a five-star rating system called the Rollover Resistance Rating (RRR). The RRR is calculated from two factors: a vehicle's static stability factor (SSF) and a dynamic rollover test. The SSF, which is determined from static measurements of the vehicle, essentially indicates how top-heavy it is. The dynamic test simulates a driver having to make a series of sharp steering maneuvers, as can happen in an emergency. Vehicles that tip up at any speed fail the test. We believe that a vehicle that tips up in this type of situation has serious stability problems, and we will not recommend it. RRR ratings are available at *www.safercar.gov.* To see if a vehicle tipped up in the dynamic test, however, you need to click on the model's name or star ratings to get more information, then scroll down to "Rollover."

Rear-impact protection: Although "rear enders" have a low fatality rate, they have a high injury rate, especially for whiplash neck injuries. The design of a car's head restraints and seats are critical factors in how severe a whiplash injury will be. CR evaluates head restraints for all seating positions in every tested vehicle. Any problems are noted in our road-test reports. Another good source for information on rear-impact protection is the IIHS Web site, *www.iihs.org.* The institute conducts evaluations of head restraints and performs dynamic rear-impact tests that measure how well the seat/head-restraint combinations in different models protect against whiplash.

Blind zones: Every year, children are injured and killed because drivers don't see them while backing up. A contributing factor is that some larger vehicles, such as SUVs and pickups, have larger blind zones—the area behind a vehicle that the driver can't see. CR measures the blind zone of every vehicle we test and publishes the information for free at *www.ConsumerReports.org.*

Power-window switches: Some vehicles have rocker- or toggle-type power-window switches that raise the window when pressed down or forward. This is a risky design because a child who is leaning out of the open window can accidentally kneel on the switch, closing the window, and possibly be injured or even killed. A better design is a lever switch, which only raises the window when it's pulled upward. Vehicles with the riskier switches are noted in our road-test reports.

RECOMMENDED SAFETY FEATURES

Many times, buyers overlook important safety features because they aren't aware of them or don't understand their benefit. The following are ones that we recommend you consider for your vehicle.

Antilock brake system (ABS). Without antilock brakes, a vehicle's wheels can lock up (stop turning) during hard braking, particularly on slippery surfaces. When that happens, the vehicle tends to keep plowing ahead in whatever direction it was going. You can't steer, and locked wheels can cause a vehicle to slide sideways or even spin. ABS prevents the wheels from locking up. This, in turn, allows the driver to retain steering control while braking, so that the car can be maneuvered around an obstacle, if necessary. It also helps keep the vehicle from sliding and often stops it in a shorter distance on most surfaces.

Electronic stability control (ESC). CONSUMER REPORTS highly recommends you get ESC on your vehicle. ESC helps keep the vehicle on its intended path during a turn, to avoid sliding or skidding out of control. ESC is especially helpful in slippery conditions and accident-avoidance situations. With tall, top-heavy vehicles like SUVs and pickups, it can also help keep a vehicle from getting into a situation where it could roll over. Because automakers each tend to have a proprietary name for their ESC systems, however, it can be confusing for buyers to know what's what. If in doubt whether a car has it, find out before you buy.

Head-protecting side air bags. IIHS

side-impact crash tests clearly show the benefit of this feature. To date, no vehicle that was tested without head-protecting side air bags has scored higher than Poor in the test. There are two types of side bags. A standard side air bag deploys from the seat or door trim. It typically protects a person's torso, but many don't do an adequate job of protecting the head. We recommend that you look for a dedicated head-protection bag that deploys from above the side windows. The most common type is a side-curtain air bag that covers the side windows in both the front and rear, preventing occupants from hitting their heads and shielding them from flying debris. A curtain bag can also keep people from being ejected during a rollover.

Safety-belt features. While the safety belt is arguably the single most important piece of safety equipment, enhanced belt features are helping safety belts do their job more effectively. Adjustable upper anchors help position the belt across the chest instead of the neck to prevent neck injuries. They also can help keep the belt from pulling down on a tall person's shoulder, making it more comfortable.

Safety-belt pretensioners instantly retract the belts to take up slack during a frontal impact. This helps position occupants properly to take full advantage of a deploying air bag. Force limiters, a companion feature to pretensioners, manage the force that the shoulder belt builds up on the occupant's chest. After the pretensioners tighten it, force limiters let the belt pay back out a little.

Smart frontal air bags. Front air bags are now standard on all new vehicles, but some models offer an advanced, multistage system that tailors their deployment to the front occupants. Depending on the model, these "smart" systems can detect the presence and weight of the person in the front passenger seat, the driver's seat position, and whether the safety belts are fastened, and then adjust the deployment of the air bags accordingly to minimize the chance of injury to occupants or children.

Step 2: Check out the cars

A lot of vehicles look good on paper, but the test drive is the moment of truth. This is your best chance to see how a vehicle measures up to expectations, to see how well it "fits" you, and to evaluate its driving character, performance, and comfort. After all, you don't want any surprises after you've bought it.

You should make a separate visit to the dealership just for a test drive and walk-around inspection. Don't wait until the day you're ready to buy; that won't give you enough time to thoroughly evaluate the cars you're considering.

It's important that you spend as much time with the vehicle as possible, with an eye on what it will be like to live with over the long haul. Here are some tips to make your dealership test drive count:

MAXIMIZE YOUR TEST DRIVE

- Before you go to the dealership, list what you like and dislike about your current car so you can compare this with the vehicle you'll be driving. Take along a notebook so you can jot down impressions.
- If you're considering different models, test drive them all before you make a final decision. If more than one person will be driving the vehicle on a regular basis, make sure all have a chance to test drive it before you buy.
- Before you drive, evaluate the driving position and interior. Set the seat in a comfortable driving position and attach the safety belt. Make sure that you're at least 10 inches away from the steering

wheel and that you can fully depress all the pedals. Make sure that you can reach all the controls without straining and that they're easy to use and the displays are easy to see.

• Don't be rushed; take at least 30 minutes. Try to drive along a route that includes different types of road surfaces and driving conditions. If the dealership is in an unfamiliar place, scout out a route ahead of time. Take someone along to give you the passenger's viewpoint. If possible, take the test drive without a salesperson, so you can better concentrate on the vehicle.

• As you drive, make sure that you can see out well, that you can judge the ends of the vehicle, and that there are no serious blind spots. Pay attention to all of the vehicles' characteristics—how it rides, handles, accelerates, and stops, as well as how quiet it is. Take notes so you can compare the model with others that you test drive, and record your impressions of the vehicle's comfort, handling, and responsiveness.

• If you use any child-safety seats, bring them with you and take the time to install them properly so you can see how easy or difficult it is.

Step 3: Set a target price

In many ways, negotiating a good deal on a new vehicle is a game of numbers. The best way to ensure you don't get manipulated is to go in armed with accurate pricing information that lets you assess how good a salesperson's offer really is. Two key figures you need are a target price on the new vehicle and the value of your current vehicle.

PREPARE IN ADVANCE

The figure on a car's window sticker is only a suggested retail price set by the auto manufacturer. Dealerships are free to sell their vehicles at whatever price they want. An informed buyer, prepared with accurate price information, can often buy a vehicle for hundreds or thousands of dollars below the sticker price.

That's why it's important to calculate a reasonable target price before you go to the dealership to buy. To get the lowest price, you have to start with a figure that's based on how much the dealer actually paid for the vehicle. By knowing this, you'll know how much profit margin the dealership has to work with.

To figure out the dealer's real cost you need to find the dealer-invoice price, any current behind-the-scenes dealer sales incentives, and the dealer's holdback amount. Dealer-invoice prices are now so common that you can find them on many Web sites and pricing guides, but you'll have to do a little more digging to find dealer incentives and the holdback.

To point you in the right direction, CONSUMER REPORTS' New Car Price Reports do this work for you. Each report shows you all three factors: the dealer-invoice price, the amount of any national or regional dealer sales incentives, and the holdback amount. It also includes the CR Wholesale Price, which takes all of these figures into consideration to give a close approximation of the dealer's cost. Alternatively, you can look up current sales incentives and holdback amounts yourself at some auto-pricing Web sites.

A reasonable price for a vehicle is about 4 to 8 percent over the CR Wholesale Price or dealer's cost, depending on how popular the model is.

It can also be helpful to check your target price against those offered by dealerships affiliated with auto-buying Web sites. On these sites, you can ask for a price quote on a vehicle that's configured the way you want it and one or more dealerships will reply by e-mail. The services are free and you aren't under any obligation to buy. CarsDirect.com will also give you a no-haggle price that their contracted dealerships have agreed to honor.

You can compare these quotes against the target price range you calculated based on the dealer's cost. Usually, the quotes will be higher. But if, by chance, a quote is lower than your figure, this gives you more leverage with which to bargain.

Another point of comparison could be so-called transaction prices posted on some auto-buying Web sites. These are intended to reflect the average of what other buyers are actually paying for new vehicles. These prices are available on sites such as Autobytel and Edmunds.com, which posts its True Market Value price.

Since these transaction prices are an average of nationwide sales prices, keep in mind that some actual prices were higher and some were lower. These prices also may not be accurate for your area. By having a target price based on the dealer's cost, you may be able to do better than those transaction prices. At the very least, during your negotiating process, it's comforting to know approximately how much you should be paying.

Be informed: Get top dollar for your current car

Whether you trade in your current vehicle or sell it yourself, it's important to know its current cash value. This depends on a number of factors, including the vehicle's age, mileage, condition, trim level, optional equipment, and the region in which it's being sold. For any used car there are two prices to consider: retail and wholesale. The retail price is what you would expect to pay for the car if you were buying it at a dealership and is likely the most you should expect to get if you sold it yourself. The wholesale price is essentially its trade-in value. It is notably lower than the retail price.

Find the book value

You can get a basic idea of a vehicle's value from printed pricing guides and Web sites that provide used-car prices. The first figure you'll see when you look up a vehicle in these pricing guides is the car's base value. To get a more accurate figure, you must factor in any options as well as the vehicle's mileage and condition. Some Web sites let you do this online and then give you adjusted figures.

To help, CR offers Used Car Price Reports that are tailored to specific models. Each report gives you the retail and wholesale/trade-in value of the model and walks you through the process of adjusting the value according to options, mileage, and condition.

What are others asking?

You can often get a better fix on how much a vehicle is worth in your region by checking the classified ads and dealer ads in local newspapers, classified-ad publications, and Web sites that specialize in used-car sales. Look for vehicles that are similar to yours in terms of model year, mileage, trim level, options, and condition. But remember that the listed prices are only the asking prices, not necessarily what people are paying. You should assume that all such prices are negotiable.

Step 4: Shop for financing before you visit the dealer

You might be a whiz at getting a low price on a new car, but if you don't choose your financing carefully, you could lose everything you saved on the vehicle's purchase price and more. It's critical that you comparison shop and get preapproved for an auto loan before you go to the dealership to buy the vehicle. Otherwise, not only is your choice of loans restricted to what the dealership can offer you, but many dealers do what's called "interest-rate bumping," in which they mark up the interest rate over what you actually qualify for. Overall, this can cost you hundreds or even thousands of dollars more over the term of the loan.

SHOP FOR THE BEST TERMS

Compare interest rates at various financial institutions, such as banks, thrifts, and credit unions, as well as the dealership. Getting preapproved for a loan allows you to keep the financial arrangements out of the vehicle-price negotiations at the dealership. The figure to focus on is the annual percentage rate (APR). You can get a quick read on the terms that various banks are offering at *www.bankrate.com.*

Try to keep the length of the loan as short as possible. A three-year loan costs you far less overall than a four- or five-year loan at the same interest rate. But you need to balance the total cost of the loan against a monthly payment you can afford.

THE INCENTIVE GAME

Some automakers have been regularly offering aggressive low-interest financing incentives on many models, but there are catches of which you should be aware:

- Some low rates are available only for 36-month loans, meaning the payments will be quite high.
- Without a stellar credit record, you may not qualify. Always phone the dealership before you visit to learn what credit score qualifies a borrower for the lowest financing rate and, if you don't qualify, what the next best rate would be.
- You often have to make a choice between a low interest rate and a cash rebate. You will have to run the numbers both ways to see which offer saves you the most money. You'll find an auto-financing calculator that lets you make these types of comparisons in the Wheeling and Dealing section of ConsumerReports.org.
- Low-interest rates are also no bargain if they persuade you to buy a car you're not happy with. It may make better financial sense over the long term, for instance, to buy a consistently reliable model at a little higher interest than an unreliable model at 0 percent. Likewise, saving a few dollars each month on your payments may not seem worthwhile over the long run if you don't like the vehicle's performance, comfort, or other details.

Even if a dealership is offering a special financing incentive, you should still do your homework beforehand by carefully shopping around for the best loan offers. This lets you accurately evaluate the dealership's terms so you can make the best decision.

Step 5: Get the best deal

When you go to the dealership, the salesperson will likely want to focus on the vehicle's MSRP or on how much of a monthly payment you can afford.

Don't go down this road. Using the monthly payment as the focus, the salesperson will lump the whole process together, including the price for the new vehicle, the trade-in, and financing, if appropriate. This gives him or her more latitude to give you a "good price" in one

Know the pros and cons before you lease

Whether leasing is right for you depends on your lifestyle, expectations, and budget. When leasing a vehicle, you usually get lower monthly payments and a lower down payment, and you avoid any resale or trade-in hassles. Leasing can also let you drive a higher-priced, better-equipped vehicle for the same monthly payment you'd be making to buy a less-expensive model. But leasing makes sense only if you stay within the annual mileage (typically 12,000 miles), can keep the car until the end of the lease (to avoid early-termination penalties), maintain the car well to avoid "excess wear-and-tear" charges, and plan to trade in your car every two or three years anyway.

Many leasers end up paying more than they have to because they aren't familiar with the leasing process and don't try to negotiate the vehicle's price. Here are some tips:

1. Negotiate the purchase price of the vehicle as if you were going to buy. Once you have a firm price, then bring up your desire to lease.

2. Other negotiable elements include the mileage limit, the down payment, and the purchase-option price, or how much you'll have to pay if you want to buy the vehicle at the end of the lease.

3. Avoid lease terms that extend past the vehicle's basic warranty.

4. The four-digit "money factor" is roughly equivalent to a loan's annual percentage rate. To translate this into a percentage rate, multiply the money factor by 2,400.

5. Buy extra miles up front if there's a risk of running over the standard allotment. Excessive mileage at the lease's end is typically charged at a higher rate.

6. Protect yourself with gap insurance. In case you have an accident that totals the car, this covers the difference between an insurance settlement and the actual payoff for the car. In some cases, gap insurance is included in the lease. If it's extra, we recommend that you shop around. Prices can vary dramatically, so get a number of quotes. If your own insurance company provides it, that could be your best bet.

7. Understand your end-of-lease options, such as turning in the vehicle and walking away, purchasing the car, or rolling into another lease.

area while making up for it in another. In the end, this could cost you more overall.

Instead, insist on negotiating one thing at a time. Your first priority is to settle on the lowest price you can get on the new vehicle. Only after you've locked that in should you begin to discuss a trade-in or financing.

SET THE GROUND RULES

When you first meet the salesperson, you should set the tone of your negotiations by politely explaining the following:

- You have carefully researched the vehicle you want and have taken a test drive.
- You know exactly what trim level and options you want, have researched the price for that configuration and know what the dealership paid for it.
- You have already calculated what you are prepared to pay. Reassure him that your offer will include a fair profit.
- If he or she can meet your target price

you'll be ready to buy today; if not, you intend to visit other dealerships.

If the salesperson asks about a trade-in, say that you have investigated various options for selling your old car and that you might be open to a trade-in—but only after you've agreed on the new vehicle's price.

When he or she asks how you'll pay for the vehicle, let him know that you are preapproved for a loan, but you may be willing to consider financing through the dealership—provided the rate is competitive and you can come to terms on the purchase price of the new car.

HOW TO NEGOTIATE EFFECTIVELY

When negotiating a vehicle's price, you've got two arrows in your quill:

• Your target price, based on what the dealer paid for the vehicle

• Competing bids from other local dealerships or car-buying Web sites

The price you end up with will likely be somewhere between the two. You can start by showing the salesperson your rock-bottom target price. But don't disclose your competitive bids, which are the upper range of what's acceptable. Otherwise, the salesperson will focus on undercutting that higher figure by a token amount instead of working off of the lower figure.

For example, the CR Wholesale Price for a 2005 Chevrolet Tahoe LS 4x4 is $30,205. Add a 4 to 8 percent markup to that ($31,4132 to $32,621), and that's where you begin your negotiations. Tell the salesperson your 4 percent figure and that you want the lowest markup over that price you can get. Inch up if necessary, but don't go over the lowest competing bid.

Only if the negotiations have stalled, and the salesperson is willing to let you walk out the door, should you show him your lowest competing price, as a way of letting him know that he isn't yet in the ballpark. If the salesperson and you can agree on an acceptable price, you could proceed to wrap up the deal. If not, you can go to another dealership, now armed with the price that the first dealership gave you.

Never negotiate under pressure. Salespeople's favorite customers are those who seem to be in a rush, since they tend to be the ones who buy a more expensive car than they set out to, or don't negotiate down the price. In addition, a salesperson may tell you that someone else is very interested in the same car and is coming by later to look at it—a common sales tactic. Even if it is true, you should never feel that you have to make any deal immediately; there are always other cars out there.

TIME TO TALK TRADE-IN

Once you've settled on a price, discuss financing and any trade-in separately. This makes it easier to get the best deal at every step of the transaction.

When discussing a trade-in, you should get the full wholesale value for your current car in trade-in allowance. To help shore up your case, you should have printouts from several pricing sources. This diffuses any attempt by the salesman to pull out a used-car pricing book with which he can "prove" that your figures are too high.

Remember, if the trade-in negotiations become too burdensome, you can always take the car elsewhere or sell it yourself, which will likely reap you a higher price anyway. If, however, you're dependent on the trade-in to make the downpayment you want, these alternatives will mean that you'll have to sell your current car before you can sign the contract for your new one.

EXTENDED WARRANTIES

An extended warranty is one that takes effect after your factory warranty expires, and can cost hundreds of dollars. Most new cars today come with at least a three-year/36,000-mile bumper-to-bumper factory warranty. So, if you trade in your vehicle every five years or so, or if you lease your new vehicle under a typical 3-year lease with a 12,000-mile-per-year mileage allowance, buying an extended warranty would be a waste of money.

As a general rule, if the model you're buying has an above-average reliability record—earning a very good or excellent CONSUMER REPORTS' predicted reliability rating (see the vehicle reviews on page 154)—it's probably not worth spending the money for an extended warranty. If the model has a below-average record, and you plan to keep the vehicle well past the factory warranty period, it may be worth buying the coverage.

If you do decide that an extended warranty is for you, don't feel pressured to buy a warranty the same day you buy the vehicle. You can usually buy a plan any time before the basic warranty expires. We suggest sticking to a plan offered by the automaker. Third-party coverage varies enormously in quality, coverage, and price.

Review any service plan carefully to find out what is and isn't covered, who must perform repairs, and how to file a claim. If you're buying from a dealer, always negotiate the price. And make sure the plan is transferable if you sell the car.

Don't waste money on unnecessary extras

Dealerships often try to get you to buy extra services that are usually overpriced. Don't waste your money. What could cost the dealer about $90 can cost you $1,000 or more. These can include:

Rustproofing and undercoating. Today's vehicles are manufactured with good corrosion protection. In fact, according to CR's reliability surveys, rust problems have almost vanished in modern vehicles.

Fabric protection. If you buy a vehicle with cloth seats, you may want to spend a few bucks for a can of fabric protector and apply it yourself.

Paint sealant. This is little more than a vastly overpriced wax. You can easily purchase a good protectant from any auto-parts store and apply it yourself.

VIN etching. This is a service in which the vehicle identification number is etched into the vehicle's windows to deter theft. Some states require that a dealer offers it to you, but none require that you buy it. It's not unusual to find a charge for VIN etching already printed on the purchase agreement, as if it's assumed that you will pay for this service. This has been the case for several vehicles that we've bought for testing. We recommend that you refuse this charge. Even if you decide you want VIN etching, you can have it done less expensively elsewhere, of even do it yourself with a kit that costs about $25.

Dealer prep fees. Inquire about any fees that the dealership is charging you for preparing the vehicle for you. The manufacturer pays the dealership to prepare the vehicle for you; you shouldn't be charged for this service.

Don't accept those unnecessary services and fees. If the items are on the bill of sale, put a line through them.

REVIEWS OF THE 2006 MODELS

This rundown of all the major 2006 models can start you on your search for a new car. You'll find a capsule summary of each model, often based on recent road tests that are applicable to this year's models.

Most models include CONSUMER REPORTS' predicted reliability rating, an indication of how problematic we expect a model to be, based on our annual subscriber surveys where we ask vehicle owners about any serious problems they've had with their vehicles in the previous 12 months. This data allows us to predict how this year's models are likely to hold up.

Recommended models (✓) not only tested well, but have shown average or better reliability and performed at least adequately if crash-tested or included in a government rollover test. Recommended models that have performed especially well in both IIHS crash tests and at least one government crash test are designated with a ✓ (circled).

Entries include, where available, the date of the last road test for that model published in CONSUMER REPORTS magazine. These road-test reports are also available to subscribers of our Web site, *www.ConsumerReports.org.*

The 2006 cars, trucks, SUVs & minivans

Predicted reliability is a judgment based on our annual reliability survey data. New or recently redesigned models are marked "New." NA means data not available.

Better ⟵⟶ Worse: ⊜ ⊖ ○ ◒ ●

	Model	Predicted reliability	Description/with last road test date
✓	**Acura MDX**	⊖	One of our top-rated SUVs, the MDX is a well-designed car-based SUV that can hold seven passengers. Ride and handling are competent. The interior is flexible, with a third-row seat that folds flat into the cargo floor. **Sep. 2003**
	Acura RDX	NEW	This car-based SUV will share the same platform as the next-generation Honda CR-V, and it most likely will use a V6 engine. It joins the BMW X3 in the upscale small SUV sub-category.
✓	**Acura RL**	⊖	The all-wheel-drive RL is powered by a 300-hp V6. The powertrain is polished, but ride and handling don't stand out. The less expensive TL has similar interior room, and the RL's driver interaction system isn't particularly intuitive. **Sep. 2005**
✓	**Acura RSX**	⊖	This two-door coupe is enjoyable and affordable. The quicker Type-S uses a six-speed manual and revs higher than the base model. Handling is agile but the ride is stiff, choppy, and noisy in the Type-S. **Dec. 2005**
✓ (circled)	**Acura TL**	⊖	The TL provides a near-ideal blend of comfort, convenience, and sportiness. Handling is taut and agile, and the engine delivers quick acceleration. The ride is firm yet comfortable and quiet. **Feb. 2004**

Model	Predicted reliability	Description/with last road test date
✓ **Acura TSX**	◓	The TSX four-door features a smooth-revving engine and slick transmission. Handling is agile but the ride is a bit stiff. Good crash results and reliability round out the package. **Nov. 2004**
Audi A3	NA	The new A3 four-door hatchback has a tasteful interior and a good amount of space. The 200-hp, turbocharged 2.0-liter four-cylinder engine is quick. An AWD version with a 3.2-liter V6 arrives for 2006. **To be tested.**
✓ **Audi A4**	○	The A4 handles nimbly. The 2.0T is noisy and the 3.2 V6 is refined. The low speed ride is a bit firm. The comfortable interior is cramped in the rear. AWD is available, as are wagon and convertible models. **To be tested**
Audi A6	◒	The redesigned A6 sedan offers a 3.2-liter V6 and a 4.2-liter V8 with standard all-wheel drive. The ride is firm yet comfortable, but is no match for the Mercedes-Benz E-Class. A wagon version is available with the V6. **Sep. 2005**
Audi A8	●	Audi's flagship features a strong V8, AWD, and an aluminum body. The roomy interior is well-crafted. It is quiet and agile, but the ride is unremarkable for a luxury car. A V12 engine is optional. **Nov. 2003**
Audi S4	●	The high-performance version of the A4 uses a 340-hp, 4.2-liter V8. AWD is standard. The ride is stiff, and handling is quite capable. Wagon and convertible versions are available. Unlike the A4, reliability has been poor. **Sep. 2004**
Audi TT	◒	The TT is available as a convertible or coupe. The interior is nicely detailed and AWD is available. The ride is stiff and less sporty than a Porsche Boxster's. A smooth 3.2-liter V6 and turbocharged four-cylinder engines are offered. **Jun. 2002**
BMW 3 Series	NEW	The redesigned sedan has agile handling, a supple ride, and smooth six-cylinder engines. The revised interior is comfortable and luxurious. Coupe and convertible models use the older body style. **To be tested.**
✓ **BMW 5 Series**	○	The 5 Series is impressive and frustrating. We found the iDrive control system tedious to use. Handling is agile, and the ride is comfortable and quiet. The automatic transmission and engine are smooth. The six-cylinder model has had average reliability; the V8 is still poor. **Jun. 2004**
BMW 6 Series	NA	The 6 Series shares a platform with the 5 Series. The standard engine is a smooth and punchy 4.4-liter V8. A convertible version is also available and a limited-production, high-performance V10-powered M6 is new. **To be tested.**
BMW 7 Series	●	The 7 Series is stately, quiet, fast, and agile. The iDrive control system and other ergonomic quirks make the driving experience frustrating and annoying instead of comforting and soothing. The ride is steady and the cabin is comfortable. **Nov. 2003**
✓ **BMW M3**	○	The M3 has agile handling and virtually non-existent body roll, and it balanced at its very high limits. Some may find the ride stiff. The 3.2-liter engine is smooth and powerful. The sport seats provide excellent support. **Sep. 2004**

	Model	Predicted reliability	Description/with last road test date
✓	**BMW X3**	○	The X3 is loosely based on the previous-generation 3 Series, but with a roomier rear seat. The ride is firm, but handling is agile. All-wheel drive with traction- and stability-control systems endows it with good snow traction. **Dec. 2004**
✓	**BMW X5**	○	The X5 delivers an impressive drivetrain and comfortable front seats. The ride is choppy. All engines deliver spirited acceleration. The six-cylinder model has average reliability, but the V8 is below average. **Apr. 2005**
✓	**BMW Z4**	○	The Z4 is a sporty two-seat convertible, but it lacks agility. The cabin is roomy, and the 3.0-liter six-cylinder is strong. Electronic stability control and traction control are standard. The power-operated top is simple to use. **Oct. 2005**
✓	**Buick LaCrosse**	⊖	The LaCrosse is quiet and comfortable yet offers fairly responsive handling. The interior is well-constructed. Rear-seat room is tight. The 3.8-liter V6 engine is thirsty and sounds coarse. The 3.6-liter V6 is more refined, but expensive. **Mar. 2005**
	Buick Lucerne	NEW	The Lucerne comes with a standard 3.8-liter V6; a 4.6-liter, 275-hp V8 is optional. In our test of the LaCrosse we found the V6 to be thirsty and coarse-sounding. **To be tested.**
	Buick Rainier	○	The Rainier is the upscale version of the Chevrolet TrailBlazer. It comes with a 4.2-liter six-cylinder or a 5.3-liter V8. The permanently engaged AWD system has no low range, making it more suited for slippery roads than for off-roading.
✓	**Buick Rendezvous**	○	This minivan-based SUV features an independent suspension, optional all-wheel drive, and room for seven. Handling is secure, but reluctant. Acceleration is so-so and the interior feels cheap. **Oct. 2001**
	Buick Terraza	●	The Terraza is powered by a 3.5-liter, 200-hp V6 engine. Removing the second-row seats is cumbersome. The third-row seat only folds flat on the floor. Handling is reluctant, interior fit and finish is insubstantial, and the ride is stiff and noisy.
✓	**Cadillac CTS**	○	This sports sedan feels agile and taut but has pesky oversights. Power is provided by a 2.8-liter V6, a smooth 3.6-liter V6, or a 400-hp V8 in the sporty CTS-V. Acceleration is quick and the transmission is very smooth. **Sep. 2004**
	Cadillac DTS	NEW	The DTS is a freshening of the DeVille. It offers the smooth and powerful 4.6-liter, 291-hp Northstar V8 and a 275-hp V8. Accommodations are ample and luxurious, and the rear seat roomy and comfortable. **To be tested.**
	Cadillac Escalade	○	Essentially a Chevrolet Tahoe, this SUV is powerful. Luxury details mix with cheap plastic materials. The EXT is a plush version of the Chevrolet Avalanche; the ESV is based on the Suburban. A redesign is due for 2006.
	Cadillac SRX	●	The upscale SRX is the first car-based SUV from Cadillac. This tall wagon is powered by a smooth V8 or a V6. Handling is agile and secure. The ride is taut yet supple. The optional power-folding third-row seat operates slowly. **Mar. 2004**

Model	Predicted reliability	Description/with last road test date
✓ **Cadillac STS**	○	The rear-drive STS uses a 3.6-liter V6 or the 4.6-liter Northstar V8. All-wheel drive is optional. The ride is firm yet supple. Handling is taut and agile and the cabin is quiet, but the rear seat isn't as sumptuous as the class leaders. **Sep. 2005**
Cadillac XLR	NA	The XLR is based on the Corvette, but uses the smooth Northstar V8 and a five-speed automatic. It is quick and handles quite well. The more powerful XLR-V uses a supercharged 440-hp V8 and six-speed automatic. **To be tested.**
✓ **Chevrolet Avalanche**	○	This crew-cab pickup version of the Suburban has an innovative midgate that allows long items to extend into the rear-passenger compartment. The ride is comfortable. The four-wheel-drive system can remain engaged indefinitely, a plus. **Sep. 2002**
Chevrolet Aveo	○	The Aveo sedan and hatchback are Daewoos rebadged as Chevrolets. They handle clumsily but are ultimately secure. Acceleration and fuel economy are unimpressive for an economy car. Fit and finish is adequate. **Aug. 2004**
Chevrolet Cobalt	●	The 2.2-liter four-cylinder is a bit noisy and not fuel-efficient. A more powerful 2.4-liter and a supercharged 2.0-liter are available. ABS and traction control are available on uplevel trim lines. We recommend the optional side curtain air bags; without them the Cobalt scored Poor in the IIHS side-crash test. **Dec. 2005**
Chevrolet Colorado	●	The Colorado's five-cylinder engine is unrefined, lacks punch, and has worse fuel-economy than competing V6s. Handling is sound but unexceptional. The ride is unsettled, and the body constantly quivers. Overall it trails the competition. **Jul. 2005**
Chevrolet Corvette	●	The Corvette is powered by a 6.0-liter, 400-hp V8. Performance is impressive. The ride is comfortable, and handling is capable but less agile than other sports cars. The Z06 returns with 505 hp. **Oct. 2005**
Chevrolet Equinox	◒	The Equinox has a roomy rear seat that can move fore and aft to increase passenger or cargo room. Interior quality is subpar, and the V6 is noisy and unrefined. Handling is clumsy but secure. Tip-ups in the government rollover tests are a negative. **Oct. 2004**
Chevrolet HHR	NEW	The HHR is a five-passenger raised wagon based on the same platform as the Cobalt. Power comes from 2.2- and 2.4-liter four-cylinder engines. Visibility is compromised by the retro styling cues. **To be tested.**
Chevrolet Impala	NEW	The Impala is freshened for 2006. The new model has engines ranging from a 3.5-liter V6 to a 5.3-liter V8 in the SS. It offers seating for up to six-passengers. Side-curtain air bags are standard. **To be tested.**
Chevrolet Malibu	◒	This sedan offers easy interior access and a comfortable ride. The V6 delivers quick acceleration and 23 mpg overall in the sedan. Side curtain air bags are a must for crash protection. The Maxx is a four-door hatchback with more rear-seat room. Reliability of the Maxx is average; the sedan is below average. **Jan. 2004**

	Model	Predicted reliability	Description/with last road test date
	Chevrolet Monte Carlo	NEW	The Monte Carlo is freshened for 2006, and offers engines ranging from a 3.5-liter V6 to a 5.3-liter V8, all driving the front wheels. Side air bags will be optional. GM claims that the interior will be upgraded and improved over the previous-generation model. **To be tested.**
	Chevrolet SSR	NA	The SSR is a pickup truck with a retractable hardtop. The V8 engine is rated at 400 hp with the manual. Evoking the styling of Chevy trucks from the 1950s, this two-seater is about nostalgia and open-topped motoring, but not much else.
	Chevrolet Silverado 1500	◒	The Silverado is beginning to lose ground to newer competitors. The optional four-wheel drive is a selectable full-time system, a plus. Extended-cab versions have a usable rear seat, a rarity in this class. Look for a redesigned Silverado in 2006. **Jul. 2005**
✓	**Chevrolet Suburban**	○	The Suburban can seat nine people, hold their luggage, and still tow a heavy trailer. The turning circle is wide. Seating is comfortable, and the ride is quiet and well-controlled. A redesign is due for 2006. **Nov. 2005**
✓	**Chevrolet Tahoe**	○	This SUV is similar to the Suburban but with less cargo room. Eight can ride, but those in the third seat will be very uncomfortable. It boasts an impressive towing capability. The steering is vague, and the brakes are so-so. A redesign arrives for 2006. **Nov. 2002**
	Chevrolet TrailBlazer	◒	This SUV is quiet and spacious, with a compliant low-speed ride, but has sloppy handling, uncomfortable seats, ill-fitting trim, and too much wind noise. A longer EXT model has a third-row seat. IIHS crash-test results are unimpressive. **Aug. 2003**
	Chevrolet Uplander	●	This minivan is powered by a coarse 3.5-liter, 200-hp V6. Removing the second-row seats is cumbersome. The folding third-row seat only folds flat on the floor. Handling is reluctant, interior fit and finish is insubstantial, and the ride is stiff and noisy. **Mar. 2005**
	Chrysler 300	●	The RWD 300 offers two V6 engines in base trims and a powerful V8 in the 300C and SRT8. AWD is optional. Interior materials are OK, but the cabin doesn't stand out in this class. The claustrophobic cabin and limited outward visibility are detractions. Reliability of the V8 is poor; the V6 is average. **Jan. 2005**
✓	**Chrysler Crossfire**	○	Based on the old Mercedes-Benz SLK, this rear-drive two-seater has a strong engine, but handling lacks finesse. The ride is stiff, visibility is poor, and there's too much wind noise. A convertible and a supercharged SRT6 are available. **Dec. 2003**
✓	**Chrysler PT Cruiser**	○	This tall wagon has a versatile interior and secure, predictable handling. Acceleration with the two turbocharged engines is quick. The ride is somewhat stiff, and the cabin is a bit noisy, with wind noise particularly evident in the convertible version. **Jun. 2005**
	Chrysler Pacifica	◒	The Pacifica combines the characteristics of an SUV, a minivan, and a wagon. Ride and handling are capable, but the powertrain falls a bit short. Access is easy, and the third row folds flat when not needed. A five-passenger version is available. **Aug. 2003**

Model	Predicted reliability	Description/with last road test date
Chrysler Sebring	○	The Sebring suffers from too much road noise, lack of agility, and a stiff ride. Emergency handling is secure, and braking is competent. The four-cylinder is slow and thirsty. The convertible suffers from body shake. The IIHS side-crash score is Poor. **Jun. 2005**
Chrysler Town & Country	◒	The Town & Country has a roomy interior and optional flat-folding seats. It is pleasant to drive but the 3.8-liter V6 isn't very smooth or fuel-efficient. The minivan rides well enough with a light load and handles securely. **Mar. 2005**
Dodge Caliber	NEW	This four-door hatchback will replace the small Dodge Neon sedan. The Caliber, developed jointly with Mitsubishi, has a raised seating position to give occupants a better view out over the hood and make cabin access easier. **To be tested.**
Dodge Caravan/ Grand Caravan	◒	The Grand Caravan has a roomy interior and optional flat-folding seats. It is pleasant to drive but the 3.8-liter V6 isn't very smooth or fuel-efficient. The minivan rides well enough with a light load and handles securely. **Mar. 2005**
Dodge Charger	NEW	The Charger is the sedan version of the Magnum wagon. The Magnum V6 we tested was a sound car, but it didn't shine in any particular area. Visibility is compromised by the styling. Ride and handling are so-so. **To be tested.**
Dodge Dakota	◒	Our tested Dakota equipped with the 4.7-liter V8 accelerated slower than many V6 pickups and returned just 14 mpg. The ride is buoyant. The Dakota lacks agility and suffers from pronounced body roll and slow steering. Interior quality could be better. **Jul. 2005**
Dodge Durango	◒	The Durango straddles the midsized and large SUV classes. It handles soundly and securely, and the ride is compliant. The cabin is fairly quiet, but the engine is a bit noisy. The third-row seat is usable. Fit and finish falls short. **Mar. 2004**
✓ **Dodge Magnum**	○	The Magnum wagon is powered by two V6 engines in the lower-priced trims, or a V8 in the RT model. All-wheel drive is optional. Outward visibility is compromised by the styling. **Dec. 2004**
Dodge Neon	○	This small sedan handles securely, brakes well, and has a relatively roomy interior. But the ride is stiff and uncomfortable and the cabin noisy. The four-speed automatic is mediocre. **Mar. 2003**
Dodge Ram 1500	○	The Ram falls short of the competition, with a jittery ride and cumbersome handling. The engines are strong but noisy and thirsty, particularly the 11-mpg Hemi V8. The Mega Cab option increases interior room in crew-cab models. **Jul. 2004**
Dodge Stratus	○	The Stratus feels a bit rough and underdeveloped. Acceleration with the V6 is quick, but the ride and handling fall short. The four-cylinder is slow, noisy, and thirsty. The cabin is noisy, and access is difficult. **May 2004**
✓ **Ford Crown Victoria**	○	A big, old-fashioned sedan, the Crown Victoria's jiggly ride and engine noise reveal how dated the car is. Braking and emergency handling are fairly good. Rear leg room is less generous than you might expect, but the trunk is cavernous. **Feb. 2003**

Model	Predicted reliability	Description/with last road test date
Ford Escape	⊖	The Escape has a roomy interior and a spacious rear bench. Handling is relatively nimble, and the brakes are strong. Fuel economy is disappointing. The hybrid is noisy on the highway but returned 26 mpg in our tests. The Hybrid has above-average reliability; the regular version is average. Because of a tip-up in the gov't rollover test, we do not recommend the non-Hybrid Escape. **Aug. 2005**
Ford Expedition	●	This large SUV has a well-designed interior with flexible seating and a handy fold-down split third seat. Ride and handling are commendable, but the available engines are slow and thirsty. Reliability since the 2003 redesign has been poor. **Nov. 2002**
Ford Explorer	NEW	The fully independent suspension improved the ride, handling, and access. A third-row seat is available. The base V6 is noisy and unrefined. The optional V8 is quicker but thirsty. Stability control is standard. A freshening arrives for 2006.
Ford Explorer Sport Trac	NEW	This crew-cab truck features a truncated pickup bed and five-person cabin. The ride is stiff and choppy. Handling is secure and relatively responsive. A redesign arrives in mid-2006.
Ford F-150	◒	Ford significantly improved the F-150, including towing and payload capacities and crashworthiness. The rear gate is relatively light. The part-time 4WD system can't be used on dry pavement. The F-150 is quieter now, steers better, and rides more comfortably than the old model, but the engine is noisy. **Jul. 2004**
✓ **Ford Five Hundred**	○	The Five Hundred (and its Mercury Montego twin) is a large sedan with elevated seating positions to improve outward vision and access. The lackluster V6 engine is mated to either a six-speed automatic or a continuously variable transmission (CVT). Front-wheel drive is standard, with AWD optional. **Jan. 2005**
✓ **Ford Focus**	○	All versions of the Focus tested very well. It's agile, spacious, and fun to drive. It is also available in wagon and hatchback models. Overall crash protection is good. We recommend only the Focus with side air bags. **May 2005**
Ford Freestar	○	The Freestar is a freshened Windstar minivan. Like its competitors, it features a flat-folding third-row seat. The two V6 engines are still noisy and road noise is pronounced. Handling is more responsive, but the ride is unsettled. Crash-test results are impressive. **Mar. 2004**
Ford Freestyle	●	This is a wagon version of the Five Hundred. Second- and third-row seats fold flat. FWD models come with a six-speed automatic, while the AWD models use a CVT. Reliability of the AWD model is poor, but the FWD model is average. **Sep. 2005**
Ford Fusion	NEW	This midsized sedan is based on the Mazda6. Power comes from either a 160-hp, 2.3-liter four-cylinder or a 221-hp, 3.0-liter V6. First impressions indicate it is roomy, agile, and competent. **To be tested.**
✓ **Ford Mustang**	○	The new Mustang offers a 210-hp V6 or a 300-hp V8. The suspension still uses a live rear axle. Handling is nimble but lacks finesse at its limits. Interior materials look good but are insubstantial. The convertible is free of body shake. **Apr. 2005**

	Model	Predicted reliability	Description/with last road test date
	Ford Ranger	○	The Ranger and similar Mazda B-Series are long in the tooth. The ride is stiff and choppy. The Explorer Sport Trac is a crew-cab version of the Ranger.
✓	**Ford Taurus**	○	The Taurus is roomy and comfortable but showing its age. The ride is decent and the rear seat spacious. Handling is sound. The optional V6 performs well but isn't as responsive or quiet as the competition. **Jan. 2004**
	GMC Canyon	●	The Canyon's five-cylinder engine is unrefined, lacks punch, and has worse fuel-economy than competing V6s. Handling is sound but unexceptional. The ride is unsettled, and the body constantly quivers. Overall it trails the competition. **Jul. 2005**
	GMC Envoy	◓	This midsized SUV, twin of the Chevrolet TrailBlazer, is spacious, with a fairly comfortable ride and a spirited inline-Six. Handling is a bit ponderous and can be tricky at the limit. Wind noise is pronounced. The longer XL model has a third seat. **Sep. 2001**
	GMC Sierra 1500	◓	The Sierra is a full-sized pickup like the Chevrolet Silverado. The optional four-wheel drive is a selectable full-time system. The Denali version has a handy four-wheel-steering option. Extended-cab versions have a usable rear seat. A redesign is due for 2006. **Jul 2004**
✓	**GMC Yukon**	○	This is a twin of the Chevrolet Tahoe. Eight can ride, but it is tight in the third row. Towing capability is impressive. The ride is quiet. All models now feature standard electronic stability control. A redesign is due for 2006. **Nov. 2002**
✓	**GMC Yukon XL**	○	Formerly called the GMC Suburban, this is of the largest SUVs offered. It can accommodate up to nine people and tow a heavy trailer. It's quiet and comfortable, and handles well. The 5.3-liter V8 engine is powerful but thirsty. A redesign is due for 2006.
(✓)	**Honda Accord**	⊜	The Accord features agile handling and a steady, compliant ride. The cabin is roomy, and controls are intuitive. The four-cylinder is smooth, and the V6 is relatively fuel efficient. The hybrid V6 returned 25 mpg in our testing. Stability control is standard on V6 models for 2006. **May 2005**
(✓)	**Honda CR-V**	⊜	One of the better car-based SUVs, the CR-V has a supple and controlled ride. The rear seat is roomy. Road noise is pronounced. Crash-test results are impressive. ABS and electronic stability control are standard. **Aug. 2005**
	Honda Civic	NEW	Redesigned for 2006 the Civic has more power along with standard ABS and side-curtain air bags. The new Si promises to be more sporty than the outgoing model. The Hybrid model promises more power as well. **To be tested.**
✓	**Honda Element**	⊜	This small SUV is based on the CR-V. Styling is boxy, with rear doors that are hinged at the rear and no middle roof pillar, creating a huge loading port. We recommend only the Element with side air bags. **Jun. 2003**
	Honda Fit	NEW	The Fit is a small four-door hatchback with a tall roofline for added interior room. The 1.5-liter engine is tuned for economy, and a

	Model	Predicted reliability	Description/with last road test date
			continuously variable transmission is likely to be an option, boosting fuel economy even more. **To be tested.**
	Honda Insight	NA	This lightweight two-seater has a three-cylinder engine and a 13-hp electric motor that assists the gas engine. Handling is secure but not nimble. A stiff, uncomfortable ride and intrusive interior noise are major trade-offs for the car's excellent economy. **Dec. 2000**
✓	**Honda Odyssey**	○	The redesigned Odyssey has good interior flexibility and impressive fit and finish. The third row folds into the floor in sections. Handling is still agile and precise, and the ride is supple and steady. The 255-hp V6 is smooth, punchy, and quiet. **Mar. 2005**
✓	**Honda Pilot**	⊖	The Pilot is a car-based SUV that can hold eight passengers. Ride and handling are competent. The interior is flexible, with a third-row seat that folds flat. Road noise is pronounced. All trim levels have standard stability control. **Apr. 2005**
✓	**Honda Ridgeline**	⊜	This crew-cab pickup has a supple and steady ride. Its 5-foot-long composite cargo bed features an all-weather, lockable trunk. The AWD system is permanent. Stability control is standard and handling is agile for a pickup. **Jul. 2005**
✓	**Honda S2000**	⊜	This rear-drive roadster's 2.2-liter four-cylinder delivers an impressive 240 hp, and the six-speed manual is outstanding. Handling is precise, and tire grip is outstanding, but the ride is hard and noisy. Stability control is standard for 2006. **Oct. 2005**
	Hummer H2	●	The H2 is based on the Chevy Tahoe and has a more usable interior than the H1. Ride and handling are fairly civilized, with exceptional off-road ability. The short windshield and wide roof pillars make the view out wanting. The H2 SUT is a pickup version.
	Hummer H3	NEW	The H3 is based on the Chevrolet Colorado/GMC Canyon. A coarse 3.5-liter, 220-hp inline five-cylinder engine provides tepid acceleration and so-so fuel economy. Off-roading is terrific, but access, visibility, and ride comfort come up short. **Nov. 2005**
	Hyundai Accent	NEW	The Accent offers basic transportation in sedan or a two-door hatchback. The ride is choppy but relatively quiet. It is now powered by a 1.6-liter four-cylinder engine. **To be tested.**
	Hyundai Azera	NEW	This sedan replaces the XG350. Power comes from a 3.8-liter, 256-hp V6 mated to a five-speed automatic. The cabin is larger and more tastefully appointed than the XG350's. A comprehensive list of safety features are standard. **To be tested.**
✓	**Hyundai Elantra**	○	The Elantra rides quietly and handles securely, but lacks agility. A four-door hatchback is also available. IIHS offset-crash results are Good, but side-crash scores are Poor. ABS brakes can be very difficult to find. **May 2005**
	Hyundai Santa Fe	○	This car-based SUV has a supple, quiet ride and handles securely, if not nimbly. Acceleration and fuel economy are not impressive. Fit and finish are good. A steeply raked windshield makes the cockpit feel a bit confining. We no longer recommend the Santa Fe because of tip-ups in the government rollover tests.

Model	Predicted reliability	Description/with last road test date
Hyundai Sonata	NEW	The redesigned 2006 Sonata features new, more powerful engines and better interior quality. Interior room and access have been improved. Comprehensive safety gear, including stability control, is standard. **To be tested.**
✓ **Hyundai Tiburon**	○	The GT V6 version of this sporty coupe delivers refined power. The ride is stiff, but handling is not so agile. The car feels nose-heavy, and the steering isn't particularly quick. Even average-height drivers will have to duck under the low roof. **Oct. 2002**
Hyundai Tucson	●	The Tucson is smaller than the Santa Fe but has similar interior space. The V6 is refined, but thirsty. Handling is secure, but lacks agility. The ride is compliant. Overall, the Tucson scores higher than the Santa Fe. **Aug. 2005**
✓ **Infiniti FX**	⊜	The FX drives like a sports sedan. The FX45 has a V8, but even the V6 FX35 is quick. Handling is nimble, but the stiff ride transmits bumps and pavement flaws to the passengers. The cabin feels snug, partly because of the high doorsills and low roof. **Sep. 2003**
✓ **Infiniti G35**	⊖	The G35's 3.5-liter V6 provides abundant power, and the firm, steady ride provides capable handling. The power seat controls are not intuitive. AWD is offered on the G35X sedan. **Jul. 2003**
✓ **Infiniti M35/M45**	⊜	The 2006 M35 is a roomy, contemporary design that is competitive in its class. The 3.5-liter V6 is strong. Ride and handling are quite capable, and the plush interior is well-constructed. The audio and navigation functions are relatively easy to master. **Sep. 2005**
Infiniti Q45	NA	Nissan's flagship sedan competes against the Lexus LS430. The engine is smooth and quiet. But ride and handling aren't very impressive, and rear-seat room is tight.
Infiniti QX56	●	This is Infiniti's version of the Nissan Armada. The V8 in our tested Armada was smooth and powerful, linked to a slick five-speed automatic. Handling was quite responsive. The ride was quite stiff, and engine noise was pronounced. Reliability is extremely poor.
Isuzu Ascender	NA	This midsized SUV is essentially a rebadged Chevrolet TrailBlazer. The TrailBlazer we tested was spacious, with a comfortable low-speed ride and a spirited inline six-cylinder, but emergency handling was sloppy and braking mediocre. **Aug. 2003**
Isuzu i-Series	NEW	Isuzu's new i-Series midsized pickup trucks are rebadged versions of the Chevrolet Colorado and GMC Canyon. The i-280 is a rear-drive, extended-cab truck with a 2.8-liter four-cylinder. The i-350 is similar to the Colorado crew-cab we recently tested. **Jul. 2005**
Jaguar S-Type	●	The S-Type shares a platform with the Lincoln LS. The V8 is strong and smooth, the V6 much less so. The interior is cramped, and the trunk is small. The overall experience is more run-of-the-mill than luxurious. **Jun. 2004**
Jaguar X-Type	◒	Based on the European Ford Mondeo, this entry-level Jag comes with standard all-wheel drive and a 3.0-liter V6 engine. It targets the Audi A4 and BMW 3 Series but lacks their refinement and driving enjoyment. **Mar. 2002**

	Model	Predicted reliability	Description/with last road test date
	Jaguar XJ8	◒	The XJ8 features an aluminum body and offers a bit more interior room. The classy styling remains. The powertrain is strong, but the ride isn't luxurious. Handling is nimble, but steering is light. A long-wheelbase model is available. **Nov. 2003**
	Jaguar XK8	NA	The XK8 carries on the long tradition of Jaguar coupes and convertibles. The V8 and five-speed automatic are smooth. Handling is not sports-car agile, but relatively athletic. The cabin is furnished with plenty of wood and leather. A redesign arrives soon. **To be tested.**
	Jeep Commander	NEW	The Commander is built on the same platform as the new Grand Cherokee, but is longer, taller, and wider. It offers seating for seven. Power comes from a 3.7-liter V6 and two V8s: a 4.7-liter and the ubiquitous 5.7-liter Hemi. **To be tested.**
	Jeep Grand Cherokee	●	The redesigned Grand Cherokee features an independent front suspension and modern rack-and-pinion steering. Handling is more precise and the ride is improved. The base engine is a lackluster 3.7-liter V6. Fit and finish isn't on par with its competitors, and rear-seat space is only slightly improved. A third-row seat isn't available. ESC is standard for 2006. **Nov. 2005**
✓	**Jeep Liberty**	○	The Liberty has independent front suspension and a modern rack-and-pinion steering setup for more precise handling on and off road, but the ride is still jittery. The cockpit is narrow, and access is awkward. The diesel version is slow and noisy and gets only 18 mpg overall. **Aug. 2005**
	Jeep Wrangler	○	The Wrangler is small and crude, with a hard, noisy ride. Handling is primitive, and the driving position is unpleasant. Nevertheless, it remains popular with off-road enthusiasts. The long-wheelbase Unlimited model improves rear seating room. **Aug. 2005**
✓	**Kia Amanti**	⊖	The Amanti has a soft, buoyant ride, but has clumsy handling, although its optional ESC keeps it secure. The V6 delivers only adequate performance, and its 18-mpg fuel economy is unexceptional. The interior boasts impressive fit and finish **Jan. 2005**
	Kia Optima	⊖	The Optima provides a lot of features for a competitive price. It has a comfortable ride and a quiet cabin but lackluster handling. The V6 is smooth but averaged just 20 mpg overall. A redesign arrives in spring 2006. **Jan. 2004**
	Kia Rio	NEW	The Rio is one of the lowest-priced cars sold in the U.S. A five-door wagon model named the Cinco is also available. The 10-year/100,000-mile powertrain warranty is one of the few selling points. A 1.6-liter engine from the Hyundai Accent is standard. 2006 brings a redesign. **To be tested.**
	Kia Sedona	NEW	The Sedona is relatively refined, with good fit and finish. It isn't very nimble and corners reluctantly. The ride is stiff and jiggly, and the van's heavy weight hinders acceleration and fuel economy—only 16 mpg overall. A redesign arrives for 2006. **To be tested.**

Model	Predicted reliability	Description/with last road test date
Kia Sorento	◒	The Sorento competes among small SUVs but is larger than most competitors. Acceleration is spirited but fuel economy is abysmal. The roomy interior has good fit and finish. The ride is stiff, and handling is clumsy though ultimately secure. **Jun. 2004**
Kia Spectra	NA	The Spectra is available as a sedan or a hatchback. It is relatively comfortable and quiet but lacks agility and has mediocre fuel economy. Side- and head-protection air bags are standard, but ABS may be hard to find. **Aug. 2004**
Kia Sportage	●	The Sportage is a rebadged Hyundai Tucson. A four-cylinder front-wheel drive and a five-speed manual are standard. It is relatively roomy and comfortable, but lacks agility. ABS, stability control, and head-protection air bags are all standard. **Aug. 2005**
Land Rover LR3	●	The LR3 uses a smooth, Jaguar-derived V8, but the engine is taxed with moving a heavy vehicle. Cabin access and interior quality have been improved. The ride is comfortable but handling is lumbering. Off-road capability is terrific. **Nov. 2005**
Land Rover Range Rover	●	The Range Rover delivers smooth, strong acceleration, and a very comfortable ride, although handling isn't agile. It also features a height-adjustable air suspension and luxury amenities. The seats are very comfortable, and the wood and leather interior is upscale.
Land Rover Range Rover Sport	NEW	Despite the name this luxury midsized SUV is really based on the new LR3. Power comes from standard 4.4-liter, 300-hp V8. A supercharged 4.2-liter V8 is optional. Off-road capability should be acceptable with the proper tires, but the Sport is geared more for on-road performance.
✓ **Lexus ES330**	⊖	The ES330 is quiet and comfortable with a smooth and powerful V6. Handling is lackluster with pronounced body lean. The lack of a telescoping steering wheel is a significant omission. Crash-test results are impressive. **Feb. 2004**
✓ **Lexus GS300/GS430**	⊜	The redesigned GS features a new V6 engine and optional AWD. The 4.3-liter V8 is quick. Both have a six-speed automatic transmission and a host of safety and high-tech features. The cockpit is tight, and handling isn't sporty. **Sep. 2005**
✓ **Lexus GX470**	⊖	The GX470 is based on the Toyota 4Runner, and combines comfort, luxury, and off-road capability. It's smaller than the LX470 but offers a third seat. The ride is comfortable and quiet, but it gets unsettled. Cornering lacks agility but is ultimately secure. **Mar. 2004**
Lexus IS250/IS350	NEW	The redesigned Lexus IS seems more luxurious and comfortable than the previous generation. It is taut and agile, and might better compete with the BMW 3 Series and Audi A4. The IS350 is very quick; AWD is available with the IS250. **To be tested.**
✓ **Lexus LS430**	⊜	Lexus' flagship is one of the world's finest luxury sedans. The engine and transmission are extremely smooth, and passengers are pampered with every imaginable convenience. The ride is smooth, supple, and quiet. **Nov. 2003**

Model	Predicted reliability	Description/with last road test date
Lexus LX470	⊖	This luxury SUV, based on the Toyota Land Cruiser, features a height-adjustable suspension and a well-equipped interior. The engine and transmission are smooth, and the ride is comfortable and quiet. It's capable off-road and civilized on pavement.
✓ **Lexus RX400h**	⊜	The new RX400h combines gas and electric engines to produce 268 hp. Acceleration is impressive and seamless, while returning 23 mpg overall. Typical Lexus characteristics include a beautifully finished interior, a quiet cabin, and a comfortable ride. **Nov. 2005**
✓ **Lexus RX330**	⊖	The RX330 has a comfortable and quiet ride, and AWD traction for bad weather and light off-road use. The V6 is smooth and responsive, and handling is secure. Attention to detail is impressive. **Sep. 2003**
Lexus SC430	⊜	This luxury car features a metal roof that retracts into the trunk at the touch of a button. The rear seat is tiny. The 300-hp, 4.3-liter V8 is smooth. Expect quiet, smooth, powerful acceleration. Handling is less sporty than in some competing models, however. **To be tested.**
Lincoln LS	●	The LS is a capable rear-drive sedan with a smooth powertrain, agile handling, and a firm ride. The V6 model has been discontinued; the V8 carries on for one more year. Reliability has dropped to below average. **Jul. 2003**
Lincoln Mark LT	NEW	The Mark LT is based on the new Ford F-150 pickup, which we found to ride more comfortably, handle more nimbly, and have a quieter, better-trimmed interior than the previous version. The Mark LT sports a luxurious interior, but the 4WD system is part-time only.
Lincoln Navigator	●	The Navigator features a fully independent suspension and a comfortable, power-operated split third-row seat that folds flat into the floor. The cabin is quiet, steering is responsive, and ride and handling are improved. Reliability since the redesign has been poor.
✓ **Lincoln Town Car**	○	The Town Car has a smooth ride and acceptable handling. The front seats are soft and poorly shaped. The rear fits three with ease, and the trunk is very large. Crash-test results are impressive. **Feb. 2003**
Lincoln Zephyr	NEW	The Zephyr midsized sedan is the upscale sibling of the Ford Fusion and Mercury Milan. The Lincoln is powered by a 221-hp, 3.0-liter V6 mated to a six-speed automatic transmission. **To be tested.**
Lotus Elise	NA	This mid-engined roadster is super-quick due to its light weight. Power comes from a high-revving four-cylinder from Toyota. Highlights include a spartan driver-focused interior, difficult cabin access, race car agility, and unpredictable handling at its extremely high cornering limits. **Oct. 2005**
Mazda B-Series	○	This compact pickup is a Ford Ranger with a Mazda nameplate. Handling is quite good for a truck, but the ride is stiff and jiggly. The 4.0-liter V6 is a welcome option. The rear seats in the extended-cab version are tight.

Model	Predicted reliability	Description/with last road test date
Mazda CX-7	NEW	The CX-7 SUV, based on the Mazda6 platform, is a sporty SUV similar to the Nissan Murano. It will be focused towards ride comfort and agility when it goes on sale. Expect pricing to start at around $30,000.
Mazda MPV	◒	The MPV minivan is smaller and narrower than most competitors. Handling is secure, but the ride is stiff. The V6 is lackluster. The interior is well finished, but the flat-folding third row is uncomfortable and hard to access. Reliability has declined. **Oct. 2003**
Mazda MX-5	NEW	The redesigned 2006 MX-5 is longer, wider, and just a bit taller than the previous Miata. Power will come from a 2.0-liter, 170-hp four-cylinder shifting through a standard six-speed manual or a paddle-shifting six-speed automatic. **To be tested.**
✓ **Mazda RX-8**	○	The RX-8 revived the rotary engine in Mazda sports cars. It is an agile and fun coupe that revs exceptionally smoothly, and the ride is impressive for a sports car. The rear-hinged rear doors make back seat access relatively easy. Fuel economy is disappointing. **Dec. 2003**
Mazda Tribute	○	The car-based Tribute is a twin of the Ford Escape. The 2005 freshening made it a bit quieter, and interior quality is improved. Because of a tip-up in the government rollover test, we do not recommend the non-hybrid Escape and its siblings. **Oct. 2004**
✓ **Mazda3**	⊖	The standard 2.0-liter, four-cylinder engine is relatively quick and sparing with fuel; the 2.3-liter version is strong and refined. Handling is precise and sporty. Interior quality is very good. We recommend the curtain air bags. Without them the Mazda3 received a Poor rating in the IIHS side-crash test. **Aug. 2004**
Mazda5	NEW	This six-passenger small minivan is based on the Mazda3 and provides the utility of a minivan with easy maneuverability, all at an affordable price and with good fuel economy. The second- and third-row seats can be folded when not in use. **To be tested.**
Mazda6	◒	The Mazda6 offers nimble handling and a firm ride. The V6 comes with a six-speed automatic. The four-cylinder doesn't feel punchy or refined. Wagon and hatchback versions are available. The 6 scored Poor in the IIHS side-crash test without its optional side air bags. Reliability of the wagon is above average; the sedan is below average. **May 2003**
Mercedes-Benz C-Class	◒	The C-Class comes in sedan and wagon body styles. They offer quick acceleration, a quiet, comfortable ride, and agile, secure handling. All-wheel drive is optional. The seats are comfortable and supportive, but the rear is tight. **To be tested.**
Mercedes-Benz CLK	●	The C-Class coupe accelerates quickly, handles well, and rides comfortably. The available engines are powerful. Rear seating is reasonably hospitable. A convertible is available. Steering feel has improved. The V6 is nice, but the 5.0-liter V8 is muscular.

Model	Predicted reliability	Description/with last road test date
Mercedes-Benz CLS	NEW	The CLS is a four-door sedan with a swoopy, streamlined roof and seating for just four passengers. Even so, rear-seat room is tight, and the angle of the roof cuts into head room. The luxurious and comfortable CLS delivers powerful performance and agile handling.
Mercedes-Benz E-Class	●	The E-Class is a pleasure to drive, blending spirited acceleration and respectable fuel economy. The strong 3.5-liter V6 is mated to a seven-speed automatic. Seat comfort and driving position are first class. Wagon, diesel, and all-wheel-drive models are also available. Reliability has been poor. **Jun. 2004**
Mercedes-Benz M-Class	NEW	The redesigned M-Class uses unibody construction, but seats just five. The seven-speed automatic isn't very responsive. The ride is comfortable and quiet. Handling is capable but lacks agility. Second-row seats are very comfortable. **Nov. 2005**
Mercedes-Benz R-Class	NEW	The three-row R-Class shares the same AWD platform with the redesigned M-Class, which only features seating for five. The R-Class offers easy access and comfortable seating for six passengers. **To be tested.**
Mercedes-Benz S-Class	●	The S-Class is stately and advanced with smooth, powerful engines. Handling is agile, and the ride is comfortable. The sumptuous rear is roomy. We can't recommend the S-Class because of below-par reliability. A redesign arrives for 2006. **Nov. 2003**
Mercedes-Benz SLK	◒	This roadster features an folding hardtop and a strong 3.5-liter V6. The manual shifter and clutch are more user-friendly than in the first-generation SLK. Handling is more agile than the previous version, yet the ride is relatively comfortable. **Oct. 2005**
✓ **Mercury Grand Marquis**	○	A big, old-fashioned sedan, the Grand Marquis' ride is jiggly, and engine noise is pronounced. Braking and emergency handling are fairly good. Rear leg room is less generous than you might expect. Crash-test results are impressive. **Feb. 2003**
Mercury Mariner	⊖	The Mariner is a twin of the Ford Escape. The Escape's handling is relatively nimble, and the rear seat is roomy. Interior trim was upgraded, and it is now quieter and more comfortable. Because of a tip-up in the government rollover test, we do not recommend the non-Hybrid Escape and its siblings. **Oct. 2004**
Mercury Milan	NEW	The Milan, based on the Mazda6, is a twin of the Ford Fusion. Power comes from a 160-hp, 2.3-liter four-cylinder or a 221-hp, 3.0-liter V6. The four-cylinder offers a five-speed manual or automatic. The V6 uses a six-speed automatic. **To be tested.**
✓ **Mercury Montego**	○	The Montego (and its Ford Five Hundred twin) is a large sedan with elevated seating positions to improve outward vision and access. The lackluster V6 engine has to work hard to move the Montego. Front-wheel drive is standard, with AWD optional. **Jan. 2005**
Mercury Monterey	○	This upscale version of the Ford Freestar uses a noisy 4.2-liter V6 and features a flat-folding third-row seat. Handling is more responsive, but the ride is unsettled. Fit and finish is poor. Crash-test results are impressive. **Mar. 2004**

Model	Predicted reliability	Description/with last road test date
Mercury Mountaineer	NEW	The Mountaineer is a more-expensive Ford Explorer. The coarse 4.0-liter V6 performs adequately. Our tested 4.6-liter V8 was more powerful but noisy and thirsty. The ride is firm and controlled, and handling is sound. ESC is standard for 2005. A 2006 freshening arrives in the fall. **To be tested.**
✓ **Mini Cooper**	○	The Mini features extremely agile handling and is fun to drive, but the ride is choppy. The rear is very tight and some controls are confusing. The convertible top is easy to use. The base engine lacks oomph, but the supercharged Cooper S is strong. Reliability remained below average. **Jun. 2005**
Mitsubishi Eclipse	NEW	A powerful engine in the GT trim is this coupe's major appeal. The cockpit is very cramped. Handling lacks agility. The four-cylinder engine is noisy and the manual transmission is clunky. The ride is stiff and busy. **Dec. 2005**
✓ **Mitsubishi Endeavor**	◒	The Endeavor is a midsized car-based SUV. Power comes from a 3.8-liter V6. Front- and all-wheel-drive versions are available. The Endeavor rides reasonably well, but cornering isn't particularly agile. **Aug. 2003**
✓ **Mitsubishi Galant**	◒	The redesigned Galant arrived for 2004. Engine choices include a weak four-cylinder and a powerful V6 that overwhelms the front wheels. The ride is not very comfortable. Handling is secure but not particularly agile. The interior is roomy but bland, with disappointing fit and finish. **May 2004**
Mitsubishi Lancer	◒	Mitsubishi's small sedan falls short of the competition—and offers no price advantage, either. Handling is clumsy, the ride unsettled, and the interior noisy. The Lancer received a Poor in the IIHS side-crash test. **Jul. 2002**
Mitsubishi Lancer Evolution	NA	This turbocharged, all-wheel-drive version of the Lancer sedan competes well with the Subaru Impreza WRX STi. The car is super fast, agile, and fun, but has a harsh ride. For 2006 horsepower increased to 286 and the suspension is revised slightly. **Dec. 2003**
Mitsubishi Montero	NA	The Montero is a pleasant SUV that's marred by clumsy and disconcerting handling. The standard stability-control system helps, but it scores a poor rating in our emergency-handling tests. It will be discontinued after the 2006 model year. **Aug. 2003**
✓ **Mitsubishi Outlander**	●	The Outlander is available with either front- or all-wheel drive, powered by a 2.4-liter four-cylinder. The ride is reasonably comfortable and secure but with pronounced body lean. Cargo volume is relatively small. The Outlander received a Poor rating in the IIHS side-crash test when tested without side air bags. **Jun. 2003**
Mitsubishi Raider	NEW	This reskinned Dodge Dakota offers two Dodge engines, a 3.7-liter V6 or a 4.7-liter, 230-hp V8. Extended- and crew-cab body styles will be offered. We found the Dakota's ride buoyant and front head room limited, and it suffered from excessive body roll and lacked agility. **Jul. 2005**

	Model	Predicted reliability	Description/with last road test date
✓	**Nissan 350Z**	○	The 350Z is a two-seater powered by a smooth-revving 3.5-liter V6. The manual gearbox feels slightly notchy. Handling is agile, and the stiff ride has been improved. A convertible with a power-operated top is available. **Oct. 2005**
✓	**Nissan Altima**	○	The Altima is roomy, with strong engines and secure handling, but a stiff and jittery ride. The front seats are comfortable, but the rear seat lacks support. 2005 brought improved interior fit and finish. The Altima received a Poor rating in the IIHS side-crash test without the optional curtain air bags. **Feb. 2005**
	Nissan Armada	●	This large SUV has seating for eight. Power comes from a 5.6-liter V8 engine mated to a five-speed automatic. Two- and four-wheel drive versions are available, and it features an independent rear suspension. First-year reliability has been poor. **Mar. 2004**
✓	**Nissan Frontier**	○	The redesigned Frontier is quick and nimble, with a stiff, though tolerable, ride. The 265-hp, 4.0-liter V6 is strong and smooth. Optional stability control is a plus. The tailgate is very heavy. **Jul. 2005**
(✓)	**Nissan Maxima**	○	The Maxima's powerful V6 is quick but produces torque steer. Handling is improved from the previous model, though the ride is stiff and jiggly. The wide turning circle is a nuisance. **Jul. 2003**
✓	**Nissan Murano**	⊖	This car-based SUV offers roomy seating for five in a sporty package. The spring-loaded rear seat can be folded by flipping a lever. The V6 delivers strong performance. Handling is fairly nimble, but the ride is stiff. Reliability has been above average. **Apr. 2005**
✓	**Nissan Pathfinder**	○	The redesigned Pathfinder features a new V6, independent-rear suspension, and third-row seat. The 270-hp, 4.0-liter V6 is smooth and strong. The ride is stiff, though handing is responsive. The third-row seat is tolerable for short trips. Stability control is standard. **Nov. 2005**
	Nissan Quest	●	The Quest is a capable, competitively priced minivan powered by a 240-hp, 3.5-liter V6. Both the second- and third-row seats fold flat into the floor. Ride and handling are good. The center-mounted gauges and cluttered controls are a nuisance and reliability has been poor. Crash-test results are impressive. **Oct. 2003**
	Nissan Sentra	⊖	The Sentra is a solid small sedan with a refined, efficient powertrain, decent handling, and a well-designed interior. But ride comfort, braking, and rear-seat room fall short. Reliability has remained below average. The Sentra received a Poor rating in the IIHS side-crash test.
	Nissan Titan	●	The Titan is powerful and has a comfortable ride. The engine is strong but loud. The cargo bed is smaller than competing trucks, and the 1,105-pound payload capacity is meager. Safety features include optional ESC and curtain air bags. Reliability has dropped to well below average. **Jul. 2004**

Model	Predicted reliability	Description/with last road test date
Nissan Xterra	NA	The redesigned Xterra retains its off-road capability but is more civilized. The strong 4.0-liter, 265-hp V6 delivers quick acceleration but just 17 mpg. The four-wheel-drive system is still part-time. The spartan interior looks rugged and is well assembled. ESC and side- and head-protection air bags are available. **Aug. 2005**
✓ **Pontiac G6**	○	The G6 shares the Chevrolet Malibu's platform. The coarse-sounding V6 provides ample power and acceptable fuel economy. The base G6 lacks agility and tire grip, and the ride is a bit stiff. The coupelike styling impedes rear access and visibility. **Feb. 2005**
Pontiac GTO	◒	The GTO is quick, and its engine is muscular. Handling is entertaining at its limits. The manual shifter isn't slick, and the clutch is heavy. The ride is fairly compliant. The seats are comfortable, and the interior is well-made. **Sep. 2004**
Pontiac Grand Prix	⊖	The Grand Prix's ride, rear-seat comfort, and 20 mpg fuel economy trail the competition. The V6 is fairly quick but noisy. Taller drivers wished for more head room. The rear seats are very cramped. Reliability of the supercharged model is poor. **Jan. 2004**
Pontiac Montana SV6	●	This minivan is powered by a 3.5-liter, 200-hp V6. Removing the second-row seats is cumbersome. The folding third-row seat only folds flat on the floor. Handling is reluctant, interior fit and finish is insubstantial, and the ride is stiff and noisy. This minivan isn't competitive in the category. **Mar. 2005**
Pontiac Solstice	NEW	This rear-wheel drive, affordable two-seat roadster is meant to compete with the Mazda MX-5. It's powered by a 2.4-liter, 170-hp four-cylinder engine. A five-speed manual is the only transmission offered. Saturn will also get a version named the Sky. **To be tested.**
Pontiac Torrent	NEW	This is Pontiac's version of the Chevrolet Equinox. We found the Equinox's moveable rear seat roomy. Interior quality is subpar, and the V6 is noisy and unrefined. Handling is clumsy and a tip-up by the Equinox in the government rollover test is another negative. **To be tested.**
✓ **Pontiac Vibe**	⊖	The Vibe is a roomy small wagon with good cabin and cargo access. Handling and ride are OK, but the engine is noisy. All-wheel drive is optional. This is a sensible alternative to a small SUV. Stability control is optional for 2005. **Aug. 2002**
Porsche Boxster	NA	This roadster's handling and braking are superb, and the ride is firm but not punishing. It is relatively quick and fun to drive. The two trunks give it a bit of practicality. The power top can be operated at low speeds . **Oct. 2005**
Porsche Cayenne	●	The Cayenne is a midsized, luxury car-based design with all-wheel drive. Low-range gearing and advanced electronics promise some off-road capability. It comes with a choice of engines and available adjustable ride height. Poor reliability is a disappointment.
Porsche Cayman	NEW	Porsche based the Cayman coupe on the Boxster. Power comes from a mid-mounted, flat-six engine that produces 295 hp, positioning it between the Boxster and 911. A six-speed manual is standard, and the five-speed Tiptronic is optional.

Model	Predicted reliability	Description/with last road test date
Saab 9-2X	NA	This thinly disguised Subaru Impreza wagon has a traditional Saab nose, but the rest of the vehicle is virtually identical to the Impreza. All-wheel drive and the Subaru's adequate four-cylinder are standard. The WRX's turbo engine comes in the Aero trim line. **To be tested.**
Saab 9-3	●	The 9-3 sedan is available with two turbocharged engines. Handling has been improved, with quick, direct steering and taut body control. The rear seat is cramped and the ride is stiff. A convertible and wagon is available. Reliability continues to be well below average. **Jul. 2003**
✓ **Saab 9-5**	○	The 9-5 has unimpressive ride and handling. Front seats are comfortable, and the rear is relatively roomy. The wagon is competent and well-designed but lacks a third-seat option. Excellent crash-test results are a plus. **Feb. 2004**
Saab 9-7X	NA	Saab's SUV is a Chevrolet TrailBlazer with upgraded interior and exterior appointments, and a revised suspension. The AWD system is permanent and lacks a low range. Reliability of the TrailBlazer has been poor, and offset crash-test results are unimpressive.
Saturn Aura	NEW	Based on the same platform as the Pontiac G6 the Aura should bring some European flair to Saturn. The optional engine will be the 3.6-liter V6 that performed well in our tested Cadillac STS. The Aura goes on sale in late 2006.
Saturn Ion	○	The Ion as an acceptable ride and handling is capable, but steering feel is inconsistent. The noisy engine returned less-than-exceptional fuel economy. The cramped interior feels cheap. The Ion received a Poor rating in the IIHS side-crash test. **May 2005**
Saturn Relay	●	The Relay is powered by a 3.5-liter, 200-hp V6 engine. Removing the second-row seat is cumbersome. The folding third-row seat only folds flat on the floor. Handling is reluctant, interior trim is insubstantial, and the ride is stiff and noisy. **Mar. 2005**
Saturn Sky	NEW	New for 2006, the Sky is Saturn's version of the Pontiac Solstice roadster. The rear-drive, two-seat Sky will be powered by a 2.4-liter four-cylinder engine that produces about 170 hp. A five-speed manual will be the only transmission offered initially. Antilock brakes will be optional.
Saturn Vue	●	The Vue has light steering and the AWD system is slow to engage. Interior fit and finish are sub-par, and the front and rear seats lack support. A Poor in the IIHS side-crash test when tested without the optional curtain air bags and tip-ups in government rollover tests are negatives. **Oct. 2004**
✓ **Scion tC**	○	The tC coupe is the third Scion model. Power comes from a 160-hp, 2.4-liter four-cylinder engine. It drives nicely but isn't particularly sporty. Rear seat room is generous for a coupe, and there is a lot of standard equipment for the money. **Dec. 2005**
Scion xA	⊖	The xA is a small four-door hatchback powered by a 1.5-liter, 108-hp four-cylinder. Handling is nimble, but the ride is stiff and choppy. Acceleration is so-so and the engine is buzzy, but the xA is affordable and gets good mileage. The cargo area is small. **Aug. 2004**

Model	Predicted reliability	Description/with last road test date
✓ **Scion xB**	⊖	The xB is a small, tall, slab-sided wagon powered a 1.5-liter, 108-hp four-cylinder. It is very space efficient. Antilock brakes and stability control are standard. High levels of wind and engine noise, and the stiff, choppy ride, make the xB fatiguing on long drives. **Aug. 2004**
✓ **Subaru B9 Tribeca**	⊖	Subaru's first SUV is designed to carry seven people, but the second and third rows are cramped. The standard 250-hp, 3.0-liter engine struggles to pull the Tribeca, and the transmission doesn't downshift readily. Interior appointments are impressive. **Nov. 2005**
✓ **Subaru Baja**	⊖	The Baja is a small pickup with four full-sized doors. A removable partition between cabin and cargo bed adds to its versatility. A 210-hp turbocharged model is available. **Jun. 2003**
(✓) **Subaru Forester**	⊜	The Forester has a tall and roomy cargo area and a controlled, compliant ride. Handling is relatively responsive, and acceleration and rear-seat room have improved. For mid-2005 Subaru revised some styling cues and boosted engine power. **Jun. 2003**
✓ **Subaru Impreza**	⊜	The small Impreza delivers good handling and a quiet, comfortable ride. The line includes the Outback Sport small wagon that rides more stiffly and doesn't handle as well as the regular Impreza. A score of Good in the IIHS offset-crash test is a plus. **Jul. 2002**
✓ **Subaru Impreza WRX/STi**	⊖	The WRX/WRX STi has race-car-like handling and a relatively good ride. The WRX's engine provides quick and effortless acceleration. The ferociously quick 300-hp WRX STi has performance numbers the same as vehicles costing twice as much. **Dec. 2003**
✓ **Subaru Legacy**	⊖	The Legacy has a supple ride, agile handling, and precise steering. The standard engine is sluggish with the automatic. The GT's 250-hp turbocharged engine is quick but thirsty. Stability control is not available on the Legacy. **Nov. 2004**
✓ **Subaru Outback**	⊖	This SUV alternative has good steering feel and a supple ride. The standard engine with the automatic transmission is not quick. The Outback XT uses a powerful 250-hp turbocharged engine, but fuel economy suffers. Interior quality is improved. Stability control is available only in the Outback 3.0 VDC. **Dec. 2004**
Suzuki Aerio	○	The Aerio features a tall roofline designed to increase head room and improve outward visibility. It's available in sedan and four-door wagon/hatchback versions. The Aerio received a Poor rating in the IIHS side-crash test. **Mar. 2003**
Suzuki Forenza	NA	The Forenza does not compete well in its class. Acceleration is slow and fuel economy just so-so. The ride is stiff and not well-controlled. Interior fit and finish is good, and the rear seat is roomy. It received a Poor rating in the IIHS side-crash test. **Aug. 2004**
Suzuki Grand Vitara	NEW	The redesigned Grand Vitara became a car-based SUV for 2006. Itis designed for on-road refinement and light off-roading. The interior is roomy. **May 2002**

Model	Predicted reliability	Description/with last road test date
✓ **Suzuki XL-7**	○	This truck-based SUV is hampered by a crude, unresponsive automatic and a stiff ride. Handling is vague but secure. The extended-length XL-7 has a small third-row seat. **To be tested.**
Suzuki Verona	NA	The Verona has reluctant handling, but the ride is fairly comfortable. The engine is quiet but lackluster, and the automatic transmission is hesitant to downshift. Fit and finish is relatively good, but the driving position is compromised. **May 2004**
✓ **Toyota 4Runner**	⊖	The 4Runner is roomy and has an optional third-row seat. This credible off-roader offers hill-descent control and a system that prevents roll-back on slow, steep ascents. Electronic Stability Control is standard. **Aug. 2003**
✓ **Toyota Avalon**	○	The redesigned Avalon has a limo-like rear seat and impressive interior. The ride is very comfortable and quiet, but tends to float at highway speeds. Handling is responsive but far from sporty. The quiet 280-hp, 3.5-liter V6 feels smooth and punchy. **Sep. 2005**
Ⓥ **Toyota Camry**	⊖	The Camry is quiet, refined, and roomy, but it's difficult for some to find a comfortable driving position. Both engines are smooth and responsive. Cabin controls are logical. We recommend the optional curtain air bags; without them the Camry scored Poor in the IIHS side-crash test. A redesign is due for 2006. **Feb. 2005**
✓ **Toyota Camry Solara**	⊖	The Solara's standard 157-hp four-cylinder is acceptable; the optional 225-hp V6 is smooth. The ride is comfortable, but handling is not sporty. The rear seat is relatively roomy. The convertible suffered from body shake, but the top is well-insulated. **Jun. 2005**
Ⓥ **Toyota Corolla**	⊖	This small car has a roomy, high-quality interior. The engine delivers responsive performance and excellent fuel economy, but is a bit boomy. ESC is optional. Without the optional curtain air bags the Corolla rated Poor in the IIHS side-crash test. **Jul. 2002**
✓ **Toyota Echo**	⊖	The Echo is a surprisingly roomy small car. The 1.5-liter engine provides very good fuel economy. Handling is fairly responsive and secure, but body roll is pronounced. Antilock brakes can be hard to find. A redesign called Yaris arrives in 2006**. Dec. 2000**
Toyota FJ Cruiser	NEW	This small SUV is based on the 4Runner and arrives in early 2006. Power comes from a 4.0-liter, 245-hp V6. Two- and four-wheel drive versions will be available. A five-speed automatic is available with both, but a five-speed manual is available only on 4WD models. ESC will be standard. **To be tested.**
✓ **Toyota Highlander**	⊖	This SUV is roomy, quiet, comfortable, and well designed. It uses the same platform as the Lexus RX330 but less expensive. Excellent offset-crash results as well as outstanding reliability round out this highly rated SUV. The hybrid returned 22 mpg overall in our tests. **Dec. 2004/Nov. 2005**
✓ **Toyota Land Cruiser**	⊖	This big, expensive SUV uses a quiet 4.7-liter V8 and has a smooth ride. The interior offers lots of room and a third seat. It combines plushness and quality with off-road ability. Standard ESC and a permanently engaged 4WD system are major advantages. **Mar. 2001**

Model	Predicted reliability	Description/with last road test date
✓ **Toyota Matrix**	◍	The Matrix is a roomy small wagon that's easy to get people and cargo into and out of. Handling and ride are acceptable, but the engine is noisy and the driving position is not ideal. All-wheel drive and stability control are optional. **Aug. 2002**
✓ **Toyota Prius**	◍	Toyota's hybrid returned an excellent 44 mpg in our tests. Acceleration is comparable to most family sedans. Access is easy and the interior is well-put-together. The unusual controls and displays take some getting used to. **May 2004**
Toyota RAV4	NEW	The RAV4 has a flexible interior layout, easy access, nimble handling, and standard stability control. The four-cylinder accelerates adequately. We recommend the optional curtain air bags. A redesign, including a V6 engine, arrives for 2006. **To be tested.**
✓ **Toyota Sequoia**	◓	The Sequoia competes against the Nissan Armada, Ford Expedition, and Chevrolet Tahoe. It is roomier than the Land Cruiser, but doesn't ride as comfortably. It boasts a V8 powertrain and a third-row seat. 2005 brought more power and a five-speed automatic. **Nov. 2002**
✓ **Toyota Sienna**	◓	The Sienna rides very comfortably and quietly. The third seat folds flat into the floor. The 3.3-liter V6 engine is smooth and strong. Handling is secure, predictable, and responsive. Crash-test results are impressive. AWD is available, but readers report high tire wear with the runflat tires. **Mar. 2005**
✓ **Toyota Tacoma**	○	The redesigned Tacoma has improved steering and interior trim. The 4.0-liter V6 provides strong performance. The ride trails some competitors and the driving position is too low. Payload capacity is relatively small. We highly recommend the optional ESC for added safety. **Jul. 2005**
✓ **Toyota Tundra**	◍	The Tundra's V8 is smooth and quiet. 2005 brings a new 4.0-liter V6. The ride is civilized, the cabin is quiet and roomy in the crew cab, and fit and finish is top-notch. The extended-cab model has a cramped rear seat. ESC can be very hard to find. **Jul. 2004**
Volkswagen Golf	NEW	The Golf's responsive but noisy 2.0-liter four-cylinder and easy-shifting manual perform well together. The front seats offer good, firm support, but the rear is cramped. A redesign arrives for '06. **To be tested.**
Volkswagen Jetta	NEW	Volkswagen has evolved the new Jetta into a more upscale sedan. A 2.5-liter, 150-hp five-cylinder engine is standard. A 200-hp, 2.0-liter turbo and a diesel are also available. The new Jetta rides comfortably and handles better than the previous generation. The interior is considerably roomier. **To be tested.**
Volkswagen New Beetle	●	The New Beetle rides and handles well. The front seats are supportive, but the rear is cramped. The power-operated convertible top is well-insulated from wind noise. Reliability is below average and the Beetle scored a Poor in the IIHS side-crash test. **Jun. 2005**

Model	Predicted reliability	Description/with last road test date
Volkswagen Passat	NEW	The Passat, one of the better family sedans, has been redesigned. It is larger and roomier, and offers many safety features. A 2.0-liter turbocharged four-cylinder is standard. A 3.6-liter V6 is available, as are wagon and AWD versions. **To be tested.**
Volkswagen Phaeton	NA	The Phaeton is Volkswagen's first large, premium-luxury cruiser. Engines include a 4.2-liter V8 and an optional 6.0-liter 12-cylinder. All-wheel drive is standard. This heavy and plush sedan rides on an adjustable air suspension.
Volkswagen Touareg	●	Volkswagen's first SUV has features such as low-range gearing and a locking center differential, making it one of the few car-based SUVs that's capable off road. The V6 is thirsty and underpowered, and the V8 is stronger but expensive. The interior is elegant but not so roomy. **Sep. 2003**
✓ **Volvo S40**	○	The S40 sedan corners fairly nimbly but has a stiff ride. The standard 2.4-liter engine sounds raspy. A stronger turbocharged engine powers the T5. The interior is well finished. The front seats are supportive, but the rear seat is very tight. All-wheel drive is available. **Nov. 2004**
✓ **Volvo S60**	⊖	The S60 is neither luxurious nor sporty. The interior is fairly quiet and the front seats are comfortable. The ride is stiff and handling is secure, but not particularly agile. The rear seat is cramped. The confusing radio controls have been improved. **Feb. 2004**
✓ **Volvo S80**	○	Volvo's front- or all-wheel-drive flagship performs well. It's roomy, quiet, and comfortable. A turbocharged five-cylinder with optional AWD is the only available engine for 2006. **Jun. 2004**
Volvo V50	●	The V50 is the wagon version of the S40. It corners fairly nimbly but has a stiff ride. The standard 2.4-liter engine sounds raspy. A stronger turbocharged engine powers the T5. The front seats are supportive, but the rear seat is very tight. All-wheel drive is available. **Dec. 2004**
✓ **Volvo V70/XC70**	○	The V70 is spacious, with comfortable seats. The all-wheel-drive XC70 Cross Country model is an SUV alternative that rides and handles more roughly than the V70. AWD is also available on the fast V70R. **Jul. 2001**
Volvo XC90	●	This seven-seater SUV has all-wheel drive and a third row that folds flat. It features a stability-control system that detects an impending rollover and reacts to stop it. The ride is more comfortable than in the XC70. Power comes from a turbocharged five-cylinder or a V8. **Sep. 2003**

RATING THE 2006 MODELS

Included here are Ratings on more than 200 vehicles that CR has recently tested. Within each category, vehicles are ranked by their overall test score. Recommended models (✓) not only tested well, but have shown average or better reliability and performed at least adequately if crash-tested or included in a government rollover test. Recommended models that performed especially well in both IIHS crash tests and at least one government crash test are designated with a (Ⓥ).

Predicted reliability is our forecast of how well a new car will likely hold up, based on data from our 2005 subscriber survey.

Accident avoidance reflects how capable a vehicle is in helping you avoid an accident through braking, emergency handling, or accelerating out of harm's way. The crash protection rating is given only to vehicles that have been in both IIHS tests and at least one government crash test. Split results indicate whether the vehicle was tested in the IIHS side-crash test with or without side and/or curtain air bags. Overall fuel economy is based on CR's real-world tests.

Better ⟵⟶ Worse

⊜ ⊖ ○ ◒ ●

	Make & model	Version tested	Price as tested	Road test score (0–100; P F G VG E)	Survey results: Predicted reliability	Safety: Accident avoidance	Safety: Crash protection w/wo	Fuel economy: Overall MPG
	SMALL CARS (AUTOMATIC TRANSMISSION)							
✓	**Ford Focus**	ZX4 SES	$19,080		○	⊜	—/○	24
✓	**Mazda3**	i	18,190		⊖	⊜	—/○	27
✓	**Toyota Prius**	-	23,490		⊜	○	—	44
Ⓥ	**Toyota Corolla**	LE	17,545		⊜	○	⊜/○	29
✓	**Hyundai Elantra**	GT	17,589		○	⊖	○	24
	Kia Spectra	EX	16,185		NA	○	◒	25
✓	**Subaru Impreza**	2.5 RS	20,470		⊜	⊖	—	22
✓	**Scion xB**	-	14,995		⊖	⊖	—	30
	Suzuki Aerio	LX	16,494		○	○	—	25
	Chevrolet Cobalt	LS	17,350		●	○	⊜/○	23
	Mitsubishi Lancer	ES	16,574		⊖	○	—/○	26
	Scion xA	-	14,445		⊖	⊖	—	30

	Make & model	Version tested	Price as tested	Road test score (0–100; P F G VG E)	Survey results: Predicted reliability	Safety: Accident avoidance	Safety: Crash protection w/wo	Fuel economy: Overall MPG
	SMALL CARS (AUTOMATIC TRANSMISSION)							
	Saturn Ion	3	$18,415		○	○	◒/◒	25
	Suzuki Forenza	S	14,794		NA	○	—	24
	Chevrolet Aveo	LS	14,005		○	○	—	28
	Dodge Neon	SXT	17,285		○	⊖	—/◒	24
	SMALL CARS (MANUAL TRANSMISSION)							
✓	Mazda3	i	$17,290		⊖	⊜	—/○	30
	Kia Spectra	EX	15,185		NA	○	◒	28
✓	Scion xB	-	14,245		⊖	⊖	—	32
	Scion xA	-	13,045		⊖	⊖	—	31
	Suzuki Forenza	S	13,994		NA	○	—	27
	Honda Insight	-	21,045		NA	⊖	—	51
	Chevrolet Aveo	LS	13,045		○	○	—	27
	ROADSTERS							
	Porsche Boxster	Base	$49,075		NA	⊜	—	22
	Mercedes Benz SLK	SLK350	53,950		◒	⊜	—	21
	Chevrolet Corvette	Base	57,520		●	⊜	—	21
✓	Nissan 350Z	Grand Touring	42,800		○	⊜	—	20
✓	Honda S2000	-	33,665		⊜	⊜	—	25
✓	BMW Z4	3.0i	46,070		○	⊜	—	26
	Audi TT	Quattro	42,320		◒	⊜	—	22
	Lotus Elise	-	45,545		NA	⊖	—	29
	SPORTS/SPORTY CARS							
	Audi S4	-	$50,870		●	⊜	⊜	20
✓	BMW M3	-	56,495		○	⊜	—	19
✓	Subaru Impreza	WRX STi	32,870		⊖	⊜	—	20
✓	Mazda RX-8	-	31,305		○	⊜	—	18
✓	Cadillac CTS-V	-	52,685		○	⊜	—	17
	Mitsubishi Lancer	Evolution	29,094		NA	⊜	—	20

	Make & model	Version tested	Price as tested	Road test score (0–100; P F G VG E)	Survey results: Predicted reliability	Safety: Accident avoidance	Safety: Crash protection w/wo	Fuel economy: Overall MPG
	SPORTS/SPORTY CARS							
✓	**Subaru Impreza**	WRX	$25,470		⊖	⊖	—	21
✓	**Ford Mustang**	GT (V8)	29,020		○	⊜	—	20
✓	**Mini Cooper**	Base	18,295		○	⊖	—	30
✓	**Acura RSX**	Base	20,845		⊖	○	—	28
	Chevrolet Cobalt	SS	24,135		●	⊖	—	23
✓	**Scion tC**	-	17,115		○	○	—	26
	Pontiac GTO	-	34,295		◒	⊖	—	17
✓	**Chrysler Crossfire**	Coupe	29,920		○	⊜	—	22
✓	**Hyundai Tiburon**	GT (V6)	21,389		○	⊖	—	22
	Mitsubishi Eclipse	GS (4-cyl.)	21,764		New	○	—	23
	CONVERTIBLES (MANUAL TRANSMISSION)							
✓	**Mini Cooper**	S	$29,820		○	⊜	—	25
	Volkswagen New Beetle	GLS 1.8T	27,950		●	⊖	—	24
✓	**Chrysler PT Cruiser**	GT turbo	29,305		○	⊖	—	22
	CONVERTIBLES (AUTOMATIC TRANSMISSION)							
✓	**Toyota Camry Solara**	XLE (V6)	$31,087		⊖	⊖	—	21
	Ford Mustang	Premium (V6)	28,070		●	⊖	—	20
	Chrysler Sebring	Limited (V6)	32,715		○	○	—	21
	UPSCALE SEDANS							
(✓)	**Acura TL**	-	$33,670		⊖	⊜	⊜	23
(✓)	**Lexus ES330**	-	35,715		⊖	⊖	⊜	22
✓	**Acura TSX**	-	29,760		⊖	⊜	—	23
✓	**Cadillac CTS**	-	39,425		○	⊖	—	20
	Saab 9-3	Aero	36,845		●	⊜	—	21
✓	**Infiniti G35**	-	34,960		⊖	⊖	—	20
	Jaguar X-Type	3.0	39,120		◒	⊜	⊖	19
(✓)	**Saab 9-5**	Arc	38,865		○	⊖	⊖	21
(✓)	**Volvo S60**	2.5T	34,980		⊖	○	⊖	22

	Make & model	Version tested	Price as tested	Road test score (0–100: P, F, G, VG, E)	Survey results: Predicted reliability	Safety: Accident avoidance	Safety: Crash protection w/wo	Fuel economy: Overall MPG
	FAMILY SEDANS							
(✓)	**Honda Accord**	Hybrid (V6)	$30,655		⊜	⊜	⊜	25
(✓)	**Toyota Camry**	XLE (V6)	27,680		⊜	⊜	⊖/○	20
(✓)	**Honda Accord**	EX (V6)	27,365		⊖	⊖	⊜	23
(✓)	**Honda Accord**	EX (4-cyl.)	23,515		⊜	⊖	⊜	24
(✓)	**Toyota Camry**	LE (4-cyl.)	22,065		⊜	○	⊖/○	24
✓	**Subaru Legacy**	2.5 GT (4-cyl.)	30,370		⊖	⊖	—	18
(✓)	**Nissan Maxima**	3.5 SE (V6)	33,080		○	⊖	⊖	21
✓	**Nissan Altima**	3.5 SE (V6)	28,280		○	⊜	—/○	20
✓	**Mazda6**	i (4-cyl.)	21,930		○	⊜	—/○	23
	Mazda6	s (V6)	27,790		◒	⊜	—/○	20
✓	**Toyota Prius**	(4-cyl.)	23,490		⊜	○	—	44
	Chevrolet Malibu	Base (4-cyl.)	21,125		◒	⊖	⊖/○	24
	Chevrolet Malibu	LS (V6)	22,960		◒	○	⊖/○	23
✓	**Nissan Altima**	2.5 S (4-cyl.)	24,380		○	⊖	—/○	23
(✓)	**Mitsubishi Galant**	GTS (V6)	27,094		⊖	⊖	⊜	20
(✓)	**Volvo S40**	2.4i (5-cyl.)	29,145		○	⊖	⊖	23
(✓)	**Mitsubishi Galant**	ES (4-cyl.)	20,944		⊖	⊖	⊜	23
	Kia Optima	EX (V6)	22,745		⊖	○	◒	20
✓	**Ford Taurus**	SES (V6)	25,445		○	○	—	22
	Chrysler Sebring	Touring (V6)	23,140		○	⊖	—/◒	21
	Dodge Stratus	ES (V6)	22,585		○	⊖	—/◒	21
✓	**Pontiac G6**	Base (V6)	23,080		○	○	—	21
	Suzuki Verona	LX (6-cyl.)	19,794		NA	⊖	○	20
	Pontiac Grand Prix	GT (V6)	28,255		⊖	○	—	20
	Chrysler Sebring	(4-cyl.)	21,080		○	⊖	—/◒	21
	Dodge Stratus	SXT (4-cyl.)	20,620		○	⊖	—/◒	21

	Make & model	Version tested	Price as tested	Road test score (0–100: P F G VG E)	Survey results: Predicted reliability	Safety: Accident avoidance	Safety: Crash protection w/wo	Fuel economy: Overall MPG
	LARGE SEDANS							
✓	**Toyota Avalon**	XLS	$33,070		○	⊖	—	22
✓	**Ford Five Hundred**	SEL (FWD)	24,905		○	○	—	21
✓	**Mercury Montego**	Luxury (FWD)	25,105		○	○	—	21
✓	**Ford Five Hundred**	SEL (AWD)	29,115		○	○	—	20
✓	**Mercury Montego**	Luxury (AWD)	29,080		○	○	—	20
	Chrysler 300	C (V8)	37,480		●	⊖	—	16
✓	**Chrysler 300**	Touring (V6)	30,255		○	⊖	—	19
✓	**Buick LaCrosse**	CXL	31,450		⊖	○	—	18
✓	**Kia Amanti**	-	29,740		⊖	○	—	18
✓	**Lincoln Town Car**	Signature	42,715		○	○	—	17
✓	**Ford Crown Victoria**	LX	30,900		○	○	—	16
✓	**Mercury Grand Marquis**	LSE	32,765		○	○	—	16
	LUXURY SEDANS							
✓	**Infiniti M35**	X (V6,AWD)	$50,240		⊜	⊜	—	18
✓	**Lexus LS430**	-	69,534		⊜	⊖	—	19
	Mercedes-Benz S-Class	S430	83,800		●	⊜	—	18
	Mercedes-Benz E-Class	E320	54,086		●	⊜	—	20
✓	**BMW 5 Series**	530i	55,370		○	⊜	—	20
	Audi A6	3.2	50,820		◒	⊖	—	21
✓	**Cadillac STS**	V6	50,335		○	⊜	—	19
	Audi A8	L	76,470		●	⊖	—	17
✓	**Acura RL**	-	49,670		○	○	—	18
	Jaguar S-Type	4.2	54,795		●	⊜	—	19
✓	**Jaguar XJ8**	Vanden Plas	73,295		○	⊜	—	19
✓	**Lexus GS300**	AWD	51,859		⊜	⊖	—	20
✓	**Volvo S80**	T6	49,200		○	⊜	—	19
	BMW 7 Series	745Li	84,145		●	⊖	—	18

	Make & model	Version tested	Price as tested	Road test score (0–100; P F G VG E)	Survey results: Predicted reliability	Safety: Accident avoidance	Safety: Crash protection w/wo	Fuel economy: Overall MPG
	MINIVANS							
✓	**Honda Odyssey**	EX	$32,610		○	⊖	—	19
✓	**Toyota Sienna**	XLE	34,909		⊖	○	—	19
	Nissan Quest	3.5 SL	26,430		●	○	—	18
✓	**Mazda MPV**	ES	32,340		○	⊖	—	19
	Chrysler Town & Country	Limited	37,115		◒	○	—	17
	Dodge Grand Caravan	SXT	34,140		◒	○	—	17
✓	**Ford Freestar**	SEL	33,285		○	○	—	17
✓	**Mercury Monterey**	Luxury	35,610		○	○	—	17
	Chevrolet Uplander	LS	27,205		●	○	—	17
	Pontiac Montana SV6	-	25,660		●	○	—	17
	Saturn Relay	3	30,895		●	○	—	17
	WAGONS AND HATCHBACKS							
✓	**Ford Focus**	ZXW SE	$20,490		○	⊖	—	23
✓	**Subaru Outback**	2.5i	28,670		⊖	○	—	21
✓	**Mazda6**	s	25,840		⊖	⊖	—	19
✓	**Pontiac Vibe**	Base (FWD)	21,155		⊖	○	—	26
✓	**Toyota Matrix**	XR (AWD)	20,095		⊜	⊖	—	24
✓	**Ford Focus**	ZX5	18,750		○	⊜	—	24
✓	**Chevrolet Malibu Maxx**	LS (V6)	24,085		○	○	—	21
	Volvo V50	T5 (AWD)	35,270		●	⊖	—	20
✓	**Chrysler PT Cruiser**	Limited	23,250		○	○	—	18
✓	**Subaru Impreza**	Outback Sport	20,370		⊜	⊖	—	22
✓	**Dodge Magnum**	SXT	29,630		○	○	—	19
✓	**Scion xB**	-	14,995		⊖	⊖	—	30

	Make & model	Version tested	Price as tested	Road test score (0–100: P F G VG E)	Survey results: Predicted reliability	Safety: Accident avoidance	Safety: Crash protection w/wo	Fuel economy: Overall MPG
	COMPACT PICKUPS							
✓	**Honda Ridgeline**	RTS	$30,590		⊜	○	—	15
✓	**Nissan Frontier**	LE (V6)	30,010		○	○	—	15
✓	**Toyota Tacoma**	Base TRD (V6)	29,210		○	⊖	—	17
	Dodge Dakota	SLT (4.7)	29,970		◒	○	—	14
	Chevrolet Colorado	LS Z71 (5-cyl.)	30,500		●	◒	—	16
	GMC Canyon	SLE Z71 (5-cyl.)	30,080		●	◒	—	16
	FULL-SIZED PICKUPS							
✓	**Toyota Tundra**	SR5 (4.7)	$33,459		⊜	○	—	14
✓	**Chevrolet Avalanche**	1500	43,690		○	○	—	13
	Ford F-150	XLT (5.4)	35,940		◒	○	—	14
	Nissan Titan	SE (5.6)	36,370		●	○	—	13
✓	**Chevrolet Silverado 1500**	Z71 (5.3)	35,610		○	○	—	14
✓	**GMC Sierra 1500**	SLT (5.3)	39,500		○	○	—	14
	Dodge Ram 1500	SLT (5.7)	36,015		○	○	—	11
	Dodge Ram 1500	SLT (4.7)	33,995		○	◒	—	12
	SMALL SPORT-UTILITY VEHICLES							
✓ (circled)	**Subaru Forester**	2.5 X	$22,670		⊜	⊖	⊜	21
✓ (circled)	**Honda CR-V**	EX	24,065		⊜	⊖	⊜	21
✓	**Pontiac Vibe**	(AWD)	22,610		⊖	⊖	—	24
✓	**Toyota Matrix**	XR (AWD)	20,095		⊜	⊖	—	24
	Hyundai Tucson	GLS (V6)	22,154		●	⊖	—	18
	Kia Sportage	EX (V6)	22,290		●	⊖	—	18
✓	**Ford Escape Hybrid**	(AWD)	31,210		⊖	○	⊜/◒	26
✓	**Mercury Mariner Hybrid**	(AWD)	31,910		⊖	○	⊜/◒	26
✓	**Subaru Baja**	-	23,570		⊖	⊖	—	20
	Ford Escape	XLT (V6)	26,745		○	○	⊜/◒	18
	Mazda Tribute	s (V6)	27,020		○	○	⊜/◒	18
	Mercury Mariner	Luxury (V6)	26,445		⊜	○	⊜/◒	18

	Make & model	Version tested	Price as tested	Road test score (0–100; P F G VG E)	Survey results: Predicted reliability	Safety: Accident avoidance	Safety: Crash protection w/wo	Fuel economy: Overall MPG
	SMALL SPORT-UTILITY VEHICLES							
✓	Honda Element	EX	$22,240		⊜	⊖	—/○	20
	Nissan Xterra	S	27,660		NA	○	—	17
✓	Mitsubishi Outlander	XLS	24,524		⊜	○	—/○	20
	Saturn Vue	(V6)	26,810		●	○	—/○	19
	Chevrolet Equinox	LT	26,360		◒	○	—	17
✓	Suzuki XL-7	EX	28,394		○	○	—	17
	Kia Sorento	LX	24,865		◒	○	—	15
✓	Jeep Liberty	Sport (V6)	24,310		○	○	—	15
	Jeep Liberty	Limited (turbodiesel)	29,955		NA	○	—	18
	Jeep Wrangler	Unlimited (6-cyl.)	28,735		○	◒	—/○	14
	MIDSIZED SPORT-UTILITY VEHICLES							
✓	Toyota Highlander Hybrid	Limited	$39,885		⊜	○	—	22
✓	Lexus RX Hybrid	400h	49,883		⊜	○	—	23
✓	Lexus RX330	-	44,833		⊖	⊖	—	18
✓	Honda Pilot	EX-L	34,835		⊖	⊖	—	17
✓	BMW X5	3.0i	49,370		○	⊖	—	17
✓	Toyota Highlander	Limited (V6)	35,155		⊜	⊖	—	19
✓	Nissan Murano	SL	36,240		⊖	⊖	—	19
	Cadillac SRX	(V8)	53,730		●	⊖	—	16
	Ford Freestyle	SEL (AWD)	32,675		◒	○	—	18
✓	Acura MDX	Touring	43,045		⊖	○	—	17
✓	Infiniti FX35	(V6)	39,960		⊜	⊖	—	18
	Mercedes Benz M-Class	ML350	48,880		New	⊖	—	16
✓	BMW X3	2.5i	40,195		○	⊖	—	17
✓	Lexus GX470	-	51,787		⊖	⊖	—	15
✓	Mitsubishi Endeavor	XLS	32,394		⊖	○	—	17
✓	Toyota 4Runner	SR5 (V6)	33,330		⊖	⊖	—	16

	Make & model	Version tested	Price as tested	Road test score (0–100; P F G VG E)	Survey results: Predicted reliability	Safety: Accident avoidance	Safety: Crash protection w/wo	Fuel economy: Overall MPG
	MIDSIZED SPORT-UTILITY VEHICLES							
	Chrysler Pacifica	Touring	$33,995		◒	⊖	—	16
✓	**Subaru B9 Tribeca**	Limited	36,550		⊖	⊖	—	16
	Volvo XC90	T6	46,815		●	○	—	15
✓	**Nissan Pathfinder**	LE	36,160		○	○	—	15
	Land Rover LR3	SE (V8)	50,150		●	○	—	13
	Volkswagen Touareg	(V6)	43,645		●	○	—	15
	Dodge Durango	Limited 5.7 (V8)	39,620		◒	○	—	12
✓	**Buick Rendezvous**	CXL	36,242		○	○	—	16
	Jeep Grand Cherokee	Laredo 4.7 (V8)	35,500		●	○	—	14
	Mitsubishi Montero	Limited	36,394		NA	○	—	14
	Chevrolet TrailBlazer	LS	33,775		◒	○	—	15
	GMC Envoy	SLE	34,935		◒	○	—	15
	Chevrolet TrailBlazer	EXT LT	36,875		◒	◒	—	13
	GMC Envoy	XL SLT	39,750		◒	◒	—	13
	Hummer H3	-	36,915		New	○	—	14
	LARGE SPORT-UTILITY VEHICLES							
	Nissan Armada	LE	$43,370		●	○	—	13
✓	**Toyota Sequoia**	Limited	46,705		⊖	○	—	15
✓	**Chevrolet Suburban**	LT	49,720		○	◒	—	13
✓	**GMC Yukon XL**	SLT	50,405		○	◒	—	13
	Ford Expedition	Eddie Bauer	47,335		●	◒	—	12
	Dodge Durango	Limited 5.7 (V8)	39,620		◒	○	—	12
✓	**Chevrolet Tahoe**	LT	48,175		○	○	—	13
✓	**GMC Yukon**	SLT	48,835		○	○	—	13

THE BEST AND WORST USED CARS

This year 54 models made our **CR Good Bets** list of typically reliable models that have performed well in our road tests, compared with 50 last year. There are seven new entries on the list.

But our 2004 list of **CR Bad Bets**, models that are considered especially risky buys because they have exhibited several years of below-average reliability, has grown to 34 models from 21 in 2003. There are 15 new entries on the list.

CR Good Bets and CR Bad Bets are based on our larger lists of **Reliable Used Cars** and **Used Cars to Avoid**. These comprehensive lists give you a rundown of all the models that were found, from our data, to be above or below average in reliability.

These lists are based on data from our 2004 subscriber survey, which covered 1997-2004 models and for which we received 810,000 responses. Owners reported on any serious problems they had with their cars, minivans, SUVs, and pickup trucks in the previous year.

CR Good Bets and CR Bad Bets include only the models for which we have sufficient data for at least three model years. Models that were new in 2003 or 2004 do not appear. Problems with the engine, engine cooling, transmission, and drive system were weighted more heavily than other problems. The abbreviations 2WD, 4WD, and AWD stand for two-, four-, and all-wheel drive, respectively.

To view the detailed reliability history charts on which these lists are based, see page 191.

CR Good Bets: The best of both worlds

These are models that have performed well in CONSUMER REPORTS road tests over the years and have proved to have several or more years of better-than-average overall reliability. They are listed alphabetically.

Acura Integra	Honda Prelude	Mazda Millenia	Toyota 4Runner
Acura MDX	Honda S2000	Mazda MX-5 Miata	Toyota Avalon
Acura RL	Infiniti G20	Mazda Protegé	Toyota Camry
Acura RSX	Infiniti I30, I35	Mercury Grand Marquis	Toyota Camry Solara
Acura TL	Infiniti Q45	Mercury Tracer	Toyota Celica
Buick Regal	Infiniti QX4	Mitsubishi Galant	Toyota Corolla
Chevrolet/Geo Prizm	Lexus ES300, ES330	Nissan Altima	Toyota Echo
Chrysler PT Cruiser	LexusGS300/GS400, GS430	Nissan Maxima	Toyota Highlander
Ford Crown Victoria	Lexus IS300	Nissan Pathfinder	Toyota Land Cruiser
Ford Escort	Lexus LS400, LS430	Subaru Forester	Toyota Prius
Honda Accord	Lexus RX300, RX330	Subaru Impreza	Toyota RAV4
Honda Civic	Lincoln Town Car	Subaru Legacy	Toyota Sequoia
Honda CR-V	Mazda 626	Subaru Outback	Toyota Sienna
Honda Odyssey			Toyota Tundra

Reliable used cars

The following are all 1997 through 2004 models that showed better-than-average reliability in our latest survey. They are listed by price group and alphabetically within groups. Price ranges are what you'd be likely to pay for a typically equipped car with average mileage. All prices are rounded to the nearest $1,000.

LESS THAN $4,000

Chevrolet/Geo Prizm '97-98
Ford Escort '97, '99
Mazda B-Series (2WD) '97, **Protegé** '97-98
Mercury Tracer '97, '99
Nissan Sentra '97-98

$4,000-$6,000

Buick Century '97-98
Chevrolet Prizm '99-01
Ford Crown Victoria '98, **Ranger (2WD)** '97-98
Honda Civic '97-98
Mazda 626 '98, **B-Series (2WD)** '98-99, **Protegé** '99-00
Nissan Altima '97-98, **Frontier** '98, **Pickup** '97, **Sentra** '99
Saturn SL Sedan '02, **SW Wagon** '99
Subaru Impreza '97-98
Toyota Corolla '97-99, **Echo** '00

$6,000-$8,000

Acura Integra '97-98
Buick Century '01, **Regal** '99
Chevrolet Prizm '02
Ford Crown Victoria '99, **Escort** '02, **F-150** '97, **Mustang** '98-99, **Ranger (2WD)** '99-00
Honda Accord '97, **Civic** '99-00, **CR-V** '97
Infiniti I30 '97
Mazda 626 '00, **B-Series (2WD)** '00-01, **Millenia** '98, **MX-5 Miata** '97, **Protegé** '01
Mercury Grand Marquis '98-99
Mitsubishi Eclipse '00, **Galant** '99-00, **Lancer** '02
Nissan Altima '99-00, **Frontier** '99, **Maxima** '97
Saturn SC Coupe '02
Subaru Legacy/Outback (4-cyl.) '97-98
Toyota Avalon '97, **Camry** '97-98, **Celica** '97, **Corolla** '00-01, **Echo** '01-02, **RAV4** '97-99, **T100** '97, **Tacoma** '97

$8,000-$10,000

Acura CL '97-99, **Integra** '99, **TL** '97-98
Buick Century '02, **Regal** '01
Chrysler PT Cruiser '01
Ford Crown Victoria '00, **F-150** '98-99, **Focus** '03, **Ranger (2WD)** '01
Honda Accord '98-99, **Civic** '01, **CR-V** '98-99, **Odyssey** '97-98, **Prelude** '97-98
Hyundai Elantra '03
Infiniti G20 '99, **I30** '98-99
Lincoln Town Car '97-98
Mazda 626 '01, **Millenia** '99, **MX-5 Miata** '99, **Protegé** '02
Mercury Grand Marquis '00
Mitsubishi Galant '01-02
Nissan Altima '01, **Maxima** '98-99, **Pathfinder** '97-98
Saturn L-Series (4-cyl.) '02
Subaru Impreza '00, **Legacy/Outback (4-cyl.)** '99
Toyota 4Runner '97, **Avalon** '98, **Camry** '99, **Camry Solara** '99, **Corolla** '02, **Echo** '03, **Sienna** '98, **T100** '98, **Tacoma** '98-99

$10,000-$12,000

Acura Integra '00-01, **RL** '97, **TL** '99
Buick Century '03
Chrysler PT Cruiser '02
Ford Crown Victoria '02, **Focus** '04
Honda Accord '00, **Civic** '02, **CR-V** '00, **Insight** '00
Hyundai Elantra '04
Infiniti G20 '00, **Q45** '97, **QX4** '98
Lexus ES300 '97-98
Lincoln Town Car '99
Mazda 626 '02, **Millenia** '00, **MPV** '00-01, **MX-5 Miata** '00, **Protegé** '03
Mitsubishi Eclipse '01-02, **Galant** '03, **Montero Sport** '01
Nissan Frontier '00, **Pathfinder** '99, **Xterra** '00
Saturn L-Series (4-cyl.) '03
Subaru Impreza '01
Toyota 4Runner '98, **Avalon** '99, **Camry** '00-01, **Celica** '00, **Corolla** '03, **RAV4** '00, **Sienna** '99, **Tacoma** '00
Volvo S70 '99

$12,000-$14,000

Acura RL '98
Buick Regal '02
Chevrolet Impala '03
Chrysler PT Cruiser '03
Ford F-150 '00, **Mustang** '02

Honda Accord '01, **Civic** '03, **CR-V** '01
Hyundai Sonata '03
Infiniti I30 '00, **QX4** '99
Lexus ES300 '99
Lincoln Town Car '00
Mazda Millenia '01, **MX-5 Miata** '01
Mercury Grand Marquis '02
Mitsubishi Outlander '03
Nissan Frontier '01, **Maxima** '00-01, **Pathfinder** '00
Pontiac Grand Am '03-04, **Vibe** '03
Scion xB '04
Subaru Forester '01, **Impreza** '02
Toyota 4Runner '99, **Camry Solara** '00, **Celica** '01, **Corolla** '04, **RAV4** '01, **Sienna** '00, **Tundra** '00
Volvo S70 '00

$14,000-$16,000

Acura RL '99, **RSX** '02, **TL** '00
Buick Regal '03
Chrysler PT Cruiser '04
Ford F-150 '01
Honda Accord '02, **Civic** '04, **Odyssey** '00, **Prelude** '01
Hyundai Santa Fe '02, **Sonata** '04
Infiniti G20 '02, **Q45** '99
Mazda 3 '04, **Millenia** '02, **MX-5 Miata** '02-03
Mitsubishi Montero Sport '02
Nissan Frontier '02, **Maxima** '02
Pontiac Vibe '04
Subaru Forester '02, **Impreza** '03
Toyota Avalon '00, **Camry** '02, **Camry Solara** '01, **Celica** '02, **Land Cruiser** '97, **Matrix** '03-04, **RAV4** '02, **Sienna** '01, **Tacoma** '01-02

$16,000-$18,000

Acura RL '00, **RSX** '03, **TL** '01
Chevrolet Impala '04
Ford Escape '03, **F-150** '02
Honda CR-V '02, **Element** '03-04, **S2000** '00
Infiniti I30 '01
Lexus ES300 '00, **GS300/GS400** '98, **LS400** '97-98, **RX300** '99
Lincoln Town Car '01
Mazda Tribute '03
Nissan Altima '04, **Frontier** '03, **Pathfinder** '01, **Xterra** '02
Subaru Impreza '04, **Legacy/Outback (4-cyl.)** '03
Toyota 4Runner '00 **Avalon** '01, **Camry** '03, **Camry Solara** '02, **Celica** '03, **Prius** '01, **RAV4** '03-04, **Sienna** '02, **Tacoma** '03-04, **Tundra** '01

$18,000-$20,000

Ford Escape '04, **F-150** '03, **Mustang** '04
Honda Accord '03-04, **CR-V** '03-04, **Odyssey** '01
Hyundai Santa Fe '03-04
Infiniti I35 '02
Lexus ES300 '01, **GS300/GS400** '99, **IS300** '01
Mazda Tribute '04
Mitsubishi Endeavor '04
Nissan Maxima '03, **Pathfinder** '02
Subaru Forester '03-04, **Legacy/Outback (4-cyl.)** '04, **Outback (6-cyl.)** '01-02
Toyota Avalon '02, **Camry** '04, **Camry Solara**'03, **Highlander** '01, **Land Cruiser** '98, **Prius** '02-03, **Tundra** '02

$20,000-$24,000

Acura RSX '04, **TL** '03
BMW 3 Series (AWD) '01
Honda Odyssey '04, **S2000** '01-02
Infiniti I35 '03, **QX4** '01
Lexus GS300/GS400 '00 **IS300** '02, **LS400** '99, **RX300** '00
Lincoln Town Car '02
Nissan Maxima '04, **Pathfinder** '03-04
Porsche Boxster '99
Subaru Outback (6-cyl.) '03
Toyota 4Runner '01-02, **Avalon** '03-04, **Highlander** '02-03, **Land Cruiser** '99, **Prius** '04, **Tundra** '03-04

$24,000-$28,000

Acura MDX '01, **RL** '02, **TSX** '04
BMW 3 Series '02
Honda Odyssey '03, **Pilot** '03-04, **S2000** '03
Infiniti QX4 '02
Lexus ES300 '02, **GS300/GS430** '01, **IS300** '03, **LS400** '00, **LX470** '99, **RX300** '01
Nissan Murano '03-04
Saab 9-5 '04
Subaru Outback (6-cyl.) '04
Toyota 4Runner '03-04, **Highlander** '04, **Land Cruiser** '00, **Sequoia** '01

$28,000 and up

Acura MDX '02-04, **RL** '04
BMW 5 Series '01-03
Infiniti FX '03-04, **G35** '04
Lexus ES300 '03, **GS300/GS430** '02-04, **LS430** '01-04, **LX470** '00-03, **RX300/RX330** '02-04, **SC430** '02-03
Toyota Land Cruiser '01-03, **Sequoia** '02, '04

CR Bad Bets: Be especially careful

These models have shown several years of much-worse-than-average overall reliability in their 1997 to 2004 models. They are listed alphabetically.

Audi A6
BMW 7 Series
Chevrolet Astro
Chevrolet Blazer
Chevrolet Express 1500
Chevrolet S-10 (4WD)
Chevrolet TrailBlazer
Chrysler Town & Country (AWD)
Dodge Dakota (4WD)
Dodge Grand Caravan (AWD)
Dodge Neon
Ford Windstar
GMC Envoy
GMC Jimmy
GMC Safari
GMC Savana 1500
GMC Sonoma (4WD)
Jaguar S-Type
Jaguar X-Type
Jeep Grand Cherokee
Land Rover Discovery
Lincoln Navigator
Mercedes-Benz C-Class (V6)
Mercedes-Benz CLK
Mercedes-Benz M-Class
Mercedes-Benz S-Class
Oldsmobile Bravada
Oldsmobile Cutlass
Plymouth Neon
Pontiac Aztek
Saturn Vue
Volkswagen Golf
Volkswagen Jetta
Volkswagen New Beetle
Volvo S80

Used cars to avoid

Here are all the models that showed below-average reliability in our 2004 survey. They are listed alphabetically by make, model, and year.

Audi A4 (4-cyl.) '98-00, '02, **A4 (V6)** '97-00, '02-03, **A6/Avant** '99, **A6/Allroad** '01, '03, **A6 3.0** '98, '02, **A6** '00, **TT** '01-02

BMW 3 Series '04, **5 Series** '04, **7 Series** '97-98, '00, '02-03, **X5** '01, '04

Buick Century '04, **LeSabre** '04, **Park Avenue** '98, '04, **Rainier** '04, **Rendezvous** '02

Cadillac Catera '98, **CTS** '03, **DeVille** '97, '00-02, '04, **Escalade** '03, **Seville** '97, '99-03, **SRX** '04

Chevrolet Astro '97-03, **Avalanche** '02, **Blazer** '97-03, **C1500** '97, **Camaro** '97, '99, '01, **Cavalier Coupe & Convertible** '99-00, **Cavalier** '03, **Corvette** '00-02, '04, **Express 1500** '97-03, **Impala** '01, **K1500** 97-98, **Lumina** '97, '99, **Malibu** '97-01, '04, **Monte Carlo** '99, **S-10** '97-98, '00-03, **Silverado 1500 (4WD)** '02-03, **Suburban** '97-99, **Tahoe** '97-99, **TrailBlazer** '02-04, **Venture** '97-01, **Venture (reg.)** '02

Chrysler 300M '99, '03-04, **Cirrus** '97, **Concorde** '97-99, '02, **LHS** '97, '99, **Sebring Convertible** '97, '01, '03-04, **Sebring Sedan** '02, '04, **Town & Country** '97, '00-02, **Town & Country (AWD)** '98-99, **Voyager** '01-02

Dodge Caravan '97-98, '01-02, **Caravan (4-cyl.)** '99, **Caravan (V6)** '00, **Dakota (2WD)** '97-99, **Dakota (4WD)** '98-02, '04, **Durango** '98-00, **Grand Caravan** '97, '00-02, **Grand Caravan (AWD)** '98-99, **Intrepid** '97-99, **Neon** '97-02, **Ram 1500** '97, '02, **Ram 1500 (4WD)** '98-01, **Ram Van/Wagon 1500** '99, **Stratus (4-cyl.)** '98-00, **Stratus Sedan**

(V6) '97, '02, '04
Ford Contour (V6) '97-98, **Escape** '01, **Excursion** '01, '03, **Expedition** '03-04, **Explorer** '00, **Explorer (4WD)** '98, '02, **F-150 (4WD)** '04, **Focus** '00-01, **Focus Wagon** '04, **Ranger (4WD)** '97, '01-02, '04, **Windstar** '97-01

GMC Envoy '02-04, **Jimmy** '97-01, **Sierra 1500** '97, **Sierra 1500 (4WD)** '98, '02-03, **Sonoma** '97-98, '00-03, **Safari** '97-03, **Savana 1500** '97-03, **Suburban** '97-99, **Yukon** '97-99

Honda Passport '97-99

Hyundai Sonata '00, **Tiburon** '03, **XG350** '04

Infiniti M45 '03

Isuzu Rodeo '97-99

Jaguar S-Type '00-01, '03, **XJ Series** '98, '00, **X-Type** '02-03

Jeep Grand Cherokee '97-02, **Wrangler** '98, '03

Kia Sedona '02

Land Rover Discovery '00-01, '03, **Freelander** '02

Lexus GX470 '03

Lincoln Aviator '03-04, **LS** '00, '03, **Mark VIII** '98, **Navigator** '02-04

Mazda B-Series (4WD) '97, '01-02, '04, **MPV** '03-04, **RX-8** '04, **Tribute** '01, **Mazda6** '03-04

Mercedes-Benz C-Class (4-cyl.) '02, **C-Class (V6)** '01-04, **CLK** '99-00, '02-04, **E-Class** '99, '01-04, **E-Class (AWD)** '00, **M-Class** '98-04, **S-Class** '00, '02-03, **SL** '03

Mercury Cougar '99-01, **Mountaineer** '00, **Mountaineer (4WD)** '98, '02, **Mystique (V6)** '97-98

Mini Cooper '02-03

Mitsubishi Eclipse '97

Nissan 350Z '03, **Armada** '04, **Frontier** '04, **Quest** '04, **Sentra** '02-03

Oldsmobile 88 '98, **Alero** '99-01, **Aurora** '97, '01, **Bravada** '97-00, '02, **Cutlass** '97-99, **Cutlass Supreme** '97, **Silhouette** '97-01

Plymouth Breeze '98-00, **Grand Voyager** '97, '00, **Voyager** '97-98, **Voyager (4-cyl.)** '99, **Voyager (V6)** '00, **Neon** '97-00

Pontiac Aztek '01-03, **Bonneville** '98-02, **Firebird** '97, '99, '01, **Grand Am** '97-01, **Grand Prix** '97-98, **Grand Prix SC** '99-01, '04, **Sunfire Coupe & Convertible** '99-00, 03, **Trans Sport/Montana** '97-'01, **Montana (reg.)** '02

Porsche Boxster '01, '03, **Cayenne** '04

Saab 9-3 '03-04, **9-5** '99

Saturn Ion '03, **L-Series (V6)** '00-02, **SW Wagon** '00, **Vue** '02-04

Volkswagen Cabrio '99, '01-02, **EuroVan** '03, **Golf** '97- 03, **Jetta** '97-03, **New Beetle** '98-04, **Passat (4-cyl.)** '98-99, '01-02, **Passat (V6)** '97, '99-01, '04, **Passat (AWD)** '00-01, '04, **Passat W8** '03, **Touareg** '04

Volvo 960 '97, **V70/Cross Country** '98, '01, **Cross Country** '99-00, **V70** '02, **XC70** '03, **S60 (AWD)** '04, **S80** '99-03, **S90/V90** '97-98, **XC90** '03-04

DETAILED RELIABILITY

In the following pages, CONSUMER REPORTS provides you with reliability information on more than 200 vehicle models. Based on 810,000 responses to our 2004 annual subscriber survey, these charts show you how 1997 through 2004 models are holding up regarding 14 trouble spots.

To check a model's overall reliability, look at the Reliability Verdict. A key is included below.

To identify the most reliable models, look for those with a ✔, which means they had above-average reliability overall. Be wary of models with an ✘—they showed below-average reliability overall.

The Reliability Verdict is calculated from the problem rates for the 14 trouble spots and compared with the average for that model year. Extra weight is given to the engine, cooling system, transmission, and drive-system ratings.

To assess a model in more detail, look at the individual ratings for each of the 14 trouble spots. Refer to the "Trouble-Spot Ratings" key, below, to see each model's strengths and weaknesses.

To see whether a model's problems are unusually high or the result of normal aging, compare its trouble-spot ratings with those for an average model in the chart below. You'll see that older models generally have more problems than newer ones, and some trouble spots pose more problems than others.

The 2004 models were generally less than six months old at the time of the survey, with an average of about 3,000

How to read the charts

Reliability History

TROUBLE SPOTS	The Average Model							
	97	98	99	00	01	02	03	04
Engine	○	○	○	⊖	⊖	⊜	⊜	⊜
Cooling	○	○	⊖	⊖	⊜	⊜	⊜	⊜
Fuel	○	○	○	○	⊖	⊖	⊜	⊜
Ignition	⊖	⊖	⊖	⊖	⊜	⊜	⊜	⊜
Transmission	○	⊖	⊖	⊖	⊖	⊖	⊜	⊜
Electrical	◒	◒	◒	○	○	○	⊖	⊜
Air conditioning	○	○	⊖	⊖	⊖	⊖	⊜	⊜
Suspension	○	○	⊖	⊖	⊖	⊖	⊜	⊜
Brakes	◒	◒	○	○	○	⊖	⊖	⊜
Exhaust	⊖	⊖	⊜	⊜	⊜	⊜	⊜	⊜
Paint/trim/rust	○	⊖	⊖	⊖	⊖	⊖	⊜	⊜
Body Integrity	○	○	○	○	○	○	○	⊖
Power equipment	○	○	○	○	○	○	⊖	⊜
Body hardware	○	○	○	○	○	⊖	⊖	⊜
RELIABILITY VERDICT	–	–	–	–	–	–	–	–

RELIABILITY VERDICTS

Black check ✔
Better-than-average overall reliability.

Black dash –
Average overall reliability.

Black ✘
Below-average overall reliability.

TROUBLE-SPOT RATINGS

Scores for the individual trouble spots represent the percentage of survey respondents who reported problems occurring in the 12 months from April 1, 2003, through March 31, 2004, that were deemed serious because of cost, failure, compromised safety, or downtime.

- ⊜ 2.0% or less
- ⊖ 2.0% to 5.0%
- ○ 5.0% to 9.3%
- ◒ 9.3% to 14.8%
- ● More than 14.8%

miles. New vehicles should have few problems, so a score of ⊖ or worse is below average for most. A ○ may be cause for concern. With older vehicles, a ○ can be average; scores of ◒ or ● may not be unusual in categories such as electrical, brakes, and air conditioning.

Why does it look reliable but rate an ✘?

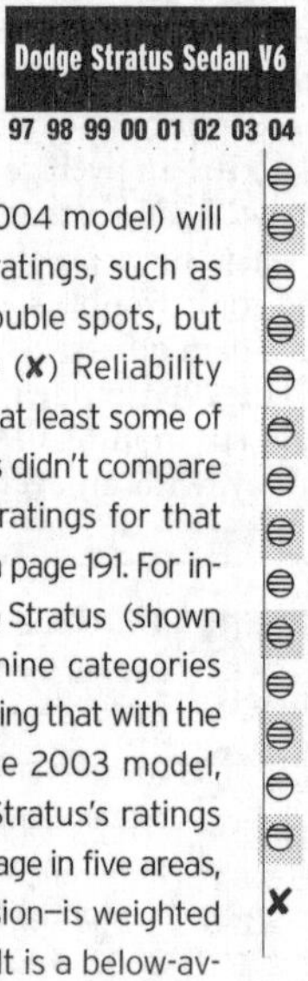

This is a frequently asked question about our reliability charts. Sometimes a newer vehicle (especially a 2004 model) will have seemingly high ratings, such as ⊜ and ⊖, in the 14 trouble spots, but gets a below-average (✘) Reliability Verdict. That's because at least some of the trouble-spot ratings didn't compare well with the average ratings for that model year, as shown on page 191. For instance, the 2004 Dodge Stratus (shown here) was rated ⊜ in nine categories and ⊖ in five. By comparing that with the ratings for the average 2003 model, you can see that the Stratus's ratings are worse than the average in five areas, one of which—transmission—is weighted more heavily. The result is a below-average (✘) Reliability Verdict.

What the trouble spots include

ENGINE: Pistons, rings, valves, block, heads, bearings, camshafts, gaskets, supercharger, turbocharger, cam belts and chains, oil pumps.

COOLING: Radiator, heater core, water pump, thermostat, hoses, intercooler, and plumbing.
FUEL: Fuel injection, computer and sensors, fuel pump, tank, emissions controls, check-engine light.
IGNITION: Spark plugs, coil, distributor, electronic ignition, sensors and modules, timing.
TRANSMISSION: Transaxle, gear selector and linkage, coolers, and lines. (We no longer provide separate data for manual transmissions since survey responses in this area are so few.)
ELECTRICAL: Starter, alternator, battery, horn, gauges, lights, wiring, and wiper motor.
AIR CONDITIONING: Compressor, condenser, evaporator, expansion valves, hoses, dryer, fans, electronics.
SUSPENSION: Steering linkage, power-steering gear, pump, coolers and lines, alignment and balance, springs and torsion bars, ball joints, bushings, shocks and struts, electronic or air suspension.
BRAKES: Hydraulic system, linings, rotors and drums, power boost, antilock system, parking brake, linkage.
EXHAUST: Manifold, muffler, catalytic converter, pipes.
PAINT/TRIM/RUST: Fading, discoloring, chalking, peeling, cracking paint; loose exterior trim or moldings; rust.
BODY INTEGRITY: Seals, weather stripping, air and water leaks, wind noise, rattles and squeaks.
POWER EQUIPMENT: Electronically operated accessories such as mirrors, sunroof, windows, door locks and seats, cruise control, audio system, navigational system.
BODY HARDWARE: Manual mirrors, sunroof; window, door, seat mechanisms; locks; safety belts; loose interior trim; glass defects.

Acura CL

TROUBLE SPOTS	97	98	99	00	01	02	03	04
Engine	⊖	⊖	⊜		⊜	⊜	⊖	
Cooling	⊜	⊜	⊜		⊜	⊜	⊜	
Fuel	⊖	⊜	⊖		⊜	⊜	⊜	
Ignition	⊖	⊜	⊖		⊜	⊜	⊜	
Transmission	⊖	⊜	⊖		●	◒	⊖	
Electrical	◒	○	○		⊖	⊖	⊖	
A/C	○	⊜	⊖		⊜	⊜	⊜	
Suspension	⊖	⊖	⊜		⊜	⊜	⊜	
Brakes	○	○	◒		○	⊖	⊜	
Exhaust	⊖	⊖	⊖		⊜	⊜	⊜	
Power equip.	●	◒	○		⊜	⊖	⊜	
Paint/trim/rust	⊖	⊖	⊜		⊖	⊖	⊜	
Integrity	⊖	⊜	⊖		○	○	⊖	
Hardware	⊖	⊜	⊖		⊖	⊖	⊜	
RELIABILITY VERDICT	✔	✔	✔		–	–	–	

Acura Integra, RSX

TROUBLE SPOTS	97	98	99	00	01	02	03	04
Engine	⊜	⊜	⊜	⊜	⊜	⊜	⊜	⊜
Cooling	○	○	⊖	⊜	⊜	⊜	⊜	⊜
Fuel	⊜	⊜	⊜	⊜	⊖	⊜	⊜	⊜
Ignition	⊜	⊜	⊜	⊜	⊜	⊜	⊜	⊜
Transmission	⊜	⊜	⊜	⊜	⊖	⊜	⊜	⊜
Electrical	⊜	⊖	⊜	⊜	⊖	⊖	⊜	⊜
A/C	⊖	⊜	⊖	⊜	⊖	⊜	⊜	⊜
Suspension	⊜	⊜	⊜	⊜	⊜	⊜	⊜	⊜
Brakes	○	⊖	○	⊜	⊖	⊖	⊖	⊜
Exhaust	○	⊖	⊖	⊜	⊜	⊜	⊜	⊜
Power equip.	○	⊖	⊖	⊖	○	⊜	⊜	⊜
Paint/trim/rust	⊖	⊖	⊜	⊜	○	⊖	⊜	⊜
Integrity	⊖	⊖	⊖	⊖	⊖	○	⊖	⊖
Hardware	⊖	⊖	⊖	⊖	⊖	⊖	⊜	⊜
RELIABILITY VERDICT	✔	✔	✔	✔	✔	✔	✔	✔

Acura MDX

TROUBLE SPOTS	97	98	99	00	01	02	03	04
Engine					⊜	⊜	⊜	⊜
Cooling					⊜	⊜	⊜	⊜
Fuel					⊖	⊜	⊜	⊜
Ignition					⊜	⊜	⊜	⊜
Transmission					⊖	⊖	⊜	⊜
Electrical					⊖	⊜	⊜	⊜
A/C					⊖	⊜	⊜	⊜
Suspension					⊖	⊖	⊜	⊜
Brakes					⊖	⊖	⊖	⊜
Exhaust					⊜	⊜	⊜	⊜
Power equip.					⊖	⊖	⊜	⊜
Paint/trim/rust					⊜	⊜	⊜	⊜
Integrity					⊖	⊖	⊖	⊖
Hardware					⊖	⊜	⊜	⊜
RELIABILITY VERDICT					✔	✔	✔	✔

Acura R

TROUBLE SPOTS	97	98	99	00	01	02	03	04
Engine	⊖	⊜	⊜	⊜	Insufficient data	⊜	Insufficient data	⊜
Cooling	⊖	⊖	⊖	⊜		⊜		⊜
Fuel	⊖	⊖	○	⊖		⊜		⊜
Ignition	⊜	⊜	⊜	⊜		⊖		⊜
Transmission	⊖	⊜	⊖	⊜		⊜		⊜
Electrical	⊖	⊖	⊖	⊖		⊖		⊜
A/C	⊖	⊖	⊜	⊜		⊜		⊜
Suspension	○	⊖	⊖	⊜		⊜		⊜
Brakes	◒	○	⊖	⊖		⊜		⊜
Exhaust	⊜	⊜	⊜	⊜		⊜		⊜
Power equip.	○	○	◒	⊖		⊖		⊜
Paint/trim/rust	○	⊜	⊖	⊜		⊜		⊖
Integrity	⊖	⊜	⊖	⊖		⊜		⊜
Hardware	⊖	⊖	○	⊖		⊜		⊜
RELIABILITY VERDICT	✔	✔	✔	✔		✔		✔

Acura TL

TROUBLE SPOTS	97	98	99	00	01	02	03	04
Engine	⊖	⊜	⊜	⊜	⊜	⊜	⊜	⊜
Cooling	⊖	⊜	⊜	⊜	⊜	⊜	⊜	⊜
Fuel	⊖	⊖	⊖	⊜	⊜	⊜	⊜	⊜
Ignition	⊜	⊜	⊖	⊜	⊜	⊜	⊜	⊜
Transmission	⊖	⊖	⊖	○	◒	◒	⊖	⊜
Electrical	◒	○	⊖	⊜	⊖	⊜	⊜	⊜
A/C	⊖	⊜	⊜	⊜	⊜	⊜	⊜	⊜
Suspension	⊖	⊖	⊜	⊜	⊜	⊜	⊜	⊖
Brakes	○	⊜	⊖	○	⊖	⊖	⊜	⊜
Exhaust	⊖	○	⊜	⊜	⊜	⊜	⊜	⊜
Power equip.	○	⊜	⊖	⊜	⊜	⊖	⊖	⊖
Paint/trim/rust	⊜	⊖	⊖	⊖	⊜	⊖	⊜	⊜
Integrity	⊖	⊜	⊖	⊖	⊖	⊖	⊖	⊖
Hardware	⊖	⊖	⊜	⊖	⊖	⊖	⊖	⊜
RELIABILITY VERDICT	✔	✔	✔	✔	✔	–	✔	–

Acura TSX

TROUBLE SPOTS	97	98	99	00	01	02	03	04
Engine								⊜
Cooling								⊜
Fuel								⊖
Ignition								⊖
Transmission								⊖
Electrical								⊖
A/C								⊜
Suspension								⊖
Brakes								⊜
Exhaust								⊜
Power equip.								⊖
Paint/trim/rust								⊖
Integrity								⊖
Hardware								⊖
RELIABILITY VERDICT								✔

Audi A4 4-cyl. AWD

TROUBLE SPOTS	97	98	99	00	01	02	03	04
Engine	Insufficient data	◒	◒	◒	○	○	⊜	⊜
Cooling		○	⊖	⊖	⊜	⊜	⊜	⊜
Fuel		○	○	◒	○	○	⊜	⊜
Ignition		⊖	○	⊖	●	◒	⊖	⊜
Transmission		⊖	⊜	⊖	⊜	⊜	⊜	⊜
Electrical		◒	◒	◒	◒	●	⊖	⊜
A/C		⊖	⊖	⊖	⊜	⊜	⊜	⊜
Suspension		◒	◒	⊖	⊖	⊜	⊜	⊜
Brakes		◒	●	○	○	⊖	⊜	⊜
Exhaust		⊜	⊖	⊖	⊜	⊜	⊜	⊜
Power equip.		○	○	○	○	○	⊖	⊜
Paint/trim/rust		○	⊖	⊜	⊜	⊜	⊜	⊜
Integrity		◒	○	⊖	⊜	⊖	⊜	⊜
Hardware		○	○	⊖	⊖	○	⊖	⊜
RELIABILITY VERDICT		✘	✘	✘	–	✘	–	–

Audi A4 V

TROUBLE SPOTS	97	98	99	00	01	02	03	04
Engine	○	●	◒	○	○	⊜	⊜	⊜
Cooling	●	◒	◒	◒	⊖	⊖	⊜	⊜
Fuel	○	○	○	○	○	○	⊖	⊜
Ignition	⊖	⊖	⊖	⊜	⊖	◒	⊖	⊜
Transmission	⊖	○	⊖	⊖	⊜	⊜	⊖	⊜
Electrical	◒	◒	◒	◒	○	●	○	⊖
A/C	◒	⊖	⊖	⊜	⊜	⊖	⊖	⊜
Suspension	●	●	○	⊖	⊖	⊜	⊜	⊜
Brakes	○	◒	◒	◒	○	⊖	⊜	⊜
Exhaust	○	⊖	⊜	○	⊜	⊖	⊜	⊜
Power equip.	◒	○	○	◒	◒	◒	○	⊜
Paint/trim/rust	○	◒	⊖	⊜	⊜	⊜	⊜	⊜
Integrity	○	◒	○	⊖	⊖	⊜	⊖	⊖
Hardware	○	○	○	⊖	○	⊖	⊖	⊜
RELIABILITY VERDICT	✘	✘	✘	✘	–	✘	✘	✔

Audi A6 sedan 2.7T	97	98	99	00	01	02	03	04
Engine				●	○	⊖	⊜	Insufficient data
Cooling				◒	⊜	⊜	⊜	
Fuel				◒	○	⊖	⊖	
Ignition				⊜	⊜	⊜	⊖	
Transmission				○	⊜	⊜	⊜	
Electrical				◒	○	○	⊖	
A/C				⊜	⊜	○	⊜	
Suspension				○	⊜	⊖	⊖	
Brakes				◒	●	○	⊜	
Exhaust				⊖	⊜	⊜	⊖	
Power equip.				◒	○	○	◒	
Paint/trim/rust				⊖	⊜	⊖	⊜	
Integrity				○	⊖	○	○	
Hardware				⊖	○	⊖	○	
RELIABILITY VERDICT				✗	✗	–	✗	

Audi A6 sedan 3.0	97	98	99	00	01	02	03	04
Engine	Insufficient data	●	◒	○	○	⊖	⊖	
Cooling		○	○	◒	⊜	⊖	⊜	
Fuel		◒	○	○	⊖	○	⊜	
Ignition		⊖	⊜	⊖	⊜	◒	⊖	
Transmission		⊖	○	⊖	⊜	⊖	⊜	
Electrical		●	●	◒	○	●	○	
A/C		○	⊖	⊖	⊜	⊖	⊜	
Suspension		●	◒	◒	⊖	⊖	⊖	
Brakes		◒	◒	○	○	●	○	
Exhaust		⊜	⊜	⊖	⊜	⊖	⊜	
Power equip.		●	●	◒	◒	◒	◒	
Paint/trim/rust		⊖	⊖	⊜	⊜	⊜	⊜	
Integrity		○	○	⊖	○	⊖	⊜	
Hardware		◒	○	⊖	○	⊖	⊜	
RELIABILITY VERDICT		✗	✗	✗	–	✗	✗	

Audi TT	97	98	99	00	01	02	03	04
Engine				⊖	⊖	⊜	Insufficient data	Insufficient data
Cooling				⊖	⊖	⊖		
Fuel				◒	◒	⊜		
Ignition				⊜	○	○		
Transmission				⊖	⊜	⊜		
Electrical				●	●	●		
A/C				○	⊜	⊖		
Suspension				⊖	⊜	⊖		
Brakes				○	⊜	⊜		
Exhaust				⊜	⊜	⊜		
Power equip.				◒	◒	○		
Paint/trim/rust				⊜	⊜	⊖		
Integrity				◒	◒	◒		
Hardware				○	○	◒		
RELIABILITY VERDICT				–	✗	✗		

BMW 3 Series	97	98	99	00	01	02	03	04
Engine	⊖	⊖	⊖	⊜	⊜	⊜	⊜	⊜
Cooling	◒	◒	⊖	⊖	⊖	⊜	⊜	⊜
Fuel	◒	○	⊖	⊖	⊖	⊜	⊜	⊖
Ignition	⊜	⊖	⊖	⊜	⊜	⊜	⊜	⊜
Transmission	⊜	⊜	⊖	⊖	⊜	⊜	⊖	⊖
Electrical	◒	●	◒	○	○	○	○	⊖
A/C	◒	○	○	○	⊖	⊜	⊜	⊜
Suspension	⊖	⊖	○	○	⊖	⊜	⊜	⊜
Brakes	○	○	○	○	⊖	⊖	⊜	⊜
Exhaust	⊖	⊖	⊜	⊜	⊜	⊜	⊜	⊜
Power equip.	○	●	◒	◒	◒	○	⊜	⊜
Paint/trim/rust	⊖	⊖	⊖	⊜	⊜	⊜	⊜	⊜
Integrity	○	○	○	◒	○	○	⊜	⊖
Hardware	○	○	○	○	○	○	⊖	⊖
RELIABILITY VERDICT	–	–	–	–	–	✓	–	✗

BMW 5 Series	97	98	99	00	01	02	03	04
Engine	○	⊖	⊖	⊜	⊖	⊜	⊜	⊜
Cooling	●	◒	○	○	⊖	⊜	⊜	⊜
Fuel	⊖	⊖	⊖	⊖	⊖	⊖	⊜	⊜
Ignition	⊜	⊖	⊜	⊜	⊜	⊜	⊖	⊜
Transmission	⊖	⊖	⊖	⊜	⊜	⊜	⊜	⊜
Electrical	●	◒	○	◒	◒	○	⊖	⊖
A/C	○	○	○	○	○	⊜	⊜	⊜
Suspension	○	○	⊖	⊖	⊜	⊜	⊜	⊜
Brakes	○	○	○	○	⊜	⊖	⊜	⊜
Exhaust	⊖	○	⊜	⊜	⊜	⊜	⊜	⊜
Power equip.	●	◒	○	○	○	⊖	⊜	○
Paint/trim/rust	⊖	⊜	⊖	⊖	⊖	⊜	⊜	⊜
Integrity	○	○	⊖	○	○	⊖	⊜	⊜
Hardware	◒	◒	○	⊖	⊖	⊖	⊜	⊖
RELIABILITY VERDICT	–	–	–	–	✓	✓	✓	✗

BMW 7 Series	97	98	99	00	01	02	03	04
Engine	◒	◒	Insufficient data	⊖	⊜	⊖	⊖	Insufficient data
Cooling	●	●		●	⊖	⊜	⊖	
Fuel	○	◒		○	⊜	○	⊖	
Ignition	⊜	⊖		⊜	⊜	◒	⊖	
Transmission	⊜	⊖		⊖	⊜	⊜	⊖	
Electrical	●	●		◒	○	●	●	
A/C	○	◒		○	○	⊖	⊖	
Suspension	◒	◒		○	⊖	⊜	○	
Brakes	◒	◒		⊖	⊜	⊖	⊖	
Exhaust	○	◒		⊜	⊜	⊜	⊜	
Power equip.	◒	●		●	○	●	●	
Paint/trim/rust	⊖	⊖		⊜	⊖	⊖	⊜	
Integrity	◒	◒		○	○	⊖	○	
Hardware	○	◒		○	○	○	○	
RELIABILITY VERDICT	✗	✗		✗	–	✗	✗	

BMW X5	97	98	99	00	01	02	03	04
Engine				Insufficient data	⊜	⊜	⊜	⊜
Cooling					○	⊜	⊜	⊜
Fuel					⊖	⊖	⊖	⊜
Ignition					⊜	⊜	⊜	⊜
Transmission					⊖	⊜	⊖	⊖
Electrical					●	◒	○	⊖
A/C					○	⊖	⊜	⊜
Suspension					○	⊖	⊜	⊜
Brakes					○	⊖	⊜	⊜
Exhaust					⊜	⊜	⊜	⊜
Power equip.					●	◒	○	⊖
Paint/trim/rust					⊖	⊖	⊜	⊜
Integrity					◒	○	⊖	⊖
Hardware					●	◒	⊖	⊖
RELIABILITY VERDICT					✗	–	–	✗

BMW Z3, Z4	97	98	99	00	01	02	03	04
Engine	⊖	⊖	⊖	⊖	⊜	Insufficient data	⊜	Insufficient data
Cooling	○	⊖	○	⊖	○		⊜	
Fuel	◒	○	⊖	○	⊖		⊖	
Ignition	⊖	⊜	⊜	⊜	⊜		⊜	
Transmission	⊖	⊜	⊜	⊖	⊜		⊜	
Electrical	○	◒	●	○	○		○	
A/C	◒	○	○	○	○		⊜	
Suspension	○	⊜	⊜	⊜	⊜		⊜	
Brakes	⊖	⊜	⊖	⊖	○		⊜	
Exhaust	⊖	○	⊜	⊜	⊜		⊜	
Power equip.	●	○	●	○	○		⊖	
Paint/trim/rust	●	○	◒	⊜	⊖		⊖	
Integrity	●	○	◒	○	○		⊖	
Hardware	◒	○	◒	●	○		⊖	
RELIABILITY VERDICT	–	✓	–	–	–		–	

Key to symbols as used below: ⊜ = fully lined circle, ⊖ = partly lined circle, ○ = open circle, ◒ = half-black circle, ● = black circle.

TROUBLE SPOTS	Buick Century 97	98	99	00	01	02	03	04	Buick LeSabre 97	98	99	00	01	02	03	04
Engine	⊖	○	◒	⊖	⊖	⊜	⊜	⊜	○	◒	○	⊖	⊖	⊖	⊜	⊜
Cooling	○	○	◒	⊖	⊜	⊜	⊜	⊜	◒	◒	○	⊖	⊖	⊖	⊖	⊜
Fuel	○	○	○	⊖	⊖	⊖	⊜	⊖	◒	◒	○	○	⊖	⊜	⊜	⊜
Ignition	⊖	⊜	⊖	⊜	⊜	⊜	⊜	⊜	⊖	⊖	⊖	⊖	⊜	⊜	⊜	⊜
Transmission	⊖	⊜	⊜	◒	⊖	⊜	⊜	⊜	○	○	○	⊖	○	⊜	⊜	⊜
Electrical	●	○	○	○	○	⊖	⊜	⊜	◒	◒	○	◒	○	⊖	⊖	⊖
A/C	⊖	⊜	⊖	⊖	⊜	⊜	⊜	⊜	○	⊖	⊜	⊜	⊜	⊜	⊜	⊜
Suspension	○	⊖	○	⊖	⊖	⊜	⊜	⊖	○	⊖	⊖	○	○	⊖	⊜	⊜
Brakes	◒	○	◒	○	⊖	⊖	⊜	⊜	◒	◒	◒	○	○	⊖	⊜	⊜
Exhaust	⊜	⊜	⊜	⊜	⊜	⊜	⊜	⊜	⊖	⊖	⊜	⊜	⊜	⊜	⊜	⊜
Power equip.	◒	◒	◒	○	⊖	⊖	⊜	⊖	○	○	○	●	○	○	⊖	⊖
Paint/trim/rust	○	⊖	⊖	⊖	⊜	⊜	⊜	⊖	⊖	⊖	⊖	⊖	⊖	⊜	⊜	⊜
Integrity	○	⊖	○	⊖	⊖	⊖	⊖	⊖	⊖	○	○	○	○	○	⊖	⊖
Hardware	⊖	⊖	○	⊖	⊜	⊖	⊜	⊖	⊖	⊖	⊖	⊖	⊖	⊜	⊜	⊖
RELIABILITY VERDICT	✔	✔	-	-	✔	✔	✔	✘	-	-	-	-	-	-	✔	✘

TROUBLE SPOTS	Buick Park Avenue 97	98	99	00	01	02	03	04	Buick Regal 97	98	99	00	01	02	03	04
Engine	◒	◒	⊖	⊖	⊜	⊜	⊜	⊜	◒	◒	⊖	⊖	⊜	⊜	⊜	Insufficient data
Cooling	○	○	⊜	⊖	⊖	⊖	⊜	⊜	◒	○	⊜	⊖	⊖	⊖	⊜	
Fuel	○	◒	◒	○	⊖	⊜	⊜	⊜	⊖	⊖	⊖	⊖	⊖	⊜	⊜	
Ignition	⊖	⊖	⊖	⊖	⊜	⊜	⊜	⊜	⊖	⊖	⊜	⊜	⊜	⊜	⊜	
Transmission	○	○	○	⊖	⊖	⊜	⊜	⊜	○	⊜	⊖	⊖	⊖	⊜	⊜	
Electrical	●	◒	◒	◒	◒	○	⊖	⊖	●	◒	◒	○	○	○	⊖	
A/C	○	⊖	⊖	⊖	⊜	⊜	⊜	⊜	○	○	○	⊖	⊜	⊜	⊜	
Suspension	○	○	○	⊖	○	⊖	⊖	⊖	◒	○	⊖	⊖	○	⊖	⊜	
Brakes	◒	◒	◒	◒	○	⊖	⊖	⊜	◒	○	○	○	○	⊖	⊜	
Exhaust	⊜	⊜	⊜	⊜	⊜	⊜	⊜	⊜	⊜	⊜	⊜	⊜	⊜	⊜	⊜	
Power equip.	◒	◒	◒	◒	○	○	⊖	⊖	◒	◒	◒	○	○	⊖	⊖	
Paint/trim/rust	○	⊖	⊖	⊖	⊜	⊜	⊜	⊜	⊖	⊖	⊖	⊖	⊜	⊜	⊜	
Integrity	○	○	○	⊖	○	○	⊖	○	◒	○	○	○	⊖	⊖	⊖	
Hardware	◒	◒	◒	◒	○	○	⊖	⊜	○	⊖	○	⊖	⊖	⊜	⊜	
RELIABILITY VERDICT	-	✘	-	-	-	-	-	✘	✘	-	✔	-	✔	✔	✔	

TROUBLE SPOTS	Buick Rendezvous 97	98	99	00	01	02	03	04	Cadillac Catera, CTS 97	98	99	00	01	02	03	04
Engine						⊜	⊜	⊜	Insufficient data	●	Insufficient data	Insufficient data	Insufficient data		⊜	⊜
Cooling						⊜	⊜	⊜		●					⊖	⊜
Fuel						⊖	⊖	⊜		◒					⊖	⊜
Ignition						⊜	⊜	⊜		○					⊜	⊜
Transmission						⊖	⊜	⊜		◒					⊜	⊜
Electrical						○	○	⊜		●					○	⊜
A/C						○	⊜	⊜		○					⊜	⊜
Suspension						⊖	⊜	⊜		○					⊖	⊜
Brakes						⊖	⊖	⊜		◒					⊜	⊜
Exhaust						⊜	⊜	⊜		⊜					⊜	⊜
Power equip.						○	⊖	⊖		◒					○	⊜
Paint/trim/rust						⊜	⊜	⊜		⊖					⊖	⊜
Integrity						○	⊖	⊜		⊖					○	⊜
Hardware						○	⊖	⊜		◒					⊖	⊜
RELIABILITY VERDICT						✘	-	✔		✘					✘	✔

TROUBLE SPOTS	Cadillac DeVille 97	98	99	00	01	02	03	04	Cadillac Escalade 97	98	99	00	01	02	03	04
Engine	◒	○	○	○	◒	⊖	⊖	⊜			Insufficient data	Insufficient data		⊜	⊜	⊜
Cooling	●	○	⊖	○	⊖	○	⊜	⊜						⊜	⊜	⊜
Fuel	●	○	○	◒	○	○	⊖	⊜						⊜	⊜	⊜
Ignition	◒	⊖	⊖	○	⊖	⊖	⊖	⊜						⊜	⊜	⊜
Transmission	⊖	○	⊖	○	⊖	⊜	⊜	⊜						⊖	⊖	⊜
Electrical	●	●	◒	◒	○	○	○	⊜						○	○	⊜
A/C	●	●	○	○	⊖	⊖	⊜	⊜						⊜	⊖	⊜
Suspension	○	○	○	○	○	○	⊖	⊜						⊖	⊖	⊜
Brakes	◒	◒	◒	◒	○	○	⊖	⊜						⊖	⊜	⊜
Exhaust	⊜	⊜	⊜	⊖	⊜	⊜	⊜	⊜						⊜	⊜	⊜
Power equip.	◒	◒	○	◒	○	○	⊖	⊖						○	○	○
Paint/trim/rust	○	○	○	⊖	⊜	⊜	⊜	⊜						⊖	⊜	⊜
Integrity	○	○	○	○	⊖	⊖	⊖	⊖						○	⊖	⊖
Hardware	⊖	⊖	⊖	○	⊖	⊖	⊖	⊖						○	⊖	⊜
RELIABILITY VERDICT	✘	-	-	✘	✘	✘	-	✘						-	✘	✔

Cadillac SRX

Trouble spots	97	98	99	00	01	02	03	04
Engine								⊜
Cooling								⊜
Fuel								⊜
Ignition								⊜
Transmission								⊜
Electrical								⊜
A/C								⊜
Suspension								⊜
Brakes								⊜
Exhaust								⊜
Power equip.								⊖
Paint/trim/rust								⊜
Integrity								⊖
Hardware								⊖
RELIABILITY VERDICT								✗

Cadillac Seville

Trouble spots	97	98	99	00	01	02	03	04
Engine	●	◒	◒	○	○	⊖	⊖	
Cooling	◒	○	○	⊖	⊖	⊜	⊜	
Fuel	◒	○	○	○	○	⊖	⊖	
Ignition	○	⊜	○	○	⊖	⊖	⊜	
Transmission	⊖	⊖	⊖	⊖	⊜	⊜	⊜	
Electrical	●	◒	◒	◒	◒	◒	○	
A/C	●	○	○	⊖	⊖	⊖	⊜	
Suspension	◒	◒	○	◒	●	◒	○	
Brakes	○	◒	◒	◒	◒	◒	⊖	
Exhaust	⊜	⊜	⊜	⊖	⊜	⊜	⊜	
Power equip.	◒	◒	○	○	◒	◒	○	
Paint/trim/rust	⊖	⊜	⊖	○	⊜	⊖	⊜	
Integrity	○	◒	◒	◒	◒	○	⊖	
Hardware	○	○	○	○	⊖	○	○	
RELIABILITY VERDICT	✗	-	✗	✗	✗	✗	✗	

Chevrolet (Geo) Prizm

Trouble spots	97	98	99	00	01	02	03	04
Engine	⊜	⊜	⊜	⊖	⊜	⊜		
Cooling	⊜	⊜	⊜	⊜	⊜	⊜		
Fuel	⊜	⊖	⊖	○	⊖	⊜		
Ignition	⊜	⊜	⊜	⊜	⊜	⊜		
Transmission	⊜	⊜	⊜	⊜	⊜	⊜		
Electrical	○	○	⊖	⊖	⊖	⊖		
A/C	⊜	○	⊖	⊖	⊜	⊜		
Suspension	⊜	⊖	⊖	⊜	⊖	⊖		
Brakes	⊜	⊜	⊖	⊖	⊜	⊖		
Exhaust	⊜	⊜	⊜	⊜	⊜	⊜		
Power equip.	⊖	⊜	⊜	⊜	⊜	⊜		
Paint/trim/rust	○	⊖	⊖	⊜	⊖	⊜		
Integrity	○	⊖	⊖	⊖	⊖	⊖		
Hardware	○	○	○	⊜	⊜	⊖		
RELIABILITY VERDICT	✓	✓	✓	✓	✓	✓		

Chevrolet (Geo) Tracker

Trouble spots	97	98	99	00	01	02	03	04
Engine	○	Insufficient data	○	⊖	○	⊖	⊜	Insufficient data
Cooling	⊖		⊜	⊜	⊜	⊜	⊜	
Fuel	◒		○	○	⊖	⊜	⊜	
Ignition	⊜		⊖	⊜	⊖	⊜	⊖	
Transmission	○		○	⊜	⊖	⊜	⊜	
Electrical	○		○	○	⊖	⊖	⊖	
A/C	○		◒	○	○	⊜	⊖	
Suspension	⊜		⊖	⊜	⊖	⊜	⊜	
Brakes	○		○	○	○	⊖	⊖	
Exhaust	○		⊖	⊜	⊜	⊜	⊜	
Power equip.	⊜		⊖	○	⊖	○	⊜	
Paint/trim/rust	◒		○	○	○	⊖	⊜	
Integrity	●		◒	◒	○	○	⊖	
Hardware	○		⊖	○	⊜	⊜	⊖	
RELIABILITY VERDICT	-		-	-	-	✓	-	

Chevrolet Astro

Trouble spots	97	98	99	00	01	02	03	04
Engine	◒	○	⊖	⊖	○	⊖	⊜	Insufficient data
Cooling	◒	◒	○	⊖	⊜	⊜	⊜	
Fuel	●	◒	◒	○	⊜	⊖	⊜	
Ignition	⊖	○	⊖	⊜	⊜	⊖	⊜	
Transmission	◒	◒	◒	⊖	⊜	⊖	⊖	
Electrical	●	●	●	●	○	◒	⊖	
A/C	●	●	○	⊖	⊖	⊜	⊜	
Suspension	◒	◒	○	○	○	○	○	
Brakes	◒	●	◒	●	◒	◒	○	
Exhaust	⊖	⊖	⊜	⊖	⊜	⊖	⊜	
Power equip.	●	●	●	●	◒	●	⊖	
Paint/trim/rust	○	◒	○	⊖	○	⊖	⊜	
Integrity	●	●	●	●	◒	●	●	
Hardware	●	●	●	●	●	◒	○	
RELIABILITY VERDICT	✗	✗	✗	✗	✗	✗	✗	

Chevrolet Avalanche

Trouble spots	97	98	99	00	01	02	03	04
Engine						⊜	⊜	⊜
Cooling						⊜	⊜	⊜
Fuel						⊖	⊜	⊜
Ignition						⊜	⊜	⊜
Transmission						⊖	⊜	⊜
Electrical						⊖	⊖	⊜
A/C						⊖	⊖	⊜
Suspension						⊖	⊖	⊜
Brakes						○	⊜	⊜
Exhaust						⊜	⊜	⊜
Power equip.						○	⊖	⊜
Paint/trim/rust						○	⊖	⊜
Integrity						◒	○	⊜
Hardware						○	⊖	⊖
RELIABILITY VERDICT						✗	-	-

Chevrolet Blazer

Trouble spots	97	98	99	00	01	02	03	04
Engine	◒	○	○	○	○	⊖	⊜	Insufficient data
Cooling	●	◒	◒	⊖	⊖	⊜	⊖	
Fuel	●	○	○	○	○	⊖	⊖	
Ignition	○	⊖	⊖	⊖	⊖	⊜	⊜	
Transmission	●	◒	○	○	○	⊖	⊖	
Electrical	●	●	●	●	●	◒	○	
A/C	●	◒	○	⊖	⊖	⊖	⊖	
Suspension	◒	◒	◒	◒	○	○	⊖	
Brakes	●	◒	◒	◒	○	○	⊖	
Exhaust	⊖	⊖	⊖	⊖	⊖	⊜	⊜	
Power equip.	◒	◒	○	◒	○	○	⊖	
Paint/trim/rust	○	⊜	○	○	⊖	○	⊜	
Integrity	◒	●	●	◒	◒	◒	◒	
Hardware	●	●	◒	◒	○	○	○	
RELIABILITY VERDICT	✗	✗	✗	✗	✗	✗	✗	

Chevrolet Camaro

Trouble spots	97	98	99	00	01	02	03	04
Engine	◒	⊖	○	⊖	⊖	⊜		
Cooling	●	⊖	○	⊜	⊜	⊜		
Fuel	◒	○	○	○	⊖	⊜		
Ignition	○	⊖	⊖	⊜	⊖	⊜		
Transmission	○	○	⊖	⊖	○	⊖		
Electrical	●	●	●	◒	◒	⊖		
A/C	○	○	⊖	⊖	⊜	⊜		
Suspension	⊖	⊖	○	⊖	⊖	⊖		
Brakes	○	◒	●	○	◒	◒		
Exhaust	⊖	⊜	⊖	○	⊖	⊜		
Power equip.	●	○	●	◒	◒	○		
Paint/trim/rust	⊖	⊖	⊜	○	⊜	⊜		
Integrity	◒	○	●	◒	●	◒		
Hardware	⊖	○	⊖	○	○	⊖		
RELIABILITY VERDICT	✗	-	✗	-	✗	-		

Chevrolet Cavalier Sedan

TROUBLE SPOTS	97	98	99	00	01	02	03	04
Engine	○	⊖	○	○	○	⊖	⊖	Insufficient data
Cooling	○	○	⊖	⊖	⊖	⊖	⊖	
Fuel	○	○	○	○	○	○	⊖	
Ignition	⊖	○	◒	⊖	⊖	⊖	⊖	
Transmission	⊖	⊖	⊖	⊖	⊖	⊖	⊖	
Electrical	◒	●	◒	◒	◒	○	◒	
A/C	◒	○	⊖	⊖	⊖	⊖	⊖	
Suspension	○	○	⊖	○	○	⊖	⊖	
Brakes	◒	●	◒	◒	◒	○	⊖	
Exhaust	⊖	⊖	⊖	⊖	⊖	⊖	⊖	
Power equip.	○	○	○	○	⊖	○	⊖	
Paint/trim/rust	○	○	○	⊖	○	⊖	⊖	
Integrity	○	○	○	◒	◒	○	○	
Hardware	○	○	○	○	○	⊖	⊖	
RELIABILITY VERDICT	-	-	-	-	-	-	✗	

Chevrolet Corvette

TROUBLE SPOTS	97	98	99	00	01	02	03	04
Engine	Insufficient data	⊖	⊖	⊖	⊖	⊖	⊖	⊖
Cooling		⊖	⊖	⊖	⊖	⊖	⊖	⊖
Fuel		○	⊖	◒	○	◒	⊖	⊖
Ignition		⊖	⊖	⊖	⊖	⊖	⊖	⊖
Transmission		◒	⊖	⊖	⊖	⊖	⊖	⊖
Electrical		●	●	●	●	●	⊖	⊖
A/C		◒	⊖	⊖	⊖	⊖	⊖	⊖
Suspension		⊖	○	◒	⊖	⊖	⊖	⊖
Brakes		○	○	⊖	○	⊖	⊖	⊖
Exhaust		⊖	○	⊖	⊖	⊖	⊖	⊖
Power equip.		●	◒	●	●	○	⊖	⊖
Paint/trim/rust		⊖	⊖	⊖	⊖	⊖	⊖	⊖
Integrity		●	○	◒	◒	◒	○	○
Hardware		○	⊖	◒	◒	⊖	⊖	⊖
RELIABILITY VERDICT		-	✓	✗	✗	✗	-	✗

Chevrolet Impala

TROUBLE SPOTS	97	98	99	00	01	02	03	04
Engine				⊖	⊖	⊖	⊖	⊖
Cooling				○	○	⊖	⊖	⊖
Fuel				○	⊖	⊖	⊖	⊖
Ignition				⊖	⊖	⊖	⊖	⊖
Transmission				⊖	○	⊖	⊖	⊖
Electrical				○	○	○	⊖	⊖
A/C				⊖	⊖	⊖	⊖	⊖
Suspension				◒	◒	⊖	⊖	⊖
Brakes				◒	◒	○	⊖	⊖
Exhaust				⊖	⊖	⊖	⊖	⊖
Power equip.				○	⊖	⊖	⊖	⊖
Paint/trim/rust				⊖	⊖	⊖	⊖	⊖
Integrity				○	○	⊖	⊖	⊖
Hardware				⊖	⊖	⊖	⊖	⊖
RELIABILITY VERDICT				-	✗	-	✓	✓

Chevrolet Malibu

TROUBLE SPOTS	97	98	99	00	01	02	03	04
Engine	●	◒	◒	○	○	⊖	⊖	⊖
Cooling	◒	●	●	○	○	⊖	⊖	⊖
Fuel	◒	○	○	◒	○	⊖	⊖	⊖
Ignition	○	⊖	⊖	⊖	⊖	⊖	⊖	⊖
Transmission	⊖	⊖	⊖	⊖	⊖	⊖	⊖	⊖
Electrical	●	●	●	●	●	⊖	⊖	⊖
A/C	◒	●	◒	◒	⊖	⊖	⊖	⊖
Suspension	●	◒	○	⊖	⊖	⊖	⊖	○
Brakes	●	●	●	●	●	●	○	⊖
Exhaust	⊖	⊖	⊖	⊖	⊖	⊖	⊖	⊖
Power equip.	○	○	○	⊖	○	⊖	⊖	⊖
Paint/trim/rust	○	○	○	⊖	⊖	⊖	⊖	⊖
Integrity	◒	◒	○	○	⊖	⊖	⊖	⊖
Hardware	○	○	○	⊖	○	⊖	⊖	⊖
RELIABILITY VERDICT	✗	✗	✗	✗	✗	-	✓	✗

Chevrolet Monte Carlo

TROUBLE SPOTS	97	98	99	00	01	02	03	04
Engine	◒	○	○	⊖	⊖	⊖	⊖	Insufficient data
Cooling	○	○	●	○	○	⊖	⊖	
Fuel	●	◒	◒	○	○	⊖	⊖	
Ignition	⊖	⊖	⊖	⊖	⊖	⊖	⊖	
Transmission	○	⊖	⊖	○	⊖	⊖	⊖	
Electrical	◒	●	◒	○	◒	○	⊖	
A/C	○	○	⊖	⊖	⊖	⊖	⊖	
Suspension	●	◒	⊖	○	○	⊖	⊖	
Brakes	◒	●	◒	○	○	○	⊖	
Exhaust	⊖	⊖	⊖	⊖	⊖	⊖	⊖	
Power equip.	◒	◒	◒	◒	○	○	⊖	
Paint/trim/rust	○	○	⊖	⊖	⊖	⊖	⊖	
Integrity	○	○	○	⊖	⊖	⊖	⊖	
Hardware	○	◒	○	⊖	⊖	⊖	⊖	
RELIABILITY VERDICT	-	-	✗	-	-	-	✓	

Chevrolet S-10 V6 2WD, Colorado

TROUBLE SPOTS	97	98	99	00	01	02	03	04
Engine	○	○	⊖	⊖	⊖	⊖	⊖	⊖
Cooling	◒	◒	○	⊖	⊖	⊖	⊖	⊖
Fuel	◒	⊖	◒	⊖	○	⊖	⊖	⊖
Ignition	⊖	⊖	⊖	⊖	⊖	⊖	⊖	⊖
Transmission	○	○	⊖	⊖	⊖	⊖	⊖	⊖
Electrical	●	●	○	○	○	○	○	⊖
A/C	●	●	◒	○	⊖	⊖	⊖	⊖
Suspension	⊖	⊖	⊖	⊖	⊖	⊖	⊖	⊖
Brakes	◒	○	○	○	◒	⊖	⊖	⊖
Exhaust	⊖	⊖	⊖	⊖	⊖	⊖	⊖	⊖
Power equip.	⊖	⊖	⊖	⊖	⊖	⊖	⊖	⊖
Paint/trim/rust	⊖	○	⊖	⊖	⊖	⊖	⊖	⊖
Integrity	●	●	◒	○	◒	◒	○	⊖
Hardware	○	●	◒	◒	◒	○	⊖	⊖
RELIABILITY VERDICT	✗	✗	-	-	-	-	✗	✓

Chevrolet Silverado 1500 2WD

TROUBLE SPOTS	97	98	99	00	01	02	03	04
Engine			⊖	⊖	⊖	⊖	⊖	⊖
Cooling			⊖	⊖	⊖	⊖	⊖	⊖
Fuel			◒	○	⊖	⊖	⊖	⊖
Ignition			⊖	⊖	⊖	⊖	⊖	⊖
Transmission			⊖	⊖	⊖	⊖	⊖	⊖
Electrical			○	○	○	⊖	⊖	⊖
A/C			⊖	⊖	⊖	⊖	⊖	⊖
Suspension			⊖	⊖	○	○	○	⊖
Brakes			●	○	○	⊖	⊖	⊖
Exhaust			⊖	⊖	⊖	⊖	⊖	⊖
Power equip.			○	○	⊖	⊖	⊖	⊖
Paint/trim/rust			⊖	⊖	⊖	⊖	⊖	⊖
Integrity			◒	○	○	○	○	⊖
Hardware			○	⊖	○	⊖	⊖	⊖
RELIABILITY VERDICT			-	✓	✓	-	-	-

Chevrolet Silverado 1500 4WD

TROUBLE SPOTS	97	98	99	00	01	02	03	04
Engine			⊖	⊖	⊖	⊖	⊖	⊖
Cooling			⊖	⊖	⊖	⊖	⊖	⊖
Fuel			○	○	⊖	⊖	⊖	⊖
Ignition			⊖	⊖	⊖	⊖	⊖	⊖
Transmission			⊖	⊖	⊖	○	⊖	⊖
Electrical			○	○	⊖	⊖	⊖	⊖
A/C			⊖	⊖	⊖	⊖	⊖	⊖
Suspension			○	○	○	○	⊖	⊖
Brakes			●	◒	○	⊖	⊖	⊖
Exhaust			⊖	⊖	⊖	⊖	⊖	⊖
Power equip.			○	⊖	⊖	⊖	⊖	⊖
Paint/trim/rust			⊖	⊖	⊖	⊖	⊖	⊖
Integrity			◒	◒	○	○	○	⊖
Hardware			○	○	⊖	○	⊖	⊖
RELIABILITY VERDICT			-	-	-	✗	✗	-

Chevrolet Suburban	97	98	99	00	01	02	03	04
Engine	◒	○	○	⊜	⊖	⊜	⊜	⊜
Cooling	●	◒	◒	⊜	⊜	⊜	⊜	⊜
Fuel	◒	○	◒	○	○	⊖	⊖	⊜
Ignition	⊖	⊖	⊖	⊜	⊖	⊜	⊜	⊜
Transmission	◒	○	○	⊖	⊖	⊖	⊜	⊜
Electrical	●	●	●	○	○	⊖	○	⊜
A/C	●	◒	○	⊖	⊖	⊖	⊖	⊜
Suspension	◒	○	○	○	⊜	○	⊖	⊜
Brakes	●	●	●	◒	○	⊖	⊜	⊜
Exhaust	⊖	⊖	⊖	⊜	⊜	⊜	⊜	⊜
Power equip.	○	○	●	●	○	⊖	○	⊜
Paint/trim/rust	⊖	⊖	⊜	⊜	⊜	⊜	⊜	⊜
Integrity	◒	○	◒	○	○	○	⊖	⊜
Hardware	◒	◒	◒	○	○	⊖	⊖	⊜
RELIABILITY VERDICT	✗	✗	✗	-	-	-	-	-

Chevrolet Tahoe	97	98	99	00	01	02	03	04
Engine	◒	◒	○	⊖	⊜	⊜	⊜	⊜
Cooling	●	◒	○	⊖	⊜	⊜	⊜	⊜
Fuel	◒	◒	○	○	⊖	⊖	⊖	⊜
Ignition	⊖	⊖	⊖	⊜	⊜	⊜	⊜	⊜
Transmission	◒	○	⊖	⊖	⊖	⊖	⊜	⊜
Electrical	●	●	●	○	○	⊖	○	⊜
A/C	◒	○	○	⊖	⊖	⊖	⊖	⊜
Suspension	◒	◒	○	○	⊖	○	⊖	⊜
Brakes	●	●	●	◒	○	⊖	⊜	⊜
Exhaust	⊖	⊖	⊖	⊜	⊜	⊜	⊜	⊜
Power equip.	○	○	○	◒	○	⊖	○	⊜
Paint/trim/rust	⊜	⊖	⊜	⊖	⊜	⊜	⊜	⊜
Integrity	○	○	○	○	○	○	⊖	⊜
Hardware	○	○	○	○	○	⊖	⊖	⊜
RELIABILITY VERDICT	✗	✗	✗	-	-	-	-	-

Chevrolet TrailBlazer	97	98	99	00	01	02	03	04
Engine						⊖	⊜	⊜
Cooling						⊜	⊜	⊜
Fuel						⊖	⊖	⊜
Ignition						⊖	⊜	⊜
Transmission						⊖	⊜	⊜
Electrical						●	○	⊖
A/C						⊖	◒	⊜
Suspension						⊖	⊜	⊜
Brakes						⊖	⊜	⊜
Exhaust						⊜	⊜	⊜
Power equip.						◒	⊖	⊖
Paint/trim/rust						⊖	⊖	⊜
Integrity						◒	◒	⊖
Hardware						○	○	⊖
RELIABILITY VERDICT						✗	✗	✗

Chevrolet Venture (ext.) 2WD	97	98	99	00	01	02	03	04
Engine	●	●	●	○	○	⊜	⊜	⊜
Cooling	●	◒	●	○	⊖	⊜	⊜	⊜
Fuel	◒	○	○	○	⊖	⊖	⊜	⊜
Ignition	⊜	⊖	⊜	⊜	⊜	⊜	⊜	⊜
Transmission	○	⊖	◒	○	○	⊜	⊜	⊜
Electrical	●	◒	◒	●	◒	⊖	⊖	⊜
A/C	○	○	⊖	⊖	○	⊖	⊜	⊜
Suspension	◒	○	⊖	○	○	⊖	⊜	⊜
Brakes	◒	◒	●	◒	◒	⊖	⊜	⊜
Exhaust	⊜	⊜	⊜	⊜	⊜	⊜	⊜	⊜
Power equip.	●	●	●	●	◒	○	○	⊖
Paint/trim/rust	○	⊖	⊖	⊖	⊖	⊜	⊜	⊜
Integrity	●	◒	◒	◒	◒	◒	○	⊖
Hardware	●	◒	◒	◒	○	○	⊖	⊖
RELIABILITY VERDICT	✗	✗	✗	✗	✗	-	-	-

Chrysler (Plymouth) Voyager V6	97	98	99	00	01	02	03	04
Engine	◒	◒	○	⊖	⊜	⊜	⊜	
Cooling	◒	○	⊖	⊖	⊜	⊜	⊜	
Fuel	○	⊖	⊖	⊖	⊖	⊜	⊜	
Ignition	⊖	⊖	⊖	⊖	⊜	⊜	⊜	
Transmission	◒	◒	●	●	⊖	○	⊖	
Electrical	●	◒	○	○	◒	○	⊖	
A/C	●	◒	○	○	○	⊖	⊜	
Suspension	○	○	○	⊖	◒	○	⊜	
Brakes	●	●	●	●	◒	○	⊖	
Exhaust	⊜	⊜	⊜	⊜	⊜	⊜	⊜	
Power equip.	○	○	○	○	●	○	⊖	
Paint/trim/rust	○	⊖	⊖	⊖	⊖	⊖	⊖	
Integrity	◒	○	○	○	○	○	⊖	
Hardware	○	○	○	○	○	⊖	⊖	
RELIABILITY VERDICT	✗	✗	-	✗	✗	✗	-	

Chrysler 300M	97	98	99	00	01	02	03	04
Engine			⊖	⊜	⊜	⊖	⊜	⊜
Cooling			⊖	⊜	⊜	⊜	⊜	⊜
Fuel			⊖	⊖	⊖	⊖	⊖	⊜
Ignition			⊖	⊜	⊜	⊜	⊖	⊜
Transmission			◒	⊖	⊖	⊖	○	⊜
Electrical			●	○	○	⊖	⊖	⊜
A/C			●	○	⊖	⊖	⊜	⊜
Suspension			○	○	⊖	⊜	⊜	⊜
Brakes			○	○	○	○	⊜	⊜
Exhaust			⊜	⊜	⊜	⊜	⊜	⊜
Power equip.			●	●	○	○	⊖	⊖
Paint/trim/rust			⊖	⊖	⊖	⊖	⊖	⊖
Integrity			◒	●	○	○	○	⊖
Hardware			◒	◒	⊖	⊖	⊖	⊖
RELIABILITY VERDICT			✗	-	✓	-	✗	✗

Chrysler Cirrus	97	98	99	00	01	02	03	04
Engine	◒	○	⊖	⊖				
Cooling	◒	⊖	⊜	⊜				
Fuel	◒	⊖	○	○				
Ignition	⊖	⊜	⊖	⊖				
Transmission	◒	○	◒	◒				
Electrical	◒	⊖	○	○				
A/C	◒	○	⊖	⊖				
Suspension	◒	○	○	○				
Brakes	●	◒	◒	◒				
Exhaust	⊜	⊜	⊜	⊜				
Power equip.	○	○	○	○				
Paint/trim/rust	○	○	○	⊖				
Integrity	○	○	⊖	○				
Hardware	○	⊖	⊖	○				
RELIABILITY VERDICT	✗	✓	-	-				

Chrysler Concorde	97	98	99	00	01	02	03	04
Engine	○	○	⊖	⊖	⊖	⊖	⊖	⊜
Cooling	●	○	○	⊜	⊖	⊜	⊜	⊜
Fuel	◒	○	⊖	⊖	⊖	○	⊜	⊜
Ignition	⊖	⊖	⊖	⊖	⊜	⊜	⊜	⊜
Transmission	○	◒	◒	⊖	⊖	○	⊖	⊜
Electrical	○	●	◒	○	⊜	⊖	⊖	⊜
A/C	●	●	●	◒	⊜	⊖	⊜	⊜
Suspension	◒	○	○	○	⊖	⊖	⊜	⊜
Brakes	◒	◒	⊖	○	⊜	⊖	⊜	⊜
Exhaust	⊜	⊖	⊜	⊜	⊜	⊜	⊜	⊜
Power equip.	⊖	●	●	●	⊜	⊖	⊜	⊜
Paint/trim/rust	◒	◒	○	○	⊖	⊖	⊖	⊜
Integrity	○	●	●	◒	⊖	○	⊖	⊖
Hardware	○	◒	◒	○	⊖	○	⊜	⊜
RELIABILITY VERDICT	✗	✗	✗	-	✓	✗	-	-

Chrysler PT Cruiser

TROUBLE SPOTS	97	98	99	00	01	02	03	04
Engine					⊜	⊜	⊜	⊜
Cooling					⊖	⊜	⊜	⊜
Fuel					⊖	⊖	⊖	⊖
Ignition					⊜	⊜	⊖	⊜
Transmission					⊖	⊖	⊖	⊜
Electrical					○	⊖	⊖	⊜
A/C					⊜	⊜	⊜	⊜
Suspension					○	⊖	⊜	⊜
Brakes					◒	○	⊜	⊜
Exhaust					⊜	⊜	⊜	⊜
Power equip.					⊖	⊜	⊜	⊜
Paint/trim/rust					⊖	⊜	⊜	⊜
Integrity					⊖	⊖	⊜	⊜
Hardware					⊖	⊜	⊜	⊜
RELIABILITY VERDICT					✔	✔	✔	✔

Chrysler Pacifica

TROUBLE SPOTS	97	98	99	00	01	02	03	04
Engine								⊜
Cooling								⊜
Fuel								⊖
Ignition								⊜
Transmission								⊜
Electrical								⊖
A/C								⊜
Suspension								⊜
Brakes								⊜
Exhaust								⊜
Power equip.								⊖
Paint/trim/rust								⊜
Integrity								⊖
Hardware								⊖
RELIABILITY VERDICT								-

Chrysler Sebring Convertible

TROUBLE SPOTS	97	98	99	00	01	02	03	04
Engine	○	○	⊖	⊜	⊖	⊜	⊜	⊜
Cooling	◒	⊖	⊖	⊜	⊜	⊜	⊜	⊜
Fuel	○	⊖	⊖	⊖	⊖	⊜	⊖	⊜
Ignition	⊖	⊖	⊖	⊖	⊜	⊜	⊜	⊜
Transmission	○	⊖	○	◒	⊜	○	○	⊖
Electrical	●	●	◒	○	◒	⊜	○	⊜
A/C	◒	○	○	○	⊖	⊖	⊜	⊜
Suspension	⊖	○	⊖	⊖	○	⊜	⊜	⊜
Brakes	●	◒	●	◒	○	⊜	⊜	⊜
Exhaust	⊖	⊜	⊜	⊜	⊜	⊜	⊜	⊜
Power equip.	◒	○	○	○	◒	⊖	○	⊖
Paint/trim/rust	○	○	○	⊖	⊖	⊖	⊖	⊜
Integrity	◒	◒	◒	◒	●	◒	◒	○
Hardware	○	○	⊖	○	○	○	⊖	⊖
RELIABILITY VERDICT	✗	-	-	-	✗	-	✗	✗

Chrysler Sebring Sedan

TROUBLE SPOTS	97	98	99	00	01	02	03	04
Engine					⊖	⊖	⊜	⊜
Cooling					⊖	⊜	⊜	⊜
Fuel					⊖	⊜	⊖	⊖
Ignition					⊜	⊜	⊜	⊜
Transmission					⊜	○	○	⊖
Electrical					◒	○	⊖	⊖
A/C					○	⊖	⊜	⊜
Suspension					⊖	⊖	⊖	⊜
Brakes					○	○	⊖	⊜
Exhaust					⊜	⊜	⊜	⊜
Power equip.					○	⊜	⊖	⊜
Paint/trim/rust					⊜	⊖	⊜	⊜
Integrity					○	⊖	○	⊖
Hardware					⊜	⊜	⊜	⊖
RELIABILITY VERDICT					-	✗	-	✗

Chrysler Town & Country (ext.) 2WD

TROUBLE SPOTS	97	98	99	00	01	02	03	04
Engine	○	◒	⊖	⊖	⊜	⊜	⊜	⊜
Cooling	◒	⊖	⊖	⊖	⊜	⊜	⊜	⊜
Fuel	○	⊖	⊖	⊖	⊖	⊖	⊜	⊜
Ignition	⊖	⊖	⊖	⊖	⊜	⊜	⊜	⊜
Transmission	◒	◒	●	●	⊖	○	⊖	⊜
Electrical	●	◒	◒	○	◒	○	⊖	⊜
A/C	◒	◒	○	○	◒	○	⊜	⊜
Suspension	○	○	○	⊖	◒	○	⊖	⊜
Brakes	◒	●	◒	◒	◒	○	⊖	⊜
Exhaust	⊜	⊜	⊜	⊜	⊜	⊜	⊜	⊜
Power equip.	◒	○	○	○	●	○	⊖	⊜
Paint/trim/rust	○	⊖	⊖	⊖	⊖	⊜	⊜	⊜
Integrity	◒	○	○	○	○	⊜	⊖	⊖
Hardware	○	○	○	○	○	○	⊖	⊜
RELIABILITY VERDICT	✗	-	-	✗	✗	✗	-	-

Dodge Caravan V6

TROUBLE SPOTS	97	98	99	00	01	02	03	04
Engine	◒	◒	○	⊖	⊜	⊜	⊜	⊜
Cooling	◒	○	⊖	⊖	⊜	⊜	⊜	⊜
Fuel	○	⊖	⊖	⊖	⊖	⊜	⊜	⊜
Ignition	⊖	⊖	⊖	⊖	⊜	⊜	⊜	⊜
Transmission	◒	◒	●	●	⊖	○	⊖	⊜
Electrical	●	◒	○	○	◒	○	⊖	⊜
A/C	●	◒	○	○	○	⊖	⊜	⊜
Suspension	○	○	○	⊖	◒	○	⊜	⊜
Brakes	●	●	●	●	◒	○	⊖	⊜
Exhaust	⊜	⊜	⊜	⊜	⊜	⊜	⊜	⊜
Power equip.	○	○	○	○	●	○	⊖	⊖
Paint/trim/rust	○	⊖	⊖	⊖	⊖	⊖	⊖	⊜
Integrity	◒	○	○	○	○	○	⊖	⊜
Hardware	○	○	○	○	○	⊖	⊖	⊜
RELIABILITY VERDICT	✗	✗	-	✗	✗	✗	-	-

Dodge Dakota 2WD

TROUBLE SPOTS	97	98	99	00	01	02	03	04
Engine	◒	○	○	⊖	⊖	⊜	⊜	⊜
Cooling	◒	◒	◒	⊖	⊖	⊜	⊜	⊜
Fuel	◒	○	○	○	○	⊖	⊖	⊜
Ignition	○	○	⊖	⊜	⊜	⊜	⊜	⊜
Transmission	○	◒	○	○	○	⊜	⊜	⊜
Electrical	○	○	⊖	○	○	⊜	⊖	⊜
A/C	●	●	○	⊖	⊖	⊖	⊜	⊜
Suspension	◒	◒	○	○	○	○	⊖	⊜
Brakes	◒	◒	◒	◒	○	◒	⊖	⊜
Exhaust	◒	◒	◒	⊜	⊜	⊜	⊜	⊜
Power equip.	⊜	⊖	⊖	◒	⊖	⊜	⊜	⊜
Paint/trim/rust	◒	○	⊖	⊜	⊜	⊜	⊜	⊜
Integrity	○	○	⊜	⊖	⊖	⊜	○	⊖
Hardware	○	⊖	⊖	⊖	⊜	⊜	⊖	⊜
RELIABILITY VERDICT	✗	✗	✗	-	-	-	-	-

Dodge Dakota 4WD

TROUBLE SPOTS	97	98	99	00	01	02	03	04
Engine	○	⊖	○	⊜	⊜	⊜	⊜	⊜
Cooling	◒	○	◒	⊖	⊖	⊖	⊜	⊜
Fuel	○	○	○	○	○	⊖	⊖	⊜
Ignition	⊖	⊖	⊖	⊖	⊜	⊜	⊜	⊜
Transmission	⊖	◒	○	○	○	⊖	⊖	⊜
Electrical	○	○	○	⊖	○	○	⊖	⊖
A/C	●	◒	⊖	⊖	⊖	⊖	⊜	⊜
Suspension	◒	●	●	◒	○	○	⊖	⊖
Brakes	◒	●	◒	●	●	◒	⊖	⊜
Exhaust	⊖	○	◒	⊜	⊜	⊜	⊜	⊜
Power equip.	⊜	⊖	⊖	○	⊖	⊜	⊖	⊜
Paint/trim/rust	○	○	○	⊖	⊜	⊜	⊖	⊖
Integrity	⊖	○	○	○	⊜	⊜	⊖	○
Hardware	⊜	○	⊖	⊖	⊖	⊜	⊜	⊖
RELIABILITY VERDICT	-	✗	✗	✗	✗	✗	-	✗

Dodge Durango

TROUBLE SPOTS	97	98	99	00	01	02	03	04
Engine		○	◒	⊖	⊜	⊜	⊜	⊜
Cooling		◒	◒	⊖	⊖	⊜	⊜	⊜
Fuel		○	○	⊖	⊖	⊖	⊜	⊜
Ignition		⊖	⊖	⊜	⊜	⊜	⊜	⊜
Transmission		◒	◒	○	○	⊖	⊖	⊜
Electrical		○	◒	○	○	⊖	○	⊜
A/C		●	○	⊖	○	○	⊖	⊜
Suspension		●	◒	◒	○	⊖	⊖	⊜
Brakes		◒	●	◒	◒	○	⊖	⊜
Exhaust		⊜	⊜	⊜	⊜	⊜	⊜	⊜
Power equip.		●	●	◒	○	⊖	⊖	⊜
Paint/trim/rust		⊖	⊖	⊖	⊜	⊖	⊖	⊜
Integrity		⊖	○	○	○	⊖	○	⊜
Hardware		○	○	◒	⊖	⊖	⊖	⊜
RELIABILITY VERDICT		✗	✗	✗	–	–	–	–

Dodge Grand Caravan V6 2WD

TROUBLE SPOTS	97	98	99	00	01	02	03	04
Engine	○	◒	⊖	⊖	⊜	⊜	⊜	⊜
Cooling	◒	⊖	⊖	⊖	⊜	⊜	⊜	⊜
Fuel	○	⊖	⊖	⊖	⊖	⊖	⊜	⊜
Ignition	⊖	⊖	⊖	⊖	⊜	⊜	⊜	⊜
Transmission	◒	◒	●	●	⊖	○	⊖	⊜
Electrical	●	◒	◒	○	◒	○	⊖	⊜
A/C	◒	◒	○	○	◒	○	⊜	⊜
Suspension	○	○	○	⊖	◒	○	⊖	⊜
Brakes	◒	●	◒	◒	◒	○	⊖	⊜
Exhaust	⊜	⊜	⊜	⊜	⊜	⊜	⊜	⊜
Power equip.	◒	○	○	○	●	○	⊖	⊜
Paint/trim/rust	○	⊖	⊖	⊖	⊖	⊜	⊜	⊜
Integrity	◒	○	○	○	○	⊖	⊖	⊖
Hardware	○	○	○	○	○	○	⊖	⊜
RELIABILITY VERDICT	✗	–	–	✗	✗	✗	–	–

Dodge Intrepid

TROUBLE SPOTS	97	98	99	00	01	02	03	04
Engine	◒	○	○	○	⊖	⊜	⊜	⊜
Cooling	●	○	○	⊜	⊖	⊜	⊜	⊜
Fuel	◒	○	○	⊖	○	⊖	⊜	⊜
Ignition	○	⊖	⊖	⊜	⊖	⊖	⊖	⊜
Transmission	○	○	◒	○	⊖	⊖	⊖	⊜
Electrical	◒	●	◒	○	○	⊖	⊜	⊜
A/C	◒	◒	●	○	⊖	⊜	⊜	⊜
Suspension	●	○	⊖	⊖	⊜	⊖	⊖	⊜
Brakes	◒	◒	○	○	○	⊖	⊖	⊜
Exhaust	⊖	⊖	⊜	⊜	⊜	⊜	⊜	⊜
Power equip.	○	●	●	●	○	⊖	⊖	⊜
Paint/trim/rust	●	◒	⊖	⊖	⊖	⊜	⊜	⊜
Integrity	◒	◒	○	●	○	⊖	⊖	⊖
Hardware	⊖	○	◒	◒	⊖	⊖	⊜	⊜
RELIABILITY VERDICT	✗	✗	✗	–	–	✓	–	✓

Dodge Neon

TROUBLE SPOTS	97	98	99	00	01	02	03	04
Engine	●	●	●	⊖	⊖	⊜	⊜	Insufficient data
Cooling	◒	○	⊖	○	⊖	⊖	⊜	
Fuel	○	◒	◒	⊖	○	⊖	⊜	
Ignition	⊖	○	⊖	⊖	⊖	⊜	⊜	
Transmission	○	○	⊖	⊖	⊖	○	⊖	
Electrical	◒	◒	◒	◒	◒	◒	⊜	
A/C	●	●	○	○	⊜	⊜	⊜	
Suspension	○	○	⊖	○	⊖	⊖	⊖	
Brakes	◒	○	◒	◒	◒	◒	⊖	
Exhaust	⊜	⊖	⊜	⊜	⊖	⊜	⊜	
Power equip.	⊖	○	○	◒	○	⊖	⊜	
Paint/trim/rust	●	◒	⊖	○	⊖	⊜	⊜	
Integrity	●	●	◒	◒	◒	○	○	
Hardware	◒	◒	○	◒	⊖	⊖	⊜	
RELIABILITY VERDICT	✗	✗	✗	✗	✗	✗	✓	

Dodge Ram 1500 2WD

TROUBLE SPOTS	97	98	99	00	01	02	03	04
Engine	○	○	⊖	⊜	⊜	⊜	⊜	⊜
Cooling	○	○	○	⊖	⊜	⊖	⊜	⊜
Fuel	◒	○	○	⊖	⊖	⊖	⊜	⊖
Ignition	○	○	⊖	⊜	⊜	⊜	⊜	⊜
Transmission	◒	◒	○	◒	◒	⊖	⊜	⊖
Electrical	○	⊖	○	○	⊖	○	⊖	⊖
A/C	◒	◒	○	○	○	○	⊜	⊜
Suspension	○	⊖	⊖	⊖	⊖	○	⊜	⊜
Brakes	◒	◒	◒	○	○	⊖	○	⊖
Exhaust	○	⊖	○	⊖	⊜	⊜	⊜	⊜
Power equip.	⊖	⊖	⊖	⊖	⊖	⊖	⊜	⊖
Paint/trim/rust	◒	○	⊖	⊖	⊖	⊖	⊖	⊖
Integrity	○	○	⊖	○	○	○	⊖	⊜
Hardware	⊖	○	○	⊖	⊖	○	⊜	⊜
RELIABILITY VERDICT	✗	–	–	–	–	✗	–	–

Dodge Ram 1500 4WD

TROUBLE SPOTS	97	98	99	00	01	02	03	04
Engine	○	○	○	⊖	⊖	⊜	⊜	⊜
Cooling	○	○	○	⊜	⊖	⊜	⊜	⊜
Fuel	◒	○	○	⊖	⊖	⊖	⊜	⊜
Ignition	○	⊖	○	○	⊖	⊜	⊜	⊜
Transmission	◒	◒	◒	○	◒	⊖	⊖	⊜
Electrical	◒	○	⊖	○	⊖	○	⊜	⊜
A/C	○	○	○	○	⊖	⊖	⊜	⊜
Suspension	◒	○	○	◒	○	⊖	⊖	⊜
Brakes	○	◒	◒	◒	○	○	◒	⊖
Exhaust	⊖	⊜	○	⊜	⊜	⊜	⊜	⊜
Power equip.	⊖	○	⊜	⊖	⊖	○	⊜	⊜
Paint/trim/rust	○	○	○	○	⊖	⊖	⊜	⊜
Integrity	○	○	○	○	⊖	○	⊖	⊜
Hardware	○	⊖	⊖	⊖	⊖	○	⊜	⊜
RELIABILITY VERDICT	✗	✗	✗	✗	✗	✗	–	✓

Dodge Stratus Sedan V6

TROUBLE SPOTS	97	98	99	00	01	02	03	04
Engine	◒	○	⊖	⊖	⊖	⊖	⊜	⊜
Cooling	◒	⊖	⊜	⊜	⊖	⊜	⊜	⊜
Fuel	◒	⊖	○	○	⊖	⊜	⊖	⊖
Ignition	⊖	⊜	⊖	⊖	⊜	⊜	⊜	⊜
Transmission	◒	○	◒	◒	⊖	○	○	⊖
Electrical	◒	⊖	○	○	◒	○	⊖	⊖
A/C	◒	○	⊖	⊖	○	⊖	⊜	⊜
Suspension	◒	○	○	○	⊖	⊖	⊖	⊜
Brakes	●	◒	◒	◒	○	○	⊖	⊜
Exhaust	⊜	⊜	⊜	⊜	⊜	⊜	⊜	⊜
Power equip.	○	○	○	○	○	⊜	⊖	⊜
Paint/trim/rust	○	○	○	⊖	⊜	⊖	⊜	⊜
Integrity	○	○	⊖	○	○	⊖	○	⊖
Hardware	○	⊖	⊖	○	⊖	⊖	⊜	⊖
RELIABILITY VERDICT	✗	✓	–	–	–	✗	–	✗

Ford Contour 4-cyl.

TROUBLE SPOTS	97	98	99	00	01	02	03	04
Engine	◒	⊖	⊖					
Cooling	⊖	⊖	⊖					
Fuel	◒	○	○					
Ignition	○	⊖	⊖					
Transmission	○	○	⊖					
Electrical	●	◒	○					
A/C	○	○	⊖					
Suspension	○	○	○					
Brakes	●	◒	◒					
Exhaust	○	⊜	⊜					
Power equip.	◒	○	⊜					
Paint/trim/rust	⊖	⊖	○					
Integrity	◒	◒	●					
Hardware	○	○	○					
RELIABILITY VERDICT	–	–	–					

Ford Crown Victoria

TROUBLE SPOTS	97	98	99	00	01	02	03	04
Engine	⊖	⊜	⊜	⊖	⊖	⊜	⊜	⊜
Cooling	○	⊜	⊜	⊜	⊜	⊜	⊜	⊜
Fuel	○	⊖	⊜	○	○	⊖	⊜	⊜
Ignition	⊖	⊜	⊜	⊜	⊜	⊜	⊜	⊜
Transmission	⊖	⊖	⊜	⊖	⊜	⊜	⊜	⊜
Electrical	○	○	○	○	○	⊖	⊖	⊖
A/C	⊜	⊜	⊜	⊖	⊜	⊜	⊜	⊜
Suspension	○	○	○	⊜	⊖	⊖	⊖	⊜
Brakes	◒	⊖	○	○	⊜	⊖	⊖	⊜
Exhaust	⊖	⊜	⊜	⊜	⊜	⊜	⊜	⊜
Power equip.	◒	○	⊜	○	○	⊜	⊜	⊜
Paint/trim/rust	⊖	⊜	⊜	⊜	⊜	⊖	⊜	⊜
Integrity	○	⊖	⊖	○	○	○	○	○
Hardware	○	⊜	⊖	⊜	⊖	⊖	⊖	⊜
RELIABILITY VERDICT	-	✓	✓	✓	-	✓	-	✗

Ford Escape

TROUBLE SPOTS	97	98	99	00	01	02	03	04
Engine					⊖	⊖	⊜	⊜
Cooling					⊖	⊜	⊜	⊜
Fuel					○	○	⊖	⊜
Ignition					⊖	⊜	⊜	⊜
Transmission					○	⊖	⊜	⊜
Electrical					○	○	⊜	⊜
A/C					⊜	⊖	⊜	⊖
Suspension					⊖	⊖	⊜	⊜
Brakes					◒	○	⊜	⊜
Exhaust					⊜	⊜	⊜	⊜
Power equip.					⊖	⊖	⊜	⊜
Paint/trim/rust					⊜	⊜	⊜	⊖
Integrity					◒	◒	○	⊖
Hardware					◒	○	⊜	⊜
RELIABILITY VERDICT					✗	-	✓	✓

Ford Escort, ZX2

TROUBLE SPOTS	97	98	99	00	01	02	03	04
Engine	○	⊜	⊖	⊖	⊖	⊜	Insufficient data	
Cooling	◒	○	⊜	⊖	⊜	⊜		
Fuel	○	⊖	⊖	○	○	⊜		
Ignition	⊜	⊖	⊜	⊜	⊖	⊜		
Transmission	⊜	⊖	⊖	○	⊖	⊖		
Electrical	○	○	○	○	○	⊜		
A/C	○	◒	○	○	⊜	⊜		
Suspension	◒	○	○	⊖	⊜	⊜		
Brakes	○	◒	○	○	○	⊖		
Exhaust	⊖	⊖	⊜	⊜	⊖	⊜		
Power equip.	⊖	⊜	⊜	⊜	⊖	⊜		
Paint/trim/rust	⊖	⊖	⊖	⊜	⊜	⊜		
Integrity	○	○	○	⊖	○	⊖		
Hardware	⊜	⊖	⊖	○	○	⊜		
RELIABILITY VERDICT	✓	-	✓	-	-	✓		

Ford Excursion

TROUBLE SPOTS	97	98	99	00	01	02	03	04
Engine				⊖	○	○	◒	Insufficient data
Cooling				⊜	⊜	⊜	⊖	
Fuel				⊖	○	⊖	○	
Ignition				⊖	⊜	⊜	⊜	
Transmission				⊖	○	⊜	⊖	
Electrical				○	◒	⊖	○	
A/C				⊜	⊖	⊜	○	
Suspension				○	⊜	○	⊖	
Brakes				◒	○	○	⊖	
Exhaust				⊜	⊜	⊜	⊖	
Power equip.				◒	◒	○	○	
Paint/trim/rust				⊜	⊖	⊜	⊖	
Integrity				○	◒	⊜	⊖	
Hardware				○	○	⊖	○	
RELIABILITY VERDICT				-	✗	-	✗	

Ford Expedition

TROUBLE SPOTS	97	98	99	00	01	02	03	04
Engine	⊖	⊖	○	⊖	⊖	⊜	⊜	⊜
Cooling	⊜	⊜	⊜	⊜	⊜	⊜	⊜	⊜
Fuel	○	⊜	⊜	⊖	⊖	⊖	⊜	⊜
Ignition	⊖	○	⊜	⊖	⊜	⊜	⊜	⊜
Transmission	⊖	⊖	⊜	⊖	⊜	⊖	⊖	⊜
Electrical	◒	◒	◒	◒	○	○	○	⊜
A/C	○	○	⊖	⊖	⊜	⊖	⊖	⊜
Suspension	◒	○	○	○	⊖	⊖	⊖	⊜
Brakes	◒	○	◒	◒	⊜	⊖	⊖	⊖
Exhaust	⊜	⊜	⊜	⊜	⊜	⊜	⊜	⊜
Power equip.	○	◒	◒	○	○	○	◒	⊜
Paint/trim/rust	○	⊜	⊜	⊖	○	⊜	⊖	⊜
Integrity	○	○	○	○	○	○	◒	⊖
Hardware	○	○	○	○	○	⊜	○	⊖
RELIABILITY VERDICT	✓	-	-	-	-	-	✗	✗

Ford Explorer 2WD

TROUBLE SPOTS	97	98	99	00	01	02	03	04
Engine	○	⊖	⊖	⊖	⊜	⊜	⊜	⊜
Cooling	○	⊖	⊖	○	○	⊜	⊜	⊜
Fuel	○	○	○	◒	⊖	⊖	⊜	⊜
Ignition	⊖	⊖	⊖	⊖	⊖	⊜	⊜	⊜
Transmission	⊖	⊖	⊖	⊖	⊖	⊖	⊜	⊜
Electrical	○	◒	●	●	○	○	⊖	⊖
A/C	●	◒	⊖	⊖	⊖	○	⊖	⊜
Suspension	○	○	⊖	⊖	⊖	⊖	⊜	⊜
Brakes	◒	○	○	○	○	⊖	⊜	⊜
Exhaust	⊖	⊜	⊜	⊜	⊜	⊜	⊜	⊜
Power equip.	◒	◒	◒	◒	○	○	○	⊜
Paint/trim/rust	○	⊜	⊖	⊖	⊖	⊖	⊜	⊜
Integrity	○	○	○	○	◒	○	⊖	⊖
Hardware	◒	◒	○	○	○	○	⊖	⊜
RELIABILITY VERDICT	-	-	-	✗	-	-	-	-

Ford Explorer 4WD

TROUBLE SPOTS	97	98	99	00	01	02	03	04
Engine	○	○	○	⊖	⊖	⊜	⊜	⊜
Cooling	○	○	⊖	○	⊖	⊜	⊜	⊜
Fuel	○	○	○	○	⊖	⊖	⊖	⊜
Ignition	⊖	⊖	⊖	⊖	⊖	⊜	⊜	⊜
Transmission	○	○	○	○	⊖	○	⊖	⊜
Electrical	○	●	◒	◒	○	○	⊖	⊜
A/C	●	◒	⊖	⊜	⊜	⊖	⊜	⊜
Suspension	○	◒	○	○	⊖	⊖	⊜	⊜
Brakes	◒	◒	◒	◒	○	⊖	⊖	⊜
Exhaust	⊖	⊜	⊜	⊜	⊜	⊜	⊜	⊜
Power equip.	○	◒	◒	○	⊖	○	⊖	⊖
Paint/trim/rust	○	⊖	○	⊖	⊖	⊜	⊖	⊜
Integrity	○	○	○	○	○	○	○	⊜
Hardware	○	◒	○	◒	○	○	⊜	⊜
RELIABILITY VERDICT	-	✗	-	✗	-	✗	-	-

Ford Explorer Sport Trac

TROUBLE SPOTS	97	98	99	00	01	02	03	04
Engine					⊜	⊜	⊜	⊜
Cooling					⊜	⊜	⊜	⊜
Fuel					○	○	⊖	⊜
Ignition					⊜	⊜	⊜	⊜
Transmission					⊖	⊖	⊜	⊜
Electrical					○	⊖	⊖	⊜
A/C					⊜	⊜	⊜	⊜
Suspension					⊖	⊖	⊖	⊜
Brakes					○	○	⊖	⊜
Exhaust					⊜	⊜	⊜	⊜
Power equip.					○	⊖	⊖	⊜
Paint/trim/rust					⊜	⊖	⊜	⊜
Integrity					⊖	◒	⊖	⊖
Hardware					⊖	○	⊖	⊖
RELIABILITY VERDICT					-	-	-	-

Ford F-150 2WD

TROUBLE SPOTS	97	98	99	00	01	02	03	04
Engine	○	⊖	⊖	⊜	⊜	⊜	⊜	⊜
Cooling	○	⊜	⊜	⊜	⊜	⊜	⊜	⊜
Fuel	○	⊖	⊖	⊖	⊖	⊖	⊜	⊜
Ignition	⊖	⊖	⊖	⊖	⊖	⊜	⊜	⊜
Transmission	⊜	⊖	⊖	⊜	⊖	⊜	⊜	⊜
Electrical	◒	◒	○	⊖	⊖	⊖	⊜	⊖
A/C	⊖	⊖	⊖	⊖	⊖	⊜	⊜	⊜
Suspension	○	⊖	⊖	⊜	⊜	⊜	⊜	⊜
Brakes	◒	○	○	○	⊖	⊜	⊜	⊜
Exhaust	⊜	⊜	⊜	⊜	⊜	⊜	⊜	⊜
Power equip.	○	⊖	⊖	⊖	⊖	⊖	⊜	⊜
Paint/trim/rust	⊖	⊖	⊖	⊖	⊖	⊜	⊜	⊜
Integrity	○	⊖	⊖	⊖	○	⊖	⊖	⊖
Hardware	⊖	⊖	⊖	○	⊖	⊖	⊜	⊜
RELIABILITY VERDICT	✔	✔	✔	✔	✔	✔	✔	–

Ford F-150 4WD

TROUBLE SPOTS	97	98	99	00	01	02	03	04
Engine	⊖	⊖	○	⊜	⊖	⊜	⊜	⊜
Cooling	⊖	⊜	⊜	⊖	⊜	⊜	⊜	⊜
Fuel	○	○	⊖	⊖	⊖	⊜	⊜	⊜
Ignition	⊖	⊖	⊖	⊖	⊖	⊜	⊜	⊜
Transmission	○	⊖	⊖	⊖	⊖	⊜	⊜	⊜
Electrical	◒	◒	◒	⊖	⊖	⊖	⊜	⊜
A/C	⊖	⊖	⊖	⊖	⊜	⊜	⊜	⊜
Suspension	○	○	⊖	⊖	⊖	⊖	⊜	⊜
Brakes	◒	◒	◒	◒	○	⊖	⊜	⊜
Exhaust	⊖	⊜	⊜	⊜	⊜	⊜	⊜	⊜
Power equip.	○	○	○	○	⊖	⊖	⊜	⊜
Paint/trim/rust	⊖	⊖	⊖	⊖	⊖	⊖	⊖	⊖
Integrity	○	○	○	⊖	⊖	⊖	○	⊖
Hardware	⊖	○	⊖	⊖	⊖	⊖	⊜	⊜
RELIABILITY VERDICT	✔	✔	–	✔	✔	✔	✔	✘

Ford Focus Sedan

TROUBLE SPOTS	97	98	99	00	01	02	03	04
Engine				⊖	⊜	⊜	⊜	⊜
Cooling				⊜	⊜	⊜	⊜	⊜
Fuel				●	●	○	⊖	⊜
Ignition				○	⊖	⊜	⊜	⊜
Transmission				⊖	⊖	⊖	⊜	⊜
Electrical				◒	○	⊖	⊜	⊜
A/C				⊖	⊜	⊖	⊜	⊜
Suspension				○	○	⊖	⊜	⊜
Brakes				●	◒	○	⊖	⊜
Exhaust				⊜	⊜	⊜	⊜	⊜
Power equip.				◒	○	⊖	⊜	⊜
Paint/trim/rust				⊖	⊖	⊖	⊜	⊜
Integrity				◒	○	○	⊖	⊖
Hardware				◒	○	○	⊖	⊜
RELIABILITY VERDICT				✘	✘	–	✔	✔

Ford Mustang

TROUBLE SPOTS	97	98	99	00	01	02	03	04
Engine	⊖	⊜	⊖	⊖	⊜	⊜	⊜	⊜
Cooling	◒	⊖	⊜	⊜	⊜	⊜	⊜	⊜
Fuel	○	◒	⊖	○	○	⊜	⊜	⊜
Ignition	○	⊖	⊜	⊖	⊖	⊜	⊜	⊜
Transmission	○	⊖	⊜	⊖	⊖	⊜	⊜	⊜
Electrical	○	○	○	⊖	⊖	⊖	⊖	⊜
A/C	○	⊖	⊖	⊜	⊜	⊖	⊜	⊜
Suspension	⊖	⊖	⊖	⊖	⊖	⊜	⊖	⊖
Brakes	◒	○	○	○	⊖	⊜	⊜	⊜
Exhaust	⊜	⊜	⊖	⊖	⊜	⊜	⊜	⊜
Power equip.	⊖	⊖	⊖	○	○	○	○	⊜
Paint/trim/rust	○	⊖	⊖	⊖	○	⊖	⊖	⊜
Integrity	○	◒	○	◒	○	○	◒	⊜
Hardware	○	○	○	○	○	⊜	⊖	⊜
RELIABILITY VERDICT	–	✔	✔	–	–	✔	–	✔

Ford Ranger 2WD

TROUBLE SPOTS	97	98	99	00	01	02	03	04
Engine	⊖	⊖	⊖	⊖	⊖	⊖	⊖	⊜
Cooling	⊖	⊜	⊜	⊜	⊜	⊜	⊜	⊜
Fuel	◒	○	○	○	⊖	⊖	⊜	⊜
Ignition	⊖	⊖	⊖	⊖	⊜	⊖	⊜	⊜
Transmission	⊖	⊖	○	⊖	⊜	⊖	⊖	⊜
Electrical	●	●	◒	○	○	○	⊜	⊜
A/C	◒	○	⊜	⊖	⊖	⊜	⊜	⊜
Suspension	⊖	○	⊜	⊜	⊖	⊖	⊜	⊜
Brakes	○	○	○	⊖	○	○	⊜	⊜
Exhaust	⊖	⊜	⊜	⊜	⊜	⊜	⊜	⊜
Power equip.	⊖	⊖	⊖	⊖	⊖	⊖	⊜	⊜
Paint/trim/rust	⊖	⊖	⊖	⊖	⊜	⊖	⊜	⊜
Integrity	○	○	⊜	⊜	⊜	⊖	⊖	⊜
Hardware	○	○	⊜	○	⊜	⊖	⊖	⊜
RELIABILITY VERDICT	✔	✔	✔	✔	✔	–	–	–

Ford Ranger 4WD

TROUBLE SPOTS	97	98	99	00	01	02	03	04
Engine	○	⊖	⊖	⊖	⊖	⊜	⊜	⊜
Cooling	◒	○	⊖	⊖	⊜	⊜	⊜	⊜
Fuel	◒	○	○	⊖	○	⊖	⊜	⊜
Ignition	⊖	⊖	⊜	⊖	⊖	⊜	⊜	⊜
Transmission	○	○	○	⊖	○	○	⊜	⊜
Electrical	●	●	◒	○	○	⊖	⊖	⊖
A/C	◒	○	⊜	⊜	⊜	⊜	⊜	⊜
Suspension	⊜	○	○	○	○	⊖	⊜	⊜
Brakes	◒	◒	●	◒	○	⊖	⊖	⊜
Exhaust	⊜	⊜	⊜	⊜	⊜	⊜	⊜	⊜
Power equip.	⊖	○	⊖	⊖	○	⊖	⊜	⊖
Paint/trim/rust	⊜	⊖	⊖	⊖	⊜	⊜	⊖	⊖
Integrity	○	○	⊖	○	○	○	⊖	○
Hardware	○	○	⊖	⊖	○	○	⊜	⊖
RELIABILITY VERDICT	✘	–	–	–	✘	✘	✔	✘

Ford Taurus Sedan

TROUBLE SPOTS	97	98	99	00	01	02	03	04
Engine	○	⊖	⊖	⊖	⊖	⊜	⊖	⊜
Cooling	○	○	○	⊜	⊜	⊜	⊜	⊜
Fuel	○	○	○	○	○	⊖	⊖	⊜
Ignition	⊖	⊖	⊜	⊖	⊖	⊜	⊜	⊜
Transmission	◒	○	○	⊖	⊖	⊖	⊜	⊜
Electrical	●	●	◒	◒	○	○	⊖	⊜
A/C	○	○	⊖	⊖	⊖	⊖	⊜	⊜
Suspension	○	○	◒	○	○	⊖	⊜	⊜
Brakes	◒	●	●	◒	◒	○	⊖	⊜
Exhaust	⊖	⊜	⊜	⊜	⊜	⊜	⊜	⊜
Power equip.	◒	○	○	⊖	⊖	⊖	⊜	⊜
Paint/trim/rust	⊖	⊖	⊖	⊖	⊜	⊜	⊜	⊜
Integrity	○	○	○	○	○	○	⊖	⊖
Hardware	○	○	⊖	⊖	⊖	⊖	⊖	⊜
RELIABILITY VERDICT	–	–	–	–	–	–	–	–

Ford Thunderbird

TROUBLE SPOTS	97	98	99	00	01	02	03	04
Engine	⊖					⊜	⊜	Insufficient data
Cooling	●					⊜	⊜	
Fuel	○					⊜	⊜	
Ignition	⊖					⊜	⊖	
Transmission	⊜					⊜	⊜	
Electrical	○					⊖	○	
A/C	⊖					⊖	⊖	
Suspension	○					⊜	⊖	
Brakes	◒					⊖	⊜	
Exhaust	⊖					⊜	⊜	
Power equip.	◒					⊖	⊖	
Paint/trim/rust	○					○	⊜	
Integrity	⊖					○	●	
Hardware	○					○	⊜	
RELIABILITY VERDICT	–					✔	–	

Ford Windstar, Freestar

TROUBLE SPOTS	97	98	99	00	01	02	03	04
Engine	◒	○	◒	○	⊖	⊜	⊜	⊜
Cooling	◒	⊖	⊖	⊜	⊜	⊜	⊜	⊜
Fuel	●	◒	●	◒	○	⊖	⊜	⊜
Ignition	○	⊖	○	⊖	⊜	⊜	⊜	⊜
Transmission	◒	◒	●	◒	⊖	⊖	⊜	⊜
Electrical	●	●	●	◒	◒	○	⊖	⊖
A/C	◒	○	○	⊖	⊖	⊜	⊜	⊜
Suspension	●	●	●	◒	○	⊖	⊖	⊜
Brakes	●	●	◒	◒	○	⊖	⊜	⊜
Exhaust	⊖	⊜	⊖	⊜	⊜	⊜	⊜	⊜
Power equip.	●	●	●	◒	●	◒	○	⊖
Paint/trim/rust	○	○	○	○	○	⊜	⊜	⊜
Integrity	●	◒	◒	◒	◒	○	⊖	⊖
Hardware	◒	◒	◒	◒	◒	○	⊖	⊖
RELIABILITY VERDICT	✗	✗	✗	✗	✗	-	-	-

GMC Jimmy, Envoy

TROUBLE SPOTS	97	98	99	00	01	02	03	04
Engine	◒	○	○	○	○	⊖	⊜	⊜
Cooling	●	◒	◒	⊖	⊖	⊜	⊜	⊜
Fuel	●	○	○	○	○	⊖	⊖	⊜
Ignition	○	⊖	⊖	⊖	⊖	⊖	⊜	⊜
Transmission	●	◒	○	○	○	⊖	⊜	⊜
Electrical	●	●	●	●	●	●	○	⊖
A/C	●	◒	○	⊖	⊖	⊖	◒	⊜
Suspension	◒	◒	◒	◒	○	⊖	⊜	⊜
Brakes	●	◒	◒	◒	○	⊖	⊜	⊜
Exhaust	⊖	⊖	⊖	⊖	⊖	⊜	⊜	⊜
Power equip.	◒	◒	○	◒	○	◒	⊖	⊖
Paint/trim/rust	○	⊖	○	○	⊖	⊖	⊖	⊖
Integrity	◒	●	●	◒	◒	◒	◒	⊖
Hardware	●	●	◒	◒	○	○	○	⊖
RELIABILITY VERDICT	✗	✗	✗	✗	✗	✗	✗	✗

GMC New Sierra 1500 4WD

TROUBLE SPOTS	97	98	99	00	01	02	03	04
Engine			⊖	⊜	⊜	⊖	⊜	⊜
Cooling			⊜	⊜	⊜	⊜	⊜	⊜
Fuel			○	○	⊖	⊜	⊜	⊜
Ignition			⊜	⊜	⊜	⊜	⊜	⊜
Transmission			⊖	⊖	⊖	○	⊖	⊜
Electrical			○	○	⊖	⊖	⊖	⊜
A/C			⊜	⊜	⊜	⊜	⊖	⊜
Suspension			○	○	○	○	⊖	⊜
Brakes			●	◒	○	⊖	⊜	⊜
Exhaust			⊜	⊜	⊜	⊜	⊜	⊜
Power equip.			○	⊖	⊖	⊖	⊖	⊜
Paint/trim/rust			⊖	⊖	⊜	⊖	⊜	⊜
Integrity			◒	◒	○	○	○	⊖
Hardware			○	○	⊜	○	⊖	⊖
RELIABILITY VERDICT			-	-	-	✗	✗	-

GMC S-15 Sonoma V6 2WD, Canyon

TROUBLE SPOTS	97	98	99	00	01	02	03	04
Engine	○	○	⊜	⊖	⊖	⊜	⊜	⊜
Cooling	◒	◒	○	⊖	⊜	⊖	⊜	⊜
Fuel	◒	⊖	◒	⊖	○	⊜	⊜	⊜
Ignition	⊖	⊜	⊖	⊖	⊜	⊜	⊜	⊜
Transmission	○	○	⊖	⊖	⊖	⊜	⊜	⊜
Electrical	●	●	○	○	○	○	○	⊜
A/C	●	●	◒	○	⊜	⊜	⊜	⊜
Suspension	⊖	⊖	⊖	⊖	⊖	⊖	⊖	⊜
Brakes	◒	○	○	○	◒	⊖	⊖	⊜
Exhaust	⊜	⊜	⊜	⊜	⊜	⊜	⊜	⊜
Power equip.	⊜	⊖	⊖	⊖	⊜	⊜	⊖	⊜
Paint/trim/rust	⊖	○	⊖	⊖	⊜	⊖	⊖	⊜
Integrity	●	●	◒	○	◒	◒	○	⊖
Hardware	○	●	◒	◒	◒	○	⊜	⊜
RELIABILITY VERDICT	✗	✗	-	-	-	-	✗	✓

GMC Safari

TROUBLE SPOTS	97	98	99	00	01	02	03	04
Engine	◒	○	⊖	⊖	○	⊖	⊜	Insufficient data
Cooling	◒	◒	○	⊖	⊜	⊜	⊜	
Fuel	●	◒	◒	○	⊖	⊖	⊜	
Ignition	⊖	○	⊖	⊜	⊜	⊖	⊜	
Transmission	◒	◒	◒	⊖	⊖	⊖	⊖	
Electrical	●	●	●	●	○	◒	⊖	
A/C	●	●	○	⊖	⊖	⊜	⊜	
Suspension	◒	◒	○	○	○	○	○	
Brakes	◒	●	◒	●	◒	◒	○	
Exhaust	⊖	⊖	⊜	⊖	⊜	⊖	⊜	
Power equip.	●	●	●	●	◒	●	⊖	
Paint/trim/rust	○	◒	○	⊖	○	⊖	⊜	
Integrity	●	●	●	●	◒	●	●	
Hardware	●	●	●	●	●	◒	○	
RELIABILITY VERDICT	✗	✗	✗	✗	✗	✗	✗	

GMC Suburban, Yukon XL

TROUBLE SPOTS	97	98	99	00	01	02	03	04
Engine	◒	○	○	⊜	⊖	⊜	⊜	⊜
Cooling	●	◒	◒	⊜	⊜	⊜	⊜	⊜
Fuel	◒	○	◒	○	○	⊖	⊖	⊜
Ignition	⊖	⊖	⊖	⊜	⊖	⊜	⊜	⊜
Transmission	◒	○	○	⊖	⊖	⊖	⊜	⊜
Electrical	●	●	●	○	○	⊖	○	⊜
A/C	●	◒	○	⊖	⊖	⊖	⊖	⊜
Suspension	◒	○	○	○	⊖	○	⊖	⊜
Brakes	●	●	●	◒	○	⊖	⊜	⊜
Exhaust	⊖	⊖	⊖	⊜	⊜	⊜	⊜	⊜
Power equip.	○	○	●	●	○	⊖	○	⊜
Paint/trim/rust	⊖	⊖	⊜	⊜	⊜	⊜	⊜	⊜
Integrity	◒	○	◒	○	○	○	⊖	⊜
Hardware	◒	◒	◒	○	○	⊜	⊜	⊜
RELIABILITY VERDICT	✗	✗	✗	-	-	-	-	-

Honda Accord 4-cyl.

TROUBLE SPOTS	97	98	99	00	01	02	03	04
Engine	⊖	⊜	⊜	⊜	⊜	⊜	⊜	⊜
Cooling	⊖	⊜	⊜	⊜	⊜	⊜	⊜	⊜
Fuel	⊜	○	⊖	⊖	⊜	⊜	⊜	⊜
Ignition	⊜	⊖	⊖	⊜	⊜	⊜	⊜	⊜
Transmission	⊜	⊖	⊜	⊖	○	⊜	⊜	⊜
Electrical	⊖	⊖	⊖	⊖	⊜	⊜	⊜	⊜
A/C	○	⊜	⊜	⊜	⊜	⊜	⊜	⊜
Suspension	⊜	⊜	⊜	⊜	⊜	⊜	⊜	⊜
Brakes	⊖	○	⊖	⊖	⊖	⊜	○	⊜
Exhaust	○	○	⊖	⊜	⊜	⊜	⊜	⊜
Power equip.	○	⊖	⊖	⊜	⊜	⊜	⊜	⊜
Paint/trim/rust	⊖	⊖	⊖	⊖	⊜	⊜	⊜	⊜
Integrity	⊖	⊖	⊖	⊖	⊖	⊖	⊖	⊖
Hardware	⊖	⊖	⊖	⊖	⊜	⊜	⊜	⊜
RELIABILITY VERDICT	✓	✓	✓	✓	✓	✓	✓	✓

Honda CR-V

TROUBLE SPOTS	97	98	99	00	01	02	03	04
Engine	⊜	⊜	⊜	⊜	⊜	⊜	⊜	⊜
Cooling	⊜	⊜	⊜	⊜	⊜	⊜	⊜	⊜
Fuel	⊜	⊖	⊜	⊜	⊜	⊖	⊜	⊜
Ignition	⊖	⊜	⊜	⊜	⊜	⊜	⊜	⊜
Transmission	⊜	⊜	⊜	⊜	⊜	⊜	⊜	⊜
Electrical	⊖	⊖	⊖	⊜	⊜	⊖	⊜	⊜
A/C	⊖	⊜	⊜	⊜	⊜	⊜	⊜	⊜
Suspension	⊖	⊖	⊜	⊜	⊜	⊜	⊜	⊜
Brakes	⊖	⊖	⊖	⊖	⊖	⊖	⊜	⊜
Exhaust	⊜	⊜	⊜	⊜	⊜	⊜	⊜	⊜
Power equip.	⊖	⊖	⊖	⊜	⊜	⊜	⊜	⊜
Paint/trim/rust	⊖	○	⊜	⊜	⊜	⊜	⊜	⊜
Integrity	⊖	⊖	⊖	⊖	⊖	⊖	⊖	⊜
Hardware	⊖	⊖	⊖	⊜	⊜	⊖	⊖	⊜
RELIABILITY VERDICT	✓	✓	✓	✓	✓	✓	✓	✓

Honda Civic

TROUBLE SPOTS	97	98	99	00	01	02	03	04
Engine	⊜	⊜	⊜	⊜	⊜	⊜	⊜	⊜
Cooling	⊜	⊜	⊜	⊜	⊜	⊜	⊜	⊜
Fuel	⊖	⊖	⊖	⊜	⊜	⊜	⊜	⊜
Ignition	⊜	⊜	⊜	⊜	⊜	⊜	⊜	⊜
Transmission	⊖	⊜	⊜	⊜	⊜	⊜	⊜	⊜
Electrical	⊖	⊖	⊖	⊖	⊖	⊖	⊜	⊜
A/C	⊖	⊖	⊖	⊜	⊜	⊜	⊜	⊜
Suspension	⊜	⊜	⊜	⊜	○	⊖	⊜	⊜
Brakes	⊖	⊖	⊖	⊜	⊖	⊖	⊜	⊜
Exhaust	○	○	○	⊖	⊜	⊜	⊜	⊜
Power equip.	⊖	⊖	⊖	⊖	⊖	⊜	⊜	⊜
Paint/trim/rust	⊖	⊖	⊖	⊖	⊖	⊖	⊜	⊜
Integrity	○	⊖	⊖	⊖	○	○	⊖	⊜
Hardware	⊖	⊖	⊖	⊖	⊖	⊖	⊜	⊜
RELIABILITY VERDICT	✔	✔	✔	✔	✔	✔	✔	✔

Honda Element

TROUBLE SPOTS	97	98	99	00	01	02	03	04
Engine							⊜	⊜
Cooling							⊜	⊜
Fuel							⊜	⊜
Ignition							⊜	⊜
Transmission							⊜	⊜
Electrical							⊜	⊜
A/C							⊜	⊜
Suspension							⊜	⊜
Brakes							⊜	⊜
Exhaust							⊜	⊜
Power equip.							⊜	⊜
Paint/trim/rust							⊜	⊜
Integrity							○	⊜
Hardware							⊖	⊖
RELIABILITY VERDICT							✔	✔

Honda Odyssey

TROUBLE SPOTS	97	98	99	00	01	02	03	04
Engine	⊜	⊖	⊜	⊜	⊜	⊖	⊜	⊜
Cooling	⊜	⊜	⊜	⊜	⊜	⊜	⊜	⊜
Fuel	⊜	⊖	⊖	⊖	⊖	⊜	⊜	⊜
Ignition	⊖	⊜	⊖	⊜	⊜	⊜	⊜	⊜
Transmission	⊜	⊖	◒	⊖	○	○	⊜	⊜
Electrical	⊖	⊖	○	⊖	⊖	⊖	⊖	⊜
A/C	⊖	⊖	⊖	⊜	⊜	⊜	⊜	⊜
Suspension	⊜	⊜	⊖	⊜	⊜	⊜	⊜	⊜
Brakes	○	◒	○	○	○	⊜	⊜	⊜
Exhaust	⊜	⊖	⊖	⊜	⊜	⊜	⊜	⊜
Power equip.	⊖	⊖	◒	◒	◒	○	⊖	⊜
Paint/trim/rust	⊖	⊜	⊖	⊜	⊜	⊜	⊜	⊜
Integrity	⊖	⊖	○	○	○	○	⊖	⊖
Hardware	⊖	⊖	◒	◒	○	⊜	⊜	⊜
RELIABILITY VERDICT	✔	✔	-	✔	✔	-	✔	✔

Honda Pilot

TROUBLE SPOTS	97	98	99	00	01	02	03	04
Engine							⊜	⊜
Cooling							⊜	⊜
Fuel							⊜	⊜
Ignition							⊜	⊜
Transmission							⊜	⊜
Electrical							⊖	⊜
A/C							⊜	⊜
Suspension							⊜	⊜
Brakes							⊜	⊜
Exhaust							⊜	⊜
Power equip.							⊜	⊜
Paint/trim/rust							⊜	⊜
Integrity							⊖	⊖
Hardware							⊖	⊜
RELIABILITY VERDICT							✔	✔

Honda Prelude

TROUBLE SPOTS	97	98	99	00	01	02	03	04
Engine	○	○	Insufficient data	Insufficient data	○			
Cooling	⊖	⊜			⊜			
Fuel	⊖	⊖			⊜			
Ignition	⊜	⊜			⊜			
Transmission	⊖	⊜			⊖			
Electrical	⊖	⊖			⊖			
A/C	⊖	⊜			⊜			
Suspension	○	⊜			⊜			
Brakes	○	⊜			⊜			
Exhaust	⊖	⊜			⊜			
Power equip.	⊜	⊜			⊜			
Paint/trim/rust	○	⊖			⊖			
Integrity	⊖	○			○			
Hardware	⊖	⊖			⊜			
RELIABILITY VERDICT	✔	✔			✔			

Honda S2000

TROUBLE SPOTS	97	98	99	00	01	02	03	04
Engine				⊜	○	⊜	⊜	Insufficient data
Cooling				⊜	⊜	⊜	⊜	
Fuel				⊜	⊜	⊜	⊜	
Ignition				⊜	⊜	⊜	⊜	
Transmission				⊜	○	⊜	⊜	
Electrical				⊜	⊖	⊜	⊜	
A/C				⊜	⊜	⊜	⊜	
Suspension				⊜	⊜	⊜	⊜	
Brakes				⊜	⊜	⊜	⊜	
Exhaust				⊜	⊜	⊜	⊜	
Power equip.				⊜	⊖	◒	⊜	
Paint/trim/rust				⊖	⊜	⊜	⊜	
Integrity				⊖	◒	○	⊜	
Hardware				⊖	⊖	⊖	⊜	
RELIABILITY VERDICT				✔	✔	✔	✔	

Hummer H2

TROUBLE SPOTS	97	98	99	00	01	02	03	04
Engine							⊜	Insufficient data
Cooling							⊜	
Fuel							⊜	
Ignition							⊜	
Transmission							⊜	
Electrical							⊖	
A/C							⊜	
Suspension							⊖	
Brakes							⊜	
Exhaust							⊜	
Power equip.							○	
Paint/trim/rust							⊜	
Integrity							○	
Hardware							⊖	
RELIABILITY VERDICT							-	

Hyundai Accent

TROUBLE SPOTS	97	98	99	00	01	02	03	04
Engine	Insufficient data	Insufficient data	Insufficient data	Insufficient data	⊖	⊜	⊜	Insufficient data
Cooling					⊜	⊜	⊜	
Fuel					○	⊖	⊜	
Ignition					⊖	⊜	⊜	
Transmission					○	○	⊖	
Electrical					⊖	○	⊖	
A/C					⊖	⊜	⊜	
Suspension					⊜	⊜	⊜	
Brakes					○	◒	⊜	
Exhaust					⊜	⊜	⊜	
Power equip.					⊖	⊜	⊜	
Paint/trim/rust					⊖	⊖	⊜	
Integrity					○	⊖	○	
Hardware					○	⊖	⊜	
RELIABILITY VERDICT					-	-	✔	

Hyundai Elantra

Trouble spots	97	98	99	00	01	02	03	04
Engine	Insufficient data	Insufficient data	⊖	⊖	⊜	⊜	⊜	⊜
Cooling			⊜	⊖	⊜	⊜	⊜	⊜
Fuel			⊖	○	○	⊖	⊜	⊜
Ignition			⊖	○	⊖	⊜	⊜	⊜
Transmission			◒	○	⊜	⊖	⊜	⊜
Electrical			○	○	◒	⊖	⊜	⊜
A/C			⊜	⊜	⊜	⊜	⊜	⊜
Suspension			⊜	⊜	⊖	⊜	⊖	⊜
Brakes			○	⊖	○	○	⊖	⊜
Exhaust			○	⊜	⊜	⊜	⊜	⊜
Power equip.			◒	◒	○	⊖	⊜	⊜
Paint/trim/rust			○	○	○	○	⊖	⊖
Integrity			○	○	○	○	⊖	⊖
Hardware			○	○	○	⊖	⊖	⊜
RELIABILITY VERDICT			-	-	-	-	✓	✓

Hyundai Santa Fe

Trouble spots	97	98	99	00	01	02	03	04
Engine					⊖	⊜	⊜	⊜
Cooling					⊜	⊜	⊜	⊜
Fuel					◒	⊖	⊖	⊜
Ignition					⊖	⊜	⊜	⊜
Transmission					⊖	⊖	⊖	⊜
Electrical					◒	⊖	⊜	⊜
A/C					⊖	⊜	⊜	⊜
Suspension					⊖	⊜	⊜	⊜
Brakes					○	⊜	⊖	⊖
Exhaust					⊜	⊜	⊜	⊜
Power equip.					○	⊖	⊜	⊜
Paint/trim/rust					⊖	⊖	⊜	⊜
Integrity					○	⊖	⊖	⊜
Hardware					⊖	⊖	⊖	⊜
RELIABILITY VERDICT					-	✓	✓	✓

Hyundai Sonata

Trouble spots	97	98	99	00	01	02	03	04
Engine	Insufficient data	Insufficient data	Insufficient data	⊖	⊖	⊜	⊜	⊜
Cooling				⊜	⊜	⊜	⊜	⊜
Fuel				◒	○	○	⊜	⊜
Ignition				⊖	⊜	⊜	⊜	⊜
Transmission				⊖	⊖	⊜	⊜	⊜
Electrical				○	○	○	⊜	⊜
A/C				⊜	⊜	⊜	⊜	⊜
Suspension				⊖	⊜	⊜	⊜	⊜
Brakes				◒	○	⊖	⊜	⊜
Exhaust				⊜	⊜	⊜	⊜	⊜
Power equip.				●	◒	○	⊜	⊜
Paint/trim/rust				◒	◒	○	⊖	⊜
Integrity				○	⊜	⊜	⊜	⊜
Hardware				○	⊖	⊜	⊖	⊜
RELIABILITY VERDICT				✗	-	-	✓	✓

Hyundai XG300, XG350

Trouble spots	97	98	99	00	01	02	03	04
Engine					⊖	⊖	⊜	⊜
Cooling					⊜	⊜	⊜	⊜
Fuel					○	◒	⊖	⊜
Ignition					⊜	⊜	⊜	⊜
Transmission					○	⊜	⊜	⊜
Electrical					●	○	⊖	⊜
A/C					⊖	⊖	⊜	⊜
Suspension					⊖	⊖	⊜	⊜
Brakes					⊖	⊖	⊜	⊜
Exhaust					⊜	⊜	⊜	⊜
Power equip.					○	⊜	⊜	⊖
Paint/trim/rust					⊜	⊜	⊖	⊖
Integrity					○	⊖	⊜	⊖
Hardware					⊖	⊖	○	⊖
RELIABILITY VERDICT					-	-	✓	✗

Infiniti FX

Trouble spots	97	98	99	00	01	02	03	04
Engine							⊜	⊜
Cooling							⊜	⊜
Fuel							⊜	⊜
Ignition							⊜	⊜
Transmission							⊜	⊜
Electrical							⊖	⊜
A/C							⊜	⊜
Suspension							⊜	⊜
Brakes							⊖	⊜
Exhaust							⊜	⊜
Power equip.							○	⊖
Paint/trim/rust							⊖	⊜
Integrity							⊖	⊜
Hardware							○	⊜
RELIABILITY VERDICT							✓	✓

Infiniti G20

Trouble spots	97	98	99	00	01	02	03	04
Engine			⊜	⊜	Insufficient data	⊜		
Cooling			⊜	⊜		⊜		
Fuel			⊜	⊖		⊜		
Ignition			⊜	⊜		⊜		
Transmission			⊜	⊖		⊜		
Electrical			○	◒		⊜		
A/C			⊜	⊜		⊜		
Suspension			○	⊜		⊜		
Brakes			⊖	⊖		⊜		
Exhaust			⊜	⊜		⊜		
Power equip.			⊖	⊜		⊜		
Paint/trim/rust			⊖	⊖		⊜		
Integrity			⊖	⊖		⊖		
Hardware			⊖	⊜		⊜		
RELIABILITY VERDICT			✓	✓		✓		

Infiniti G35

Trouble spots	97	98	99	00	01	02	03	04
Engine							⊜	⊜
Cooling							⊜	⊜
Fuel							⊜	⊜
Ignition							⊜	⊜
Transmission							⊜	⊜
Electrical							⊖	⊜
A/C							⊜	⊜
Suspension							⊜	⊜
Brakes							◒	⊜
Exhaust							⊜	⊜
Power equip.							⊖	⊜
Paint/trim/rust							⊜	⊜
Integrity							⊖	⊖
Hardware							⊜	⊜
RELIABILITY VERDICT							-	✓

Infiniti I30, I35

Trouble spots	97	98	99	00	01	02	03	04
Engine	⊖	⊖	⊜	⊜	⊜	⊜	⊜	Insufficient data
Cooling	⊜	⊜	⊜	⊜	⊜	⊜	⊜	
Fuel	⊖	⊖	○	⊖	⊖	⊖	⊜	
Ignition	⊖	⊜	○	⊖	⊜	⊜	⊜	
Transmission	⊖	⊜	⊜	⊜	⊜	⊜	⊜	
Electrical	○	○	⊖	⊖	⊖	⊜	⊖	
A/C	⊖	⊖	⊖	⊜	⊜	⊜	⊜	
Suspension	⊖	⊖	⊜	⊜	⊜	⊜	⊜	
Brakes	◒	◒	○	○	○	⊜	⊖	
Exhaust	⊜	⊜	⊜	⊜	⊜	⊜	⊜	
Power equip.	⊖	⊖	⊖	⊖	⊖	⊖	⊖	
Paint/trim/rust	⊖	⊖	⊖	⊜	⊜	⊜	⊜	
Integrity	⊜	○	⊜	⊖	⊖	⊖	⊖	
Hardware	⊜	⊖	⊜	⊖	⊖	⊜	⊜	
RELIABILITY VERDICT	✓	✓	✓	✓	✓	✓	✓	

Infiniti Q45

TROUBLE SPOTS	97	98	99	00	01	02	03	04
Engine	⊜		⊜			⊖		
Cooling	⊜		⊜			⊜		
Fuel	⊖		○			⊜		
Ignition	⊜		⊖			⊜		
Transmission	⊜		⊜			⊖		
Electrical	⊖	Insufficient data	⊜	Insufficient data	Insufficient data	⊖	Insufficient data	Insufficient data
A/C	⊜		⊖			⊖		
Suspension	○		⊖			⊖		
Brakes	◒		⊖			⊖		
Exhaust	⊜		⊜			⊜		
Power equip.	⊜		⊜			⊖		
Paint/trim/rust	⊜		⊖			⊖		
Integrity	⊖		⊖			⊜		
Hardware	⊜		⊜			⊖		
RELIABILITY VERDICT	✔		✔			–		

Infiniti QX4

TROUBLE SPOTS	97	98	99	00	01	02	03	04
Engine		⊖	⊜		⊜	⊜		
Cooling		⊜	⊖		⊜	⊜		
Fuel		⊖	⊖		⊖	⊜		
Ignition		⊜	⊜		⊜	⊜		
Transmission		⊖	⊜		⊜	⊜		
Electrical	Insufficient data	⊜	⊖	Insufficient data	⊜	⊖	Insufficient data	
A/C		⊖	⊖		⊖	⊜		
Suspension		⊖	⊖		⊜	⊖		
Brakes		○	○		○	⊖		
Exhaust		○	⊜		⊜	⊖		
Power equip.		⊖	⊖		○	⊖		
Paint/trim/rust		⊖	⊜		⊜	⊜		
Integrity		⊖	⊖		⊖	⊖		
Hardware		⊖	⊜		⊖	⊜		
RELIABILITY VERDICT		✔	✔		✔	✔		

Isuzu Rodeo

TROUBLE SPOTS	97	98	99	00	01	02	03	04
Engine	◒	◒	◒	○	⊖	⊖		
Cooling	◒	⊖	⊜	⊜	⊜	⊜		
Fuel	○	◒	●	●	○	⊖		
Ignition	⊖	○	⊖	⊖	⊜	⊜		
Transmission	⊖	⊖	○	○	⊖	⊖		
Electrical	●	●	◒	○	○	○	Insufficient data	Insufficient data
A/C	○	◒	○	○	⊖	⊜		
Suspension	⊖	○	○	⊖	⊖	⊜		
Brakes	◒	●	●	○	○	◒		
Exhaust	⊖	⊖	⊖	⊜	⊜	⊜		
Power equip.	◒	⊖	⊖	⊖	⊖	⊜		
Paint/trim/rust	◒	○	○	⊖	⊜	⊖		
Integrity	●	◒	◒	○	○	○		
Hardware	○	○	○	○	⊖	⊖		
RELIABILITY VERDICT	✘	✘	✘	–	–	–		

Jaguar S-Type

TROUBLE SPOTS	97	98	99	00	01	02	03	04
Engine				○	⊜		⊜	
Cooling				◒	⊖		⊜	
Fuel				⊖	⊖		⊖	
Ignition				⊖	⊖		⊜	
Transmission				◒	○		◒	
Electrical				●	◒	Insufficient data	◒	Insufficient data
A/C				○	⊜		○	
Suspension				⊖	⊖		○	
Brakes				○	○		◒	
Exhaust				⊜	⊜		⊜	
Power equip.				◒	◒		◒	
Paint/trim/rust				⊜	⊜		⊜	
Integrity				◒	○		○	
Hardware				◒	◒		○	
RELIABILITY VERDICT				✘	✘		✘	

Jaguar X-Type

TROUBLE SPOTS	97	98	99	00	01	02	03	04
Engine						⊖	⊜	⊜
Cooling						◒	⊖	⊜
Fuel						○	⊖	⊜
Ignition						⊜	⊜	⊜
Transmission						●	⊖	⊜
Electrical						◒	⊖	⊜
A/C						⊖	⊖	⊜
Suspension						○	⊜	⊜
Brakes						○	⊖	⊜
Exhaust						⊜	⊜	⊜
Power equip.						○	⊖	⊜
Paint/trim/rust						⊖	⊜	⊜
Integrity						●	○	⊜
Hardware						●	⊖	⊜
RELIABILITY VERDICT						✘	✘	–

Jeep Cherokee

TROUBLE SPOTS	97	98	99	00	01	02	03	04
Engine	⊖	⊖	⊖	⊖	⊖			
Cooling	◒	⊖	⊖	⊜	⊖			
Fuel	◒	○	⊖	⊖	○			
Ignition	⊜	⊖	⊜	⊖	⊖			
Transmission	⊖	⊖	⊖	⊜	⊖			
Electrical	●	◒	◒	⊖	○			
A/C	●	●	○	○	○			
Suspension	○	⊖	⊖	○	⊖			
Brakes	◒	◒	◒	◒	◒			
Exhaust	⊜	⊖	⊜	⊜	⊜			
Power equip.	○	◒	●	○	○			
Paint/trim/rust	◒	○	○	○	⊖			
Integrity	○	○	○	○	○			
Hardware	○	○	○	○	○			
RELIABILITY VERDICT	–	–	–	–	–			

Jeep Grand Cherokee 4WD

TROUBLE SPOTS	97	98	99	00	01	02	03	04
Engine	○	⊖	⊖	⊖	⊖	⊜	⊜	⊜
Cooling	◒	○	○	⊖	⊜	⊜	⊜	⊜
Fuel	◒	○	○	⊖	⊖	⊖	⊖	⊜
Ignition	⊖	⊖	⊖	⊖	⊜	⊜	⊜	⊜
Transmission	◒	◒	◒	○	○	⊖	⊖	⊜
Electrical	◒	◒	◒	○	○	○	⊜	⊜
A/C	●	◒	○	⊖	⊖	⊖	⊖	⊜
Suspension	○	◒	○	⊖	○	⊖	⊖	⊖
Brakes	●	●	●	●	●	●	○	⊜
Exhaust	○	○	⊜	⊜	⊜	⊜	⊜	⊜
Power equip.	◒	◒	●	◒	◒	⊖	⊖	⊜
Paint/trim/rust	⊖	⊖	⊖	⊖	⊖	⊜	⊜	⊜
Integrity	○	○	◒	○	○	⊖	⊖	⊖
Hardware	○	○	○	○	⊖	⊖	⊜	⊜
RELIABILITY VERDICT	✘	✘	✘	✘	✘	✘	–	–

Jeep Liberty

TROUBLE SPOTS	97	98	99	00	01	02	03	04
Engine						⊜	⊜	⊜
Cooling						⊜	⊜	⊜
Fuel						⊜	⊜	⊜
Ignition						⊜	⊜	⊜
Transmission						⊖	⊖	⊜
Electrical						⊖	⊜	⊜
A/C						⊜	⊜	⊜
Suspension						○	⊖	⊜
Brakes						○	○	⊜
Exhaust						⊜	⊜	⊜
Power equip.						⊖	⊜	⊖
Paint/trim/rust						⊖	⊜	⊜
Integrity						⊖	⊖	⊜
Hardware						⊖	⊜	⊜
RELIABILITY VERDICT						–	–	–

Jeep Wrangler

Trouble spots	97	98	99	00	01	02	03	04
Engine	⊖	⊖	⊖	⊖	⊖	⊜	⊜	⊜
Cooling	◒	◒	○	○	⊜	⊜	⊜	⊜
Fuel	○	○	⊜	⊖	○	⊖	⊜	⊜
Ignition	⊖	⊖	⊜	⊖	⊖	⊜	⊜	⊜
Transmission	○	○	⊜	○	⊜	⊜	⊖	⊜
Electrical	◒	●	◒	⊖	○	⊖	⊖	⊜
A/C	◒	◒	○	⊖	⊜	⊖	⊜	⊜
Suspension	○	○	⊖	⊖	⊖	⊖	⊜	⊜
Brakes	⊖	○	⊖	○	○	⊖	⊜	⊜
Exhaust	●	◒	○	⊜	⊜	⊜	⊜	⊜
Power equip.	⊜	⊜	⊜	⊜	⊜	⊜	⊜	⊜
Paint/trim/rust	○	○	◒	◒	○	○	⊖	⊖
Integrity	◒	◒	○	○	○	○	○	⊖
Hardware	○	○	○	○	◒	○	⊖	⊜
RELIABILITY VERDICT	-	✗	-	-	-	-	✗	-

Kia Sedona

Trouble spots	97	98	99	00	01	02	03	04
Engine						⊖	⊜	Insufficient data
Cooling						⊜	⊜	
Fuel						○	⊖	
Ignition						⊜	⊜	
Transmission						⊜	⊖	
Electrical						◒	○	
A/C						○	⊖	
Suspension						○	⊜	
Brakes						⊖	⊖	
Exhaust						⊜	⊜	
Power equip.						◒	⊖	
Paint/trim/rust						◒	⊖	
Integrity						◒	○	
Hardware						●	○	
RELIABILITY VERDICT						✗	-	

Kia Sorento

Trouble spots	97	98	99	00	01	02	03	04
Engine							⊜	⊜
Cooling							⊜	⊜
Fuel							⊖	⊜
Ignition							⊜	⊜
Transmission							⊜	⊜
Electrical							⊖	⊜
A/C							⊜	⊜
Suspension							⊜	⊜
Brakes							⊖	⊜
Exhaust							⊜	⊜
Power equip.							⊜	⊜
Paint/trim/rust							○	⊜
Integrity							○	⊜
Hardware							⊖	⊜
RELIABILITY VERDICT							-	✓

Land Rover Discovery

Trouble spots	97	98	99	00	01	02	03	04
Engine	Insufficient data	Insufficient data	Insufficient data	◒	○	Insufficient data	○	Insufficient data
Cooling				◒	⊖		⊜	
Fuel				○	○		⊜	
Ignition				○	○		⊜	
Transmission				◒	⊖		⊖	
Electrical				◒	◒		⊖	
A/C				○	○		⊜	
Suspension				⊖	○		⊜	
Brakes				●	●		○	
Exhaust				⊖	⊜		⊜	
Power equip.				◒	○		○	
Paint/trim/rust				⊖	⊖		⊜	
Integrity				◒	●		◒	
Hardware				●	◒		○	
RELIABILITY VERDICT				✗	✗		✗	

Land Rover Freelander

Trouble spots	97	98	99	00	01	02	03	04
Engine						⊖	Insufficient data	Insufficient data
Cooling						⊖		
Fuel						○		
Ignition						⊖		
Transmission						○		
Electrical						●		
A/C						◒		
Suspension						○		
Brakes						●		
Exhaust						⊜		
Power equip.						●		
Paint/trim/rust						⊖		
Integrity						◒		
Hardware						◒		
RELIABILITY VERDICT						✗		

Lexus ES300, ES330

Trouble spots	97	98	99	00	01	02	03	04
Engine	⊖	⊜	⊜	⊜	⊜	⊜	⊜	⊜
Cooling	⊜	⊜	⊜	⊜	⊜	⊜	⊜	⊜
Fuel	⊖	⊖	⊖	⊖	⊜	⊜	⊜	⊜
Ignition	⊜	⊜	⊜	⊜	⊜	⊜	⊜	⊜
Transmission	⊜	⊜	⊜	⊜	⊜	⊖	⊜	⊖
Electrical	⊖	⊖	○	⊖	⊖	⊜	⊜	⊜
A/C	⊜	⊜	⊜	⊜	⊜	⊜	⊜	⊜
Suspension	○	⊖	⊖	⊜	⊜	⊜	⊜	⊜
Brakes	⊖	⊖	⊖	○	○	◒	⊖	⊜
Exhaust	⊜	⊜	⊜	⊜	⊜	⊜	⊜	⊜
Power equip.	⊖	⊖	⊜	⊜	⊜	⊖	⊖	⊜
Paint/trim/rust	⊖	⊜	⊖	⊖	⊖	⊜	⊜	⊖
Integrity	⊖	⊜	⊜	⊜	⊖	⊖	⊖	⊖
Hardware	⊖	⊜	⊖	⊜	⊖	⊜	⊜	⊜
RELIABILITY VERDICT	✓	✓	✓	✓	✓	✓	✓	-

Lexus GS300/GS400, GS430

Trouble spots	97	98	99	00	01	02	03	04
Engine	Insufficient data	⊜	⊜	⊜	⊜	⊜	⊜	⊜
Cooling		⊜	⊜	⊜	⊜	⊜	⊜	⊜
Fuel		⊖	⊖	⊜	⊜	⊜	⊜	⊜
Ignition		⊜	⊜	⊜	⊜	⊜	⊜	⊜
Transmission		⊜	⊜	⊜	⊜	⊜	⊜	⊜
Electrical		⊖	⊖	⊖	⊖	⊜	⊜	⊜
A/C		⊜	⊜	⊜	⊜	⊜	⊜	⊜
Suspension		⊖	⊜	⊖	⊖	⊖	⊜	⊜
Brakes		⊖	⊖	⊖	⊖	⊜	⊜	⊜
Exhaust		⊜	⊜	⊜	⊜	⊜	⊜	⊜
Power equip.		○	○	⊜	⊖	⊜	⊜	⊜
Paint/trim/rust		⊖	⊜	⊜	⊜	⊜	⊜	⊜
Integrity		○	⊖	⊜	⊖	⊖	⊖	⊜
Hardware		⊖	⊜	⊜	⊖	⊜	⊖	⊜
RELIABILITY VERDICT		✓	✓	✓	✓	✓	✓	✓

Lexus GX470

Trouble spots	97	98	99	00	01	02	03	04
Engine							⊜	⊜
Cooling							⊜	⊜
Fuel							⊜	⊜
Ignition							⊜	⊜
Transmission							⊜	⊜
Electrical							⊜	⊜
A/C							⊜	⊜
Suspension							⊖	⊜
Brakes							⊜	⊜
Exhaust							⊜	⊜
Power equip.							○	⊜
Paint/trim/rust							⊜	⊜
Integrity							○	⊜
Hardware							⊖	⊜
RELIABILITY VERDICT							✗	✓

Lexus IS300

TROUBLE SPOTS	97	98	99	00	01	02	03	04
Engine					⊜	⊜	⊜	Insufficient data
Cooling					⊜	⊜	⊜	
Fuel					⊜	⊜	⊜	
Ignition					⊜	⊜	⊜	
Transmission					⊜	⊜	⊜	
Electrical					⊜	⊜	⊜	
A/C					⊖	⊜	⊜	
Suspension					⊜	⊖	⊜	
Brakes					⊖	⊜	⊜	
Exhaust					⊜	⊜	⊜	
Power equip.					⊖	⊖	⊜	
Paint/trim/rust					⊜	⊖	⊖	
Integrity					⊜	⊖	⊜	
Hardware					⊜	⊖	⊜	
RELIABILITY VERDICT					✔	✔	✔	

Lexus LS400, LS430

TROUBLE SPOTS	97	98	99	00	01	02	03	04
Engine	⊜	⊜	⊜	⊜	⊜	⊜	⊜	⊜
Cooling	⊜	⊜	⊜	⊜	⊜	⊜	⊜	⊜
Fuel	⊜	⊖	⊜	⊜	⊜	⊜	⊜	⊖
Ignition	⊜	⊜	⊜	⊜	⊜	⊜	⊜	⊜
Transmission	⊜	⊜	⊜	⊜	⊜	⊜	⊜	⊜
Electrical	⊖	⊖	○	⊖	⊖	⊜	⊜	⊜
A/C	⊖	⊜	⊜	⊜	⊜	⊜	⊜	⊜
Suspension	⊖	⊖	⊖	⊖	⊜	⊜	⊜	⊜
Brakes	⊖	⊖	⊖	⊜	⊖	⊖	⊜	⊜
Exhaust	⊜	⊜	⊜	⊜	⊜	⊜	⊜	⊜
Power equip.	⊖	⊜	⊖	⊖	○	⊖	⊜	⊖
Paint/trim/rust	⊜	⊜	⊜	⊜	⊜	⊜	⊜	⊜
Integrity	⊜	⊖	⊖	⊜	⊖	⊜	⊜	⊜
Hardware	⊜	⊖	⊖	⊜	⊖	⊜	⊜	⊜
RELIABILITY VERDICT	✔	✔	✔	✔	✔	✔	✔	✔

Lexus LX450, LX470

TROUBLE SPOTS	97	98	99	00	01	02	03	04
Engine	Insufficient data	Insufficient data	⊜	⊖	⊜	⊜	⊜	Insufficient data
Cooling			⊜	⊜	⊜	⊜	⊜	
Fuel			⊖	⊜	⊜	⊜	⊜	
Ignition			⊖	⊜	⊜	⊜	⊜	
Transmission			⊜	⊜	⊜	⊜	⊜	
Electrical			⊖	○	⊖	⊜	⊜	
A/C			⊜	⊖	⊜	⊜	⊖	
Suspension			⊜	⊖	⊖	⊜	⊖	
Brakes			○	○	○	⊖	⊖	
Exhaust			⊜	⊜	⊖	⊜	⊜	
Power equip.			○	◒	○	⊖	⊖	
Paint/trim/rust			⊖	⊖	⊜	⊜	⊜	
Integrity			⊖	⊖	⊖	⊜	⊖	
Hardware			⊜	⊖	⊜	⊖	⊜	
RELIABILITY VERDICT			✔	✔	✔	✔	✔	

Lexus RX300, RX330

TROUBLE SPOTS	97	98	99	00	01	02	03	04
Engine			⊖	⊖	⊜	⊜	⊜	⊜
Cooling			⊜	⊜	⊜	⊜	⊜	⊜
Fuel			⊖	⊖	⊜	⊜	⊜	⊜
Ignition			⊜	⊜	⊜	⊜	⊜	⊜
Transmission			⊖	⊜	⊜	⊜	⊜	⊜
Electrical			○	⊖	⊜	⊜	⊜	⊜
A/C			⊜	⊜	⊜	⊜	⊜	⊜
Suspension			⊖	⊜	⊜	⊜	⊜	⊜
Brakes			⊖	⊜	⊖	⊖	⊜	⊜
Exhaust			⊖	⊜	⊜	⊜	⊜	⊜
Power equip.			⊖	⊜	⊜	⊜	⊜	⊜
Paint/trim/rust			⊖	⊜	⊜	⊜	⊜	⊜
Integrity			⊖	⊖	⊖	⊜	⊖	⊖
Hardware			⊖	⊜	⊜	⊜	⊜	⊜
RELIABILITY VERDICT			✔	✔	✔	✔	✔	✔

Lexus SC300/SC400, SC430

TROUBLE SPOTS	97	98	99	00	01	02	03	04
Engine	Insufficient data	Insufficient data	Insufficient data	Insufficient data		⊜	⊜	Insufficient data
Cooling						⊜	⊜	
Fuel						⊜	⊜	
Ignition						⊜	⊜	
Transmission						⊜	⊜	
Electrical						⊖	⊖	
A/C						⊜	⊜	
Suspension						⊖	⊖	
Brakes						⊜	⊜	
Exhaust						⊜	⊜	
Power equip.						⊖	⊜	
Paint/trim/rust						⊜	⊜	
Integrity						○	⊜	
Hardware						⊖	⊖	
RELIABILITY VERDICT						✔	✔	

Lincoln Aviator

TROUBLE SPOTS	97	98	99	00	01	02	03	04
Engine							⊜	⊜
Cooling							⊜	⊜
Fuel							⊜	⊜
Ignition							⊜	⊜
Transmission							⊖	⊜
Electrical							○	⊖
A/C							⊖	⊜
Suspension							⊖	⊜
Brakes							⊖	⊜
Exhaust							⊜	⊜
Power equip.							◒	⊖
Paint/trim/rust							⊜	⊖
Integrity							⊖	○
Hardware							⊖	⊖
RELIABILITY VERDICT							✘	✘

Lincoln Continental

TROUBLE SPOTS	97	98	99	00	01	02	03	04
Engine	⊖	⊖	⊜	⊜	⊜	⊜		
Cooling	⊖	⊖	⊖	⊜	⊜	⊜		
Fuel	○	○	○	⊖	⊖	⊜		
Ignition	○	○	⊖	⊜	⊜	⊜		
Transmission	○	⊖	○	⊖	○	⊜		
Electrical	●	◒	○	○	○	⊖		
A/C	◒	⊖	⊖	⊖	⊖	⊖		
Suspension	●	◒	●	○	○	⊖		
Brakes	◒	○	◒	◒	○	⊜		
Exhaust	⊖	⊜	⊜	⊜	⊜	⊜		
Power equip.	◒	◒	◒	◒	○	○		
Paint/trim/rust	⊖	⊖	⊖	⊖	⊜	⊜		
Integrity	◒	○	⊖	○	○	⊜		
Hardware	◒	○	⊖	○	○	○		
RELIABILITY VERDICT	–	–	–	–	–	✔		

Lincoln LS

TROUBLE SPOTS	97	98	99	00	01	02	03	04
Engine				○	○	⊜	⊜	⊜
Cooling				⊖	⊜	⊜	⊜	⊜
Fuel				⊖	⊜	⊖	⊜	⊜
Ignition				⊖	⊖	⊜	⊖	⊜
Transmission				○	⊜	⊖	◒	⊖
Electrical				○	○	○	○	⊜
A/C				○	⊖	⊖	⊖	⊜
Suspension				○	⊖	⊖	⊖	⊜
Brakes				○	⊖	⊖	⊖	⊜
Exhaust				⊜	⊜	⊜	⊜	⊜
Power equip.				●	●	○	⊖	⊖
Paint/trim/rust				⊖	⊖	⊖	⊖	⊖
Integrity				◒	○	○	○	⊖
Hardware				◒	○	⊖	⊖	⊖
RELIABILITY VERDICT				✘	–	–	✘	–

Lincoln Navigator

TROUBLE SPOTS	97	98	99	00	01	02	03	04
Engine		○	⊖	⊖	⊖	⊖	⊜	⊜
Cooling		⊜	⊜	⊜	⊜	⊖	⊜	⊜
Fuel		◒	⊖	⊖	⊜	⊖	⊜	⊜
Ignition		⊖	⊖	⊖	⊖	⊖	⊜	⊜
Transmission		⊖	○	○	⊖	○	⊜	⊜
Electrical		○	◒	○	○	○	◒	○
A/C		◒	⊖	⊖	⊖	○	○	⊖
Suspension		◒	○	◒	⊖	○	⊖	⊖
Brakes		◒	○	◒	○	○	⊜	⊜
Exhaust		⊜	⊜	⊜	⊜	⊖	⊜	⊜
Power equip.		◒	◒	⊖	○	◒	●	○
Paint/trim/rust		⊖	○	○	⊜	⊖	⊖	⊖
Integrity		○	◒	⊖	⊖	◒	◒	○
Hardware		○	○	○	○	○	○	○
RELIABILITY VERDICT		–	–	–	–	✗	✗	✗

Lincoln Town Car

TROUBLE SPOTS	97	98	99	00	01	02	03	04
Engine	⊖	⊜	⊖	⊜	⊖	⊜	⊜	⊜
Cooling	⊖	⊜	⊜	⊜	⊜	⊜	⊜	⊜
Fuel	○	⊖	⊖	⊖	○	⊖	⊜	⊜
Ignition	⊖	⊜	⊖	⊖	⊖	⊜	⊜	⊜
Transmission	⊖	⊖	⊖	⊜	⊜	⊜	⊜	⊜
Electrical	○	◒	○	○	○	⊖	⊖	⊜
A/C	○	⊖	⊖	⊖	○	⊜	⊖	⊜
Suspension	○	◒	⊖	⊜	⊖	⊖	⊖	⊜
Brakes	◒	○	⊜	○	⊜	⊜	⊖	⊜
Exhaust	⊖	⊜	⊜	⊜	⊜	⊜	⊜	⊜
Power equip.	◒	●	◒	○	○	○	○	⊜
Paint/trim/rust	○	⊜	⊜	⊖	⊖	⊜	⊖	⊜
Integrity	⊖	○	○	○	⊖	○	○	⊖
Hardware	⊖	⊖	○	⊜	⊜	⊜	⊖	⊜
RELIABILITY VERDICT	✓	✓	✓	✓	✓	✓	–	–

Mazda 626, Mazda6

TROUBLE SPOTS	97	98	99	00	01	02	03	04
Engine	○	○	⊖	⊜	⊜	⊜	⊜	⊜
Cooling	○	○	⊖	⊖	⊜	⊜	⊖	⊜
Fuel	◒	○	○	⊖	⊜	⊜	○	⊜
Ignition	○	⊜	⊜	⊜	⊖	⊜	⊜	⊜
Transmission	○	○	○	⊖	⊖	⊖	⊜	⊜
Electrical	○	○	○	⊖	⊖	⊜	⊜	⊖
A/C	⊜	⊖	○	○	⊖	⊜	⊜	⊜
Suspension	○	⊖	⊖	○	⊖	⊖	⊜	⊜
Brakes	○	⊖	○	○	⊜	⊖	○	⊜
Exhaust	◒	⊜	⊖	⊜	⊜	⊜	⊜	⊜
Power equip.	⊖	⊜	⊖	⊖	⊖	⊖	⊖	⊜
Paint/trim/rust	⊖	⊖	⊖	⊖	⊖	⊜	⊖	⊜
Integrity	⊖	◒	○	○	⊖	⊖	○	⊖
Hardware	⊖	⊖	⊖	⊜	⊖	⊖	⊖	⊖
RELIABILITY VERDICT	–	✓	–	✓	✓	✓	✗	✗

Mazda B-Series 4WD

TROUBLE SPOTS	97	98	99	00	01	02	03	04
Engine	○	⊖	⊖	⊖	⊖	⊜	⊜	⊜
Cooling	◒	○	⊖	⊖	⊜	⊜	⊜	⊜
Fuel	◒	○	○	⊖	○	⊖	⊜	⊜
Ignition	⊖	⊖	⊜	⊖	⊖	⊜	⊜	⊜
Transmission	○	○	○	⊖	○	○	⊜	⊜
Electrical	●	●	◒	○	○	⊖	⊖	⊖
A/C	◒	○	⊜	⊜	⊜	⊜	⊜	⊜
Suspension	⊜	○	○	○	○	⊖	⊜	⊜
Brakes	◒	◒	●	◒	○	⊖	⊖	⊜
Exhaust	⊜	⊜	⊜	⊜	⊜	⊜	⊜	⊜
Power equip.	⊖	○	⊖	⊖	○	⊖	⊜	⊖
Paint/trim/rust	⊜	⊖	⊖	⊖	⊜	⊜	⊖	⊖
Integrity	○	○	⊜	○	○	○	⊖	○
Hardware	○	○	⊖	⊖	○	○	⊜	⊖
RELIABILITY VERDICT	✗	–	–	–	✗	✗	✓	✗

Mazda MPV

TROUBLE SPOTS	97	98	99	00	01	02	03	04
Engine	Insufficient data	Insufficient data		⊖	⊜	⊖	⊜	⊜
Cooling				⊜	⊜	⊜	⊜	⊜
Fuel				⊖	⊖	○	⊜	⊜
Ignition				⊖	⊜	⊜	⊜	⊜
Transmission				⊖	⊜	⊖	○	◒
Electrical				⊖	⊖	⊖	⊜	⊜
A/C				⊜	⊜	⊜	⊜	⊜
Suspension				⊖	⊖	⊖	⊜	⊜
Brakes				⊖	⊖	⊖	⊖	⊜
Exhaust				⊖	⊜	⊖	⊜	⊜
Power equip.				⊖	⊜	⊖	⊖	⊖
Paint/trim/rust				⊜	⊜	⊜	⊜	⊜
Integrity				⊖	⊖	⊖	⊖	⊜
Hardware				○	⊖	⊖	⊜	⊜
RELIABILITY VERDICT				✓	✓	–	✗	✗

Mazda MX-5 Miata

TROUBLE SPOTS	97	98	99	00	01	02	03	04
Engine	⊜		⊜	⊜	⊜	⊜	⊖	Insufficient data
Cooling	⊖		⊖	⊜	⊜	⊜	⊜	
Fuel	⊜		◒	○	⊖	⊜	⊖	
Ignition	⊜		⊖	⊜	⊜	⊜	⊜	
Transmission	⊜		⊜	⊖	⊖	⊖	⊜	
Electrical	⊖		○	⊖	⊜	⊜	⊖	
A/C	⊖		⊜	⊜	⊜	⊖	⊜	
Suspension	⊜		⊜	⊜	⊜	⊖	⊜	
Brakes	⊖		⊜	⊜	⊜	⊖	⊜	
Exhaust	⊜		○	⊜	⊜	⊜	⊜	
Power equip.	⊜		⊖	⊜	⊖	⊖	⊜	
Paint/trim/rust	○		⊜	⊜	⊖	⊜	⊜	
Integrity	⊖		⊖	○	⊖	○	⊖	
Hardware	⊖		⊜	⊜	⊖	⊜	⊜	
RELIABILITY VERDICT	✓		✓	✓	✓	✓	✓	

Mazda Millenia

TROUBLE SPOTS	97	98	99	00	01	02	03	04
Engine	Insufficient data	⊖	⊖	⊖	⊜	⊜		
Cooling		⊜	⊜	⊜	⊜	⊜		
Fuel		●	◒	○	⊖	⊖		
Ignition		⊜	⊖	○	⊜	⊜		
Transmission		⊖	⊜	○	⊜	⊜		
Electrical		⊖	○	⊖	⊖	⊜		
A/C		⊜	⊖	⊜	⊖	⊜		
Suspension		○	⊖	⊜	⊜	⊜		
Brakes		⊜	⊜	⊜	⊖	⊜		
Exhaust		⊖	⊖	○	⊜	⊜		
Power equip.		◒	○	○	⊖	⊖		
Paint/trim/rust		○	⊖	⊜	⊖	⊖		
Integrity		⊖	⊜	⊖	⊖	⊖		
Hardware		⊜	⊖	⊜	⊜	⊖		
RELIABILITY VERDICT		✓	✓	✓	✓	✓		

Mazda ProtÈgÈ, Mazda3

TROUBLE SPOTS	97	98	99	00	01	02	03	04
Engine	⊖	⊖	⊖	⊖	⊜	⊜	⊜	⊜
Cooling	○	⊜	⊖	⊖	⊜	⊜	⊜	⊜
Fuel	◒	○	○	○	⊜	⊜	⊜	⊜
Ignition	⊜	⊜	⊖	⊖	⊜	⊜	⊜	⊜
Transmission	⊜	⊖	⊖	⊜	⊜	⊜	⊜	⊜
Electrical	◒	○	○	⊖	⊖	⊜	⊜	⊜
A/C	○	○	⊜	⊜	⊜	⊜	⊜	⊜
Suspension	⊖	⊜	○	⊖	⊜	⊜	⊜	⊜
Brakes	◒	◒	⊜	⊖	⊖	⊖	⊜	⊖
Exhaust	◒	◒	⊖	⊖	⊜	⊜	⊜	⊜
Power equip.	⊜	⊖	○	○	○	⊜	⊜	⊜
Paint/trim/rust	○	⊜	⊖	⊜	⊜	⊜	⊜	⊜
Integrity	○	○	○	○	⊖	⊖	⊖	⊜
Hardware	○	◒	⊖	⊖	⊜	⊜	⊜	⊜
RELIABILITY VERDICT	✓	✓	✓	✓	✓	✓	✓	✓

Mazda RX-8

Trouble spots	97	98	99	00	01	02	03	04
Engine								⊖
Cooling								⊜
Fuel								⊖
Ignition								⊖
Transmission								⊖
Electrical								⊜
A/C								⊖
Suspension								⊜
Brakes								⊜
Exhaust								⊜
Power equip.								⊜
Paint/trim/rust								⊜
Integrity								⊜
Hardware								⊜
RELIABILITY VERDICT								✗

Mazda Tribute

Trouble spots	97	98	99	00	01	02	03	04
Engine					⊖	⊖	⊜	⊜
Cooling					⊖	⊜	⊜	⊜
Fuel					○	○	⊖	⊜
Ignition					⊖	⊜	⊜	⊜
Transmission					○	⊖	⊜	⊜
Electrical					○	○	⊜	⊜
A/C					⊜	⊖	⊜	⊜
Suspension					⊖	⊖	⊜	⊜
Brakes					◒	○	⊜	⊜
Exhaust					⊜	⊜	⊜	⊜
Power equip.					⊖	⊖	⊜	⊜
Paint/trim/rust					⊜	⊜	⊜	⊜
Integrity					◒	◒	○	⊖
Hardware					◒	○	⊜	⊜
RELIABILITY VERDICT					✗	–	✓	✓

Mercedes-Benz C-Class V6

Trouble spots	97	98	99	00	01	02	03	04
Engine	Insufficient data	Insufficient data	◒	Insufficient data	⊖	⊜	⊜	⊜
Cooling			⊜		⊖	⊜	⊜	⊜
Fuel			●		◒	○	⊜	⊜
Ignition			⊜		○	⊜	⊜	⊜
Transmission			○		⊖	⊖	⊜	⊖
Electrical			●		●	●	◒	⊖
A/C			○		○	○	⊖	⊜
Suspension			⊖		○	○	⊖	⊜
Brakes			⊖		○	○	⊖	⊜
Exhaust			⊜		⊜	⊜	⊜	⊜
Power equip.			○		●	●	◒	⊖
Paint/trim/rust			⊜		⊜	⊜	⊜	⊜
Integrity			○		○	○	⊖	⊜
Hardware			⊖		◒	◒	⊜	⊜
RELIABILITY VERDICT			–		✗	✗	✗	✗

Mercedes-Benz CLK

Trouble spots	97	98	99	00	01	02	03	04
Engine		Insufficient data	◒	○	⊜	⊖	⊖	⊜
Cooling			⊖	⊖	⊜	⊜	⊜	⊜
Fuel			◒	◒	○	⊖	⊖	⊜
Ignition			⊜	⊖	⊖	⊖	⊜	⊜
Transmission			○	⊖	⊜	⊜	⊖	⊖
Electrical			◒	●	◒	◒	○	⊖
A/C			○	○	⊜	⊖	⊜	⊜
Suspension			○	⊖	⊜	⊖	⊜	⊜
Brakes			○	○	⊖	⊜	⊜	⊜
Exhaust			⊖	⊜	⊖	⊖	⊜	⊜
Power equip.			○	◒	●	●	◒	○
Paint/trim/rust			⊜	○	⊜	⊖	⊜	⊖
Integrity			◒	○	○	◒	○	⊜
Hardware			◒	◒	●	◒	◒	⊖
RELIABILITY VERDICT			✗	✗	–	✗	✗	✗

Mercedes-Benz E-Class

Trouble spots	97	98	99	00	01	02	03	04
Engine	◒	○	○	⊖	⊖	⊜	⊜	⊜
Cooling	⊖	⊜	⊜	⊜	⊜	⊜	⊜	⊜
Fuel	○	◒	○	○	⊖	⊖	⊖	⊜
Ignition	⊖	○	⊜	⊜	⊖	⊜	⊜	⊜
Transmission	○	⊖	○	⊖	○	⊜	⊜	⊜
Electrical	●	●	●	●	◒	◒	◒	○
A/C	●	◒	○	○	◒	◒	⊖	⊖
Suspension	◒	⊖	⊖	⊖	○	⊖	⊜	⊖
Brakes	○	○	○	○	○	⊜	⊜	⊜
Exhaust	⊖	⊜	⊖	⊖	⊖	⊖	⊜	⊜
Power equip.	●	●	●	●	◒	○	◒	○
Paint/trim/rust	⊖	○	⊖	⊖	⊖	⊜	⊜	⊜
Integrity	○	○	○	○	○	⊖	⊜	⊖
Hardware	◒	◒	○	○	○	○	⊜	⊜
RELIABILITY VERDICT	–	–	✗	–	✗	✗	✗	✗

Mercedes-Benz M-Class

Trouble spots	97	98	99	00	01	02	03	04
Engine		○	○	○	⊖	⊖	⊜	⊜
Cooling		⊖	⊖	⊖	○	◒	⊜	⊜
Fuel		●	●	◒	◒	○	⊖	⊜
Ignition		⊖	⊖	⊖	⊖	⊖	⊜	⊖
Transmission		○	○	○	○	⊖	⊜	⊜
Electrical		◒	◒	◒	●	◒	○	⊜
A/C		⊖	⊖	⊖	○	⊖	⊜	⊜
Suspension		○	○	●	◒	○	⊖	⊖
Brakes		◒	◒	●	●	●	⊖	⊜
Exhaust		⊖	⊖	○	⊜	⊜	⊜	⊜
Power equip.		●	●	●	●	◒	○	⊖
Paint/trim/rust		○	○	○	○	⊖	⊖	⊜
Integrity		●	◒	●	●	◒	○	⊖
Hardware		●	◒	●	●	◒	○	⊖
RELIABILITY VERDICT		✗	✗	✗	✗	✗	✗	✗

Mercedes-Benz S-Class

Trouble spots	97	98	99	00	01	02	03	04
Engine	Insufficient data	Insufficient data	Insufficient data	⊖	⊜	⊖	⊜	Insufficient data
Cooling				⊜	⊜	⊖	⊜	
Fuel				○	⊖	⊖	⊜	
Ignition				⊖	⊖	⊜	⊜	
Transmission				⊖	⊖	⊖	⊜	
Electrical				●	●	●	○	
A/C				○	⊖	○	⊖	
Suspension				◒	⊜	○	⊖	
Brakes				◒	○	○	⊖	
Exhaust				⊜	⊜	⊜	⊜	
Power equip.				●	○	●	●	
Paint/trim/rust				⊖	⊜	⊜	⊖	
Integrity				○	⊜	○	⊖	
Hardware				○	⊖	○	○	
RELIABILITY VERDICT				✗	–	✗	✗	

Mercedes-Benz SLK

Trouble spots	97	98	99	00	01	02	03	04
Engine		○	⊜	Insufficient data	⊖	⊖	Insufficient data	Insufficient data
Cooling		○	⊜		⊖	⊜		
Fuel		◒	○		○	⊜		
Ignition		⊜	⊜		⊜	⊜		
Transmission		○	⊜		⊖	⊜		
Electrical		●	◒		◒	○		
A/C		⊜	○		⊖	⊖		
Suspension		○	⊖		⊖	⊜		
Brakes		⊜	⊖		⊖	⊜		
Exhaust		⊜	⊜		○	○		
Power equip.		○	○		⊖	⊖		
Paint/trim/rust		⊜	⊖		⊜	⊖		
Integrity		○	◒		◒	○		
Hardware		○	○		○	○		
RELIABILITY VERDICT		–	✓		–	–		

Mercury Cougar

Trouble spots	97	98	99	00	01	02	03	04
Engine	⊖		○	⊖	⊖	Insufficient data		
Cooling	◒		⊖	⊖	○			
Fuel	◒		◒	●	●			
Ignition	⊜		⊖	○	⊜			
Transmission	⊖		⊖	⊜	⊖			
Electrical	○		●	●	⊖			
A/C	⊜		○	○	⊖			
Suspension	⊖		○	⊖	⊖			
Brakes	⊖		◒	○	○			
Exhaust	⊖		○	⊖	⊜			
Power equip.	⊜		◒	◒	⊖			
Paint/trim/rust	○		⊖	⊖	⊖			
Integrity	⊖		◒	◒	◒			
Hardware	⊖		◒	○	⊖			
RELIABILITY VERDICT	✓		✗	✗	✗			

Mercury Grand Marquis

Trouble spots	97	98	99	00	01	02	03	04
Engine	⊖	⊜	⊜	⊖	⊖	⊜	⊜	⊜
Cooling	○	⊜	⊜	⊜	⊜	⊜	⊜	⊜
Fuel	○	⊖	⊖	○	○	⊖	⊜	⊜
Ignition	⊖	⊖	⊖	⊖	⊖	⊜	⊜	⊖
Transmission	⊖	⊖	⊜	⊖	⊖	⊜	⊜	⊜
Electrical	○	○	○	○	○	⊖	⊖	⊖
A/C	⊖	⊖	⊖	⊖	⊖	⊜	⊜	⊜
Suspension	○	○	○	⊖	⊖	⊖	⊖	⊜
Brakes	◒	⊖	○	○	⊖	⊖	⊖	⊜
Exhaust	⊖	⊜	⊜	⊜	⊜	⊜	⊜	⊜
Power equip.	◒	○	⊖	○	○	⊖	⊖	⊜
Paint/trim/rust	⊖	⊜	⊜	⊖	⊖	⊖	⊖	⊜
Integrity	○	⊖	⊖	○	○	○	○	○
Hardware	○	⊖	⊖	⊖	⊖	⊖	⊖	⊜
RELIABILITY VERDICT	-	✓	✓	✓	-	✓	-	✗

Mercury Mountaineer 4WD

Trouble spots	97	98	99	00	01	02	03	04
Engine	○	○	○	⊖	⊖	⊜	⊜	⊜
Cooling	○	○	⊖	○	⊖	⊜	⊜	⊜
Fuel	○	○	○	○	⊖	⊖	⊖	⊜
Ignition	⊖	⊖	⊖	⊖	⊖	⊜	⊜	⊜
Transmission	○	○	○	○	⊖	○	⊖	⊜
Electrical	○	●	◒	◒	○	○	⊖	⊜
A/C	●	◒	⊖	⊜	⊜	⊖	⊜	⊜
Suspension	○	◒	○	○	⊖	⊖	⊜	⊜
Brakes	◒	◒	◒	◒	○	⊖	⊖	⊜
Exhaust	⊖	⊖	⊜	⊜	⊜	⊜	⊜	⊜
Power equip.	○	◒	◒	○	⊖	○	⊖	⊖
Paint/trim/rust	○	⊖	○	⊖	⊖	⊖	⊖	⊜
Integrity	○	○	○	○	○	○	○	⊜
Hardware	○	◒	○	◒	○	○	⊖	⊜
RELIABILITY VERDICT	-	✗	-	✗	-	✗	-	-

Mercury Mystique V6

Trouble spots	97	98	99	00	01	02	03	04
Engine	⊖	○	⊖	⊖				
Cooling	●	○	⊜	⊖				
Fuel	●	●	◒	●				
Ignition	○	⊖	⊖	⊖				
Transmission	○	◒	⊖	⊖				
Electrical	●	●	○	○				
A/C	◒	○	○	⊖				
Suspension	○	○	⊜	○				
Brakes	◒	◒	○	○				
Exhaust	○	◒	⊖	⊜				
Power equip.	◒	○	⊜	⊜				
Paint/trim/rust	○	○	⊖	⊖				
Integrity	◒	◒	◒	●				
Hardware	○	○	○	⊖				
RELIABILITY VERDICT	✗	✗	-	-				

Mercury Sable Sedan

Trouble spots	97	98	99	00	01	02	03	04
Engine	○	⊖	⊖	⊖	⊖	⊜	⊖	⊜
Cooling	○	○	○	⊜	⊜	⊜	⊜	⊜
Fuel	○	○	○	○	○	⊖	⊖	⊜
Ignition	⊖	⊖	⊜	⊖	⊖	⊜	⊜	⊜
Transmission	◒	○	○	⊖	⊖	⊖	⊜	⊜
Electrical	●	●	◒	◒	○	○	⊖	⊜
A/C	○	○	⊖	⊖	⊖	⊖	⊜	⊜
Suspension	○	○	◒	○	○	⊖	⊜	⊜
Brakes	◒	●	●	◒	◒	○	⊖	⊜
Exhaust	⊖	⊜	⊜	⊜	⊜	⊜	⊜	⊜
Power equip.	◒	○	○	⊖	⊖	⊖	⊜	⊜
Paint/trim/rust	⊖	⊖	⊖	⊖	⊜	⊜	⊜	⊜
Integrity	○	○	○	○	○	○	⊜	⊖
Hardware	○	○	⊖	⊖	⊖	⊖	⊖	⊜
RELIABILITY VERDICT	-	-	-	-	-	-	-	-

Mercury Villager, Monterey

Trouble spots	97	98	99	00	01	02	03	04
Engine	⊖	⊖	⊜	⊜	⊜	⊜		⊜
Cooling	⊖	⊖	⊜	⊜	⊜	⊖		⊜
Fuel	◒	○	○	⊖	⊖	⊖		⊜
Ignition	⊖	⊜	⊜	⊜	⊜	⊜		⊜
Transmission	⊖	⊖	⊜	⊜	⊜	⊜		⊜
Electrical	◒	◒	◒	◒	○	○		⊖
A/C	◒	◒	○	⊖	⊖	⊖		⊜
Suspension	○	○	○	○	⊖	○		⊜
Brakes	◒	◒	○	○	⊖	⊖		⊜
Exhaust	⊖	⊜	⊜	⊜	⊜	⊜		⊜
Power equip.	●	●	●	◒	◒	○		⊖
Paint/trim/rust	⊖	⊖	⊖	⊖	⊖	⊖		⊜
Integrity	◒	◒	○	○	◒	◒		⊖
Hardware	●	●	○	○	●	◒		⊖
RELIABILITY VERDICT	-	-	-	✓	-	-		-

Mini Cooper

Trouble spots	97	98	99	00	01	02	03	04
Engine						⊜	⊜	⊜
Cooling						◒	⊖	⊜
Fuel						⊖	⊖	⊜
Ignition						⊜	⊜	⊜
Transmission						○	⊖	⊜
Electrical						○	○	⊜
A/C						⊜	⊜	⊜
Suspension						⊖	⊜	⊜
Brakes						⊜	⊜	⊜
Exhaust						⊜	⊜	⊜
Power equip.						○	○	⊜
Paint/trim/rust						⊜	⊜	⊜
Integrity						◒	○	⊖
Hardware						◒	○	⊖
RELIABILITY VERDICT						✗	✗	-

Mitsubishi Eclipse

Trouble spots	97	98	99	00	01	02	03	04
Engine	●	○	Insufficient data	⊖	⊜	⊜	⊜	Insufficient data
Cooling	○	⊖		⊜	⊜	⊜	⊜	
Fuel	◒	⊜		⊜	⊜	⊖	⊜	
Ignition	⊖	⊖		⊜	⊜	⊜	⊜	
Transmission	⊜	⊖		⊜	⊜	⊜	⊜	
Electrical	◒	○		⊖	⊖	⊖	⊖	
A/C	○	⊖		⊜	⊜	⊜	⊖	
Suspension	⊖	⊖		⊖	⊖	⊖	⊜	
Brakes	◒	⊖		○	○	⊜	⊖	
Exhaust	⊜	⊜		⊜	⊜	⊜	⊜	
Power equip.	◒	◒		○	○	○	⊖	
Paint/trim/rust	○	⊜		○	⊜	⊜	⊖	
Integrity	●	◒		○	○	○	⊖	
Hardware	◒	◒		○	○	◒	⊖	
RELIABILITY VERDICT	✗	-		✓	✓	✓	-	

Mitsubishi Endeavor

Trouble spots	97	98	99	00	01	02	03	04
Engine								⊜
Cooling								⊜
Fuel								⊜
Ignition								⊜
Transmission								⊜
Electrical								⊜
A/C								⊜
Suspension								⊜
Brakes								⊜
Exhaust								⊜
Power equip.								⊜
Paint/trim/rust								⊜
Integrity								⊜
Hardware								⊜
RELIABILITY VERDICT								✓

Mitsubishi Galant

Trouble spots	97	98	99	00	01	02	03	04
Engine	○	Insufficient data	⊖	⊜	⊜	⊜	⊜	
Cooling	○		⊜	⊜	⊜	⊜	⊜	
Fuel	⊖		⊖	⊜	⊖	⊖	⊜	
Ignition	⊖		⊖	⊜	⊜	⊜	⊜	
Transmission	●		⊜	⊜	⊜	⊜	⊜	
Electrical	◒		○	⊖	○	⊜	⊖	
A/C	○		⊖	⊜	⊖	⊜	⊖	
Suspension	○		○	⊖	⊖	⊜	⊜	
Brakes	◒		●	◒	○	○	⊖	
Exhaust	⊖		⊜	⊜	⊖	⊜	⊜	
Power equip.	◒		⊜	⊜	⊖	⊜	⊜	
Paint/trim/rust	●		○	○	⊖	⊖	⊜	
Integrity	●		○	○	○	⊖	⊖	
Hardware	○		○	○	○	⊖	⊖	
RELIABILITY VERDICT	✗		✓	✓	✓	✓	✓	

Mitsubishi Outlander

Trouble spots	97	98	99	00	01	02	03	04
Engine							⊜	Insufficient data
Cooling							⊜	
Fuel							⊜	
Ignition							⊜	
Transmission							⊜	
Electrical							⊜	
A/C							⊜	
Suspension							⊜	
Brakes							⊖	
Exhaust							⊜	
Power equip.							⊜	
Paint/trim/rust							⊜	
Integrity							⊖	
Hardware							⊖	
RELIABILITY VERDICT							✓	

Nissan 350Z

Trouble spots	97	98	99	00	01	02	03	04
Engine							⊜	⊜
Cooling							⊜	⊜
Fuel							⊜	⊜
Ignition							⊜	⊜
Transmission							⊖	⊜
Electrical							⊖	⊜
A/C							⊜	⊜
Suspension							●	⊜
Brakes							⊖	⊜
Exhaust							⊜	⊜
Power equip.							◒	⊜
Paint/trim/rust							⊖	⊜
Integrity							○	⊖
Hardware							⊖	⊜
RELIABILITY VERDICT							✗	✓

Nissan Altima 4-cyl.

Trouble spots	97	98	99	00	01	02	03	04
Engine	○	⊖	⊖	⊖	⊜	⊖	⊜	⊜
Cooling	⊖	⊖	⊜	⊜	⊜	⊖	⊖	⊜
Fuel	⊖	⊖	⊜	⊜	⊜	○	⊖	⊜
Ignition	⊜	⊜	⊜	⊜	⊜	⊖	⊜	⊜
Transmission	⊖	⊖	⊜	⊜	⊜	⊜	⊜	⊜
Electrical	◒	○	⊖	○	⊖	○	⊖	⊜
A/C	⊖	⊜	⊜	⊖	⊜	⊖	⊜	⊜
Suspension	○	⊖	⊖	⊖	⊜	⊖	⊜	⊜
Brakes	○	○	○	○	⊖	⊖	⊜	⊜
Exhaust	○	⊜	⊜	⊜	⊜	⊖	⊖	⊜
Power equip.	⊖	○	⊖	○	●	⊖	⊜	⊜
Paint/trim/rust	◒	⊖	⊖	⊖	⊖	⊖	⊜	⊜
Integrity	○	◒	○	○	○	○	⊖	⊖
Hardware	○	⊖	⊜	⊖	○	⊖	⊖	⊜
RELIABILITY VERDICT	✓	✓	✓	✓	✓	✗	–	✓

Nissan Armada

Trouble spots	97	98	99	00	01	02	03	04
Engine								⊜
Cooling								⊜
Fuel								⊜
Ignition								⊜
Transmission								⊜
Electrical								⊖
A/C								⊜
Suspension								⊜
Brakes								○
Exhaust								⊜
Power equip.								⊖
Paint/trim/rust								⊖
Integrity								◒
Hardware								○
RELIABILITY VERDICT								✗

Nissan Maxima

Trouble spots	97	98	99	00	01	02	03	04
Engine	⊖	⊜	⊖	⊜	⊜	⊜	⊜	⊜
Cooling	⊜	⊜	⊜	⊜	⊜	⊜	⊜	⊜
Fuel	○	⊖	○	○	○	⊖	⊜	⊜
Ignition	⊖	⊜	◒	○	⊜	⊜	⊜	⊜
Transmission	⊖	⊜	⊜	⊜	⊜	⊜	⊜	⊜
Electrical	◒	○	○	⊖	⊖	⊖	⊜	⊜
A/C	⊖	⊖	⊖	⊜	⊜	⊜	⊜	⊜
Suspension	⊖	⊖	⊖	⊜	⊜	⊖	⊜	⊖
Brakes	○	○	◒	◒	○	⊖	⊜	⊜
Exhaust	⊖	⊜	⊜	⊜	⊜	⊜	⊜	⊜
Power equip.	⊖	⊖	⊖	⊖	⊖	○	○	⊖
Paint/trim/rust	⊖	⊖	⊖	⊖	⊜	⊖	⊖	⊜
Integrity	⊖	⊖	⊖	⊖	⊖	⊜	○	⊖
Hardware	⊜	⊜	⊜	⊜	⊖	⊖	⊜	⊜
RELIABILITY VERDICT	✓	✓	✓	✓	✓	✓	✓	✓

Nissan Murano

Trouble spots	97	98	99	00	01	02	03	04
Engine							⊜	⊜
Cooling							⊜	⊜
Fuel							⊜	⊜
Ignition							⊜	⊜
Transmission							⊜	⊜
Electrical							⊖	⊜
A/C							⊜	⊜
Suspension							⊖	⊖
Brakes							⊜	⊜
Exhaust							⊜	⊜
Power equip.							⊖	⊜
Paint/trim/rust							⊜	⊜
Integrity							○	⊜
Hardware							⊖	⊖
RELIABILITY VERDICT							✓	✓

Nissan Pathfinder

TROUBLE SPOTS	97	98	99	00	01	02	03	04
Engine	⊖	⊖	⊜	⊜	⊜	⊜	⊜	⊜
Cooling	⊖	⊜	⊜	⊜	⊜	⊜	⊜	⊜
Fuel	○	⊖	⊖	⊖	○	⊖	⊜	⊜
Ignition	⊜	⊜	⊜	⊜	⊖	⊜	⊜	⊜
Transmission	⊖	⊖	⊜	⊜	⊜	⊜	⊜	⊜
Electrical	⊖	⊜	⊖	○	⊖	⊖	⊜	⊖
A/C	⊖	⊜	⊖	⊖	⊜	⊜	⊜	⊜
Suspension	◒	○	○	⊖	⊖	⊜	⊜	⊜
Brakes	○	○	○	⊖	⊜	⊜	⊜	⊜
Exhaust	●	◒	⊜	⊜	⊜	⊖	⊜	⊜
Power equip.	⊖	⊖	⊖	⊖	○	○	⊖	⊜
Paint/trim/rust	⊖	⊖	⊖	⊖	⊜	⊖	⊜	⊜
Integrity	○	⊖	⊖	⊖	⊖	⊖	⊖	⊜
Hardware	⊜	⊖	⊖	⊜	⊖	⊖	⊖	⊜
RELIABILITY VERDICT	✔	✔	✔	✔	✔	✔	✔	✔

Nissan Pickup, Frontier

TROUBLE SPOTS	97	98	99	00	01	02	03	04
Engine	⊜	⊜	⊖	⊜	⊜	⊜	⊜	⊜
Cooling	⊜	⊜	⊜	⊖	⊜	⊜	⊜	⊜
Fuel	○	⊖	⊖	⊖	⊖	⊜	⊜	⊜
Ignition	⊖	⊖	⊜	⊜	⊜	⊜	⊜	⊜
Transmission	⊖	⊖	⊖	⊜	⊜	⊜	⊜	⊜
Electrical	⊖	○	○	⊖	⊖	⊜	⊜	⊖
A/C	⊖	○	⊖	⊖	⊖	⊜	⊜	⊜
Suspension	⊖	○	⊜	⊖	⊖	⊜	⊜	⊖
Brakes	⊖	○	○	⊖	⊖	⊖	⊜	⊖
Exhaust	⊖	⊜	⊜	⊖	⊜	⊜	⊜	⊜
Power equip.	⊜	⊖	⊜	⊖	○	⊜	⊜	⊜
Paint/trim/rust	⊖	○	⊜	⊖	○	⊖	⊜	⊜
Integrity	○	◒	⊜	○	○	○	⊖	⊖
Hardware	⊖	⊖	⊜	⊖	⊖	⊖	⊖	⊜
RELIABILITY VERDICT	✔	✔	✔	✔	✔	✔	✔	✘

Nissan Quest

TROUBLE SPOTS	97	98	99	00	01	02	03	04
Engine	⊖	⊖	⊜	⊜	⊜	⊜		⊜
Cooling	⊖	⊖	⊜	⊜	⊜	⊜		⊜
Fuel	◒	○	○	⊖	⊖	⊖		⊖
Ignition	⊖	⊜	⊜	⊜	⊜	⊜		⊜
Transmission	⊖	⊖	⊜	⊜	⊜	⊜		⊜
Electrical	◒	◒	◒	◒	○	○		⊖
A/C	◒	◒	○	⊖	⊖	⊜		⊜
Suspension	○	○	○	○	⊖	○		⊜
Brakes	◒	◒	○	○	⊖	⊜		⊜
Exhaust	⊖	⊜	⊜	⊜	⊜	⊜		⊜
Power equip.	●	●	●	◒	◒	○		○
Paint/trim/rust	⊖	⊖	⊖	⊖	⊖	⊖		⊖
Integrity	◒	◒	○	○	◒	◒		●
Hardware	●	●	○	○	●	◒		◒
RELIABILITY VERDICT	-	-	-	✔	-	-		✘

Nissan Sentra

TROUBLE SPOTS	97	98	99	00	01	02	03	04
Engine	⊖	⊖	⊖	○	○	○	⊖	⊜
Cooling	⊜	⊜	⊜	⊖	⊜	⊜	⊜	⊜
Fuel	○	⊖	⊜	◒	○	◒	⊖	⊜
Ignition	⊖	⊖	⊜	⊖	⊖	○	⊖	⊜
Transmission	⊜	⊜	⊜	⊜	⊜	⊜	⊖	⊜
Electrical	◒	◒	○	◒	○	○	⊖	⊖
A/C	○	○	⊜	⊖	⊖	⊖	⊖	⊜
Suspension	⊖	⊖	⊖	⊖	○	⊜	⊜	⊜
Brakes	◒	○	○	○	⊖	⊖	⊜	⊜
Exhaust	⊖	⊖	⊜	⊖	⊜	⊖	⊖	⊜
Power equip.	⊖	⊖	○	⊜	○	⊖	⊖	⊜
Paint/trim/rust	○	⊖	○	⊖	⊜	⊖	⊖	⊜
Integrity	◒	○	◒	○	○	◒	○	⊖
Hardware	○	○	⊜	⊖	⊖	⊖	⊖	⊖
RELIABILITY VERDICT	✔	✔	✔	-	-	✘	✘	-

Nissan Titan

TROUBLE SPOTS	97	98	99	00	01	02	03	04
Engine								⊜
Cooling								⊜
Fuel								⊜
Ignition								⊜
Transmission								⊜
Electrical								⊜
A/C								⊜
Suspension								⊜
Brakes								⊖
Exhaust								⊜
Power equip.								⊖
Paint/trim/rust								⊖
Integrity								⊖
Hardware								⊖
RELIABILITY VERDICT								-

Nissan Xterra

TROUBLE SPOTS	97	98	99	00	01	02	03	04
Engine				⊜	⊜	⊜	⊜	Insufficient data
Cooling				⊖	⊜	⊜	⊜	
Fuel				⊖	⊖	⊜	⊜	
Ignition				⊜	⊜	⊜	⊜	
Transmission				⊜	⊜	⊜	⊜	
Electrical				⊖	○	⊜	⊜	
A/C				◒	⊖	⊖	⊜	
Suspension				⊜	⊖	⊖	⊜	
Brakes				○	⊖	⊖	⊜	
Exhaust				⊖	⊜	⊜	⊜	
Power equip.				⊖	●	○	⊖	
Paint/trim/rust				⊖	○	⊖	⊜	
Integrity				○	⊖	○	⊖	
Hardware				⊖	○	⊖	⊖	
RELIABILITY VERDICT				✔	-	✔	-	

Oldsmobile Alero

TROUBLE SPOTS	97	98	99	00	01	02	03	04
Engine			◒	○	⊖	⊖	⊜	Insufficient data
Cooling			●	○	⊖	⊜	⊜	
Fuel			⊖	◒	○	⊖	⊖	
Ignition			⊖	⊖	⊖	⊖	⊜	
Transmission			⊜	⊜	⊜	⊜	⊜	
Electrical			●	●	●	○	○	
A/C			○	◒	⊖	⊜	⊜	
Suspension			◒	○	○	⊖	⊜	
Brakes			●	●	●	◒	○	
Exhaust			⊜	⊜	⊜	⊜	⊜	
Power equip.			◒	◒	◒	○	⊜	
Paint/trim/rust			○	⊖	⊜	⊜	⊜	
Integrity			◒	◒	◒	◒	○	
Hardware			○	○	○	⊖	⊜	
RELIABILITY VERDICT			✘	✘	✘	-	✔	

Oldsmobile Aurora

TROUBLE SPOTS	97	98	99	00	01	02	03	04
Engine	◒	○	Insufficient data		⊜	⊜	Insufficient data	
Cooling	●	◒			⊜	⊜		
Fuel	●	⊖			○	⊜		
Ignition	◒	⊜			⊖	⊜		
Transmission	○	⊖			○	⊖		
Electrical	●	●			◒	○		
A/C	●	●			○	⊖		
Suspension	◒	○			◒	◒		
Brakes	○	○			⊜	⊖		
Exhaust	⊜	⊜			⊜	⊜		
Power equip.	●	◒			○	⊖		
Paint/trim/rust	○	○			⊖	⊜		
Integrity	◒	◒			◒	◒		
Hardware	○	⊖			⊖	⊖		
RELIABILITY VERDICT	✘	-			✘	-		

Oldsmobile Bravada

TROUBLE SPOTS	97	98	99	00	01	02	03	04
Engine	●	○	◒	○	Insufficient data	⊖	Insufficient data	Insufficient data
Cooling	●	◒	○	⊖		⊜		
Fuel	●	○	○	◒		⊖		
Ignition	○	⊖	⊜	⊖		⊖		
Transmission	○	⊖	○	◒		⊖		
Electrical	●	●	●	●		●		
A/C	●	◒	○	⊖		⊜		
Suspension	○	◒	◒	◒		○		
Brakes	○	◒	○	○		⊖		
Exhaust	⊖	⊜	⊜	⊖		⊜		
Power equip.	○	◒	○	◒		●		
Paint/trim/rust	⊖	⊖	◒	○		○		
Integrity	●	○	●	◒		◒		
Hardware	◒	○	◒	○		○		
RELIABILITY VERDICT	✗	✗	✗	✗		✗		

Oldsmobile Intrigue

TROUBLE SPOTS	97	98	99	00	01	02	03	04
Engine		◒	⊖	⊜	⊖	⊜		
Cooling		○	⊖	⊜	⊖	⊜		
Fuel		⊖	○	○	⊖	⊖		
Ignition		⊜	⊖	⊖	⊖	⊜		
Transmission		○	○	⊜	○	⊜		
Electrical		◒	◒	●	◒	○		
A/C		○	○	○	⊜	⊜		
Suspension		◒	○	◒	○	⊖		
Brakes		◒	○	○	⊖	⊖		
Exhaust		⊜	⊜	⊜	⊜	⊜		
Power equip.		◒	◒	○	○	⊖		
Paint/trim/rust		⊖	⊖	⊜	⊖	⊖		
Integrity		◒	○	○	⊖	○		
Hardware		○	⊖	⊖	⊖	⊖		
RELIABILITY VERDICT		-	-	-	-	✓		

Pontiac Aztek

TROUBLE SPOTS	97	98	99	00	01	02	03	04
Engine					○	⊜	⊖	Insufficient data
Cooling					⊖	⊖	⊜	
Fuel					⊖	⊖	⊜	
Ignition					⊖	⊜	⊜	
Transmission					○	⊜	⊜	
Electrical					●	◒	⊖	
A/C					●	⊖	⊖	
Suspension					⊖	⊖	⊖	
Brakes					○	⊖	○	
Exhaust					⊜	⊜	⊜	
Power equip.					○	○	○	
Paint/trim/rust					⊖	⊜	⊜	
Integrity					○	⊖	○	
Hardware					○	○	○	
RELIABILITY VERDICT					✗	✗	✗	

Pontiac Bonneville

TROUBLE SPOTS	97	98	99	00	01	02	03	04
Engine	◒	●	◒	⊖	⊖	⊖	⊜	Insufficient data
Cooling	◒	◒	○	○	○	○	⊖	
Fuel	○	◒	○	⊖	○	⊖	⊜	
Ignition	○	⊖	⊖	⊖	⊜	⊜	⊜	
Transmission	○	○	○	⊖	⊖	⊜	⊖	
Electrical	◒	◒	○	◒	○	○	⊜	
A/C	◒	○	⊖	⊖	⊜	⊖	⊜	
Suspension	⊖	⊖	⊖	●	●	◒	⊖	
Brakes	○	○	◒	◒	○	⊖	⊖	
Exhaust	⊖	⊖	⊖	⊜	⊜	⊜	⊜	
Power equip.	⊖	○	○	●	◒	◒	⊜	
Paint/trim/rust	⊖	○	○	⊖	⊖	⊖	⊜	
Integrity	○	○	◒	◒	◒	●	○	
Hardware	⊖	⊖	⊖	○	⊖	○	⊜	
RELIABILITY VERDICT	-	✗	✗	✗	✗	✗	-	

Pontiac Grand Am

TROUBLE SPOTS	97	98	99	00	01	02	03	04
Engine	◒	○	◒	○	⊖	⊜	⊜	⊜
Cooling	●	◒	◒	○	⊖	⊜	⊜	⊜
Fuel	◒	○	○	◒	◒	⊖	⊜	⊜
Ignition	○	○	⊖	⊖	⊖	⊜	⊜	⊜
Transmission	⊖	⊖	⊖	⊜	⊜	⊜	⊜	⊜
Electrical	●	●	●	●	●	○	⊜	⊜
A/C	◒	⊖	○	○	⊖	⊜	⊜	⊜
Suspension	○	⊖	○	○	○	⊖	⊜	⊜
Brakes	●	●	●	●	●	◒	⊖	○
Exhaust	○	⊖	⊜	⊜	⊜	⊜	⊜	⊜
Power equip.	●	◒	●	●	○	○	⊜	⊜
Paint/trim/rust	○	○	○	○	○	⊖	⊜	⊜
Integrity	◒	◒	●	◒	◒	○	○	⊜
Hardware	◒	○	◒	◒	○	⊖	⊜	⊜
RELIABILITY VERDICT	✗	✗	✗	✗	✗	-	✓	✓

Pontiac Grand Prix

TROUBLE SPOTS	97	98	99	00	01	02	03	04
Engine	◒	◒	⊖	⊖	⊖	⊜	⊖	⊜
Cooling	●	◒	○	○	⊖	⊖	⊖	⊜
Fuel	○	○	⊖	⊖	⊖	⊖	⊜	⊜
Ignition	⊖	⊖	⊖	⊖	⊜	⊜	⊜	⊜
Transmission	⊖	○	○	⊖	○	⊜	⊜	⊜
Electrical	●	●	○	◒	○	⊖	⊜	⊜
A/C	◒	○	◒	⊖	⊖	⊜	⊜	⊜
Suspension	◒	○	⊖	○	○	⊜	⊜	⊜
Brakes	○	○	○	○	○	⊖	⊖	⊜
Exhaust	⊜	⊜	⊜	⊜	⊜	⊜	⊜	⊜
Power equip.	●	●	●	○	○	○	⊜	⊜
Paint/trim/rust	○	⊖	⊖	⊜	⊖	⊖	⊖	⊜
Integrity	◒	◒	○	○	○	○	⊖	⊜
Hardware	○	○	○	⊖	⊖	⊖	⊜	⊜
RELIABILITY VERDICT	✗	✗	-	-	-	-	-	✓

Pontiac Sunfire Coupe & Conv.

TROUBLE SPOTS	97	98	99	00	01	02	03	04
Engine	○	⊖	○	⊖	○	⊜	⊜	Insufficient data
Cooling	◒	○	○	○	⊖	⊜	⊜	
Fuel	○	○	⊖	○	○	⊖	⊖	
Ignition	○	○	◒	⊖	⊜	⊜	⊜	
Transmission	⊖	⊖	⊖	⊖	⊜	⊖	⊜	
Electrical	◒	●	●	●	◒	○	◒	
A/C	●	○	○	○	⊖	⊜	○	
Suspension	◒	⊖	⊖	○	⊖	⊖	⊖	
Brakes	◒	◒	◒	●	◒	◒	○	
Exhaust	⊖	⊜	⊖	⊖	⊜	⊜	⊜	
Power equip.	○	○	○	◒	⊖	○	⊜	
Paint/trim/rust	○	○	⊖	◒	⊜	⊜	⊖	
Integrity	◒	◒	◒	◒	○	◒	○	
Hardware	◒	○	◒	○	⊖	○	⊖	
RELIABILITY VERDICT	-	-	✗	✗	-	-	✗	

Pontiac TransSport, Montana (ext.)

TROUBLE SPOTS	97	98	99	00	01	02	03	04
Engine	●	●	●	○	○	⊜	⊜	⊜
Cooling	●	◒	●	○	⊖	⊜	⊜	⊜
Fuel	◒	○	○	○	⊖	⊖	⊜	⊜
Ignition	⊜	⊖	⊜	⊜	⊜	⊜	⊜	⊜
Transmission	○	⊖	◒	○	○	⊜	⊜	⊜
Electrical	●	◒	◒	●	◒	⊖	⊖	⊜
A/C	○	○	⊖	⊖	○	⊖	⊜	⊜
Suspension	◒	○	⊖	○	○	⊖	⊜	⊜
Brakes	◒	◒	●	◒	◒	⊖	⊜	⊜
Exhaust	⊜	⊜	⊜	⊜	⊜	⊜	⊜	⊜
Power equip.	●	●	●	●	◒	○	○	⊖
Paint/trim/rust	○	⊖	⊖	⊖	⊖	⊜	⊜	⊜
Integrity	●	◒	◒	◒	◒	◒	○	⊖
Hardware	●	◒	◒	◒	○	○	⊖	⊖
RELIABILITY VERDICT	✗	✗	✗	✗	✗	-	-	-

Pontiac Vibe

Trouble spots	97	98	99	00	01	02	03	04
Engine							⊜	⊜
Cooling							⊜	⊜
Fuel							⊜	⊜
Ignition							⊜	⊜
Transmission							⊜	⊜
Electrical							⊖	⊜
A/C							⊜	⊜
Suspension							⊜	⊜
Brakes							⊜	⊜
Exhaust							⊜	⊜
Power equip.							⊜	⊜
Paint/trim/rust							⊖	⊜
Integrity							○	⊖
Hardware							⊖	⊖
RELIABILITY VERDICT							✓	✓

Porsche Boxster

Trouble spots	97	98	99	00	01	02	03	04
Engine	Insufficient data	Insufficient data	○	◒	◒	○	○	Insufficient data
Cooling			⊖	⊜	⊖	⊜	⊜	
Fuel			●	○	⊖	⊜	⊖	
Ignition			⊜	⊜	⊖	⊜	⊜	
Transmission			⊜	⊜	○	⊖	⊜	
Electrical			○	⊖	○	⊖	○	
A/C			⊜	⊜	⊜	⊜	⊜	
Suspension			⊜	⊖	⊜	⊜	⊜	
Brakes			⊜	⊜	⊜	⊜	⊜	
Exhaust			⊜	⊜	⊖	⊜	⊜	
Power equip.			⊜	⊖	○	⊜	○	
Paint/trim/rust			⊜	⊜	⊜	⊜	⊜	
Integrity			⊜	⊖	○	◒	○	
Hardware			⊖	⊖	○	⊖	⊖	
RELIABILITY VERDICT			✓	-	✗	-	✗	

Saab 9-3

Trouble spots	97	98	99	00	01	02	03	04
Engine			◒	○	○	⊜	⊜	⊜
Cooling			⊖	⊜	⊜	⊖	⊜	⊜
Fuel			⊖	⊖	○	⊖	⊖	⊖
Ignition			⊖	○	○	⊖	⊜	⊜
Transmission			⊜	⊜	⊜	⊜	⊖	⊖
Electrical			◒	◒	◒	○	◒	⊖
A/C			◒	⊖	⊖	⊖	⊜	⊜
Suspension			○	⊖	⊜	⊖	⊖	⊜
Brakes			○	○	○	⊖	○	⊖
Exhaust			○	⊖	⊖	⊜	⊜	⊜
Power equip.			◒	○	⊖	○	◒	○
Paint/trim/rust			○	⊖	⊜	⊖	⊜	⊜
Integrity			○	○	○	○	○	⊜
Hardware			○	○	⊜	○	○	⊜
RELIABILITY VERDICT			-	-	-	-	✗	✗

Saab 9-5

Trouble spots	97	98	99	00	01	02	03	04
Engine			●	○	○	⊖	⊜	⊜
Cooling			⊖	⊜	⊖	⊖	⊜	⊜
Fuel			○	⊖	⊖	⊜	⊜	⊜
Ignition			○	○	○	⊖	⊜	⊜
Transmission			⊖	⊖	⊜	⊖	⊖	⊜
Electrical			●	●	●	○	⊖	⊜
A/C			○	⊖	⊖	⊖	⊖	⊜
Suspension			⊖	○	⊖	⊜	⊜	⊜
Brakes			○	⊖	○	⊖	⊜	⊜
Exhaust			⊖	⊖	⊜	⊜	⊜	⊜
Power equip.			○	○	○	⊖	⊖	⊜
Paint/trim/rust			⊖	⊜	⊖	⊜	⊜	⊜
Integrity			⊖	⊖	⊖	⊖	⊖	⊜
Hardware			⊖	⊖	⊖	⊖	⊖	⊜
RELIABILITY VERDICT			✗	-	-	-	-	✓

Saturn L-Series, L300 4-cyl.

Trouble spots	97	98	99	00	01	02	03	04
Engine				⊜	⊖	⊜	⊜	Insufficient data
Cooling				⊖	⊜	⊜	⊜	
Fuel				⊖	⊖	⊖	⊜	
Ignition				○	⊖	⊖	⊖	
Transmission				⊜	⊜	⊜	⊜	
Electrical				◒	◒	○	○	
A/C				○	⊖	⊜	⊖	
Suspension				○	○	○	⊖	
Brakes				○	○	⊜	⊜	
Exhaust				⊜	⊜	⊜	⊜	
Power equip.				○	○	⊖	⊖	
Paint/trim/rust				⊖	⊜	⊜	⊜	
Integrity				◒	○	○	⊖	
Hardware				○	⊜	⊖	⊜	
RELIABILITY VERDICT				-	-	✓	✓	

Saturn SL, Ion

Trouble spots	97	98	99	00	01	02	03	04
Engine	◒	○	○	○	⊖	⊜	⊜	⊜
Cooling	○	○	⊖	○	⊖	⊜	⊜	⊜
Fuel	◒	○	⊖	⊖	⊖	⊜	⊖	⊖
Ignition	○	⊖	⊖	⊖	⊖	⊖	⊜	⊜
Transmission	⊖	⊖	⊖	⊖	⊖	⊜	⊖	⊖
Electrical	●	◒	○	◒	○	⊖	○	⊖
A/C	⊖	⊖	⊖	⊖	⊜	⊜	⊖	⊜
Suspension	⊖	⊖	⊖	⊖	⊖	⊜	⊜	⊜
Brakes	○	○	○	○	⊖	⊜	⊜	⊜
Exhaust	⊖	○	○	○	⊜	⊜	⊜	⊜
Power equip.	○	○	○	○	○	⊖	⊖	⊜
Paint/trim/rust	⊖	⊖	⊖	⊜	⊜	⊜	⊜	⊜
Integrity	◒	○	○	○	○	⊖	◒	⊖
Hardware	○	○	○	⊖	○	⊖	○	⊖
RELIABILITY VERDICT	-	-	-	-	-	✓	✗	-

Saturn Vue

Trouble spots	97	98	99	00	01	02	03	04
Engine						⊖	⊜	⊜
Cooling						○	⊜	⊜
Fuel						○	⊖	⊜
Ignition						⊜	⊜	⊜
Transmission						⊖	⊖	⊜
Electrical						○	⊖	⊜
A/C						⊖	⊜	⊜
Suspension						○	○	⊜
Brakes						○	⊜	⊜
Exhaust						⊜	⊜	⊜
Power equip.						⊖	⊖	⊜
Paint/trim/rust						⊜	⊜	⊜
Integrity						◒	○	⊖
Hardware						○	⊖	⊜
RELIABILITY VERDICT						✗	✗	✗

Scion xB

Trouble spots	97	98	99	00	01	02	03	04
Engine								⊜
Cooling								⊜
Fuel								⊜
Ignition								⊜
Transmission								⊜
Electrical								⊜
A/C								⊜
Suspension								⊜
Brakes								⊜
Exhaust								⊜
Power equip.								⊜
Paint/trim/rust								⊜
Integrity								⊖
Hardware								⊖
RELIABILITY VERDICT								✓

Subaru Baja — TROUBLE SPOTS	97	98	99	00	01	02	03	04
Engine							⊜	Insufficient data
Cooling							⊜	
Fuel							⊜	
Ignition							⊜	
Transmission							⊜	
Electrical							⊖	
A/C							⊜	
Suspension							⊜	
Brakes							⊖	
Exhaust							⊜	
Power equip.							⊜	
Paint/trim/rust							⊜	
Integrity							○	
Hardware							⊜	
RELIABILITY VERDICT							✓	

Subaru Forester — TROUBLE SPOTS	97	98	99	00	01	02	03	04
Engine		◒	◒	⊖	⊜	⊜	⊜	⊜
Cooling		⊖	○	⊜	⊖	⊜	⊜	⊜
Fuel		⊖	⊖	○	⊖	○	⊜	⊜
Ignition		⊜	⊖	⊖	⊜	⊜	⊜	⊖
Transmission		⊖	○	⊖	⊜	⊜	⊜	⊜
Electrical		○	○	⊖	⊖	⊜	⊜	⊜
A/C		⊖	⊖	⊜	⊜	⊜	⊜	⊜
Suspension		⊖	⊖	⊜	⊜	⊜	⊜	⊜
Brakes		○	⊖	⊖	⊖	⊖	⊜	⊜
Exhaust		⊖	⊜	⊖	⊜	⊜	⊜	⊜
Power equip.		⊖	⊖	⊜	⊜	⊜	⊜	⊜
Paint/trim/rust		⊜	⊖	⊖	⊖	⊜	⊜	⊖
Integrity		⊖	⊜	⊖	⊖	⊜	⊖	⊜
Hardware		⊜	⊜	⊖	⊖	⊖	⊜	⊜
RELIABILITY VERDICT		-	-	-	✓	✓	✓	✓

Subaru Impreza — TROUBLE SPOTS	97	98	99	00	01	02	03	04
Engine	○	○	⊖	⊜	⊖	⊜	⊜	⊜
Cooling	⊖	⊜	⊖	⊜	⊜	⊜	⊜	⊜
Fuel	⊖	⊖	⊖	○	⊖	⊖	⊜	⊜
Ignition	⊜	⊜	⊖	⊖	⊜	⊜	⊜	⊜
Transmission	⊜	⊜	⊖	⊜	⊜	⊖	⊜	⊜
Electrical	○	○	⊖	⊖	⊖	⊜	⊖	⊜
A/C	○	⊜	⊖	⊜	⊖	⊜	⊜	⊜
Suspension	⊖	⊖	⊜	⊜	⊜	⊜	⊜	⊜
Brakes	○	○	○	⊖	⊖	⊖	⊜	⊜
Exhaust	⊜	⊜	⊖	⊖	⊜	⊜	⊜	⊜
Power equip.	⊖	⊖	⊖	⊖	⊖	⊖	⊜	⊜
Paint/trim/rust	○	⊜	⊖	⊖	⊜	⊖	⊜	⊜
Integrity	○	○	○	○	○	⊜	⊖	⊜
Hardware	⊖	⊖	⊜	⊖	⊖	⊖	⊖	⊜
RELIABILITY VERDICT	✓	✓	-	✓	✓	✓	✓	✓

Subaru Legacy/Outback 4-cyl. — TROUBLE SPOTS	97	98	99	00	01	02	03	04
Engine	◒	◒	○	⊖	⊖	⊖	⊜	⊜
Cooling	⊖	⊖	⊜	○	⊖	⊜	⊜	⊜
Fuel	⊖	⊖	⊖	○	⊖	⊖	⊜	⊜
Ignition	⊖	⊜	⊖	⊜	⊜	⊜	⊜	⊜
Transmission	⊖	⊖	⊖	⊖	⊜	⊖	⊜	⊜
Electrical	◒	○	○	⊖	⊖	⊜	⊜	⊜
A/C	⊖	⊖	⊖	⊜	⊜	⊜	⊜	⊜
Suspension	⊖	⊖	⊜	⊖	⊜	⊜	⊜	⊜
Brakes	◒	○	○	○	◒	○	⊜	⊜
Exhaust	⊖	⊜	⊜	⊜	⊜	⊜	⊜	⊜
Power equip.	⊖	⊖	⊖	⊖	⊜	⊜	⊜	⊜
Paint/trim/rust	⊖	⊖	⊖	⊖	⊜	⊖	⊜	⊜
Integrity	⊖	⊖	⊖	○	○	○	○	⊖
Hardware	⊖	⊖	⊖	⊖	⊖	⊖	⊜	⊜
RELIABILITY VERDICT	✓	✓	✓	-	-	-	✓	✓

Suzuki Sidekick, Vitara, XL-7 — TROUBLE SPOTS	97	98	99	00	01	02	03	04
Engine	○	Insufficient data	○	⊖	○	⊜	⊜	Insufficient data
Cooling	⊖		⊜	⊜	⊜	⊜	⊜	
Fuel	◒		○	○	⊜	⊜	⊜	
Ignition	⊜		⊖	⊜	⊖	⊜	⊜	
Transmission	○		○	⊜	⊜	⊜	⊜	
Electrical	○		○	○	⊖	⊜	⊖	
A/C	○		◒	○	○	⊖	⊜	
Suspension	⊜		⊖	⊖	⊖	⊜	⊜	
Brakes	○		○	○	○	⊖	⊖	
Exhaust	○		⊖	⊜	⊜	⊜	⊜	
Power equip.	⊜		⊖	○	⊜	○	⊜	
Paint/trim/rust	◒		○	○	○	⊜	⊜	
Integrity	●		◒	◒	○	○	⊖	
Hardware	○		⊖	○	⊜	⊜	⊜	
RELIABILITY VERDICT	-		-	-	-	✓	-	

Toyota 4Runner V6 — TROUBLE SPOTS	97	98	99	00	01	02	03	04
Engine	⊜	⊜	⊜	⊜	⊜	⊜	⊜	⊜
Cooling	⊖	⊖	⊜	⊜	⊜	⊜	⊜	⊜
Fuel	⊜	⊜	⊖	⊖	⊜	⊜	⊖	⊜
Ignition	⊜	⊜	⊜	⊜	⊜	⊜	⊜	⊜
Transmission	⊜	⊜	⊜	⊜	⊜	⊜	⊜	⊜
Electrical	○	○	⊖	⊖	⊜	⊜	⊜	⊜
A/C	⊜	⊜	⊜	⊜	⊜	⊜	⊜	⊜
Suspension	⊖	⊖	⊜	⊜	⊜	⊜	⊜	⊜
Brakes	○	⊖	⊖	⊖	⊖	⊖	⊜	⊜
Exhaust	⊜	⊜	⊜	⊜	⊜	⊜	⊜	⊜
Power equip.	○	○	⊖	⊖	⊜	⊜	⊖	⊜
Paint/trim/rust	⊖	⊖	⊜	⊖	⊜	⊜	⊜	⊜
Integrity	⊖	⊜	⊜	⊖	⊜	◒	○	⊜
Hardware	⊖	⊖	⊜	⊖	⊜	⊖	○	⊜
RELIABILITY VERDICT	✓	✓	✓	✓	✓	✓	✓	✓

Toyota Avalon — TROUBLE SPOTS	97	98	99	00	01	02	03	04
Engine	⊖	⊖	⊜	⊜	⊜	⊜	⊜	⊜
Cooling	⊜	⊜	⊜	⊜	⊜	⊜	⊜	⊜
Fuel	⊖	⊖	○	⊖	⊖	⊜	⊜	⊜
Ignition	⊜	⊖	⊜	⊜	⊜	⊜	⊜	⊜
Transmission	⊜	⊜	⊜	⊜	⊜	⊜	⊜	⊜
Electrical	⊖	○	⊖	⊖	⊖	⊜	⊜	⊜
A/C	⊜	○	⊜	⊜	⊜	⊜	⊜	⊜
Suspension	●	◒	◒	⊖	⊖	⊜	⊜	⊖
Brakes	○	⊖	⊖	⊖	⊖	⊖	⊜	⊜
Exhaust	⊜	⊜	⊜	⊜	⊜	⊜	⊜	⊜
Power equip.	⊖	⊖	⊖	⊜	⊜	⊜	⊜	⊜
Paint/trim/rust	⊖	⊖	⊖	⊜	⊜	⊜	⊜	⊜
Integrity	○	○	○	⊖	⊖	⊖	⊜	⊜
Hardware	⊖	⊖	⊖	⊜	⊖	⊜	⊜	⊜
RELIABILITY VERDICT	✓	✓	✓	✓	✓	✓	✓	✓

Toyota Camry 4-cyl. — TROUBLE SPOTS	97	98	99	00	01	02	03	04
Engine	○	⊖	⊖	⊜	⊜	⊜	⊜	⊜
Cooling	⊖	⊖	⊖	⊖	⊜	⊜	⊜	⊜
Fuel	⊖	⊖	⊖	⊖	⊖	⊜	⊜	⊜
Ignition	⊜	⊜	⊜	⊜	⊜	⊜	⊜	⊜
Transmission	⊜	⊜	⊜	⊜	⊜	⊜	⊜	⊜
Electrical	○	○	○	⊖	⊜	⊜	⊜	⊜
A/C	⊜	⊜	⊜	⊜	⊜	⊜	⊜	⊜
Suspension	◒	○	○	⊖	⊜	⊖	⊜	⊜
Brakes	○	○	○	○	⊜	⊜	⊜	⊜
Exhaust	⊖	⊜	⊜	⊜	⊜	⊜	⊜	⊜
Power equip.	⊖	⊖	⊖	⊖	⊖	⊖	⊜	⊜
Paint/trim/rust	⊖	⊜	⊖	⊖	⊜	⊖	⊜	⊜
Integrity	⊖	⊖	⊖	⊖	⊜	○	⊖	⊜
Hardware	⊖	⊜	⊖	⊖	⊜	⊖	⊜	⊜
RELIABILITY VERDICT	✓	✓	✓	✓	✓	✓	✓	✓

Toyota Camry Solara

TROUBLE SPOTS	97	98	99	00	01	02	03	04
Engine			⊖	⊜	⊜	⊜	⊜	⊜
Cooling			⊜	⊜	⊜	⊜	⊜	⊜
Fuel			○	⊖	⊖	⊜	⊜	⊜
Ignition			⊜	⊜	⊜	⊜	⊜	⊜
Transmission			⊜	⊜	⊜	⊜	⊜	⊜
Electrical			⊖	⊖	⊖	⊖	⊖	⊖
A/C			⊜	⊜	⊜	⊜	⊜	⊜
Suspension			○	⊖	⊜	⊜	⊜	⊖
Brakes			⊖	⊖	⊜	⊜	⊖	⊜
Exhaust			⊜	⊜	⊜	⊜	⊜	⊜
Power equip.			⊖	⊖	⊜	⊜	⊜	⊜
Paint/trim/rust			⊖	⊖	⊜	⊜	⊜	⊜
Integrity			⊖	⊖	○	⊖	○	○
Hardware			⊖	⊖	⊖	⊖	⊖	⊜
RELIABILITY VERDICT			✔	✔	✔	✔	✔	–

Toyota Celica

TROUBLE SPOTS	97	98	99	00	01	02	03	04
Engine	○	Insufficient data	Insufficient data	○	⊜	⊜	⊜	Insufficient data
Cooling	⊜			⊖	⊜	⊜	⊜	
Fuel	⊖			⊖	⊖	⊜	○	
Ignition	⊜			⊜	⊜	⊜	⊜	
Transmission	⊜			⊜	⊜	⊜	⊜	
Electrical	⊖			⊖	⊜	⊖	⊜	
A/C	⊖			⊜	⊜	⊜	⊜	
Suspension	⊜			⊜	⊜	⊜	⊜	
Brakes	⊖			⊖	⊜	⊖	⊜	
Exhaust	⊜			⊜	⊜	⊜	⊜	
Power equip.	◒			⊜	⊖	⊜	⊜	
Paint/trim/rust	○			⊖	⊜	⊜	⊜	
Integrity	○			○	○	○	⊖	
Hardware	⊖			⊖	⊜	⊜	⊖	
RELIABILITY VERDICT	✔			✔	✔	✔	✔	

Toyota Corolla

TROUBLE SPOTS	97	98	99	00	01	02	03	04
Engine	⊜	⊖	⊖	⊖	⊜	⊜	⊜	⊜
Cooling	⊜	⊜	⊜	⊜	⊜	⊜	⊜	⊜
Fuel	⊜	⊖	⊜	⊖	⊜	⊜	⊜	⊜
Ignition	⊜	⊜	⊜	⊜	⊜	⊜	⊜	⊜
Transmission	⊜	⊜	⊜	⊜	⊜	⊜	⊜	⊜
Electrical	◒	⊖	⊖	⊖	⊖	⊜	⊜	⊜
A/C	⊜	⊖	⊜	⊜	⊜	⊜	⊜	⊜
Suspension	⊖	⊖	⊖	⊖	⊜	⊜	⊜	⊜
Brakes	○	○	⊖	⊖	⊖	⊖	⊜	⊜
Exhaust	⊜	⊜	⊜	⊜	⊜	⊜	⊜	⊜
Power equip.	⊖	⊖	⊖	⊖	⊜	⊜	⊜	⊜
Paint/trim/rust	○	⊖	⊜	⊖	⊖	⊜	⊜	⊜
Integrity	⊖	○	⊖	⊖	⊖	⊖	⊖	⊜
Hardware	○	○	⊖	⊖	⊖	⊖	⊜	⊜
RELIABILITY VERDICT	✔	✔	✔	✔	✔	✔	✔	✔

Toyota Echo

TROUBLE SPOTS	97	98	99	00	01	02	03	04
Engine				⊜	⊜	⊜	⊜	Insufficient data
Cooling				⊜	⊜	⊜	⊜	
Fuel				⊜	⊜	⊜	⊜	
Ignition				⊜	⊜	⊜	⊜	
Transmission				⊜	⊜	⊜	⊜	
Electrical				⊜	⊜	⊜	⊜	
A/C				⊜	⊜	⊜	⊖	
Suspension				⊜	⊜	⊜	⊜	
Brakes				⊖	⊖	⊜	⊜	
Exhaust				⊜	⊜	⊜	⊜	
Power equip.				⊜	⊜	⊜	⊜	
Paint/trim/rust				⊖	⊖	⊜	⊜	
Integrity				⊖	⊜	⊜	⊖	
Hardware				⊜	⊜	⊜	⊜	
RELIABILITY VERDICT				✔	✔	✔	✔	

Toyota Highlander

TROUBLE SPOTS	97	98	99	00	01	02	03	04
Engine					⊜	⊜	⊜	⊜
Cooling					⊜	⊜	⊜	⊜
Fuel					⊖	⊜	⊜	⊜
Ignition					⊜	⊜	⊜	⊜
Transmission					⊜	⊜	⊜	⊜
Electrical					⊜	⊜	⊜	⊜
A/C					⊜	⊜	⊜	⊜
Suspension					⊜	⊜	⊜	⊜
Brakes					⊖	⊜	⊜	⊜
Exhaust					⊜	⊜	⊜	⊜
Power equip.					⊜	⊜	⊜	⊜
Paint/trim/rust					⊜	⊜	⊜	⊜
Integrity					⊖	⊖	⊖	⊜
Hardware					⊜	⊜	⊜	⊜
RELIABILITY VERDICT					✔	✔	✔	✔

Toyota Land Cruiser

TROUBLE SPOTS	97	98	99	00	01	02	03	04
Engine	⊖	⊜	⊜	⊜	⊜	⊜	⊜	Insufficient data
Cooling	⊖	⊜	⊜	⊜	⊜	⊜	⊜	
Fuel	⊜	⊖	⊜	⊖	⊜	⊜	⊜	
Ignition	⊖	⊖	⊜	⊜	⊜	⊜	⊜	
Transmission	⊜	⊜	⊜	⊜	⊜	⊜	⊜	
Electrical	○	○	⊖	⊖	⊖	⊜	⊜	
A/C	⊖	⊜	⊜	⊖	⊜	⊜	⊜	
Suspension	⊖	⊜	⊜	⊜	⊜	⊜	⊖	
Brakes	◒	◒	⊖	⊖	○	⊖	⊜	
Exhaust	⊜	◒	⊜	⊖	⊜	⊜	⊜	
Power equip.	⊖	◒	○	○	⊜	⊜	⊜	
Paint/trim/rust	⊜	⊖	⊜	⊜	⊜	⊖	⊜	
Integrity	⊖	○	⊖	⊖	⊖	⊜	⊖	
Hardware	⊜	⊜	○	⊖	⊜	⊖	⊜	
RELIABILITY VERDICT	✔	✔	✔	✔	✔	✔	✔	

Toyota Matrix

TROUBLE SPOTS	97	98	99	00	01	02	03	04
Engine							⊜	⊜
Cooling							⊜	⊜
Fuel							⊜	⊜
Ignition							⊜	⊜
Transmission							⊜	⊜
Electrical							⊖	⊜
A/C							⊜	⊜
Suspension							⊜	⊜
Brakes							⊜	⊜
Exhaust							⊜	⊜
Power equip.							⊜	⊜
Paint/trim/rust							⊖	⊜
Integrity							○	⊖
Hardware							⊖	⊜
RELIABILITY VERDICT							✔	✔

Toyota Prius

TROUBLE SPOTS	97	98	99	00	01	02	03	04
Engine					⊜	⊜	⊜	⊜
Cooling					⊜	⊜	⊜	⊜
Fuel					○	⊖	⊜	⊜
Ignition					⊜	⊜	⊜	⊜
Transmission					⊜	⊜	⊜	⊜
Electrical					○	○	○	⊜
A/C					⊜	⊜	⊜	⊜
Suspension					○	○	⊜	⊜
Brakes					⊜	⊜	⊜	⊜
Exhaust					⊜	⊜	⊜	⊜
Power equip.					⊜	⊜	⊜	⊜
Paint/trim/rust					⊜	⊜	⊜	⊜
Integrity					⊜	⊜	⊜	⊜
Hardware					⊜	⊜	⊜	⊜
RELIABILITY VERDICT					✔	✔	✔	✔

Toyota RAV4

Trouble spots	97	98	99	00	01	02	03	04
Engine	○	⊖	⊖	⊜	⊜	⊜	⊜	⊜
Cooling	⊜	⊖	⊜	⊜	⊜	⊜	⊜	⊜
Fuel	⊖	○	⊖	⊖	⊖	⊜	⊜	⊜
Ignition	⊖	⊜	⊜	⊜	⊜	⊜	⊜	⊜
Transmission	⊜	⊜	⊜	⊜	⊜	⊜	⊜	⊜
Electrical	⊖	⊖	⊖	⊖	⊖	⊜	⊜	⊜
A/C	⊜	⊜	⊜	⊜	⊜	⊜	⊜	⊜
Suspension	⊖	⊜	⊖	⊜	⊜	⊜	⊜	⊜
Brakes	○	○	⊖	⊖	○	⊜	⊜	⊜
Exhaust	⊖	⊖	⊖	⊖	⊖	⊜	⊜	⊜
Power equip.	⊜	⊖	⊖	⊜	⊜	⊜	⊜	⊜
Paint/trim/rust	⊖	⊜	⊜	⊜	⊖	⊖	⊜	⊜
Integrity	⊖	○	⊖	⊖	◒	○	○	⊖
Hardware	⊖	○	⊖	⊜	⊖	⊖	⊜	⊜
RELIABILITY VERDICT	✔	✔	✔	✔	✔	✔	✔	✔

Toyota Sequoia

Trouble spots	97	98	99	00	01	02	03	04
Engine					⊜	⊜	⊜	⊜
Cooling					⊜	⊜	⊜	⊜
Fuel					⊜	⊜	⊜	⊜
Ignition					⊜	⊜	⊜	⊜
Transmission					⊜	⊜	⊜	⊜
Electrical					○	⊖	○	⊜
A/C					⊖	⊖	⊜	⊜
Suspension					⊜	⊜	⊜	⊜
Brakes					◒	◒	⊖	⊜
Exhaust					⊜	⊜	⊜	⊜
Power equip.					⊖	⊖	⊖	⊜
Paint/trim/rust					⊜	⊖	⊜	⊜
Integrity					⊖	⊖	⊖	⊜
Hardware					⊖	⊖	⊖	⊜
RELIABILITY VERDICT					✔	✔	–	✔

Toyota Sienna

Trouble spots	97	98	99	00	01	02	03	04
Engine		⊖	⊖	⊖	⊜	⊜	⊜	⊜
Cooling		⊜	⊜	⊜	⊜	⊜	⊜	⊜
Fuel		⊜	⊖	⊜	⊖	⊜	⊜	⊖
Ignition		⊜	⊜	⊜	⊜	⊜	⊜	⊜
Transmission		⊖	⊖	⊖	⊜	⊜	⊜	⊜
Electrical		○	○	⊖	⊖	⊖	⊜	⊜
A/C		⊖	⊖	⊜	⊜	⊜	⊜	⊜
Suspension		⊖	⊖	⊜	⊜	⊜	⊖	⊜
Brakes		◒	○	○	○	○	⊖	⊜
Exhaust		⊜	⊜	⊜	⊜	⊜	⊜	⊜
Power equip.		○	○	○	○	⊖	⊖	⊜
Paint/trim/rust		⊖	⊖	⊜	⊜	⊜	⊜	⊜
Integrity		◒	⊖	⊜	⊜	⊖	⊖	⊖
Hardware		●	◒	○	○	○	○	⊜
RELIABILITY VERDICT		✔	✔	✔	✔	✔	–	✔

Toyota T100, Tundra

Trouble spots	97	98	99	00	01	02	03	04
Engine	⊜	⊖		⊜	⊜	⊜	⊜	⊜
Cooling	⊖	⊜		⊜	⊜	⊜	⊜	⊜
Fuel	⊖	⊜		○	○	⊜	⊖	⊜
Ignition	⊜	⊜		⊜	⊜	⊜	⊜	⊜
Transmission	⊜	⊖		⊜	⊜	⊜	⊜	⊜
Electrical	○	⊖		⊖	⊖	⊜	⊖	⊜
A/C	⊜	○		⊜	⊜	⊜	⊜	⊜
Suspension	⊖	○		⊜	⊜	⊜	⊜	⊜
Brakes	⊖	⊜		◒	◒	○	⊜	⊜
Exhaust	⊖	⊜		⊖	⊖	⊜	⊜	⊜
Power equip.	⊜	⊖		⊖	⊜	⊜	⊜	⊜
Paint/trim/rust	⊖	⊜		⊖	⊜	⊜	⊜	⊜
Integrity	⊜	⊖		⊖	⊖	⊖	⊜	⊜
Hardware	⊖	○		⊖	⊜	⊜	⊜	⊜
RELIABILITY VERDICT	✔	✔		✔	✔	✔	✔	✔

Toyota Tacoma

Trouble spots	97	98	99	00	01	02	03	04
Engine	⊜	⊜	⊜	⊜	⊜	⊜	⊜	⊜
Cooling	⊖	⊖	⊜	⊜	⊜	⊜	⊜	⊜
Fuel	⊖	⊖	⊜	⊜	⊜	⊜	⊜	⊜
Ignition	⊜	⊜	⊜	⊜	⊜	⊜	⊜	⊜
Transmission	⊜	⊜	⊜	⊜	⊜	⊜	⊜	⊜
Electrical	○	⊖	⊖	⊖	⊜	⊜	⊜	⊜
A/C	⊖	⊜	⊜	⊜	⊜	⊜	⊜	⊜
Suspension	⊖	⊖	⊖	⊖	⊖	⊜	⊜	⊜
Brakes	○	⊖	⊖	⊖	⊖	⊖	⊜	⊜
Exhaust	⊖	⊜	⊜	⊜	⊜	⊜	⊜	⊜
Power equip.	⊜	⊜	⊜	⊜	⊜	⊜	⊜	⊜
Paint/trim/rust	⊖	⊜	⊖	⊖	○	⊖	⊜	⊜
Integrity	⊖	⊖	⊜	⊖	○	○	○	⊜
Hardware	⊖	⊖	⊜	⊜	⊖	⊜	⊜	⊜
RELIABILITY VERDICT	✔	✔	✔	✔	✔	✔	✔	✔

Volkswagen Golf 4-cyl.

Trouble spots	97	98	99	00	01	02	03	04
Engine	○	○	○	○	○	⊖	⊖	⊜
Cooling	○	○	⊖	⊖	⊜	⊜	⊜	⊜
Fuel	◒	○	●	●	◒	⊖	⊜	⊜
Ignition	○	◒	⊖	⊖	⊖	⊜	⊜	⊜
Transmission	○	⊜	⊖	⊜	⊖	⊖	⊖	⊜
Electrical	●	●	●	●	●	◒	○	○
A/C	◒	○	○	⊖	⊖	⊜	⊜	⊜
Suspension	⊖	⊖	⊖	⊖	⊜	⊜	⊜	⊜
Brakes	○	○	○	◒	◒	⊖	⊖	⊜
Exhaust	◒	◒	○	⊜	⊜	⊜	⊜	⊜
Power equip.	◒	●	●	●	◒	●	⊖	⊜
Paint/trim/rust	●	●	○	○	○	⊖	⊜	⊜
Integrity	●	●	◒	◒	◒	◒	○	⊜
Hardware	●	◒	●	●	○	○	○	⊜
RELIABILITY VERDICT	✘	✘	✘	✘	✘	✘	✘	–

Volkswagen Jetta 4-cyl. Turbo

Trouble spots	97	98	99	00	01	02	03	04
Engine				◒	○	○	⊖	Insufficient data
Cooling				○	⊖	⊖	⊜	
Fuel				●	●	○	⊖	
Ignition				●	●	●	○	
Transmission				⊜	⊖	⊖	⊜	
Electrical				◒	●	●	○	
A/C				⊖	⊖	⊜	⊜	
Suspension				⊜	⊜	⊜	⊜	
Brakes				◒	◒	⊖	⊜	
Exhaust				⊖	⊖	⊜	⊜	
Power equip.				●	●	●	⊖	
Paint/trim/rust				⊖	⊖	⊜	⊜	
Integrity				◒	◒	◒	⊖	
Hardware				◒	●	◒	○	
RELIABILITY VERDICT				✘	✘	✘	–	

Volkswagen New Beetle

Trouble spots	97	98	99	00	01	02	03	04
Engine		◒	⊖	○	⊖	⊖	⊜	⊜
Cooling		◒	○	⊖	○	⊜	⊜	⊜
Fuel		◒	◒	◒	○	○	⊜	⊜
Ignition		⊖	⊖	○	⊖	⊖	⊜	⊜
Transmission		⊖	⊖	⊜	⊖	⊖	⊖	⊜
Electrical		●	●	●	●	●	○	⊖
A/C		◒	◒	⊖	⊜	⊖	⊜	⊜
Suspension		⊖	⊜	⊜	⊜	⊜	⊜	⊜
Brakes		◒	◒	◒	○	○	⊜	⊜
Exhaust		⊖	○	⊖	⊖	⊜	⊜	⊜
Power equip.		●	●	●	◒	●	◒	○
Paint/trim/rust		○	○	⊖	⊖	⊖	⊖	⊜
Integrity		●	◒	◒	○	◒	○	⊜
Hardware		●	●	●	◒	◒	○	○
RELIABILITY VERDICT		✘	✘	✘	✘	✘	✘	✘

Volkswagen Passat 4-cyl.

Trouble spots	97	98	99	00	01	02	03	04
Engine	Insufficient data	●	◒	○	◒	○	⊜	⊜
Cooling		○	○	○	⊖	⊜	⊜	⊜
Fuel		◒	◒	●	◒	○	⊖	⊜
Ignition		◒	○	⊖	◒	●	○	⊜
Transmission		⊖	⊖	⊜	⊜	⊜	⊜	⊜
Electrical		●	●	◒	◒	◒	○	⊖
A/C		⊖	⊖	⊜	⊖	⊜	⊜	⊜
Suspension		●	○	⊖	⊜	⊜	⊜	⊜
Brakes		◒	◒	○	○	⊖	⊖	⊜
Exhaust		⊜	⊜	⊖	⊜	⊜	⊜	⊜
Power equip.		●	◒	○	○	○	⊖	⊜
Paint/trim/rust		⊖	⊖	⊖	⊖	⊖	⊜	⊜
Integrity		◒	◒	⊖	○	○	⊖	⊜
Hardware		●	◒	○	○	⊖	⊜	⊜
RELIABILITY VERDICT		✗	✗	–	✗	✗	–	–

Volkswagen Passat V6 AWD

Trouble spots	97	98	99	00	01	02	03	04
Engine				◒	○	⊜	⊜	⊜
Cooling				○	⊖	⊜	⊜	⊜
Fuel				◒	○	⊖	⊜	⊜
Ignition				⊖	⊜	⊜	⊜	⊜
Transmission				⊖	⊜	⊜	⊜	◒
Electrical				◒	◒	◒	⊖	⊜
A/C				⊜	⊖	⊖	⊜	⊜
Suspension				○	⊖	⊜	⊜	⊜
Brakes				⊖	◒	○	⊖	⊖
Exhaust				○	⊜	⊜	⊜	⊜
Power equip.				○	○	○	⊖	⊖
Paint/trim/rust				⊖	⊖	⊖	⊖	⊖
Integrity				○	○	○	⊖	⊜
Hardware				⊖	○	⊖	⊖	⊖
RELIABILITY VERDICT				✗	✗	–	✓	✗

Volkswagen Touareg

Trouble spots	97	98	99	00	01	02	03	04
Engine								⊜
Cooling								⊜
Fuel								⊜
Ignition								⊜
Transmission								⊜
Electrical								◒
A/C								⊜
Suspension								⊖
Brakes								⊜
Exhaust								⊜
Power equip.								◒
Paint/trim/rust								⊜
Integrity								○
Hardware								○
RELIABILITY VERDICT								✗

Volvo Cross Country XC70

Trouble spots	97	98	99	00	01	02	03	04
Engine		◒	○	⊖	⊖	⊜	⊜	⊜
Cooling		○	⊖	⊖	⊖	⊜	⊜	⊜
Fuel		◒	●	◒	○	⊜	⊖	⊜
Ignition		⊖	⊖	⊖	⊖	⊜	⊜	⊜
Transmission		⊖	⊖	⊖	○	⊖	⊖	⊜
Electrical		●	●	◒	●	◒	○	⊖
A/C		◒	○	⊖	⊖	⊜	⊜	⊜
Suspension		◒	◒	○	○	⊖	○	⊜
Brakes		●	○	○	○	⊜	⊜	⊜
Exhaust		⊖	⊜	⊜	⊜	⊜	⊜	⊜
Power equip.		◒	◒	◒	◒	○	⊖	⊜
Paint/trim/rust		⊖	⊖	⊜	○	⊜	⊜	⊜
Integrity		◒	○	○	○	⊖	⊖	⊜
Hardware		●	○	◒	◒	○	⊖	⊜
RELIABILITY VERDICT		✗	✗	✗	✗	–	✗	–

Volvo S40/V40

Trouble spots	97	98	99	00	01	02	03	04
Engine				○	⊜	⊜	⊜	⊜
Cooling				⊖	⊜	⊜	⊜	⊜
Fuel				○	○	⊖	○	⊜
Ignition				⊜	⊜	⊜	⊜	⊜
Transmission				⊜	⊖	⊜	⊜	⊜
Electrical				●	○	○	○	⊜
A/C				⊖	⊖	⊜	⊖	⊜
Suspension				○	⊜	⊖	⊜	⊜
Brakes				●	●	◒	⊖	⊜
Exhaust				⊜	⊜	⊜	⊜	⊜
Power equip.				⊖	○	⊖	⊜	⊜
Paint/trim/rust				○	⊜	⊖	⊖	⊜
Integrity				○	⊜	⊖	⊖	⊜
Hardware				○	⊜	⊖	⊖	⊜
RELIABILITY VERDICT				–	–	–	–	✓

Volvo S60

Trouble spots	97	98	99	00	01	02	03	04
Engine					⊜	⊜	⊜	⊜
Cooling					⊜	⊜	⊜	⊜
Fuel					⊖	⊖	⊜	⊖
Ignition					⊜	⊜	⊜	⊜
Transmission					○	⊜	⊜	⊜
Electrical					◒	○	⊖	⊜
A/C					⊖	⊖	⊜	⊜
Suspension					○	⊖	⊖	⊖
Brakes					⊖	⊖	⊜	⊜
Exhaust					⊜	⊜	⊜	⊜
Power equip.					○	○	⊖	⊜
Paint/trim/rust					○	⊜	⊜	⊖
Integrity					○	⊖	⊜	⊖
Hardware					○	○	⊖	⊜
RELIABILITY VERDICT					–	–	✓	–

Volvo S80

Trouble spots	97	98	99	00	01	02	03	04
Engine			◒	○	⊖	⊖	⊖	⊜
Cooling			○	○	⊖	⊜	⊜	⊜
Fuel			●	●	⊖	⊖	⊖	⊜
Ignition			⊖	⊖	⊖	⊜	⊜	⊜
Transmission			◒	○	⊜	⊖	○	⊜
Electrical			●	●	●	◒	⊖	⊖
A/C			⊖	⊖	⊖	⊜	⊜	⊜
Suspension			●	●	○	⊖	⊖	⊖
Brakes			◒	○	○	⊖	⊜	⊜
Exhaust			⊖	⊜	⊜	⊜	⊜	⊜
Power equip.			◒	◒	○	◒	⊖	⊜
Paint/trim/rust			⊖	⊖	○	⊖	⊜	⊜
Integrity			◒	◒	◒	◒	⊖	⊜
Hardware			◒	◒	○	○	⊖	⊜
RELIABILITY VERDICT			✗	✗	✗	✗	✗	–

Volvo XC90

Trouble spots	97	98	99	00	01	02	03	04
Engine							⊖	⊜
Cooling							⊖	⊜
Fuel							⊖	⊜
Ignition							⊜	⊜
Transmission							○	⊜
Electrical							○	⊜
A/C							⊖	⊜
Suspension							○	⊜
Brakes							○	⊖
Exhaust							⊜	⊜
Power equip.							◒	⊖
Paint/trim/rust							⊖	⊜
Integrity							◒	⊖
Hardware							◒	⊖
RELIABILITY VERDICT							✗	✗

PRODUCT RATINGS AND BRAND RELIABILITY

The product rating and brand reliability information that follows is designed to help you zero in on the model you want to buy. Start by reading the general buying advice for the product you're interested in. The page numbers for these reports are noted on each Ratings page. Then turn to the Ratings chart to get the big picture in terms of performance.

The Quick Picks highlight the best models for most people plus models that may be especially suited to you family's needs. The Recommendations provide additional detail on features and performance for individual models. Use the key numbers to move easily between the charts and the other information.

CONSUMER REPORTS checked to make sure most of the products rated in this Buying Guide were still available when the book was published. However, depending on how long after publication you use this book, you may find a rating for a product that is no longer available. Or, you may not find a rating for a model that is available because it hadn't been tested as of publication. Models similar to the tested models, when they exist, are also listed. Such models differ in features, not essential performance, according to the manufacturers.

Besides checking for similar models, you can also refer to the brand reliability charts. Most products today are pretty reliable, but some brands have been more reliable than others.

Every year we survey readers on repairs and on problems they encounter with household products. From their responses, we derive the percentage of a brand's products that have been repaired or had a serious problem. The reliability graphs that accompany the ratings give brand repair rates for 12 product categories. Over the 30-plus years we've surveyed brand reliability, our findings have been consistent, though they are not infallible predictors.

A brand's repair history includes data on many models, some of which may have been more or less reliable than others. And surveys of a brand's past models can't anticipate design or manufacturing changes in its new models. Still, you can improve your chances of getting a trouble-free product by getting a brand that has been reliable in the past.

Product categories include appliances such as washers and ranges, electronic products such as TV sets and digital cameras, and lawn mowers and tractors. Note that repair histories for different products are not directly comparable.

Because the quality of technical support may be the deciding factor when you're shopping for a desktop or laptop computer, we include a recent assessment of the manufacturers' technical support as well.

Ratings and Reliability

CONTENTS

QUICK GUIDE

AIR CONDITIONERS

All the air conditioners in our tests should keep you cool. Top-scoring models perform the most efficiently and quietly.

The Ratings rank models by overall performance within size groups. Once you determine the right size, consider that the more off-center your window, the more it matters that the unit blow air where you need it. Buy the highest-rated model within your budget that meets this need and that has other attributes you may favor, such as a top score for noise.

Safety plugs are required by Underwriters Laboratories on units made after July 2004. In the Ratings, the following models have these plugs: GE (1), Frigidaire (3), Haier (9), Goldstar (12), Frigidaire (16), GE (17), Goldstar (21), LG (22), Friedrich (26), Frigidaire (30), GE (32), GE (33), Fedders (35), LG (36). The others, carryover models from recent tests, do not, though all similar models do.

Excellent | Very good | Good | Fair | Poor

Within types, in performance order. Gray key numbers indicate Quick Picks.

Key number	Brand & model (Similar models, in small type, comparable to tested model.)	Price	Overall score (0–100; P F G VG E)	Test results: Comfort	Noise	Brownout	Ease of use	Features: Btu/hr.	EER	Weight (lbs.)	Window width (in.)	Remote control
	5,000 TO 6,000 BTU/HR. (COOLING: 100-300 SQ. FT.)											
1	**GE** AGM06LH	$180		Excellent	Excellent	Excellent	Very good	6000	10.7	22-36	59	•
2	**Sharp** AF-S60FX	240		Excellent	Very good	Excellent	Very good	6000	10.7	22-36	50	•
3	**Frigidaire** FAA067P7 (Lowes) **CR Best Buy**	130		Excellent	Very good	Excellent	Good	6000	10.7	23-36	49	•
4	**Kenmore (Sears)** 72059 D 75052	180		Excellent	Very good	Excellent	Very good	5700	11.2	23-34	48	•
5	**Friedrich** X Star XQ05J10 D X Star XQ05L10	365		Excellent	Very good	Excellent	Good	5400	10.7	25-42	69	
6	**Kenmore (Sears)** 72056 D 75051	130		Excellent	Very good	Good	Very good	5300	10.8	23-34	49	•
7	**Whirlpool** ACQ068MP ACQ068PR	175		Excellent	Very good	Excellent	Very good	6000	11	26-39	57	•
8	**LG** LP6000ER D BP6000ER, GP6000ER	280		Excellent	Very good	Excellent	Good	6000	10.7	25-41	47	•
9	**Haier** HWR06XC5 Amana ACB065R, HEC CR06BC5	160		Excellent	Good	Excellent	Good	6000	9.7	23-33	45	•
10	**Kenmore (Sears)** 73069 D 75062	220		Excellent	Good	Excellent	Good	6000	10.7	25-40	47	•
11	**Panasonic** Deluxe D CW-XC55HU	160		Excellent	Good	Good	Very good	5200	10.8	23-36	48	•
12	**Goldstar** WG6005R	150		Excellent	Very good	Fair	Very good	6000	9.7	22-36	46	•

Excellent / Very good / Good / Fair / Poor

Within types, in performance order. Gray key numbers indicate Quick Picks.

Key number	Brand & model (Similar models, in small type, comparable to tested model.)	Price	Overall score (0–100; P F G VG E)	Test results: Comfort	Noise	Brownout	Ease of use	Features: Btu/hr.	EER	Weight (lbs.)	Window width (in.)	Remote control
5,000 TO 6,000 BTU/HR. (COOLING: 100-300 SQ. FT.) *continued*												
13	**Whirlpool** Value Series ACD502PR	$110		Excellent	Very good	Excellent	Good	5000	9.7	17-38	48	
14	**Fedders** X Series A6X06F2A Maytag M6X06F2C, X Series A6X06F2C	180		Excellent	Good	Excellent	Very good	6000	9.7	24-38	48	•
15	**Fedders** X Series A6X05F2B D Maytag M6X05F2D, X Series A6X05F2D	195		Excellent	Fair	Excellent	Excellent	5200	9.7	24-37	42	•
7,000 TO 8,200 BTU/HR. (COOLING: 250-550 SQ. FT.)												
16	**Frigidaire** FAA087P7 (Lowes) **CR Best Buy**	160		Excellent	Very good	Excellent	Good	8000	10.8	23-36	53	•
17	**GE** AGM08LH	240		Excellent	Excellent	Excellent	Very good	8000	10.8	22-36	64	•
18	**LG** LW8000ER D LB8000ER	260		Excellent	Very good	Excellent	Very good	8200	10.9	23-38	65	•
19	**Sharp** AF-S80FX	310		Excellent	Good	Excellent	Very good	8000	10.8	22-36	54	•
20	**Fedders** Q Series D Maytag M7Q08F2B, Q Series A7Q08F2B	230		Excellent	Good	Excellent	Very good	8000	10.8	24-36	66	•
21	**Goldstar** WG8005R	170		Excellent	Very good	Fair	Very good	8000	9.8	22-36	60	•
22	**LG** LWHD8000R	170		Excellent	Very good	Fair	Very good	8000	9.8	22-36	58	•
23	**Friedrich** Quietmaster Electronic D Quietmaster Electronics SS08L10	590		Very good	Fair	Excellent	Good	8200	11	26-43	108	•
24	**Whirlpool** ACQ088XP D ACQ088MR	210		Excellent	Fair	Excellent	Very good	8000	10.8	26-40	57	•
25	**Panasonic** Deluxe CW-XC84 D Deluxe CW-XC85HU	245		Excellent	Good	Fair	Fair	7800	10.8	22-34	62	•
9,800 TO 12,500 BTU/HR. (COOLING: 350-950 SQ. FT.)												
26	**Friedrich** SS10L10-A	700		Excellent	Excellent	Excellent	Good	10400	12.0	28-42	109	•
27	**Kenmore (Sears)** 74107 D 75101	300		Excellent	Very good	Excellent	Good	10000	10.8	27-39	80	•
28	**LG** LW1000ER	300		Excellent	Very good	Excellent	Good	10000	11	28-39	79	•
29	**Panasonic** Deluxe CW-XC104HU Deluxe CW-XC105HU	265		Excellent	Very good	Excellent	Fair	9800	10.8	27-39	81	•
30	**Frigidaire** FAC107P1 (Lowes) **CR Best Buy**	195		Excellent	Good	Excellent	Good	10000	10.8	23-36	78	•
31	**Kenmore** (Sears) 76129 D 75132	370		Excellent	Good	Excellent	Very good	12300	10.8	28-41	86	•
32	**GE** AGW10A AGH10AH, AGQ10AH	270		Excellent	Very good	Fair	Very good	10000	9.8	25-36	71	•
33	**GE** AGM12AH	350		Excellent	Very good	Good	Very good	12000	10.8	27-39	82	•

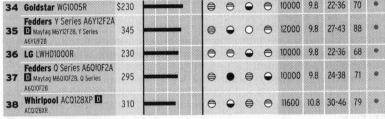

Key number	Brand & model (Similar models, in small type, comparable to tested model.)	Price	Overall score (0–100; P F G VG E)	Test results: Comfort	Test results: Noise	Test results: Brownout	Test results: Ease of use	Features: Btu/hr.	Features: EER	Features: Weight (lbs.)	Features: Window width (in.)	Features: Remote control
	9,800 TO 12,500 BTU/HR. (COOLING: 350-950 SQ. FT.)											
34	**Goldstar** WG1005R	$230		E	VG	F	VG	10000	9.8	22-36	70	•
35	**Fedders** Y Series A6Y12F2A [D] Maytag M6Y12F2B, Y Series A6Y12F2B	345		E	F	G	VG	12000	9.8	27-43	88	•
36	**LG** LWHD1000R	230		VG	VG	F	VG	10000	9.8	22-36	68	•
37	**Fedders** Q Series A6Q10F2A [D] Maytag M6Q10F2B, Q Series A6Q10F2B	295		E	P	E	F	10000	9.8	24-38	71	•
38	**Whirlpool** ACQ128XP [D] ACQ128XR	310		VG	F	E	VG	11600	10.8	30-46	79	•

[D] Discontinued, but similar model available.

See report, page 83. Based on tests posted to Consumer Reports.org in August 2005, with updated prices and availability.

Guide to the Ratings

Overall score is based mainly on comfort, noise, and energy efficiency. **Comfort** is how well temperature and humidity are controlled at the low-cool setting. The best performers held temperatures to within one-and-a-half degrees of the setpoint. **Noise** is based on the judgment of indoor noise at the low-cool setting, and combines an objective measurement of noise level using a decibel meter with a subjective assessment of noise quality (how annoying or grating the particular sounds were). **Brownout** gauges the unit's ability to run and restart during extreme heat and low voltage. **Ease of use** reflects control-panel layout, including the clarity of its markings, as well as how easy and intuitive the controls were to operate. **Price** is approximate retail price.

Quick Picks

Efficient, quiet, and CR Best Buys:

3 Frigidaire, $130
16 Frigidaire, $160
30 Frigidaire, $195

All do a better job directing air to the left.

If quiet is paramount:

1 GE, $180
17 GE, $240
27 Kenmore (Sears), $300

Both GEs are difficult to install. The Kenmore is somewhat louder than the Friedrich SS10L10-A (26), but far less expensive. It's a good choice if you want air blown to the right as are the Haier HWR06XC5 (9) and the LG LW8000ER (18).

CAMCORDERS

You can expect a digital camcorder to deliver very good video, as our Ratings scores demonstrate. Many of the digital camcorders that record directly onto small DVD discs were ranked at or near the top of the Ratings. However, that doesn't automatically make them the best choice. As the Ratings show, most DVD models were not markedly better than many camcorders that use MiniDV tape. The MiniDV camcorders win on price, making them the type that most people should consider first. The DVD models are for people who want ease of playback above all else.

Most camcorders weigh about a pound, give or take a few ounces. As camcorders get smaller and lighter, image-stabilization features become more important. A lightweight camcorder is harder to hold steady than a heavy one. Fortunately, most did an excellent job of minimizing the shakes.

Nearly all these camcorders turned in fair or poor performance when we tested them in low light. Two Canon models, the Canon Elura 85 (3) and the Canon Elura 60 (17), a Panasonic, the Panasonic PV-GS65 (24) and the Sony DCR-DVD101 (29) were better than the rest.

Analog camcorders are a dying breed. Three models remain in the Ratings, and none is in the same league as the digitals. Their picture quality is only fair, comparable with that of a rental videotape.

The Ratings rank models strictly on performance. Quick Picks considers other factors such as features, reliability, and value.

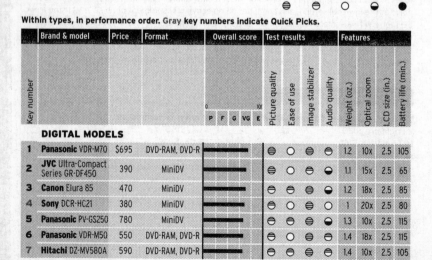

Excellent / Very good / Good / Fair / Poor

Within types, in performance order. Gray key numbers indicate Quick Picks.

Key number	Brand & model	Price	Format	Overall score (0–100: P F G VG E)	Test results: Picture quality	Ease of use	Image stabilizer	Audio quality	Features: Weight (oz.)	Optical zoom	LCD size (in.)	Battery life (min.)
	DIGITAL MODELS											
1	**Panasonic** VDR-M70	$695	DVD-RAM, DVD-R		Excellent	Good	Excellent	Very good	1.2	10x	2.5	105
2	**JVC** Ultra-Compact Series GR-DF450	390	MiniDV		Excellent	Good	Very good	Fair	1.1	15x	2.5	65
3	**Canon** Elura 85	470	MiniDV		Very good	Very good	Excellent	Fair	1.2	18x	2.5	85
4	**Sony** DCR-HC21	380	MiniDV		Very good	Good	Excellent	Good	1	20x	2.5	80
5	**Panasonic** PV-GS250	780	MiniDV		Very good	Very good	Excellent	Fair	1.3	10x	2.5	115
6	**Panasonic** VDR-M50	550	DVD-RAM, DVD-R		Very good	Good	Excellent	Very good	1.4	18x	2.5	115
7	**Hitachi** DZ-MV580A	590	DVD-RAM, DVD-R		Very good	Very good	Excellent	Very good	1.4	10x	2.5	105

Key number	Brand & model	Price	Format	Overall score (0–100: P F G VG E)	Picture quality	Ease of use	Image stabilizer	Audio quality	Weight (oz.)	Optical zoom	LCD size (in.)	Battery life (min.)
	DIGITAL MODELS											
8	**Canon** ZR200	$370	MiniDV		⊖	⊖	⊜	◒	1.1	20x	2.4	85
9	**Sony** DCR-HC90	785	MiniDV		⊖	○	⊖	⊖	1.1	10x	2.7	80
10	**Canon** Optura 50	635	MiniDV		⊖	○	⊜	◒	1.3	10x	2.5	75
11	**Sony** DCR-HC20	430	MiniDV		⊖	○	⊜	◒	1	10x	2.5	110
12	**JVC** Everio Series GZ-MC100	900	External Memory		⊖	◒	⊜	◒	0.7	10x	1.8	65
13	**Sony** DCR-IP1	990	MicroMV		⊖	○	⊜	○	0.6	10x	2	90
14	**Sony** DCR-PC55	625	MiniDV		⊖	○	⊜	◒	0.8	10x	3	95
15	**Sony** DCR-TRV480	335	D8		⊖	○	⊜	◒	2	20x	2.5	80
16	**JVC** Compact Series GR-D270	315	MiniDV		⊖	○	⊖	◒	1.1	25x	2.5	65
17	**Canon** Elura 60	375	MiniDV		○	⊖	⊜	◒	1.2	14x	2.5	90
18	**Panasonic** PV-GS31	370	MiniDV		○	○	⊖	◒	1	26x	2.5	85
19	**Panasonic** PV-GS55	500	MiniDV		⊖	○	⊖	⊖	0.8	10x	2.5	NS
20	**Panasonic** PV-GS120	640	MiniDV		○	○	○	⊖	1.2	10x	2.5	125
21	**Sony** DCR-DVD201	655	DVD-RAM, DVD-R		○	○	⊜	◒	1.2	10x	2.5	105
22	**Sony** DCR-PC109	640	MiniDV		⊖	○	⊜	○	1	10x	2.5	100
23	**JVC** GR-D93US	370	MiniDV		⊖	○	○	◒	1.4	10x	2.5	65
24	**Panasonic** PV-GS65	520	MiniDV		○	○	⊖	◒	1.1	10x	2.5	80
25	**Canon** Elura 70	500	MiniDV		○	⊖	⊜	○	1.4	18x	2.5	190
26	**Canon** ZR85	345	MiniDV		○	◒	○	◒	1.2	20x	2.5	85
27	**JVC** GR-D230U	390	MiniDV		○	○	⊖	◒	1.2	10x	2.5	80
28	**Samsung** SC-D103	295	MiniDV		○	○	◒	⊖	1.2	18x	2.5	90
29	**Sony** DCR-DVD101	605	DVD-RAM, DVD-R		○	○	⊜	○	1.2	10x	2.5	120
30	**JVC** GR-DX77U	350	MiniDV		○	○	⊜	○	1.2	12x	2.5	75
31	**Panasonic** PV-GS9	265	MiniDV		○	○	⊖	◒	1	20x	2.5	105
32	**Canon** ZR80	320	MiniDV		○	⊖	○	◒	1.2	18x	2.5	85
	ANALOG MODELS											
33	**Sony** CCD-TRV138	235	Hi8		○	○	0	⊖	2	20x	2.5	115
34	**Sony** CCD-TRV128	210	Hi8		◒	○	0	⊖	2	20x	2.5	115
35	**Panasonic** PV-L354D	210	VHS-C		◒	⊖	⊖	●	2.4	20x	2.5	40

See report, page 23. Based on tests posted to ConsumerReports.org in July 2005, with updated prices and availability.

Guide to the Ratings

Overall score is based mainly on picture quality; ease of use, image stabilizing, and audio quality carried less weight. **Picture quality** is based on the judgments of trained panelists who viewed static images shot in good light at standard speed (SP) for tape and fine mode for DVDs. **Ease of use** takes into account ergonomics, weight, how accurately the viewfinder frames scenes, and contrast in the LCD viewer. **Image stabilizer** indicates how well that circuitry worked. **Audio quality** represents accuracy using the built-in microphone, plus freedom from noise and flutter. **Weight** includes battery and tape or disk. **Optical zoom range** is as stated by the manufacturer. **LCD size** is measured diagonally. **Battery life** is as stated by the manufacturer, using the LCD viewer. Turning off the viewer typically extends battery life by 10 to 40 minutes on a charge. NS indicates that the manufacturer did not provide the specification for battery life. **Price** is approximate retail.

Expect these camcorders to have: Tape counter, backlight-compensation switch, manual aperture control, high-speed manual shutter, manual white balance, simple switch for manual focus, audio dub, tape-position memory, audio fade, transitional effects, S-video signal out, and video fade.

Quick Picks

Best values in digital tape:

4 Sony, $380

15 Sony, $335 **CR Best Buy**

The Sony DCR-HC21 (4) weighs just a pound and is among the lowest-priced digital camcorders we tested. Although very good overall, its sound quality was only good; that may not matter much for recording speech, but you may notice it with music. The Sony DCR-TRV480 (15) offers more features and better image stabilization—though it, too, has mediocre sound quality. JVC also has some high-scoring, low-priced models; however, Sony has been the most reliable brand among digital camcorders.

Best value in a DVD camcorder:

7 Hitachi, $590

This is one of the least expensive DVD camcorders we tested; its straightforward controls also made it one of the easiest to use. We don't have enough data to judge the reliability of DVD camcorders.

Brand Repair History

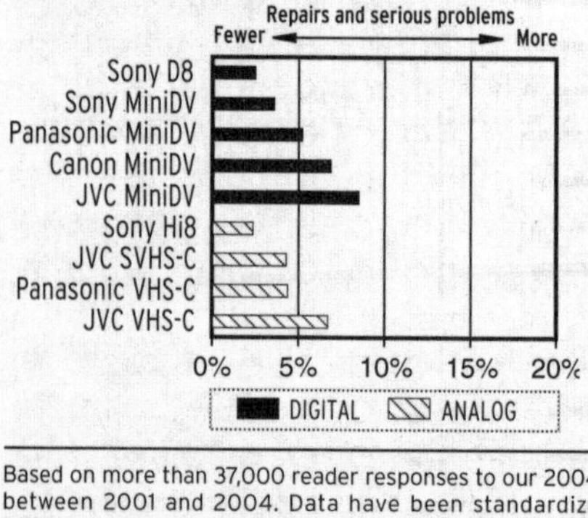

The graph shows the percentage of digital and analog camcorders that have been repaired or developed a serious problem that was not repaired. We don't have enough reader data to judge the reliability of DVD camcorders. Models within a brand may vary, and design and manufacturing changes may affect reliability. Nevertheless, you can improve your chances of getting a trouble-free camcorders if you choose a brand that has been reliable in the past.

Based on more than 37,000 reader responses to our 2004 Annual Questionnaire about camcorders bought new between 2001 and 2004. Data have been standardized to eliminate differences linked to age and use. Differences in score of less than 3 points aren't meaningful.

CELL PHONES

We've grouped the tested phones by carriers to make it easier for you to find a phone once you've settled on a company for service. Overall, the phones are closely matched in voice quality and sensitivity. We found GSM phones have better talk time compared with CDMA phones, except for the Sharp TM-150. GSM phones also tend to offer more advanced features for the money, like Bluetooth, but they lack analog backup.

The phones' weights range from 3.1 ounces, for the Siemens CF62T, to 6.3 ounces for the PalmOne Treo 650. All measure about 4 inches long.

The Ratings rank phones strictly on performance. Quick Picks considers other factors, such as coverage and value.

Excellent · Very good · Good · Fair · Poor

Within types, in performance order. Gray key numbers indicate Quick Picks.

Key number	Brand & model	Price	Overall score (0–100; P F G VG E)	Listening	Talking	Talk time (hr.)	Sensitivity	Ease of use	Speakerphone	Std. headset connector	Camera	Analog backup
	VERIZON PHONES *These work on Verizon's CDMA digital network.*											
1	**LG** VX8000	$150		Good	Very good	4 1/4	Very good	Very good	•	•	M	
2	**LG** VX7000	100		Good	Very good	4	Good	Very good		•	S	
3	**Samsung** SCH-a790	430		Good	Very good	3 1/4	Very good	Very good		•	S	
4	**Kyocera** SE47	40		Fair	Good	3 3/4	Excellent	Good	•	•		
5	**LG** VX3200	40		Good	Very good	3 1/4	Good	Very good	•	•		•
6	**Samsung** SCH-a650	20		Good	Very good	3 1/2	Good	Good		•		•
7	**Motorola** V710	100		Fair	Very good	3 1/4	Very good	Very good		•	M	•
	SPRINT PCS PHONES *These work on Sprint's CDMA digital network.*											
8	**Samsung** MM-A700	200		Good	Very good	4 1/4	Very good	Very good		•	M	•
9	**PalmOne** Treo 650	420		Good	Good	4 1/4	Very good	Very good	•	•	S	
10	**LG** PM-325	40		Good	Good	3 1/4	Very good	Good		•	S	•
11	**Sanyo** PM-8200	50		Good	Very good	2 3/4	Very good	Very good	•	•	S	•
12	**Nokia** 6016i	0		Good	Good	3 1/4	Very good	Good	•	•		•
13	**Motorola** V60v	70		Good	Very good	2 1/2	Good	Good		•		•

Within types, in performance order. Gray **key numbers indicate Quick Picks.**

Key number	Brand & model	Price	Overall score (0–100: P F G VG E)	Performance: Listening	Performance: Talking	Performance: Talk time (hr.)	Performance: Sensitivity	Performance: Ease of use	Features: Speakerphone	Features: Std. headset connector	Features: Camera	Features: Analog backup
	CINGULAR AND T-MOBILE PHONES *These work on GSM digital networks.*											
14	**Samsung** SGH p735 (T-Mobile)	$500		○	○	6¼	⊖	⊖			M	
15	**Motorola** Razr V3 GSM (Cingular)	200		○	○	5¼	⊖	⊖	●		S	
16	**Nokia** 6010 (Cingular, T-Mobile)	20		○	○	6¾	⊖	3				
17	**Siemens** CF62T (T-Mobile)	0		○	⊖	4¾	⊜	○	●			
18	**Nokia** 6620 (Cingular)	200		○	○	4½	⊜	○	●		S	
19	**Nokia** 6820 (Cingular)	100		○	○	5¼	⊜	◒		●	S	
20	**Siemens** C61 (Cingular)	10		○	⊖	4½	⊜	○	●			
21	**Nokia** 6230 (Cingular)	0		○	○	5½	⊖	○	●		S	
22	**Sony** Ericsson Z500a (Cingular)	50		○	⊖	5	⊖	○	●		S	
23	**Sharp** TM150 (T-Mobile)	100		○	○	3¼	⊜	⊖		●	M	

See report, page 117. Based on tests in Consumer Reports in February 2005, with updated prices and availaibility.

Guide to the Ratings

Overall score is based mainly on voice quality and talk time. **Listening** rates voice quality for those calling you; **talking** rates voice quality for your speech. Listening and talking tests were conducted in noisy and quiet environments using live phone calls. **Talk time** is the average time for calls you should expect, based on our tests with strong and weak signals. **Sensitivity** is a measure of a phone's voice quality when a call is placed using a weak signal. The scores are applicable only within a Ratings group, not between groups. **Ease of use** takes in the design of the display and keypad and the ease with which we could program and access speed-dial numbers, redial, send or receive text messages, and the like. **Price** is the approximate price for a phone purchased in the spring of 2005 with a 1 or 2 year contract. Prices don't include rebates or special offers.

Quick Picks

Best for Verizon (CDMA):

1 LG VX8000, $150
6 Samsung SCH-a650, $20

The LG is a good choice for a multimedia phone. It features a high resolution camera, speakerphone, one of the easiest-to-read keypads we've seen in all lighting conditions, and a display that's easily readable except in bright light. It's also compatible with Verizon's high speed EV-DO network, which allows access to Verizon's VCast TV service. Its main drawback is the lack of analog backup.

The Samsung is a good choice for an inexpensive phone. It has good battery life for a CDMA phone, plus analog backup. Its keypad is a bit hard to read in dim light and its display is hard to read in bright light. It lacks a second display you can read with the case closed.

Best for Sprint (CDMA):

8 Samsung MM-A700, $200
10 LG PM-325, $40

The Samsung is a good choice for a high-end phone. It has an easy-to-use keypad viewable in all lighting conditions. The display is bright and easy to see in low and normal lighting, but somewhat difficult in bright light. It also features a high-resolution camera that lets you record short videos. A voice command feature lets you call anyone in your phone book without having to program the voice dialing function; you can dial a number simply by speaking the digits. Its four-way jog dial can be programmed with shortcuts to frequently used functions. The phone is compatible with Sprint's TV service.

The LG is a good choice for an inexpensive phone. Its keypad is easy to use and readable in all lighting conditions, and the display is viewable everywhere except in bright light. It has a compact sliding case: The keypad slides down while on a call, extending the microphone and putting it closer to your mouth when you're speaking. The result is very good voice quality when listening, and good voice quality when talking, comparable to some folding case phone designs. It also has a built-in VGA-resolution camera and is Bluetooth compatible. But the Bluetooth connection only supports headsets and handsfree devices; you can't use it to transfer pictures or other digital data. The average talk-time battery life of 3¼ hours is less than with other CDMA phones.

Both phones are tri-mode; they can connect digitally in both the cellular and PCS bands and have analog backup. This allows users to make calls on roaming networks when outside Sprint's network.

COMPUTERS, desktops and laptops

Below you'll find the results of surveys in which we asked subscribers about whether their computer has needed repair and what their experience was if they sought technical support—two very important things to consider when choosing which manufacturer you want to buy your next computer from. Computer models tested by CONSUMER REPORTS were no longer available at the time this Buying Guide was published.

Desktops

In order of reader score.

Excellent | Very good | Good | Fair | Poor

Manufacturer	Reader score (0–100)	Solved problem	Waiting on phone	Support staff	Web support
Apple	81	Excellent	Excellent	Excellent	Excellent
Dell	57	Very good	Good	Good	Good
Gateway	56	Good	Very good	Very good	Good
HP	51	Good	Good	Good	Good
Sony	51	Good	Good	Good	–
Compaq	45	Fair	Fair	Fair	Good

Note: (-) indicates insufficient sample size. Based on nearly 8,000 desktop computers bought before January 2005. eMachines and IBM had insufficient sample size.

Laptops

In order of reader score.

Manufacturer	Reader score (0–100)	Solved problem	Waiting on phone	Support staff	Web support
Apple	84	Excellent	Excellent	Excellent	Excellent
IBM	69	Very good	Excellent	Very good	–
Toshiba	58	Fair	Good	Good	Good
Dell	57	Very good	Fair	Fair	Good
Gateway	55	Good	Fair	Good	–
HP	54	Good	Good	Good	Good
Compaq	48	Fair	Poor	Fair	Fair
Sony	46	Poor	Fair	Fair	–

Based on more than 4,500 laptops bought before December 2004.

TECH SUPPORT

We conducted two surveys of subscribers to ConsumerReports.org on their most recent experiences with manufacturers' technical support. We asked the subscribers to tell us which manufacturers did the best job of answering questions quickly and correctly. For desktop computers, the survey covered September 2003 through January 2005; for laptops, the survey covered September 2003 to December 2004. The charts on page 232 give the specifics.

If everyone was completely satisfied, the reader score would be 100; 80 would mean respondents were very satisfied, on average; 60, fairly well satisfied. In both surveys, differences of 6 or more points are meaningful.

Solved problem indicates how many people said the manufacturer solved their problem. **Waiting on phone** refers to time waiting and other phone-system problems. **Support staff** is primarily based on how knowledgeable phone representatives seemed and whether they communicated clearly. **Web support** indicates subscribers' experiences going online to get help.

Because of differences in timing and methodology, the charts are not directly comparable.

BRAND REPAIR HISTORY

We surveyed subscribers to Consumer Reports.org, our Web site, who own a desktop or laptop computer, asking about their experiences with the hardware. We got responses for more than 140,0000 desktop and laptop computers. The charts below show the percentage ever needing a repair or having a serious problem. Any brand's repair history includes models that have been more or less reliable than others. Design or manufacturing changes, which we cannot anticipate, may also affect a brand's repair record. Still, you increase your chances of getting a reliable desktop or laptop by choosing from brands that have proven reliable in the past. Gateway was among the more repair-prone brands of desktop; Gateway and Compaq were among the more repair-prone brands of laptop.

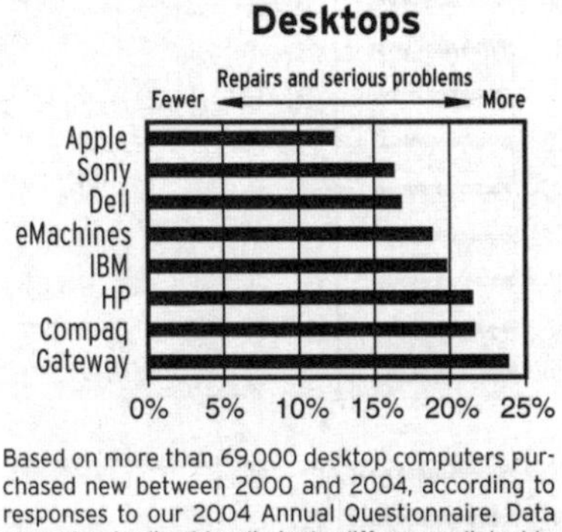

Based on more than 69,000 desktop computers purchased new between 2000 and 2004, according to responses to our 2004 Annual Questionnaire. Data were standardized to eliminate differences linked to age and use. Differences of 4 or more points are meaningful.

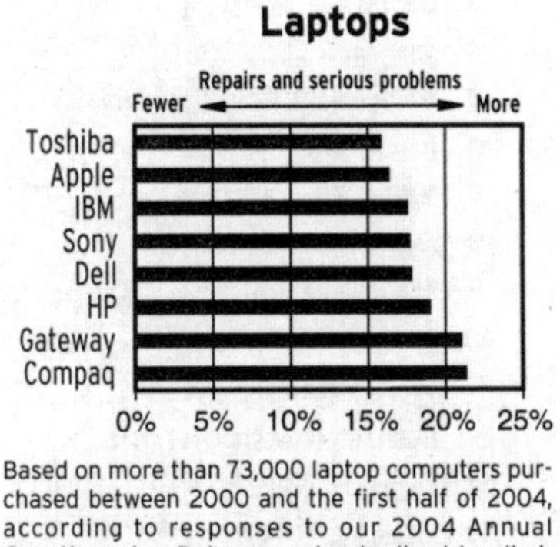

Based on more than 73,000 laptop computers purchased between 2000 and the first half of 2004, according to responses to our 2004 Annual Questionnaire. Data were standardized to eliminate differences linked to age and usage. Differences of 3 or more points are meaningful.

COOKTOPS & WALL OVENS

All of the electric cooktops performed well overall, but paying more doesn't guarantee a better cooktop. While the best gas models cost $1,200 or more, so did some lesser performers. Indeed, several capable gas cooktops we tested cost well below $1,000, though they typically sacrifice style and convenience features. Electric and gas cooktops can't match the quick heating and instant response of induction models, which can cost $2,000 or more.

Electric wall ovens are another appliance where price can have little to do with performance. While the top-scoring Thermador cost the most, several models cooked nearly as well for hundreds of dollars less.

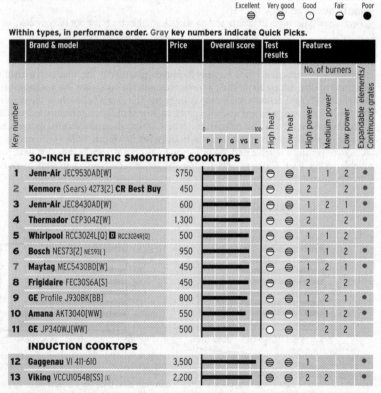

Excellent ⊜ Very good ⊖ Good ○ Fair ◒ Poor ●

Within types, in performance order. Gray key numbers indicate Quick Picks.

Key number	Brand & model	Price	Overall score (0–100: P F G VG E)	Test results: High heat	Test results: Low heat	Features: No. of burners: High power	Features: No. of burners: Medium power	Features: No. of burners: Low power	Features: Expandable elements/ Continuous grates
	30-INCH ELECTRIC SMOOTHTOP COOKTOPS								
1	**Jenn-Air** JEC9530AD[W]	$750		Very good	Excellent	1	1	2	•
2	**Kenmore** (Sears) 4273[2] **CR Best Buy**	450		Very good	Excellent	2		2	•
3	**Jenn-Air** JEC8430AD[W]	600		Very good	Excellent	1	2	1	•
4	**Thermador** CEP304Z[W]	1,300		Very good	Excellent	2		2	•
5	**Whirlpool** RCC3024L[Q] D RCC3024R[Q]	500		Very good	Excellent	1	1	2	
6	**Bosch** NES73[2] NES93[ ]	950		Very good	Excellent	1	1	2	•
7	**Maytag** MEC5430BD[W]	450		Very good	Excellent	1	2	1	•
8	**Frigidaire** FEC30S6A[S]	450		Very good	Excellent	2		2	
9	**GE** Profile J930BK[BB]	800		Very good	Excellent	1	2	1	•
10	**Amana** AKT3040[WW]	550		Very good	Very good	1	1	2	•
11	**GE** JP340WJ[WW]	500		Good	Excellent		2	2	
	INDUCTION COOKTOPS								
12	**Gaggenau** VI 411-610	3,500		Excellent	Excellent	1			•
13	**Viking** VCCU1054B[SS] [1]	2,200		Excellent	Excellent	2	2		•

See report, page 53. Based on tests in Consumer Reports in November 2005.

In performance order. Gray **key numbers indicate Quick Picks.**

Key number	Brand & model	Price	Overall score (0–100; P F G VG E)	Test results: High heat	Test results: Low heat	Features: No. of burners: High power	Features: No. of burners: Medium power	Features: No. of burners: Low power	Features: Expandable elements/ Continuous grates
	36-INCH GAS COOKTOPS								
14	**Dacor** Preference PGM365	$1,470		⊖	⊜	3	2		•
15	**GE** Monogram ZGU375NSD[SS]	1,400		○	⊜	1	4		•
16	**GE** Profile JGP975WEK[WW]	1,200		○	⊜	1	2	2	•
17	**DCS** CT-365SS	1,350		⊖	⊖	1	4		•
18	**Jenn-Air** JGC8536AD[S]	950		⊖	⊖	2	1	2	•
19	**Maytag** MGC6536BD[W] **CR Best Buy**	650		○	⊜	1	3	1	•
20	**Thermador** SGSX365Z[S]	1,400		○	⊖	1	4		•
21	**Fisher & Paykel** GC912M	1,260		⊖	○	1	2	2	•
22	**Jenn-Air** JGC9536AD[W]	1,000		⊖	○	2	1	2	•
23	**GE** JGP637WEJ[WW]	650		○	⊖	1	2	2	
24	**KitchenAid** Pro Line KGCV465M[SS]	2,100		⊖	○	3		2	•

D *Discontinued, but similar model is available. Price is for similar model.* [1] *Includes two conventional smoothtop electric burners.*

In performance order. Gray **key numbers indicate Quick Picks.**

Key number	Brand & model	Price	Overall score (0–100; P F G VG E)	Test results: Baking	Test results: Broiling	Test results: Capacity	Features: Covered element	Features: Convection
	WALL OVENS							
1	**Thermador** C301B[W]	$2,200		⊖	⊜	⊖	•	•
2	**Jenn-Air** JJW8530DD[W]	1,250		⊖	⊖	⊖	•	
3	**Jenn-Air** JJW9530DD[W] [1]	1,650		⊖	⊖	⊖	•	•
4	**GE** Profile JT915WF[WW] [1]	1,500		⊖	⊖	○	•	•
5	**Maytag** MEW6530DD[W] [1]	1,100		⊖	⊖	○		•
6	**GE** JTP20WF[WW]	850		○	⊖	⊖		
7	**Kenmore** (Sears) 4907[2] [1]	1,500		⊖	⊖	◒	•	•
8	**KitchenAid** Superba KEBC107K[WH]	1,500		⊖	⊖	⊖	•	•

[1] *Has auto-conversion for convection temperatures.*

Guide to the Ratings

Overall score for cooktops is mainly cooktop performance at high and low heat; for wall ovens, score includes capacity, baking, and broiling, as well as self-cleaning (not shown; all tested models were good or better). **High heat,** for cooktops, denotes how quickly the highest-powered cooktop element or burner heated water to near-boiling. **Low heat** for cooktops reflects how well the lowest-powered cooktop element or burner melted and held chocolate without scorching and how well the most powerful element or burner, set on low, held tomato sauce below a boil. **Capacity,** for wall ovens, is our measurement of usable space. **Baking** reflects whether cakes and cookies baked on two racks were evenly browned. **Broiling** denotes even browning of a pan of burgers and high-heat searing ability. **For cooktops:** number of elements or burners cover the following categories: **High** is more than 2,000 watts for electric, 11,000 Btu/hr. for gas. **Medium:** more than 1,500 to 2,000 watts for electric, more than 6,500 to 11,000 Btu/hr. for gas. **Low:** 1,500 watts or less for electric, 6,500 Btu/hr. or less for gas. **Price** is approximate retail. Under **cooktop features, expandable elements** means that at least one element has two or more settings for electric models; **continuous grates** for gas cooktops denotes grates that allow you to slide heavy pots without lifting them. Note that scores have changed since our last report because of a change in our testing benchmarks, based on induction cooktops' faster heating. Under **wall oven features, covered element** denotes a smooth, easy-to-clean surface above the element; **convection** denotes fan(s) to circulate heated air for faster cooking.

Quick Picks

ELECTRIC COOKTOPS

Best for most; fine overall:

2 Kenmore, $450, **CR Best Buy**

7 Maytag, $450

Both offer stainless trim and cooked nearly as well as the top-scoring Jenn-Air (1) for less. A 3,000-watt burner and slightly faster heating on high give the Kenmore an edge.

GAS COOKTOPS

Best for most; fine overall:

18 Jenn-Air, $950

19 Maytag, $650, **CR Best Buy**

The Jenn-Air has stainless trim and fast heating. The lower-priced Maytag trades some heating speed for better simmering. Consider the GE (23) if you can live without continuous grates.

WALL OVENS

Best for most; fine overall:

4 GE, $1,500

5 Maytag, $1,100

6 GE, $850

All three are capable and come from reliable brands. Paying more for the GE (4) buys a covered bottom element and convection. The lower-priced Maytag lacks a covered element; the GE (6) also sacrifices convection, but costs less.

CORDLESS PHONES

All the phones with excellent scores for voice quality use analog transmission. But the best digital models had very good scores and offer better security and slightly longer range. Interference problems are more likely to occur with both digital and analog phones that use the 2.4-gigahertz frequency band, though some (including some Quick Picks) are designed to minimize them.

With similar phones and phone-answerers, the phone performance should be like that of the tested model. Phone-answerer versions of tested phones should perform like the answerer of the same brand.

The Ratings list products strictly by performance. Quick Picks considers factors such as features and value.

Excellent | Very good | Good | Fair | Poor

Within types, in performance order. Gray key numbers indicate Quick Picks.

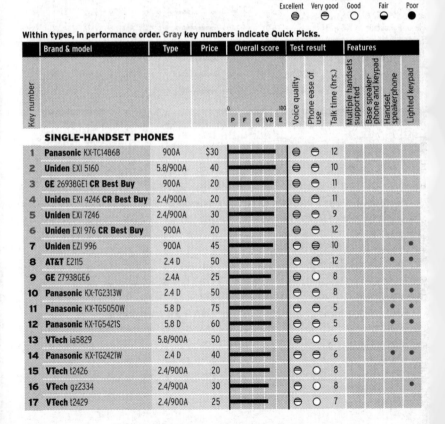

Key number	Brand & model	Type	Price	Overall score (0–100: P F G VG E)	Test result: Voice quality	Test result: Phone ease of use	Test result: Talk time (hrs.)	Features: Multiple handsets supported	Features: Base speaker-phone and keypad	Features: Handset speakerphone	Features: Lighted keypad
	SINGLE-HANDSET PHONES										
1	**Panasonic** KX-TC1486B	900A	$30		Excellent	Very good	12				
2	**Uniden** EXI 5160	5.8/900A	40		Excellent	Very good	10				
3	**GE** 26938GE1 **CR Best Buy**	900A	20		Excellent	Very good	11				
4	**Uniden** EXI 4246 **CR Best Buy**	2.4/900A	20		Excellent	Very good	11				
5	**Uniden** EXI 7246	2.4/900A	30		Excellent	Very good	9				
6	**Uniden** EXI 976 **CR Best Buy**	900A	20		Excellent	Very good	12				
7	**Uniden** EZI 996	900A	45		Very good	Excellent	10				●
8	**AT&T** E2115	2.4 D	50		Very good	Very good	12			●	●
9	**GE** 27938GE6	2.4A	25		Excellent	Good	8				
10	**Panasonic** KX-TG2313W	2.4 D	50		Very good	Very good	8			●	●
11	**Panasonic** KX-TG5050W	5.8 D	75		Very good	Very good	5			●	●
12	**Panasonic** KX-TG5421S	5.8 D	60		Very good	Very good	5			●	●
13	**VTech** ia5829	5.8/900A	50		Excellent	Good	6				
14	**Panasonic** KX-TG2421W	2.4 D	40		Very good	Very good	6			●	●
15	**VTech** t2426	2.4/900A	20		Very good	Good	8				
16	**VTech** gz2334	2.4/900A	30		Very good	Good	8				●
17	**VTech** t2429	2.4/900A	25		Very good	Good	7				

Key number	Brand & model	Type	Price	Overall score (0–100; P F G VG E)	Test results: Voice quality	Test results: Phone ease of use	Talk time (hrs.)	Features: Multiple handsets supported	Features: Base speaker-phone and keypad	Features: Handset speakerphone	Features: Lighted keypad
	MULTIPLE-HANDSET CAPABLE PHONES										
18	**Uniden** DXI 986-2 **CR Best Buy**	900A	$35		⊜	⊖	12	2 (1)			
19	**Uniden** DXI 7286-2 **CR Best Buy**	2.4/900A	50		⊜	⊖	9	2 (1)			
20	**VTech** ev 2625	2.4 D	60		⊖	⊖	11	2 (1)		•	•
21	**GE** 25840GE3	5.8/900A	60		⊜	⊖	8	2 (1)			
22	**Panasonic** KX-TG2700S	2.4 D	75		⊖	⊖	7	8	•	•	•
23	**Uniden** DCT 646-2	2.4 D	65		⊖	⊖	9	4 (1)		•	•
24	**Panasonic** KX-TG5423M	5.8 D	140		⊖	⊖	5	3 (2)		•	•
25	**Uniden** DMX 776	2.4 D	80		⊖	⊖	9	4		•	
26	**VTech** VT20-2431	2.4 D	140		⊖	⊖	10	8	•	•	•
27	**GE** 25831GE3	5.8/2.4 D	100		⊖	○	6	4 (1)		•	
28	**Motorola** MD751	5.8/2.4 D	80		○	⊖	7	8		•	•

Key numbers	Brand & model	Type	Price	Overall score (0–100; P F G VG E)	Test results: Voice quality	Phone ease of use	Talk time (hrs.)	Message quality	Answerer ease of use	Greeting quality	Recording time (mins.)	Features: Multiple handsets supported	Features: Mailboxes
	SINGLE-HANDSET PHONES WITH AN ANSWERER												
29	**Uniden** CXAI 5198	5.8/900A	$75		⊜	⊖	10	○	⊜	⊖	12		1
30	**AT&T** 1465	2.4/900A	40		⊖	⊖	8	⊖	⊜	⊖	20		1
31	**VTech** 2151	900A	25		⊖	○	8	⊖	⊖	⊖	20		1
32	**Uniden** EXAI 5580	5.8/900A	50		⊜	⊖	10	○	⊖	○	12		1
33	**GE** 27958GE1	2.4A	65		⊖	⊖	11	○	○	◒	16		1
34	**VTech** VT9152	900A	20		⊖	○	5	⊖	⊖	⊖	14		1
	MULTIPLE-HANDSET CAPABLE PHONES WITH AN ANSWERER												
35	**VTech** i5867	5.8/2.4D	110		⊖	⊖	10	⊖	⊖	⊖	31	8	3
36	**AT&T** E5965C	5.8/2.4D	135		⊖	⊖	7	⊖	⊖	⊖	30	8	1
37	**Uniden** ELBT 595	5.8D	250		⊖	⊖	7	⊖	⊖	⊖	14	10	1
38	**AT&T** E5925B	5.8/2.4D	130		⊖	⊖	6	⊖	⊜	⊖	20	2 (1)	1
39	**Radio Shack** TAD-3880	5.8D	100		⊖	⊖	7	⊖	⊖	⊜	14	10	1

Key numbers	Brand & model	Type	Price	Overall score (0–100; P F G VG E)	Voice quality	Phone ease of use	Talk time (hrs.)	Message quality	Answerer ease of use	Greeting quality	Recording time (mins.)	Multiple handsets supported	Mailboxes
	MULTIPLE-HANDSET CAPABLE PHONES WITH AN ANSWERER												
40	**AT&T** E5630	5.8/2.4D	$95		⊖	⊖	6	⊖	⊜	⊖	20	4	1
41	**Uniden DXAI** 5188-2	5.8/900A	100		⊜	⊜	10	○	⊖	○	12	2 (1)	1
42	**VTech** ia5859	5.8/900A	100		⊜	○	6	⊖	⊖	○	20	2 (1)	3
43	**Motorola** MD681	5.8/2.4D	115		⊖	⊖	7	⊖	○	⊖	30	6	3
44	**Panasonic** KX-TG5240M	5.8D	130		⊖	⊖	5	⊖	⊖	○	15	4	3
45	**Panasonic** KX-TG5452M	5.8D	125		⊖	⊖	5	⊖	⊖	○	19	2 (1)	1
46	**VTech** ip 5850	5.8/2.4D	120		⊖	⊖	6	⊖	⊖	⊖	20	2 (1)	3
47	**AT&T** 2256	2.4D	80		⊖	⊖	17	⊖	⊖	⊖	20	2 (1)	3
48	**AT&T** E2725B	2.4D	80		⊖	⊖	8	⊖	⊜	⊖	20	2 (1)	1
49	**Uniden** DXAI 4288-2	2.4/900A	50		⊜	⊖	11	○	⊖	○	12	2 (1)	1
50	**Panasonic** KX-TG2770S	2.4D	125		⊖	⊖	7	⊖	⊖	○	15	8	3
51	**Uniden** TRU 8885-2	5.8D	150		⊖	⊖	7	⊖	○	⊖	14	10 (1)	1
52	**Panasonic** KX-TG2344B	2.4D	90		⊖	⊖	8	⊖	⊖	○	14	2 (1)	1
53	**Panasonic** KX-TG2432B	2.4D	80		⊖	⊖	6	⊖	⊖	○	14	2 (1)	1
54	**Uniden** DXAI 5588-2	5.8/900A	75		⊜	⊖	10	○	⊖	○	12	2 (1)	1
55	**Uniden** DCT 6485-2	2.4D	110		⊖	⊖	9	○	○	○	12	4 (1)	1
56	**GE** 25833GE3	5.8/2.4D	80		⊖	○	6	○	⊖	○	24	4	3
57	**GE** 21028GE3	2.4D	80		⊖	○	8	○	⊖	○	24	4 (1)	3

See report, page 120. Based on tests in Consumer Reports in October 2005, with updated prices and availability.

Guide to the Ratings

For both phones and phone-answerers: Overall score mainly covers voice quality, ease of use, unobstructed range, electrical surge protection, and privacy. **Type** is as follows: 900=900 MHz; 2.4=2.4 GHz; 5.8=5.8 GHz; A=analog; D=digital spread spectrum. As noted, some phones use two frequency bands. **Voice quality** covers listening and talking, as judged by trained panelists. **Ease of use** includes handset comfort and weight, talk time, setup and control accessibility, clarity of labels, and the presence of useful features. **Talk time** is based on continuous-use tests with fully charged batteries. **Features** identify enhancements that provide versatility. **Multiple handsets supported** is the manufacturer stated maximum number of handsets that can be registered to a phone.

Guide to the Ratings *continued*

The number of additional handsets and charging cradles included are indicated in parentheses. **Price** is approximate retail. **All tested phones have** 1-yr. warranty, flash to answer call-waiting, handset earpiece volume control, handset ringer, at least 10 memory-dial slots, last-number redial, and low-battery indicator. **Most models have** caller ID and are wall-mountable. **For models with answering machines:** The overall score also considers message and greeting voice quality, answerer ease of use, and recording time. For answerer, **message** and **greeting** voice **quality** were judged by trained panelists. **Answerer ease of use** mainly includes readability of labels, accessibility of controls, setup, and ability to play new messages first and not erase unplayed ones. **Recording time** is based on tests using continuous speech. **Features** identifies enhancements to answerer versatility, such as the number of separate mailboxes. **All tested answerers have** call screening, day/time stamp, remote access, selectable number of rings, repeat, and message skip.

Quick Picks

PHONE-ONLY MODELS

Best values for a small home:

1 Panasonic, $30
2 Uniden, $40
3 GE $20, **CR Best Buy**
4 Uniden, $20, **CR Best Buy**
5 Uniden, $30
6 Uniden, $20, **CR Best Buy**

As the best single-handset phones tested, all performed with excellent voice quality, very good ease of use, and 9 to 12 hours of continuous talk time. One other, more specialized choice: the Uniden EZI 996 (7) has features for the hearing- or sight-impaired.

Best values for most homes:

18 Uniden, $35, **CR Best Buy**
19 Uniden, $50, **CR Best Buy**
20 VTech, $60
21 GE, $60

All come with two handsets. The Unidens and the GE had excellent voice quality. The VTech has handset-to-handset talk, is wireless-home-network friendly, and uses AAA rechargeable batteries.

Best value for a large home:

24 Panasonic $140

This 5.8-GHz model includes three handsets; with most other models, those could send the price above $175.

PHONES WITH ANSWERER

Best values for a small home:

29 Uniden, $75
30 AT&T, $40
31 VTech, $25
32 Uniden, $50

These single-handset models are light on phone features. The Uniden (29) has a corded phone that works during power outages. The Unidens had better phone voice quality, the AT&T and VTech the better answerer.

Best values for most homes:

36 AT&T, $135
47 AT&T, $80
48 AT&T, $80
49 Uniden, $50
54 Uniden, $75

The Unidens and the AT&Ts (47, 48) include an additional handset with a charging cradle. The AT&T (36) has a full array of features and the ability to function during power outages. The AT&Ts (36, 48) are home-network friendly. The Unidens had better phone voice quality, the AT&Ts the better answerer.

Best value for a large home:

55 Uniden, $110

This 2.4-GHz model lets you create a three-phone system for about $140—only a little more than the cost with the lower-rated GE (57), which has fewer features.

DIGITAL CAMERAS

Based on our judgments of uncropped 8x10-inch prints, all the cameras produced images that were very good or excellent. But if we had used only a small portion of the original image and enlarged it to 8x10, the higher-megapixel cameras would have produced better results than the others. Camera size and shape can vary considerably, even within a category.

The Ratings list models by overall performance. Quick Picks considers factors such as features and price.

Excellent ⊜ Very good ⊖ Good ○ Fair ◒ Poor ●

Within types, in performance order. Gray key numbers indicate Quick Picks.

Key number	Brand & model	Price	Overall score (0–100: P F G VG E)	Print quality	Megapixels	Weight (oz.)	Flash range (ft.)	Battery life (shots)	Next-shot delay (sec.)	Optical zoom	Manual controls	Charger	AA batteries	Wide angle	Image stabilizer
	COMPACT CAMERAS *For people who want the basics at a low price.*														
1	**Canon** PowerShot A510 **CR Best Buy**	$180		⊜	3	8	11	300	2	4x	•		•		
2	**Kodak** EasyShare Z700	250		⊜	4	10	12	200	2	5x	•	•	•		
3	**Olympus** C-5500 Sport Zoom	250		⊜	5	12	12	340	5	5x	•		•		•
4	**Olympus** Stylus 500 Digital	270		⊜	5	7	14	140	2	3x		•			
5	**Olympus** Stylus 410 Digital	210		⊜	4	7	12	360	2	3x		•			
6	**Kodak** EasyShare DX7630	290		⊜	6	10	14	400	3	3x	•	•			
7	**Kodak** EasyShare CX7530	210		⊜	5	9	12	240	2	3x			•		
8	**Kodak** EasyShare CX7430 **CR Best Buy**	180		⊜	4	8	12	520	2	3x			•		
9	**Pentax** Optio 750Z	430		⊜	7	9	17	170	4	5x	•	•			
10	**HP** PhotoSmart R717	300		⊜	6	7	16	80	2	3x	•	•			
11	**Olympus** C-60 Zoom	280		⊜	6	8	11	400	2	3x	•	•			
12	**Kodak** EasyShare LS753	310		⊜	5	6	10	400	1	2.8x		•			
13	**Kodak** EasyShare LS743	240		⊜	4	6	10	400	2	2.8x		•			
14	**Canon** PowerShot A95	270		⊜	5	12	14	650	2	3x	•		•		
15	**Olympus** D-580 Zoom **CR Best Buy**	160		⊜	4	8	11	600	2	3x			•		
16	**HP** PhotoSmart R707	250		⊜	5	7	9	320	3	3x	•	•			
17	**Panasonic** Lumix DMC-LC70	260		⊖	4	8	16	320	2	3x			•		
18	**Canon** PowerShot S500	360		⊜	5	8	11	320	3	3x		•			
19	**Olympus** Camedia C-5000 Zoom	220		⊖	5	10	12	40	3	3x	•	•			

Excellent ⊜ Very good ⊖ Good ○ Fair ◒ Poor ●

Within types, in performance order. Gray key numbers indicate Quick Picks.

Key number	Brand & model	Price	Overall score (0–100; P F G VG E)	Print quality	Megapixels	Weight (oz.)	Flash range (ft.)	Battery life (shots)	Next-shot delay (sec.)	Optical zoom	Manual controls	Charger	AA batteries	Wide angle	Image stabilizer
	COMPACT CAMERAS *continued*														
20	**Olympus** D-425	$140		Excellent	4	6	10	260	2	none			•		
21	**HP** PhotoSmart M307	150		Excellent	3	6	9	85	4	3x			•		
22	**Samsung** Digimax A5	230		Excellent	5	8	10	100	6	3x	•		•		
23	**Olympus** Stylus 300 Digital	200		Very good	3	7	12	170	2	3x		•			
24	**Sony** Cyber-shot DSC-W1	300		Very good	5	9	11	240	4	3x	•	•	•		
25	**Fujifilm** FinePix S3100	220		Very good	4	14	11	220	3	6x	•		•		
26	**Olympus** D-540 Zoom	150		Very good	3	7	11	460	5	3x			•		
27	**Sony** Cyber-shot DSC-P72	200		Very good	3	9	12	260	3	3x		•	•		
28	**Fujifilm** FinePix A340	190		Very good	4	7	11	340	4	3x			•		
29	**Casio** Elixim EX-P600	430		Very good	6	9	10	260	4	4x	•	•			
30	**Samsung** V-700	380		Very good	7	7	10	180	5	3x	•	•			
31	**Olympus** D-595	200		Very good	5	7	12	180	4	3x	•		•		
32	**Sony** CD Mavica MVC-CD500	530		Very good	5	21	16	55	2	3x	•	•			
33	**Sony** CD Mavica MVC-CD350	350		Very good	3	18	8	120	2	3x		•			
34	**Kodak** EasyShare CX7300	90		Very good	3	7	8	240	2	none			•		
35	**Bell + Howell** 10.0 Digital Camera	300		Very good	5	7	10	190	14	3x	•		•		
	SUBCOMPACT CAMERAS *For people who need a camera that fits in a purse or pocket.*														
36	**Canon** PowerShot SD500 Digital ELPH	450		Excellent	7	7	16	160	2	3x		•			
37	**Canon** PowerShot SD300	310		Excellent	4	5	11	140	1	3x		•			
38	**Pentax** Optio SV	320		Excellent	5	6	14	100	9	5x	•	•			
39	**Sony** Cyber-shot DSC-L1	240		Excellent	4	5	7	260	2	3x		•			
40	**Sony** Cyber-shot DSC-M1	460		Excellent	5	8	6	160	4	3x		•			
41	**Canon** PowerShot S410	320		Excellent	4	8	11	380	2	3x		•			
42	**Sony** Cyber-shot DSC-P100	310		Excellent	5	7	11	460	3	3x	•	•			
43	**Casio** Exilim EX-Z55	310		Excellent	5	6	9	400	2	3x		•			
44	**Sony** Cyber-shot DSC-P150	340		Excellent	7	6	11	420	2	3x	•	•			
45	**Sony** Cyber-shot DSC-T33	330		Excellent	5	5	5	180	1	3x		•			
46	**Fujifilm** FinePix F450	300		Excellent	5	6	12	150	4	3.4x		•			
47	**Sony** Cyber-shot DSC-P73	210		Excellent	4	8	11	560	4	3x	•	•	•		

Key number	Brand & model	Price	Overall score (0–100: P F G VG E)	Test results: Print quality	Megapixels	Weight (oz.)	Flash range (ft.)	Battery life (shots)	Next-shot delay (sec.)	Optical zoom	Features: Manual controls	Charger	AA batteries	Wide angle	Image stabilizer
	SUBCOMPACT CAMERAS *For people who need a camera that fits in a purse or pocket.*														
48	**Pentax** Optio S4i	$280		⊖	4	4	11	150	3	3x		●			
49	**Sony** Cyber-shot DSC-T1	330		⊜	5	6	5	120	4	3x		●			
50	**Nikon** Coolpix 7900	350		⊖	7	6	15	220	2	3x		●			
51	**Fujifilm** FinePix Z1	340		⊖	5	5	10	170	2	3x		●			
52	**Nikon** Coolpix 5200	340		⊖	5	6	15	120	3	3x		●			
53	**Konica Minolta** DiMAGE X50	280		⊖	5	5	6	240	3	2.8x		●			
54	**Canon** PowerShot SD10	300		⊜	4	4	7	110	2	none		●			
55	**Olympus** Stylus Verve	200		⊖	4	5	9	55	2	2x		●			
56	**Nikon** Coolpix S1	340		⊖	5	5	8	200	2	3x		●			
57	**Casio** Exilim EX-S100	230		⊖	3	5	8	110	3	2.8x		●			
58	**Pentax** Optio WP	300		⊖	5	5	8	180	4	3x		●			
59	**Panasonic** Lumix DMC-FX7	340		⊖	5	5	13	45	7	3x		●			●
	ADVANCED COMPACT CAMERAS *For people who need more than the basics.*														
60	**Nikon** Coolpix 8400	750		⊜	8	17	20	180	5	3.5x	●	●		●	
61	**Canon** PowerShot G6	540		⊜	7	17	16	850	2	4x	●	●			
62	**Fujifilm** FinePix E550	300		⊜	6	9	15	300	1	4x	●	●	●		
63	**Olympus** C-7070 Wide Zoom	390		⊜	7	18	12	750	2	4x	●	●		●	●
64	**Fujifilm** FinePix S7000	480		⊜	6	21	28	60	2	6x	●		●		
65	**Olympus** C-8080 Wide Zoom	570		⊜	8	27	19	120	3	5x	●	●		●	
66	**Canon** PowerShot Pro1	640		⊜	8	23	16	110	3	7x	●	●		●	
67	**Canon** PowerShot S60	360		⊜	5	10	14	260	2	3.6x	●	●		●	
68	**Sony** Cyber-shot DSC-V3	530		⊜	7	14	10	300	1	4x	●	●			
69	**Olympus** C-5060 Wide Zoom	450		⊜	5	18	12	560	2	4x	●			●	
70	**Canon** PowerShot S70	440		⊜	7	10	14	140	2	3.6x	●	●		●	
71	**Sony** Cyber-shot DSC-F828	800		⊜	8	33	15	110	4	7x	●	●		●	
	SUPER-ZOOM CAMERAS *For people who need an extremely versatile zoom lens.*														
72	**Panasonic** Lumix DMC-FZ20S	450		⊜	5	22	23	280	1	12x	●	●			●
73	**Panasonic** Lumix DMC-FZ5	420		⊜	5	14	15	300	1	12x	●	●			●
74	**Kodak** EasyShare DX6490	340		⊜	4	14	16	60	2	10x	●	●			
75	**Nikon** Coolpix 8700	650		⊜	8	19	13	140	3	8x	●	●			

Excellent | Very good | Good | Fair | Poor

Within types, in performance order. Gray **key numbers indicate Quick Picks.**

Key number	Brand & model	Price	Overall score (0–100; P F G VG E)	Print quality	Megapixels	Weight (oz.)	Flash range (ft.)	Battery life (shots)	Next-shot delay (sec.)	Optical zoom	Manual controls	Charger	AA batteries	Wide angle	Image stabilizer
	SUPER-ZOOM CAMERAS *continued*														
76	**Olympus** C-765 Ultra Zoom	$270		Excellent	4	11	15	130	2	10x	•	•			
77	**Canon** PowerShot S1IS	270		Excellent	3	17	14	180	3	10x	•		•		•
78	**Konica Minolta** DiMAGE Z5	400		Very good	5	16	7	420	3	12x	•		•		•
79	**Konica Minolta** DiMAGE Z2	300		Very good	4	14	10	280	3	10x	•		•		

See report, page 26. Based on tests in Consumer Reports in November 2005.

Guide to the Ratings

Overall score is based mainly on print quality, weight, and the presence of useful features. **Print quality** is based on expert judgments using 8x10-inch prints made with each camera's best resolution and compression settings and printed on a high-rated inkjet printer. **Megapixels** is the resolution in millions of pixels (picture elements). **Weight,** in ounces, includes battery and memory card. **Flash range,** in feet, is the maximum claimed range for a well-lighted subject. **Battery life** is the number of high-resolution photos taken with the batteries supplied, if the camera uses a proprietary size, or with rechargeable nickel-metal hydrides for those using AAs; half the shots used flash, and the zoom lens was racked in and out. **Next-shot delay** is the time, in seconds, the camera needs to ready itself for the next photo. **Optical zoom** refers to the range of focal lengths. **Manual controls** refers to settings that let you adjust shutter speed and lens opening. **Charger** is for the batteries. **AA batteries** denotes cameras that use that size, which are much more widely available than proprietary batteries. **Wide angle** shows which have a lens that can zoom as wide as a 28 mm lens. **Image stabilizer** shows which have this steadying feature. **Price** is approximate retail.

Quick Picks

Best values for most people; all are CR Best Buys:

1 Canon, $180
8 Kodak, $180
15 Olympus, $160

All have excellent print quality and are very low priced for 3- or 4-megapixel compacts. The Canon has manual controls and a 4x zoom but is the bulkiest. The Kodak and Olympus have long battery life, but they both lack manual controls.

For additional flexibility:

2 Kodak, $250
3 Olympus, $250
14 Canon, $270

All have excellent print quality, manual controls, and 4- or 5-megapixel resolution. The Kodak and Olympus both have a 5x zoom lens. The latter has an image stabilizer but also a long next-shot delay. The Canon has very long battery life.

For a camera that fits in a purse:

37 Canon, $310
39 Sony, $240
50 Nikon, $350

All of these are small and light, with excellent or very good print quality and good battery life, but they lack manual controls. The Canon has a short next-shot delay. The Sony is low-priced for a subcompact, but its flash range is just 7 feet. The Nikon is relatively high priced but has 7-megapixel resolution.

For an advanced compact camera:

62 Fujifilm, $300
63 Olympus, $390
67 Canon, $360

All have excellent print quality and manual controls. The low-priced Fujifilm is relatively light, with a short next-shot delay. The bulky Olympus has 7-megapixel resolution, very long battery life, a very wide-angle lens, and image stabilizer. The Canon is low-priced, with a very wide-angle lens.

For a long zoom range, consider:

73 Panasonic, $420
76 Olympus, $270
77 Canon, $270

The Panasonic has a 12x zoom and image stabilizer, excellent battery life, and a short next-shot delay. The Olympus is low-priced and relatively light, with a 10x zoom. But its battery life was the among the lowest for super-zoom models. The 3-megapixel Canon is low-priced and has a 10x zoom and stabilizer, but also a long next-shot delay. It records video up to the memory card's limit, as can the high-priced Sony (40), not a Quick Pick.

Brand Repair History

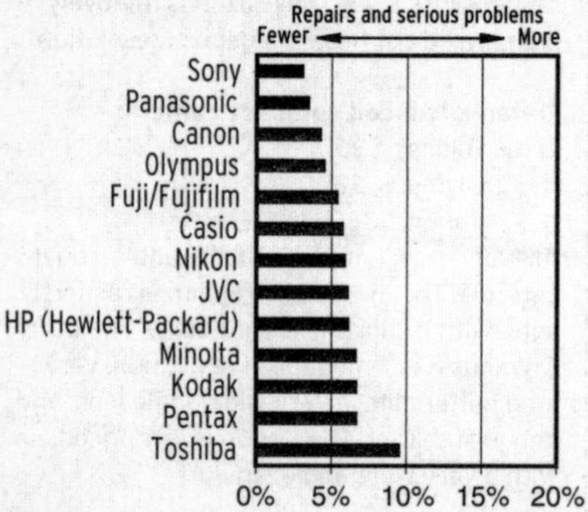

This graph shows the percentage of digital cameras that have been repaired or developed a serious problems that wasn't repaired. Models within a brand may vary, and design and manufacturing changes may affect repair history. Our results for Minolta may not apply to Konica Minolta digital cameras. Megapixel count does not affect reliability, we have found. You can improve your chances of getting a trouble-free camera by choosing a brand that has been reliable.

Based on 167,335 reader responses to our 2004 Annual Questionnaire about digital cameras bought new between 2001 and 2004. Data have been standardized to eliminate differences linked to age and usage. Differences of less than 4 points aren't meaningful.

DISHWASHERS

There are plenty of very capable dishwashers on the market, as our tests bear out. We put 10 full place settings of extremely soiled dishes, glasses, and flatware into the dishwasher without prerinsing, then let them sit overnight before washing them. Most of the models we tested did an excellent job despite these challenging conditions.

You can get this high level of performance on some models priced as low as $350, but figure on paying closer to $500 to get excellent washing plus quiet operation and convenience features such as an adjustable top rack and tines that fold down to make room for large items.

You'll typically pay about $600 or more for a dishwasher with a stainless-steel tub. This type of tub won't discolor over time as a plastic tub might, but plastic tubs are perfectly serviceable and likely to last for the life of your dishwasher. Many of the dishwashers we tested are available with a stainless exterior finish for about $100 more than a white model. Hidden controls, which make for a clutter-free exterior, are usually offered on dishwashers that cost $800 and up.

If you live in an area where water and energy costs are high, factor those ongoing costs into your choice. A more expensive model that is frugal with both may wind up costing you less than a cheaper model over the long haul.

Excellent · Very good · Good · Fair · Poor

In performance order. Gray key numbers indicate Quick Picks.

Key number	Brand & model	Price	Overall score (0–100; P F G VG E)	Test results: Washing	Energy use	Noise	Loading flexibility	Ease of use	Cycle time (hr:min)	Features: Sensor	Self-cleaning filter	Stainless-steel tub	Hidden controls	Ample flatware slots	Adjustable upper rack	Stainless/SS-look option
1	**Bosch** SHU66C0[2]	$875		Excellent	Very good	Excellent	Very good	Very good	1:45	•		•		•	•	•
2	**Bosch** SHU43C0[2]	570		Excellent	Very good	Excellent	Very good	Good	1:45	•		•		•	•	•
3	**Kenmore (Sears)** 1603[2] **CR Best Buy**	550		Excellent	Very good	Excellent	Very good	Excellent	1:55	•	•			•	•	•
4	**Kenmore (Sears)** Elite 1626	850		Excellent	Very good	Excellent	Very good	Excellent	2:00	•	•	•			•	•
5	**Bosch** Deluxe SHX46L0[2]	790		Excellent	Very good	Very good	Very good	Very good	2:00	•		•	•	•	•	•
6	**Siemens** SL84A30[5]	900		Excellent	Very good	Excellent	Very good	Good	1:50	•		•	•	•	•	•
7	**Kenmore (Sears)** Elite 1630[3]	1,020		Excellent	Very good	Very good	Very good	Very good	1:45	•		•		•	•	•
8	**Miele** G894SCi	1,450		Excellent	Very good	Very good	Very good	Very good	2:15			•		•	•	•
9	**Whirlpool Gold** GU2400XTP[Q] **CR Best Buy**	500		Excellent	Very good	Very good	Very good	Excellent	2:05	•	•			•	•	•

Excellent (E) · Very good (VG) · Good (G) · Fair (F) · Poor (P)

In performance order. Gray key numbers indicate Quick Picks.

Key number	Brand & model	Price	Overall score (0–100; P F G VG E)	Washing	Energy use	Noise	Loading flexibility	Ease of use	Cycle time (hr:min)	Sensor	Self-cleaning filter	Stainless-steel tub	Hidden controls	Ample flatware slots	Adjustable upper rack	Stainless/SS-look option
10	**Maytag** MDB7600AW[W]	485		E	G	VG	E	E	2:00	●	●			●	●	●
11	**Maytag** MDB8600AW[W]	575		E	G	VG	VG	E	1:50	●	●			●		●
12	**Whirlpool** DU1100XTP[Q] **CR Best Buy**	410		E	VG	VG	G	VG	1:55	●	●			●		●
13	**Frigidaire Gallery** GLD3450RD[S]	600		E	VG	G	VG	E	1:50	●	●		●	●	●	
14	**Whirlpool** DU1050XTP[Q]	415		E	VG	VG	F	VG	2:05		●					●
15	**Maytag** MDB5600AW[W]	395		E	G	VG	VG	E	2:15	●	●					●
16	**Fisher & Paykel** DD603[W]	1,260		E	VG	VG	VG	VG	1:55				●	●		●
17	**Frigidaire** Gallery GLD2450RD[S]	375		E	VG	G	VG	E	1:40	●	●			●	●	
18	**GE** GSD6900J[WW]	475		E	G	G	E	E	2:00	●	●			●	●	●
19	**Maytag** MDB8750AW[W]	560		E	F	G	VG	E	2:25	●	●	●		●		●
20	**Samsung** DB5710DT	650		E	F	G	VG	E	2:25	●	●	●		●		●
21	**Whirlpool** DU945PWP[Q]	320		E	G	F	F	VG	1:55		●				●	●
22	**Jenn-Air** JDB2150AWP	970		E	F	G	VG	E	2:30	●	●	●		●		●
23	**Frigidaire** GLD2250RD[S]	400		VG	VG	G	G	E	1:30		●			●		
24	**Frigidaire** FDB2310L[C]	365		G	VG	G	G	E	1:40		●			●		●
25	**Hotpoint** HDA3700G[WW]	270		VG	VG	F	F	VG	1:35		●					
26	**Whirlpool** DU850SWP[Q]	280		G	VG	G	F	G	1:25		●					●
27	**Haier** ESD200	400		F	E	G	G	G	1:40			●			●	
28	**Kenmore (Sears)** 1516[2]	285		F	E	G	G	VG	1:20		●			●		●
29	**Frigidaire** FDB710L[C]	240		F	VG	G	G	VG	1:25		●					

See report, page 56. Based on tests posted to ConsumerReports.org in July 2005, with updated prices and availability.

Guide to the Ratings

Overall score is based mainly on washing, but also factors in noise, energy and water use, loading, and more. **Washing** was tested using our standard, very dirty, full load. Because we switched to an enzyme-based detergent for our tests, Ratings for models that appear here and in archived reports may differ. **Energy use** is for a normal cycle. The largest portion is needed for heating water, both at the water heater and in the machine. **Noise** was judged during fill, wash, and drain, mainly by a listening panel. **Loading flexibility** reflects the ability to hold extra place settings and oversized items such as platters up to 13½ in. long and Pilsner-type glasses up to 10 in. high. **Ease of use** considers convenience of controls and other factors (lower-scoring models often lack a self-cleaning filter). **Cycle time** (hr:min) is based on a normal cycle including heated dry, where that feature is available. Under **brand and model**, bracketed letters or numbers are color codes. **Price** is approximate retail.

Quick Picks

Best for most; top performance and flexibility at a reasonable price:

3 Kenmore (Sears), $550, **CR Best Buy**
9 Whirlpool, $500, **CR Best Buy**
10 Maytag, $485
12 Whirlpool, $410, **CR Best Buy**
15 Maytag, $395

All these models did an excellent job cleaning our very dirty dishes and are from reliable brands. Noise isn't an issue with any of them—the Kenmore was the quietest, but the other four did very well in our noise test. The Maytag (10) was the most flexible for loading oversized and odd-shaped items. It and the Maytag (15) used a bit more energy than the other three.

If you're willing to pay more for a stainless tub and extra cleaning oomph:

4 Kenmore (Sears), $850

In addition to a stainless tub, the Kenmore has a special TurboZone in the bottom rack for heavily soiled items. It was effective at removing baked-on food in our tests. While the Bosch SHU43C0[2] (2) includes a stainless tub for less, it has been more repair-prone than Kenmore in our survey.

Recommendations

1 BOSCH SHU66C0[2] High-priced but excellent at washing dishes and very quiet, with a stainless-steel tub. It has a manual-clean filter. Similar models: SHV66A0, SHY66C0, SHI66A0.

2 BOSCH SHU43C0[2] Excellent at washing dishes and very quiet. Similar model: SHU53A0.

3 KENMORE (SEARS) 1603[2] **A CR Best Buy** Excellent at washing dishes and very quiet. Uses less water than most in the normal cycle. Similar models: 1601, 1602, 1701, 1702, 1703.

4 KENMORE (SEARS) Elite 1626 The high price gets you excellent washing performance with a special zone for tough soil, plus very quiet operation, and a stainless steel tub. Uses less water than most in the normal cycle. Similar models: 1605, 1627, 1628, 1629, 1726, 1728.

5 BOSCH Deluxe SHX46L0[2] Excellent at washing dishes and very quiet, this pricey model has hidden controls. It has a manual-clean filter.

Recommendations

6 SIEMENS SL84A30[5] Excellent at washing dishes and very quiet, this pricey model has hidden controls and a stainless-steel tub. It has a manual-clean filter. Discontinued, but similar model SHX46A0 may be available.

7 KENMORE (SEARS) Elite 1630[3] Excellent at washing dishes, this quiet dishwasher (made by Bosch) has a stainless-steel tub, but it's pricey. It has a manual-clean filter. Similar model: 1730.

8 MIELE G894SCi Quiet and excellent at washing dishes, but among the highest-priced. Has a stainless-steel tub. Uses less water than most in the normal cycle. Long cycle time. Similar model: G694Sci.

9 WHIRLPOOL Gold GU2400XTP[Q] **A CR Best Buy** Quiet and excellent at washing dishes. Similar models: GU2500XTP, GU2548XTP, GU2600XTP.

10 MAYTAG MDB7600AW[W] Quiet and excellent at washing dishes, a top choice for many consumers. Uses more water than most in the normal cycle. Similar models: MDBF750AW, MDBH970AW, MDBTT79AW.

11 MAYTAG MDB8600AW[W] Quiet and excellent at washing dishes. Has third rack at bottom, which allows loading of items such as platters. Center rack is adjustable. Similar model: MDB9600AW.

12 WHIRLPOOL DU1100XTP[Q] **A CR Best Buy** Quiet and excellent at washing dishes, a top choice for consumers seeking competence and value. Uses less water than most in the normal cycle. Similar models: DU1145XTP, DU1148XTP, DUL240XTP.

13 FRIGIDAIRE Gallery GLD3450RD[S] Excellent at washing dishes but a little noisy. Has partially hidden controls. Uses less water than most in the normal cycle. Similar model: GLD2860RD.

14 WHIRLPOOL DU1050XTP[Q] A basic, low-priced model that's quiet and excellent at washing dishes. A real value for typical use, but not the best choice if you want maximum loading flexibility. Uses less water than most in the normal cycle.

15 MAYTAG MDB5600AW[W] Excellent at washing dishes. Long cycle time. Uses less water than most in the normal cycle. Discontinued, but similar models MDB6600AW, MDBH950AW, MDBTT59AW may be available.

16 FISHER & PAYKEL DD603[W] Excellent at washing dishes but pricey; has two drawers that can be used separately. It has partially hidden controls and a manual-clean filter. No heated-dry option. Although we lack sufficient historical data to include Fisher & Paykel in our reliability charts, its repair rate over the past few years has been significantly higher than that of other brands.

17 FRIGIDAIRE Gallery GLD2450RD[S] Excellent at washing dishes but a little noisy. Cycle time is shorter than most.

18 GE GSD6900J[WW] Excellent at washing dishes but a little noisy. Uses more water than most in the normal cycle.

19 MAYTAG MDB8750AW[W] Excellent at washing dishes, with a stainless-steel tub, but a little noisy. Uses more energy and water than most in the normal cycle. Cycle time is longer than most.

20 SAMSUNG DB5710DT Excellent at washing dishes, with a stainless-steel tub and exterior finish, but a little noisy. Uses more energy and water than most in the normal cycle. Cycle time is longer than most.

Recommendations

21 WHIRLPOOL DU945PWP[Q] Excellent at washing dishes and low-priced, but noisy and not the best choice if you want maximum loading flexibility. Uses more water than most in the normal cycle. Similar models: DU930PWP, DU948PWP, DUL140PP.

22 JENN-AIR JDB2150AWP This pricey pro-style model has a stainless-steel finish and tub and was excellent at washing dishes, but it's a little noisy. Uses more energy and water than most in the normal cycle. Cycle time is longer than most.

23 FRIGIDAIRE GLD2250RD[S] Very good at washing dishes but a little noisy. Uses less water than most in the normal cycle. Cycle time is shorter than most. Similar model: FDBB1940DB.

24 FRIGIDAIRE FDB2310L[C] Just okay at washing dishes and a little noisy. You can get better performance for the same price or a little more.

25 HOTPOINT HDA3700G[WW] This basic, low-priced machine was very good at washing dishes but noisy. Cycle time is shorter than most.

26 WHIRLPOOL DU850SWP[Q] Low-priced but just okay at washing dishes and a little noisy. You can get better performance for not much more money.

27 HAIER ESD200 Low-priced for a model with a stainless-steel tub but only fair at washing dishes and a little noisy. You can get better performance for the same price or less.

28 KENMORE (SEARS) 1516[2] A basic, low-priced model that's only fair at washing dishes and a little noisy. You can get better performance for not much more money.

29 FRIGIDAIRE FDB710L[C] A basic, low-priced model that's only fair at washing dishes and a little noisy. You can get better performance for not much more money. Similar model: FDB750R.

Brand Repair History

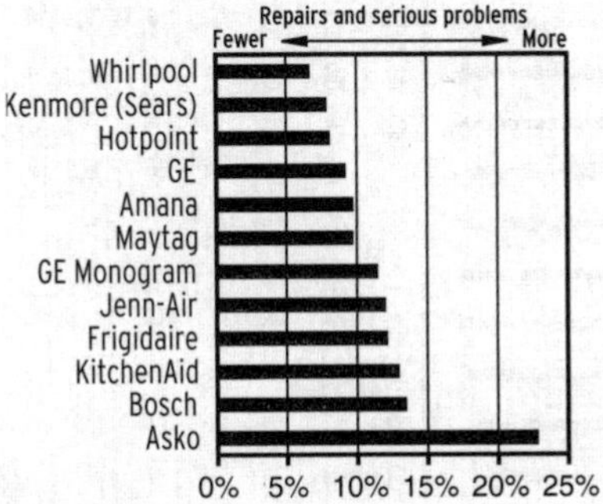

Choosing a brand with a good repair history can improve your odds of getting a reliable model. The graph shows the percentage of dishwashers bought new between 1999 and 2004 that were repaired or had a serious problem. Asko has been the most repair-prone of these 12 brands. While we lack enough historical data to include Fisher & Paykel, its repair rate over the past few years has been significantly higher than for other brands.

Data are based on more than 122,000 responses to our 2004 Annual Questionnaire and are standardized to eliminate differences linked to age and usage. Differences of less than 3 points aren't meaningful.

DRYERS

Dryers judged excellent for drying were noticeably better than lower-rated units at leaving a load damp for ironing and for drying delicates at low heat. Those that earned very good scores for drying should also satisfy most consumers. Because there are so many models at all prices that can do an excellent or very good job drying your laundry, there's no reason to settle for lower performance.

Capacity isn't much of an issue under normal circumstances. All the tested dryers can hold a typical wash load. One with excellent capacity would be best for items such as comforters. Those rated excellent or very good for noise are quiet; those scoring lower are noisier and could be disruptive if the laundry room is near a living area.

Many models in the Ratings have moisture sensors, which are better than thermostats at determining when laundry is dry, and extended tumble (also called cooldown), useful for reducing wrinkles.

Paying more for a dryer may get you a more stylish design, additional cycle options (which we don't consider necessary), or fancier controls, such as touchscreens with onscreen menus. It won't necessarily get you better performance, though.

Excellent / Very good / Good / Fair / Poor

Within types, in performance order. Gray key numbers indicate Quick Picks.

Key number	Brand & model	Price	Overall score (0–100: P F G VG E)	Test results: Drying performance	Test results: Capacity	Test results: Noise	Features: Stainless-steel drum	Features: Porcelain top	Features: Removable drying rack	Features: Custom programs
1	**Kenmore (Sears)** Elite 6506[2]	$700		Excellent	Excellent	Excellent		•	•	•
2	**GE** Profile DPSB620EC[WW]	580		Excellent	Excellent	Excellent	•		•	•
3	**Kenmore (Sears)** Elite 6697[2]	550		Excellent	Excellent	Excellent		•	•	
4	**Kenmore (Sears)** Elite HE4 8586[2]	880		Excellent	Excellent	Excellent		•	•	•
5	**Maytag** Neptune MCE8000AY[W]	1,000		Excellent	Excellent	Very good			•	
6	**Kenmore (Sears)** Elite 6692[2]	430		Very good	Excellent	Excellent			•	
7	**Whirlpool** Duet GEW9250P[W]	800		Excellent	Excellent	Very good		•	•	•
8	**LG** DL-E5932[W]	800		Very good	Excellent	Very good	•	•	•	•
9	**Whirlpool** LEQ8000J[Q] **CR Best Buy**	380		Very good	Excellent	Very good				
10	**Whirlpool** Gold GEW9868K[Q]	650		Very good	Excellent	Excellent		•	•	
11	**Whirlpool** Gold GEW9878J[Q]	530		Very good	Excellent	Very good				

Key number	Brand & model	Price	Overall score (0–100: P F G VG E)	Test results: Drying performance	Test results: Capacity	Test results: Noise	Features: Stainless-steel drum	Features: Porcelain top	Features: Removable drying rack	Features: Custom programs
12	**Bosch** Nexxt premium WTMC6300US	$800		VG	VG	VG	•	•	•	•
13	**GE** Profile Harmony DPGT750EC[WW]	800		VG	E	E	•		•	•
14	**Bosch** Nexxt WTMC3300US	700		VG	VG	VG	•	•	•	
15	**KitchenAid** Superba Ensemble KEHS01PMT	1,200		VG	E	E		•		
16	**Frigidaire** Gallery GLER642A[S] **CR Best Buy**	310		VG	VG	VG			•	
17	**Kenmore (Sears)** 6683[2]	380		VG	E	G			•	
18	**Maytag** Atlantis MDE8400AY[W]	570		VG	E	E		•	•	
19	**Frigidaire** Gallery GLEQ642A[S]	380		VG	VG	VG			•	
20	**LG** DL-E2514[W]	600		VG	E	VG			•	
21	**GE** Profile DPXH46EA[WW]	450		VG	VG	G			•	
22	**GE** DWSR405EB[WW]	400		G	E	VG			•	
23	**Fisher & Paykel** Smartload DEGX1	780		VG	VG	G	•			•
24	**Estate by Whirlpool** TEDS840J[Q]	370		G	E	G				
25	**Hotpoint** NWSR483EB[WW]	330		G	E	VG				
26	**Miele** Touchtronic T1303	1,080		VG	P	E				
27	**Roper** RES7745P[Q]	280		VG	VG	F				
28	**Admiral** LNC7764A[W]	325		G	E	G				
29	**Roper** REX4634K[Q]	200		G	VG	G				

See report, page 59. Based on tests posted to ConsumerReports.org in June 2005, with updated prices and availability.

Guide to the Ratings

Overall score is based primarily on drying performance, drum volume and noise. The **drying performance** score combines performance on four types of laundry loads of different sizes and fabric mixes: A 12-lb. load, predominantly cotton, representing a family's large weekly load; an 8-lb. load of all-cotton items; an 8-lb. load of cotton/polyester blend clothing; and a 3-lb. load of synthetic delicates, women's pajamas, nightgowns, bras and underwear. Among the models we tested, the **capacity** of the drum volume varied from about 5 to 7.5 cu. ft. **Noise** score was determined by a panel of judges who listened while machines dried an 8-pound load, measuring both sound quality and volume. Under **brand and model**, bracketed letters or numbers are color codes. **Price** is approximate retail price.

Quick Picks

For excellent drying, large capacity, and very quiet operation at a good price:

2 GE, $580

3 Kenmore (Sears), $550

Both were excellent at drying, very quiet, and large enough to handle oversized items such as comforters. The GE Profile has a slightly larger door opening than the Kenmore (Sears), which improves access.

Very good and great values; both are CR Best Buys:

9 Whirlpool, $380

16 Frigidaire, $310

The Whirlpool is large enough for oversized items such as comforters. The Frigidaire Gallery has slightly less capacity but is big enough for most wash loads. The two did especially well drying our largest test load, but temperatures in the delicate cycle in the Whirlpool were a bit warmer than we consider ideal.

A bit more expensive than our Best Buys, but still a well-priced, solid performer:

6 Kenmore (Sears), $430

Very good at drying and quiet, this model is large enough for oversized items. It did especially well drying our largest test load, but the delicate cycle is a bit warmer than we consider ideal.

An excellent but high-priced dryer that has a separate cabinet for air-drying garments:

5 Maytag, $1,000

The standard dryer on the Maytag Neptune is excellent and quiet, with a drum large enough to fit items such as comforters. What's unique about this model is that above the dryer it has a separate armoire-like cabinet for air-drying wet clothes and refreshing dry garments. The cabinet worked well in our tests. The design makes this model big—twice as tall as a standard dryer and a few inches wider. Reliability ratings for Maytag dryers may not apply to this model as it uses a new technology for which we have insufficient reliability data.

Recommendations

1 KENMORE (SEARS) Elite 6506[2] Spacious and very quiet, this model excelled in our drying tests. The low temperature of its delicate cycle treats lingerie and knits with TLC. The drum can handle bulky items such as comforters. A signal alerts you when clothes are damp-dry so you can remove them for ironing. Similar model: 6508. Gas equivalents: 7506, 7508.

2 GE Profile DPSB620EC[WW] Spacious and very quiet, this model excelled in our drying tests. The low temperature of its delicate cycle treats lingerie and knits with TLC. The drum can handle bulky items such as comforters, and the large door opening makes it easy to load and unload. A signal alerts you when clothes are damp-dry so you can remove them for ironing. Gas equivalent: DPSB620GC.

3 KENMORE (SEARS) Elite 6697[2] Spacious and very quiet, this model excelled in our drying tests. The drum is large enough to handle bulky items such as comforters. Similar models: 6698, 6699. Gas equivalents: 7697, 7698, 7699.

4 KENMORE (SEARS) Elite HE4 8586[2] Spacious and very quiet, this high-priced model excelled in our drying tests. The low temperature of its delicate cycle treats lingerie and knits with TLC. The drum can handle bulky items such as comforters, and the door opening makes it easy to load and unload. A signal alerts

Recommendations

you when clothes are damp-dry so you can remove them for ironing. Similar model: HE4 8587. Gas equivalents: HE4 9586, HE4 9587.

5 **MAYTAG** Neptune MCE8000AY[W] This high-priced model combines a spacious, quiet dryer with a unique heated cabinet on top for air-drying garments. It excelled in our drying tests and is well-suited to drying lingerie and knits because its low temperature in the delicate cycle treats such garments gently. A signal alerts you when clothes are damp-dry so you can remove them for ironing. Gas equivalent: MCG8000A.

6 **KENMORE (SEARS)** Elite 6692[2] Spacious and very quiet, this model did very well in our drying tests, though the delicate cycle is a bit warmer than we consider ideal. It did a fine job drying our largest test load, and the drum can handle bulky items such as comforters. Similar models: 6694, 6696. Gas equivalents: 7692, 7694, 7696.

7 **WHIRLPOOL** Duet GEW9250P[W] This spacious, quiet model excelled in our drying tests, but it's high-priced. The drum can handle bulky items such as comforters, and the door opening makes it easy to load and unload. Gas equivalent: GGW9250P.

8 **LG** DL-E5932[W] This spacious, quiet model did very well in our drying tests, but it's high-priced. The low temperature of its delicate cycle treats lingerie and knits with TLC. The drum can handle bulky items such as comforters. A signal alerts you when clothes are damp-dry so you can remove them for ironing. Gas equivalent: DL-G5932.

9 **WHIRLPOOL** LEQ8000J[Q] **A CR Best Buy** Quiet and spacious, this low-priced model did very well in our drying tests, though the delicate cycle is a bit warmer than we consider ideal. It did a fine job drying our largest test load, and the drum can handle bulky items such as comforters. Gas equivalent: LGQ8000J.

10 **WHIRLPOOL** Gold GEW9868K[Q] Spacious and very quiet, this model did very well in our drying tests. It did a fine job drying our largest test load, and the drum can handle bulky items such as comforters. Gas equivalent: GGW9868K.

11 **WHIRLPOOL** Gold GEW9878J[Q] Quiet and spacious, this dryer did very well in our drying tests, though the delicate cycle is a bit warmer than we consider ideal. It did a fine job drying our largest test load, and the drum can handle bulky items such as comforters. Discontinued, but similar model GEW9878P may be available. Gas equivalent: GGW9878P.

12 **BOSCH** Nexxt premium WTMC6300US This high-priced dryer is quiet and did very well in our drying tests, though the delicate cycle is a bit warmer than we consider ideal. The drum can handle most loads, and the large door opening makes it easy to load and unload. A signal alerts you when clothes are damp-dry so you can remove them for ironing. Gas equivalent: WTMC6500US.

13 **GE** Profile Harmony DPGT750EC[WW] Spacious and very quiet, this high-priced model did very well in our drying tests, and it has a unique feature that receives cycle information from the matching washer. The low temperature of its delicate cycle treats lingerie and knits with TLC. The drum can handle bulky items such as comforters, and the door opening makes it easy to load and unload. The matching washer sends an electronic signal indicating which wash cycle was used so the dryer can choose the correct set-

Recommendations

ting. While this feature worked in our tests, it doesn't seem especially useful. Gas equivalent: DPGT750GC.

14 BOSCH Nexxt WTMC3300US This quiet model did very well in our drying tests. The drum can handle most wash loads, and the door opening makes it easy to load and unload. Similar model: Seimens Ultra Sense WTXD5300US. Gas equivalent: Siemens Ultra Sense WTXD5500UC.

15 KITCHENAID Superba Ensemble KEHS01PMT Spacious and very quiet, this high-priced model did very well in our drying tests. The drum can handle bulky items such as comforters, and the large door opening makes it easy to load and unload. Gas equivalent: KGHS01PMT.

16 FRIGIDAIRE Gallery GLER642A[S] **A CR Best Buy** This quiet, low-priced model did very well in our drying tests. It did a fine job drying our largest test load, and the drum can handle most wash loads. Gas equivalent: GLGR642A.

17 KENMORE (SEARS) 6683[2] This spacious, low-priced dryer did very well in our drying tests, but it's rather noisy and the delicate cycle is a bit warmer than we consider ideal. The drum can handle bulky items such as comforters. Similar models: 6684, 6686. Gas equivalents: 7683, 7684, 7686.

18 MAYTAG Atlantis MDE8400AY[W] Spacious and very quiet, this model did very well in our drying tests and is well-suited to drying delicates because its low temperature in that cycle treats lingerie and knits gently. The drum can handle bulky items such as comforters, and the door opening makes it easy to load and unload. Gas equivalent: MDG8400A.

19 FRIGIDAIRE Gallery GLEQ642A[S] This quiet, low-priced dryer did very well in our drying tests. The drum can handle most wash loads. Gas equivalent: GLGQ642A.

20 LG DL-E2514[W] Spacious and quiet, this dryer did very well in our drying tests. The drum can handle bulky items such as comforters. Gas equivalent: DL-G2524.

21 GE Profile DPXH46EA[WW] This model did very well in our drying tests, but it's rather noisy and the delicate cycle is a bit warmer than we consider ideal. It did a fine job drying our largest test load, and the drum can handle most wash loads. Similar model: DSXH43EA. Gas equivalents: DPXH46GA, DSXH43GA.

22 GE DWSR405EB[WW] This low-priced dryer is spacious and quiet, but it was only mediocre in our tests and the delicate cycle is a bit warmer than we consider ideal. The drum can handle bulky items such as comforters, and the door opening makes it easy to load and unload. Gas equivalent: DWSR405GB.

23 FISHER & PAYKEL Smartload DEGX1 This unique top-loading dryer did very well in our drying tests, but it's rather noisy and the delicate cycle is a bit warmer than we consider ideal. The drum can handle most wash loads, and the door opening makes it easy to load and unload. Gas equivalent: DGGX1.

24 ESTATE BY WHIRLPOOL TEDS840J[Q] This basic, low-priced dryer has no moisture sensor, a feature we strongly recommend, and it was mediocre in our tests. It's rather noisy, and the delicate cycle is a bit warmer than we consider ideal. The drum can handle bulky items such as comforters. Discontinued, but similar model TEDS840P may be available.

Recommendations

25 HOTPOINT NWSR483EB[WW] This basic, low-priced dryer has no moisture sensor, a feature we strongly recommend, and it was mediocre in our tests. Also, the delicate cycle is a bit warmer than we consider ideal. On the plus side, it's quiet, the drum can handle bulky items such as comforters, and the large door opening makes it easy to load and unload. Gas equivalent: NWSR483GB.

26 MIELE Touchtronic T1303 This very quiet, compact dryer did very well in our drying tests and is fine for drying small loads, but it's high-priced. Its low temperature in the delicate cycle treats clothing gently.

27 ROPER RES7745P[Q] This basic, low-priced model did very well in our drying tests, and Roper has been more reliable than most brands of electric dryers, but it's rather noisy and it has no moisture sensor, a feature we strongly recommend. Also, the delicate cycle is a bit warmer than we consider ideal. The drum can handle most wash loads, and the door opening makes it easy to load and unload. Gas equivalent: RGS7745P.

28 ADMIRAL LNC7764A[W] This basic, low-priced dryer has no moisture sensor, a feature we strongly recommend, and it was mediocre in our tests. It's also rather noisy. The drum is large enough to handle bulky items such as comforters. Discontinued, but similar model ADE7000 may be available. Gas equivalent: ADG7000.

29 ROPER REX4634K[Q] This basic, low-priced dryer has no moisture sensor, a feature we strongly recommend, and it was mediocre in our tests. It's also rather noisy. On the plus side, Roper has been more reliable than most brands of electric dryers. The drum can handle most wash loads. Discontinued, but similar model REX5634P may still be available.

Brand Repair History

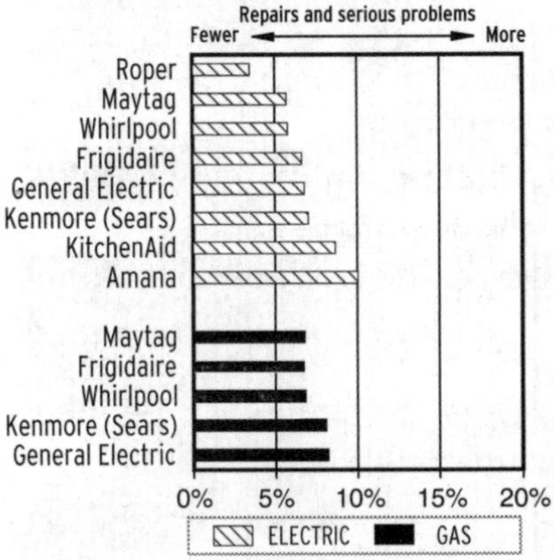

Reliability is especially important with workhorse appliances like washers and dryers. Choosing a brand with a good repair history can improve your odds of getting a reliable model. This graph shows the percentage of full-sized dryers that have ever been repaired or had a serious problem, according to our 2004 Annual Questionnaire. Note that models within a brand may vary, and design and manufacturing changes may affect reliability.

Among electric dryers, Amana was one of the more repair-prone brands. No brand stood out as more repair-prone among gas dryers.

Data are based on more than 122,000 responses to our 2004 Annual Questionnaire and are standardized to eliminate differences linked to age and usage. Differences of less than 3 points aren't meaningful.

FREEZERS

Most freezers, except those we've noted in the Ratings as Not Acceptable, performed to a high standard in our tests. After you've decided whether a chest freezer or an upright unit would better meet your needs, choose a model based on size, capacity, energy efficiency, and noise. A power-on light can also be a handy feature.

The Ratings list models by performance within types. Quick Picks highlights models you might want to consider first, based on performance, features, and price.

Excellent · Very good · Good · Fair · Poor

Within types, in performance order. Gray key numbers indicate Quick Picks.

Key number	Brand & model (Similar models, in small type, comparable to tested model.)	Price	Overall score (0–100; P F G VG E)	Test results: Temperature performance	Energy efficiency	Noise	Ease of use	Features: Power-on light	Interior light	Easy-to-access controls	Claimed capacity (cu. ft.)	HxWxD (in.)
	CHESTS, MANUAL-DEFROST *Economical, but defrosting can be a chore.*											
1	**Whirlpool** EH150FXM[Q]	$460		Excellent	Excellent	Very good	Fair				14.8	35x47x30
2	**Amana** AQC1526AE[W] Wood's C15WC01E[ ]	400		Excellent	Excellent	Very good	Fair		●		14.8	35x47x29
3	**Kenmore** (Sears) 1492[2] Frigidaire FFC0923D[ ], FFC09K0D[ ], LFFC0924D[ ], GE FCM9DM	265		Very good	Very good	Very good	Fair	●	●		8.8	35x42 x24
4	**Haier** HCM073PA[W]	225		Excellent	Very good	Fair	Fair	●		●	7.3	33x42x23
5	**Holiday** (Lowe's) LCM070LB	175		Excellent	Very good	Good	Fair	●		●	7.0	32x38x24
6	**Frigidaire** FFC0723D[W] FFC07K0D[ ]	225		Excellent	Very good	Good	Fair	●			7.2	35x36x24
7	**Frigidaire** FFC1311D[W] FFC13K0D[ ], FFC13C3A[ ], Kenmore (Sears) 1434[ ]	330		Very good	Excellent	Good	Fair				12.9	35x43x30
	CHEST, SELF-DEFROST *Makes defrosting easier but at a cost.*											
8	**Frigidaire** AFFC1466D[W] LFFC1466D[ ]	450		Very good	Very good	Fair	Good	●	●	●	13.8	36x48x30
	UPRIGHTS, MANUAL-DEFROST *Saves on floor space but requires defrosting.*											
9	**GE** FUM17DRR[WH] Frigidaire FFU1724D[ ], Kenmore (Sears) 2472[ ]	465		Very good	Very good	Good	Good		●	●	17.1	66x32x27
10	**Maytag** MQU1554AE[W] **CR Best Buy** Amana AQU1525AE[ ], Wood's V15WB01E[ ]	365		Very good	Excellent	Fair	Good		●	●	15.2	61x30x28
11	**Whirlpool** EV150FXM[Q]	460		Good	Very good	Good	Good	●		●	15.2	61x30x31
	UPRIGHTS, SELF-DEFROST *Most expensive but also most convenient.*											
12	**Frigidaire** FFU1764D[W] FFU17FK0D[ ], LFFU1765D[ ], AFFU1766D[ ], Kenmore (Sears) 2475[ ]	500		Very good	Good	Fair	Very good	●	●		16.7	66x32x27

Within types, in performance order. Gray key numbers indicate Quick Picks.

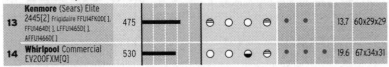

Key number	Brand & model (Similar models, in small type, comparable to tested model.)	Price	Overall score (0–100; P F G VG E)	Test results: Temperature performance	Energy efficiency	Noise	Ease of use	Features: Power-on light	Interior light	Easy-to-access controls	Claimed capacity (cu. ft.)	HxWxD (in.)
	UPRIGHTS, SELF-DEFROST *continued*											
13	**Kenmore** (Sears) Elite 2445[2] Frigidaire FFU14FK0D[ ], FFU1464D[ ], LFFU1465D[ ], AFFU1466D[ ]	475		⊖	○	○	⊖	•	•		13.7	60x29x29
14	**Whirlpool** Commercial EV200FXM[Q]	530		○	○	◒	⊖	•	•	•	19.6	67x34x31
	NOT ACCEPTABLE *Two samples of each reached very high temperatures.*											
15	**Kenmore** (Sears) 1340[1]	225		●	○	○	◒	•			4.8	33x27x29
16	**GE** FUM5SN[WW]	345		●	●	⊖	◒			•	4.7	34x22x24

See report, page 63. Based on tests in Consumer Reports in October 2005, with updated prices and availability.

Guide to the Ratings

Overall score is based on temperature performance, energy efficiency, ease of use, and noise. **Temperature performance** combines results of several tests that measured how closely the manufacturer's recommended settings matched the ideal temperature of 0° F and how well a model kept optimum temperatures in all parts of the freezer despite constant changes in room temperatures ranging from 55° F to 110° F. **Energy efficiency** reflects energy use for the usable volume (our measurement) based on average energy costs. **Noise** reflects measured and panel judgments. **Ease of use** considers controls, lighting, defrosting, and general convenience. **Claimed capacity** is as labeled by manufacturer. We found that usable space in self-defrost uprights was about 20 percent less than labeled; manual-defrost uprights about 15 percent less; chest freezers about 5 percent less. Under **brand and model**, letters or numbers in brackets are color codes. **Price** is approximate retail.

Quick Picks

If you need a lot of storage:

1 Whirlpool, $460 (chest)

10 Maytag, $365, **CR Best Buy** (upright)

Both offer excellent energy efficiency. The Whirlpool chest freezer has better temperature performance, while the Maytag upright provides more convenient storage.

If storage isn't a priority for you:

5 Holiday, $175 (chest)

A good value, this small chest freezer does an excellent job at keeping food frozen and includes a power-on light.

If you live in an area that is prone to brownouts and blackouts:

7 Frigidaire, $330 (chest)

This manual-defrost chest freezer model performed very well in our power-outage tests and is also very energy-efficient. One drawback: It lacks a power-on light.

If you want a self-defrosting model:

12 Frigidaire, $500 (upright)

This medium-sized upright combines very good performance with convenient features such as interior and power-on lights.

GAS GRILLS

When it comes to gas grills, what you pay may have little to do with how well they cook. The best often cost $400 to $500, not $1,000 or more. Several grills that sell for $200 or less outperformed models that cost several times that price.

A number of grills occasionally flared up when we loaded them with fatty foods, including some with systems designed to siphon away grease. Tested models that flared up include the Kenmore (3, 25), Napoleon (9), Ducane (11, 15), Brinkmann (12, 16), George Foreman (18), Frigidaire (20), Viking (26), Kirkland (28), Coleman (30), and BBQ Grillware (37).

The Ratings rank gas grills by overall score. See our Quick Picks for grills that offer high performance and value.

Excellent ⊜ Very good ⊖ Good ○ Fair ◓ Poor ●

Within types, in performance order. Gray **key numbers indicate Quick Picks.**

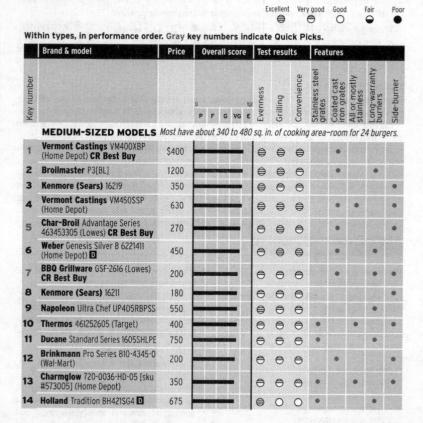

Key number	Brand & model	Price	Overall score (0–100: P F G VG E)	Test results: Evenness	Test results: Grilling	Test results: Convenience	Features: Stainless steel grates	Features: Coated cast iron grates	Features: All or mostly stainless	Features: Long-warranty burners	Features: Side-burner
MEDIUM-SIZED MODELS	*Most have about 340 to 480 sq. in. of cooking area–room for 24 burgers.*										
1	**Vermont Castings** VM400XBP (Home Depot) **CR Best Buy**	$400		Excellent	Excellent	Excellent		•			
2	**Broilmaster** P3[BL]	1200		Excellent	Excellent	Very good		•		•	
3	**Kenmore (Sears)** 16219	350		Excellent	Very good	Very good					•
4	**Vermont Castings** VM450SSP (Home Depot)	630		Excellent	Excellent	Excellent		•	•		•
5	**Char-Broil** Advantage Series 463453305 (Lowes) **CR Best Buy**	270		Very good	Excellent	Very good		•			•
6	**Weber** Genesis Silver B 6221411 (Home Depot) D	450		Very good	Excellent	Excellent		•		•	
7	**BBQ Grillware** GSF-2616 (Lowes) **CR Best Buy**	200		Very good	Very good	Very good		•		•	•
8	**Kenmore (Sears)** 16211	180		Very good	Very good	Very good					•
9	**Napoleon** Ultra Chef UP405RBPSS	550		Excellent	Very good	Very good				•	
10	**Thermos** 461252605 (Target)	400		Very good	Very good	Very good	•		•		•
11	**Ducane** Standard Series 1605SHLPE	750		Very good	Very good	Very good	•			•	
12	**Brinkmann** Pro Series 810-4345-0 (Wal-Mart)	200		Very good	Very good	Very good		•			•
13	**Charmglow** 720-0036-HD-05 [sku #573005] (Home Depot)	350		Very good	Very good	Very good	•		•		•
14	**Holland** Tradition BH421SG4 D	675		Excellent	Good	Good	•			•	

Key number	Brand & model	Price	Overall score (0–100; P F G VG E)	Test results: Evenness	Test results: Grilling	Test results: Convenience	Features: Stainless steel grates	Features: Coated cast iron grates	Features: All or mostly stainless	Features: Long-warranty burners	Features: Side-burner
	MEDIUM-SIZED MODELS *Most have about 340 to 480 sq. in. of cooking area–room for 24 burgers.*										
15	**Ducane** Standard Series 1305SHLPE	$650		VG	VG	VG	•			•	
16	**Brinkmann** Pro Series 2200 810-2200-0 (Wal-Mart) [D]	175		VG	VG	VG		•		•	
17	**Char-Broil** 7000 Quickset 463728504 [D]	160		VG	VG	G					•
18	**George Foreman** GBQ440	425		VG	G	VG		•	•		
19	**Uniflame Wellington** NSG3902B (Wal-Mart)	250		G	VG	E		•			•
20	**Frigidaire** Gallery GL30LKEC	1,100		G	G	VG	•		•		•
21	**BBQ Pro** Deluxe 24" [item #116396] (K-Mart)	350		P	G	VG		•	•	•	•
	LARGE MODELS *Most have almost 500 sq. in. or more of cooking area–room for 30 burgers or more.*										
22	**Great Outdoors** Pinnacle TG-560 (Lowes) **CR Best Buy**	500		E	E	VG	•		•		•
23	**Char-Broil** Commercial Series 463251705 (Lowes) **CR Best Buy**	500		E	E	E	•		•	•	•
24	**Weber** Summit Gold A 5260001 [D]	1,300		E	VG	E	•		•	•	
25	**Kenmore (Sears)** 16329	700		E	G	VG	•		•	•	•
26	**Viking** T Series VGBQ300-2RTL	3,200		VG	VG	VG			•		
27	**Jenn-Air** 720-0061LP (Lowes)	650		VG	VG	E	•		•	•	•
28	**Kirkland Signature** (Costco) [item# 778627] 720-0108	800		G	E	E	•		•		•
29	**Aussie** Bonza 4 7462	500		VG	VG	VG		•			
30	**Coleman** Back Home Select 6000 994-7A726	720		G	G	VG	•		•	•	•
	SMALL MODELS *Most have about 330 sq. in or less of cooking area–room for 15 burgers.*										
31	**Weber** Genesis Silver A 6711001	400		VG	VG	VG				•	
32	**Char-Broil** Quickset 463631705 (Wal-Mart) [1]	130		VG	VG	G					
33	**Fiesta** Advantis 1000 EZA30030 [1]	135		VG	VG	G					
34	**Aussie** Bushman Elite 772	130		G	VG	G				•	
	PORTABLE MODELS *Most have about 200 sq. in or less of cooking area–room for 10 burgers.*										
35	**Weber** Q 396001 [2]	170		E	E	VG		•			
36	**Weber** Baby Q 386001	130		G	G	G		•			
37	**BBQ** Grillware 720-0001	100		VG	G	G	•		•		

[D] Discontinued, but similar model is available. [1] Price includes propane tank. [2] $265 with optional cart and adapter for large tank.

See report, page 88. Based on tests in Consumer Reports in June 2005, with updated prices and availability.

Guide to the Ratings

Overall score denotes performance, features, and convenience. We tested **evenness** at high and low settings with temperature sensors, then combined scores. We verified results by searing 18 to 24 burgers on the high setting of the best and worst grills for 1½ minutes. **Low-temperature grilling** is the ability to cook chicken and fish on the low setting without burning. **Features** and **convenience** includes construction and materials, accessory burners, shelves, rack space, and ease of use. **Price** is approximate retail.

Most grills have: A lifetime warranty for castings, three to five years for burners, and two to five years for other parts. Steel triangles or plates to distribute heat. A painted-steel cart. Natural-gas conversion kit (or similar model made for gas). No propane tank (costs $25 to $30 extra). **Most medium-sized grills have:** Two to four burners, compared with three to six for large grills and one or two for small and portable grills, based on the size of the cooking area.

Quick Picks

Best for most; all are high-scoring medium-sized grills; all are CR Best Buys:

1 Vermont Castings, $400
5 Char-Broil, $270
7 BBQ Grillware, $200

Top performance and shelf space make the Vermont Castings a fine choice. The Char-Broil adds a side burner, griddle, more cooking space, and better searing, though it lacks a fully rolling cart. Consider the BBQ Grillware for its fine searing and long-warranty burners.

If you often cook for a crowd; both are CR Best Buys:

22 Great Outdoors, $500
23 Char-Broil, $500

Both deliver lots of cooking space for the price and are mostly stainless steel. Though both stained the most in our salt-spray tests, the stains weren't severe. Between the two, better searing, more shelf space, and an infrared rotisserie burner give the Great Outdoors an edge in convenience, while better grates and long-warranty burners make the Char-Broil better-built overall.

For smaller groups and tailgating:

35 Weber $170

The portable Weber offers ample performance and cooking space. It costs $265 with a cart and adapter for a larger tank, but that's still less than some small grills. The Char-Broil (32) and Fiesta (33) are cheaper, though their carts were less sturdy than others. You'll need a potholder to grip the Char-Broil's hot handle.

LAWN MOWERS

Many self-propelled gasoline-powered mowers scored at least a very good, as brands such as Craftsman, Honda, Lawn-Boy, and Toro create new designs with better decks and controls. The best self-propelled models typically include easy mode changes and bag removal, and comfortable handlebars. Six of our top 10 self-propelled models cost less than $500.

For smaller lawns, you'll find more top push mowers for less as retailers such as Home Depot, Lowe's, and Sears compete for your dollar. The best in this test cut evenly and proved easy to start, maneuver, and control. They also bagged competently, courtesy of rear-mounted collection bags, which tend to fill more completely than the side-mounted bags they've displaced on most models. Good gas-powered and corded electric push mowers cost around $200, though you'll still pay a premium for cordless electric models.

Excellent · Very good · Good · Fair · Poor

Within types, in performance order. Gray key numbers indicate Quick Picks.

Key number	Brand & model	Price	Overall score (0–100; P F G VG E)	Test results: Evenness	Mulching	Bagging	Side discharging	Handling	Ease of use	Features: Rear Bag	Easy Mode Change	Deck Size (in.)	Engine Power (hp)
	SELF-PROPELLED MOWERS												
1	**Honda** HRX217HXA	$700		Very good	Excellent	Excellent	Good	Very good	Excellent	•	•	21	6.5
2	**Toro** Super Recycler 20055	520		Very good	Very good	Very good	Excellent	Excellent	Excellent	•	•	21	NA
3	**John Deere** JX75	910		Very good	Very good	Very good	Excellent	Excellent	Excellent	•	•	21	6.75
4	**Lawn-Boy** 10685	380		Very good	Good	Very good	Very good	Excellent	Excellent	•	•	21	6.5
5	**Lawn-Boy** 10695	450		Very good	Good	Very good	Very good	Excellent	Excellent	•	•	21	5.5
6	**Toro** Recycler 20041 **CR Best Buy**	400		Very good	Good	Very good	Very good	Excellent	Excellent	•	•	22	NA
7	**Lawn-Boy** 10684	340		Very good	Good	Very good	Very good	Excellent	Excellent	•	•	21	6.5
8	**Husqvarna** 55R21HV	480		Good	Good	Very good	Good	Very good	Excellent	•	•	21	5.5
9	**John Deere** JS63C	590		Very good	Good	Good	Very good	Excellent	Very good	•		21	6.75
10	**Craftsman (Sears)** 37669	300		Good	Good	Very good	Very good	Very good	Very good	•	•	21	5.5
11	**Cub Cadet** SR621 12A-977A	460		Very good	Very good	Very good	Very good	Fair	Very good	•	•	21	6.5
12	**Husqvarna** 5521CHV	350		Good	Good	Good	Good	Very good	Very good	•	•	21	5.5
13	**Ariens** LM21S (911514)	600		Good	Good	Very good	Very good	Good	Excellent	•	•	21	6.75
14	**Troy-Bilt** 12AV839N	350		Good	Good	Very good	Good	Very good	Good	•	•	21	7

Within types, in performance order. Gray key numbers indicate Quick Picks.

Key number	Brand & model	Price	Overall score (0–100; P F G VG E)	Test results: Evenness	Mulching	Bagging	Side discharging	Handling	Ease of use	Features: Rear Bag	Easy Mode Change	Deck Size (in.)	Engine Power (hp)
	SELF-PROPELLED MOWERS												
15	**Craftsman (Sears)** 37657	$330		○	○	○	○	⊖	○	•	•	22	6.75
16	**Craftsman (Sears)** 37706	300		○	○	◒	○	⊖	⊖	•	•	21	6.5
17	**Craftsman (Sears)** 37709	380		○	○	○	○	⊖	⊖	•	•	21	6.5
18	**Craftsman (Sears)** 37794	480		○	○	○	○	⊖	⊖	•	•	21	5.5
19	**Ariens** 911097	490		○	◒	⊖	◒	⊖	⊜	•	•	21	5.5
20	**Troy-Bilt** 12AV566N	300		○	○	○	○	⊖	○	•	•	21	6.75
21	**Toro** Recycler 20016	320		⊖	○	⊖	○	○	○	•	•	22	6.5
22	**Honda** Harmony II HRS216SDA	415		⊖	⊖	●	⊖	○	○		•	21	5.5
23	**Yard-Man** 12A-556Q	330		○	○	○	NA	⊖	○	•	•	21	6.5
24	**Yard Man** 12A-568Q	290		○	○	○	○	⊖	○	•	•	21	5.5
25	**Snapper** RP217018BV	550		○	○	⊖	○	○	○	•		21	7
26	**Murray** 226111x92	215		○	○	NA	○	○	○	•	•	21	5.5
27	**Bolens** 12A-264E	230		○	○	NA	◒	○	○		•	22	4.5
	GAS-POWERED PUSH MODELS												
28	**Lawn-Boy** 10683	$320		⊖	○	⊖	⊖	○	⊖	•	•	21	6.5
29	**Lawn-Boy** Gold Series 10654	330		⊖	○	⊖	○	○	⊖	•	•	22	5.5
30	**Troy-Bilt** 11A-436 **A CR Best Buy**	200		○	○	○	○	⊖	○	•	•	21	6.5
31	**Craftsman (Sears)** 38885	230		○	⊖	◒	NA	⊖	○	•	•	21	6.5
32	**Weed Eater** 961360001	160		○	○	○	NA	⊖	○	•	•	21	4.5
33	**Yard-Man** 11A435D **CR Best Buy**	200		○	○	○	○	⊖	○	•	•	21	6.5
34	**Bolens** 11A-414E	160		○	○	○	NA	⊖	○	•	•	21	4.5
35	**MTD** Pro 11A588Q	200		○	○	○	NA	⊖	○	•	•	21	5.5
36	**Honda** Harmony II HRS216PDA	365		⊖	○	●	⊜	○	⊖			21	5.5
37	**Craftsman (Sears)** 38766	140		○	○	NA	○	⊖	○		•	22	4.5
38	**Murray** Select 204210x8	160		○	◒	◒	NA	⊖	○	•	•	20	4.5

Excellent ⊜ Very good ⊖ Good ○ Fair ◒ Poor ●

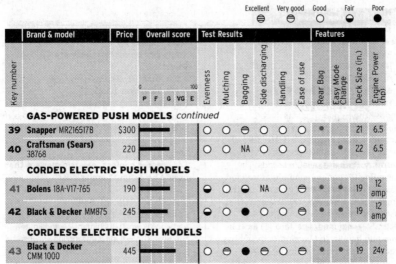

Key number	Brand & model	Price	Overall score (0–100; P F G VG E)	Evenness	Mulching	Bagging	Side discharging	Handling	Ease of use	Rear Bag	Easy Mode Change	Deck Size (in.)	Engine Power (hp)
	GAS-POWERED PUSH MODELS *continued*												
39	**Snapper** MR216517B	$300		○	○	⊖	○	○	○	•		21	6.5
40	**Craftsman (Sears)** 38768	220		○	○	NA	○	○	○		•	22	6.5
	CORDED ELECTRIC PUSH MODELS												
41	**Bolens** 18A-V17-765	190		◒	○	◒	NA	○	⊖	•	•	19	12 amp
42	**Black & Decker** MM875	245		◒	○	●	○	○	⊖	•	•	19	12 amp
	CORDLESS ELECTRIC PUSH MODELS												
43	**Black & Decker** CMM 1000	445		○	⊖	●	⊖	○	⊖	•	•	19	24v

See report, page 92. Based on tests posted to ConsumerReports.org in June 2005, with updated prices and availability.

Guide to the Ratings

Overall score is based mainly on cutting performance, handling, and ease of use. **Evenness** shows cutting performance for two or three modes; scores notably better or worse in any mode are called out in the recommendations. **Mulching** reflects how completely the mower distributed the clippings over the lawn's surface. **Bagging** denotes how many clippings the bag held before it filled or the chute clogged. **Side discharging** shows how evenly clippings were dispersed in this mode. **Handling** includes ease of operating the drive controls (for self-propelled), pushing and pulling, making U-turns, and maneuvering in tight spots. **Ease of use** includes ease of starting the engine, operating the blade-stopping controls, shifting speeds (for self-propelled), and adjusting the cutting height. **Price** is approximate retail price. The price includes the cost of the bag and mulch kit, when not included with the mower.

Quick Picks

Best for most; versatile mowing:

1 Honda, $700
2 Toro, $520
4 Lawn-Boy, $380
6 Toro, $400, **CR Best Buy**
10 Craftsman (Sears), $300

Choose the Honda (1) for its superb mulching and bagging, and the ability to tailor both for tall or wet grass, the Toro (2) for its fine side-discharging and five-year warranty. Both are reliable brands. The Lawn-Boy (4) performs nearly as well for less and costs only slightly more than the single-speed Lawn-Boy (7). The brand has historically been repair-prone but was recently redesigned. The Toro (6) lacks a swing-up handle and bag interlock but has electric starting for slightly more. Also consider the front-drive Craftsman (Sears) for flat, midsized lawns.

Best choices for those with small, relatively flat properties; both are CR Best Buys:

30 Troy-Bilt, $200
33 Yard-Man, $200

Nimble handling and a low price make the Troy-Bilt and Yard-Man fine values. Also consider the Craftsman (Sears) 38885 (31) if mulching is a priority.

For greener choices; electric mowers that create no exhaust emissions:

41 Bolens, $190
43 Black & Decker, $445

Consider the Black & Decker if cord-free convenience is worth its high price and limited run time, the Bolens if entangling shrubs aren't a concern.

Recommendations

SELF-PROPELLED MOWERS

1 **HONDA** HRX217HXA Excellent. Top performance and premium features, though pricey. Among the more reliable brands. A unique Versamow System allows partial bagging and mulching simultaneously. Has an infinitely variable hydrostatic transmission. Plastic deck.

2 **TORO** Super Recycler 20055 Excellent. A top-performing, well-rounded mower with a relatively long warranty. Among the more reliable brands. Aluminum deck.

3 **JOHN DEERE** JX75 Excellent. Top performance and premium features, but pricey. Some key features cost extra. Blade-brake clutch. Aluminum deck.

4 **LAWN-BOY** 10685 Very good. Fine performance and value with unique features. While Lawn-Boy has been among the more-repair prone brands of self-propelled mowers, its mowers have been redesigned and are now built by Toro. We will monitor whether these changes affects Lawn-Boy's reliability. Has tilt-up handlebar. Collection-bag interlock eliminates hinged inner flap.

5 **LAWN-BOY** 10695 Very good. Fine performance with unique features. While Lawn-Boy has been among the more-repair prone brands of self-propelled mowers, its mowers have been redesigned and are now built by Toro. We will monitor whether these changes affects Lawn-Boy's reliability. Has tilt-up handlebar. Collection bag interlock eliminates the hinged inner flap.

Recommendations

6 TORO Recycler 20041 **A CR Best Buy** Very good. Fine performance and value. Among the more reliable brands. Has electric start. Similar models: Lawn-Boy Gold Series 10655, Recycler 20017.

7 LAWN-BOY 10684 Very good. Fine performance with unique features, but only one ground speed. While Lawn-Boy has been among the more-repair prone brands of self-propelled mowers, its mowers have been redesigned and are now built by Toro. We will monitor whether these changes affects Lawn-Boy's reliability. Collection bag interlock eliminates the hinged inner flap.

8 HUSQVARNA 55R21HV Very good. A fine choice if bagging is your mowing mode of choice.

9 JOHN DEERE JS63C Very good. A relatively pricey mower. Some attachments cost extra. Has swivel wheels. Bag hard to empty.

10 CRAFTSMAN (Sears) 37669 Very good. Fine performance and value though front-drive makes it a dubious choice for steep slopes.

11 CUB CADET SR621 12A-977A Very good. A well-rounded mower compromised by handling flaws. Difficult to push, pull, and do lap turns. Bag difficult to empty.

12 HUSQVARNA 5521CHV Very good. A fine, relatively inexpensive mower, but basic. Only one ground speed. Front-drive makes this a dubious choice for steep slopes.

13 ARIENS LM21S (911514) Very good. A very good, if pricey, choice for bagging and side-discharging. Difficult lap turns. Bag hard to empty. Front-drive make this a dubious choice for steep slopes.

14 TROY-BILT 12AV839N Very good. A fine, relatively inexpensive choice if bagging is your mode of choice. No handlebar adjustment.

15 CRAFTSMAN (Sears) 37657 Very good. A fine, relatively inexpensive choice. Has fuel preserving cap.

16 CRAFTSMAN (Sears) 37706 Good. A good, inexpensive choice if bagging isn't a priority. Has fuel preserving cap.

17 CRAFTSMAN (Sears) 37709 Good. A good choice overall. Has fuel preserving cap.

18 CRAFTSMAN (Sears) 37794 Good. A good choice overall.

19 ARIENS 911097 Good. A good choice, provided bagging is your mowing mode of choice.

20 TROY-BILT 12AV566N Good. Relatively inexpensive, but front-drive makes this a dubious choice for steep slopes. No handlebar adjustment.

21 TORO Recycler 20016 Good. Relatively inexpensive, but front-drive makes this a dubious choice for steep slopes. Among the more reliable brands. Lap turns difficult.

22 HONDA Harmony II HRS216SDA Good. A good choice, provided bagging isn't a priority. Among the more reliable brands. Some attachments cost extra. Only one ground speed. Side bag. Blade change to bag.

23 YARD-MAN 12A-556Q Good. Its unique stainless-steel deck lacks a side-discharge mode—a potential problem in tall grass. Only one ground speed. No handlebar adjustment. Front-drive makes this a dubious choice for steep slopes.

Recommendations

24 YARD-MAN 12A-568Q Good. Only one ground speed. Difficult handlebar adjustment. Front-drive make this a dubious choice for steep slopes.

25 SNAPPER RP217018BV Good. A good, if pricey, choice for bagging. Difficult to use wheel drive control.

26 MURRAY 226111x92 Good. Inexpensive, but lacks a bagging mode. Front-drive makes this a dubious choice for steep slopes.

27 BOLENS 12A-264E Good. Inexpensive, but lacks a side-discharge mode—a potential problem in tall grass. Only one ground speed. Uncomfortable handle grip.

GAS-POWERED PUSH MODELS

28 LAWN-BOY 10683 Very good. A top performer, but pricey for a push mower. While Lawn-Boy has been the most-repair prone brand of push mowers, its mowers have been redesigned and are now built by Toro. We will monitor whether these changes affects Lawn-Boy's reliability. Collection-bag interlock eliminates spring-loaded inner flap.

29 LAWN-BOY Gold Series 10654 Very good. Expensive for a push mower. While Lawn-Boy has been the most-repair prone brand of push mowers, its mowers have been redesigned and are now built by Toro. We will monitor whether these changes affect Lawn-Boy's reliability. Similar deck to Lawn-Boy Series 10655 and Toro 20031. Mulching and bagging attachments included. Has Honda engine. Handlebar can swing up for easier bag removal and storage, but scratches the paint at the base of the handlebars. Engine starter rope has large, padded handle. Bag has padded handle.

30 TROY-BILT 11A-436 **A CR Best Buy** Very good. Fine performance and value. Pushing, and U-turns especially easy. Bag inconvenient to empty.

31 CRAFTSMAN (Sears) 38885 Good. A good, Inexpensive choice if bagging isn't a priority. Has fuel preserving cap. Excessive play in handlebar. Uncomfortable handlebar grip.

32 WEED EATER 961360001 Good. Inexpensive, but lacks a side-discharge mode—a potential problem in tall grass. Excessive play in handlebar. Uncomfortable handlebar grip.

33 YARD-MAN 11A435D **A CR Best Buy** Good. Fine performance and value. Pushing and U-turns especially easy. Bag inconvenient to empty. Cut height hard to adjust.

34 BOLENS 11A-414E Good. Inexpensive, but lacks a side-discharge mode—a potential problem in tall grass. Pushing and U-turns especially easy. Uncomfortable handlebar grip.

35 MTD PRO 11A588Q Good. Inexpensive, but lacks a side-discharge mode—a potential problem in tall grass. Uncomfortable handlebar grip. Available only at Sam's Club warehouse stores.

36 HONDA Harmony II HRS216PDA Good. Top side-discharging performance, but you pay for it. Some attachments cost extra. Side bag. Bagging requires blade change.

37 CRAFTSMAN (Sears) 38766 Good. Inexpensive, but lacks a side-discharge mode—a potential problem in tall grass. Has fuel preserving cap. Excess play in handlebar. Uncomfortable handle grip.

38 MURRAY Select 204210x8 Good. There are better choices. Mulching and bagging only fair. Lacks a side-discharge mode—a potential problem in tall grass. Bag inconvenient to empty. Cut height hard to adjust. Uncomfortable handle.

39 SNAPPER MR216517B Good. Pricey for a push mower. Requires tools for mode changes. Discontinued, but similar model MR216518B is available.

40 CRAFTSMAN (Sears) 38768 Good. An unexceptional performer. Lacks a bagging mode. Excessive play in handlebar. Uncomfortable handlebar grip.

CORDED ELECTRIC PUSH MODELS

41 BOLENS 18A-V17-765 Good. A good corded-electric choice for small properties where clippings are mostly mulched. Lacks a side-discharge mode—a potential problem in tall grass. Cord hard to keep out of the way while mowing.

42 BLACK & DECKER MM875 Good. A good corded-electric choice for small properties where clippings are mostly mulched or side-discharged. Cord hard to keep out of the way while mowing.

CORDLESS ELECTRIC PUSH MODELS

43 BLACK & DECKER CMM 1000 Good. A good, if pricey, cordless choice for small properties, provided bagging isn't a priority. Run time per battery charge is relatively short.

Brand Repair History

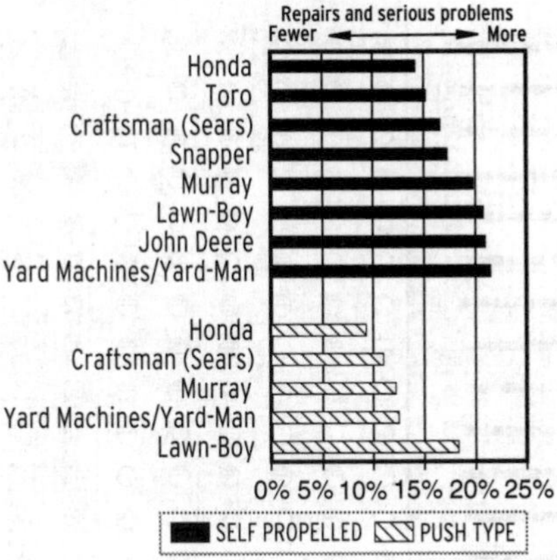

Self-propelled mowers continue to be more repair-prone than push types. While models within a brand may vary, and changes in design or manufacturer may affect reliability, you can improve your odds of getting a trouble-free mower by choosing a reliable brand. The graphs show the percentage of mowers that have ever been repaired or had a serious problem. Lawn-Boy, which has historically been the most repair-prone push-mower brand, has recently redesigned all of its walk-behind mowers and now builds them in the same plant as models from Toro. We will monitor whether these changes affect Lawn-Boy's reliability.

Based on 36,944 responses to our 2004 Annual Questionnaire for self-propelled and push mowers bought new between 2000 and 2004. Data have been standardized to eliminate differences linked to age and usage. Differences of less than 5 points are not meaningful.

LAWN TRACTORS

Nearly all of these machines are at least adequate at side-discharging clippings—the most-used mowing mode by far. Top-scoring models add more even cutting and better bagging overall.

Several top-performing, automatic-drive models cost $1,800 or less as major retailers work with manufacturers to cut costs. Indeed, low-priced automatic-drive tractors leave little reason to buy a gear-drive model. But you'll still spend $4,000 for a top-scoring zero-turn-radius model.

Excellent (E) · Very good (VG) · Good (G) · Fair (F) · Poor (P)

Within types, in performance order. Gray **key numbers indicate Quick Picks.**

Key number	Brand & model	Price	Overall score (0–100; P F G VG E)	Test results: Eveness	Side discharging	Mulching	Bagging	Handling	Ease of use	Features: Deck size (in.)	Engine Power (hp)
	AUTOMATIC-DRIVE MODELS										
1	**John Deere** L111 **CR Best Buy**	$1,800		VG	VG	G	E	E	VG	42	20
2	**John Deere** L108 **CR Best Buy**	1,600		VG	VG	G	E	E	VG	42	18.5
3	**Cub Cadet** 13AL11C	1,600		G	VG	VG	E	E	VG	42	18.5
4	**John Deere** LT160	2,600		VG	VG	G	E	VG	VG	42	16
5	**Simplicity** Regent 16hp 44"	2,800		G	G	VG	E	E	VG	44	16
6	**Toro** Wheel Horse 16-38 HXL	2,200		G	G	E	G	E	VG	38	16
7	**Troy-Bilt** 13AJ609G **CR Best Buy**	1,400		G	VG	VG	E	VG	VG	42	18.5
8	**Kubota** T1670 40"	3,000		F	VG	G	E	E	VG	40	15
9	**Cub Cadet** 13AQ11CP	2,000		G	VG	VG	F	VG	VG	50	26
10	**John Deere** L120	2,200		G	G	G	E	E	VG	48	20
11	**Yard-Man** 13AN791G **CR Best Buy**	995		G	VG	VG	VG	VG	G	42	17.5
12	**Craftsman (Sears)** 2757	1,800		G	VG	G	VG	VG	VG	48	24
13	**Husqvarna** YTH1542XP	2,000		VG	VG	G	G	VG	VG	42	15
14	**Cub Cadet** LT1045 13AX11CB	1,700		G	G	VG	F	VG	VG	46	20
15	**Craftsman (Sears)** 27564	1,500		G	G	G	G	VG	VG	42	18.5
	GEAR-DRIVE MODELS										
16	**John Deere** L100 5 Speed	1,500		VG	G	VG	E	VG	VG	42	17
17	**Craftsman (Sears)** 27537	1,100		G	G	G	G	F	G	42	17.5

Key number	Brand & model	Price	Overall score (0–100; P F G VG E)	Evenness	Side discharging	Mulching	Bagging	Handling	Ease of use	Deck size (in.)	Engine Power (hp)
	ZERO-TURN-RADIUS MODELS										
18	**Snapper** ZT18440KH	$4,000		○	⊖	⊖	⊜	⊖	⊖	44	18
19	**Cub Cadet** 15HP Z-Force 44-53AA5D2L	4,000		○	○	⊖	○	⊖	○	44	15
20	**Ariens** 915065 1540	3,100		○	○	⊖	◒	⊖	○	40	15
21	**Husqvarna** Z4217	2,700		○	○	○	○	⊖	○	42	17.5
22	**Toro** 1642Z Timecutter	3,000		○	●	⊖	◒	○	○	42	16

See report, page 95. Based on tests posted to ConsumerReports.org in August 2005, with updated prices and availability.

Guide to the Ratings

Overall score is based on a combination of performance, handling, and ease of use. **Evenness** is how close the tractors came to even, carpet-like mowing. **Side discharging** is how evenly clippings were dispersed from the side-discharge chute. **Mulching** is how finely and evenly clippings were cut and dispersed in this mode. **Bagging** measures effective capacity of the grass bag, determined when bag was full or when the chute clogged and clippings weren't being collected. **Handling** includes clutching or drive engagement, braking, steering, turn radius, and stability. **Ease of use** is a composite score that includes leg room and seat and steering-wheel comfort, as well as ease of blade engagement, cut-height adjustment, parking brake engagement, bag removal, and cutting-mode changes. **Price** is approximate retail.

Quick Picks

Best for most; versatile mowing at a reasonable price; all are CR Best Buys:

1 John Deere, $1,800
2 John Deere, $1,600
7 Troy-Bilt, $1,400
11 Yard-Man, $995

Less horsepower and lack of a cruise control are all that distinguish the John Deere L108 (2) from the John Deere L111 (1). Consider the Troy-Bilt if you're willing to trade a hydrostatic drive for a belt-and-pulley system that's slightly less smooth. Also consider the low-priced Yard-Man if you don't mind trading a foot-pedal drive for a lever and can live with a less-supportive seat.

For large, wide-open spaces:

12 Craftsman (Sears), $1,800

The Craftsman has a wide, 48-inch mowing deck that saves time in open areas. Also consider the 48-inch John Deere L120 (10) if you're willing to pay a bit more for better bagging. While the 50-inch Cub Cadet 13AQ11CP (9) is even wider, it has been among the more repair-prone brands.

For lawns with lots of obstacles:

18 Snapper, $4,000

The Snapper performs well and offers responsive control via a more refined drive system. While Snapper riding mowers have been repair-prone, our data may not apply to its zero-turn-radius mowers.

Recommendations

AUTOMATIC-DRIVE MODELS

1 **JOHN DEERE** L111 **A CR Best Buy** Very good overall. Briggs & Stratton engine. Has cruise control and hour meter. Must change blades to bag. Reverse-cut interlock. Bag $310. Mulch cover included. Similar model: L118.

2 **JOHN DEERE** L108 **A CR Best Buy** Very good overall. Briggs & Stratton engine. Lacks cruise control and hour meter. Must change blades to bag. Has reverse-cut interlock. Bag $310. Mulch cover included.

3 **CUB CADET** 13AL11C Very good overall, but among the more repair-prone brands. Excellent bagging and handling. Briggs & Stratton engine. Automatic drive with foot-operated speed control. Electric blade engagement. Comfortable steering wheel. Cruise control. Won't cut in reverse. Bag $300. Mulch kit included. Similar model: 13BX11CG.

4 **JOHN DEERE** LT160 Very good. Kohler engine. High brake pedal awkward. Must change blade to mulch. Must engage override switch to cut in reverse. Bag $445. Mulch kit included.

5 **SIMPLICITY** Regent 16hp 44" Very good overall. Excellent bagging and handling. Kohler engine. Hydrostatic drive with foot-operated speed control. Electric blade engagement. Deck has a fan attachment to improve grass bagging, also useful for leaf pickup. Must change blade to mulch and bag. Bag with fan assist $400. Mulch kit $135.

6 **TORO** Wheel Horse 16-38 HXL Very good. A top pick for mulching, but Toro has been among the more repair-prone brands. Smooth drive engagement. Precise steering and comfortable steering wheel. Briggs & Stratton engine. High brake pedal awkward. Must engage override switch to cut in reverse. Bag $340. Mulch kit included.

7 **TROY-BILT** 13AJ609G **A CR Best Buy** Very good in discharge and mulching and excellent for bagging. Briggs & Stratton engine. Pedal drive (not a true hydrostatic—requires shifting from forward to reverse) with foot-operated speed control. Fuel level visible from seat. Cruise control. Bag $300. Mulch kit included. Similar model: Yard Man 13AT605G.

8 **KUBOTA** T1670 40" Very good overall, but evenness is only Fair. Excellent bagging and handling. Kohler engine. Automatic drive with foot-operated speed control. Must change blade to mulch. Bag $454. Mulch kit $180.

9 **CUB CADET** 13AQ11CP Very good overall, but among the more repair-prone brands of tractor mowers. Only fair for bagging. Cut evenness has a slight ridge, characteristic of three-blade decks. Large 50" deck. Kohler engine. Hydrostatic drive with foot-operated speed control. Electric blade engagement. Comfortable steering wheel. Must change blades to bag. Has reverse-cut interlock. Hour meter. Pressurized engine oil. Bag $300. Mulch cover included. Similar model: Yard-Man 13AU615P.

10 **JOHN DEERE** L120 Very good overall, with a 48-in. cutting width. Cruise control. Electric blade engagement. Comfortable seat. Briggs & Stratton engine. High brake pedal awkward. Must change blade to bag. Must engage override switch to cut in reverse. 3 blades. Bag $295. Mulch kit included.

11 **YARD-MAN** 13AN791G **A CR Best Buy** Very good overall; among the lowest-priced hydrostatic models. Briggs & Stratton engine. Seat less comfortable

Recommendations

than most. Has reverse-cut interlock. No pressurized engine oil. Bag $300. Mulch cover included. Similar model: MTD Pro 13AO791G.

12 CRAFTSMAN (Sears) 2757 Very good overall. 48" deck. Briggs & Stratton engine. Mulching good. Comfortable steering wheel. High back seat. Hydrostatic drive with fender lever control. Electric blade engagement. Must change blades to mulch. Has reverse-cut interlock. Pressurized engine oil. Fuel level visible from the seat. Amp meter. Bag $320. Mulch kit $50. Similar model: Husqvarna YTH2448.

13 HUSQVARNA YTH1542XP Very good. Fine overall. Electric blade engagement. Kawasaki engine. Bag kit $310. Mulch cover included.

14 CUB CADET LT1045 13AX11CB Very good overall, but among the more repair-prone brands of tractor mowers. Only fair for bagging. Cut evenness has a slight ridge, characteristic of three-blade decks. Large 46" deck. Kohler engine. Hydrostatic drive with foot-operated speed control. Electric blade engagement. Comfortable steering wheel. Has reverse-cut interlock. Hour meter. Pressurized engine oil. Bag $300. Mulch cover included. Similar model: White Outdoor 13A4616H.

15 CRAFTSMAN (Sears) 27564 Good overall. Briggs & Stratton engine. Evenness and all cutting modes only good. Comfortable steering wheel. Hydrostatic drive with fender lever control. Electric blade engagement. Must change blades to mulch. Has reverse cut interlock. Pressurized engine oil. Fuel level visible from the seat. Amp meter. Bag $290. Mulch kit $50. Similar model: 27562.

GEAR-DRIVE MODELS

16 JOHN DEERE L100 5 Speed A very good gear-drive tractor. Briggs & Stratton engine. Must change blade to bag. Must engage override switch to cut in reverse. Bag $285. Mulch kit included.

17 CRAFTSMAN (Sears) 27537 Good overall. Briggs & Stratton engine. Handling only fair. Evenness in all cutting modes only good. Manual gear drive. Has reverse-cut interlock. Seat less comfortable than most. Must change blades to mulch. No pressurized engine oil. No cup holder. Bag $290. Mulch kit $50. Similar models: 27575, 27581.

ZERO-TURN-RADIUS MODELS

18 SNAPPER ZT18440KH Very good overall; best of the zero-turn-radius models tested. While Snapper riding mowers have been repair-prone, our data may not apply to the zero-turn-radius models. Has separate hydraulic pump and motors for better steering control and balance. Excellent bagging due to fan assist. Kohler engine. Electric blade engagement. Must change blades to bag. Bag $840. Mulch plate included. Similar model: Simplicity ZT1844.

19 CUB CADET 15HP Z-Force 44-53AA5D2L A good zero-turn machine. Electric blade engagement. Kawasaki engine. Awkward parking brake and cut-height adjustment. Bag $349. Mulch kit included. Repair history data may not apply to zero-turn-radius models.

20 ARIENS 915065 1540 Good overall. Zero-turn-radius model. Bagging uses a fan assist, but is only fair. Briggs & Stratton engine. Electric blade engagement. Must change blades to mulch. Pressurized engine oil. Bag $750. Mulch kit $80.

Recommendations

21 HUSQVARNA Z4217 Good overall. Zero-turn-radius model. Kohler engine. Electric blade engagement. Pressurized engine oil. Bag $500. Mulch kit $65.

22 TORO 1642Z Timecutter Good. A tight-turning model that's Poor for side-discharge and only Fair for bagging; Toro has been among the more repair-prone brands. Briggs & Stratton engine. Auto drive controlled by twin levers, one for each wheel. Levers do not return to the neutral position when released. Electric blade engagement. Seat lacks arm rests. Bag $400. Mulch kit $70. Similar model: Lawn Boy Z330 LX.

Brand Repair History

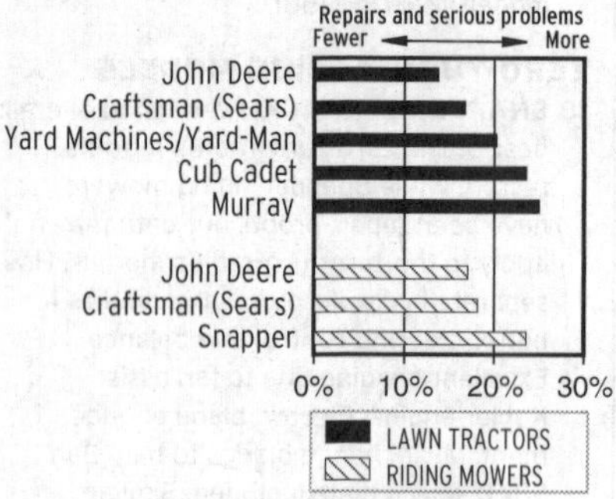

Lawn tractors and riding mowers are among the most repair-prone products. But choosing a brand with a good repair history can improve your odds of getting a trouble-free model. The graphs show the percentage by brand of tractors and riders that were ever repaired or had a serious problem. Cub Cadet and Murray continue to be among the more repair-prone tractor brands. Note that our data for riding mowers may not apply to zero-turn-radius models, which have a different design. Snapper has been the most repair-prone riding-mower brand. Note also that models within a brand may vary, and changes in design or manufacture may affect reliability.

Based on 14,210 responses to our 2004 Annual Questionnaire for lawn tractors and riding mowers bought new between 2000 and 2004. Data have been standardized to eliminate differences linked to age and usage. Differences of less than 5 points are not meaningful.

MICROWAVE OVENS

Competent performance overall makes most of these models safe bets. The best are also adept at auto-defrosting, though some deliver more usable cooking space. One model, the over-the-range Maytag MMV5207AA[B], does that by trading a turntable for a tray that moves from side to side to accept larger platters while keeping food moving for even cooking.

Note that midsized countertop models are not included in the chart below because the majority of models from our last test are no longer available.

The Ratings rank models by overall performance. Begin by deciding on the type you want and, among countertop models, considering the space you have on your counter. Quick Picks indicate models that deliver notable strengths and value.

Excellent ⊜ | Very good ⊖ | Good ○ | Fair ◒ | Poor ●

Within types, in performance order. Gray key numbers indicate Quick Picks.

Key number	Brand & model	Price	Overall score (0–100; P F G VG E)	Watts	Capacity: Claimed (cu. ft.)	Capacity: Measured (cu. ft.)	Test results: Turntable diameter (in.)	Heating evenness	Auto defrost	Ease of use	Features: Convection mode	Sensor	Detailed prompts	Stainless/SS-look option
	LARGE COUNTERTOP MODELS													
1	**GE** JE1860[W]H	$165		1100	1.8	1.2	13.5	⊖	⊖	⊜		•	•	•
2	**GE** JE1460[B]F **CR Best Buy**	120		1150	1.4	1	11.8	⊖	⊖	⊖		•	•	
3	**GE** Profile JE2160[B]F	170		1200	2.1	1.5	15.3	⊖	⊖	⊖		•	•	•
4	**KitchenAid** KCMS145J[BL]	350		1100	1.4	1	12.2	⊖	⊖	⊖		•	•	•
5	**Sharp** Carousel R-428J[K]	130		1200	1.6	1	13.1	⊖	⊖	⊖		•	•	
6	**Frigidaire** Professional PLMB209D[CA]	280		1200	2	1.3	14.6	○	⊖	⊖		•	•	•
7	**Jenn-Air** JMC9158AA[B]	450		1000	1.5	1.2	12.2	○	⊖	⊖	•	•	•	•
8	**Amana** AMC5143AA[B]	120		1100	1.4	1	13.4	○	⊖	⊖		•		•
9	**LG** LMH1517CV	400		1000	1.5	1.2	12	⊖	⊖	⊖	•	•	•	
10	**Sharp** R530E[S]	250		1200	2	1.3	14.6	○	⊜	◒		•		•
11	**Sharp** Carousel R-121[0]	250		1100	1.5	1	13.3	⊖	○	⊖		•		
12	**Haier** MWG100214T[WW]	85		1000	1.4	0.9	12.3	○	◒	○				
	OVER-THE-RANGE MODELS													
13	**Whirlpool** Gold GH4155XP[B] **CR Best Buy**	400		1000	1.5	0.7	11.5	⊖	⊜	⊜		•	•	•
14	**GE** Profile Spacemaker JVM2070[B]	500		1100	2	1.1	13.5	⊖	⊖	⊜		•	•	•

Within types, in performance order. Gray key numbers indicate Quick Picks.

Key number	Brand & model	Price	Overall score (0–100; P F G VG E)	Watts	Capacity: Claimed (cu. ft.)	Test results: Measured (cu. ft.)	Turntable diameter (in.)	Heating evenness	Auto defrost	Ease of use	Features: Convection mode	Sensor	Detailed prompts	Stainless/ SS-look option
	OVER-THE-RANGE MODELS *continued*													
15	**Maytag** MMV5207AA[B]	$450		1100	2	1.7	14.75 x12	⊖	⊖	⊜		●	●	●
16	**Kenmore (Sears)** Elite 6379[9]	800		1100	1.7	0.8	11.5	⊖	⊜	⊖		●	●	●
17	**Maytag** MMV6178AA[B]	760		950	1.7	0.9	12.7	⊖	⊖	⊜	●	●	●	●
18	**Samsung** SMH7178[STD] **CR Best Buy**	350		1100	1.7	1.1	13.5	⊖	⊜	⊖		●	●	●
19	**Panasonic** Genius NN-H264[B]F	300		1200	1.9	0.8	11.6	○	⊖	⊜		●	●	●
20	**Samsung** Pro Gourmet SMV9165[SC]	585		1500	1.6	0.9	12.8	○	⊖	⊜	●		●	●
21	**Whirlpool** Gold GH6177XP[B]	700		1100	1.7	0.9	11.4	○	⊜	⊖		●	●	●
22	**Amana** AMV5206AA[B]	420		1150	2	0.9	11.4	⊖	⊜	⊖		●	●	●
23	**KitchenAid** Ultima Cook KHHS179L[BL]	800		1100	1.7	0.9	11.4	⊖	⊖	⊖		●	●	●
24	**Whirlpool** MH3185XP[B]	400		1000	1.8	0.9	11.4	⊖	○	⊜		●	●	●
25	**Frigidaire** Gallery GLMV169D[B]	300		1000	1.6	0.8	11.7	⊖	⊖	⊖		●	●	●
26	**GE** Profile Spacemaker JVM1850[B]F	375		1000	1.8	0.9	13.5	⊖	⊖	⊖		●	●	●
27	**GE** Spacemaker JVM1650[B]	320		1000	1.6	0.8	13	○	○	⊖		●	●	●
28	**Kenmore (Sears)** Elite 8080[9]	450		1150	2	0.9	11.3	○	⊖	○		●	●	●

See report, page 66. Based on tests posted to ConsumerReports.org in July 2005, with updated prices and availability.

Guide to the Ratings

Overall score is based mainly on evenness of heating, ease of use, and auto-defrosting ability. **Watts** is the manufacturer's figure. In general, the more watts an oven offers, the greater its cooking power—and the faster your food will be cooked. That said, differences in claimed wattage of 100 watts or less are unlikely to result in significant differences in performance. **Claimed capacity** (cu. ft.) is as listed on the product or packaging. **Measured capacity** (cu. ft.) is the usable space based on our measurements, and excludes the corner spaces for models with rotating turntables. **Turntable diameter** (in.) is the measured diameter of the oven's turntable, rounded down to the nearest half-inch. **Heating evenness** reflects how evenly a model reheated a dish of cold mashed potatoes. **Auto defrost** is based on how well the automatic-defrost program defrosted one pound of frozen ground chuck. **Ease of use** includes how easy it is to set the microwave without referring to the instructions. Bracketed letters or numbers indicate color. **Price** is approximate retail price.

Quick Picks

Best countertop for most; all-around performers:

1 GE, $165
2 GE, $120, **CR Best Buy**

Among large ovens, the well-equipped GE JE1860[W]H (1) is one of the few countertop models with a turntable on/off switch. The lower-priced GE JE1460[B]F (2) is a bit smaller but did nearly as well. While the GE Profile JE2160[B]F (3) is appealingly spacious, it reheated some foods to lower temperatures than other models.

If you're willing to pay for convection:

7 Jenn-Air, $450

The large Jenn-Air JMC9158AA[B] is pricey but costs little more than the convection-equipped LG LMH1517CV (9) and adds stainless styling and a power-level display.

Best over-the-range models for most; all-around performers:

13 Whirlpool, $400, **CR Best Buy**
15 Maytag, $450
18 Samsung, $350, **CR Best Buy**

All three are fine values. The Whirlpool Gold GH4155XP[B] offers fine performance and controls though it's relatively small. Consider the sliding-tray Maytag MMV5207AA[B] for its cooking space, or the low-priced Samsung SMH7178[STD] if you can live without a power-level display.

Recommendations

LARGE COUNTERTOP MODELS

1 **GE** JE1860[W]H Very good. Has turntable on/off. Child lock. Optional kit allows wall or cabinet mount.

2 **GE** JE1460[B]F **A CR Best Buy** Very good. Has child lock.

3 **GE PROFILE** JE2160[B]F Very good. Has child lock. Optional kit allows wall or cabinet mount. Reheat feature did not heat up food adequately.

4 **KITCHENAID** KCMS145J[BL] Very good. Sensor reheat. Child lock. Shortcut keys. Optional kit allows wall or cabinet mount.

5 **SHARP CAROUSEL** R-428J[K] Very good. Sensor reheat. Built-in installation. Child lock. Shortcut keys. Optional kit allows wall or cabinet mount.

6 **FRIGIDAIRE** Professional PLMB209D[CA] Very good. Stainless steel look. Sensor reheat. Child lock. Shortcut keys. Optional kit allows wall or cabinet mount. Similar model: Gallery GLMB209D.

7 **JENN-AIR** JMC9158AA[B] Very good. Sensor reheat. Convection feature. Displays power level being used. Has door handle. Has metal oven rack. Child lock. Shortcut keys. Optional kit allows wall or cabinet mount.

8 **AMANA** AMC5143AA[B] Very good. Sensor reheat. Child lock. Shortcut keys. Optional kit allows wall or cabinet mount.

9 **LG** LMH1517CV Good. Sensor reheat. Convection feature. Has door handle. Child lock. Shortcut keys. Oven light does not go on when door is opened. Power level can't be checked. Optional kit allows wall or cabinet mount.

Recommendations

10 SHARP R530E[S] Good. Sensor reheat did not heat up some foods as well as others. Built-in installation. Child lock. Shortcut keys. Power level can't be checked. You may need instructions for some settings. Optional kit allows wall or cabinet mount.

11 SHARP Carousel R-121[0] Good. Controls across the bottom of door. Child lock.

12 HAIER MWG100214T[WW] Good, but lacks sensor. Turntable on/off. Child lock. Shortcut keys. Oven light does not go on when door is opened. No automatic program for reheating a plate of food. You may need instructions for some settings.

OVER-THE-RANGE MODELS

13 WHIRLPOOL GOLD GH4155XP[B] **A CR Best Buy** Very good. Turntable on/off. Child lock. A major 2002 recall resulted in a much higher than average repair rate for this brand's OTR ovens.

14 GE Profile Spacemaker JVM2070[B]H Very good. Turntable on/off. Child lock. Similar model: JVM2050.

15 MAYTAG MMV5207AA[B] Very good. Sensor reheat. Unique rectangular tray moves side to side. Displays power level being used. Has door handle. Has metal oven rack. Child lock. Shortcut keys. Night light can be set to turn on, off automatically. Has defrost tray.

16 KENMORE (Sears) Elite 6379[9] Very good. Has supplemental halogen or quartz bulbs for browning or crisping foods, so as to "speed cook" foods normally cooked in an oven or skillet. In our tests, however, the extra speed-cooking features didn't deliver enough to justify their extra cost. Turntable on/off. Child lock. A major 2002 recall resulted in a much higher than average repair rate for this brand's OTR ovens.

17 MAYTAG MMV6178AA[B] Very good. Sensor reheat. Convection feature. Displays power level being used. Has door handle. Turntable on/off. Child lock. Shortcut keys. Night light can be set to turn on, off automatically.

18 SAMSUNG SMH7178[STD] **A CR Best Buy** Very good. Sensor reheat. Has door handle. Has metal oven rack. Turntable on/off. Child lock. Shortcut keys.

19 PANASONIC GENIUS NN-H264[B]F Very good. Sensor reheat. Displays power level being used. Has metal oven rack. Turntable on/off. Child lock. Shortcut keys.

20 SAMSUNG PRO GOURMET SMV9165[SC] Very good. Sensor reheat. Convection feature. Displays power level being used. Has door handle. Turntable on/off. Child lock. Shortcut keys.

21 WHIRLPOOL GOLD GH6177XP[B] Very good. Has supplemental halogen or quartz bulbs for browning or crisping foods, so as to "speed cook" foods normally cooked in an oven or skillet. In our tests, however, the extra speed-cooking features didn't deliver enough to justify their extra cost. Displays power level being used. Has door handle. Has metal oven rack. Turntable on/off. Child lock. Shortcut keys. Sensor night-light turns on and off automatically. A major 2002 recall resulted in a much higher than average repair rate for this brand's OTR ovens. Similar model: GH6178XP.

22 AMANA AMV5206AA[B] Very good. Sensor reheat. Displays power level being used. Has door handle. Has metal oven rack. Turntable on/off. Child lock. Shortcut keys. Night light can be set to turn on, off automatically.

Recommendations

23 KITCHENAID Ultima Cook KHHS179L[BL] Very good. Sensor reheat. Has supplemental halogen or quartz bulbs for browning or crisping foods, so as to "speed cook" foods normally cooked in an oven or skillet. In our tests, however, the extra speed-cooking features didn't deliver enough to justify their extra cost. Displays power level being used. Has door handle. Has metal oven rack. Turntable on/off. Child lock. Shortcut keys. Sensor night-light turns on and off automatically.

24 WHIRLPOOL MH3185XP[B] Very good. Sensor reheat. Displays power level being used. Has door handle. Has metal oven rack. Turntable on/off. Child lock. Shortcut keys. No automatic program for reheating a plate of food. You may need instructions for some settings. A major 2002 recall resulted in a much higher than average repair rate for this brand's OTR ovens. Similar model: MH3184XP.

25 FRIGIDAIRE Gallery GLMV169D[B] Very good. Sensor reheat. Has door handle. Turntable on/off. Child lock. Shortcut keys. Noisy vent fan, even at low setting. Similar model: Professional PLMV169D.

26 GE Profile Spacemaker JVM1850[B]F Very good. Turntable on/off. Child lock. Noisy vent fan even at low setting. Discontinued, but similar model JVM1870 is available.

27 GE Spacemaker JVM1650[B]B Very good. Relatively quiet during oven operation, but vent fan noisy. Turntable on/off. Child lock. Optional kit allows wall or cabinet mount. Similar model: JVM1640.

28 KENMORE (Sears) Elite 8080[9] Very good. Sensor reheat. Has door handle. Has metal oven rack. Dial Controls. Child lock. Shortcut keys. Night light can be set to turn on, off automatically. Power level can't be checked. A major 2002 recall resulted in a much higher than average repair rate for this brand's OTR ovens.

Brand Repair History

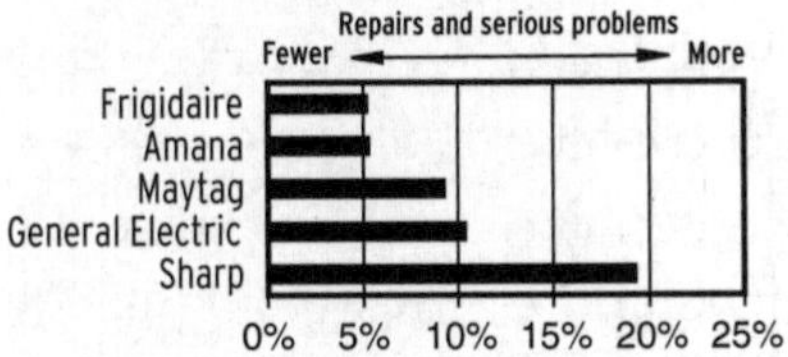

Choosing an oven with a good repair history can improve your odds of getting a reliable model. The graph shows the percentage of nonconvection, over-the-range (OTR) ovens bought new between 2000 and 2004 that have ever been repaired or had a serious problem that wasn't repaired. Among those brands, Sharp has been more repair-prone than the others. While we lack data for OTR convection ovens as a group, reliability for the GE brand has been comparable between convection and nonconvection ovens. Note, however, that models within a brand may vary, and our data cannot always anticipate design or manufacturing changes.

The graph doesn't include Kenmore or Whirlpool. Our analysis indicated that a major recall in 2002 resulted in misleadingly high repair rates for those brands, which have otherwise had average repair rates in our survey.

Data are based on 27,595 reader responses to our 2004 Annual Questionnaire about over-the-range ovens. Data are standardized to eliminate differences linked to age and usage. Differences of fewer than 4 points are not meaningful.

PDAs

The Ratings tell you which models were easiest to use, had the longest battery life, and performed best overall. The table also indicates the models' major features. Quick Picks highlights good values that our experts consider full-featured or especially well-designed.

Excellent ⊜ Very good ⊖ Good ○ Fair ◒ Poor ●

Within types, in performance order. Gray key numbers indicate Quick Picks.

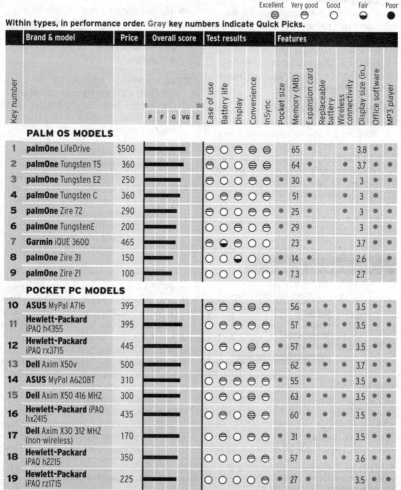

Key number	Brand & model	Price	Overall score (0–100: P F G VG E)	Ease of use	Battery life	Display	Convenience	InSync	Pocket size	Memory (MB)	Expansion card	Replaceable battery	Wireless connectivity	Display size (in.)	Office software	MP3 player
	PALM OS MODELS															
1	**palmOne** LifeDrive	$500		⊖	○	⊖	⊜	⊜		65	●		●	3.8	●	●
2	**palmOne** Tungsten T5	360		⊖	○	○	⊜	⊜		64	●		●	3.7	●	●
3	**palmOne** Tungsten E2	250		⊖	○	○	⊖	⊖	●	30	●		●	3	●	●
4	**palmOne** Tungsten C	360		○	⊖	⊖	○	⊖		51	●		●	3	●	
5	**palmOne** Zire 72	290		⊖	○	○	⊖	⊖	●	25	●		●	3	●	●
6	**palmOne** TungstenE	200		○	○	⊖	○	⊖	●	29	●			3	●	●
7	**Garmin** iQUE 3600	465		⊖	◒	⊖	○	○		23	●			3.7	●	●
8	**palmOne** Zire 31	150		○	○	◒	○	○	●	14	●			2.6		●
9	**palmOne** Zire 21	100		○	○	○	○	○	●	7.3				2.7		
	POCKET PC MODELS															
10	**ASUS** MyPal A716	395		⊖	⊖	⊖	⊜	⊖		56	●	●	●	3.5	●	●
11	**Hewlett-Packard** iPAQ h4355	395		○	⊖	⊖	⊖	⊖		57	●	●	●	3.5	●	●
12	**Hewlett-Packard** iPAQ rx3715	445		○	⊖	○	⊜	⊖	●	57	●	●	●	3.5	●	●
13	**Dell** Axim X50v	500		○	○	⊖	⊜	⊖		62	●	●	●	3.7	●	●
14	**ASUS** MyPal A620BT	310		○	⊖	⊖	⊖	⊖	●	55	●		●	3.5	●	●
15	**Dell** Axim X50 416 MHZ	300		○	⊖	○	⊜	⊖		63	●	●	●	3.5	●	●
16	**Hewlett-Packard** iPAQ hx2415	435		○	⊖	○	⊜	⊖		60	●	●	●	3.5	●	●
17	**Dell** Axim X30 312 MHZ (non-wireless)	170		○	⊖	○	⊖	⊖	●	31	●	●		3.5	●	●
18	**Hewlett-Packard** iPAQ h2215	350		○	○	○	⊖	⊖	●	57	●	●	●	3.6	●	●
19	**Hewlett-Packard** iPAQ rz1715	225		○	○	○	○	⊖	●	27	●			3.5	●	●

See report, page 134. Based on tests posted to ConsumerReports.org in July 2005, with updated prices and availability.

Guide to the Ratings

Overall score is based primarily on ease of use, battery life, and display. **Ease of use** considers overall design, navigation, and built-in software. **Battery life** is how long fully charged models lasted with continuous use. (For battery life and display, we scored monochrome and color models differently.) For color units: ⊜ 15 hours or more; ⊖ 8 to 15 hours; ○ 4 to 8 hours; ◒ less than 4 hours. **Display** is readability in low and normal room light and in sunlight. **Convenience** considers battery type, expansion capability, and software. **In sync** indicates how easily the PDA can be synchronized with a computer. **Price** is approximate retail.

Quick Picks

For a basic organizer at a good price:

3 palmOne, $250
15 Dell, $300

The palmOne and the Dell are well-priced yet offer plenty. Both have Bluetooth capability and let you view pictures, listen to music, and see daily tasks at a glance. The palmOne Tungsten E2 retains all of your data automatically in its nonvolatile memory, even when the battery has drained completely. The Dell Axim X50 series includes a task-switcher program that lets you manage multiple tasks better than other Pocket PCs, and it supports multiple memory cards. Another unit, the palmOne Zire 21 (9), is the only monochrome unit tested. It's low-priced and fine for to-do lists and contacts.

For a full-featured Palm OS unit:

1 palmOne, $500
2 palmOne, $360

The palmOne LifeDrive (1) is the closest thing we've seen to a "laptop replacement" in a PDA. It has an internal 3.7GB hard drive and lets you view and store photos, listen to music, manage e-mail, and edit documents and spreadsheets. You can access the hard drive via a desktop computer. Like the LifeDrive, the palmOne Tungsten T5 (2) combines the versatility of typical Palm OS models with the drag-and-drop convenience of the Pocket PC. It has 64 MB of user memory, plus another 161 MB that a connected Windows computer can recognize as an external drive. Both models have Bluetooth capability, and the LifeDrive has Wi-Fi as well.

For a Windows look and feel in a PDA:

11 Hewlett-Packard, $395
13 Dell, $500

The Hewlett-Packard is well-designed and has Wi-Fi and Bluetooth capability. It squeezes a usable keyboard and easily readable display into a slim case. The Dell Axim X50v (13) is similar to the Dell Axim X50 416 MHZ (15) but has a faster processor, more nonvolatile memory, and a larger display that is very readable, even in bright sunlight. It also has both Wi-Fi and Bluetooth capability.

For a portable navigation system:

7 Garmin, $465

The Garmin iQUE 3600 is the only unit tested to include a GPS-equipped navigation system. It was easy to use, though its battery life was lacking.

Recommendations

PALM OS MODELS

1 **palmOne** LifeDrive Very good. A worthy laptop replacement for travelers. Combines the ease of use of Palm OS with the drag-and-drop convenience of Pocket PC. Easily readable display. Overall design better than most, and basic organizer functions easy to use. Has picture viewer, expense tracker, eBook Reader, and LED alarm. Can record voice memos. But too bulky to fit in a shirt pocket. Doesn't include backup program. New e-mail program is less reliable than previous versions. 3.7GB hard drive for storage. 6.8 oz.

2 **palmOne** Tungsten T5 Very good. Combines the ease of use of Palm OS with the drag-and-drop convenience of Pocket PC. Overall design better than most, and basic organizer functions easy to use. Has picture viewer, expense tracker, and eBook Reader. Office software installed in ROM. But too bulky to fit in a shirt pocket. Doesn't include backup program. 161 MB flash memory for storage. 5.2 oz.

3 **palmOne** Tungsten E2 Very good. Overall design better than most, and basic organizer functions easy to use. All memory is nonvolatile, which prevents data loss even if battery dies. Fits easily in a shirt pocket. Has picture viewer, expense tracker, and eBook Reader. Doesn't include backup program. 26 MB flash memory for storage. 4.7 oz.

4 **palmOne** Tungsten C Very good; a fine choice for viewing and editing documents, accessing e-mail, and wireless Web surfing. Has one of the most readable screens we've seen, plus picture viewer, expense tracker, eBook reader, and LED and vibrating alarms. Basic organizer functions easy to use. But too bulky to fit in a shirt pocket. Doesn't include backup program. 6.3 oz.

5 **palmOne** Zire 72 Good. Overall design better than most, and basic organizer functions easy to use. Fits easily in a shirt pocket. Has picture viewer, expense tracker, eBook Reader, and LED alarm. Can record voice memos. Doesn't include backup program. 4.8 oz.

6 **palmOne** TungstenE Good. A fine choice for Palm users looking to upgrade. Easily readable display. Improved datebook software lets you see daily tasks at a glance. Basic organizer functions easy to use. Has expense-tracker software, picture viewer, and eBook reader. Fits easily in a shirt pocket. Doesn't include backup program. Battery life not as good as most others tested. 4.6 oz.

7 **GARMIN** iQUE 3600 Good. A good organizer with GPS capability. Well-conceived design, with large, easily readable display. Basic organizer functions easy to use, and user interface better than most. Has handy jog dial, eBook reader, and LED and vibrating alarms. Can record voice memos. Lacks e-mail and backup software. Not much battery life for GPS functionality. Too bulky to fit in a shirt pocket. 5.8 oz.

8 **palmOne** Zire 31 Good overall, though display is difficult to read. Basic organizer functions easy to use. Fits easily in a shirt pocket. Has picture viewer, expense tracker, and eBook Reader. But doesn't include backup program or e-mail program. 4.1 oz.

9 **palmOne** Zire 21 Good, but there are better choices. Basic organizer functions easy to use. Fits easily in a shirt pocket. Has expense tracker and eBook reader. But doesn't include e-mail or backup programs. Disappointing battery life for a monochrome-display PDA. Display lacks backlight and is difficult to read. No external memory card. 3.9 oz.

Recommendations

POCKET PC MODELS

10 ASUS MyPal A716 Very good; a fine choice if you want to add peripherals. Overall design better than most, with easily readable display. User interface better than most. Has picture viewer, eBook reader, printed manual, and LED alarm. Can record voice memos. But too bulky to fit in a shirt pocket. 25 MB flash memory for storage. 7.2 oz.

11 HEWLETT-PACKARD iPAQ h4355 Very good; a fine organizer with laptop-like functionality and an easily readable display. Slim case design incorporates many features. User interface better than most. Has built-in keyboard, picture viewer, eBook reader, and LED alarm. Can record voice memos. But too bulky to fit in a shirt pocket. 3 MB flash memory for storage. 5.9 oz. Similar model: iPAQ h4350.

12 HEWLETT-PACKARD iPAQ rx3715 Very good. Overall design and user interface better than most, and basic organizer functions easy to use. Has picture viewer and LED alarm. Can record voice memos. Fits easily in a shirt pocket. 96 MB flash memory for storage. 5.7 oz. Similar model: iPAQ rx3115.

13 DELL AXIM X50v Very good, with a display that's easily readable even in bright sunlight. User interface better than most. Has picture viewer, printed manual, and LED alarm. Can record voice memos. 91 MB flash memory for storage. 6 oz.

14 ASUS MyPal A620BT Very good, with easily readable display. User interface better than most. Fits easily in a shirt pocket. Has picture viewer, eBook reader, printed manual, and LED alarm. Can record voice memos. 31 MB flash memory for storage. 5.2 oz. Similar model: ASUS MyPal A620.

15 DELL Axim X50 416 MHZ Very good. User interface better than most. Has picture viewer, printed manual, and LED alarm. Can record voice memos. 31 MB flash memory for storage. 5.7 oz. Similar model: Dell Axim X50 520 MHZ.

16 HEWLETT-PACKARD iPAQ hx2415 Very good. Overall design better than most, and basic organizer functions easy to use. Has picture viewer and LED alarm. Can record voice memos. But too bulky to fit in a shirt pocket. 22 MB flash memory for storage. 6.1 oz. Similar model: Hewlett-Packard iPAQ hx2410.

17 DELL Axim X30 312 MHZ (nonwireless) Very good, with a better user interface than most. Fits easily in a shirt pocket. Has LED alarm, printed manual, and picture viewer. Can record voice memos. 3 MB flash memory for storage. 4.7 oz. Similar models: Dell Axim X30 624 MHz, Dell Axim X30 312 MHZ (Wi-Fi).

18 HEWLETT-PACKARD iPAQ h2215 Good, with a lot of capability in a small case; a fine choice if you want to add peripherals. User interface better than most. Basic organizer functions easy to use. Fits easily in a shirt pocket. Has picture viewer and eBook reader. Can record voice memos. 4 MB flash memory for storage. 5.1 oz.

19 HEWLETT-PACKARD iPAQ rz1715 Good, with a better user interface than most. Fits easily in a shirt pocket. Has LED alarm and picture viewer. Can record voice memos. But doesn't include backup program. 10 MB flash memory for storage. 4.4 oz.

PRINTERS

A standard inkjet remains the best all-purpose printer, and one model, the Canon Pixma iP8500, has even outpaced the inkjet-based 4x6 photo printers for snapshot speed. Multifunction inkjets are worth a look if you need to fit multiple functions into a small space. And 4x6 printers are best for the casual digital-camera user who cares more for convenience and speed than for print quality and flexibility.

There's no connection between price and print quality. The CR Best Buy Canon has low per-page costs. Supplies can make even low-priced units costly to own over time.

The Ratings rank models by performance. Quick Picks highlights models you might consider first based on how they scored and on other factors, such as price and features.

Excellent | Very good | Good | Fair | Poor

Within types, in performance order. Gray key numbers indicate Quick Picks.

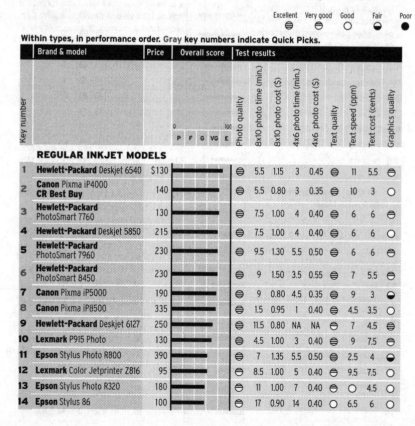

Key number	Brand & model	Price	Overall score (0–100; P F G VG E)	Photo quality	8x10 photo time (min.)	8x10 photo cost ($)	4x6 photo time (min.)	4x6 photo cost ($)	Text quality	Text speed (ppm)	Text cost (cents)	Graphics quality
	REGULAR INKJET MODELS											
1	**Hewlett-Packard** Deskjet 6540	$130		Excellent	5.5	1.15	3	0.45	Excellent	11	5.5	Very good
2	**Canon** Pixma iP4000 **CR Best Buy**	140		Excellent	5.5	0.80	3	0.35	Excellent	10	3	Good
3	**Hewlett-Packard** PhotoSmart 7760	130		Excellent	7.5	1.00	4	0.40	Excellent	6	6	Very good
4	**Hewlett-Packard** Deskjet 5850	215		Excellent	7.5	1.00	4	0.40	Excellent	6	6	Good
5	**Hewlett-Packard** PhotoSmart 7960	230		Excellent	9.5	1.30	5.5	0.50	Excellent	6	6	Very good
6	**Hewlett-Packard** PhotoSmart 8450	230		Excellent	9	1.50	3.5	0.55	Excellent	7	5.5	Very good
7	**Canon** Pixma iP5000	190		Excellent	9	0.80	4.5	0.35	Excellent	9	3	Fair
8	**Canon** Pixma iP8500	335		Excellent	1.5	0.95	1	0.40	Excellent	4.5	3.5	Good
9	**Hewlett-Packard** Deskjet 6127	250		Excellent	11.5	0.80	NA	NA	Very good	7	4.5	Excellent
10	**Lexmark** P915 Photo	130		Excellent	4.5	1.00	3	0.40	Excellent	9	7.5	Very good
11	**Epson** Stylus Photo R800	390		Excellent	7	1.35	5.5	0.50	Excellent	2.5	4	Fair
12	**Lexmark** Color Jetprinter Z816	95		Very good	8.5	1.00	5	0.40	Very good	9.5	7.5	Good
13	**Epson** Stylus Photo R320	180		Very good	11	1.00	7	0.40	Very good	Good	4.5	Good
14	**Epson** Stylus 86	100		Very good	17	0.90	14	0.40	Good	6.5	6	Good

Key number	Brand & model	Price	Overall score (0–100; P F G VG E)	Photo quality	8x10 photo time (min.)	8x10 photo cost ($)	4x6 photo time (min.)	4x6 photo cost ($)	Text quality	Text speed (ppm)	Text cost (cents)	Graphics quality
	REGULAR INKJET MODELS *continued*											
15	**Epson** Stylus Photo R200	$100		⊜	11	1.00	7	0.40	○	2.5	4.5	○
16	**Epson** Stylus Photo R300M	150		⊜	11	1.00	7.5	0.40	○	2.5	4.5	○
	MULTIFUNCTION INKJET MODELS											
17	**Hewlett-Packard** PhotoSmart 2710	390		⊖	5.5	1.15	3	0.45	⊜	9	5.5	⊖
18	**Canon** Pixma All in One MP780	300		⊜	6	0.80	3	0.35	⊜	10	3	○
19	**Hewlett-Packard** PSC 1350	120		⊜	20.5	1.00	10.5	0.40	⊜	5.5	6	⊖
20	**Canon** MultiPASS MP370	150		⊖	6.5	0.85	4	0.35	⊜	8	6.5	⊖
21	**Hewlett-Packard** PSC 1315	100		⊖	20	1.00	10.5	0.40	⊜	6	6	⊖
22	**Dell** Photo All in One 962	130		⊜	8.5	1.00	4.5	0.40	⊜	10.5	8	⊖
23	**Epson** Stylus Photo RX500	235		⊜	10	1.00	7	0.40	⊖	3	4.5	○
24	**Lexmark** X5270	100		⊜	8.5	1.00	5	0.40	⊖	9	7.5	◒
25	**Epson** Stylus All in One CX6600	195		⊖	17.5	0.90	7.5	0.35	⊖	6.5	4	○
26	**Lexmark** P6250 Photo	160		⊜	4.5	1.00	3	0.40	⊜	3	7.5	⊖
27	**Epson** Stylus CX4600	110		○	20	0.85	14.5	0.35	⊖	3	7.5	○
	4X6 PHOTO MODELS											
28	**Hewlett-Packard** PhotoSmart 245	190		⊜	NA	NA	2.5	0.35	0	NA	NA	0
29	**Hewlett-Packard** PhotoSmart 375	190		⊜	NA	NA	1.5	0.35	0	NA	NA	0
30	**Canon** Selphy CP400	150		⊖	NA	NA	1.5	0.50	0	NA	NA	0
31	**Sony** Picturestation DPP-EX50	175		⊖	NA	NA	1	0.45	0	NA	NA	0
32	**Sony** DPP-FP30	150		⊖	NA	NA	1.5	0.40	0	NA	NA	0
33	**Olympus** P-10 Digital Photo Printer	140		⊖	NA	NA	1	0.60	0	NA	NA	0
34	**Canon** Selphy DS700	185		○	NA	NA	1.5	0.55	0	NA	NA	0
35	**Epson** PictureMate	200		⊖	NA	NA	2.5	0.20	0	NA	NA	0
36	**Dell** Photo Printer 540	130		○	NA	NA	1	0.50	0	NA	NA	0
37	**Lexmark** P315	130		○	NA	NA	3	0.30	0	NA	NA	0
38	**Polaroid** PP46d Digital Photo Printer	210		⊖	NA	NA	3	0.60	0	NA	NA	0
39	**Kodak** EasyShare Printer Dock Plus	185		○	NA	NA	1	0.55	0	NA	NA	0

Excellent ⊜ Very good ⊖ Good ○ Fair ◒ Poor ●

Within types, in performance order. Gray **key numbers indicate Quick Picks.**

Key number	Brand & model	Price	Overall score (0–100; P F G VG E)	Photo quality	8x10 photo time (min.)	8x10 photo cost ($)	4x6 photo time (min.)	4x6 photo cost ($)	Text quality	Text speed (ppm)	Text cost (cents)	Graphics quality
	4X6 PHOTO MODELS *continued*											
40	**Kodak** EasyShare Printer Dock	$140		○	NA	NA	2	0.55	0	NA	NA	0
41	**Olympus** P-S100	200		○	NA	NA	1.5	0.60	0	NA	NA	0
42	**Canon** CP-330	255		○	NA	NA	1.5	0.50	0	NA	NA	0

See report, page 136. Based on tests in Consumer Reports in May 2005, with updated prices and availability.

Guide to the Ratings

Overall score is based mainly on speed and text/photo quality. For multifunction models, only printing is scored. **Photo quality** reflects a color snapshot's appearance. **8x10 time** measures, to the nearest half-minute, the time to print an 8x10-inch color photo at the best-quality setting. **4x6 time** measures the time to print a borderless 4x6-inch color photo. **Text quality** is for clarity and crispness of black text. **Text speed** measures pages per minute (ppm) for a 10-page document at default settings. **Graphics quality** assesses output such as greeting cards and charts. **Cost** is estimated for one black text page (for ink and plain paper), one 8x10-inch color photo (ink and glossy 8½x11-inch paper), or one 4x6-inch color photo (ink or, for dye-sublimation 4x6 printers, ribbon and glossy 4x6-inch paper). **Price** is approximate retail. All but one model print borderless photos.

All tested models work with Windows XP and 2000; all but the Dell (22, 36) support Windows ME and 98; most support Mac OS. All standard-size printers can hold at least 100 sheets or 10 envelopes; the 4x6 photo printers hold at least 20 ready-cut, 4x6-inch photo sheets.

Quick Picks

Top choices if you frequently print text and photos:

1 Hewlett-Packard, $130

2 Canon, $140 **CR Best Buy**

Consider the Hewlett-Packard Deskjet 6540 and the Canon Pixma iP4000 for fast, first-rate photos and text. The Canon's low cost-per-page makes it a good value if you print lots of text. Neither supports memory cards, but the Canon accepts images via cable from cameras supporting the PictBridge standard.

Smart choices for photographers:

3 Hewlett-Packard, $130

6 Hewlett-Packard, $230

8 Canon, $335

Excellent photos, memory-card support, PictBridge, and an LCD for previewing and cropping make the Hewlett-Packard

Quick Picks

PhotoSmart 7760 (3) and the Hewlett-Packard PhotoSmart 8450 (6) good choices for camera buffs. None of the tested inkjets, including 4x6-inch models, could match the speed of the Canon Pixma iP8500, which produced excellent photos. The Canon holds eight ink cartridges. The HP 8450 holds three multicolor cartridges; the 7760, two. For the best-quality photos from both models, HP recommends swapping out the black-ink cartridge for photo ink. Some users may find this inconvenient.

For printing limited to 4x6 photos:

28 Hewlett-Packard, $190
29 Hewlett-Packard, $190

Overall, standard-sized inkjets produced better photos and cost less to buy and use than printers limited to 4x6 snapshots. The Hewlett-Packard PhotoSmart 245 (28) and Hewlett-Packard PhotoSmart 375 (29) were the only 4x6 printers to receive an excellent score for photo quality. Photo quality for the 245 was slightly better, but the newer 375 offers PictBridge support, a trimmer package, and faster printing. Another inkjet, the Epson PictureMate (35), costs only 20 cents per photo but scored lower in photo quality. If print speed is paramount, consider the Sony Picturestation DPP-EX50 (31), among the highest-rated dye-sublimation models.

For a multifunction printer:

17 Hewlett-Packard, $390
18 Canon, $300

While relatively pricey, the Hewlett-Packard and Canon were the best all-around performers among multifunction models, with fine text and photo printing at high speeds. Both feature a built-in fax modem, as does the Dell Photo All in One 962 (22). But the Canon offers the best text and 8x10-inch photo costs of its category. Both the 1,200-dot-per-inch HP and the 2,400-dpi Canon were judged very good for scan quality and speed.

RANGES

You'll find style and performance at a reasonable price among the nearly 50 ranges we tested. Several $400 to $800 stoves outcooked much pricier models, yet offer stainless trim, dual elements, and other features. Spending more buys more style, convection, and, for gas ranges, burners rated at 15,000 Btu/hr. and above.

More firepower doesn't necessarily mean better cooking. Pro-style models such as the Viking (35, 47, 48), DCS (37), and Dacor (46) were among the lower scorers, despite their high-heat burners. Our survey data also show that Viking and Thermador gas ranges and Dacor dual-fuel models have been repair-prone.

The Ratings list models by overall performance. Quick Picks highlights models that deliver performance and value.

Excellent ⊜ Very good ⊖ Good ○ Fair ◒ Poor ●

Within types, in performance order. Gray key numbers indicate Quick Picks.

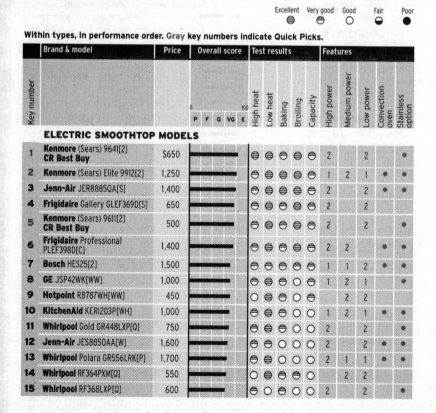

Key number	Brand & model	Price	Overall score (0–100; P F G VG E)	Test results: High heat	Low heat	Baking	Broiling	Capacity	Features: High power	Medium power	Low power	Convection oven	Stainless option
	ELECTRIC SMOOTHTOP MODELS												
1	**Kenmore** (Sears) 9641[2] **CR Best Buy**	$650		Excellent	Excellent	Very good	Excellent	Very good	2		2		●
2	**Kenmore** (Sears) Elite 9912[2]	1,250		Very good	Excellent	Excellent	Excellent	Very good	1	2	1	●	●
3	**Jenn-Air** JER8885QA[S]	1,400		Very good	Excellent	Excellent	Excellent	Very good	2		2	●	●
4	**Frigidaire** Gallery GLEF369D[S]	650		Very good	Excellent	Very good	Excellent	Very good	2		2		
5	**Kenmore** (Sears) 9611[2] **CR Best Buy**	500		Very good	Excellent	Very good	Excellent	Very good	2		2		●
6	**Frigidaire** Professional PLEF398D[C]	1,400		Very good	Excellent	Very good	Excellent	Very good	2	2		●	●
7	**Bosch** HES25[2]	1,500		Very good	Very good	Very good	Very good	Very good	1	1	2	●	●
8	**GE** JSP42WK[WW]	1,000		Very good	Excellent	Very good	Good	Very good	1	2	1		●
9	**Hotpoint** RB787WH[WW]	450		Good	Excellent	Very good	Good	Very good		2	2		
10	**KitchenAid** KERI203P[WH]	1,000		Very good	Excellent	Very good	Good	Good	1	2	1	●	●
11	**Whirlpool** Gold GR448LXP[Q]	750		Very good	Excellent	Very good	Good	Good	2		2		●
12	**Jenn-Air** JES8850AA[W]	1,600		Very good	Very good	Good	Good	Good	2		2	●	●
13	**Whirlpool** Polara GR556LRK[P]	1,700		Very good	Excellent	Good	Good	Good	2	1	1	●	●
14	**Whirlpool** RF364PXM[Q]	550		Good	Excellent	Very good	Very good	Good		2	2		
15	**Whirlpool** RF368LXP[Q]	600		Very good	Good	Very good	Good	Good	2		2		●

Key number	Brand & model	Price	Overall score (0–100; P F G VG E)	Test results: High heat	Low heat	Baking	Broiling	Capacity	Features: High power	Medium power	Low power	Convection oven	Stainless option
	ELECTRIC SMOOTHTOP MODELS *continued*												
16	**Sharp** Insight KB-3300J[W]	$1,300		⊖	⊖	⊖	○	◒	1	1	2		•
17	**Viking** VESC306-4B[SS]	4,000		⊖	⊜	⊖	○	◒	1	2	1	•	•
	ELECTRIC-COIL MODELS												
18	**Kenmore** (Sears) 9421[2] **CR Best Buy**	530		⊖	⊜	⊖	⊜	⊜	2		2		•
19	**GE** JBP35WH[WW]	450		⊖	⊜	○	⊜	⊜	2		2		•
20	**Hotpoint** RB757WH[WW] **CR Best Buy**	450		⊖	⊜	⊖	○	⊖	2		2		
21	**Maytag** MER5555QA[W]	525		○	⊜	⊖	⊖	⊖	2		2		
	GAS MODELS												
22	**Hotpoint** RGB745WEH[WW] **CR Best Buy**	550		○	⊜	⊖	⊜	⊖	1	2	1		
23	**GE** JGBP85WEJ[WW]	850		⊖	⊖	⊖	⊖	⊖	1	2	1		•
24	**Thermador** PG304BS	4,100		⊖	⊜	○	⊖	⊖	4			•	•
25	**GE** Profile JGBP918WEK1[WW] [1]	1,600		⊖	⊜	⊖	○	⊖	1	2	2	•	•
26	**Jenn-Air** JGS8750AD[W]	1,500		⊖	⊖	⊖	⊜	○	1	2	1		•
27	**Maytag** MGR5875QD[W]	1,150		○	⊖	⊖	⊖	⊖	2	2	1	•	•
28	**Whirlpool** Gold GS470LEM[Q]	1,000		○	⊜	○	⊖	⊖	2	1	1		
29	**Whirlpool** SF368LEP[Q]	600		○	⊜	⊖	○	⊖	1	2	1		•
30	**Frigidaire** Gallery GLGF386D[S]	700		⊖	⊖	⊖	○	⊖	2	2	1	•	•
31	**Maytag** MGR5751AD[W] [D]	550		○	⊜	⊖	○	⊖	1	3			•
32	**Frigidaire** FGF366D[S]	700		⊖	⊖	⊖	○	⊖	1	3			•
33	**GE** Profile JGB900WEF[WW]	1,000		○	○	⊖	⊖	⊖	1	2	1		•
34	**Kenmore** (Sears) 7881[2]	900		○	○	⊖	○	○	2	2	1		•
35	**Viking** VGSC3064B[SS]	3,900		⊜	◒	⊖	⊜	◒	4			•	•
36	**Bosch** HGS25[2]	1,550		○	○	⊖	⊖	⊖	2	1	1	•	•
37	**DCS** RGSC-305	3,700		⊖	⊜	⊖	○	○	5			•	•
38	**Kenmore** (Sears) Elite 7936[2]	1,350		○	○	⊜	○	○	2	2	1	•	•
39	**GE** JGBP26WEH[WW]	750		○	●	⊖	⊖	⊖		4			
	DUAL-FUEL MODELS												
40	**KitchenAid** KDRP407H[SS]	3,400		⊜	⊖	⊜	⊜	○	4			•	•
41	**GE** Profile J2B918WEK1[WW] [1] **CR Best Buy**	1,700		⊖	⊜	⊖	○	⊖	1	2	2	•	•

Excellent / Very good / Good / Fair / Poor

Within types, in performance order. Gray key numbers indicate Quick Picks.

Key number	Brand & model	Price	Overall score (0–100; P F G VG E)	Test results: High heat	Low heat	Baking	Broiling	Capacity	Features: High power	Medium power	Low power	Convection oven	Stainless option
	DUAL-FUEL MODELS												
42	**Jenn-Air** JDS8850AA[S]	$2,150		Good	Excellent	Good	Very good	Good	1	2	1	•	•
43	**Kenmore** (Sears) Elite 7938[2] **CR Best Buy**	1,550		Very good	Good	Very good	Very good	Good	2	2	1	•	•
44	**Wolf** DF304	5,200		Good	Very good	Very good	Very good	Good	3	1		•	•
45	**Jenn-Air** JDS9860AA[W]	2,000		Fair	Very good	Very good	Excellent	Good		4		•	•
46	**Dacor** ERD30S06[BK]	3,800		Good	Excellent	Very good	Fair	Good	4			•	•
47	**Viking** VDSC3054B[SS]	3,800		Good	Excellent	Good	Very good	Fair	4			•	•
48	**Viking** VDSC3074B[SS]	4,000		Good	Excellent	Good	Very good	Fair	4			•	•

[1] *Has dual ovens.*

See report, page 67. Based on tests in Consumer Reports in November 2005.

Guide to the Ratings

Overall score reflects cooktop performance, oven capacity, baking, broiling, and self-cleaning, as well as surface temperature and other safety issues. **High heat** denotes how quickly the highest-powered cooktop element or burner heated water to near-boiling. **Low heat** reflects how well the lowest-powered cooktop element or burner melted and held chocolate without scorching and how well the most powerful element or burner, set on low, held tomato sauce below a boil. Oven **capacity** is our measurement of usable space. **Baking** reflects whether cakes and cookies baked on two racks were evenly browned. **Broiling** denotes even browning of a pan of burgers and high-heat searing ability. We also evaluated self-cleaning; scores were good or better except for the Vikings (17, 47, 48), DCS (37), GE Profile (41), and Wolf (44), which were fair. **High** is more than 2,000 watts for electric, 11,000 Btu/hr. for gas. **Medium:** more than 1,500 to 2,000 watts for electric, more than 6,500 to 11,000 Btu/hr. for gas. **Low:** 1,500 watts or less for electric, 6,500 Btu/hr. or less for gas. **Price** is approximate retail. Under **brand and model,** brackets show color codes. **All tested ranges:** Are 30 inches wide. Have a self-cleaning oven and oven light. Note that scores have changed since our last report because of a change in our test benchmarks for heating speed.

Quick Picks

ELECTRIC RANGES

Best for most; fine performance at relatively low price; all are CR Best Buys:

1 Kenmore, $650
5 Kenmore, $500
18 Kenmore, $530
20 Hotpoint, $450

Both Kenmore smoothtops (1, 5) have dual elements. The Kenmore (1) has a warming element, a warming drawer, and faster heating. Among coil-tops, a larger oven and better broiling set the Kenmore (18) apart from the Hotpoint (20).

For added style:

2 Kenmore, $1,250

Paying more for the Kenmore buys you convection, a warming drawer, and a triple element with up to 2,700 watts, along with superb baking and broiling.

GAS RANGES

Best for most; performance and value:

22 Hotpoint, $550, **CR Best Buy**
23 GE, $850

The high-scoring Hotpoint is our top pick among gas ranges for high performance at a no-frills price. Paying more for the GE buys you faster heating, continuous cast-iron grates, a warming drawer, and available stainless-steel trim.

DUAL-FUEL RANGES

For a gas cooktop and electric oven, two CR Best Buys:

41 GE, $1,700
43 Kenmore, $1,550

Both of these premium models include high-end features such as continuous cast-iron grates and convection for far less than most dual-fuel ranges. Between the two, the GE provided better simmering and a second oven for cooking two dishes at different temperatures. The Kenmore delivered better broiling and oven cleaning in our tests.

Brand Repair History

Gas ranges and dual-fuel ranges

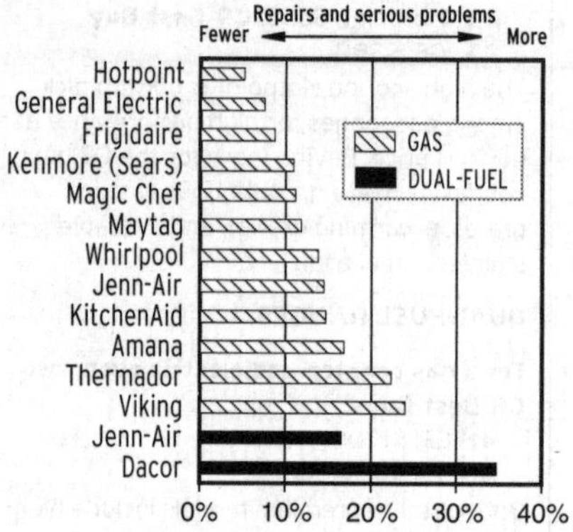

Electric ranges

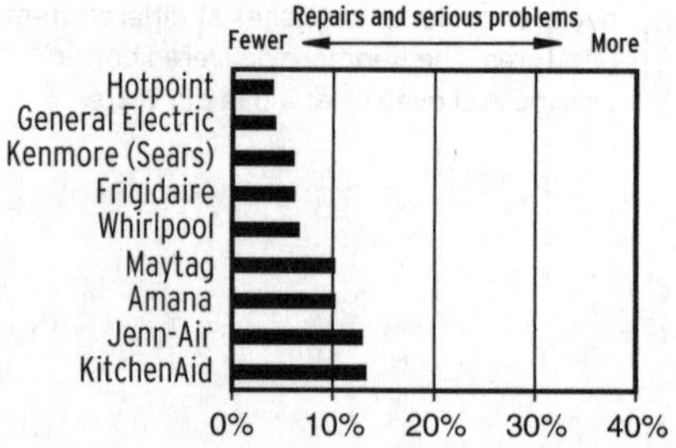

Based on more than 78,000 responses to our 2004 Annual Questionnaire, representing 49,702 electric ranges and 28,426 gas and dual-fuel ranges. Data have been standardized to eliminate differences linked to age. For electric ranges, differences of less than 3 points aren't meaningful. For gas and dual-fuel ranges, differences of less than 4 points aren't meaningful. Because gas and electric ranges were analyzed separately, results can't be compared. Repair rates for different models may vary, and changes in design and manufacture can affect reliability.

Choosing a brand with a good repair history can improve your odds of getting a reliable range. Don't look to price as an indicator of reliability, judging by the experiences of our subscribers. Several high-priced brands in the survey had more repairs than most. Jenn-Air and KitchenAid were the most repair-prone electric ranges. Among gas ranges, Thermador and Viking were the most trouble-prone. Dacor dual-fuel ranges were by far the most repair-prone of any type of range. We've experienced problems ourselves with some of the Viking and Dacor ranges we've purchased for testing.

We have enough data to comment only on Dacor and Jenn-Air dual-fuel ranges, but data we've collected on other brands suggest that dual-fuel models as a group have tended to be slightly more repair-prone than gas models. If you are considering a dual-fuel range, note that GE, Kenmore, and Frigidaire have been reliable brands of gas and electric ranges, and the limited data we have on their dual-fuel models do not suggest major repair issues to date.

The graphs show the percentage of gas, dual-fuel, and electric ranges bought new between 2000 and early 2004 that were ever repaired or had a serious problem that wasn't repaired.

REFRIGERATORS

Nearly any refrigerator will keep your milk chilled and your ice cream frozen. Top-scoring models of each type tend to deliver the most even, consistent temperatures while often providing more energy efficiency and usable space. Some of the best of these models also cost less than many lower-scoring performers and include adjustable, spill-proof glass shelves, pull-out bins and shelves in the fridge and freezer, and filtered water dispensers. But you'll typically pay extra for added storage flexibility and stainless or faux-stainless finishes (about $200).

The Ratings rank models by performance, within types. Check Quick Picks for models that offer lots of performance, features, and other strengths for the price. You'll find them arranged by width, since most refrigerators are bought as replacements to fit a specific space.

Excellent ⊜ Very good ⊖ Good ○ Fair ◒ Poor ●

Within types, in performance order. Gray key numbers indicate Quick Picks.

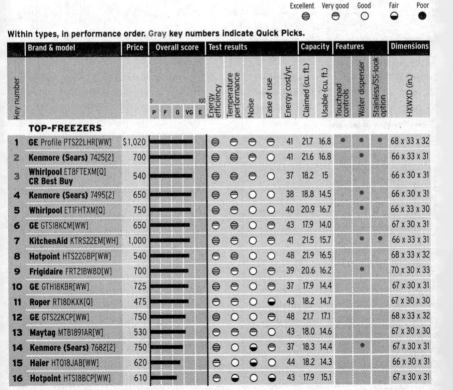

Key number	Brand & model	Price	Overall score (0–100; P F G VG E)	Test results: Energy efficiency	Temperature performance	Noise	Ease of use	Energy cost/yr.	Capacity: Claimed (cu. ft.)	Usable (cu. ft.)	Features: Touchpad controls	Water dispenser	Stainless/SS-look option	Dimensions: HXWXD (in.)
	TOP-FREEZERS													
1	**GE** Profile PTS22LHR[WW]	$1,020		Excellent	Very good	Very good	Very good	41	21.7	16.8	●	●	●	68 x 33 x 32
2	**Kenmore (Sears)** 7425[2]	700		Excellent	Excellent	Very good	Good	41	21.6	16.8		●		66 x 33 x 31
3	**Whirlpool** ET8FTEXM[Q] **CR Best Buy**	540		Excellent	Excellent	Very good	Good	37	18.2	15				66 x 30 x 31
4	**Kenmore (Sears)** 7495[2]	650		Excellent	Very good	Good	Good	38	18.8	14.5		●		66 x 30 x 31
5	**Whirlpool** ET1FHTXM[Q]	750		Excellent	Very good	Good	Good	40	20.9	16.7		●		66 x 33 x 30
6	**GE** GTS18KCM[WW]	650		Very good	Excellent	Good	Very good	43	17.9	14.0				67 x 30 x 31
7	**KitchenAid** KTRS22EM[WH]	1,000		Excellent	Very good	Good	Very good	41	21.5	15.7		●	●	66 x 33 x 31
8	**Hotpoint** HTS22GBP[WW]	540		Very good	Excellent	Good	Good	48	21.9	16.5				68 x 33 x 32
9	**Frigidaire** FRT21BW8D[W]	700		Excellent	Very good	Good	Very good	39	20.6	16.2		●		70 x 30 x 33
10	**GE** GTH18KBR[WW]	725		Excellent	Very good	Good	Very good	37	17.9	14.4				67 x 30 x 31
11	**Roper** RT18DKXK[Q]	475		Very good	Very good	Good	Fair	43	18.2	14.7				67 x 30 x 30
12	**GE** GTS22KCP[WW]	750		Excellent	Good	Good	Very good	48	21.7	17.1				68 x 33 x 32
13	**Maytag** MTB1891AR[W]	530		Very good	Very good	Very good	Good	43	18.0	14.6				67 x 30 x 30
14	**Kenmore (Sears)** 7682[2]	750		Excellent	Good	Fair	Very good	37	18.3	14.4		●		67 x 30 x 31
15	**Haier** HTQ18JAB[WW]	620		Very good	Good	Fair	Good	44	18.2	14.3				66 x 30 x 31
16	**Hotpoint** HTS18BCP[WW]	610		Very good	Fair	Good	Fair	43	17.9	15.1				67 x 30 x 31

Within types, in performance order. Gray key numbers indicate Quick Picks.

Key number	Brand & model	Price	Overall score (0–100; P F G VG E)	Test results: Energy efficiency	Test results: Temperature performance	Test results: Noise	Test results: Ease of use	Test results: Energy cost/yr.	Capacity: Claimed (cu. ft.)	Capacity: Usable (cu. ft.)	Features: Touchpad controls	Features: Water dispenser	Features: Stainless/SS-look option	Dimensions: HXWXD (in.)
BOTTOM-FREEZERS (INCLUDING FRENCH-DOOR MODELS)														
17	**LG** LRFC25750[WW] Note: This product has been recalled.	$1,650		⊜	⊜	⊜	⊖	45	25	17.1	•		•	70 x 36 x 32
18	**Amana** ABB2222DE[W] **CR Best Buy**	980		⊜	⊜	○	⊖	44	21.9	16.5	•		•	70 x 33 x 31
19	**Amana** AFD2535DE[W]	1,650		⊜	⊜	○	⊖	46	25.1	17.5	•	•	•	70 x 36 x 32
20	**Kenmore (Sears)** Elite Trio 7552[2]	1,800		⊜	⊜	○	⊖	46	24.8	18.1	•	•	•	70 x 36 x 32
21	**Kenmore (Sears)** Elite Trio 7554[2] Note: This product has been recalled.	1,800		⊜	⊖	⊜	⊖	45	25.0	16.8	•	•	•	69 x 36 x 32
22	**Maytag** MFF2557HE[W]	1,430		⊜	⊜	○	⊖	46	24.8	16.7	•		•	70 x 36 x 32
23	**Kenmore (Sears)** 7500[2] **CR Best Buy**	750		⊖	⊜	⊖	⊖	47	19.7	15.2	•			68 x 30 x 32
24	**GE** GBS20KBR[WW]	895		⊖	⊜	○	⊖	41	19.5	13.3				68 x 30 x 32
25	**GE** Profile PDS22MCR[WW]	1,375		⊖	⊜	○	⊖	42	22.3	13.9	•			69 x 33 x 33
26	**Kenmore (Sears)** 7528[2]	1,150		⊖	⊜	⊖	⊖	45	22.4	13.7	•		•	69 x 33 x 32
27	**Whirlpool** Gold GB9SHKXM[Q]	855		⊖	⊖	○	⊖	43	18.5	13.1				67 x 30 x 31
28	**Fisher & Paykel** E522B	1,050		○	⊖	⊜	◒	47	17.2	12.8	•		•	67 x 32 x 28
SIDE-BY-SIDES (INCLUDING CABINET-DEPTH MODELS)														
29	**Amana** ASD2628HE[W]	1,350		⊜	⊜	○	⊖	53	25.6	15.8	•	•	•	71 x 36 x 31
30	**GE** GSH25JFR[WW] **CR Best Buy**	1,040		⊖	⊜	⊖	⊖	55	25.0	16.5		•		70 x 36 x 33
31	**Kenmore (Sears)** 5538[2] **CR Best Buy**	1,120		○	⊜	⊖	⊖	52	21.9	13.1	•	•		67 x 33 x 31
32	**Kenmore (Sears)** 5653[2] **CR Best Buy**	1,200		⊖	⊖	⊜	⊖	56	25.4	16.1	•	•	•	70 x 36 x 32
33	**Maytag** MSD2657HE[W]	1,400		⊜	⊖	○	⊖	53	25.6	16	•	•	•	70 x 36 x 31
34	**GE** Profile Arctica PSH23PGR[WW]	2,460		○	⊖	⊜	⊖	53	22.5	13.4	•	•	•	71 x 36 x 28
35	**LG** LRSC26960[TT]	2,050		⊖	⊖	⊜	⊖	51	25.5	14.7	•	•	•	70 x 36 x 34
36	**Maytag** MZD2667HE[W]	1,550		⊖	⊖	⊖	⊖	56	25.6	16.5	•	•	•	71 x 36 x 31
37	**GE** Profile PSS26NGP[WW]	1,850		⊖	⊖	⊖	⊖	56	25.5	16.2	•	•	•	70 x 36 x 33
38	**KitchenAid** KSRS25CN[WH]	1,800		⊖	⊖	⊖	⊖	56	25.4	16.8	•	•	•	70 x 36 x 33
39	**Jenn-Air** JCD2290HE[W]	1,930		⊖	⊜	○	⊖	49	21.6	12.8	•	•	•	71 x 36 x 27
40	**Kenmore (Sears)** 5522[2]	1,350		○	⊜	⊖	⊖	52	21.8	14.1	•	•		67 x 33 x 31
41	**Whirlpool** Gold GC3SHEXN[Q]	2,000		⊖	⊖	⊖	⊜	50	23.1	13.8	•	•	•	69 x 36 x 28

Excellent, Very good, Good, Fair, Poor

Key number	Brand & model	Price	Overall score (0–100; P F G VG E)	Test results: Energy efficiency	Test results: Temperature performance	Test results: Noise	Test results: Ease of use	Test results: Energy cost/yr.	Capacity: Claimed (cu. ft.)	Capacity: Usable (cu. ft.)	Features: Touchpad controls	Features: Water dispenser	Features: Stainless/SS-look option	Dimensions: HXWXD (in.)
SIDE-BY-SIDES (INCLUDING CABINET-DEPTH MODELS)														
42	**Amana** ASD2624HE[W]	$1,100		Very good	Very good	Good	Very good	56	25.6	16.1		•		71 x 36 x 31
43	**LG** LRSC26980[TT]	3,200		Very good	Very good	Very good	Very good	55	25.3	14.5	•	•	•	70 x 36 x 34
44	**Frigidaire** Gallery GHSC239D[W]	1,790		Very good	Very good	Very good	Very good	53	22.6	13.9	•	•		70 x 36 x 28
45	**GE** Profile Artica PSC25PSS[SS]	3,200		Good	Very good	Very good	Very good	55	24.6	13.3	•	•	•	72 x 36 x 28
46	**Kenmore (Sears)** 5470[3]	1,050		Excellent	Very good	Very good	Good	56	26	17.2		•	•	70 x 36 x 33
47	**KitchenAid** KSRD22FK[WH]	1,300		Very good	Very good	Very good	Very good	52	21.9	13.2		•	•	67 x 33 x 31
48	**KitchenAid** Superba KSCS25IN[WH]	2,400		Very good	Good	Excellent	Excellent	55	24.5	14.9	•	•	•	72 x 36 x 28
49	**Whirlpool** Gold GD5SHAXM[Q]	1,350		Very good	Very good	Good	Very good	56	25.5	16.7		•		70 x 36 x 31
50	**Electrolux** Icon E23CS80D[SS]	2,300		Very good	Very good	Very good	Very good	53	22.6	13.7	•	•	•	70 x 36 x 28
51	**Admiral** LSD2615HE[W]	800		Excellent	Good	Good	Good	56	25.6	17.4		•		71 x 36 x 32
52	**Samsung** RS2534[WW]	990		Very good	Good	Very good	Very good	61	25.2	18.2	•	•		70 x 36 x 33
53	**Hotpoint** HSS25GFP[WW]	850		Good	Very good	Very good	Good	65	25	16.7		•		70 x 36 x 32
54	**Kenmore (Sears)** Elite 4430[2]	2,000		Very good	Good	Very good	Very good	53	22.5	13.3	•	•	•	70 x 36 x 28
55	**Whirlpool** ED2VHGXM[Q]	900		Good	Very good	Good	Very good	52	21.8	12.9		•		67 x 33 x 31
56	**Samsung** Select Series RS2630[WW]	950		Very good	Fair	Excellent	Very good	65	26.0	17.7	•	•	•	70 x 36 x 34
57	**GE** GSS20IEM[WW]	970		Good	Good	Good	Very good	59	19.9	13.3		•		68 x 32 x 32
58	**GE** GSC23LGQ[WW]	1,820		Good	Good	Very good	Very good	62	22.6	13.6	•	•		70 x 36 x 28
BUILT-INS (INCLUDING BOTTOM-FREEZER AND SIDE-BY-SIDE MODELS)														
59	**Sub-Zero** 650/F	4,500		Very good	Excellent	Good	Good	46	20.6	15.4	•		•	84 x 37 x 26
60	**KitchenAid** KSSC42QM[SS]	5,815		Very good	Very good	Excellent	Very good	55	25.3	17.6	•	•	•	84 x 42 x 26
61	**Viking** DFSB423	5,300		Very good	Very good	Very good	Very good	59	24	16.6	•		•	83 x 43 x 25
62	**Jenn-Air** JS42FWD[W]	4,650		Good	Excellent	Very good	Very good	66	26	14.5	•	•	•	84 x 42 x 27
63	**Viking** DFBB363	4,700		Very good	Excellent	Good	Very good	51	20.3	15.0			•	84 x 36 x 25
64	**Thermador** KBUDT4270A	5,280		Good	Very good	Very good	Very good	65	25.2	15.9	•	•	•	84 x 41 x 26
65	**GE** Monogram ZISS420DR[SS]	6,500		Good	Very good	Excellent	Very good	56	26.1	14.9	•	•	•	85 x 43 x 26
66	**GE** Profile PSB42LSR[BV]	6,200		Very good	Good	Very good	Very good	55	25.2	16.6	•	•	•	84 x 42 x 26
67	**Sub-Zero** 650G	6,000		Very good	Excellent	Very good	Fair	52	20.8	15.4	•		•	84 x 36 x 25
68	**Sub-Zero** 680	5,600		Very good	Very good	Good	Very good	63	23.7	16.9	•	•	•	84 x 43 x 26

See report, page 71. Based on tests posted to ConsumerReports.org in July 2005, with updated prices and availability.

Guide to the Ratings

Overall score gives the most weight to energy efficiency and temperature performance, then to noise and ease of use. **Energy efficiency** reflects electricity consumption (as stated on the Energy Guide) per cubic foot of measured usable storage space. **Temperature performance** indicates how a refrigerator performed at different room temperatures, including high heat, and how uniformly it maintained 37 degrees in the main space and 0 degrees in the freezer. **Noise** was gauged by a sound meter and panelists. **Ease of use** assesses features and design including layout, controls, and lighting. **Energy cost/yr.** Is cost in dollars, based on the 2003 average national electricity rate of 8.41 cents/kwh (kilowatt hours). Your cost will vary depending on the rate for electricity in your area. **Claimed (cu. ft.)** is the manufacturer's estimate of the volume, in cubic feet, of interior space. **Usable (cu. ft.)** is the volume, in cubic feet, of usable interior space, based on our measurements. We included ice-makers in the storage measurements for top-freezer and bottom-freezer models, but not for side-by-sides. **Price** is approximate retail price.

Quick Picks

Small; 30 inches wide; both are CR Best Buys:

3 Whirlpool, $540
23 Kenmore (Sears), $750

Among top-freezers, the Whirlpool offers superb performance and ample space for its size and price. Among bottom-freezers, the Kenmore (Sears) is a strong, low-priced performer. While not very spacious, it has half shelves, controlled keepers, and other features. Also consider the top-freezer Kenmore (Sears) 7495[2] (4) if you don't mind a bit more noise.

Midsized; 33 inches wide:

2 Kenmore (Sears), $700
18 Amana, $980, **CR Best Buy**
31 Kenmore (Sears), $1,120

Among top-freezers, the Kenmore (Sears) (2) is relatively spacious, energy-efficient, and well-equipped. The bottom-freezer Amana delivers fine performance and value, though it's relatively noisy. Its bottom freezer has a door plus pull-out bins inside. The Kenmore (Sears) (31) is a top performer among side-by-side models and features a digital temperature display, though its energy efficiency is unexceptional.

Large; 36 inches wide:

17 LG, $1,650
30 GE, $1,040
32 Kenmore (Sears), $1,200, **CR Best Buy**
34 GE, $2,460
41 Whirlpool, $2,000

The bottom-freezer LG is especially quiet and has curved-front French doors for the refrigerator and a full-extension freezer drawer. However, we have no repair history for this brand. Models sold between May 2004 and May 2005 were subject to a recall. Features include a temperature-controlled meatkeeper and digital temperature displays. Among side-by-side models, the GE (30) was among the best for temperature performance and is a fine value. The side-by-side Kenmore (Sears) (32) did nearly as well and is especially quiet, with a removable freezer-door bin for easy access to ice. Willing to pay more for cabinet-depth? The GE (34) and Whirlpool Gold include through-the-door ice and water, a temperature-controlled meatkeeper, and digital displays of temperature and settings for fridge and

Quick Picks

freezer. The GE was quiet, but has a smallish freezer. The Whirlpool has a bit less space in the fridge but more in the freezer, along with a removal freezer-door bin. Built-in models cost even more and, as a group, appear to be more repair-prone than free-standing units (we have enough survey data to comment only on Sub-Zero). If you still want one, consider the 37-inch-wide Sub-Zero 650/F (59) bottom-freezer model, which offers ample space and high performance at a relatively low price.

Recommendations

TOP-FREEZERS

1 GE Profile PTS22LHR[WW] Very good but pricey top-freezer with excellent energy efficiency. Has a water filter and digital display of temperature settings and actual compartment temperatures. Discontinued, but similar model PTS22LHS is still available.

2 KENMORE (Sears) 7425[2] Very good overall, with excellent energy efficiency. Has water filter and internal water dispenser. Similar model: 7426.

3 Whirlpool ET8FTEXM[Q] **A CR Best Buy** Very good overall, with excellent energy efficiency. No pull-out shelves or freezer light.

4 KENMORE (Sears) 7495[2] Very good overall, with excellent energy efficiency. Has water filter and internal water dispenser. Similar models: 6495, 7496.

5 WHIRLPOOL ET1FHTXM[Q] A very good model with excellent energy efficiency. Has a water filter. Has no freezer light or pull-out shelves.

6 GE GTS18KCM[WW] Very good overall, but no pull-out shelves. Discontinued, but similar model GTS18KCP is available.

7 KITCHENAID KTRS22EM[WH] A very good but pricey top-freezer with excellent energy efficiency. Manufacturer's settings left internal temperatures too warm. Has a water filter.

8 HOTPOINT HTS22GBP[WW] Very good overall and low-priced for this type of refrigerator. No spillproof shelves, pull-out shelves, or light in freezer.

9 FRIGIDAIRE FRT21BW8D[W] A relatively inexpensive, energy efficient top-freezer with a dispenser on the door for filtered water. Door is nonreversible.

10 GE GTH18KBR[WW] A very good model with excellent energy efficiency. Meat keeper was too warm. No pull-out shelves.

11 ROPER RT18DKXK[Q] A very good, low-priced model, though spartan. No freezer light, spillproof shelves, or pull-out shelves. Single control for fridge and freezer.

12 GE GTS22KCP[WW] A very good model with excellent energy efficiency. No pull-out shelves.

13 MAYTAG MTB1891AR[W] A basic, inexpensive top-freezer. Tested price includes optional icemaker.

14 KENMORE (Sears) 7682[2] Unexceptional temperature performance and relatively noisy operation hamper this top-freezer. Features include a dispenser on the door for filtered water.

Recommendations

15 HAIER HTQ18JAB[WW] Good overall, but noisy. Manufacturer's recommended settings kept both refrigerator and freezer too warm. Single control for both refrigerator and freezer. No pull-out shelves. Similar models: HTQ18JAA, HTQ18JABR.

16 HOTPOINT HTS18BCP[WW] Good overall. Manufacturer's recommended setting kept freezer too warm. Single control for both refrigerator and freezer. No spill-proof shelves, pull-out-shelves, or light in freezer. Similar model: HTS18BBP.

BOTTOM-FREEZERS (INCLUDING FRENCH-DOOR MODELS)

17 LG LRFC25750[WW] An excellent French-door bottom-freezer with excellent energy efficiency and very quiet. Curved front doors. Door open alarm. Digital display of temperature settings. Bottom-freezer with pullout-drawer freezer door. Ice cube size adjuster. Models sold between May 2004 and May 2005 were subject to a recall. Go to *us.lge.com* or *www.sears.com* to determine whether your refrigerator is subject to recall.

18 AMANA ABB222ZDE[W] **CR Best Buy** A very good low-priced bottom-freezer. Excellent energy efficiency.

19 AMANA AFD2535DE[W] A very good French-door bottom-freezer with excellent energy efficiency. Water filter. Bottom-freezer with pull out drawer type freezer door.

20 KENMORE (Sears) Elite Trio 7552[2] A very good French-door bottom-freezer with excellent energy efficiency. Water filter. Bottom-freezer with pullout-drawer freezer door. Similar model: 7553.

21 KENMORE (Sears) Elite Trio 7554[2] This pricey, French-door bottom-freezer offers an array of features that include dispenser on the door for filtered water and a pull-out freezer drawer. It's also relatively quiet, though other, less expensive models did better in temperature performance. Models sold between May 2004 and May 2005 were subject to a recall. Go to *us.lge.com* or *www.sears.com* to determine whether your refrigerator is subject to recall.

22 MAYTAG MFF2557HE[W] Though relatively noisy, this full-featured, French-door bottom-freezer offers excellent energy efficiency and temperature performance.

23 KENMORE (Sears) 7500[2] **A CR Best Buy.** A very good low-priced bottom-freezer. Curved front doors. Door open alarm.

24 GE GBS20KBR[WW] Though basic, this fine-performing refrigerator is among the least-expensive bottom-freezer models and features a curved front and a swing-open freezer door. Tested with optional icemaker, which isn't reflected in the price.

25 GE Profile PDS22MCR[WW] Digital controls and displays for refrigerator and freezer temperature settings are this moderately priced model's notable features, though it's relatively noisy.

26 KENMORE (Sears) 7528[2] Very good. Curved front doors. Door open alarm. Bottom-freezer with pull out drawer type freezer door. Similar model: 7529.

27 WHIRLPOOL Gold GB9SHKXM[Q] While inexpensive for a bottom-freezer refrigerator, you'll find better performers at comparable lower prices. Features include a swing-open freezer door. Tested with optional icemaker, which isn't reflected in the price.

Recommendations

28 FISHER & PAYKEL E522B An exceptionally quiet, but relatively basic bottom-freezer with swing-open freezer door. It lacks a freezer light and an icemaker, and the door is nonreversible. This model is available only in a stainless-steel finish. Discontinued, but similar model E522B is available.

SIDE-BY-SIDES (INCLUDING CABINET-DEPTH MODELS)

29 AMANA ASD2628HE[W] Very good with excellent energy efficiency. Beverage chiller on door.

30 GE GSH25JFR[WW] **A CR Best Buy** This low-priced side-by-side offers fine performance and value. Pluses include quiet operation and convenience features such as a built-in water filter on the water dispenser, pull-out shelves, and a temperature-controlled deli drawer. Similar model: GSL25JFR.

31 KENMORE (Sears) 5538[2] **A CR Best Buy** Very good overall. Made more than 7 lbs. of ice per day. Has digital display and water filter. Similar model: 5539.

32 KENMORE (Sears) 5653[2] **A CR Best Buy** This low-priced side-by-side offers fine performance and value. Pluses include exceptionally quiet operation and many features found on models that cost hundreds of dollars more. It also makes lots of ice.

33 MAYTAG MSD2657HE[W] Very good with excellent energy efficiency. Crank adjusting shelf. Maytag has been among the more repair-prone brands of side-by-side refrigerators.

34 GE Profile Arctica PSH23PGR[WW] Very good cabinet-depth side-by-side model with excellent noise score. Digital display of temperature settings and actual compartment temperatures.

35 LG LRSC26960[TT] Very good, but pricey. Excellent noise score. Smooth stainless-look curved front doors. Door open alarm. Controls on front door. Ice cube size adjuster. Digital displays on front door. Digital display of temperature settings.

36 MAYTAG MZD2667HE[W] Very good unique side-by-side with zig-zag doors. Crank adjusting shelf. Maytag has been among the more repair-prone brands of side-by-side refrigerators.

37 GE Profile PSS26NGP[WW] Very good overall. Has water filter, curved doors, and door alarm. Discontinued, but similar model PSS26NGS is still available.

38 KITCHENAID KSRS25CN[WH] Very good but pricey. Made more than 7 lbs. of ice per day. Smooth curved front doors. Ice bin on freezer door for easy access and removal. Digital display of temperature settings.

39 JENN-AIR JCD2290HE[W] Very good cabinet-depth side-by-side model. Beverage chiller on door. Crank adjusting shelf. But the Jenn-Air freestanding side-by-side brand has been among the more repair-prone brands of side-by-side refrigerators.

40 KENMORE (Sears) 5522[2] Very good overall. Made more than 7 lbs. of ice per day. Has water filter, ice bin on door, and digital display of temperature settings. Discontinued, but similar models 5616 and 5617 are available.

41 WHIRLPOOL Gold GC3SHEXN[Q] This cabinet-depth, side-by-side model offers solid performance and has an array of features. Major ones include through-the-door ice and water, temperature-controlled deli drawers, touchpad controls, and digital displays of temperature set-

Recommendations

tings. It also makes lots of ice, and an ice bin on freezer door makes the ice easier to take out.

42 AMANA ASD2624HE[W] Very good overall. Has water filter.

43 LG LRSC26980[TT] Very good but pricey. Smooth stainless-look curved front doors. Door open alarm. Controls on front door. Digital displays on front door. Ice cube size adjuster. Digital display of temperature settings. Built-in 15-inch LCD TV and radio on front door.

44 FRIGIDAIRE Gallery GHSC239D[W] A fully featured, relatively inexpensive cabinet-depth side-by-side model, though Frigidaire has been among the more repair-prone brands of side-by-side refrigerators.

45 GE Profile Artica PSC25PSS[SS] This pricey cabinet-depth side-by-side is available only in stainless steel and is relatively inefficient on energy. But its price buys an array of features that include a beverage chiller on door, digital temperature displays, and dual evaporators that help prevent odor migration between compartments.

46 KENMORE (Sears) 5470[3] Very good and well-priced stainless-steel model with few features. Excellent energy efficiency. Meatkeeper was too warm.

47 KITCHENAID KSRD22FK[WH] Very good.

48 KITCHENAID Superba KSCS25IN[WH] Unexceptional temperature performance hampers this quiet cabinet-depth side-by-side model.

49 WHIRLPOOL Gold GD5SHAXM[Q] Very good overall. Has water filter and-beverage-chiller compartment on door. Ice bin on freezer door for easy access and removal. Discontinued, but similar model GD5SHAXN is available.

50 ELECTROLUX Icon E23CS80D[SS] Very good coated stainless steel cabinet-depth side-by-side model. Digital display of temperature settings and actual compartment temperatures. Door-open, power-loss, and high-internal-temperature alarm indicator lights inside refrigerator. Crank adjusting shelf. Discontinued, but similar model E23CS78E is available.

51 ADMIRAL LSD2615HE[W] Though inexpensive and energy-efficient, this basic side-by-side's temperature performance was unexceptional.

52 SAMSUNG RS2534[WW] Very good and well-priced with dual evaporators. Internal temperature variation higher than most. Door open alarm. Controls on front door. Digital displays on front door. Digital display of temperature settings. Discontinued, but similar model RS253BA is available.

53 HOTPOINT HSS25GFP[WW] Very good overall and low-priced for its type. Has water filter but no spillproof or pull-out shelves.

54 KENMORE (Sears) Elite 4430[2] A very good cabinet-depth side-by-side model. Digital display of temperature settings and actual compartment temperatures. Door-open, power-loss, and high-internal-temperature alarm indicator lights inside refrigerator. Crank adjusting shelf. Discontinued, but similar model 4438 is available.

55 WHIRLPOOL ED2VHGXM[Q] Very good and well-priced.

56 SAMSUNG Select Series RS2630[WW] Temperature performance that's only

Recommendations

fair hampers this inexpensive and quiet side-by-side. Temperatures in different sections of the refrigerator and freezer varied more than most others.

57 GE GSS20IEM[WW] Good overall and low-priced for its type. But meatkeeper too warm, internal temperature variations higher than most, and manufacturer's recommended setting left freezer much too cold. No spillproof shelves. Discontinued, but similar model GSS20IEP is available.

58 GE GSC23LGQ[WW] Good cabinet-depth side-by-side model. Has water filter. Discontinued, but similar models GSC23LGR and GSC23LSR are available.

BUILT-INS (INCLUDING BOTTOM-FREEZER AND SIDE-BY-SIDE MODELS)

59 SUB-ZERO 650/F Very good built-in, bottom-freezer model. Bottom freezer pulls open like a drawer. Needs custom panels at extra cost. But Sub-Zero has been the most repair-prone brand of top- and bottom-freezer refrigerators.

60 KITCHENAID KSSC42QM[SS] This pricey, stainless-steel built-in is quiet and includes touchpad controls and digital temperature displays. But it lacks stainless shelves.

61 VIKING DFSB423 Very good built-in, side-by-side model. Has door alarm. Needs custom panels at extra cost. Similar models: DDSB423, VCSB423SS.

62 JENN-AIR JS42FWD[W] Very good built-in side-by-side model. Has water filter, door alarm, and crank-adjustable shelf. Needs custom panels at extra cost.

63 VIKING DFBB363 Very good model. Bottom-freezer opens like a drawer. Needs custom panels at extra cost. Stainless option costs about $700 more. Similar models: DDBB363, DTBB363, VCBB363.

64 THERMADOR KBUDT4270A Very good built-in side-by-side model. Has water filter, ice bin on door, and digital controls (actual temperature). No spillproof shelves. Needs custom panels at extra cost. Similar models: KBUDT4250A, KBUDT4260A, KBUIT4250A, KBUIT4260A, KBUIT4270A.

65 GE Monogram ZISS420DR[SS] Very good built-in side-by-side. Very quiet. Has water filter, door alarm and digital displays with temperature settings and actual compartment temperatures.

66 GE Profile PSB42LSR[BV] Pricey and fully featured, this built-in side-by-side delivered unexceptional temperature performance.

67 SUB-ZERO 650G This relatively narrow, 36-inch built-in bottom-freezer model is quiet and energy-efficient, and has a pull-out drawer along with a glass-door refrigerator compartment. But Sub-Zero has been the most repair-prone brand of top- and bottom-freezer refrigerators. The glass refrigerator door precludes door shelves. This model also lacks some features you'll find on lower priced models, such as a temperature-controlled meat-keeper and humidity-controlled crispers.

68 SUB-ZERO 680 Very good built-in, side-by-side model. Has water filter. No spillproof shelves. Storage compartment for meats too warm. Needs custom panels at extra cost. But Sub-Zero has been among the more repair-prone brands of side-by-side refrigerators. Discontinued, but similar model 685F is available.

Brand Repair History

Choosing a brand with a good repair history can improve your odds of getting a reliable model. The graphs show the percentage of full-sized refrigerators that have ever been repaired or had a serious problem. Models within a brand may vary, and changes in design or manufacture may affect reliability. Adding an icemaker increases the odds of repairs. Sub-Zero, Frigidaire, Jenn-Air, and Maytag were among the more repair-prone brands of side-by-sides. Sub-Zero was also the most repair-prone brand of bottom- and top-freezers. We have enough data to list only Sub-Zero among built-in, bottom-freezer models. But our data suggest that, as a category, these bottom-freezers have had higher repair rates than freestanding models.

Side-by-sides with icemaker and dispenser

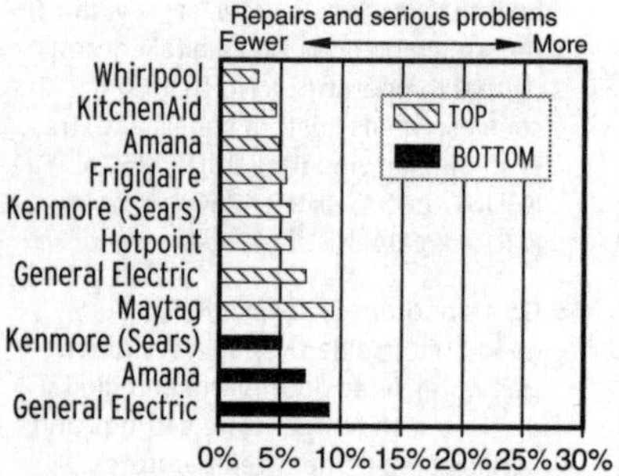

Top- and bottom-freezers without icemakers

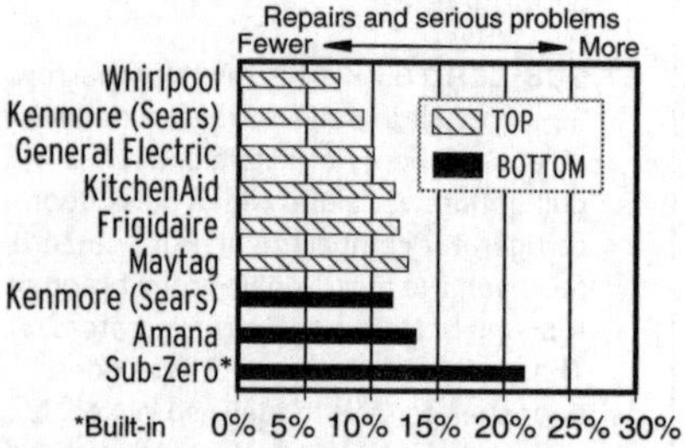

*Built-in

Top- and bottom-freezers with icemakers

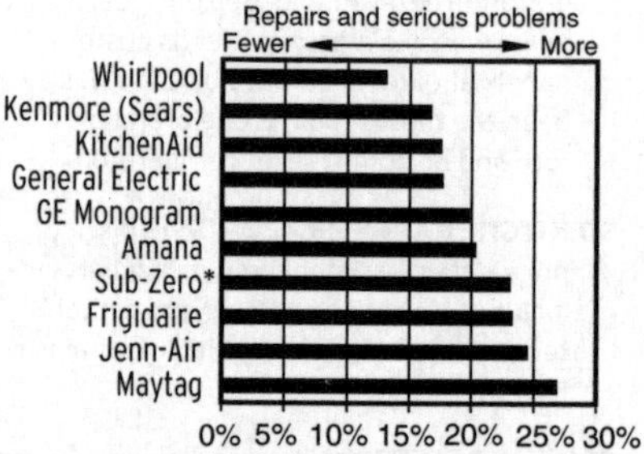

*Built-in & icemaker only

Based on nearly 86,000 responses to our 2004 Annual Questionnaire for models bought new between 2000 and 2004. Data have been standardized to eliminate differences linked to age. Note that differences of 4 points or more are meaningful.

TVS, LCDS

The Ratings list models by performance. Quick Picks highlights sets you might want to consider based not only on test scores but also on factors such as price, features, and computer compatibility.

Excellent ⊜ Very good ⊖ Good ○ Fair ◒ Poor ●

Within types, in performance order. Gray key numbers indicate Quick Picks.

Key number	Brand & model	Price	Overall score (0–100; P F G VG E)	Size (in.)	Test results: Picture quality: HD programming	DVD playback	Regular TV via high-quality input	Regular TV via basic input	Sound quality	Ease of use	Features: Digital-tuning options	Rear inputs: Component-video	S-video
	Most models are wide-screen. Unless noted below, all have 12-mo. parts and labor warranty.												
	HIGH-DEFINITION SETS												
1	**Sony** LCD Wega KLV-32M1	$2,200		32	⊖	⊖	⊖	◒	⊖	○		1	2
2	**Sharp** Aquos LC-26GD4U	1,600		26	⊖	⊖	⊖	◒	⊜	⊖	2	2	1
3	**Panasonic** Viera TC-26LX50	1,500		26	⊖	⊖	○	○	⊖	◒		2	2
4	**Sony** LCD Wega KLV-S23A10	1,300		23	⊖	⊖	⊖	○	○	◒		1	2
5	**Toshiba** TheaterWide HD 26HL84	1,350		26	○	⊖	⊖	◒	⊖	○		2	3
6	**Panasonic** Viera TC-32LX50	2,000		32	⊖	○	○	○	⊖	◒		2	2
7	**LG** 37LP1D	3,500		37	○	○	○	○	⊖	○	2	2	1
8	**Samsung** LN-R268W	1,250		26	○	⊖	○	◒	⊖	○		2	1
9	**Samsung** LN-R328W	1,700		32	○	⊖	○	◒	⊜	○		2	1
10	**LG** 26LX1D	1,500		26	○	○	○	○	○	○	2	2	1
11	**LG** 32LX1D	2,200		32	○	○	○	◒	○	○	2	2	1
12	**Zenith** Z32LZ5R	1,600		32	○	⊖	○	◒	○	◒		2	(1)
13	**Sharp** Aquos LC-20B9U-S	1,000		20	○	○	○	◒	○	○		2	1
14	**Zenith** Z26LZ5R	1,200		26	○	○	◒	◒	◒	◒		2	(1)
15	**Benq** DV-2680	1,150		26	◒	◒	○	◒	⊖	◒		1	2
	ENHANCED-DEFINITION SETS												
16	**JVC** LT-17X475	700		17	-	○	○	●	◒	◒		1	1
17	**Sharp** Aquos LC-20SH4U	550		20	-	◒	○	◒	◒	○		1	1
	STANDARD-DEFINITION SET												
18	**Toshiba** 20DL74	975		20	-	-	◒	●	○	◒		1	2

See report, page 45. Based on tests in Consumer Reports in November 2005.

Guide to the Ratings

Overall score is based primarily on picture quality; sound quality and ease of use are also figured in. Expert panelists evaluated picture quality for clarity and color accuracy. **HD programming** reflects display of a 1080i signal. **DVD playback** indicates how a set displayed a 480p signal, such as the output from a progressive-scan DVD player. For both, we used a component-video input. **Regular TV** scores are for a 480i signal, such as that of a regular TV program, received via **high-quality** (S-video) and **basic** (antenna or cable) inputs. Since HD and DVD images can look much better than regular TV programming, we used higher standards when judging HD and DVD content; thus, a very good score for HD indicates a better picture than a very good score for regular TV signals. **Sound quality** applies to the set's built-in speakers. **Ease of use** is our assessment of the remote control, onscreen menus, labeling of inputs, and useful features. **Size** indicates diagonal screen size in inches. **Price** is approximate retail. Models with one digital-tuning option can receive digital signals, including HD, from an antenna. Those with two are digital-cable-ready (DCR) sets that accept a CableCard; they can receive digital signals from either antenna or cable.

Quick Picks

The best choice for a primary TV:

1 Sony, $2,200

This 32-inch, wide-screen HDTV had a very good picture, even with non-HD programming (via the S-video input) and DVDs. Its viewing angle makes it best for watching straight-on. It has no computer input.

Best choices among midsized sets:

2 Sharp, $1,600
3 Panasonic, $1,500
4 Sony, $1,300

This 26-inch Sharp rivaled the Sony (1) for picture quality and had excellent sound. It has a DVI input, usable for connecting to some newer computers, and a very well-designed remote. The 26-inch Panasonic was very good with HD and DVD input, but regular TV via the S-video input was less sharp. It cannot accept computer input. The 23-inch Sony was a notch below the others in HD but matched them for DVD and regular TV. It has a VGA input for computer hookups. All have limitations in viewing angle, so they're not the best choices for viewing from the side.

If you often watch TV from an angle:

8 Samsung, $1,250
9 Samsung, $1,700

The 26-inch Samsung (8) and its 32-inch sibling (9) have very wide viewing angles, allowing leeway in where you sit. They scored good overall. Both have a VGA input.

Fine value in a smaller, non-HD set:

16 JVC, $700
17 Sharp, $550

Either would be a good choice for watching regular TV. The JVC has a 17-inch screen; the Sharp, a 20-inch.

Also worth considering are older HD sets that may still be available from Internet retailers. All have fine picture quality. Ratings are in the March 2005 or December 2004 issue.

Sony Wega KDL-32XBR950 (32-inch, with digital tuner for antenna), $2,975
Sony Wega KLV-26HG2 (26-inch), $1,650
Philips 26PF9966 (26-inch), $1,225
Philips 17PF8946 (17-inch), $600

Recommendations

HIGH-DEFINITION SETS

1 **SONY** LCD Wega KLV-32M1 This HD set displayed very good picture quality for HD, DVD playback, and regular TV through an S-video connection, but it was fair with regular TV through an antenna/cable hookup. Viewing angle not as wide as with some others, so picture may appear dimmer if you're not watching from directly in front of the set. Sound quality was very good. Its unlighted remote control, while otherwise very good, can be hard to use in dim lighting.

2 **SHARP** Aquos LC-26GD4U This HD set displayed very good picture quality for HD, DVD playback, and regular TV through an S-video connection, but it was fair with regular TV through an antenna/cable connection. An integrated HDTV, it can accept a first-generation CableCard for some digital-cable programming without the need for a cable box. (It can also receive over-the-air digital TV signals, without the need for an external decoder, if you live close enough to transmitting antennas.) Viewing angle not as wide as with some others, so picture may appear dimmer if you're not watching from directly in front of the set. Sound quality was excellent, unlike most of the LCD sets we tested.

3 **PANASONIC** Viera TC-26LX50 This HD set displayed a very good picture with HD and DVD and was good for regular TV signals. Viewing angle not as wide as with some others, so picture may appear dimmer if you're not watching from directly in front of the set. Lacks film mode (often called 3:2-pulldown compensation), which enhances picture quality on an HDTV or EDTV slightly if you watch movies with an older, non-progressive-scan DVD player or a VCR. Sound quality was very good. Its unlighted remote control, while otherwise very good, can be hard to use in dim lighting, and the onscreen menu is hard to navigate.

4 **SONY** LCD Wega KLV-S23A10 This HD set displayed a very good picture for HD, DVD playback, and regular TV through an S-video connection, and it was good for regular TV through an antenna/cable hookup. Viewing angle not as wide as with some others, so picture may appear dimmer if you're not watching from directly in front of the set. Sound quality was good but fell short of many other sets tested. Its unlighted remote control, while otherwise very good, can be hard to use in dim lighting.

5 **TOSHIBA** TheaterWide HD 26HL84 This HD set displayed a good picture for HD and was very good picture for DVD playback and regular TV through an S-video connection, but it was fair for regular TV through an antenna/cable hookup. Sound quality was very good. The remote control was very easy to use.

6 **PANASONIC** TC-32LX50 This HD set displayed a very good HD picture and was good for DVD playback and regular TV signals. Viewing angle not as wide as with some others, so picture may appear dimmer if you're not watching from directly in front of the set. Lacks film mode (often called 3:2-pulldown compensation), which enhances picture quality on an HDTV or EDTV slightly if you watch movies with an older, nonprogressive-scan DVD player or a VCR. Sound quality was very good. The remote control was very easy to use.

7 **LG** 37LP1D This HD set had good picture quality for HD, DVD playback, and regular TV. An integrated HDTV, it can accept a first-generation CableCard for some digital-cable programming without the need for a cable box. (It can also receive over-the-air digital TV signals, without the

Recommendations

need for an external decoder, if you live close enough to transmitting antennas.) Sound quality was very good. Remote control is excellent, but the rear jacks' labels are hard to read.

8 **SAMSUNG** LN-R268W Consider this model if you need a set with a wide viewing angle that doesn't make the picture look dimmer when viewed from different spots in the room. This HD set was good for HD and regular TV through an S-video connection, and very good for DVD playback but only fair for regular TV through an antenna/cable hookup. Sound quality was very good. Its unlighted remote control, while otherwise excellent, can be hard to use in dim lighting. The rear jacks' labels are hard to read.

9 **SAMSUNG** LN-R328W Consider this model if you need a set with a wide viewing angle that doesn't make the picture look dimmer when viewed from different spots in the room. This HD set was good for HD and regular TV through an S-video connection, and very good for DVD playback but only fair for regular TV through an antenna/cable hookup. Sound quality was excellent, unlike most of the LCD sets we tested. Its unlighted remote control, while otherwise excellent, can be hard to use in dim lighting. The rear jacks' labels are hard to read.

10 **LG** 26LX1D This HD set had good picture quality for HD, DVD playback, and regular TV. An integrated HDTV, it can accept a first-generation CableCard for some digital-cable programming without the need for a cable box. (It can also receive over-the-air digital TV signals, without the need for an external decoder, if you live close enough to transmitting antennas.) Sound quality was good but fell short of many other sets tested. Its unlighted remote control, while otherwise excellent, can be hard to use in dim lighting, and the rear jacks' labels are hard to read.

11 **LG** 32LX1D This HD set had good picture quality for HD, DVD playback, and regular TV through an S-video connection, but regular TV through an antenna/cable hookup was fair. An integrated HDTV, it can accept a first-generation CableCard for some digital-cable programming without the need for a cable box. (It can also receive over-the-air digital TV signals, without the need for an external decoder, if you live close enough to transmitting antennas.) Sound quality was good but fell short of many other sets tested. Its unlighted remote control, while otherwise excellent, can be hard to use in dim lighting. The rear jacks' labels are hard to read.

12 **ZENITH** Z32LZ5R This HD set's picture was good for HD and regular TV through an S-video connection, and very good for DVD playback. For regular TV through an antenna/cable hookup, it was fair. Sound quality was good but fell short of many other sets tested. Its unlighted remote control, while otherwise very good, can be hard to use in dim lighting.

13 **SHARP** Aquos LC-20B9U-S This HD set displayed a good picture for HD, DVD playback, and regular TV through an S-video connection, but regular TV through an antenna/cable hookup was fair. This set has a squarish 4:3 screen. Viewing angle not as wide as with some others, so picture may appear dimmer if you're not watching from directly in front of the set. Sound quality was good but fell short of many other sets tested. Its unlighted remote control, while otherwise excellent, can be hard to use in dim lighting.

14 **ZENITH** Z26LZ5R This HD set's HD and DVD pictures were good, but regular-TV

Recommendations

pictures were only fair. Sound quality was only fair and fell short of most other LCD sets tested. Its unlighted remote control, while otherwise very good, can be hard to use in dim lighting.

15 BENQ DV-2680 This HD set's pictures were only fair for HD, DVD playback, and regular TV through an antenna/cable connection; for regular TV through an S-video hookup, it was good. Lacks film mode (often called 3:2-pulldown compensation), which enhances picture quality on an HDTV or EDTV slightly if you watch movies with an older, nonprogressive-scan DVD player or a VCR. Sound quality was very good. Its unlighted remote control, while otherwise very good, can be hard to use in dim lighting. The onscreen menu is hard to navigate.

ENHANCED DEFINITION

16 JVC LT-17X475 This ED set displayed a good DVD picture, and regular TV through an S-video connection was also good; regular TV through an antenna/cable hookup, however, was poor. The model cannot accept an HD signal for down-converted display. This set has a squarish 4:3 screen. Sound quality was only fair and fell short of most other LCD sets tested. Its unlighted remote control, while otherwise very good, can be hard to use in dim lighting.

17 SHARP Aquos LC-20SH4U This ED set's picture was good for regular TV through an S-video connection, but it was only fair for DVD playback and regular TV through an antenna/cable hookup. The model cannot accept an HD signal for down-converted display. This set has a squarish 4:3 screen. Viewing angle not as wide as with some others, so picture may appear dimmer if you're not watching from directly in front of the set. Lacks film mode (often called 3:2-pulldown compensation), which enhances picture quality on an HDTV or EDTV slightly if you watch movies with an older, nonprogressive-scan DVD player or a VCR. Sound quality was only fair and fell short of most other LCD sets tested. Its unlighted remote control, while otherwise excellent, can be hard to use in dim lighting. The rear jacks' labels are hard to read, and the labor warranty is short at 3 months.

STANDARD DEFINITION SETS

18 TOSHIBA 20DL74 This standard-definition set's regular-TV picture was only fair from an S-video connection and poor from an antenna/cable hookup; there are better choices. This set has a squarish 4:3 screen. Viewing angle not as wide as with some others, so picture may appear dimmer if you're not watching from directly in front of the set. Sound quality was good but fell short of many other LCD sets tested. Its unlighted remote control can be hard to use in dim lighting.

TVS, PICTURE-TUBE

The best picture-tube TVs produced crisp, bright, detailed images with accurate colors and rich contrast. TVs judged excellent for picture quality came closest to that ideal. Sets with very good scores fell short in one or more of those attributes, but the differences may be subtle.

An HD model's ability to display HD is critical, but it's worth considering the other scores since you'll likely watch DVDs and regular programming through the S-video or antenna/cable input. Note that for HD sets, scores for HD and DVD images are judged on a higher scale than scores for regular TV signals.

The tested HD sets are HD-ready except for the Samsung (8), and two Sonys (28, 29) which have built-in digital tuners. Those two Sonys are digital-cable-ready sets that accept CableCards.

The Ratings list models by overall performance. The Quick Picks highlight models you might want to consider based on how they scored and on factors such as price.

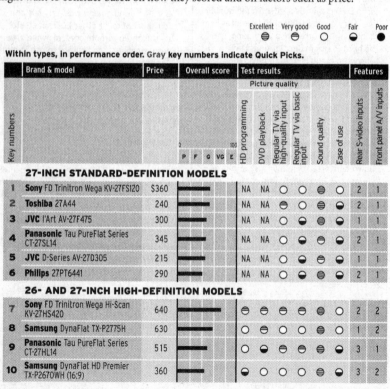

Excellent · Very good · Good · Fair · Poor

Within types, in performance order. Gray key numbers indicate Quick Picks.

Key numbers	Brand & model	Price	Overall score (0–100; P F G VG E)	Test results: Picture quality: HD programming	Picture quality: DVD playback	Picture quality: Regular TV via high-quality input	Picture quality: Regular TV via basic input	Sound quality	Ease of use	Features: Rear S-video inputs	Features: Front panel A/V inputs
	27-INCH STANDARD-DEFINITION MODELS										
1	**Sony** FD Trinitron Wega KV-27FS120	$360		NA	NA	Good	Good	Excellent	Good	2	1
2	**Toshiba** 27A44	240		NA	NA	Very good	Good	Excellent	Fair	2	1
3	**JVC** I'Art AV-27F475	300		NA	NA	Good	Fair	Excellent	Fair	1	1
4	**Panasonic** Tau PureFlat Series CT-27SL14	345		NA	NA	Good	Fair	Very good	Fair	2	1
5	**JVC** D-Series AV-27D305	215		NA	NA	Good	Fair	Very good	Fair	1	1
6	**Philips** 27PT6441	290		NA	NA	Good	Fair	Excellent	Fair	2	1
	26- AND 27-INCH HIGH-DEFINITION MODELS										
7	**Sony** FD Trinitron Wega Hi-Scan KV-27HS420	640		Very good	Very good	Very good	Very good	Excellent	Good	2	2
8	**Samsung** DynaFlat TX-P2775H	630		Good	Very good	Good	Good	Excellent	Good	1	2
9	**Panasonic** Tau PureFlat Series CT-27HL14	515		Good	Fair	Very good	Very good	Excellent	Fair	3	1
10	**Samsung** DynaFlat HD Premier TX-P2670WH (16:9)	360		Fair	Good	Good	Good	Excellent	Fair	3	2

Key numbers	Brand & model	Price	Overall score (0–100; P F G VG E)	HD picture quality	DVD picture quality	Regular TV via high-quality input	Regular TV via basic input	Sound quality	Ease of use	Rear S-video inputs	Rear component inputs
				Picture quality						Features	
	32-INCH STANDARD-DEFINITION MODELS										
11	**Toshiba** FST Black 32A43 **CR Best Buy**	350		NA	NA	○	○	⊜	⊖	1	1
12	**RCA** 32V430T	400		NA	NA	⊖	○	⊜	◒	1	1
13	**Sony** FD Trinitron Wega KV-32FS120	550		NA	NA	○	◒	⊜	○	1	1
14	**JVC** I'Art AV-32F475	450		NA	NA	⊖	○	⊜	◒	1	1
15	**JVC** D-Series AV-32D305	355		NA	NA	○	○	⊜	◒	1	1
16	**Toshiba** FST Pure 32AF44	495		NA	NA	○	◒	⊜	○	1	1
17	**Panasonic** Tau PureFlat Series CT-32SL14	500		NA	NA	○	◒	⊜	◒	1	1
	32-INCH HIGH-DEFINITION MODELS										
18	**Sony** FD Trinitron Wega Hi-Scan KV-32HS420	845		⊜	⊖	⊖	⊖	⊜	○	2	2
19	**Sony** FD Trinitron Wega KV-36FS320	800		NA	NA	⊖	◒	⊜	○	1	2
20	**JVC** I'Art AV-36F475	700		NA	NA	○	◒	⊜	◒	1	1
21	**Sony** FD Trinitron Wega KV-36FS120	820		NA	NA	⊖	◒	⊜	○	1	1
22	**Toshiba** Cinema Series 35AF44	690		NA	NA	○	◒	⊜	○	1	1
	30-INCH WIDE-SCREEN HIGH-DEFINITION MODELS										
23	**Sony** FD Trinitron Wega Hi-Scan KV-30HS420	855		⊜	⊖	⊖	⊖	⊜	○	2	2
24	**Sony** FD Trinitron Wega Hi-Scan KD-30XS955	1,070		⊜	⊜	⊖	⊖	⊜	◒	2	2
25	**Panasonic** Tau PureFlat Series CT-30WX54	750		○	⊖	○	◒	⊜	⊖	2	2
26	**Toshiba** TheaterWide HD 30HF84	720		○	⊖	○	◒	⊜	◒	2	2
27	**Philips** 30PW8402	775		○	⊖	○	◒	⊜	◒	1	2
	34-INCH WIDE-SCREEN HIGH-DEFINITION MODELS										
28	**Sony** FD Trinitron Wega HDTV KD-34XBR960	1,895		⊜	⊜	⊖	⊖	⊜	○	2	2
29	**Sony** FD Trinitron Wega Hi-Scan KD-34XS955	1,800		⊜	⊜	⊖	⊖	⊜	○	2	2
30	**Sony** FD Trinitron Wega Hi-Scan KV-34HS420	1,340		⊜	⊖	⊖	⊖	⊜	○	2	2
31	**Toshiba** TheaterWide 34HF84	1,170		⊖	○	⊖	○	⊜	◒	2	2
32	**Panasonic** Tau PureFlat Series CT-34WX54	1,070		○	○	⊖	○	⊜	○	2	2

Excellent ⊜ Very good ⊖ Good ○ Fair ◒ Poor ●

Within types, in performance order. Gray **key numbers indicate Quick Picks.**

Key numbers	Brand & model	Price	Overall score (0–100; P F G VG E)	Test results: Picture quality – HD programming	Picture quality – DVD playback	Picture quality – Regular TV via high-quality input	Picture quality – Regular TV via basic input	Sound quality	Ease of use	Features: Rear S-video inputs	Front panel A/V inputs
	36-INCH HIGH-DEFINITION MODELS										
33	**Sony** FD Trinitron Wega Hi-Scan KV-36HS420	$1,230		⊜	⊜	⊖	⊖	⊜	○	2	2
34	**Panasonic** Tau PureFlat Series CT-36HL44	1,030		⊜	⊜	⊜	⊖	⊜	◒	2	2

See report, page 45. Based on testing in Consumer Reports in March 2005, updated for price and availability.

Guide to the Ratings

Overall score is based primarily on picture quality; sound quality and ease of use are also figured in. Expert panelists evaluated picture quality for clarity and color accuracy. **HD programming** reflects display of a 1080i signal. **DVD playback** indicates how a set displayed a 480p signal, such as output from a progressive-scan DVD player. **Regular TV** scores are for a 480i signal, such as that of a regular TV program, received via **high-quality** (S-video) and **basic** (antenna/cable) inputs. HD and DVD performance are judged by higher standards than regular TV, so scores can't be compared. **Sound quality** is for built-in speakers. **Ease of use** assesses the remote control, onscreen menus, labeling of rear-jack panel, and useful features. **Price** is approximate retail.

Quick Picks

26- TO 27-INCH

For a conventional analog set:

1 Sony, $360
2 Toshiba, $240

The Sony, a flat-screen set, had good picture quality and front-panel A/V input. The Toshiba, which has a curved screen, displayed very good S-video picture quality and also accepts connections through its front panel. Both, however, have only a 3-month labor warranty.

For an HD set:

7 Sony, $640

This model had very good picture quality across the board, though it lacks special aspect-ratio settings such as zoom or stretch, has only one S-video input, and comes with a short (3-month) labor warranty. Like many HD sets tested, it has HDMI input, which may provide enhanced picture quality from newer devices with a matching digital output.

30- TO 36-INCH

For a 32-inch, conventional analog set:

11 Toshiba, $350 **CR Best Buy**
14 JVC, $450

The Toshiba offers good picture quality and very good ease of use at a low price. It has a curved screen. Among the flat-screen sets, we'd recommend the JVC, which had a better S-video picture than the Toshiba, though its remote control was hard to use in low light.

Quick Picks

For a 36-inch, conventional analog set:

19 Sony, $800

This flat-screen Sony had a very good S-video picture and includes ample inputs plus a Memory Stick slot for viewing photos taken with a compatible digital camera. Shortcomings are 30-day labor and on-site warranties and a remote control that was difficult to use in low light.

For a wide-screen HD set that will provide the best viewing experience:

23 Sony, $855
28 Sony, $1,895
29 Sony, $1,800
30 Sony, $1,340

All four of these Sony TVs were excellent with HD and very good or excellent for DVD and regular TV. The Sony (28) and Sony (29) are 34-inch digital-cable-ready sets with built-in tuners and CableCard slots, plus features such as a Memory Stick slot for viewing digital images. The Sony (28) has a longer warranty than its brandmates. The Sony (30) and Sony (23) are HD-ready models with 34-inch and 30-inch screens, respectively.

If you want to spend less for HD and are happy with the familiar squarish screen:

18 Sony, $845
33 Sony, $1,230
34 Panasonic, $1,030

The 36-inch Panasonic was excellent for picture quality nearly across the board and is well-priced for this size. The 36-inch Sony (33) and 32-inch Sony (18) were judged excellent for HD and very good or better for other content. Both have a front-panel S-video input.

Recommendations

27-INCH STANDARD DEFINITION

1 SONY FD Trinitron Wega KV-27FS120 Good, with excellent sound. Very good remote, but hard to use in low light. Lacks automatic display of active program's rating and channel block-out. Short labor warranty. Dimensions (HWD): 24x31x20 inches, 100 lbs.

2 TOSHIBA 27A44 Good, with very good S-video picture and excellent sound. Short labor warranty. To see program ratings, must push a button on remote. Dimensions (HWD): 23x30x20 inches, 82 lbs.

3 JVC I'Art AV-27F475 Good, with excellent sound, but picture via basic connection only fair. Lacks customizable channel labels and auto display of active program's rating. Dimensions (HWD): 24x33x21 inches, 95 lbs. Discontinued, but may be available.

4 PANASONIC Tau PureFlat Series CT-27SL14 Good, with very good sound, but picture via basic connection only fair. Has automatic display of active program's rating. Very good remote, but hard to use in low light. Short labor warranty. Dimensions (HWD): 24x31x20 inches, 95 lbs.

5 JVC D-Series AV-27D305 Good, with very good sound, but picture via basic connection only fair. Lacks customizable channel labels and automatic display of active program's rating. Remote control hard to use in low light. Has curved screen. Dimensions (HWD): 24x30x23 inches, 71 lbs. Discontinued, but may still be available.

6 PHILIPS 27PT6441 Good, with excellent sound, but picture via basic connection only fair. Front A/V inputs located on side. Lacks virtual surround sound, customizable channel labels, and automatic display of active program's rating. Remote control only so-so. Short labor warranty. Has curved screen. Dimensions (HWD):

20x30x20 inches, 108 lbs. Discontinued, but may still be available.

26- AND 27-INCH HIGH-DEFINITION

7 SONY FD Trinitron Wega Hi-Scan KV-27HS420 Very good, with excellent sound. Front A/V inputs include S-video. Very good remote, but hard to use in low light. Lacks special aspect-ratio settings (such as zoom or stretch), automatic display of active program's rating, and channel block-out. Short labor warranty. Dimensions (HWD): 24x31x21 inches, 111 lbs.

8 SAMSUNG DynaFlat TX-P2775H Good, with very good DVD picture and excellent sound, but had intermittent HD-decoding problem. Has integrated tuner for decoding off-air digital signals, and optical digital-audio output to receiver. Motion compensation feature worked very well. Front A/V inputs, located on side, include S-video. Very good remote, but hard to use in low light. Lacks virtual surround sound and channel block-out. To see program ratings, must push a button on remote. Dimensions (HWD): 24x30x21 inches, 105 lbs.

9 PANASONIC Tau PureFlat Series CT-27HL14 Good, with very good regular-TV pictures and excellent sound, but DVD picture only fair. Can't display an image from a 720p HD signal. Has automatic display of active program's rating. Very good remote control, but hard to use in low light. Lacks special aspect-ratio settings (such as zoom or stretch). Single S-video and component-video inputs limit connection options. Onscreen menu hard to use. Short labor warranty. Dimensions (HWD): 23x28x20 in., 100 lbs. Discontinued, but may still be available.

10 SAMSUNG DynaFlat HD Premier TX-P2670WH Good 26-in. wide-screen set, with excellent sound, but Samsung has been among the more repair-prone brands of 25- to 27-in. sets. HD picture only fair. Motion compensation feature worked very well. Has integrated tuner for decoding off-air digital signals, optical digital-audio output to receiver. Front A/V inputs, located on side, include S-video. To see program ratings, must push a button on remote. Remote very good, but hard to use in low light. Lacks virtual surround sound and channel block-out. Dimensions (HWD): 20x32x22 in., 89 lbs.

32-INCH STANDARD DEFINITION

11 TOSHIBA FST Black 32A43 **A CR Best Buy** Very good, with excellent sound. Very good remote control and excellent onscreen menu. Lacks auto volume leveler, customizable channel labels, and automatic display of active program's rating. Dimensions (HWD): 28x34x22 in., 111 lbs.

12 RCA 32V430T Good, with very good S-video picture and excellent sound, but RCA has been among the most repair-prone brands of 30-32-in. sets. Lacks automatic display of active program's rating and channel block-out. Short labor warranty. Has curved screen. Dimensions (HWD): 29x31x23 in., 120 lbs.

13 SONY FD Trinitron Wega KV-32FS120 Good, with excellent sound, but picture via basic connection only fair. Very good remote, but hard to use in low light. Lacks automatic display of active program's rating and channel block-out. Short labor warranty. Dimensions (HWD): 28x36x23 in., 166 lbs.

14 JVC I'Art AV-32F475 Good, with very good S-video picture and excellent sound. Lacks customizable channel labels and automatic display of active program's rating. Dimensions (HWD): 27x37x23 in., 141 lbs.

Recommendations

15 JVC D-Series AV-32D305 Good, with excellent sound. Lacks customizable channel labels and automatic display of active program's rating. Has a curved screen. Dimensions (HWD): 27x34x22 in., 115 lbs.

16 TOSHIBA FST Pure 32AF44 Good, with excellent sound, but picture via basic connection only fair. Front A/V inputs include S-video. Very good remote control. Lacks auto volume leveler. Dimensions (HWD): 27x35x23 in., 144 lbs. Discontinued, but may be available.

17 PANASONIC Tau PureFlat Series CT-32SL14 Good, with excellent sound, but antenna/cable picture only fair. Has automatic display of active program's rating. Front A/V inputs include S-video. Very good remote, but hard to use in low light. Dimensions (HWD): 27x35x23 in.

32-INCH HIGH-DEFINITION

18 SONY FD Trinitron Wega Hi-Scan KV-32HS420 Very good, with excellent sound and HD picture. Motion compensation feature worked well. Front A/V inputs include S-video. Very good remote, but hard to use in low light. Lacks special aspect-ratio settings, automatic display of active program's rating, and channel block-out. Short labor and in-home warranties. Dimensions (HWD): 28x36x24 in., 165 lbs.

19 SONY FD Trinitron Wega KV-36FS320 Good, with very good S-video picture and excellent sound, but picture via basic connection only fair. Has slot for viewing digital photos stored on Memory Stick media, Lacks automatic display of active program's rating and channel block-out. Short labor and in-home warranties. Dimensions (HWD): 30x40x26 in., 223 lbs.

20 JVC I'Art AV-36F475 Good, with excellent sound, but picture via basic connection only fair. Lacks customizable channel labels and automatic display of active program's rating. Dimensions (HWD): 30x41x25 in., 187 lbs

21 SONY FD Trinitron Wega KV-36FS120 Good, with very good S-video picture and excellent sound, but picture via basic connection only fair. Very good remote, but hard to use in low light. Lacks automatic display of active program's rating and channel block-out. Short labor warranty. Dimensions (HWD): 31x39x25 in., 217 lbs.

22 TOSHIBA Cinema Series 35AF44 Good 35-inch set, with excellent sound, but picture via basic connection only fair. Front A/V inputs include S-video. Remote control only so-so. Dimensions (HWD): 30x39x25 in., 154 lbs.

30-INCH WIDE-SCREEN HIGH-DEFINITION

23 SONY FD Trinitron Wega Hi-Scan KV-30HS420 Very good, with excellent sound and HD picture. Motion compensation feature worked well. Front A/V inputs include S-video. Very good remote control, but difficult to use in low light. Lacks automatic display of active program's rating and channel block-out. Short labor and in-home warranties. Dimensions (HWD): 24x36x23 in., 150 lbs.

24 SONY FD Trinitron Wega Hi-Scan KD-30XS955 Very good, with excellent HD and DVD pictures and excellent sound. Motion compensation feature worked well. Has integrated tuner for decoding off-air digital and digital-cable signals, optical digital-audio output to receiver, slot for viewing digital photos stored on Memory Stick media, and automatic display of active program's rating. Front A/V inputs include S-video. Lacks channel block-out. Short labor and in-home warranties. Dimensions (HWD): 24x36x22 in., 154 lbs.

Recommendations

25 PANASONIC Tau PureFlat Series CT-30WX54 Good, with very good DVD picture and excellent sound, but can't display an image from a 720p HD signal. Has scrolling channel preview and automatic display of active program's rating. Excellent remote control. Front A/V inputs include S-video. Has dual-tuner PIP. Dimensions (HWD): 23x36x23 in., 140 lbs. Discontinued, but may be available.

26 TOSHIBA TheaterWide HD 30HF84 **Good**, with very good DVD picture and excellent sound, but picture via basic connection only fair. Front A/V inputs include S-video. Very good remote control, but onscreen menu hard to use. Dimensions (HWD): 22x32x23 in., 88 lbs.

27 PHILIPS 30PW8402 Good, with very good DVD picture and excellent sound, but picture via basic connection only fair. Can't display an image from a 720p HD signal. Front A/V inputs, located on side, include S-video. Short labor warranty. Dimensions (HWD): 22x36x22 in., 117 lbs. Discontinued, but may be available.

34-INCH WIDE-SCREEN HIGH-DEFINITION

28 SONY FD Trinitron Wega HDTV KD-34XBR960 Very good, with excellent HD and DVD pictures and excellent sound. Has integrated tuner for decoding off-air digital and digital-cable signals, optical digital-audio output to receiver, scrolling channel preview, slot for viewing digital photos stored on Memory Stick media. Long (2-yr.) parts and labor warranty. Front A/V inputs include S-video and FireWire. Very good remote, but hard to use in low light. Has dual-tuner PIP. Lacks customizable channel labels, automatic display of active program's rating, and channel block-out. Dimensions (HWD): 26x40x24 in., 196 lbs.

29 SONY FD Trinitron Wega Hi-Scan KD-34XS955 Very good, with excellent DVD picture and sound. Has integrated tuner for decoding off-air digital and digital-cable signals, optical digital-audio output to receiver, slot for viewing digital photos stored on Memory Stick media. Front A/V inputs include S-video. Very good remote, but hard to use in low light. Lacks customizable channel labels, automatic display of active program's rating, and channel block-out. Short labor warranty. Dimensions (HWD): 26x40x24 in., 205 lbs.

30 SONY FD Trinitron Wega Hi-Scan KV-34HS420 Very good, with excellent sound and HD picture. Motion compensation feature worked well. Front A/V inputs include S-video. Very good remote control, but difficult to use in low light. Lacks automatic display of active program's rating and channel block-out. Short labor and in-home warranties. Dimensions (HWD): 26x40x24 in., 194 lbs.

31 TOSHIBA TheaterWide 34HF84 Good, with very good HD and S-video pictures and excellent sound. Motion compensation feature worked very well. Has scrolling channel preview. Front A/V inputs include S-video. Remote control only so-so. Has dual-tuner PIP. Dimensions (HWD): 25x34x24 in., 119 lbs.

32 PANASONIC Tau PureFlat Series CT-34WX54 Good, with very good S-video picture and excellent sound, but can't display an image from a 720p HD signal. Has scrolling channel preview and automatic display of active program's rating. Front A/V inputs include S-video. Has dual-tuner PIP. Dimensions (HWD): 25x40x24 in.

36-INCH HIGH-DEFINITION

33 SONY FD Trinitron Wega Hi-Scan KV-36HS420 Very good, with excellent HD

Recommendations

and DVD pictures and excellent sound. Motion compensation worked well. Front A/V inputs include S-video. Lacks special aspect-ratio settings (such as zoom or stretch), automatic display of active program's rating, and channel block-out. Short labor and in-home warranties. Dimensions (HWD): 31x40x25 in., 230 lbs.

34 PANASONIC Tau PureFlat Series CT-36HL44 Very good overall, with excellent HD, DVD, and S-video pictures and excellent sound, but can't display an image from a 720p HD signal. Has scrolling channel preview and automatic display of active program's rating. Front A/V inputs include S-video. Excellent selectivity. Lacks special aspect-ratio settings, virtual surround sound, Remote control only so-so. Has dual-tuner PIP. Dimensions (HWD): 30x39x24 in., 217 lbs.

Brand Repair History

25- to 27-inch

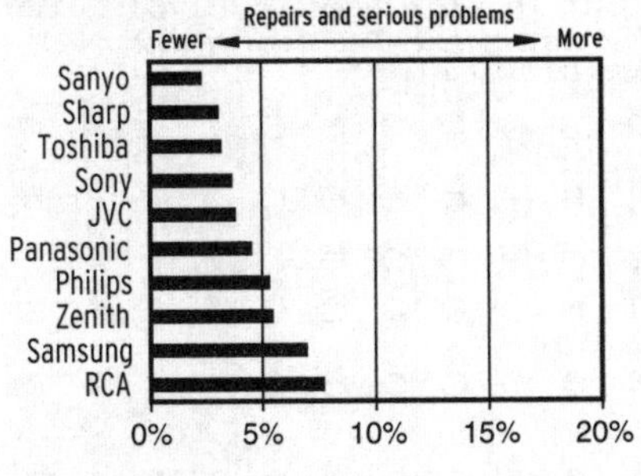

30- to 36-inch

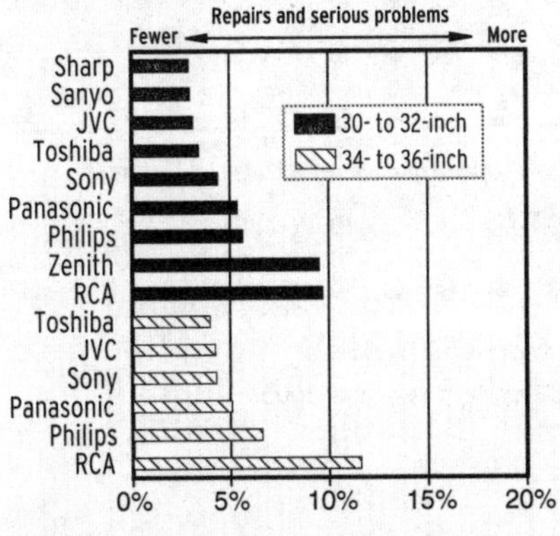

The graphs show the percentage of conventional 25- to 36-inch TV sets purchased new from 1999 through 2004 that were ever repaired or had a serious problem that was not resolved. Both graphs include digital HD sets as well as analog sets; the two types showed no significant difference in reliability. Still, we will continue to monitor HD models' repair record closely in the years to come. Of the 25- to 27-inch sets, RCA and Samsung were among the more repair-prone brands. Of the 30- to 32-inch sets, RCA and Zenith were the most repair-prone; of 34- to 36-inch sets, RCA was the most repair-prone. Data do not apply to LCD, plasma, or rear-projection TVs.

Data for 25- to 27-inch sets are based on more than 75,000 responses to our 2004 Annual Questionnaire; data for 30- to 32-inch and 34- to 36-inch sets are based on nearly 71,000 responses. Data for the two charts are not directly comparable. Repair rates for specific models may vary, and changes in design and manufacturing may affect reliability. Still, you increase your chances of getting a reliable TV by choosing among brands that have proven reliable in the past. Data have been standardized to eliminate any differences attributable to age. Differences of less than 3 percentage points are not meaningful.

TVS, PLASMA

The Ratings list models by performance. Quick Picks highlights models that you might want to consider based not only on how they scored, but also on factors such as price and features.

Excellent / Very good / Good / Fair / Poor

Within types, in performance order. Gray key numbers indicate Quick Picks.

Key number	Brand & model	Price	Overall score (0–100: P F G VG E)	Size (in.)	Test results: Picture quality: HD programming	Picture quality: DVD playback	Picture quality: Regular TV via high-quality input	Picture quality: Regular TV via basic input	Sound quality	Ease of use	Features: Digital-tuning options	Rear inputs: Component-video	Rear inputs: S-video	Full warranty (mo.)
	All models are 16:9 (wide-screen).													
	HIGH-DEFINITION SETS *All 42-inch HD models tested have 1,024x768 native resolution; the three 50-inch TVs, 1,366x768.*													
1	**Panasonic** TH-50PX50U	$4,000		50	Excellent	Excellent	Excellent	Very good	Very good	Good	2	2	2	12
2	**Panasonic** TH-42PX50U	2,800		42	Excellent	Excellent	Excellent	Very good	Very good	Good	2	2	2	12
3	**Dell** W4200HD	3,000		42	Very good	Excellent	Good	Good	Very good	Good	1	2	2	12
4	**LG** 42PX4D	3,300		42	Very good	Very good	Fair	Fair	Very good	Good	2	2	1	24
5	**Sony** Plasma Wega KDE-50XS955	4,300		50	Very good	Very good	Good	Good	Very good	Fair	2	2	2	12
6	**Pioneer** PureVision PDP-4350	4,000		43	Very good	Very good	Good	Fair	Very good	Fair	2	2	2	12
7	**LG** 50PX4DR [1]	5,000		50	Fair	Good	Fair	Fair	Very good	Good	2	2	1	24
8	**Samsung** HP-R4252	2,700		42	Fair	Fair	Fair	Poor	Excellent	Good	2	2	1	12
9	**Proview** MH-422HU	2,500		42	Fair	Fair	Fair	Poor	Fair	Fair		2	2	12
	ENHANCED-DEFINITION SETS *Both have native resolution of 852x480.*													
10	**Panasonic** TH-42PD50U	1,800		42	Good	Very good	Very good	Very good	Very good	Good	1	2	2	12
11	**Proview** MH-422SU	1,825		42	Fair	Fair	Fair	Fair	Very good	Fair		2	2	12

[1] *Has 160-gigabyte hard drive and Gemstar program guide for recording of TV content.*

See report, page 45. Based on tests in Consumer Reports in November 2005.

Guide to the Ratings

Overall score is based primarily on picture quality; sound quality and ease of use are also figured in. Trained panelists evaluated **picture quality** for clarity and color accuracy. **HD programming** reflects display of a 1080i signal. For ED sets, HD scores indicate how well they down-converted 1080i signals to 480p. **DVD playback** indicates how a set displayed a 480p signal, such as the output from a progressive-scan DVD player. For both, we used a component-video input. **Regular TV** scores are for a 480i signal, such as that of a regular TV program, received via **high-quality** (S-video) and **basic** (antenna/cable) inputs. Scores for HD programming and DVD playback are held to a higher standard than scores for regular TV. **Sound quality** is measured from the set's built-in speakers using computer-aided test equipment. **Ease of use** is our assessment of the remote control, onscreen menus, labeling of inputs, and useful features. **Full warranty** is for parts and labor. Models with one **digital-tuning option** can receive digital signals, including HD, using an antenna. Those with two are digital-cable-ready (DCR) models that accept a CableCard; they can receive digital signals through either antenna or cable. ED sets can display 480p signals from progressive-scan DVD players or from an external digital-TV tuner. **Price** is approximate retail.

Quick Picks

The best choices for an HDTV:

1 Panasonic, $4,000
2 Panasonic, $2,800

Panasonic was the performance leader across the board for plasma TVs, and these two were the top-scoring sets overall, especially for HD. Both displayed an excellent picture even with non-HD content (via the S-video input) and DVDs. They also had very good sound quality. The two sets are digital-cable-ready (DCR) TVs; when equipped with a CableCard, they can receive digital-cable signals, including HD, without a cable box. They also can get digital signals via antenna. (1) costs not much more than some major-brand 42-inch sets, making it a solid value.

If a lower price is a top priority:

10 Panasonic, $1,800

This 42-inch EDTV doesn't match the better HDTVs for HD picture quality, but its picture quality was otherwise very good, as was its sound. It's well priced for an integrated set, and it can accept digital signals via antenna. We'd choose it over the lower-rated HD sets.

Also worth considering is an older 42-inch, HD-ready model that might still be available from online retailers: the Toshiba TheaterWide HD 42HP84, $2,695. It offers a fine picture and excellent sound at a good price. (The Ratings in the March 2005 issue included this set.)

Recommendations

HIGH-DEFINITION SETS

1 **PANASONIC** TH-50PX50U This HD set is one of a select few plasma sets with excellent pictures for HD, DVD, and regular TV through an S-video connection. It also was very good for regular TV from an antenna/cable hookup. An integrated HDTV, it can accept a first-generation CableCard for some digital-cable programming without the need for a cable box. (It can also receive over-the-air digital TV signals, without the need for an external decoder, if you live close enough to transmitting antennas.) Sound quality was very good, as with nearly all the plasma sets we tested. Remote control is very good, but onscreen menu is hard to navigate.

2 **PANASONIC** TH-42PX50U This HD set is one of a select few plasma sets with excellent pictures for both HD and DVD signals. It was also excellent for regular TV through an S-video connection and very good for regular TV via an antenna/cable hookup. An integrated HDTV, it can accept a first-generation CableCard for some digital-cable programming without the need for a cable box. (It can also receive over-the-air digital TV signals, without the need for an external decoder, if you live close enough to transmitting antennas.) Sound quality was very good, as with nearly all the plasma sets we tested. Remote control is very good, but onscreen menu is hard to navigate.

3 **DELL** W4200HD This HD set had a very good HD picture and an excellent picture for DVD; for regular TV, it was good. An integrated HDTV, it can accept over-the-air digital TV signals, without the need for an external decoder, if you live close enough to transmitting antennas. Sound quality (speakers are detachable) was very good, as with nearly all the plasma sets we tested. Its unlighted remote control, while otherwise excellent, can be hard to use in dim lighting, and the parts and labor warranties are short at three months.

4 **LG** 42PX4D This HD set displayed very good HD and DVD pictures; for regular TV, it was only fair. An integrated HDTV, it can accept a first-generation CableCard for some digital-cable programming without the need for a cable box. (It can also receive over-the-air digital TV signals, without the need for an external decoder, if you live close enough to transmitting antennas.) Sound quality was very good, as with nearly all the plasma sets we tested. The parts and labor warranties are long at 24 months. Its unlighted remote control, while otherwise excellent, can be hard to use in dim lighting.

5 **SONY** Plasma Wega KDE-50XS955 This HD set displayed very good HD and DVD pictures; for regular TV, it was good. An integrated HDTV, it can accept a first-generation CableCard for some digital-cable programming without the need for a cable box. (It can also receive over-the-air digital TV signals, without the need for an external decoder, if you live close enough to transmitting antennas.) Sound quality was very good, as with nearly all the plasma sets we tested. Its unlighted remote control, while otherwise very good, can be hard to use in dim lighting, and the onscreen menu is hard to navigate.

6 **PIONEER** PureVision PDP-4350HD This HD set displayed very good HD and DVD pictures. For regular TV through an S-video connection, it was good; through an antenna/cable hookup, it was only fair. An integrated HDTV, it can accept a first-generation CableCard for some digital-cable programming without the need for a cable box. (It can also receive over-the-air digital TV signals, without the need for an

Recommendations

external decoder, if you live close enough to transmitting antennas.) Sound quality (speakers are detachable) was very good, as with nearly all the plasma sets we tested. Remote control is very good, but onscreen menu is hard to navigate.

7 LG 50PX4DR This HD set includes a built-in, 160-gigabyte hard drive and Gemstar program guide for recording of TV content. Its picture for HD and regular TV signals was only fair; its DVD picture was good. An integrated HDTV, it can accept a first-generation CableCard for some digital-cable programming without the need for a cable box. (It can also receive over-the-air digital TV signals, without the need for an external decoder, if you live close enough to transmitting antennas.) Sound quality was very good, as with nearly all the plasma sets we tested. The parts and labor warranties are long at 24 months. Its unlighted remote control, while otherwise excellent, can be hard to use in dim lighting.

8 SAMSUNG HP-R4252 This HD set tested only fair for picture quality except with regular TV through an antenna/cable connection, which was poor; there are better choices. An integrated HDTV, it can accept a first-generation CableCard for some digital-cable programming without the need for a cable box. (It can also receive over-the-air digital TV signals, without the need for an external decoder, if you live close enough to transmitting antennas.) Sound quality was excellent, a notch higher than all the other plasma sets we tested. Its unlighted remote control, while otherwise excellent, can be hard to use in dim lighting.

9 PROVIEW MH-422HU This HD set tested only fair for picture quality except with regular TV through an antenna/cable connection, which was poor; there are better choices. Sound quality (speakers are detachable) was very good, as with nearly all the plasma sets we tested. Its unlighted remote control can be hard to use in dim lighting, and onscreen menu is hard to navigate.

ENHANCED-DEFINITION SETS

10 PANASONIC TH-42PD50U This ED set displayed a good picture from down-converted HD; its picture was otherwise very good. An integrated HDTV, it can accept over-the-air digital TV signals, without the need for an external decoder, if you live close enough to transmitting antennas. Lacks film mode (often called 3:2-pulldown compensation), which enhances picture quality on an HDTV or EDTV slightly if you watch movies with an older, nonprogressive-scan DVD player or a VCR. Sound quality was very good, as with nearly all the plasma sets we tested. Remote control is very good, but onscreen menu is hard to navigate.

11 PROVIEW MH-422SU This ED set's picture was overall judged only fair; there are better choices. Sound quality (speakers are detachable) was very good, as with nearly all the plasma sets we tested. Its unlighted remote control can be hard to use in dim lighting, and the onscreen menu is hard to navigate.

TVS, REAR-PROJECTION

The Ratings list models by performance. Quick Picks highlights models that you might want to consider based not only on how they scored, but also on factors such as price and features.

Excellent ⊜ · Very good ⊖ · Good ○ · Fair ◒ · Poor ●

Within types, in performance order. Gray key numbers indicate Quick Picks.

All models are 16:9 (wide-screen) and have 12-mo. parts and labor warranty.

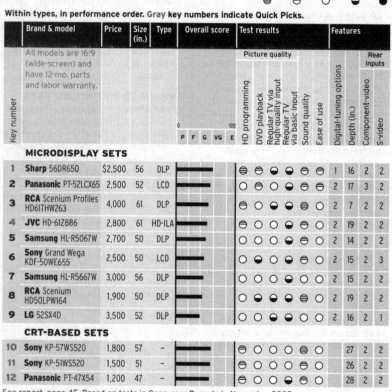

Key number	Brand & model	Price	Size (in.)	Type	Overall score (0–100: P F G VG E)	Picture quality: HD programming	Picture quality: DVD playback	Picture quality: Regular TV via high-quality input	Picture quality: Regular TV via basic input	Sound quality	Ease of use	Digital-tuning options	Depth (in.)	Rear inputs: Component-video	Rear inputs: S-video
	MICRODISPLAY SETS														
1	**Sharp** 56DR650	$2,500	56	DLP		Excellent	Very good	Fair	Fair	Very good	Very good	1	16	2	2
2	**Panasonic** PT-52LCX65	2,500	52	LCD		Good	Very good	Good	Fair	Very good	Very good	2	17	3	2
3	**RCA** Scenium Profiles HD61THW263	4,000	61	DLP		Very good	Good	Fair	Fair	Excellent	Good	2	7	2	2
4	**JVC** HD-61Z886	2,800	61	HD-ILA		Very good	Good	Good	Fair	Very good	Good	2	19	2	2
5	**Samsung** HL-R5067W	2,700	50	DLP		Good	Good	Good	Fair	Very good	Good	2	14	2	2
6	**Sony** Grand Wega KDF-50WE655	2,500	50	LCD		Good	Fair	Good	Fair	Very good	Good	2	15	2	3
7	**Samsung** HL-R5667W	3,000	56	DLP		Good	Good	Good	Fair	Good	Good	2	15	2	2
8	**RCA** Scenium HD50LPW164	1,900	50	DLP		Good	Fair	Fair	Fair	Excellent	Good	2	19	2	2
9	**LG** 52SX4D	3,500	52	DLP		Good	Good	Fair	Fair	Good	Good	2	16	2	1
	CRT-BASED SETS														
10	**Sony** KP-57WS520	1,800	57	–		Very good	Good	Good	Good	Excellent	Good		27	2	2
11	**Sony** KP-51WS520	1,500	51	–		Very good	Good	Good	Good	Very good	Good		26	2	2
12	**Panasonic** PT-47X54	1,200	47	–		Very good	Good	Good	Fair	Very good	Good		28	2	2

See report, page 45. Based on tests in Consumer Reports in November 2005.

Guide to the Ratings

Overall score is based primarily on picture quality; sound quality and ease of use are also figured in. Trained panelists evaluated **picture quality** for clarity and color accuracy. **HD programming** reflects display of a 1080i signal. **DVD playback** indicates how a set displayed a 480p signal, such as the output from a progressive-scan DVD player. For both, we used a component-video input. **Regular TV** scores are for a 480i signal, such as that of a regular TV program,

Guide to the Ratings *continued*

received via **high-quality** (S-video) and **basic** (antenna/cable) inputs. Since HD and DVD images can look much better than regular TV programming, we used higher standards when judging HD and DVD content; thus, a very good score for HD indicates a better picture than a very good score for regular TV signals. **Sound quality** is for the set's built-in speakers. **Ease of use** is our assessment of the remote control, onscreen menus, labeling of inputs, and useful features. **Size** indicates diagonal screen size, in inches. For microdisplay TVs, **type** indicates the technology the set uses. Models with one **digital-tuning option** can receive digital signals, including HD, from an antenna. Those with two are digital-cable-ready (DCR) models that accept a CableCard; they can receive digital signals from either antenna or cable. **Price** is approximate retail.

Quick Picks

Best values if you have the space:

- **10** Sony, $1,800
- **11** Sony, $1,500
- **12** Panasonic, $1,200

If you can fit a set that's at least 26 inches deep, consider these CRT-based, HD-ready models, which were very good for HD and good for regular TV and DVD. The 57-inch Sony (10) and its 51-inch sibling (11) have both automatic and manual convergence, which help when you need to perform this task. (It's an occasional necessity with CRT-based rear-projection sets, particularly after you move the TV.) Both have 3:2-pulldown compensation, which smooths action in programming that originated as film. The Panasonic, a 47-inch set, lacks 3:2-pulldown compensation, but it has both manual and automatic convergence. Consider this model if a smaller set will do and you won't hook up the TV through the antenna/cable input. It may be hard to find, since it is no longer in production. It was still available at press time.

If you prefer a slimmer set:

- **1** Sharp, $2,500
- **4** JVC, $2,800

The 56-inch Sharp was the only set tested to score excellent for HD, but it was only fair for regular TV. Like any DLP set, there's the potential problem of the rainbow effect. The 61-inch JVC uses HD-ILA technology, a variant of LCoS. It was judged very good for HD. Both these sets have a built-in digital tuner for receiving broadcast digital TV, including HD, through an antenna. When equipped with a CableCard, the JVC can also receive some digital-cable signals without the need for a cable box.

Also worth considering are older HD-ready sets we've tested. All have picture quality comparable to the above sets and may still be available from online retailers. (They have 50-inch screens except for the Toshiba, which has a 52-inch.) Ratings were in the March 2005 issue.

- Samsung HL-P5085W (DLP), $2,100
- Panasonic PT-50DL54 (DLP), $2,600
- Panasonic PT-50LC14 (LCD), $1,900
- Toshiba 52HM84 (DLP), $1,750

Recommendations

MICRODISPLAY SETS

1 SHARP 56DR650 This 56-inch, DLP-based HD set was the only tested rear-projection model to have an excellent HD picture. Its DVD picture was also very good, but the set was only fair with regular-TV content. An integrated HDTV, it can accept over-the-air digital TV signals, without the need for an external decoder, if you live close enough to transmitting antennas. Sound quality was very good, as with most of the rear-projection sets we tested. Remote control is excellent.

2 PANASONIC PT-52LCX65 This 52-inch, LCD-based HD set was good for HD and regular TV through an S-video connection, and very good for DVD playback. For regular TV through an antenna/cable hookup, it was only fair. An integrated HDTV, it can accept a first-generation CableCard for some digital-cable programming without the need for a cable box. (It can also receive over-the-air digital TV signals, without the need for an external decoder, if you live close enough to transmitting antennas.) Lacks film mode (often called 3:2-pulldown compensation), which enhances picture quality on an HDTV or EDTV slightly if you watch movies with an older, nonprogressive-scan DVD player or a VCR. Sound quality was very good, as with most of the rear-projection sets we tested. Remote control is excellent.

3 RCA Scenium Profiles HD61THW263 This 61-inch, DLP-based HD set, only 7 inches deep, displayed a very good picture for HD and was good for DVD playback. For regular TV, it was only fair. An integrated HDTV, it can accept a first-generation CableCard for some digital-cable programming without the need for a cable box. (It can also receive over-the-air digital TV signals, without the need for an external decoder, if you live close enough to transmitting antennas.) Sound quality was excellent, a notch higher than most of the other rear-projection sets we tested. Remote control is very good, but the side jacks' labels are hard to read.

4 JVC HD-61Z886 This 61-inch HD set—based on HD-ILA (JVC's variation of LCoS) technology—displayed a very good HD picture, and it was good for both DVD playback and regular TV through an S-video connection. With an antenna/cable hookup, it was only fair. An integrated HDTV, it can accept a first-generation CableCard for some digital-cable programming without the need for a cable box. (It can also receive over-the-air digital TV signals, without the need for an external decoder, if you live close enough to transmitting antennas.) Sound quality was very good, as with most of the rear-projection sets we tested. Remote control is excellent.

5 SAMSUNG HL-R5067W This 50-inch, DLP-based HD set displayed a good picture for HD, DVD playback, and regular TV through an S-video connection, but it was fair for regular TV through an antenna/cable hookup. An integrated HDTV, it can accept a first-generation CableCard for some digital-cable programming without the need for a cable box. (It can also receive over-the-air digital TV signals, without the need for an external decoder, if you live close enough to transmitting antennas.) Sound quality was very good, as with most of the rear-projection sets we tested. Its unlighted remote control, while otherwise excellent, can be hard to use in dim lighting.

6 SONY Grand Wega KDF-50WE655 This 50-inch, LCD-based HD set had a good picture for HD and regular TV through an S-video connection, but it was fair for DVD playback and regular TV through an antenna/cable hookup. An integrated HDTV, it can accept a first-generation CableCard for some digital-cable programming without the need for a cable box. (It can also receive over-the-air digital TV signals, without the need for an external decoder, if you live close enough to transmitting antennas.) Sound quality was very good, as with most of the rear-projection sets we tested. Its unlighted remote control, while otherwise excellent, can be hard to use in dim lighting.

Recommendations

7 SAMSUNG HL-R5667W This 56-inch, DLP-based HD set displayed a good picture for HD, DVD playback, and regular TV through an S-video connection, but it was fair for regular TV through an antenna/cable hookup. An integrated HDTV, it can accept a first-generation CableCard for some digital-cable programming without the need for a cable box. (It can also receive over-the-air digital TV signals, without the need for an external decoder, if you live close enough to transmitting antennas.) Sound quality was good but fell short of most other rear-projection sets tested. Its unlighted remote control, while otherwise excellent, can be hard to use in dim lighting.

8 RCA Scenium HD50LPW164 This 50-inch, DLP-based HD set had a picture that was good for HD but fair for DVD and regular TV. An integrated HDTV, it can accept a first-generation CableCard for some digital-cable programming without the need for a cable box. (It can also receive over-the-air digital TV signals, without the need for an external decoder, if you live close enough to transmitting antennas.) Sound quality was excellent, a notch higher than most of the other rear-projection sets we tested. Remote control is very good.

9 LG 52SX4D This 52-inch, DLP-based HD set had good pictures for HD and DVD playback, but was fair for regular TV. An integrated HDTV, it can accept a first-generation CableCard for some digital-cable programming without the need for a cable box. (It can also receive over-the-air digital TV signals, without the need for an external decoder, if you live close enough to transmitting antennas.) Sound quality was good but fell short of most other rear-projection sets tested. Its unlighted remote control, while otherwise excellent, can be hard to use in dim lighting.

CRT-BASED SETS

10 SONY KP-57WS520 This 57-inch, CRT-based HD set had a very good HD picture, and it was good with both DVD playback and regular TV. Lacks film mode (often called 3:2-pulldown compensation), which enhances picture quality on an HDTV or EDTV slightly if you watch movies with an older, non-progressive-scan DVD player or a VCR. Sound quality was very good, as with most of the rear-projection sets we tested. The CRT warranty is long at 24 months. Its unlighted remote control, while otherwise excellent, can be hard to use in dim lighting.

11 SONY KP-51WS520 This 51-inch, CRT-based HD set had a very good HD picture, and it was good with both DVD playback and regular TV. Sound quality was very good, as with most of the rear-projection sets we tested. The CRT warranty is long at 24 months. Its unlighted remote control, while otherwise excellent, can be hard to use in dim lighting.

12 PANASONIC PT-47X54 This 47-inch, CRT-based HD set had a very good HD picture, and it was good with both DVD playback and regular TV through an S-video connection. With regular TV through an antenna/cable hookup, it was only fair. This set cannot display 720p HD signals received through the component-video input. Lacks film mode (often called 3:2-pulldown compensation), which enhances picture quality on an HDTV or EDTV slightly if you watch movies with an older, nonprogressive-scan DVD player or a VCR. Sound quality was very good, as with most of the rear-projection sets we tested. Remote control is very good.

VACUUM CLEANERS

Carpets and floors remain a vacuum's most important challenges. The Kenmore (28) is the first canister to excel at both, and maintained good suction through the hose for cleaning with tools. But some other vacs fell down in at least one area, sometimes in surprising ways.

Examples include the Eurekas (4, 18), which did well on carpets, yet scored no better than a fair on bare floors, the easier of those tasks. We also found that you can pay top dollar without getting top performance.

Excellent · Very good · Good · Fair · Poor

Within types, in performance order. Gray key numbers indicate Quick Picks.

Key number	Brand & model	Price	Weight (lb.)	Overall score (0–100: P F G VG E)	Cleaning: Carpet	Cleaning: Bare floor	Cleaning: Tool airflow	Other results: Noise	Other results: Emissions	Other results: Ease of use	Features: Bag	Features: Brush on/off	Features: Manual pile adjustment
	UPRIGHTS *These tend to be better for carpets and are easier to store.*												
1	**Hoover** WindTunnel Self Propelled Ultra U6439-900 [1]	$250	21		Excellent	Excellent	Excellent	Fair	Excellent	Good	•	•	•
2	**Eureka** Boss Smart Vac Ultra 4870 **CR Best Buy**	140	21		Excellent	Excellent	Good	Good	Excellent	Good	•	•	•
3	**Hoover** WindTunnel Bagless U5753-900	180	21		Excellent	Excellent	Good	Fair	Excellent	Good			•
4	**Eureka** Ultra Whirlwind 4880D	200	23		Excellent	Poor	Good	Good	Excellent	Good		•	•
5	**Kirby** Ultimate G Diamond Edition [1]	1,330	24		Excellent	Excellent	Very good	Fair	Excellent	Good	•	•	•
6	**Riccar** SupraLite RSL3	330	9		Excellent	Excellent	[2]	Poor	Excellent	Very good	•		
7	**Dyson** DC15 The Ball All Floors	600	20		Very good	Excellent	Good	Good	Excellent	Good		•	
8	**Oreck** XL21-700 [3]	700	11		Very good	Excellent	Poor	Fair	Excellent	Very good	•		
9	**Hoover** WindTunnel Bagless Self Propelled U6630-900 [1]	300	24		Very good	Excellent	Good	Fair	Excellent	Good		•	•
10	**Riccar** Radiance	800	21		Excellent	Excellent	Good	Fair	Good	Good	•	•	•
11	**Bissell** Cleanview II 3576-1	80	17		Excellent	Excellent	Good	Fair	Excellent	Good			•
12	**Kenmore** (Sears) Progressive 35912	200	23		Very good	Good	Good	Good	Excellent	Good		•	•
13	**Dyson** DC07 All Floors	400	19		Good	Excellent	Very good	Fair	Excellent	Fair		•	
14	**Dyson** DC14 Complete	570	19		Good	Excellent	Good	Good	Excellent	Fair		•	
15	**Eureka** The Boss SE 5855BZ	130	21		Very good	Good	Good	Fair	Excellent	Good			•
16	**Sebo** automatic X4	750	18		Good	Excellent	Fair	Good	Excellent	Very good	•	•	

Key number	Brand & model	Price	Weight (lb.)	Overall score (0–100; P F G VG E)	Cleaning: Carpet	Cleaning: Bare floor	Cleaning: Tool airflow	Other results: Noise	Other results: Emissions	Other results: Ease of use	Features: Bag	Features: Brush on/off	Features: Manual pile adjustment
	UPRIGHTS *These tend to be better for carpets and are easier to store.*												
17	**Dirt Devil** Vision Self-Propelled M087900 [1]	$170	21		⊖	⊖	○	●	⊖	○			•
18	**Eureka** Boss 4D 5892	150	24		⊖	●	⊖	○	⊜	○		•	•
19	**Electrolux** Aptitude EL5010A	300	19		○	⊖	⊖	◒	⊜	○	•		•
20	**Miele** Powerhouse S184	380	15		⊖	⊖	◒	○	⊜	○	•	•	
21	**Dirt Devil** Jaguar (Target) M085575	50	13		⊖	⊜	○	●	⊖	○	•		
22	**Miele** ART Red Roses S938 5925521	400	14		○	⊜	●	○	⊜	◒	•	[4]	
23	**Sanyo** Performax SC-A116	125	16		○	⊖	○	◒	⊖	○	•		
24	**Bosch** Turbo Jet BUH 11700UC [D]	$235	20		○	⊜	○	◒	○	◒	•	•	
25	**Bissell** PowerForce 3522-1	50	15		○	⊜	○	◒	⊖	○	•	•	•
26	**Kenmore** (Sears) Bagless 34720	90	16		⊖	○	◒	◒	⊜	○			
27	**Sanyo** Dirt Hunter SC-F1201	150	23		●	◒	○	◒	⊜	○			•
	CANISTERS *Consider these if much of your cleaning involves drapes, upholstery, and stairs.*												
28	**Kenmore** (Sears) Progressive 25914	500	24		⊜	⊜	○	○	⊖	⊖	•	•	•
29	**Bosch** Premium Prestige Electro Duo H BSG 81360UC	800	19		⊖	⊜	⊖	⊖	⊜	⊖	•	•	
30	**Kenmore** (Sears) Progressive 25614 **CR Best Buy**	350	23		⊖	⊜	○	○	⊜	⊖	•	•	•
31	**Miele** Solaris Electro Plus 1200W S514	800	20		⊖	⊜	○	⊖	⊜	⊖	•	•	
32	**Miele** Plus 1200W S251	480	19		⊖	⊜	○	⊖	⊜	⊖	•	•	
33	**Sebo** air belt C3.1	940	26		⊜	⊜	○	○	⊜	○	•		
34	**Electrolux** Oxygen EL6988A	500	21		⊖	⊜	○	◒	⊜	⊖	•	•	•
35	**GE** (Wal-Mart) 106766	150	19		⊖	⊜	◒	○	⊖	⊖	•	•	
36	**Oreck** Dutch Tech DTX1400B	900	25		⊖	⊜	○	○	⊜	○	•	•	
37	**Riccar** 1700	1,000	27		⊖	⊖	⊖	○	⊜	○	•	•	•
38	**Aerus** Lux Guardian C154E	1,500	25		⊖	⊜	◒	○	⊜	○	•	•	
39	**Hoover** WindTunnel Plus S3639	200	22		○	⊜	⊖	○	⊖	○	•	•	
40	**Aerus** Lux Legacy C153C	1,000	22		⊖	⊜	●	○	⊜	○	•	•	
41	**Hoover** WindTunnel Bagless S3765	250	22		⊖	⊜	○	◒	○	○		•	
42	**TriStar** Mg2 A101N	1,500	23		⊖	⊖	◒	○	⊜	⊖	•	•	
43	**Sanyo** SC-X1000P	160	25		⊖	⊜	◒	◒	⊜	○		•	

Excellent · Very good · Good · Fair · Poor

Within types, in performance order. Gray key numbers indicate Quick Picks.

Key number	Brand & model	Price	Weight (lb.)	Overall score (0–100: P F G VG E)	Cleaning: Carpet	Cleaning: Bare floor	Cleaning: Tool airflow	Other results: Noise	Other results: Emissions	Other results: Ease of use	Features: Bag	Features: Brush on/off	Features: Manual pile adjustment
	CANISTERS *continued*												
44	**Filter Queen** Majestic 360 AT1100	$1,900 [5]	25		Very good	Fair	Good	Good	Very good	Very good		•	
45	**Fantom** Falcon FC251	180	22		Very good	Excellent	Poor	Fair	Very good	Good		•	
46	**Bissell** DigiPro 6900	230	21		Fair	Excellent	Fair	Fair	Excellent	Very good	•	•	•
47	**Rainbow** e-series E2	1,500	32		Good	Fair	Very good	Fair	Good	Good		•	•

[1] *Self-propelled.* [2] *Not applicable; tested model does not accept tools.* [3] *Includes mini canister for tools.* [4] *Not applicable; does not use a brush.* [5] *Total is $2,200 with Defender air cleaner.*

See report, page 112. Based on testing in Consumer Reports in October 2005, with updated prices and availability.

Guide to the Ratings

Overall score is mainly cleaning performance, ease of use, and emissions. **Carpet** is how much embedded talc and sand a vacuum lifted from medium-pile carpet. **Bare floor** is how well models vacuumed sand without dispersing it. **Tool airflow** is airflow through the hose with increasing amounts of dust-simulating wood "flour." **Noise** reflects results using a decibel meter. Models judged poor produced 85 decibels or more and should be used with hearing protection. **Emissions** denotes wood flour released while vacuuming. **Ease of use** is bag capacity and ease of pushing, pulling, carrying, and use under furniture. **Weight** for uprights denotes the body; for canisters, body, hose, and powerhead. **Price** is approximate retail.

Quick Picks

Best for most; fine all-around cleaning:

1 Hoover, $250 (upright)

2 Eureka, $140 (upright), **CR Best Buy**

28 Kenmore, $500 (canister)

30 Kenmore, $350 (canister), **CR Best Buy**

Among uprights, the self-propelled Hoover excelled in all three cleaning areas, though it's noisy. The Eureka trades some suction with tools for less noise and a lower price. Also consider the bagless Hoover (3) if you don't mind messier emptying. Among canisters, the Kenmore (28) is the highest-scoring vacuum that excelled on carpets and floors; it performed best among all vacuums. But the Kenmore (30) came close and costs less, with fewer emissions.

If lighter is worth some sacrifices:

6 Riccar, $330 (upright)

The 9-pound Riccar performed well and is far lighter than most uprights. But it doesn't accept tools, has few features, and is noisy enough to require ear protection.

If low price is a main concern:

11 Bissell, $80 (upright)

35 GE, $150 (canister)

Both of these relatively low-priced vacs cleaned carpets and floors well. Trade-offs include messier emptying and more noise for the bagless Bissell, and more frequent bag changes for the GE, based on our tests.

Recommendations

UPRIGHT VACUUMS

1 **HOOVER** WindTunnel Self Propelled Ultra U6439-900 Very good overall. Excelled at cleaning, but noisy. May not fit on some stairs. Bag: $9/3. Similar models: U6436-900, U6453-900, U6454-900

2 **EUREKA** Boss Smart Vac Ultra 4870 **A CR Best Buy**. Very good overall. Highest performance for the dollar. Excelled at most cleaning, but hard to pull. Bag: $6/3. HEPA filter: $20.

3 **HOOVER** WindTunnel Bagless U5753-900 Very good. Excellent carpet cleaning helps distinguish this very good, bagless vac. Less tippy than most with hose fully extended. Small rotating brush for stairs. HEPA filter: $30 (Replace every 3 years). Similar model: U5767-900.

4 **EUREKA** Ultra Whirlwind 4880D Very good. A very good, bagless upright, but poor on bare floors. Full bin alert. Overload protection for blower fan motor. Hose longer than most. HEPA filter. Lacks suction control. Lacks upholstery tool. Lacks headlamp. Filter: $20.

5 **KIRBY** The Ultimate G Diamond Edition Very good. A very good, self-propelled vac that has been among the more reliable brands of uprights; required fewer belt repairs than most. Easy on/off switch. Hose longer than most. On/off is by foot switch. Motor control with more than one speed. HEPA filter. Tools not stowed onboard. Lacks suction control and on/off switch for rotating brush. Pusher configuration. Comes with extra (or longer) hose and attachments. Bags: $15/9 (paper), $19/9 (HEPA), $9/2 (filtrete).

6 **RICCAR** SupraLite RSL3 Very good. Overload protection for blower fan motor. HEPA filter. Pusher configuration. Bags: $17/6. Similar model: Simplicity Freedom F3500.

7 **DYSON** DC15 The Ball All Floors Very good. Bagless. Full bin alert. Overload protection for blower fan and rotating brush motors. Hose longer than most. Lacks suction control. Lacks headlamp.

8 **ORECK** XL21-700 Very good. Overload protection for blower fan motor. Motor control with more than one speed. HEPA filter. Lacks suction control. Pusher configuration. Bags: $20/8. Bags for compact canister: $10/12 plus filter.

9 **HOOVER** WindTunnel Bagless Self Propelled U6630-900 Very good. But noisy, heavy, and tippy on stairs. HEPA filter: $30. Similar models: U6618-900, U6634-900, U6637-900.

10 **RICCAR** Radiance Very good. Full-bag alert. Suction control. Overload protection for blower fan motor. HEPA filter. Hose shorter than most. Not stable on stairs. Bags: $15/6. Similar model: Simplicity Synergy.

11 **BISSELL** CleanView II 3576-1 Very good. Bagless. Full-bin alert. Hose longer than most. HEPA filter. Lacks independent switch for rotating brush. Lacks suction control. Washable filter: $13; HEPA filter: $10. Similar model: CleanView II Plus 3576-6.

12 **KENMORE** (Sears) Progressive 35912 Very good. Bagless. Full bin alert. Overload protection for blower fan motor. Hose longer than most. HEPA filter. Lacks suction control. Tower filter: $20. Exhaust filter: $15. Similar models: 35913, 36922, 36923.

13 **DYSON** DC07 All Floors Very good. Bagless, but has confusing controls. Hose longer than most. Noisy. Hard to push and pull. No headlamp. HEPA filter (washable):

Recommendations

$17.50. Similar models: DC07 Animal, Full Gear, Full Kit, Low Reach.

14 DYSON DC14 Complete Very good. Bagless, but has confusing controls. Hose longer than most. Noisy. Hard to push and pull. No headlamp. HEPA filter (washable): $17.50. Similar models: DC14 All Floors, Animal, Full Access, Full Gear, Full Kit, Low Reach.

15 EUREKA The Boss SE 5855BZ Very good. Easy on/off switch. Overload protection for blower fan motor. Hose longer than most. On/off switch located on handle. Full-bin indication. HEPA filter. Has small powered brush for stairs. Lacks suction control and on/off switch for rotating brush. Must bend to adjust rug height. Filter: $20. Similar model: SE 5856BZ.

16 SEBO Automatic X4 Very good. But compromised by notable flaws. Full-bag alert. Overload protection for blower fan motor. Tippy with hose is extended. Unstable on stairs. Cord shorter than most. Lacks headlamp. Bags: $19/10.

17 DIRT DEVIL Vision Self-Propelled M087900 Very good. Bagless, but noisy. Hose longer than most. Had to bend to adjust rug height. No upholstery tool. Filter: $25.

18 EUREKA 4D 5892 Very good. Poor bare-floor performance compromises this bagless vac. Full bin alert. Overload protection for blower fan motor. Hose longer than most. HEPA filter. Lacks suction control. Lacks headlamp. Filter: $20.

19 ELECTROLUX Aptitude EL5010A Good. But pricey and noisy. Tippy with hose extended. Hose longer than most. Motor control has more than one speed. Had to bend to adjust rug height. No upholstery tool. Bags: $11/5. Filter: $20.

20 MIELE Powerhouse S184 Good. Some notable flaws. Full-bag alert. Hose longer than most. Motor control with more than one speed. HEPA filter. Prone to tip when hose is extended. Cord shorter than most. Lacks suction control. Unstable on stairs. Lacks upholstery tool. Bags: $15/5 Filter: $35.

21 DIRT DEVIL Jaguar M085575 (Target) Good. Inexpensive, but noisy. Cord less convenient to wrap than others. Hose and cord shorter than most. Hose isn't attached at suction end. Bag: $3/3.

22 MIELE ART Red Roses S938 5925521 Good. Some notable flaws. Retractable cord. Full-bag alert. Overload protection for blower fan motor. HEPA filter. Hose shorter than most. Cord shorter than most. Lacks suction control. Unstable on stairs. Lacks upholstery tool. Lacks headlamp.Bags: $12/5. Filter: $25-35.

23 SANYO Performax SC-A116 Good. Compromised by some notable flaws. Easy on/off switch. Lacks independent Tippy with hose extended. Lacks suction control. Bags: $12/6. Filter: $11/2.

24 BOSCH Turbo Jet BUH 11700UC Good. Just so-so on emissions. Curvy design includes front-mounted hose that we found awkward to remove. Bag: $4. Filter: $25.

25 BISSELL PowerForce 3522-1 Good. But noisy. Tippy with hose extended and unstable on stairs. Hard to push. Hose and power cord shorter than most. No overload protection. Bag: $3. Filter: $3. Discontinued, but similar model 3522-5 is available.

26 KENMORE (Sears) Bagless 34720 Good. Bagless, but noisy. Tippy on stairs and with hose extended. Hose and cord shorter than most. No upholstery tool. Tower

Recommendations

filter: $20. Exhaust filter: $14. Similar model: 34721.

27 SANYO Dirt Hunter SC-F1201 Good overall, but poor carpet cleaning and only fair cleaning on bare floors compromise this bagless vac. Full-bin alert. Overload protection for blower fan motor. Hose longer than most. HEPA filter. Lacks suction control. Filter: $40

CANISTERS

28 KENMORE (Sears) Progressive 25914 Very good. On/off switch on handle. Retractable cord. Full-bag alert. Suction control. Overload protection for blower-fan and rotating brush motor. Hose longer than most. HEPA filter. Motor control with more than one speed. Dirt sensor. Bags: $8/2. Similar model: Progressive 25915

29 BOSCH Premium Prestige Electro Duo H BSG 81360UC Very good. Retractable cord. Full-bag alert. Suction control. Overload protection for blower-fan motor. On/off switch on handle. Cord shorter than most. Lacks headlamp. Wand unstable in upright position.Bags: $15/5.

30 KENMORE (Sears) Progressive 25614 **CR Best Buy** Very good. Full-bag indication. Retractable cord. Easy on/off switch. Suction Control. Overload protection for blower-fan and rotating-brush motor. Hose longer than most. Retractable cord. On/off switch located Bags: $8/2. Similar model: Progressive 25615

31 MIELE Solaris Electro Plus 1200W S514 Very good. Quieter than most, but hard to push and pull. Cord and hose shorter than most. Bags:$15/5.

32 MIELE Plus 1200W S251 Very good. Less bulky and heavy than most. Cord shorter than most. Bags: $15/5.

33 SEBO air belt C3.1 Very good. Retractable cord. Full bag-alert. Overload protection for blower fan motor and rotating brush. Motor control with more than one speed. HEPA filter. Power cord shorter than most. Lacks suction control. Lacks headlamp. Bags: $19/10.

34 ELECTROLUX Oxygen EL6988A Very good. Better-than-average cleaning on carpet. Hose longer than most. Cord shorter than most. Difficult to detach wand-to-wand connection and wand from hose. Bags: $9/5. Similar model: Oxygen Ultra EL6989A

35 GE 106766 (Wal-Mart) Very good. Well-priced canister, with better-than-average performance on carpet. But its suction for cleaning with tools was less effective than most. Available only at Wal-Mart. Bag: $5/3. Similar model: Eureka 6852

36 ORECK Dutch Tech DTX1400B Very good. Full-bag indication. Retractable cord. Easy on/off switch. Overload protection for rotating brush motor. Hose longer than most. Motor control with more than one speed. Bags: $14/5.

37 RICCAR 1700 Very good. Retractable cord. Full-bag alert. Overload protection for blower fan and rotating brush motor. Hose longer than most. Motor control with more than one speed. HEPA filter. Lacks suction control. Wand felt heavy when using tools. Bags: $15/6. Similar model: Simplicity S36

38 AERUS Lux Guardian C154E Very good. Retractable cord. Full-bag alert. Suction control. Overload protection for blower fan and rotating brush motor. On/off switch on handle. HEPA filter. Lacks headlamp. Wand felt heavy when using tools. Bags: $22/12.

39 HOOVER WindTunnel Plus S3639 Very good. A well-rounded vac. Bag: $9/3.

40 AERUS Lux Legacy C153C Very good. Retractable cord. Full-bag alert. Overload protection for blower fan and rotating brush motor. Motor control with more than one speed. Power cord shorter than most. Lacks suction control. Wand felt heavy when using tools. Bags: $22/12.

41 HOOVER WindTunnel Bagless S3765 Very good. A canister vac with better cleaning than most on carpet. But relatively noisy. Released dust when we emptied the bin. Dirt cup filter: $17. HEPA: $15. Similar model: WindTunnel Bagless S3755

42 TRISTAR Mg2 A101N Very good. Suction control. Overload protection for blower fan motor and rotating brush motor. Less convenient to wrap cord than others. Lacks headlamp. Wand felt heavy when using tools. Bags: $15/12.

43 SANYO SC-X1000P Very good. Retractable cord. Easy on/off switch. Hose longer than most. Retractable cord. On/off is by foot switch. Full-bin indication. HEPA filter. Power cord is shorter than most. Lacks suction control. Wand unstable when placed in upright position.

44 FILTER QUEEN Majestic 360 AT1100 A good bagless vac with notable flaws. Overload protection for blower fan and rotating brush motor. Hose longer than most. Full-bin indicator. Motor control with more than one speed. Less convenient than others to wrap cord. Cord shorter than most. Lacks suction control. Unstable on stairs. Lacks headlamp. Wand felt heavy when using tools. Filters: $14/6 paper cones, 1 cloth cone.

45 FANTOM Falcon FC251 Good. Better-than average cleaning on carpet. But disconnecting the power head and wiring to change tools was very difficult. Vac also was relatively noisy, and released dust when bin was emptied. HEPA filter: $30.

46 BISSELL DigiPro 6900 Good. There are better choices, though. Noisy. Unimpressive on carpets. Hose longer than most. Cord shorter than most. Had to bend to adjust rug height. Wand unstable in upright position. Bag: $7/3.

47 RAINBOW e-series E-2 Good. Extremely high price not justified by performance, however. Among the worst on bare floors, and relatively noisy. Unusual design utilizes water to retain dust and dirt that's been picked up; that makes the machine very heavy (32 lbs.) when filled with water. Special features include the ability to pick up wet spills (not tested), an inflator for toys and a dusting brush for plants and animals. Has been among the more reliable brands of canisters.

Brand Repair History

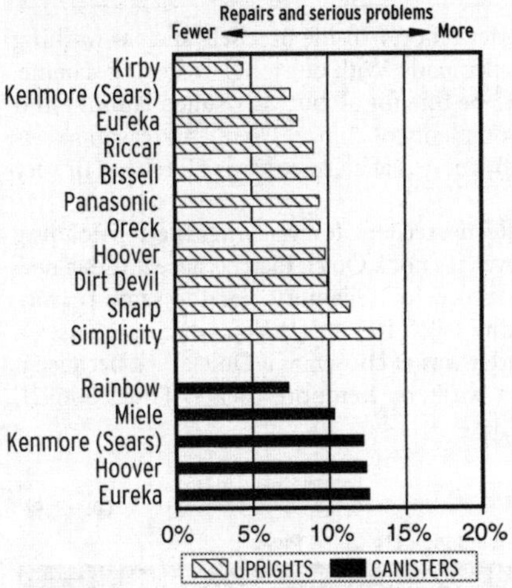

Choosing a brand with a good repair history can improve your odds of getting a reliable vacuum. This graph shows the percentage of vacuums bought new between 2000 and 2004 that have ever been repaired or had a serious problem. Simplicity was among the more repair-prone brands of uprights. Note, however, that models within a brand may vary, and changes in manufacturing and design may affect reliability. The graphs do not include broken belts, a frequent though often inexpensive-to-fix problem that was more common for uprights and for Eureka among canisters.

Data are based on more than 86,000 responses to our 2004 Annual Questionnaire. Data have been standardized to eliminate any differences linked to age or usage. Differences of less than 4 points aren't meaningful. Note that we lack sufficient data to include central vacuum systems

WASHING MACHINES

We recently updated our washing tests to better reflect real-life practices such as washing maximum loads and using less water for smaller loads. With our tougher scoring scheme, a washing score of very good or good would be fine for all but very soiled laundry and should satisfy many consumers. That gives you plenty of choice. There's no reason to settle for fair washing performance when so many models at all price levels offer good or very good results.

Only one model in the Ratings was judged excellent for washing: the top-loading Maytag Neptune TL FAV9800A[WW]. However, it's not a Quick Pick because it uses a new wash system and doesn't yet have a track record for reliability. For the same reason, we're not including the GE Profile Harmony WPGT9350C[WW], which also uses a new design. One other high-scoring top-loader wasn't chosen as a Quick Pick because it is among the more repair-prone brands of washers: Kenmore (Sears) Elite 2506[2], which is a member of the Calypso family.

Excellent | Very good | Good | Fair | Poor

Within types, in performance order. Gray key numbers indicate Quick Picks.

Key number	Brand & model	Price	Overall score (0–100; P F G VG E)	Washing performance	Energy efficiency	Water efficiency	Capacity	Gentleness	Noise	Cycle time (min.)	Stainless-steel tub	Porcelain top/lid	Auto temp. control	Auto bleach dispenser
TOP-LOADING MODELS														
1	**Maytag** Neptune TL FAV9800A[WW]	$1,300		Excellent	Very good	Excellent	Excellent	Good	Good	80	•	•	•	•
2	**Kenmore (Sears)** Elite 2506[2]	850		Very good	Very good	Very good	Excellent	Very good	Very good	70	•		•	•
3	**Whirlpool** Calypso GVW9959K[Q]	800		Very good	Very good	Good	Excellent	Very good	Very good	60	•	•	•	•
4	**GE** Profile Harmony WPGT9350C[WW]	1,000		Very good	Fair	Good	Very good	Good	Good	55	•		•	•
5	**Whirlpool** Gold GSQ9669L[W]	500		Good	Good	Very good	Very good	Very good	Good	50			•	
6	**GE** WWRE5240D[WW]	470		Good	Fair	Good	Very good	Very good	Good	50	•		•	
7	**Amana** NAV8800A[WW]	500		Good	Good	Very good	Good	Very good	Good	45	•		•	
8	**GE** WBSR3140D[WW]	300		Good	Good	Good	Very good	Very good	Fair	45				
9	**Kenmore (Sears)** 1584[2]	500		Good	Good	Good	Very good	Good	Good	40			•	
10	**Whirlpool** LSW9700P[Q]	380		Good	Good	Good	Very good	Good	Good	45			•	
11	**GE** WHSE5240D[WW]	470		Fair	Good	Good	Very good	Very good	Good	50			•	

Key number	Brand & model	Price	Overall score (0–100; P F G VG E)	Washing performance	Energy efficiency	Water efficiency	Capacity	Gentleness	Noise	Cycle time (min.)	Stainless-steel tub	Porcelain top/lid	Auto temp. control	Auto bleach dispenser
	TOP-LOADING MODELS													
12	**GE** WHRE5260E[WW]	$470		◒	⊖	◒	⊖	⊖	○	45	•		•	
13	**Kenmore (Sears)** Elite 2494[2]	580		○	◒	○	⊜	○	◒	45		•	•	•
14	**Maytag Atlantis** MAV9501E[W]	600		⊖	◒	⊖	○	◒	○	60	•	•	•	
15	**Frigidaire** FWS1339A[C]	330		◒	⊖	○	○	⊖	○	45				
16	**Kenmore (Sears)** 2685[2]	520		○	○	○	⊖	○	○	45			•	
17	**Whirlpool** Gold GSW9650L[W]	500		○	◒	⊖	○	⊖	○	50			•	•
18	**Hotpoint** VWSR4150D[WW]	350		◒	◒	○	⊖	⊖	○	45				
19	**Kenmore (Sears)** 2462[2]	330		○	◒	○	○	⊖	◒	35				
20	**Roper** RAS8333R[Q]	300		◒	○	◒	○	⊖	○	35				
	FRONT-LOADING MODELS													
21	**Kenmore (Sears)** Elite HE4t 4508[1]	1,500		⊖	⊜	⊜	⊜	○	⊖	95	•	•	•	•
22	**Whirlpool** Duet HT GHW9400P[W]	1,300		⊖	⊜	⊖	⊜	⊖	⊖	65	•	•	•	•
23	**Bosch** Nexxt Premium WFMC6400UC	1,350		⊖	⊜	⊜	⊖	○	⊖	110	•		•	•
24	**LG** WM2432H[W]	1,250		⊖	⊜	⊖	⊜	○	⊖	75	•	•	•	•
25	**Siemens** ultraSense WFXD5200UC	1,000		⊖	⊜	⊖	⊖	○	⊖	120	•	•	•	•
26	**KitchenAid** Superba KHWS01PMT	1,500		⊖	⊖	⊜	⊜	⊖	⊖	75	•	•	•	•
27	**Kenmore (Sears)** Elite HE3 4586[2]	1,100		⊖	⊖	⊖	⊜	⊖	⊖	70	•		•	•
28	**LG** WM1814C[W]	700		○	⊜	⊜	⊜	⊖	⊖	80	•		•	•
29	**LG** WM2032H[W]	1,030		⊖	⊖	⊜	⊜	⊖	⊖	80	•	•	•	•
30	**Whirlpool** Duet GHW9150P[W]	1,000		⊖	⊖	⊖	⊜	⊖	⊖	65	•		•	•
31	**Frigidaire** Gallery GLTR1670A[S]	620		○	⊖	○	○	○	⊖	60	•		•	•
32	**Miele** Touchtronic W1113	1,600		⊖	⊜	⊖	●	⊖	⊜	90	•		•	
33	**Asko** W6021	1,000		⊖	⊜	⊖	●	⊖	⊖	120	•		•	

See report, page 77. Based on tests posted to ConsumerReports.org in May 2005, with updated prices and availability.

Guide to the Ratings

Overall score is based primarily on washing ability, efficiency, capacity, and noise. **Washing performance** reflects the degree of color change to swatches of fabric that were included in an 8-pound test load of mixed cotton items using the machines' most aggressive normal cycle. The **energy efficiency** score is based on the energy needed to heat the water for 8-pound and maximum loads using a warm wash and cold rinse. We consider both gas and electric water heaters, and include electricity needed to run the washer and energy needed for drying. Washers that extract more water are scored higher. **Water efficiency** denotes how much water it took to wash our 8-pound load and each machine's maximum load. On models that didn't set the fill level automatically, we used the lowest fill setting that sufficed for the 8-pound load. We then calculated water used per pound of clothing. **Capacity** for top-loaders is based on how well the washer agitates increasingly large loads. For front-loaders, the score is based on our judgment of the maximum sized load that the washer holds. Models that earned lower scores for **gentleness** are more likely to treat your clothes roughly, causing wear and tear. **Noise** score reflects judgments by panelists during the fill, agitate, and spin cycles. **Cycle time (min.)** is our measurement of the time, rounded to the nearest five minutes, to complete the most aggressive normal cycle with our 8-pound load. (We do not use special cycle or option buttons.) **Price** is approximate retail price.

Quick Picks

For best performance at a high price:

27 Kenmore (Sears), $1,100
28 LG, $700
29 LG, $1,030
30 Whirlpool, $1,000

Capacious and quiet, these front-loaders were frugal with energy and water. The LG WM1814C[W] (28) isn't as large as the others but still holds a decent-sized load, and it costs hundreds less. (Note that we have no reliability data on LG washers.)

Good performance at modest prices:

5 Whirlpool, $500
9 Kenmore (Sears), $500
10 Whirlpool, $380

These three conventional top-loaders got laundry clean and did well in all other tests. Both the Whirlpool Gold GSQ9669L[W] (5) and Kenmore (Sears) 1584[2] (9) have been discontinued, but the similar models listed should offer comparable performance.

A value if noise isn't an issue:

8 GE, $300

This low-priced top-loader did a good job but is rather noisy. If your laundry room is in the basement or garage, it's worth considering.

Recommendations

TOP-LOADING MODELS

1 MAYTAG Neptune TL FAV9800A[WW] Very good. This unconventional top-loader did an excellent job washing clothes and holds very large loads. It uses washing disks instead of a center agitator post to move laundry around the tub. It was very efficient with water and energy and was among the best at extracting water. However, it tangled clothes and left them wrinkled, and it has a long cycle time. Low-sudsing detergent is recommended. It has touchscreen controls with a digital display of menus. Although Maytag top-loaders have been about average in reliability, that may not apply to this washer because it uses different technology.

2 KENMORE (Sears) Elite 2506[2] Very good. This unconventional top-loader, known until recently as the Kenmore

Recommendations

Calypso, uses wash plates to move laundry around the tub. It has an especially large capacity and did a very good job washing clothes. It's among the quieter, more energy- and water-efficient washers we've tested. However, it tangled clothing and left it wrinkled. Low-sudsing detergent is recommended. Kenmore Calypsos have been among the more repair-prone brands of top-loaders.

3 WHIRLPOOL Calypso GVW9959K[Q] Very good. This unconventional Calypso top-loader uses wash plates to move laundry around the tub. It has an especially large capacity and did a very good job washing clothes. It's among the quieter, more energy-efficient washers we've tested. However, it tangled clothing and left it wrinkled. Low-sudsing detergent is recommended.

4 GE Profile Harmony WPGT9350C[WW] Very good. This unconventional top-loader uses washing disks instead of a center agitator post. It can hold very large loads. It did a very good job washing clothing, but consumes more energy than most washers we tested. It has touchscreen controls with a digital display of menus. The washer electronically signals the matching dryer to indicate which wash cycle was used, and the dryer automatically chooses a corresponding setting—a unique but not especially helpful feature. Low-sudsing detergent is recommended. Although GE top-loaders have been about average in reliability, that may not apply to this washer because it uses different technology.

5 WHIRLPOOL Gold GSQ9669L[W] Good. A good choice for consumers seeking competent performance and value. It did a good job cleaning clothes, which would be fine for all but very soiled laundry, and it uses less water than conventional top-loaders. Discontinued, but similar model GST9679P may be available.

6 GE WWRE5240D[WW] Good. This low-priced machine offers competent performance and value. It did a good job cleaning clothes, which would be fine for all but very soiled laundry, but it uses more energy than most washers.

7 AMANA NAV8800A[WW] Good. This low-priced top-loader did a good job washing clothes, which would be fine for all but very soiled laundry. It has a shorter cycle time than most washers and it uses less water than most. It was among the best at extracting water from clothes at the end of the cycle.

8 GE WBSR3140D[WW] Good. A real value. It did a good job cleaning laundry, which would be fine for all but very soiled loads, and it has a short cycle time. However, it's rather noisy.

9 KENMORE (Sears) 1584[2] Good. This machine offers competent performance and value. It did a good job cleaning laundry, which would be fine for all but very soiled loads, and it has a short cycle time. Discontinued, but similar model 1685 may be available.

10 WHIRLPOOL LSW9700P[Q] Good. This low-priced conventional top-loader offers competent performance and value. It did a good job cleaning laundry, which would be fine for all but very soiled loads, and it has a short cycle time.

11 GE WHSE5240D[WW] Good. This conventional top-loader is low-priced, but it did only a fair job getting clothes clean. Many models offer better washing performance for the same price or less.

12 GE WHRE5260E[WW] Good. This conventional top-loader is low-priced, but it did only a fair job getting clothes clean. Many models offer better washing performance for the same price or less.

13 KENMORE (Sears) Elite 2494[2] Good. It did a good job cleaning laundry, which would be fine for all but very soiled loads, but costs more than other washers offering comparable or better performance. It has a large capacity and a short cycle time. However, it uses more energy than most and it's rather noisy. Discontinued, but similar models 2692 and 2694 may be available.

14 MAYTAG Atlantis MAV9501E[W] Good. This top-loader did a very good job cleaning laundry but was rough on fabric. It uses less water than conventional top-loaders but more energy. Discontinued, but similar model Atlantis MAV9504E may be available.

15 FRIGIDAIRE FWS1339A[C] Good. This machine is low-priced and Frigidaire has been among the more reliable brands of top-loaders, but it did only a fair job getting clothes clean. Many models offer better washing performance for the same price or less. Similar model: Gallery GLWS1339C.

16 KENMORE (Sears) 2685[2] Good. This machine did a good job cleaning laundry, which would be fine for all but very soiled loads. It has a short cycle time. Overall, it's a competent performer worth considering at the right price.

17 WHIRLPOOL Gold GSW9650L[W] Good. This conventional top-loader did a good job cleaning laundry, which would be fine for all but very soiled loads. It used more energy than most washers but was frugal with water. Overall, it's a competent performer worth considering at the right price. Discontinued, but similar model GSW9800P may be available.

18 HOTPOINT VWSR4150D[WW] Good. This conventional top-loader is low-priced, but it did only a fair job getting clothes clean and uses more energy than most washers. Many models offer better washing performance for the same price or less.

19 KENMORE (Sears) 2462[2] Good. This low-priced conventional top-loader did a good job cleaning laundry, which would be fine for all but very soiled loads, and it has a short cycle time. However, it was among the noisiest washers and used more energy than most washers. Still, given the price, it's worth considering if your laundry room is in the basement or garage. Discontinued, but similar models 2663, 2664, 2665 may be available.

20 ROPER RAS8333R[Q] Good. Low-priced, and Roper has been among the more reliable brands of top-loaders. However, it did only a fair job getting clothes clean and uses more water than most washers. Many models offer better washing performance for the same price or less.

FRONT-LOADING MODELS

21 KENMORE (Sears) Elite HE4t 4508[1] Very good. This front-loader has a very large capacity and is among the most frugal with both energy and water. It did a very good job washing clothes. Low-sudsing detergent is recommended. It was among the quietest models tested, but it had a rather long cycle time and is high-priced even for a front-loader. An optional 13-inch-high pedestal with a storage drawer raises the washer for easier unloading. This washer can be stacked with a companion dryer. Similar model: HE4t 4509.

22 WHIRLPOOL Duet HT GHW9400P[W] Very good. This front-loader has a very large capacity and it did a very good job washing clothes. Low-sudsing detergent is recommended. It's very efficient with

Recommendations

both water and energy and is among the quietest washers tested. An optional 13-inch-high pedestal with a storage drawer raises the washer for easier unloading.

23 BOSCH Nexxt Premium WFMC6400UC Very good. This front-loader did a very good job washing clothes. It's very efficient with both water and energy and is among the quietest washers tested. However, the model we tested sometimes would not complete the rinse and spin portion of cycle due to excessive sudsing, even though we used low-sudsing detergent, as recommended by the manufacturer. This would occur when washing with very soft water and low soil levels.

24 LG WM2432H[W] Very good. This front-loader has very large capacity, and it did a very good job washing clothes. It's very efficient with both water and energy and is among the quietest washers tested. It extracted a lot of water during the spin cycle. We don't have enough survey data to establish a track record for reliability. Low-sudsing detergent is recommended.

25 SIEMENS ultraSense WFXD5200UC Very good. This front-loader did a very good job getting clothes clean using minimal water and energy and making very little noise. But the model we tested sometimes would not complete the rinse and spin portion of cycle due to excessive sudsing, even though we used the low-sudsing detergent recommended by the manufacturer. The cycle time is rather long.

26 KITCHENAID Superba KHWS01PMT Very good. It did a very good job cleaning laundry and is frugal with both water and energy. It was especially quiet, holds very large loads, and was among the best at extracting water from clothes. However, it's high-priced even for a front-loader. An optional 13-inch high pedestal with a storage drawer raises the height for easier unloading. Low-sudsing detergent is recommended.

27 KENMORE (Sears) Elite HE3 4586[2] Very good. This front-loader holds very large loads and does a good job getting clothes clean, which should be fine for all but the most soiled laundry. It's frugal with water and energy and is very quiet. An optional 13-inch high pedestal with a storage drawer raises the height for easier unloading. Low-sudsing detergent is recommended.

28 LG WM1814C[W] Very good. Low-priced, holds very large loads, and did a good job getting clothes clean, which would be fine for all but the most soiled laundry. It's frugal with water and energy and very quiet. Low-sudsing detergent is recommended. We don't have enough survey data to establish a track record for reliability.

29 LG WM2032H[W] Very good. This front-loader holds very large loads and did a very good job getting clothes clean. It's frugal with water and energy and very quiet. It was among the best at extracting water from clothes. Low-sudsing detergent is recommended. We don't have enough survey data to establish a track record for reliability.

30 WHIRLPOOL Duet GHW9150P[W] Very good. This competent, well-priced front-loader did well on all counts. Very quiet and efficient with both water and energy, it did a very good job getting clothes clean and has a very large capacity. An optional 13-inch high pedestal with a storage drawer raises the height for easier unloading. Low-sudsing detergent is recommended.

Recommendations

31 FRIGIDAIRE Gallery GLTR1670A[S] Very good. Among the lowest-priced front-loaders, this capable model did a good job cleaning clothes, which would be fine for all but very soiled laundry. Its capacity isn't as large as that of some front-loaders, but it holds a decent-sized load—as much as many top-loaders. It's very quiet and frugal with energy. Low-sudsing detergent is recommended. Similar model: GLTF1670A.

32 MIELE Touchtronic W1113 Very good. This compact front-loader holds only small loads but fits into tight spaces. It did a very good job getting clothes clean. It's very quiet and frugal with water and energy and requires a dedicated 240-volt outlet. It has a long wash cycle but was among the best at extracting water from clothes. It's pricey even for a front-loader. Low-sudsing detergent is recommended. We have no repair data for this brand.

33 ASKO W6021 Very good. This compact front-loader holds only small loads but fits into tight spaces. It did a very good job getting clothes clean. It's very quiet and frugal with water and energy and requires a dedicated 240-volt outlet. It has a long wash cycle but was among the best at extracting water from clothes. Low-sudsing detergent is recommended. We have no repair data for this brand.

Brand Repair History

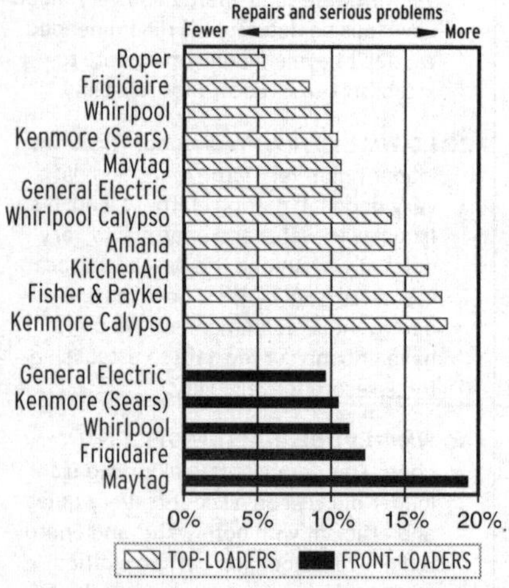

Based on 101,775 washers purchased new between 2000 and the first half of 2004. Data have been standardized to eliminate differences linked to age and usage. Differences of less than four points aren't meaningful.

Reliability is especially important with a workhorse appliance like a washer. Choosing a brand with a good repair history can improve your odds of getting a reliable model. This graph shows the percentage of full-sized washers that have ever been repaired or had a serious problem, according to our 2004 Annual Questionnaire. Note that models within a brand may vary, and design and manufacturing changes may affect reliability.

For washers in general, there was no real difference in repair rate between top- and front-loaders. In the conventional top-loader group, Fisher & Paykel and KitchenAid were among the more repair-prone brands. For the first time, we have enough data to report separately on new-technology top-loaders that use a wash system different from that of conventional top-loaders with agitators. The Kenmore (Sears) Calypso was among the less-reliable brands. (Data for GE and Maytag may not apply to the GE Profile Harmony and Maytag Neptune TL new-technology models.)
Maytag was the most repair-prone brand of front-loader, gibing with complaints in a recent class-action lawsuit charging excessive problems in its Neptune front-loaders

PRODUCT RECALLS

Products ranging from child-safety seats to chain saws are recalled when there are safety defects. Various federal agencies, such as the Consumer Product Safety Commission (CPSC), the National Highway Traffic Safety Administration (NHTSA), the U.S. Coast Guard, and the Food and Drug Administration (FDA), monitor complaints and injuries and, when there's a problem, issue a recall.

But the odds of hearing about an unsafe product are slim. Manufacturers are reluctant to issue a recall in the first place because they can be costly. And getting the word out to consumers can be haphazard. If you return the warranty card that comes with a product, however, you're more likely to receive notification on a recall for it.

A selection of the most far-reaching recalls appears monthly in CONSUMER REPORTS. Below is a listing of products recalled from December 2004 through November 2005, as reported in issues of CONSUMER REPORTS. For details on these products and hundreds more, go to our Web site, *www.ConsumerReports.org*, in order to access our free, comprehensive list of product recalls.

If you wish to report an unsafe product or get recall information, call the CPSC's hotline, 800-638-2772, or visit its Web site, *www.cpsc.gov*. Recall notices about your automobile can be obtained from a new-car dealer or by calling the NHTSA hotline at 888-327-4236 or go to *www.nhtsa.dot.gov*. Questions about food and drugs are handled by the FDA's Office of Consumer Affairs (888-463-6332, or *www.fda.gov)*.

VEHICLES & EQUIPMENT

'98-04 Audi (various models)
'01-04 BMW K and R Series motorcycles
'03-04 Buick Rendezvous
'02-03 Cadillac, Pontiac, and Oldsmobile
'04 Cadillac SRX
'04 Chrysler Pacifica
'98-00 Chrysler, Dodge, and Plymouth minivans
'01-05 Chrysler PT Cruiser
'04 Chrysler 300M and Concorde
'93-99 Chrysler cars
'94-96 Ford Bronco
'01-03 Ford Escape
'01 Ford Escape and Mazda Tribute
'97-02 Ford Expedition
'94-02 Ford F-150
'00-03 Ford Taurus and Mercury Sable
'01-03 Ford Windstar
'04 Dodge Durango
'96-01 General Motors cars
'97-99 Honda and Acura (various models)
'01-04 Honda and Acura (various models)
'02-03 Honda CR-V
'05 Honda Odyssey
'02-03 Hyundai (various models)
'01-04 Hyundai Elantra
'03-04 Jaguar with automatic transmission
'97-00 Kawasaki Prairie 300 and 400 all-terrain vehicles
'99-00 Kia
'01-04 Kia Rio and Rio Cinco
'03-05 Kia Sedona
'99-04 Land Rover Discovery II
'98-02 Lincoln Navigator
'03 Mazda6
'03-04 Mitsubishi (various models)
'99-03 Nissan Frontier and Xterra
'04 Pontiac Grand Prix
'03-04 Porsche Cayenne
'03-04 Saab 9-3
'03-04 Saturn Ion
'99-04 Suzuki Grand Vitara,
'01-04 Suzuki XL-7
'05 Volkswagen New Jetta

CHILDREN'S PRODUCTS

Arctic Flash, Arctic Wind, and Air Elegance air-hockey tables
Baby Trend "Passport" strollers sold at Babies "R" Us stores
Boston Billows and Theraline "Big V" maternity and nursing pillows
Britax Super Elite child car seats
Cosco Rock 'N Roller baby stroller
Fisher-Price battery-powered scooters and minibikes
Graco SnugRide infant car seat and carrier
Graco Travel Lite portable baby swing
Hasbro Super Soaker Monster Rocket
Plan Toys solid wood drum
"Trails End," "Cottage Retreat," and "Stages" bunk beds made by Ashley Furniture Industries

ELECTRONICS

AC adapters for Dell notebook computers
Apple iBook and PowerBook computer batteries
Apple iBook notebook computers
Batteries in LG cell phones sold through Verizon Wireless
Combination auto-air power adapter for Dell notebook computers
Guidant Corp. cardiac defibrillators
Fuji Power and A&T Fuji Power CR123A 3-volt lithium batteries
Counterfeit Kyocera cell-phone batteries

HOUSEHOLD PRODUCTS

Bachtold Whipper, DR Field & Brush Mower, and B-800 weed and brush cutters
Black Cat power washers
Bunn-O-Matic, KitchenAid, and West Bend coffeemakers
Cub Cadet Series 7000 compact tractors
Char-Broil gas barbecue grills
Euroflex multisurface steam cleaners sold on QVC cable channel
Fedders, Maytag, and Comfort-Aire air conditioners that also supply heat
GE, Kenmore, and Whirlpool dishwashers
Holmes and Bionaire tower heater fans
Lakewood Sun-Sational Deluxe Radiant electric heaters
Lasko space heaters
Murray lawn mowers and tractors
Nesco deep fryers
"Real Essence" votive candles
Tredex 6.0, TX 440, and TX 550 motorized treadmills
Turbo Power handheld hair dryers
Vicks Warm Mist humidifier
Wagner cordless drill charger base

BRAND LOCATOR

Phone numbers and Web addresses of selected manufacturers.

A		
Acura	800-382-2238	www.acura.com
ACD Systems	866-244-2237	www.acdsystems.com
Adobe	800-833-6687	www.adobe.com
Admiral	800-688-9920	www.maytag.com
Aerus (Electrolux)	800-243-9078	www.aerusonline.com
AGFA	888-988-2432	www.agfa.com
Aiwa	800-289-2492	www.us.aiwa.com
Akai	888-697-2247	www.akaiusa.com
Amana	800-843-0304	www.amana.com
AMD	800-222-9323	www.amd.com
America Online	800-827-6364	www.aol.com
Apex	909-930-1239	www.apexdigitalinc.com
Apple	800-538-9696	www.apple.com
ArcSoft	510-440-9901	www.arcsoft.com
Ariens	800-678-5443	www.ariens.com
Asko	800-898-1879	www.askousa.com
Asus	510-739-3777	usa.asus.com
AT&T	800-222-3111	www.att.com
Audi	800-367-2834	www.audiusa.com
Audiovox	800-229-1235	www.audiovox.com
B		
B&W	800-370-3740	www.bwspeakers.com
BellSouth	888-757-6500	www.bellsouth.com
BIC	888-461-4628	www.bicamerica.com
Bionaire	800-253-2764	www.bionaire.com
Bissell	800-237-7691	www.bissell.com
Black & Decker	800-544-6986	www.blackanddecker.com
BMW	800-334-4269	www.bmwusa.com
Bosch	800-921-9622	www.boschappliances.com
Bose	800-999-2673	www.bose.com
Boston Acoustics	800-246-7767	www.bostonacoustics.com
Broilmaster	800-851-3153	www.broilmaster.com
Brother	800-276-7746	www.brother.com
Buick	800-422-8425	www.buick.com
C		
Cadillac	800-333-4223	www.cadillac.com
Cambridge Soundworks	800-367-4434	www.hifi.com
Canon	800-828-4040	www.usa.canon.com
Carrier	800-227-7437	www.carrier.com
Casio	800-706-2534	www.casio.com
Cerwin-Vega	805-584-5300	www.cerwinvega.com

Char-Broil	800-241-7548	www.charbroil.com
Chevrolet	800-950-0540	www.chevrolet.com
Chrysler	800-422-4797	www.chrysler.com
Cingular	800-331-0500	www.cingular.com
Coleman	800-356-3612	www.coleman.com
Compaq	800-345-1518	www.compaq.com
CompuServe	800-336-6823	www.compuserve.com
Corel	800-772-6735	www.corel.com
Craftsman	Call local Sears store	www.sears.com
Creative Labs	800-998-1000	us.creative.com
CTX	877-688-3288	www.ctxintl.com
Cub Cadet	877-282-8684	www.cubcadet.com
Cuisinart	800-726-0190	www.cuisinart.com
D		
Dacor	800-793-0093	www.dacor.com
Daewoo	800-323-9668	www.daewoous.com
Dell	800-879-3355	www.dell.com
DeLonghi	800-322-3848	www.delonghiusa.com
Denon	973-396-0810	www.usa.denon.com
DeWalt	800-433-9258	www.dewalt.com
DirecTV	800-347-3288	www.directv.com
DirecWay	866-347-3292	www.direcway.com
Dirt Devil	800-321-1134	www.dirtdevil.com
Dish Network (EchoStar)	800-333-3474	www.dishnetwork.com
Disney Interactive	800-900-9234	disney.go.com/disneyinteractive
Dodge	800-423-6343	www.dodge.com
Ducane	800-382-2637	www.ducane.com
Dynamic Cooking Systems (DCS)	800-433-8466	www.dcsappliances.com
Dyson	866-693-9766	www.dyson.com
E		
EarthLink	800-327-8454	www.earthlink.net
Echo	800-673-1558	www.echo-usa.com
Electrolux	800-243-9078	www.electroluxusa.com
EMachines	877-566-3463	www.e4me.com
Emerson	800-909-1240	www.emersonradio.com
Envision	888-838-6388	www.envisionmonitor.com
Epson	800-463-7766	www.epson.com
Ericsson	800-374-2776	www.ericsson.com
Eureka	800-282-2886	www.eureka.com
F		
Fantom	800-668-9600	www.fantom.com
Fedders	866-629-8241	www.fedders.com
Fiesta	800-396-3838	www.fiestagasgrills.com
Fisher	818-998-7322	www.fisherav.com
Fisher & Paykel	888-936-7872	www.usa.fisherpaykel.com
Ford	800-392-3673	www.fordvehicles.com
Franklin	800-266-5626	www.franklin.com
Friedrich	800-541-6645	www.friedrich.com
Frigidaire	800-374-4432	www.frigidaire.com
Fujifilm	800-800-3854	www.fujifilm.com
Fujitsu	800-838-5487	www.fujitsupc.com
G		
Garmin	800-800-1020	www.garmin.com
Gateway	800-846-2000	www.gateway.com
GE (appliances)	800-626-2000	www.geappliances.com

GE (electronics)	800-447-1700	www.home-electronics.net
GMC	800-462-8782	www.gmc.com
Goldstar	800-243-0000	www.lgeus.com
Grizzly	570-546-9663	www.grizzly.com

H

Haier	888-764-2437	www.haieramerica.com
Hamilton Beach	800-851-8900	www.hamiltonbeach.com
Harman/Kardon	800-422-8027	www.harmankardon.com
Hewlett-Packard	800-752-0900	www.hp.com
Hitachi	800-448-2244	www.hitachi.com
Holland	800-880-9766	www.hollandgrill.com
Holmes	800-546-5637	www.holmesproducts.com
Homelite	800-242-4672	www.homelite.com
Honda (autos)	800-334-6632	www.hondacars.com
Honda (mowers)	770-497-6400	www.hondapowerequipment.com
Hoover	800-944-9200	www.hoover.com
Hotpoint	800-626-2000	www.hotpoint.com
Hughes	800-347-3288	www.hns-usa.com
Husqvarna	800-487-5962	www.usa.husqvarna.com
Hyundai	800-826-2277	www.hyundaiusa.com

I

IBM	800-426-7235	www.ibm.com
Infiniti	877-647-7266	www.infiniti.com
Infinity	516-674-4463	www.infinitysystems.com
Intel	800-628-8686	www.intel.com
Iomega	800-697-8833	www.iomega.com
Isuzu	800-726-2700	www.isuzu.com

J

Jaguar	800-452-4827	www.jaguarusa.com
Jasc	800-622-2793	www.jasc.com
JBL	516-255-4525	www.jbl.com
Jeep	800-925-5337	www.jeep.com
Jenn-Air	800-688-1100	www.jennair.com
John Deere	800-537-8233	www.deere.com
Jonsered	877-693-7729	www.usa.jonsered.com
JVC	800-252-5722	www.jvc.com

K

KDS	800-237-9988	www.kdsusa.com
Kenmore	Call local Sears store	www.sears.com
Kenwood	800-536-9663	www.kenwoodusa.com
Kia	800-333-4542	www.kia.com
Kirby	800-437-7170	www.kirby.com
KitchenAid	800-422-1230	www.kitchenaid.com
KLH	818-767-2843	www.klhaudio.com
Kodak	800-235-6325	www.kodak.com
Konica	877-462-4464	www.konica.com
Kyocera	800-421-5735	americas.kyocera.com

L

Land Rover	800-346-3493	www.landroverusa.com
Lawn-Boy	800-526-6937	www.lawnboy.com
LearningCo.com	800-395-0277	www.learningcompany.com
Lexmark	800-539-6275	www.lexmark.com
Lexus	800-872-5398	www.lexus.com
LG	800-243-0000	www.lgeus.com

Lincoln	800-521-4140	www.lincoln.com
Lotus	800-465-6887	www.lotus.com
Lucent	888-458-2368	www.lucent.com
M		
Magic Chef	800-688-1120	www.maytag.com
Magnavox	800-705-2000	www.magnavox.com
Makita	800-462-5482	www.makita.com
Maxim	800-233-9054	www.esalton.com
Maytag	800-688-9900	www.maytag.com
Mazda	800-639-1000	www.mazdausa.com
McCulloch	800-521-8559	www.mccullochpower.com
Mercedes-Benz	800-367-6372	www.mbusa.com
Mercury	800-392-3673	www.mercuryvehicles.com
Micron PC	888-719-5031	www.buympc.com
Microsoft	800-426-9400	www.microsoft.com
Microsoft Network	800-373-3676	www.msn.com
Microtek	310-687-5940	www.microtekusa.com
Miele	800-843-7231	www.mieleusa.com
Milwaukee	800-729-3878	www.milwaukeetool.com
Minolta	800-808-4888	www.minoltausa.com
Mintek	866-709-9500	www.mintekdigital.com
Mitsubishi	888-648-7820	www.mitsubishicars.com
Motorola	800-331-6456	www.motorola.com/us
MTD	800-800-7310	www.mtdproducts.com
Murray	800-224-8940	www.murray.com
N		
NEC	800-338-9549	www.necus.com
Network Associates (McAfee VirusScan)	800-338-8754	www.mcafee.com
Nextel	800-639-6111	www.nextel.com
Nikon	800-645-6689	www.nikonusa.com
Nintendo	800-255-3700	www.nintendo.com
Nissan	800-419-7520	www.nissanusa.com
Nokia	888-665-4228	www.nokiausa.com
O		
Oki	800-654-3282	www.okidata.com
Oldsmobile	800-442-6537	www.oldsmobile.com
Olympus	800-622-6372	www.olympusamerica.com
Onkyo	800-229-1687	www.onkyousa.com
Optimus	800-843-7422	www.radioshack.com
Oreck	800-989-3535	www.oreck.com
Oster	800-597-5978	www.oster.com
P		
PalmOne	800-881-7256	www.palm.com/us
Panasonic	800-211-7262	www.panasonic.com
Pentax	800-877-0155	www.pentaxusa.com
Philips	800-531-0039	www.philipsusa.com
Pioneer	800-421-1404	www.pioneerelectronics.com
Polaroid	800-432-5355	www.polaroid.com
Polk Audio	800-377-7655	www.polkaudio.com
Pontiac	800-276-6842	www.pontiac.com
Porsche	800-767-7243	us.porsche.com
Porter-Cable	800-487-8665	www.porter-cable.com
Poulan	800-238-9333	www.poulan.com
Precor	800-477-3267	www.precor.com

Precisionaire	800-800-2210	www.precisionaire.com
Proctor-Silex	800-851-8900	www.proctorsilex.com
PSB	888-772-0000	www.psbspeakers.com
Q		
Quasar	800-211-7262	www.panasonic.com
R		
RadioShack	800-843-7422	www.radioshack.com
RCA	800-336-1900	www.rca.com
Regal	262-626-2121	www.regalware.com
Regina	228-867-8507	www.reginavac.com
Remington	616-791-7325	www.remingtonchainsaw.com
ReplayTV	866-286-3662	www.replaytv.com
Research Products	800-545-2219	www.resprod.com
Rival	800-557-4825	www.rivalproducts.com
Riverdeep	319-247-3333	www.riverdeep.net
Roper	800-447-6737	www.roperappliances.com
Rowenta	781-396-0600	www.rowentausa.com
Royal	800-321-1134	wwww.dirtdevil.com
Ryobi	800-525-2579	www.ryobitools.com
S		
Saab	800-722-2872	www.saabusa.com
Sabre by John Deere	800-537-8233	www.deere.com
Salton	800-233-9054	www.esalton.com
Sampo	888-373-4360	www.sampoamericas.com
Samsung	800-726-7864	www.samsungusa.com
Sanyo	818-998-7322	www.sanyo.com
Saturn	800-522-5000	www.saturn.com
Sega	800-872-7342	www.sega.com
Sharp	800-237-4277	www.sharpusa.com
Siemens	888-777-0211	www.icm.siemens.com
Sierra	310-649 8033	www.sierra.com
Simplicity (yard equipment)	262-284-8669	www.simplicitymfg.com
Simplicity (vacuum cleaners)	888-974-6759	www.simplicityvac.com
Skil	877-754 5999	www.skiltools.com
Snapper	800-935-2967	www.snapper.com
Solo	757-245-4228	www.solousa.com
Sony	800-222-7669	www.sony.com
Southwestern Bell	800-366-0937	www.sbc.com
Sprint PCS	888-253-1315	www.sprintpcs.com
Stanley	800-788-7766	www.murray.com
Stihl	800-467-8445	www.stihlusa.com
Subaru	800-782-2783	www.subaru.com
Sub-Zero	800-222-7820	www.subzero.com
Sunbeam	800-458-8407	www.sunbeam.com
Suzuki	877-697-8985	www.suzukiauto.com
Symantec (Norton Antivirus)	800-441-7234	www.symantec.com
T		
Tappan	800-537-5530	www.frigidaire.com
TEC	800-331-0097	www.tecgasgrills.com
Technics	800-211-7262	www.panasonic.com
Thermador	800-735-4328	www.thermador.com
TiVo	877-289-8486	www.tivo.com
T-Mobile	800-866-2453	www.t-mobile.com
Toastmaster	800-947-3744	www.toastmaster.com
Toro	800-348-2424	www.toro.com

Toshiba	800-631-3811	www.toshiba.com
Toyota	800-468-6968	www.toyota.com
Trion	800-884-0002	www.trioninc.com
Troy-Bilt	800-800-7310	www.troybilt.com
U		
Ulead	800-858-5323	www.ulead.com
Umax	214-342-9799	www.umax.com
Uniden	800-297-1023	www.uniden.com
V		
Verizon Wireless	800-922-0204	www.verizonwireless.com
ViewSonic	800-688-6688	www.viewsonic.com
Viking	800-467-2643	www.vikingrange.com
Visioneer	925-251-6398	www.visioneer.com
Vivitar	805-998-0463	www.vivitar.com
Volkswagen	800-444-8987	www.vw.com
Volvo	800-458-1552	www.volvocars.us
VTech	800-595-9511	www.vtech.com
W		
Walker	800-843-7422	www.radioshack.com
Waring	800-492-7464	www.waringproducts.com
Weber	800-446-1071	www.weber.com
Weed Eater	800-554-6723	www.weedeater.com
West Bend	262-334-6949	www.westbend.com
Whirlpool	800-253-1301	www.whirlpool.com
White Outdoor	800-800-7310	www.whiteoutdoor.com
White-Westinghouse	800-374-4432	www.frigidaire.com
WinBook	800-254-7806	www.winbook.com
X		
Xerox	800-832-6979	www.xerox.com
Y		
Yamaha	800-492-6242	www.yamaha.com
Yard Machines by MTD	800-800-7310	www.mtdproducts.com
Yashica	800-421-5735	www.yashica.com
Z		
Zenith	877-993-6484	www.zenith.com
Zone Labs	415-633-4500	www.zonealarm.com

8-YEAR INDEX TO CONSUMER REPORTS

This index indicates when the last full report on a given subject was published in CONSUMER REPORTS. The index goes back as far as 1998.

In text below, **bold type** indicates Ratings reports or brand-name discussions; *italic type* indicates corrections, followups, or Updates.

A

BUYING GUIDE INDEX

Statement of Ownership, Management, and Circulation

(Required by 39 U.S.C. 3685)

1. Publication Title: Consumer Reports. 2. Publication No: 0010-7174. 3. Filing Date: September 14, 2005. 4. Issue Frequency: Monthly, except two issues in December. 5. No. of Issues Published Annually: 13. 6. Annual Subscription Price: $26.00. 7. Complete Mailing Address of Known Office of Publication: Consumers Union of United States, Inc., 101 Truman Avenue, Yonkers, New York 10703-1057. 8. Complete Mailing Address of Headquarters or General Business Office of Publisher: Consumers Union of United States, Inc., 101 Truman Avenue, Yonkers, New York 10703-1057. 9. Full Names and Complete Mailing Addresses of Publisher, Editor, and Managing Editor. Publisher: Consumers Union of United States, Inc., 101 Truman Avenue, Yonkers, New York 10703-1057. President: James A. Guest; Editor: Margot Slade; Managing Editor: Kim Kleman. 10. Owner: (If the publication is published by a nonprofit organization, its name and address must be stated.) Full Name: Consumers Union of United States, Inc., a nonprofit organization. Complete Mailing Address: 101 Truman Avenue, Yonkers, New York 10703-1057. 11. Known Bondholders, Mortgagees, and Other Security Holders Owning or Holding 1 Percent or More of Total Amount of Bonds, Mortgages, or Other Securities. If none, so state: None. 12. For Completion by Nonprofit Organizations Authorized to Mail at Special Rates: The purpose, function, and nonprofit status of this organization and the exempt status for federal income tax purposes has not changed during preceding 12 months.

15. Extent and Nature of Circulation:

	Average no. copies each issue during past 12 mo.	Actual no. copies of single issue published nearest to filing date
A. Total no. of copies (net press run)	4,621,487	4,655,683
B. Paid and/or requested circulation		
1. Paid/requested outside-county mail subscriptions stated on Form 3541	NA	NA
2. Paid in-county subscriptions stated on Form 3541	NA	NA
3. Sales through dealers, carriers, street vendors, counter sales, and other non-USPS paid distribution	117,730	90,000
4. Other classes mailed through the USPS	4,246,238	4,374,660
C. Total paid and/or requested circulation (sum of 15b(1), (2), (3), and (4))	4,363,967	4,464,660
D. Free distribution by mail (samples, complimentary, and other free)	26,392	28,298
E. Free distribution outside the mail	14,308	14,472
F. Total free distribution (sum of 15d and 15e)	40,700	42,770
G. Total distribution (sum of 15c and 15f)	4,404,668	4,507,430
H. Copies not distributed	216,819	148,253
I. TOTAL (sum of 15g and 15h)	4,621,487	4,655,683
J. Percent paid and/or requested circulation	99.08%	99.05%

17. I certify that the statements made by me above are correct and complete.

Louis J. Milani, Senior Director, Publishing Operations